WEST COAST

For the past twenty years the **West Coast Region** of the **National Conference of Synagogue Youth / NCSY** has been a major force in maintaining an influence on Jewish youth of the Pacific Coast. The educational framework we provide is unique in that we guide today's Jewish youth towards understanding a Jewish value system that is both traditional and contemporary in spirit.

Through Shabbatonim and other innovative programs, the **West Coast Region** of **NCSY** has been extremely successful in combating the escalating rate of assimilation. There are countless previously unaffiliated young Jews who are now observing Torah and Mitzvot due to the efforts of **NCSY.**

Equally important to us is the day school student. Here **NCSY** fills the vital time spent outside of school and away from home with constructive, positive Jewish experiences. **NCSY** transforms social and recreational environments into opportunities for growth.

In the past two decades, the **NCSY Experience** has provided hundreds of **NCSY**ers with the means to reach their true potential. We are resolute to expand our activities and programs as we reach out to the Jewish leaders of tomorrow. We look toward your continued support and involvement to make this possible.

WEST COAST

Rani Einziger
Richland, Washington
Regional President

Julie Freidkin
Piedmont, California
Vice President of Bay Area

Michelle Love
Calgary, Alberta
Vice President of Northwest

Samantha Rapp
Edmonton, Alberta
Vice President of Northwest

Robyn Solomon
Irvine, California
Vice President of Southland

Beth Green
Los Angeles, California
Vice President of Social Actions

Lori Shmulewitz
Santa Barbara, California
Vice President of Social Actions

Semadar Ben-Zvi
Van Nuys, California
Vice President of Education

David Genish
Los Angeles, California
Vice President of Education

Judah Glouberman
North Hollywood, California
Vice President of Education

Chana Meir
Beverly Hills, California
Vice President of Education

Felicia Himmelsein
Santa Barbara, California
Vice President of Publications

Jeanne Rothstein
Santa Barbara, California
Vice President of Publications

Jessica Morantz
Los Angeles, California
Vice President of Special Projects

Shana Parver
Los Angeles, California
Vice President of Special Projects

Rabbi Raphael B. Butler
National Director, NCSY

Rabbi Benjamin Jacoby
Regional Director
West Coast NCSY

David Kuropatwa
Director of Administration
West Coast NCSY

Steve Miller
Assistant Director of Administration
Junior NCSY Coordinator

Martin Nachimson
President
West Coast Orthodox Union

Mr. Paul Glasser
Youth Commission Chairmman
West Coast NCSY

Rabbi Alan Kalinsky
Director
West Coast Orthodox Union

ArtScroll Tanach Series®

A traditional commentary on the Books of the Bible

Rabbis Nosson Scherman/Meir Zlotowitz
General Editors

בראשית

עם פירוש נחלת יוסף

Published by

Mesorah Publications, ltd

in conjunction with

NATIONAL CONFERENCE OF SYNAGOGUE YOUTH / ORTHODOX UNION

The Family Chumash

Bereishis

GENESIS / INTRODUCTIONS, TRANSLATIONS
AND CONCISE COMMENTARY
WITH HAFTARAHS.

Translated and annotated by
Rabbi Meir Zlotowitz

Overviews and Introductions by
Rabbi Nosson Scherman

FIRST EDITION
First Impression . . . September, 1989

Published and Distributed by
MESORAH PUBLICATIONS, Ltd.
Brooklyn, New York 11232

Distributed in Israel by
MESORAH MAFITZIM / J. GROSSMAN
Rechov Harav Uziel 117
Jerusalem, Israel

Distributed in Europe by
J. LEHMANN HEBREW BOOKSELLERS
20 Cambridge Terrace
Gateshead, Tyne and Wear
England NE8 1RP

Distributed in Australia & New Zealand by
GOLD'S BOOK & GIFT CO.
36 William Street
Balaclava 3183, Vic., Australia

Distributed in South Africa by
KOLLEL BOOKSHOP
22 Muller Street
Yeoville 2198, South Africa

ARTSCROLL TANACH SERIES®
THE FAMILY CHUMASH / Bereishis
© *Copyright 1989, by MESORAH PUBLICATIONS, Ltd.*
4401 Second Avenue / Brooklyn, N.Y. 11232 / (718) 921-9000

ISBN
0-89906-012-9 (hard cover)
0-89906-013-7 (paperback)

Typography by Compuscribe at ArtScroll Studios, Ltd.

Printed in the United States of America by Noble Book Press
Bound by Sefercraft, Quality Bookbinders, Ltd. Brooklyn, N.Y.

This Chumash is dedicated
to the memory of

יוסף בן אהרן שמואל ז"ל, הי"ד

Joseph K. Miller

שנקטף בדמי ימיו י"ד טבת, תשמ"ט

Joseph K. Miller was a commanding presence,
filling a room with a highly contagious vitality and zest for life.

He was the ba'al habayis par excellence — a deeply devoted
lay leader whose highly successful professional career
often seemed to be but a convenient cover for his
indefatigable commitment to Jewish communal affairs.

One of the Orthodox Union's most respected, creative and
valuable officers, his character, vision, commitment
and integrity were both unusual and exemplary.

He loved NCSY with unmatched passion and outspoken enthusiasm.
He saw in NCSY the potential that few could imagine;
and matched that vision with the loving resolve to create, promote
and sustain dimensions of a teshuvah movement that touched
the lives of thousands. Few have done as much for NCSY;
none have done it with more love.

Joseph K. Miller's brilliant life ended in the cowardly terrorist
bombing of Pan Am Flight 103 over Lockerbie, Scotland,
on December 21, 1988.

His legacy lives on as the standard for service
in the Torah community he helped nurture.

בעל מרץ וחזון, איש אמונה ובטחון. ירא וחרד לדבר ה'.
עסק בצרכי צבור באמונה להגדיל תורה ולהאדירה.

תנצב"ה

◈§ Authors' Preface

The emergence of new generations of English-speaking Jews who are uncompromisingly loyal to the eternal traditions of Judaism is a phenomenon that would have astounded their grandparents. Furthermore, it has spawned a resurgence of Jewish life and Torah study that has led to a demand for books that present our classic Torah heritage in the vernacular, without compromise or apology. It was to help fill this need that the ArtScroll Series came into being, and it was because of this thirst that the various levels of commentary in the series have won such acceptance.

This volume, *The Family Chumash*, follows the format of *The Family Haggadah* and *The Family Megillos*. The concept is to present the popular ArtScroll translation accompanied by a concise but clear commentary that combines an exposition of the simple meaning of the text with inspirational comments, all drawn from the vast treasury of Rabbinic literature. The commentary in this Chumash is basically extracted from the acclaimed six-volume ArtScroll Bereishis/Genesis. The reader is urged to refer to that work — which is now published in two volumes — for a deeper, broader understanding of the text.

This volume includes for the first time translations of the *Haftarahs*, as well as introductory essays to every *Sidrah* and *Haftarah*. From the start of the ArtScroll Series, it has been our hope that these works would serve the reader as a springboard to further study of the sources in the original Hebrew. We are gratified that thousands of casual readers have become avid students, most of them going on to deepen their skills by studying the major commentators. Succeeding volumes of this *Chumash* will enable the reader to obtain a strong familiarity with every *Sidrah* and *Haftarah*, week by week.

We are proud that the National Conference of Synagogue Youth has joined in sponsoring this new *Chumash* project. Rabbi Raphael B. Butler, National Director, and Rabbi Moshe Krupka, coordinator, National Programs, have perceived the need for such a *Chumash* and have volunteered NCSY's support and advice in the production. It is a privilege for Mesorah Publications to be able to make this contribution to NCSY's precedent setting work.

The beauty and clarity of this book is a tribute to our colleague Rabbi Sheah Brander, whose graphic skills and consummate taste have been an indispensable factor in the success of the ArtScroll Series. One wonders if his combination of talent and Torah knowledge are duplicated in any individual.

Rabbi Shimon Golding has been an important liaison in the production of this work. Rabbi Avie Gold has done his customary meticulous and scholarly reading of the *Haftarahs*; Mrs. Faygie Weinbaum's perceptive eye has weeded out possible errors; Mrs. Esther Feierstein, Mrs. Menucha Silver, Mrs. Zissi Landau, and Bassie Goldstein have typed carefully and conscientiously; Lea Freier is a source of strength and efficiency in administration, ably assisted by Mrs. Surie Maline and Faigie Zlotowitz.

Shmuel Blitz, director of ArtScroll Jerusalem remains a vital colleague and guide; distance has not weakened the bond. We are also grateful to Sheila Tennenbaum in sales, and to the rest of the ArtScroll staff.

Finally, we express our deep gratitude to our wives, Mrs. Rochel Zlotowitz and Mrs. Chana Scherman; to Reb Sheah's wife, Mrs. Hennie Brander. Their appreciation of the importance of ArtScroll's work has led them to put it ahead of many personal needs. Their dedication to the spread of Torah — uncompromising and attractively presented — has enabled us to accomplish whatever we have in the thirteen years of ArtScroll's existence. May they be blessed with the *nachas* they cherish above all — that of בנים ובני בנים עוסקים בתורה ובמצות.

Above all, we thank Hashem Yisborach for permitting us to be the quill that records His Word, and we pledge to do everything possible to be worthy of that privilege.

Rabbi Meir Zlotowitz / Rabbi Nosson Scherman

Elul, 5749 Brooklyn, New York

In appreciation to

Stanley and Carol Klein

They are more than supporters.
They are friends, concerned friends.
The growth of countless NCSY'ers
is their personal nachas.
Because they share in the effort and the concern,
the joy is theirs, as well.

⇢❦⇢

An Overview /
The Torah — Teacher and Blueprint

ר' הוֹשַׁעְיָה רַבָּה פָּתַח: "וָאֶהְיֶה אֶצְלוֹ אָמוֹן וָאֶהְיֶה
שַׁעֲשׁוּעִים יוֹם יוֹם." אָמוֹן . . . פֶּדָגוֹג . . . דָבָר אַחֵר אָמוֹן:
אוֹמָן. הַתּוֹרָה אוֹמֶרֶת "אֲנִי הָיִיתִי כְּלִי אוּמָנוּתוֹ שֶׁל
הַקָּבָּ"ה . . . הָיָה הַקָּבָּ"ה מַבִּיט בַּתּוֹרָה וּבָרָא אֶת
הָעוֹלָם."

Rabbi Hoshayah the Great opened [the commentary on the Five Books of Moses]: I was his educator, I was His delight day by day (Proverbs 8:30). The Torah is like a skilled pedagogue ... Another interpretation: The Torah says [of itself], 'I was an artisan's tool in the hand of the Holy One, Blessed is He ... The Holy One, Blessed is He, looked into the Torah and created the world' (Bereishis Rabbah 1:1).

Pedagogue

When the Midrash begins a new subject with the term פָּתַח, *opened the discussion*, it means that we are being given an introduction that 'opens the door' to an understanding of the subject at hand. In the very first Midrashic teaching on the Torah, R' Hoshayah the Great cites a verse from *Proverbs* that 'opens the door to the Torah,' by providing us with a perspective on what the Torah is, how we are to understand its purpose, and how we can become improved and perfected by its teachings.

The Torah is a skilled pedagogue that cultivates and trains a person, the way a mother raises and nurtures her infant.

R' Hoshayah tells us that the Torah is *a skilled pedagogue* that cultivates and trains a person, the way a mother raises and nurtures her infant to independence and adulthood. In its simplest sense, this means that a careful study of the Torah can help us learn how to behave, not only in terms of obeying the commandments, but in the more mundane areas of life. The stories of the Patriarchs

---

The Overview is based on Ohr Gedaliahu, by Rabbi Gedaliah Schorr.

teach us faith, kindness, and honesty; those of Sodom, Esau, and Laban teach us the evil of depravity, cruelty, and dishonesty. The Sages find ethical, moral, and practical lessons throughout the Torah. And a lifelong immersion in the thought and dictates of the Torah develops one's character and thought processes, so that they are in consonance with the will and intellect of the Torah and its Giver.

A lifelong immersion in the thought and dictates of the Torah develops one's character and thought processes.

All people are influenced and molded by what they read and admire. Experienced teachers can easily identify the family orientation of children from their body language, inflections, and general behavior. People are what they think. And what forms their thinking is what they see, read, hear, and imitate. People are what their society admires and how the objects of that admiration behave. And they are what fashionable heroes present themselves as being. Those who strive to emulate the ideals of the Torah and its 'heroes' become different people than those who look to media heroes. It is in this sense that *Midrash Tanchuma* (*Noach*) describes Torah scholars as *b'nei Torah*, or 'children of Torah.' Since the Torah raises its students as a parent raises his children, they are truly its 'children' in a very meaningful sense.

Midrash Tanchuma describes Torah scholars as b'nei Torah, or 'children of Torah.'

Life Source

In a deeper sense, the Torah is the life source of every Jew. The Kabbalists teach that each letter in the Torah Scroll stands for an individual Jew, meaning that its holiness is the wellspring of that Jew's life. The Sages have taught that every letter of the Torah has within itself the power to bring the dead back to life, because Torah is the very source of life. Since this is so, it stands to reason that a Jew should engage in Torah study as much as he possibly can, because to do so brings him closer to and makes him more intimate with the source of his life. Again, one must decide what his ideals are and what he wishes to become. If one defines life as wealth, fashion, power, or any of the values that are so popular in modern life, then he will inevitably drift from the Torah, even if he pays lip service to its commandments. But should those be ultimate or even desirable goals? God's Torah is far more than a code of

If one defines life as wealth, fashion or power, then he will inevitably drift from the Torah.

behavior, it is a code of life. And this is why one who teaches Torah to another person's child is regarded as if he had given birth to him (*Sanhedrin* 19b). One who introduces someone to the source of all life is no less a parent than those who gave him biological existence.

Not only human beings, but the entire universe derives its continued existence from the Torah; as R' Hoshayah expressed it, God 'looked into the Torah and created the world.' It was the blueprint of Creation. The Torah existed before the universe, and God fashioned the world and its history to conform to the demands of the Torah. Because there are commandments regarding agriculture, the earth had to be hospitable to plow and seed; without crops, there could be no tithes for the priests and poor. Because there is a commandment to honor father and mother, children had to be born of parents whom they could honor; indeed, societies that take the nurturing role away from parents have crippled their children, and countries that suffer from the malaise of single-parent families have produced morally deformed children.

The Torah existed before the universe, and God fashioned the world and its history to conform to the demands of the Torah.

Purpose

In a sense, the universe is like a machine that was built for a specific purpose. Every part of its design was dictated by a particular need, and the machine is maintained only so long as its purpose remains valid. When the product it produces is discontinued, the machine is either discarded or dismantled and discarded. The universe was brought into existence as the means by which to carry out the Torah. Remove the Torah and there is no need for the universe.

Remove the Torah and there is no need for the universe.

It is in this light that we must understand the familiar teaching of the Sages that God told Israel how vital it was for them to accept the Torah at Sinai. 'If you agree to accept it — good. But if not, I will return the world to the primordial state of chaos and emptiness that existed before heaven and earth were created' (*Shabbos* 88a). Since the universe derives its claim to existence from its role as vehicle for Israel's performance of the commandments, the moment of decision when the Jewish people had to decide whether or not to accept the Torah was the verdict on the future of Creation. Psalm 136 contains twenty-six verses

the moment of decision was the verdict on the future of Creation.

enumerating God's kindness and greatness, and each verse concludes with the three words כִּי לְעוֹלָם חַסְדּוֹ, *for His kindness is forever*. As the Sages teach, these verses refer to the twenty-six generations from Creation until the Torah was given. During all that time, the world remained in existence thanks only to God's kindness. Once Israel received the Torah, however, Divine kindness was no longer necessary, because henceforth the 'soul' of the universe could be sustained through the performance of the Torah's commandments.

During all that time, the world remained in existence thanks only to God's kindness.

Torah Every-where

Judaism teaches that people must find God's will in every aspect of life. We do not accept the notion that religion is only one compartment of life, separate from any of the others. Religion is in the workplace as in the synagogue; at the table as in the study hall; in the field as at the altar. It is no less the province of the homemaker, laborer and financier than that of the saint, scholar, and priest. The rabbi has no more commandments than the porter. All are equal servants of God, beholden to perform the same commandments with the same scrupulousness.

The rabbi has no more commandments than the porter. All are equal servants of God.

It is natural, perhaps, for people to feel frustrated if their background, environment, or livelihood keeps them far from the electric adventure of intensive Torah study. Certainly it is true, as the Sages teach, that the foremost of all the commandments is Torah study, but this should neither frustrate nor excuse those who find that scholarship eludes them. To a young man who wept that his cares and responsibilities robbed him of the time to study, Reb Mendel of Kotzk replied, "How do you know that God intended you to study Torah in leisure? Perhaps you were meant *not* to have time, and to overcome that challenge by making use of the little bit of time that you can make for yourself."

"How do you know that God intended you to study Torah in leisure?"

Tree of Life

In a deeper sense, however, no one is divorced from the Torah. King Solomon said of it, עֵץ חַיִּים הִיא לַמַּחֲזִיקִים בָּהּ, *It is a tree of life for those who grasp it* (Proverbs 3:18). Whether one supports himself by the sturdy trunk of the tree or its flimsiest branch, it is the entire tree — growing from its roots, nurtured by the earth — that supports him. The insect on a leaf, the birds nesting on a branch, the slumberer on his hammock — all are supported by the entire tree, because if its roots were to be severed, the entire tree would die. Similarly, the Jew. In the kitchen, he observes the laws of *kashrus*. In the marketplace, the laws of honest dealing. On the farm, the laws of agriculture. Everywhere, the laws of sensitivity, kindness, charity, pure speech. The tree of life that is the Torah has 613 branches and countless twigs and leaves, all of them growing from the same roots. The very first of the dozens of books written by the *Chofetz Chaim* was a slim volume on the laws of weights and measures, which he composed because he noted that merchants of his home town were unaware of the basic laws of commerce. Are the laws of honest business dealings any less obligatory or holy than those of prayer and Temple offerings?

The tree of life that is the Torah has 613 branches and countless twigs and leaves, all of them growing from the same roots.

To the Jew, everything in the world is God's and everything is in the Torah. How can it be otherwise, if the Torah is the blueprint of Creation, the tree from which all emanates? Thus, there is no place for frustration in the life of the Jew, for if he conducts every area of his life according to the will of God, the entirety of the Torah supports him, and he in turn gives life to the universe.

There is no place for frustration in the life of the Jew, for he gives life to the universe.

With this to strengthen and inspire us, we turn the page to begin our study of God's blueprint and our Jewish destiny.

ספר בראשית

BEREISHIS/GENESIS

קְרִיאַת הַתּוֹרָה

The reader shows the *oleh* (person called to the Torah) the place in the Torah. The *oleh* touches the Torah with a corner of his *tallis,* or the belt or mantle of the Torah, and kisses it. He then begins the blessing, bowing at בָּרְכוּ, and straightening up at ה׳.

בָּרְכוּ אֶת יהוה הַמְבֹרָךְ.

Bless HASHEM, the blessed One.

Congregation, followed by *oleh,* responds, bowing at בָּרוּךְ, and straightening up at ה׳.

בָּרוּךְ יהוה הַמְבֹרָךְ לְעוֹלָם וָעֶד.

Blessed is HASHEM, the blessed One, for all eternity.

Oleh continues:

בָּרוּךְ אַתָּה יהוה אֱלֹהֵינוּ מֶלֶךְ הָעוֹלָם, אֲשֶׁר בָּחַר בָּנוּ מִכָּל הָעַמִּים, וְנָתַן לָנוּ אֶת תּוֹרָתוֹ. בָּרוּךְ אַתָּה יהוה, נוֹתֵן הַתּוֹרָה.
(אָמֵן.) —Cong.

בָּרוּךְ *Blessed are You, HASHEM, our God, King of the universe,* *Who selected us from all the peoples and gave us His Torah. Blessed are You, HASHEM, Giver of the Torah.*

(Cong.— *Amen.*)

After his Torah portion has been read, the *oleh* recites:

בָּרוּךְ אַתָּה יהוה אֱלֹהֵינוּ מֶלֶךְ הָעוֹלָם, אֲשֶׁר נָתַן לָנוּ תּוֹרַת אֱמֶת, וְחַיֵּי עוֹלָם נָטַע בְּתוֹכֵנוּ. בָּרוּךְ אַתָּה יהוה, נוֹתֵן הַתּוֹרָה.
(אָמֵן.) —Cong.

בָּרוּךְ *Blessed are You, HASHEM, our God, King of the universe,* *Who gave us the Torah of truth and implanted eternal life within us. Blessed are You, HASHEM, Giver of the Torah.*

(Cong.— *Amen.*)

פרשת בראשית

BEREISHIS

The Torah begins with the story of Creation, but this is not the purpose of the Book of Genesis, for even after reading how the world and its central character, man, came into existence, we still do not know the secret or even the process of Creation. Rather, as *Rashi* says, the Torah wants us to know that the world is God's and is His to apportion as He sees fit. What we do know is that man, as represented by Adam and Eve, had the mission of serving God and bringing Creation to the fulfillment of its purpose by carrying out God's commandment. They failed, and — in harbinger of Israel's later exiles after its own failures — were driven into exile.

The mission did not change, only the conditions in which it would be carried out. God punished them, but did not discard them. They could repent, because repentance preceded Creation; man could not survive without it. So it was with Cain and so it was with Lemech. Man sins, but he can come back, and God allows him the opportunity to do so.

All this is prelude to the story of Israel, because finally the failed mission of Adam and Noah was entrusted to Abraham and his offspring. This is why, according to *Ramban*, *Genesis* is called the Book of Creation: Creation is the story of the birth of Israel, and in this Book we will trace its story from the life of its first couple until their offspring develop from a family into a nation.

א א בְּרֵאשִׁית בָּרָא אֱלֹהִים אֵת הַשָּׁמַיִם וְאֵת הָאָרֶץ: בּ וְהָאָרֶץ הָיְתָה תֹהוּ וָבֹהוּ וְחֹשֶׁךְ עַל־פְּנֵי תְהוֹם וְרוּחַ אֱלֹהִים מְרַחֶפֶת עַל־פְּנֵי הַמָּיִם: ג וַיֹּאמֶר אֱלֹהִים יְהִי אוֹר וַיְהִי־אוֹר: ד וַיַּרְא אֱלֹהִים אֶת־הָאוֹר כִּי־טוֹב וַיַּבְדֵּל אֱלֹהִים בֵּין הָאוֹר וּבֵין הַחֹשֶׁךְ: ה וַיִּקְרָא אֱלֹהִים ׀ לָאוֹר יוֹם וְלַחֹשֶׁךְ קָרָא לָיְלָה וַיְהִי־עֶרֶב וַיְהִי־בֹקֶר יוֹם אֶחָד:

ו וַיֹּאמֶר אֱלֹהִים יְהִי רָקִיעַ בְּתוֹךְ הַמָּיִם וִיהִי מַבְדִּיל בֵּין מַיִם לָמָיִם: ז וַיַּעַשׂ אֱלֹהִים אֶת־הָרָקִיעַ וַיַּבְדֵּל בֵּין הַמַּיִם אֲשֶׁר מִתַּחַת לָרָקִיעַ וּבֵין הַמַּיִם אֲשֶׁר מֵעַל לָרָקִיעַ וַיְהִי־כֵן: ח וַיִּקְרָא אֱלֹהִים לָרָקִיעַ שָׁמָיִם וַיְהִי־עֶרֶב וַיְהִי־בֹקֶר יוֹם שֵׁנִי:

ט וַיֹּאמֶר אֱלֹהִים יִקָּווּ הַמַּיִם מִתַּחַת הַשָּׁמַיִם אֶל־מָקוֹם אֶחָד וְתֵרָאֶה הַיַּבָּשָׁה וַיְהִי־כֵן: י וַיִּקְרָא אֱלֹהִים ׀ לַיַּבָּשָׁה אֶרֶץ וּלְמִקְוֵה הַמַּיִם קָרָא יַמִּים וַיַּרְא אֱלֹהִים כִּי־טוֹב: יא וַיֹּאמֶר אֱלֹהִים תַּדְשֵׁא הָאָרֶץ דֶּשֶׁא עֵשֶׂב מַזְרִיעַ זֶרַע עֵץ פְּרִי עֹשֶׂה פְּרִי לְמִינוֹ אֲשֶׁר זַרְעוֹ־בוֹ עַל־הָאָרֶץ וַיְהִי־כֵן: יב וַתּוֹצֵא הָאָרֶץ דֶּשֶׁא עֵשֶׂב מַזְרִיעַ זֶרַע לְמִינֵהוּ וְעֵץ עֹשֶׂה־פְּרִי אֲשֶׁר זַרְעוֹ־בוֹ לְמִינֵהוּ וַיַּרְא אֱלֹהִים כִּי־טוֹב: יג וַיְהִי־עֶרֶב וַיְהִי־בֹקֶר יוֹם שְׁלִישִׁי: יד וַיֹּאמֶר אֱלֹהִים יְהִי מְאֹרֹת בִּרְקִיעַ הַשָּׁמַיִם

1/1. The verse does not describe the *sequence* of Creation; rather it declares that God alone is the Creator and Master of the universe. He gave the land to whom He pleased, and, according to His will, later took *Eretz Yisrael* from the Canaanites and gave it to Israel *(Rashi).*

According to *Ramban* and most other commentators, the verse begins with a general statement: *At the very first moment* (time itself being one of the objects of Creation) *God created* — from absolute nothing — *the heaven and the earth,* i.e., the upper matter and the lower matter, along with water and air — from which He fashioned the universe, as expounded in the following verses. This process reaches its ultimate meaning in the creation of Man — the prime goal of Creation.

The Torah begins with the narrative of Creation rather than with the Laws in order to establish this fundamental principal of belief.

אֱלֹהִים denotes God in His Attribute of Justice, מִדַּת הַדִּין, as Ruler, Director, Law-giver, and Judge of the world, while י־ה־ו־ה [read reverently as *'Adonoy'* and referred to in common usage as HASHEM (*The Name*)] denotes Him in His compassionate Attribute of Mercy, מִדַּת הָרַחֲמִים.

2. *Darkness* is not merely absence of light, but was a specific creation. This is clearly stated in *Isaiah* 45:7: יוֹצֵר אוֹר וּבוֹרֵא חֹשֶׁךְ, '*He who forms the light and creates darkness.'*

3. [Here begins a detailed chronology of Creation.]

5. 'God summoned the light and appointed it for duty by day, and He summoned the darkness and appointed it for duty by night' (*Pesachim* 2b).

וַיְהִי עֶרֶב וַיְהִי בֹקֶר — *And there was evening and there was morning.* The cycle of the day is complete.

Here Scripture uses the cardinal number אֶחָד, *one*, instead of the ordinal number רִאשׁוֹן, *first*, to indicate that on this day God was alone; the angels were not created until the second day (*Rashi*).

6. Second day. The heavens were created on the first day, but solidified only on the second day at this Divine command (*Rashi*).

9. Third day. God decrees boundaries for the water, making way for the development of land, vegetation, and ultimately man.

Until then the entire earth was submerged under water. Scarcely had God's words *'Let the waters be gathered'* been uttered, when mountains and hills appeared, and the waters collected in the deep-lying valleys. But the water threatened to overflow the earth until God forced it back into the sea, encircling the sea with sand (*Pirkei d'Rabbi Eliezer; Zohar*).

And let the dry land appear. This refers to the earth that was created on the first day, but which had been neither visible nor dry until the waters were commanded to assemble (*Rashbam*).

11. Organic life. *Herbage yielding seed,* i.e., it should grow its own seed within itself so that it may be planted somewhere else (*Rashi*). This refers to wheat and vegetables, which do not grow wild, but only as a result of seeding and tending (*Akeidas Yitzchak*).

14. Fourth day. The luminaries. יְהִי מְאֹרֹת — *Let there be luminaries.* — They had already been created on the first day, but were not suspended in the firmament

1 ¹ In the beginning of God's creating the heavens and the earth — ² when the earth was astonishingly empty, with darkness upon the surface of the deep, and the Divine Presence hovered upon the surface of the waters — ³ God said, 'Let there be light,' and there was light. ⁴ God saw that the light was good, and God separated between the light and the darkness. ⁵ God called to the light: 'Day,' and to the darkness He called: 'Night.' And there was evening and there was morning, one day.

⁶ God said, 'Let there be a firmament in the midst of the waters, and let it separate between water and water.' ⁷ So God made the firmament, and separated between the waters which were beneath the firmament and the waters which were above the firmament. And it was so. ⁸ God called to the firmament: 'Heaven.' And there was evening and there was morning, a second day.

⁹ God said, 'Let the waters beneath the heaven be gathered into one area, and let the dry land appear.' And it was so. ¹⁰ God called to the dry land: 'Earth,' and to the gathering of waters He called: 'Seas.' And God saw that it was good. ¹¹ God said, 'Let the earth sprout vegetation: herbage yielding seed, fruit trees yielding fruit each after its kind, containing its own seed on the earth.' And it was so. ¹² And the earth brought forth vegetation: herbage yielding seed after its kind, and trees yielding fruit, each containing its seed after its kind. And God saw that it was good. ¹³ And there was evening and there was morning, a third day.

¹⁴ God said, 'Let there be luminaries in the firmament of the heaven to separate between

לְהַבְדִּיל בֵּין הַיּוֹם וּבֵין הַלַּיְלָה וְהָיוּ לְאֹתֹת
וּלְמוֹעֲדִים וּלְיָמִים וְשָׁנִים: טו וְהָיוּ לִמְאוֹרֹת
בִּרְקִיעַ הַשָּׁמַיִם לְהָאִיר עַל־הָאָרֶץ וַיְהִי־כֵן:
טז וַיַּעַשׂ אֱלֹהִים אֶת־שְׁנֵי הַמְּאֹרֹת הַגְּדֹלִים
אֶת־הַמָּאוֹר הַגָּדֹל לְמֶמְשֶׁלֶת הַיּוֹם וְאֶת־
הַמָּאוֹר הַקָּטֹן לְמֶמְשֶׁלֶת הַלַּיְלָה וְאֵת
הַכּוֹכָבִים: יז וַיִּתֵּן אֹתָם אֱלֹהִים בִּרְקִיעַ
הַשָּׁמָיִם לְהָאִיר עַל־הָאָרֶץ: יח וְלִמְשֹׁל בַּיּוֹם
וּבַלַּיְלָה וּלְהַבְדִּיל בֵּין הָאוֹר וּבֵין הַחֹשֶׁךְ וַיַּרְא
אֱלֹהִים כִּי־טוֹב: יט וַיְהִי־עֶרֶב וַיְהִי־בֹקֶר יוֹם
רְבִיעִי:

כ וַיֹּאמֶר אֱלֹהִים יִשְׁרְצוּ הַמַּיִם שֶׁרֶץ נֶפֶשׁ חַיָּה
וְעוֹף יְעוֹפֵף עַל־הָאָרֶץ עַל־פְּנֵי רְקִיעַ הַשָּׁמָיִם:
כא וַיִּבְרָא אֱלֹהִים אֶת־הַתַּנִּינִם הַגְּדֹלִים וְאֵת
כָּל־נֶפֶשׁ הַחַיָּה ׀ הָרֹמֶשֶׂת אֲשֶׁר שָׁרְצוּ הַמַּיִם
לְמִינֵהֶם וְאֵת כָּל־עוֹף כָּנָף לְמִינֵהוּ וַיַּרְא
אֱלֹהִים כִּי־טוֹב: כב וַיְבָרֶךְ אֹתָם אֱלֹהִים
לֵאמֹר פְּרוּ וּרְבוּ וּמִלְאוּ אֶת־הַמַּיִם בַּיַּמִּים
וְהָעוֹף יִרֶב בָּאָרֶץ: כג וַיְהִי־עֶרֶב וַיְהִי־בֹקֶר יוֹם
חֲמִישִׁי:

כד וַיֹּאמֶר אֱלֹהִים תּוֹצֵא הָאָרֶץ נֶפֶשׁ חַיָּה
לְמִינָהּ בְּהֵמָה וָרֶמֶשׂ וְחַיְתוֹ־אֶרֶץ לְמִינָהּ
וַיְהִי־כֵן: כה וַיַּעַשׂ אֱלֹהִים אֶת־חַיַּת הָאָרֶץ
לְמִינָהּ וְאֶת־הַבְּהֵמָה לְמִינָהּ וְאֵת כָּל־
רֶמֶשׂ הָאֲדָמָה לְמִינֵהוּ וַיַּרְא אֱלֹהִים כִּי־טוֹב:

until the fourth day (*Chagigah* 12a). Indeed, all the potentials of heaven and earth were created on the first day but each was set in place on the day when it was so commanded (*Rashi*).

And they shall serve as signs, i.e., as omens, for when the luminaries are eclipsed, it is an ill omen for the world (*Rashi*).

16. The following verse proceeds to describe in detail how God caused each of them to shine according to its allotted time (*Radak*).

'Great' does not refer to their size, for the stars are larger than the moon. The intent, rather, is 'great' in the visible intensity of their illumination, the moon's light being stronger than that of the stars, because it is closer to the earth (*Radak; Malbim*).

18. The functions of the two luminaries are now defined. Their dominion consists of causing a distinction between the darkness and the light. The greater luminary will dominate by day and its light will be everywhere even in places where [the *direct* rays of] the sun do not reach. The smaller luminary will dominate by night — although it will do no more than relieve the darkness (*Ramban*).

20-22. Fifth day. Marine life and birds.

21. *The great sea-giants* — i.e., the gigantic fish in the sea (*Rashi*).

Abarbanel notes that this is the first time since the first day that *'created'* is used. It denotes . . . *'the living souls'* — unprecedented until then.

22. *God blessed them.* Rashi notes that they needed a special blessing because so many are reduced, hunted down, and eaten. The other animals, too, needed such a blessing, but they did not receive it so as not to include the serpent, which was destined to be cursed.

פְּרוּ וּרְבוּ — *Be fruitful and multiply.* Had the verse not added וּרְבוּ, *and multiply,* each creature would bring forth only one more — '*multiply*' implies multiple births: One should bring forth many (Rashi).

Ibn Ezra renders '*Be fruitful and multiply*' not as a command, because the power to do so was not their own, but as a Divine blessing and endowment: '*You will be fruitful and multiply.*'

24. Sixth day. Animals and man. תּוֹצֵא, *bring forth,* implies a concealed, dormant presence being transformed into existence (*Ahavas Yonasan*); for as explained earlier the potential for everything was created on the first day; it was necessary only to *bring them forth* (Rashi).

נֶפֶשׁ חַיָּה — *Living creatures.* I.e., 'Free-living, breathing beings, yielding their own species . . . The term could also include any living thing not specifically mentioned thereafter, as, for example, germs' (*R' Munk*).

25. וַיַּעַשׂ אֱלֹהִים — *God made:* i.e., he shaped them with their full volition and full-grown stature (*Chullin* 60b; *Rashi*).

the day and the night; and they shall serve as signs, and for festivals, and for days and years; [15] and they shall serve as luminaries in the firmament of the heaven to shine upon the earth.' And it was so. [16] And God made the two great luminaries, the greater luminary to dominate the day and the lesser luminary to dominate the night; and the stars. [17] And God set them in the firmament of the heaven to give light upon the earth, [18] to dominate by day and by night, and to separate between the light and between the darkness. And God saw that it was good. [19] And there was evening and there was morning, a fourth day.

[20] God said, 'Let the waters teem with creeping living creatures, and fowl that fly about over the earth across the expanse of the heavens.' [21] And God created the great sea-giants and every living being that creeps, with which the waters teemed after their kinds; and all winged fowl of every kind. And God saw that it was good. [22] God blessed them, saying, 'Be fruitful and multiply, and fill the waters in the seas; but the fowl shall increase on the earth.' [23] And there was evening and there was morning, a fifth day.

[24] God said, 'Let the earth bring forth living creatures according to their kind: cattle, and creeping things, and beasts of the land according to their kind.' And it was so. [25] God made the beast of the earth after its own kind, and the cattle after its own kind, and every creeping being of the ground after their kind. And God saw that it was good.

כו וַיֹּאמֶר אֱלֹהִים נַעֲשֶׂה אָדָם בְּצַלְמֵנוּ כִּדְמוּתֵנוּ וְיִרְדּוּ בִדְגַת הַיָּם וּבְעוֹף הַשָּׁמַיִם וּבַבְּהֵמָה וּבְכָל־הָאָרֶץ וּבְכָל־הָרֶמֶשׂ הָרֹמֵשׂ עַל־הָאָרֶץ: כז וַיִּבְרָא אֱלֹהִים ׀ אֶת־הָאָדָם בְּצַלְמוֹ בְּצֶלֶם אֱלֹהִים בָּרָא אֹתוֹ זָכָר וּנְקֵבָה בָּרָא אֹתָם: כח וַיְבָרֶךְ אֹתָם אֱלֹהִים וַיֹּאמֶר לָהֶם אֱלֹהִים פְּרוּ וּרְבוּ וּמִלְאוּ אֶת־הָאָרֶץ וְכִבְשֻׁהָ וּרְדוּ בִּדְגַת הַיָּם וּבְעוֹף הַשָּׁמַיִם וּבְכָל־חַיָּה הָרֹמֶשֶׂת עַל־הָאָרֶץ: כט וַיֹּאמֶר אֱלֹהִים הִנֵּה נָתַתִּי לָכֶם אֶת־כָּל־עֵשֶׂב ׀ זֹרֵעַ זֶרַע אֲשֶׁר עַל־פְּנֵי כָל־הָאָרֶץ וְאֶת־כָּל־הָעֵץ אֲשֶׁר־בּוֹ פְרִי־עֵץ זֹרֵעַ זָרַע לָכֶם יִהְיֶה לְאָכְלָה: ל וּלְכָל־חַיַּת הָאָרֶץ וּלְכָל־עוֹף הַשָּׁמַיִם וּלְכֹל ׀ רוֹמֵשׂ עַל־הָאָרֶץ אֲשֶׁר־בּוֹ נֶפֶשׁ חַיָּה אֶת־כָּל־יֶרֶק עֵשֶׂב לְאָכְלָה וַיְהִי־כֵן: לא וַיַּרְא אֱלֹהִים אֶת־כָּל־אֲשֶׁר עָשָׂה וְהִנֵּה־טוֹב מְאֹד וַיְהִי־עֶרֶב וַיְהִי־בֹקֶר יוֹם הַשִּׁשִּׁי: ב א וַיְכֻלּוּ הַשָּׁמַיִם וְהָאָרֶץ וְכָל־צְבָאָם: ב וַיְכַל אֱלֹהִים בַּיּוֹם הַשְּׁבִיעִי מְלַאכְתּוֹ אֲשֶׁר עָשָׂה וַיִּשְׁבֹּת בַּיּוֹם הַשְּׁבִיעִי מִכָּל־מְלַאכְתּוֹ אֲשֶׁר עָשָׂה: ג וַיְבָרֶךְ אֱלֹהִים אֶת־יוֹם הַשְּׁבִיעִי וַיְקַדֵּשׁ אֹתוֹ כִּי בוֹ שָׁבַת מִכָּל־מְלַאכְתּוֹ אֲשֶׁר־בָּרָא אֱלֹהִים לַעֲשׂוֹת: שני ד אֵלֶּה תוֹלְדוֹת הַשָּׁמַיִם וְהָאָרֶץ בְּהִבָּרְאָם בְּיוֹם עֲשׂוֹת יְהֹוָה אֱלֹהִים אֶרֶץ וְשָׁמָיִם:

26. נַעֲשֶׂה אָדָם — *Let us make man.* This preamble indicates that man was created with great deliberation and wisdom. God did not say, 'Let the earth bring forth,' as He did with other creatures; instead He attributed it to the deepest involvement of Divine Providence and wisdom (*Abarbanel*).

Targum Yonasan paraphrases: 'And God said to the ministering angels who had been created on the second day of Creation of the world, "Let us make man." '

When Moses wrote the Torah and came to this verse (*let 'us' make*), he said: 'Sovereign of the Universe! Why do You thus furnish an excuse to heretics for maintaining that there is a plurality of divinities, ח"ו?' 'Write!' God replied. 'Whoever wishes to err will err . . . Let them rather learn from their Creator who created all, yet when He came to create man He took counsel with the ministering angels' (*Midrash*).

בְּצַלְמֵנוּ — *In Our image.* In Our mold (*Rashi*) — the mold which We prepared for man — it being impossible to say that God has a 'mold' (*Sifsei Chachamim*).

כִּדְמוּתֵנוּ — *After Our likeness.* With the power of understanding and intellect (*Rashi*).

27. וַיִּבְרָא אֱלֹהִים — *So God created.* Everything else was created by a creative utterance, while man was created by [His] hands.

28. *God blessed them . . . and said . . . 'Be fruitful . . .'* *Rashi* on 8:7 comments that the phrase in our verse is a Divine *blessing*, but there it is a *command* [*Kesubos* 5a].

29-30. Most commentators group these verses together,

'it shall be yours for food and to every beast of the earth . . .' indicating that man and beast shared the same herbal diet. Man was forbidden to kill animals for food, this being permitted only after the Flood [cf. 9:3 and *Sanhedrin* 59b].

31. וְהִנֵּה טוֹב מְאֹד — *And behold it was very good.* Everything was fit for its purpose and able to act accordingly (*Rambam*).

יוֹם הַשִּׁשִּׁי — *The sixth day.* The definite article ה, *the*, before the word שִׁשִּׁי, sixth, designates that day that is distinguished among the other days of Creation as the day on which His work was completed (*Chizkuni*).

2/1. The seventh day. Sabbath. With the end of the sixth day, the heavens and earth stand before us in their final intended state in harmonious perfection.

2. *By the seventh day God completed.* God completed His work at the moment that marked the inception of the seventh day, but yet was not part of it, as the Sages commented: נִכְנַס בּוֹ כְּחוּט הַשַּׂעֲרָה, He entered into it by a hair's breadth.

3. *'Blessing'* refers to abundant [spiritual] goodness, for on Sabbath there is a renewal of physical procreative strength, and there is a greater capacity to reason and exercise the intellect. *He hallowed it* by having no work done on it as on the other days (*Ibn Ezra*).

Although God created everything in six days, it was only at the onset of the seventh day, which He blessed, that they began functioning naturally, thus attaining the goal for which they were created (*Akeidas Yitzchak*).

To make — i.e., to be self-reproductive, each according to its species (*Radak*).

²⁶ And God said, 'Let us make man in Our image, after Our likeness. They shall rule over the fish of the sea, the birds of the sky, and over the cattle, the whole earth, and every creeping thing that creeps upon the earth.' ²⁷ So God created man in His image, in the image of God He created him; male and female He created them.

²⁸ God blessed them and God said to them, 'Be fruitful and multiply, fill the earth and subdue it; and rule over the fish of the sea, the bird of the sky, and every living thing that moves on earth.'

²⁹ God said, 'Behold, I have given to you all herbage yielding seed that is upon the entire earth, and every tree that has seed-yielding fruit; it shall be yours for food. ³⁰ And to every beast of the earth, to every bird of the sky, and to everything that moves on earth, within which there is a living soul, every green herb is for food.' And it was so. ³¹ And God saw all that He had made, and behold it was very good. And there was evening and there was morning, the sixth day.

2 ¹ Thus the heaven and the earth were finished, and all their array. ² By the seventh day God completed His work which He had done, and He abstained on the seventh day from all His work which He had done. ³ God blessed the seventh day and hallowed it because on it He abstained from all His work which God created to make.

⁴ These are the products of the heaven and the earth when they were created in the day that HASHEM God made earth and heaven —

הּ וְכֹל ׀ שִׂיחַ הַשָּׂדֶה טֶרֶם יִהְיֶה בָאָרֶץ וְכָל־עֵשֶׂב הַשָּׂדֶה טֶרֶם יִצְמָח כִּי לֹא הִמְטִיר יהוה אֱלֹהִים עַל־הָאָרֶץ וְאָדָם אַיִן לַעֲבֹד אֶת־הָאֲדָמָה: וּ וְאֵד יַעֲלֶה מִן־הָאָרֶץ וְהִשְׁקָה אֶת־כָּל־פְּנֵי־הָאֲדָמָה: זּ וַיִּיצֶר יהוה אֱלֹהִים אֶת־הָאָדָם עָפָר מִן־הָאֲדָמָה וַיִּפַּח בְּאַפָּיו נִשְׁמַת חַיִּים וַיְהִי הָאָדָם לְנֶפֶשׁ חַיָּה: חּ וַיִּטַּע יהוה אֱלֹהִים גַּן בְּעֵדֶן מִקֶּדֶם וַיָּשֶׂם שָׁם אֶת־הָאָדָם אֲשֶׁר יָצָר: טּ וַיַּצְמַח יהוה אֱלֹהִים מִן־הָאֲדָמָה כָּל־עֵץ נֶחְמָד לְמַרְאֶה וְטוֹב לְמַאֲכָל וְעֵץ הַחַיִּים בְּתוֹךְ הַגָּן וְעֵץ הַדַּעַת טוֹב וָרָע: יּ וְנָהָר יֹצֵא מֵעֵדֶן לְהַשְׁקוֹת אֶת־הַגָּן וּמִשָּׁם יִפָּרֵד וְהָיָה לְאַרְבָּעָה רָאשִׁים: יא שֵׁם הָאֶחָד פִּישׁוֹן הוּא הַסֹּבֵב אֵת כָּל־אֶרֶץ הַחֲוִילָה אֲשֶׁר־שָׁם הַזָּהָב: יב וּזֲהַב הָאָרֶץ הַהִוא טוֹב שָׁם הַבְּדֹלַח וְאֶבֶן הַשֹּׁהַם: יג וְשֵׁם־הַנָּהָר הַשֵּׁנִי גִּיחוֹן הוּא הַסּוֹבֵב אֵת כָּל־אֶרֶץ כּוּשׁ: יד וְשֵׁם הַנָּהָר הַשְּׁלִישִׁי חִדֶּקֶל הוּא הַהֹלֵךְ קִדְמַת אַשּׁוּר וְהַנָּהָר הָרְבִיעִי הוּא פְרָת: טו וַיִּקַּח יהוה אֱלֹהִים אֶת־הָאָדָם וַיַּנִּחֵהוּ בְגַן־עֵדֶן לְעָבְדָהּ וּלְשָׁמְרָהּ: טז וַיְצַו יהוה אֱלֹהִים עַל־הָאָדָם לֵאמֹר מִכֹּל עֵץ־הַגָּן אָכֹל תֹּאכֵל: יז וּמֵעֵץ הַדַּעַת טוֹב וָרָע לֹא תֹאכַל מִמֶּנּוּ כִּי בְּיוֹם אֲכָלְךָ מִמֶּנּוּ מוֹת תָּמוּת: יח וַיֹּאמֶר יהוה אֱלֹהִים לֹא־טוֹב הֱיוֹת הָאָדָם

5. Since these verses lead to the incident of the Tree of Life and Tree of Knowledge, the narrative begins by describing how plant life came about (*Radak*).

For HASHEM God had not sent rain upon the earth. He had not sent rain because 'there was no man to till the soil,' and no one to recognize the utility of rain. But when man was created he recognized its importance for the world. He prayed, and rain fell, causing the trees and vegetation to spring forth (*Rashi*).

6-7. These verses describe the preliminary steps of man's creation: God caused the deep to rise, filling the clouds with water to moisten the dust, and man was created. It is similar to a kneader who first pours in water and then kneads the dough. Here, too: First, 'He watered the soil,' and then 'He formed man' (*Rashi*).

7. To make man, God used earth from all corners of the globe. This further distinguished man from animal, since it enabled him to adjust to any climate, from extreme heat to extreme cold (*Haamek Davar*).

And He blew into his nostrils the soul of life. God thus made man out of both lower [earthly] and upper [heavenly] matter: his body from the dust and his soul from the spirit (*Rashi*).

8. The Garden of Eden. God formed man outside the Garden so he saw the world of thorns and thistles. Only then did God lead him into the Garden (*Chizkuni*).

8-14. The following parenthetic verses describe in detail the Garden, which was created especially for man. This narrative is resumed in verse 15 (*Or HaChaim*).

9. The knowledge of good and bad refers to man's ability to choose the sweet even when it is harmful and reject the bitter even when it is beneficial (*Sforno*).

11. Most commentators identify *Pishon* with the Nile. *Abarbanel* comments that the Greeks identify Pishon with the River Ganges, and that Chavilah is a section of India which the Ganges surrounds, and in which there is gold.

12. *B'dolach. Rashi* to *Num.* 1:7 translates 'crystal.' According to *R' Saadiah Gaon, Ibn Ezra* and *Radak,* however, it means 'pearl.'

הַשֹּׁהַם וְאֶבֶן — *And the shoham stone.* Translations vary from *beryl* (*Targum*), to *onyx,* and *lapis lazuli.*

14. *Chidekel.* This is traditionally identified with the Tigris (*Aruch; Abarbanel*).

The Euphrates. Rashi comments that this is the most important of the four rivers on account of its connection to *Eretz Yisrael,* of which it was to be the ideal boundary, as in 15:18.

15. Man in the Garden. The narrative resumes where it left off at the end of verse 8: the details of man's entry into the Garden of Eden (*Radak; Meyuchas*).

16. The Tree of Life is not mentioned because, had man not sinned, he would have lived forever regardless, and the question of his partaking of the Tree of Life was academic (*Minchah Belulah*).

17. *For on the day you eat of it.* On that day the evil impulses of jealousy, lust, and honor will be aroused, making it impossible for you to attain the goal of spirituality on earth. Thus, eternal life will be an intolerable burden for you (*Malbim*).

⁵ Now no tree of the field was yet on the earth and no herb of the field had yet sprouted, for HASHEM God had not sent rain upon the earth and there was no man to work the soil.

⁶ A mist ascended from the earth and watered the whole surface of the soil, ⁷ and HASHEM God formed the man of dust from the ground, and He blew into his nostrils the soul of life; and man became a living being.

⁸ HASHEM God planted a garden in Eden, to the east, and placed there the man whom He had formed. ⁹ And HASHEM God caused to grow from the ground every tree that was pleasing to the sight and good for food; also the Tree of Life in the midst of the garden, and the Tree of Knowledge of Good and Bad.

¹⁰ A river issues forth from Eden to water the garden, and from there it is divided and becomes four headwaters. ¹¹ The name of the first is Pishon, the one that encircles the whole land of Chavilah, where the gold is. ¹² The gold of that land is good; b'dolach is there, and the shoham stone. ¹³ The name of the second river is Gichon, the one that encircles the whole land of Cush. ¹⁴ The name of the third river is Chidekel, the one that flows toward the east of Ashur; and the fourth river is the Euphrates.

¹⁵ HASHEM God took the man and placed him in the Garden of Eden, to work it and to guard it. ¹⁶ And HASHEM God commanded the man, saying, 'Of every tree of the garden you may freely eat; ¹⁷ but of the Tree of Knowledge of Good and Bad, you must not eat thereof; for on the day you eat of it, you shall surely die.'

¹⁸ HASHEM God said, 'It is not good that man be

לְבַדּֽוֹ אֶעֱשֶׂהּ־לּֽוֹ עֵזֶר כְּנֶגְדּֽוֹ: יט וַיִּ֫צֶר יְהֹוָ֫ה
אֱלֹהִים מִן־הָֽאֲדָמָה כָּל־חַיַּ֣ת הַשָּׂדֶה וְאֵת
כָּל־עוֹף הַשָּׁמַיִם וַיָּבֵא אֶל־הָֽאָדָם לִרְא֣וֹת
מַה־יִּקְרָא־לֽוֹ וְכֹל אֲשֶׁר יִקְרָא־לֽוֹ הָֽאָדָם
נֶפֶשׁ חַיָּה ה֣וּא שְׁמֽוֹ: *שלישי* כ וַיִּקְרָא הָֽאָדָם
שֵׁמוֹת לְכָל־הַבְּהֵמָה וּלְעוֹף הַשָּׁמַיִם וּלְכֹל
חַיַּ֣ת הַשָּׂדֶה וּלְאָדָם לֹא־מָצָא עֵזֶר כְּנֶגְדּֽוֹ:
כא וַיַּפֵּל יְהֹוָ֫ה אֱלֹהִים | תַּרְדֵּמָה עַל־הָֽאָדָם
וַיִּישָׁן וַיִּקַּח אַחַת מִצַּלְעֹתָיו וַיִּסְגֹּר בָּשָׂר
תַּחְתֶּֽנָּה: כב וַיִּ֫בֶן יְהֹוָה אֱלֹהִים | אֶת־
הַצֵּלָע אֲשֶׁר־לָקַח מִן־הָֽאָדָם לְאִשָּׁה וַיְבִאֶ֫הָ
אֶל־הָֽאָדָם: כג וַיֹּאמֶר הָֽאָדָם זֹאת הַפַּעַם
עֶצֶם מֵֽעֲצָמַי וּבָשָׂר מִבְּשָׂרִי לְזֹאת יִקָּרֵא
אִשָּׁה כִּי מֵאִישׁ לֻֽקֳחָה־זֹּֽאת: כד עַל־כֵּן
יַֽעֲזָב־אִישׁ אֶת־אָבִיו וְאֶת־אִמּֽוֹ וְדָבַק
בְּאִשְׁתּֽוֹ וְהָי֥וּ לְבָשָׂר אֶחָֽד: כה וַיִּֽהְי֤וּ שְׁנֵיהֶם
עֲרוּמִּים הָֽאָדָם וְאִשְׁתּֽוֹ וְלֹא יִתְבֹּשָֽׁשׁוּ:
ג א וְהַנָּחָשׁ הָיָה עָרוּם מִכֹּל חַיַּ֣ת הַשָּׂדֶה
אֲשֶׁר עָשָׂה יְהֹוָה אֱלֹהִים וַיֹּאמֶר אֶל־הָֽאִשָּׁה
אַף כִּֽי־אָמַר אֱלֹהִים לֹא תֹֽאכְלוּ מִכֹּל עֵץ
הַגָּן: ב וַתֹּאמֶר הָֽאִשָּׁה אֶל־הַנָּחָשׁ מִפְּרִי עֵץ־
הַגָּן נֹאכֵֽל: ג וּמִפְּרִי הָעֵץ אֲשֶׁר בְּתוֹךְ־הַגָּן
אָמַר אֱלֹהִים לֹא תֹֽאכְלוּ מִמֶּנּוּ וְלֹא תִגְּעוּ
בּֽוֹ פֶּן תְּמֻתֽוּן: ד וַיֹּאמֶר הַנָּחָשׁ אֶל־הָֽאִשָּׁה
לֹֽא־מוֹת תְּמֻתֽוּן: ה כִּי יֹדֵעַ אֱלֹהִים כִּי בְּיוֹם

18. *A helper corresponding
to him.* If man is worthy,
the woman will be 'a
helper'; if he proves to be
unworthy, she shall be
'against him' (*Yevamos* 63a;
Rashi).

19. This verse does not describe a new creation. *Rashi*
notes that the formation
spoken of here elaborates
upon the making of the animals already referred to in
1:25.

20. *The man* — endowed
by God with superior intellect, he perceived the nature
of each creature and named
it accordingly (*Radak*).

Man found animals which
would be helpful and ser-
viceable to him. They could
qualify as עֵזֶר, *help*. What
he could not find among all
the creatures that passed
before him was the כְּנֶגְדּֽוֹ,
one that would *correspond
to him* socially and intellec-
tually (*Chizkuni; Ibn Latif*).

22. Unlike man's, the basis
of woman's body was not
taken from the earth. God
built one side of man into
woman — so that the single
human being became two.
Thereby, the complete
equality of man and woman
was irrefutably demon-
strated (*R' Hirsch*).

24. The parenthetical verse
does not mean that man
should not continue to
serve or honor his parents.
It implies only a *physical*
separation; that man's at-
tachment to his wife should
be so strong that he should
move out of his parents'
house and establish a new
home with his wife (*Radak;
R' Meyuchas*).

And they shall become one flesh. Let him cling to his wife and to none other, because man and his wife are in reality one flesh as they were at the beginning of Creation (*Tur*).

. . . But that can take place only if they also become one mind, one heart, one soul . . . and if they subordinate all their strength and effort to the service of a Higher Will (*R' Hirsch*).

3/1. The serpent. The Torah does not say how much time elapsed between the creation of woman and their placement in the Garden of Eden, and their sin and expulsion. The Sages, however, tell us explicitly that *all the events related here* — including the birth of Cain and Abel — occurred on the very first day of Adam's creation.

The consensus of the commentators is that it was literally a serpent. They differ regarding what force it represented: the Evil Inclination; the Satan; or some other counterforce. According to the Midrash, before this cunning beast was cursed, it stood erect and was endowed with some faculty of communication.

3. *Nor touch it.* She added to the prohibition [which did *not* include touching], and as a result diminished from it (*Rashi*).

4. The serpent pushed her against the tree and said: 'Just as you did not die from touching it, so you will not die from eating it!' (*Midrash; Rashi*).

alone; I will make him a helper corresponding to him.' ¹⁹ Now, HASHEM God had formed out of the ground every beast of the field and every bird of the sky, and brought them to the man to see what he would call each one; and whatever man called each living creature, that remained its name. ²⁰ And the man assigned names to all the cattle and to the birds of the sky and to every beast of the field; but as for man, he did not find a helper corresponding to him.

²¹ So HASHEM God cast a deep sleep upon the man and he slept; and He took one of his sides and He filled in flesh in its place. ²² Then HASHEM God fashioned the side that He had taken from the man into a woman, and He brought her to the man. ²³ And the man said, 'This time it is bone of my bones and flesh of my flesh. This shall be called Woman, for from man was she taken.' — ²⁴ Therefore a man shall leave his father and his mother and cling to his wife and they shall become one flesh. —

²⁵ They were both naked, the man and his wife, and they were not ashamed.

3 ¹ Now the serpent was cunning beyond any beast of the field that HASHEM God had made. He said to the woman, 'Did, perhaps, God say: You shall not eat of any tree of the garden?'

² The woman said to the serpent, 'Of the fruit of any tree of the garden we may eat. ³ Of the fruit of the tree which is in the center of the garden God had said: You shall neither eat of it nor touch it, lest you die.'

⁴ The serpent said to the woman, 'You will not surely die; ⁵ for God knows that on the day

אֲכָלְכֶם מִמֶּנּוּ וְנִפְקְחוּ עֵינֵיכֶם וִהְיִיתֶם
כֵּאלֹהִים יֹדְעֵי טוֹב וָרָע: וַתֵּרֶא הָאִשָּׁה כִּי
טוֹב הָעֵץ לְמַאֲכָל וְכִי תַאֲוָה־הוּא לָעֵינַיִם
וְנֶחְמָד הָעֵץ לְהַשְׂכִּיל וַתִּקַּח מִפִּרְיוֹ וַתֹּאכַל
וַתִּתֵּן גַּם־לְאִישָׁהּ עִמָּהּ וַיֹּאכַל: וַתִּפָּקַחְנָה
עֵינֵי שְׁנֵיהֶם וַיֵּדְעוּ כִּי עֵירֻמִּם הֵם וַיִּתְפְּרוּ
עֲלֵה תְאֵנָה וַיַּעֲשׂוּ לָהֶם חֲגֹרֹת: וַיִּשְׁמְעוּ
אֶת־קוֹל יְהֹוָה אֱלֹהִים מִתְהַלֵּךְ בַּגָּן לְרוּחַ
הַיּוֹם וַיִּתְחַבֵּא הָאָדָם וְאִשְׁתּוֹ מִפְּנֵי יְהֹוָה
אֱלֹהִים בְּתוֹךְ עֵץ הַגָּן: וַיִּקְרָא יְהֹוָה אֱלֹהִים
אֶל־הָאָדָם וַיֹּאמֶר לוֹ אַיֶּכָּה: וַיֹּאמֶר אֶת־
קֹלְךָ שָׁמַעְתִּי בַּגָּן וָאִירָא כִּי־עֵירֹם אָנֹכִי
וָאֵחָבֵא: וַיֹּאמֶר מִי הִגִּיד לְךָ כִּי עֵירֹם
אָתָּה הֲמִן־הָעֵץ אֲשֶׁר צִוִּיתִיךָ לְבִלְתִּי אֲכָל־
מִמֶּנּוּ אָכָלְתָּ: וַיֹּאמֶר הָאָדָם הָאִשָּׁה
אֲשֶׁר נָתַתָּה עִמָּדִי הִוא נָתְנָה־לִּי מִן־
הָעֵץ וָאֹכֵל: וַיֹּאמֶר יְהֹוָה אֱלֹהִים לָאִשָּׁה
מַה־זֹּאת עָשִׂית וַתֹּאמֶר הָאִשָּׁה הַנָּחָשׁ
הִשִּׁיאַנִי וָאֹכֵל: וַיֹּאמֶר יְהֹוָה אֱלֹהִים ׀
אֶל־הַנָּחָשׁ כִּי עָשִׂיתָ זֹּאת אָרוּר אַתָּה
מִכָּל־הַבְּהֵמָה וּמִכֹּל חַיַּת הַשָּׂדֶה עַל־גְּחֹנְךָ
תֵלֵךְ וְעָפָר תֹּאכַל כָּל־יְמֵי חַיֶּיךָ: וְאֵיבָה ׀
אָשִׁית בֵּינְךָ וּבֵין הָאִשָּׁה וּבֵין זַרְעֲךָ וּבֵין
זַרְעָהּ הוּא יְשׁוּפְךָ רֹאשׁ וְאַתָּה תְּשׁוּפֶנּוּ
עָקֵב: אֶל־הָאִשָּׁה אָמַר הַרְבָּה

5. 'God did not prohibit this tree out of any concern for your death, but because He is aware that by eating from it you will attain extra wisdom, and become omniscient like Him.'

6. The tempter did not tell the woman to eat the fruit, but he had enveloped her in his spell. She looked on the tree with a new longing — it was good to eat, a delight to the eyes, and it would give her wisdom.

To her husband with her. She then brought it to Adam and repeated everything the serpent had told her. He was עִמָּהּ, *at one with her,* and not blameless (i.e., he was not hopelessly tempted or unreasonably deceived) and therefore liable to punishment (*Radak; Ibn Ezra*).

7. The serpent was right: they had become enlightened people. But their first realization was — that they were naked! . . . Man need not be ashamed of his body as long as it stands in the service of God . . . Otherwise he feels shame in his nakedness. This shame awakens the voice of conscience that reminds us we are not meant to be animals (*R' Hirsch*).

8. God caused His sound to be heard to afford them the opportunity of hiding (*Radak*) and also to teach etiquette: Do not look upon a man in his disgrace. God did not appear to them immediately after they sinned and felt ashamed; he waited until they had sewn figleaves together and only then did they hear *'the sound of HASHEM God.'* It also teaches that one should never enter another's home suddenly and unannounced (*Derech Eretz Rabbah* 5).

9. אַיֶּכָּה — *Where are you?* God knew where he was, but the question was merely a means of initiating a dialogue with him so he would not be terrified to repent [or: to reply], as he would be if God were suddenly to punish him. But Adam did not confess. Instead, as verse 12 shows, he hurled against God the very kindness of the gift of Eve, by implying that God was at fault for giving him that woman (*Midrash Aggadah*).

13. Since the commandment had been given only to Adam, why was Eve punished? *Ramban* explains that Eve had been included in the prohibition since she was part of him — 'bone of his bones.' Additionally, her punishment for misleading Adam and causing him to sin was greater than for her eating.

14. אֶל הַנָּחָשׁ — *To the serpent.* [I.e., regarding the serpent.] As the instigator of it, he was cursed first; then Eve, and finally Adam (*Chizkuni*).

Actually, snakes do not eat earth, but feed on living creatures. The *'eating of dust'* may be a figurative picture of creeping about on its belly, similar to *Psalms* 72:9. Or, possibly, snakes, whose tongues seem ill adapted for tasting, lack the sense of taste altogether. They eat to satisfy their hunger, but derive no enjoyment from it (*R' Hirsch*).

you eat of it your eyes will be opened and you will be like God, knowing good and bad.'

⁶ And the woman perceived that the tree was good for eating and that it was a delight to the eyes, and that the tree was desirable as a means to wisdom, and she took of its fruit and ate; and she gave also to her husband with her and he ate. ⁷ Then the eyes of both of them were opened and they realized that they were naked; and they sewed together a fig leaf and made themselves aprons.

⁸ They heard the sound of HASHEM God manifesting itself in the garden toward evening; and the man and his wife hid from HASHEM God among the trees of the garden. ⁹ HASHEM God called out to the man and said to him, 'Where are you?'

¹⁰ He said, 'I heard the sound of You in the garden, and I was afraid because I am naked, so I hid.'

¹¹ And He said, 'Who told you that you are naked? Have you eaten of the tree from which I commanded you not to eat?'

¹² The man said, 'The woman whom You gave to be with me — she gave me of the tree, and I ate.'

¹³ And HASHEM God said to the woman, 'What is this that you have done!'

The woman said, 'The serpent deceived me, and I ate.'

¹⁴ And HASHEM God said to the serpent, 'Because you have done this, accursed are you beyond all the cattle and beyond all beasts of the field; upon your belly shall you go, and dust shall you eat all the days of your life. ¹⁵ I will put enmity between you and the woman, and between your offspring and her offspring. He will pound your head, and you will bite his heel.'

¹⁶ To the woman He said, 'I will greatly increase

אַרְבֶּה עִצְּבוֹנֵךְ וְהֵרֹנֵךְ בְּעֶצֶב תֵּלְדִי בָנִים וְאֶל־אִישֵׁךְ תְּשׁוּקָתֵךְ וְהוּא יִמְשָׁל־בָּךְ: יז וּלְאָדָם אָמַר כִּי־שָׁמַעְתָּ לְקוֹל אִשְׁתֶּךָ וַתֹּאכַל מִן־הָעֵץ אֲשֶׁר צִוִּיתִיךָ לֵאמֹר לֹא תֹאכַל מִמֶּנּוּ אֲרוּרָה הָאֲדָמָה בַּעֲבוּרֶךָ בְּעִצָּבוֹן תֹּאכֲלֶנָּה כֹּל יְמֵי חַיֶּיךָ: יח וְקוֹץ וְדַרְדַּר תַּצְמִיחַ לָךְ וְאָכַלְתָּ אֶת־עֵשֶׂב הַשָּׂדֶה: יט בְּזֵעַת אַפֶּיךָ תֹּאכַל לֶחֶם עַד שׁוּבְךָ אֶל־הָאֲדָמָה כִּי מִמֶּנָּה לֻקָּחְתָּ כִּי־עָפָר אַתָּה וְאֶל־עָפָר תָּשׁוּב: כ וַיִּקְרָא הָאָדָם שֵׁם אִשְׁתּוֹ חַוָּה כִּי הִוא הָיְתָה אֵם כָּל־חָי: כא וַיַּעַשׂ יְהוָה אֱלֹהִים לְאָדָם וּלְאִשְׁתּוֹ כָּתְנוֹת עוֹר וַיַּלְבִּשֵׁם:

רביעי כב וַיֹּאמֶר | יְהוָה אֱלֹהִים הֵן הָאָדָם הָיָה כְּאַחַד מִמֶּנּוּ לָדַעַת טוֹב וָרָע וְעַתָּה | פֶּן־יִשְׁלַח יָדוֹ וְלָקַח גַּם מֵעֵץ הַחַיִּים וְאָכַל וָחַי לְעֹלָם: כג וַיְשַׁלְּחֵהוּ יְהוָה אֱלֹהִים מִגַּן־עֵדֶן לַעֲבֹד אֶת־הָאֲדָמָה אֲשֶׁר לֻקַּח מִשָּׁם: כד וַיְגָרֶשׁ אֶת־הָאָדָם וַיַּשְׁכֵּן מִקֶּדֶם לְגַן־עֵדֶן אֶת־הַכְּרֻבִים וְאֵת לַהַט הַחֶרֶב הַמִּתְהַפֶּכֶת לִשְׁמֹר אֶת־דֶּרֶךְ עֵץ הַחַיִּים: ד א וְהָאָדָם יָדַע אֶת־חַוָּה אִשְׁתּוֹ וַתַּהַר וַתֵּלֶד אֶת־קַיִן וַתֹּאמֶר קָנִיתִי אִישׁ אֶת־יְהוָה: ב וַתֹּסֶף לָלֶדֶת אֶת־אָחִיו אֶת־הָבֶל וַיְהִי־הֶבֶל רֹעֵה צֹאן וְקַיִן הָיָה עֹבֵד אֲדָמָה: ג וַיְהִי מִקֵּץ יָמִים וַיָּבֵא קַיִן

16. The Sages ordained that a man should honor his wife more than himself, and love her as himself; if he has money, he should increase his generosity to her according to his means; he should not cast fear upon her unduly and his conversation with her should be gentle — he should be prone neither to melancholy nor anger. They have similarly ordained that a wife should honor her husband exceedingly and revere him; she should arrange her affairs according to his wishes, and he should be in her eyes as if he were a prince or a king, while she behaves according to his heart's desire, and refrains from anything that is repugnant to him. This is the way of the daughters of Israel who are holy and pure in their union, and in these ways will their life together be seemly and praiseworthy (*Rambam, Hil. Ishus* 15:19-20).

20. The Torah resumes the narrative of man's naming all creatures [2:20], which had been interrupted to teach that through the giving of names Adam perceived that he was lacking a mate. Having mentioned that they were both naked and unashamed, the Torah told about the serpent, to indicate that it was due to Eve's lack of shame that the serpent desired her and attempted to deceive her (*Rashi*).

22. This translation [as opposed to the more familiar: *'behold Man has become like one of us'*] follows the commentary of *Rashi, Targum*, and *Midrash*.

Behold he is unique among the terrestrial ones, just as I am unique among the celestial ones; in that he can discriminate between good and bad, a quality not possessed by cattle and beasts (*Rashi*).

23-24. Man's expulsion from Eden.
God had originally created man outside of the Garden of Eden (see 2:9, 16), and placed him there where all his needs were supplied with a minimum of effort. He had only to till the land and guard it against wild animals. But Adam was unequal even to this light task; by his negligence he allowed the serpent to enter the garden, with calamitous results. Therefore, God returned him to his source, where he would have to toil just to provide his own sustenance (Radak; B'chor Shor).

4/1. Cain and Abel. וְהָאָדָם יָדַע אֶת חַוָּה אִשְׁתּוֹ — Now the man had known his wife Eve. The translation in the past-perfect follows Rashi: he 'had known,' i.e., the conception and birth of Cain had occurred before the sin and expulsion of Adam and Eve from Eden.

אֶת ה׳ — With HASHEM — As partners with Hashem. 'My husband and I were created by God alone, but in the birth of Cain we are partners with Him' (Rashi).

2. Because Abel feared God's curse against the ground, he turned to caring for sheep and herds (Midrash Rashi).

Although meat was still prohibited to them [see 9:3], milk, butter, wool, and the skins of dead animals were permitted to them. Abel's work consisted of shearing the sheep and milking the cows (Mizrachi).

Pirkei d'Rabbi Eliezer notes that they would exchange products with each other. (Thus the system of bartering goods and services was instituted by God from the very beginning of creation — Radak.)

your suffering and your childbearing: in pain shall you bear children. Yet your craving shall be for your husband, and he shall rule over you.''

¹⁷ To Adam He said, 'Because you listened to the voice of your wife and ate of the tree about which I commanded you saying, ''You shall not eat of it,'' accursed is the ground because of you; through suffering shall you eat of it all the days of your life. ¹⁸ Thorns and thistles shall it sprout for you, and you shall eat the herb of the field. ¹⁹ By the sweat of your brow shall you eat bread until you return to the ground, from which you were taken: For dust are you, and to dust shall you return.'

²⁰ The man called his wife's name Eve, because she had become the mother of all the living.

²¹ And HASHEM God made for Adam and his wife garments of skin, and He clothed them.

²² And HASHEM God said, 'Behold Man has become like the Unique One among Us, knowing good and bad; and now, lest he put forth his hand and take also of the tree of life, and eat and live forever!'

²³ So HASHEM God banished him from the Garden of Eden, to work the soil from which he was taken. ²⁴ And having driven out the man, He stationed at the east of the Garden of Eden the Cherubim and the flame of the ever-turning sword, to guard the way to the tree of life.

4 ¹ Now the man had known his wife Eve, and she conceived and bore Cain, saying, 'I have acquired a man with HASHEM.' ² And additionally she bore his brother Abel. Abel became a shepherd, and Cain became a tiller of the ground.

³ After a period of time, Cain brought an offering

מִפְּרִי הָאֲדָמָה מִנְחָה לַיהוָה: דוְהֶבֶל הֵבִיא
גַם־הוּא מִבְּכֹרוֹת צֹאנוֹ וּמֵחֶלְבֵהֶן וַיִּשַׁע
יהוה אֶל־הֶבֶל וְאֶל־מִנְחָתוֹ: הוְאֶל־קַיִן וְאֶל־
מִנְחָתוֹ לֹא שָׁעָה וַיִּחַר לְקַיִן מְאֹד וַיִּפְּלוּ
פָּנָיו: ווַיֹּאמֶר יהוה אֶל־קָיִן לָמָּה חָרָה לָךְ
וְלָמָּה נָפְלוּ פָנֶיךָ: זהֲלוֹא אִם־תֵּיטִיב שְׂאֵת
וְאִם לֹא תֵיטִיב לַפֶּתַח חַטָּאת רֹבֵץ וְאֵלֶיךָ
תְּשׁוּקָתוֹ וְאַתָּה תִּמְשָׁל־בּוֹ: חוַיֹּאמֶר קַיִן
אֶל־הֶבֶל אָחִיו וַיְהִי בִּהְיוֹתָם בַּשָּׂדֶה וַיָּקָם
קַיִן אֶל־הֶבֶל אָחִיו וַיַּהַרְגֵהוּ: טוַיֹּאמֶר יהוה
אֶל־קַיִן אֵי הֶבֶל אָחִיךָ וַיֹּאמֶר לֹא יָדַעְתִּי
הֲשֹׁמֵר אָחִי אָנֹכִי: יוַיֹּאמֶר מֶה עָשִׂיתָ
קוֹל דְּמֵי אָחִיךָ צֹעֲקִים אֵלַי מִן־הָאֲדָמָה:
יאוְעַתָּה אָרוּר אָתָּה מִן־הָאֲדָמָה אֲשֶׁר
פָּצְתָה אֶת־פִּיהָ לָקַחַת אֶת־דְּמֵי אָחִיךָ
מִיָּדֶךָ: יבכִּי תַעֲבֹד אֶת־הָאֲדָמָה לֹא־
תֹסֵף תֵּת־כֹּחָהּ לָךְ נָע וָנָד תִּהְיֶה בָאָרֶץ:
יגוַיֹּאמֶר קַיִן אֶל־יהוה גָּדוֹל עֲוֹנִי מִנְּשֹׂא:
ידהֵן גֵּרַשְׁתָּ אֹתִי הַיּוֹם מֵעַל פְּנֵי הָאֲדָמָה
וּמִפָּנֶיךָ אֶסָּתֵר וְהָיִיתִי נָע וָנָד בָּאָרֶץ וְהָיָה
כָל־מֹצְאִי יַהַרְגֵנִי: טווַיֹּאמֶר לוֹ יהוה לָכֵן
כָּל־הֹרֵג קַיִן שִׁבְעָתַיִם יֻקָּם וַיָּשֶׂם יהוה
לְקַיִן אוֹת לְבִלְתִּי הַכּוֹת־אֹתוֹ כָּל־מֹצְאוֹ:
טזוַיֵּצֵא קַיִן מִלִּפְנֵי יהוה וַיֵּשֶׁב בְּאֶרֶץ־נוֹד
קִדְמַת־עֵדֶן: יזוַיֵּדַע קַיִן אֶת־אִשְׁתּוֹ וַתַּהַר

3. From the subtle contrast between the simple description of Cain's offering and the more specific description of Abel's offering in the next verse (from the choicest firstlings of his flock), the Sages derive that Cain's offering was from the inferior portions of the crop, while Abel chose only the finest of his flock. Therefore Cain's sacrifice was not accepted (*Ibn Ezra; Radak*).

6. God addressed Cain to teach the way of repentance. A sinner can atone for his sins if he will but repent sincerely (*Radak*).

7. *Sin rests at the door* — At the entrance to your grave, your sin will be kept (*Rashi*). [I.e., punishment will await you in the future world unless you repent.]

If you succumb to your Evil Inclination, punishment and evil will be as everpresent as if they lived in the doorway of your house (*Sforno*).

Its desire is toward you. 'Its desire' — i.e., the goal of the Evil Inclination, which continually seeks to entice you (*Rashi*).

וְאַתָּה תִּמְשָׁל־בּוֹ — *Yet you can conquer it* — i.e., you can prevail over it if you wish (*Rashi*), for you can mend your ways and cast off your sin. Thus God taught Cain about repentance: that man can always repent and God will forgive him (*Ramban*).

8. Abel was the stronger of the two, and the expression *rose up* implies that Cain had been thrown down and lay beneath Abel. But Cain begged for mercy saying: 'We are the only two in the world. What will you tell Father if you kill me?' Abel was filled with compassion, and released his hold. Cain then *rose up and killed him* (*Midrash*).

9. *Where is Abel your bro-ther?* A rhetorical question. God knew full well where he was — He entered with him into a gentle conversa-tion to give him the oppor-tunity to confess and repent (*Rashi; Radak; Sforno*).

10. The plural form, דְּמֵי, *bloods,* means: his blood and the blood of his poten-tial descendants. Alterna-tively, this teaches that his blood [from his many wounds (*Gemara*; see above)] was splashed over the trees and stones (*Mish-nah, Sanhedrin* 37a; *Rashi*).

12. Since the earth *shall no longer yield its strength,* he would always strive to find new areas to cultivate the land. Never finding blessing, he will wander aimlessly in search of more fertile land (*B'chor Shor; Ralbag*), but the quest is futile; the land is accursed to him. He must wander about, knowing no peace, like the blood of his brother (*Tz'ror HaMor*).

15. *Before seven generations have passed he will be pun-ished.* Our rendering follows *Rashi* who interprets this as 'an abbreviated verse with an implied clause: *Whoever slays Cain* will be punished (this phrase understated, but understood); as for Cain, only *after seven gener-ations will I execute My ven-geance upon him,* when Le-mech, one of his descend-ants will arise and slay him.'

16. *The land of Nod* [נוד] = wandering] — i.e., where exiles wander . . . To the *east of Eden,* where his fa-ther had been exiled when he was driven out of the Garden [cf. 3:24]. Notably, the eastern region always forms a place of refuge for murderers, for the cities of refuge that Moses later set aside were also to the east, 'the place of sun-rise' [cf. *Deut.* 4:41] (*Rashi*).

to HASHEM of the fruit of the ground; [4] and as for Abel, he also brought of the firstlings of his flock and from their choicest. HASHEM turned to Abel and to his offering, [5] but to Cain and to his offering He did not turn. This annoyed Cain exceedingly, and his countenance fell.

[6] And HASHEM said to Cain, 'Why are you annoyed, and why has your countenance fallen? [7] Surely, if you improve yourself, you will be forgiven. But if you do not improve yourself, sin rests at the door. Its desire is toward you, yet you can conquer it.'

[8] Cain spoke with his brother Abel. And it happened when they were in the field, that Cain rose up against his brother Abel and killed him.

[9] HASHEM said to Cain, 'Where is Abel your brother?' And he said, 'I do not know. Am I my brother's keeper?' [10] Then He said, 'What have you done? Hark, the blood of your brother cries out to Me, from the ground! [11] Therefore, you are cursed more than the ground, which opened wide its mouth to receive your brother's blood from your hand. [12] When you work the ground, it shall no longer yield its strength to you. You shall become a vagrant and a wanderer on earth.'

[13] Cain said to HASHEM, 'Is my iniquity too great to be borne?' [14] Behold You have banished me this day from the face of the earth — can I be hidden from Your presence? I must become a vagrant and a wanderer on earth; whoever meets me will kill me!' [15] HASHEM said to him, 'Therefore, whoever slays Cain, before seven generations have passed he will be punished.' And HASHEM placed a mark upon Cain, so that none that meet him might kill him. [16] Cain left the presence of HASHEM and settled in the land of Nod, east of Eden.

[17] And Cain knew his wife, and she conceived

וַתֵּלֶד אֶת־חֲנוֹךְ וַיְהִי בֹּנֶה עִיר וַיִּקְרָא שֵׁם הָעִיר כְּשֵׁם בְּנוֹ חֲנוֹךְ: יח וַיִּוָּלֵד לַחֲנוֹךְ אֶת־עִירָד וְעִירָד יָלַד אֶת־מְחוּיָאֵל וּמְחִיָּיאֵל יָלַד אֶת־מְתוּשָׁאֵל וּמְתוּשָׁאֵל יָלַד אֶת־לָמֶךְ: חמישי יט וַיִּקַּח־לוֹ לֶמֶךְ שְׁתֵּי נָשִׁים שֵׁם הָאַחַת עָדָה וְשֵׁם הַשֵּׁנִית צִלָּה: כ וַתֵּלֶד עָדָה אֶת־יָבָל הוּא הָיָה אֲבִי יֹשֵׁב אֹהֶל וּמִקְנֶה: כא וְשֵׁם אָחִיו יוּבָל הוּא הָיָה אֲבִי כָּל־תֹּפֵשׂ כִּנּוֹר וְעוּגָב: כב וְצִלָּה גַם־הִוא יָלְדָה אֶת־תּוּבַל קַיִן לֹטֵשׁ כָּל־חֹרֵשׁ נְחֹשֶׁת וּבַרְזֶל וַאֲחוֹת תּוּבַל־קַיִן נַעֲמָה: כג וַיֹּאמֶר לֶמֶךְ לְנָשָׁיו עָדָה וְצִלָּה שְׁמַעַן קוֹלִי נְשֵׁי לֶמֶךְ הַאְזֵנָּה אִמְרָתִי כִּי אִישׁ הָרַגְתִּי לְפִצְעִי וְיֶלֶד לְחַבֻּרָתִי: כד כִּי שִׁבְעָתַיִם יֻקַּם־קָיִן וְלֶמֶךְ שִׁבְעִים וְשִׁבְעָה: כה וַיֵּדַע אָדָם עוֹד אֶת־אִשְׁתּוֹ וַתֵּלֶד בֵּן וַתִּקְרָא אֶת־שְׁמוֹ שֵׁת כִּי שָׁת־לִי אֱלֹהִים זֶרַע אַחֵר תַּחַת הֶבֶל כִּי הֲרָגוֹ קָיִן: כו וּלְשֵׁת גַּם־הוּא יֻלַּד־בֵּן וַיִּקְרָא אֶת־שְׁמוֹ אֱנוֹשׁ אָז הוּחַל לִקְרֹא בְּשֵׁם יהוה: ה ששי א זֶה סֵפֶר תּוֹלְדֹת אָדָם בְּיוֹם בְּרֹא אֱלֹהִים אָדָם בִּדְמוּת אֱלֹהִים עָשָׂה אֹתוֹ: ב זָכָר וּנְקֵבָה בְּרָאָם וַיְבָרֶךְ אֹתָם וַיִּקְרָא אֶת־שְׁמָם אָדָם בְּיוֹם הִבָּרְאָם: ג וַיְחִי אָדָם שְׁלֹשִׁים וּמְאַת שָׁנָה וַיּוֹלֶד בִּדְמוּתוֹ כְּצַלְמוֹ וַיִּקְרָא אֶת־שְׁמוֹ שֵׁת: ד וַיִּהְיוּ יְמֵי־אָדָם אַחֲרֵי הוֹלִידוֹ

The descendants of Cain. The term *'builder of a city'* implies that his personality is being described. Cut off from the earth, from God, and from his fellow men, Cain was left only with his own intelligence and talent which he utilized to build cities. Urban life, unlike rural life, 'cultivates' sophisticated skills in its inhabitants. The following verses list those skills (*Hirsch*).

19. *Two wives.* Such was the practice of the generation of the Flood. They would take two wives: One for childbearing and the other for pleasure. The latter would be given a sterility drug and be pampered like a bride, while the former would be bereft of companionship, and left mourning like a widow throughout her life [cf. *comm*. to *Job* 24:21] (*Midrash; Rashi*).

21. *Who handle the harp and flute.* I.e., he was the originator of the art·of music (*Radak*). He used these musical instruments for idol worship (*Rashi*).

22. *Naamah.* Her name ('lovely') is mentioned because she was the wife of Noah, and her deeds were lovely and pleasant (*Rashi*).

23-24. *Lamech's plea.* Lamech was blind and his son, Tubal-Cain, used to lead him. One day, Tubal Cain saw Cain and mistook him for an animal. He bade his father to shoot an arrow, which killed Cain. When he approached and realized it was Cain, Lamech beat his hands together [in grief] and [accidentally] struck his son, killing him. This angered his wives who denied themselves to him, and he now tried to appease them: *'Hear my voice'* — obey me and return to me (*Rashi*). [The bracketed words are from *Tanchuma*.]

24. 'If the punishment of Cain, an intentional murderer, was delayed until the seventh generation, surely my punishment will be deferred many times seven because I killed accidentally!' He used *'seventy-seven'* to denote many times seven [i.e., a long period, not meaning exactly seventy-seven] (*Rashi*).

25. Seth and his descendants.

26. *Then to call in the Name of HASHEM became profaned.* Following *Rashi* and *Midrash*, who interpret הוּחַל as לְשׁוֹן חוּלִין, meaning *'profane'*: Man and lifeless objects were called by the Name of God, and idolatry began.

5/1. Genealogy of Mankind. A new narrative begins, enumerating the generations from Adam to Noah. The genealogy traces the line through Seth, for it was through him that the human race survived; Abel dies without issue, and Cain's descendants perished (*Radak; Chizkuni*).

2. The Talmud comments that a man without a wife is not a man, for it is said, *'He created them male and female . . . and called their name Man'* [i.e., only together as man and wife is he called *'Man'*] (*Yevamos* 63a).

3. *In his likeness and his image.* The verse particularly points this out to indicate that God gave Adam, who himself was created in God's likeness, the capacity to reproduce offspring who were also in this ennobled likeness. This is not mentioned concerning Cain or Abel because, since their seed perished, the Torah did not wish to prolong the descriptions of them (*Ibn Ezra; Ramban*).

and bore Chanoch. He became a city-builder, and he named the city after his son Chanoch. [18] To Chanoch was born Irad, and Irad begot Mehujael, and Mehujael begot Methusael, and Methusael begot Lamech.

[19] Lamech took to himself two wives: the name of one was Adah, and the name of the other was Tzilah. [20] And Adah bore Jabal; he was the first of those who dwell in tents and breed cattle. [21] The name of his brother was Jubal; he was the first of all who handle the harp and flute. [22] And Tzilah, too — she bore Tuval-cain, who sharpened all cutting implements of brass and iron. And the sister of Tuval-cain was Naamah.

[23] And Lamech said to his wives, 'Adah and Tzilah, hear my voice; wives of Lamech, give ear to my speech: Have I slain a man by my wound and a child by my bruise? [24] If Cain suffered vengeance at seven generations, then Lamech at seventy-seven!'

[25] Adam knew his wife again, and she bore a son and named him Seth, because: 'God has provided me another child in place of Abel, for Cain had killed him.' [26] And as for Seth, to him also a son was born, and he named him Enosh. Then to call in the Name of HASHEM became profaned.

5 [1] This is the account of the descendants of Adam —

On the day that God created man, He made him in the likeness of God. [2] He created them male and female. He blessed them and called their name Man on the day they were created. —

[3] When Adam had lived one hundred and thirty years, he begot in his likeness and his image, and he named him Seth. [4] And the days of Adam after

אֶת־שֵׁת שְׁמֹנֶה מֵאֹת שָׁנָה וַיּוֹלֶד בָּנִים וּבָנוֹת:
ה וַיִּהְיוּ כָּל־יְמֵי אָדָם אֲשֶׁר־חַי תְּשַׁע מֵאוֹת
שָׁנָה וּשְׁלֹשִׁים שָׁנָה וַיָּמֹת: ו וַיְחִי־שֵׁת
חָמֵשׁ שָׁנִים וּמְאַת שָׁנָה וַיּוֹלֶד אֶת־אֱנוֹשׁ:
ז וַיְחִי־שֵׁת אַחֲרֵי הוֹלִידוֹ אֶת־אֱנוֹשׁ שֶׁבַע
שָׁנִים וּשְׁמֹנֶה מֵאוֹת שָׁנָה וַיּוֹלֶד בָּנִים וּבָנוֹת:
ח וַיִּהְיוּ כָּל־יְמֵי־שֵׁת שְׁתֵּים עֶשְׂרֵה שָׁנָה וּתְשַׁע
מֵאוֹת שָׁנָה וַיָּמֹת: ט וַיְחִי אֱנוֹשׁ תִּשְׁעִים
שָׁנָה וַיּוֹלֶד אֶת־קֵינָן: י וַיְחִי אֱנוֹשׁ אַחֲרֵי
הוֹלִידוֹ אֶת־קֵינָן חֲמֵשׁ עֶשְׂרֵה שָׁנָה וּשְׁמֹנֶה
מֵאוֹת שָׁנָה וַיּוֹלֶד בָּנִים וּבָנוֹת: יא וַיִּהְיוּ כָּל־יְמֵי
אֱנוֹשׁ חָמֵשׁ שָׁנִים וּתְשַׁע מֵאוֹת שָׁנָה
וַיָּמֹת: יב וַיְחִי קֵינָן שִׁבְעִים שָׁנָה וַיּוֹלֶד
אֶת־מַהֲלַלְאֵל: יג וַיְחִי קֵינָן אַחֲרֵי הוֹלִידוֹ אֶת־
מַהֲלַלְאֵל אַרְבָּעִים שָׁנָה וּשְׁמֹנֶה מֵאוֹת שָׁנָה
וַיּוֹלֶד בָּנִים וּבָנוֹת: יד וַיִּהְיוּ כָּל־יְמֵי קֵינָן עֶשֶׂר
שָׁנִים וּתְשַׁע מֵאוֹת שָׁנָה וַיָּמֹת: טו וַיְחִי
מַהֲלַלְאֵל חָמֵשׁ שָׁנִים וְשִׁשִּׁים שָׁנָה וַיּוֹלֶד
אֶת־יָרֶד: טז וַיְחִי מַהֲלַלְאֵל אַחֲרֵי הוֹלִידוֹ
אֶת־יֶרֶד שְׁלֹשִׁים שָׁנָה וּשְׁמֹנֶה מֵאוֹת שָׁנָה
וַיּוֹלֶד בָּנִים וּבָנוֹת: יז וַיִּהְיוּ כָּל־יְמֵי מַהֲלַלְאֵל
חָמֵשׁ וְתִשְׁעִים שָׁנָה וּשְׁמֹנֶה מֵאוֹת שָׁנָה
וַיָּמֹת: יח וַיְחִי־יֶרֶד שְׁתַּיִם וְשִׁשִּׁים
שָׁנָה וּמְאַת שָׁנָה וַיּוֹלֶד אֶת־חֲנוֹךְ: יט וַיְחִי־
יֶרֶד אַחֲרֵי הוֹלִידוֹ אֶת־חֲנוֹךְ שְׁמֹנֶה מֵאוֹת
שָׁנָה וַיּוֹלֶד בָּנִים וּבָנוֹת: כ וַיִּהְיוּ כָל־יְמֵי־יֶרֶד

4. *Ramban* is of the opinion that Adam, as God's handiwork, was physically perfect, and the same applied to his children. As such it was his nature to live a long time. After the Flood, however, a deterioration of the atmosphere caused a gradual shortening of life until it would appear that in the times of the Patriarchs, people lived a normal life span of seventy and eighty years, while only the most righteous ones lived longer . . .

The ten generations from Adam to Noah.

⋆§ אָדָם — *Adam*: died in 930;

⋆§ שֵׁת — *Seth*: born in the year 130 from Creation; died in 1042. After him the generations begin doing evil.

⋆§ אֱנוֹשׁ — *Enosh*: 235-1140;

⋆§ קֵינָן — *Kenan*: 325-1235;

⋆§ מְהַלַלְאֵל — *Mehalalel*: 395-1290;

⋆§ יֶרֶד — *Jared*: 460-1422;

⋆§ חֲנוֹךְ — *Chanoch*: 622-987;

⋆§ מְתוּשֶׁלַח — *Methuselah*: 687-1656;

⋆§ לֶמֶךְ — *Lamech*: 847-1651;

⋆§ נֹחַ — *Noah*: 1056-2006. Thus, Noah was born 126 years after Adam died; Lamech was the farthest descendant Adam lived to see.

begetting Seth were eight hundred years, and he begot sons and daughters. [5] All the days that Adam lived were nine hundred and thirty years; and he died.

[6] When Seth had lived one hundred and five years he begot Enosh. [7] Seth lived eight hundred and seven years after begetting Enosh, and he begot sons and daughters. [8] All the days of Seth were nine hundred and twelve years; and he died.

[9] When Enosh had lived ninety years, he begot Kenan. [10] And Enosh lived eight hundred and fifteen years after begetting Kenan, and he begot sons and daughters. [11] All the days of Enosh were nine hundred and five years; and he died.

[12] When Kenan had lived seventy years, he begot Mahalalel. [13] And Kenan lived eight hundred and forty years after begetting Mahalalel, and he begot sons and daughters. [14] All the days of Kenan were nine hundred and ten years; and he died.

[15] When Mahalalel had lived sixty-five years, he begot Jared. [16] And Mahalalel lived eight hundred and thirty years after begetting Jared, and he begot sons and daughters. [17] All the days of Mahalalel were eight hundred and ninety-five years; and he died.

[18] When Jared had lived one hundred and sixty-two years, he begot Chanoch. [19] And Jared lived eight hundred years after begetting Chanoch and he begot sons and daughters. [20] All the days of Jared came to nine hundred

שְׁתַּ֤יִם וְשִׁשִּׁים֙ שָׁנָ֔ה וּתְשַׁ֥ע מֵא֖וֹת שָׁנָ֑ה
וַיָּמֹֽת: כא וַֽיְחִ֣י חֲנ֔וֹךְ חָמֵ֥שׁ וְשִׁשִּׁ֖ים שָׁנָ֑ה
וַיּ֖וֹלֶד אֶת־מְתוּשָֽׁלַח: כב וַיִּתְהַלֵּ֨ךְ חֲנ֜וֹךְ אֶת־
הָֽאֱלֹהִ֗ים אַחֲרֵי֙ הוֹלִיד֣וֹ אֶת־מְתוּשֶׁ֔לַח שְׁלֹ֥שׁ
מֵא֖וֹת שָׁנָ֑ה וַיּ֥וֹלֶד בָּנִ֖ים וּבָנֽוֹת: כג וַיְהִ֖י כָּל־יְמֵ֣י
חֲנ֑וֹךְ חָמֵ֤שׁ וְשִׁשִּׁים֙ שָׁנָ֔ה וּשְׁלֹ֥שׁ מֵא֖וֹת שָׁנָֽה:
כד וַיִּתְהַלֵּ֥ךְ חֲנ֖וֹךְ אֶת־הָֽאֱלֹהִ֑ים וְאֵינֶ֕נּוּ כִּֽי־לָקַ֥ח
אֹת֖וֹ אֱלֹהִֽים: שביעי כה וַיְחִ֣י מְתוּשֶׁ֗לַח
שֶׁ֤בַע וּשְׁמֹנִים֙ שָׁנָ֔ה וּמְאַ֖ת שָׁנָ֑ה וַיּ֖וֹלֶד אֶת־
לָֽמֶךְ: כו וַֽיְחִ֣י מְתוּשֶׁ֗לַח אַֽחֲרֵי֙ הוֹלִיד֣וֹ אֶת־
לֶ֔מֶךְ שְׁתַּ֤יִם וּשְׁמוֹנִים֙ שָׁנָ֔ה וּשְׁבַ֥ע מֵא֖וֹת שָׁנָ֑ה
וַיּ֥וֹלֶד בָּנִ֖ים וּבָנֽוֹת: כז וַיִּֽהְיוּ֙ כָּל־יְמֵ֣י מְתוּשֶׁ֔לַח
תֵּ֤שַׁע וְשִׁשִּׁים֙ שָׁנָ֔ה וּתְשַׁ֥ע מֵא֖וֹת שָׁנָ֑ה
וַיָּמֹֽת: כח וַֽיְחִי־לֶ֔מֶךְ שְׁתַּ֥יִם וּשְׁמֹנִ֖ים
שָׁנָ֑ה וּמְאַ֣ת שָׁנָ֑ה וַיּ֖וֹלֶד בֵּֽן: כט וַיִּקְרָ֧א אֶת־שְׁמ֛וֹ
נֹ֖חַ לֵאמֹ֑ר זֶ֞ה יְנַֽחֲמֵ֤נוּ מִֽמַּעֲשֵׂ֨נוּ֙ וּמֵֽעִצְּב֣וֹן יָדֵ֔ינוּ
מִן־הָ֣אֲדָמָ֔ה אֲשֶׁ֥ר אֵֽרְרָ֖הּ יְהוָֽה: ל וַֽיְחִי־לֶ֗מֶךְ
אַֽחֲרֵי֙ הוֹלִיד֣וֹ אֶת־נֹ֔חַ חָמֵ֤שׁ וְתִשְׁעִים֙ שָׁנָ֔ה
וַֽחֲמֵ֖שׁ מֵא֣וֹת שָׁנָ֑ה וַיּ֥וֹלֶד בָּנִ֖ים וּבָנֽוֹת: לא וַֽיְהִ֣י
כָל־יְמֵי־לֶ֗מֶךְ שֶׁ֤בַע וְשִׁבְעִים֙ שָׁנָ֔ה וּשְׁבַ֥ע מֵא֖וֹת
שָׁנָ֑ה וַיָּמֹֽת: לב וַֽיְהִי־נֹ֕חַ בֶּן־חֲמֵ֥שׁ מֵא֖וֹת
שָׁנָ֑ה וַיּ֣וֹלֶד נֹ֔חַ אֶת־שֵׁ֖ם אֶת־חָ֥ם וְאֶת־יָֽפֶת:
ו א וַֽיְהִי֙ כִּֽי־הֵחֵ֣ל הָֽאָדָ֔ם לָרֹ֖ב עַל־פְּנֵ֣י הָֽאֲדָמָ֑ה
וּבָנ֖וֹת יֻלְּד֥וּ לָהֶֽם: ב וַיִּרְא֤וּ בְנֵֽי־הָֽאֱלֹהִים֙ אֶת־
בְּנ֣וֹת הָֽאָדָ֔ם כִּ֥י טֹבֹ֖ת הֵ֑נָּה וַיִּקְח֤וּ לָהֶם֙ נָשִׁ֔ים
מִכֹּ֖ל אֲשֶׁ֥ר בָּחָֽרוּ: ג וַיֹּ֣אמֶר יְהוָ֗ה לֹֽא־יָד֨וֹן רוּחִ֤י

24. Although Chanoch was a righteous man, he was liable to go astray. To avert this, God cut his life short, hence the use of the expression 'he was no more,' rather than 'he died' — i.e., he was no more in the world to complete his allotted years (Rashi).

The entire verse is paraphrased in *Targum Yonasan*: 'And Chanoch served in truth before God, and behold, he was not with the sojourners of earth, for he was withdrawn and he ascended to heaven by the word of God; and he was called Metatron, the great scribe.'

29. *This one will bring us rest.* Our rendering follows *Rashi* who relates נֹחַ, Noah, to the root נחם, *rest*: i.e., 'He will bring us rest (in the sense of 'relief') *from the toil of our hands.*' This was said [prophetically] in reference to the invention of farming tools, which was attributed to Noah. Until his time, in consequence of the curse decreed upon Adam [3:18], the earth produced thorns and thistles when one planted wheat. In Noah's days this ceased.

There was a tradition from Adam to his descendants that the curse on the earth would be in effect only during Adam's lifetime. Chronologically, Noah was the first one — in our genealogical list of leaders of the various generations — born after Adam's death. Beginning with him, the *severity of the curse would abate.* Knowing this tradition, Lamech gave him that name (*Pirkei d'Rabbi Eliezer; Abarbanel*).

6/1. Prelude to the Flood.
וַיְהִי — *And it came to pass.*
The *Talmud* notes that it is a tradition that wherever the term וַיְהִי, *and it came to pass*, occurs in Scripture, it presages trouble (*Megillah* 10b).

2. בְּנֵי הָאֱלֹהִים — *The sons of the rulers,* i.e., the sons of the princes and judges, for *Elohim* always implies rulership [cf. comm. to 1:1], as in *Exodus* 4:16 *'and you shall be his* אֱלֹהִים, *Master'* (*Rashi*).

According to many commentators, בְּנֵי הָאֱלֹהִים (lit. *'sons of God'*) are the God-fearing descendants of Seth, while the *'daughters of men'* (implying less spiritual people) are the iniquitous descendants of Cain.

The daughters of man — i.e., the daughters of the general populace (*R' Saadiah Gaon*); the multitude, the lower classes (*Rambam, Moreh* 1:14) who did not have the power to resist their superiors (*Radak*).

and sixty-two years; and he died.

²¹ When Chanoch had lived sixty-five years, he begot Methuselah. ²² Chanoch walked with God for three hundred years after begetting Methuselah; and he begot sons and daughters. ²³ All the days of Chanoch were three hundred and sixty-five years. ²⁴ And Chanoch walked with God; then he was no more, for God had taken him.

²⁵ When Methuselah had lived one hundred and eighty-seven years, he begot Lamech. ²⁶ And Methuselah lived seven hundred and eight-two years after begetting Lamech, and he begot sons and daughters. ²⁷ All the days of Methuselah were nine hundred and sixty-nine years; and he died.

²⁸ When Lamech had lived one hundred and eighty-two years, he begot a son. ²⁹ And he named him Noah saying, 'This one will bring us rest from our work and from the toil of our hands, from the ground which HASHEM had cursed.' ³⁰ Lamech lived five hundred and ninety-five years after begetting Noah, and he begot sons and daughters. ³¹ All the days of Lamech were seven hundred and seventy-seven years; and he died.

³² When Noah was five hundred years old, Noah begot Shem, Ham, and Japheth.

6 ¹ **A**nd it came to pass when man began to increase upon the ground and daughters were born to them, ² the sons of the rulers saw that the daughters of man were good and they took themselves wives from whomever they chose. ³ And HASHEM said, 'My spirit shall not

בָּאָדָם֙ לְעֹלָ֔ם בְּשַׁגַּ֖ם ה֣וּא בָשָׂ֑ר וְהָי֣וּ יָמָ֔יו מֵאָ֥ה
וְעֶשְׂרִ֖ים שָׁנָֽה: ד הַנְּפִלִ֞ים הָי֣וּ בָאָרֶץ֮ בַּיָּמִ֣ים
הָהֵם֒ וְגַ֣ם אַֽחֲרֵי־כֵ֗ן אֲשֶׁ֨ר יָבֹ֜אוּ בְּנֵ֤י הָֽאֱלֹהִים֙
אֶל־בְּנ֣וֹת הָֽאָדָ֔ם וְיָֽלְד֖וּ לָהֶ֑ם הֵ֧מָּה הַגִּבֹּרִ֛ים
אֲשֶׁ֥ר מֵֽעוֹלָ֖ם אַנְשֵׁ֥י הַשֵּֽׁם:
מפטיר ה וַיַּ֣רְא יְהֹוָ֔ה כִּ֥י רַבָּ֛ה רָעַ֥ת הָֽאָדָ֖ם בָּאָ֑רֶץ
וְכָל־יֵ֨צֶר֙ מַחְשְׁבֹ֣ת לִבּ֔וֹ רַ֥ק רַ֖ע כָּל־הַיּֽוֹם:
ו וַיִּנָּ֣חֶם יְהֹוָ֔ה כִּֽי־עָשָׂ֥ה אֶת־הָֽאָדָ֖ם בָּאָ֑רֶץ
וַיִּתְעַצֵּ֖ב אֶל־לִבּֽוֹ: ז וַיֹּ֣אמֶר יְהֹוָ֗ה אֶמְחֶ֨ה אֶת־
הָֽאָדָ֤ם אֲשֶׁר־בָּרָ֨אתִי֙ מֵעַל֙ פְּנֵ֣י הָֽאֲדָמָ֔ה
מֵֽאָדָם֙ עַד־בְּהֵמָ֔ה עַד־רֶ֖מֶשׂ וְעַד־ע֣וֹף הַשָּׁמָ֑יִם
כִּ֥י נִחַ֖מְתִּי כִּ֥י עֲשִׂיתִֽם: ח וְנֹ֕חַ מָ֥צָא חֵ֖ן בְּעֵינֵ֥י
יְהֹוָֽה:

The *Haftarah* for *Bereishis* appears on page 298

3. The warning of the Flood.

Since he is but flesh. He does not submit to My rule even though he is but flesh. How much more rebellious would man be if he were made of more durable substance! (*Rashi*).

His days shall be a hundred and twenty years. I will not inflict on mankind immediate punishment; I will grant a probationary period of 120 years in which he can repent. If they refuse, I will *then* bring a flood upon them (*Targumim; Rashi; Ramban* and most commentators).

Several commentators, however, [cited by *Ibn Ezra* and *Abarbanel*] interpret this verse as meaning that henceforth, the *average human life span*, constantly decreasing, will stabilize at not more than a hundred and twenty years.

4. The Nephilim.

הַנְּפִלִים — *The Nephilim* — i.e., Giants. They were so called because they fell [נָפְלוּ] and caused the world to fall (*Rashi*), and because the heart of whoever saw them fell in amazement at their great size (*Ibn Ezra*).

These were the offspring of the illicit union of the descended angels and Cain's daughters. They haughtily walked about committing robbery, violence, and bloodshed. They are the *Nephilim* whom the spies referred to [*Numbers* 13:33] (*Pirkei d'Rabbi Eliezer*).

6. In his penetrating discourse on the concept of God's grief and regret, *Akeidas Yitzchak* explains that this 'grief' is not contradictory to the basic Jewish belief that God foresees the future. He cites the example of one who plants a sapling for use as lumber. He tends and nurtures it, takes pride in its growth, and lovingly protects it from harm, although he knows that one day he will chop it down. When that day comes he looks back on his efforts and feels sorrow that the product of his long toil is cut down. This is in no way contradictory to his foreknowledge. Expressed in human terms, this is the 'grief' God now experienced.

7. וַיֹּאמֶר ה' — *And HASHEM said* — i.e., became determined (*Ibn Ezra*). God did not punish capriciously — only after mankind was irreversibly steeped in evil, and God was grieved to the point of changing from mercy to judgment.

8. God's *grace* made possible the salvation of Noah's family; otherwise only he would have been spared. Although Noah himself was righteous, he did not influence his generation to know God, therefore his merit was insufficient to save others. Only a righteous person who attempts to make others righteous can bring about their salvation, because there is hope that he can influence them to repent (*Sforno*).

According to the Masoretic note appearing at the end of the *Sidrah*, there are 146 verses in the *Sidrah*, corresponding to the mnemonic אֲמַצְיָ"ה and וִיחִזְקִיָּ"ה. The *Haftarah* begins with *Isaiah* 42:5: כֹּה אָמַר.

contend evermore concerning man since he is but flesh; his days shall be a hundred and twenty years.'

⁴ The Nephilim were on the earth in those days — and also afterward when the sons of the rulers would consort with the daughters of man, who would bear to them. They were the mighty who, from old, were men of devastation.

⁵ HASHEM saw that the wickedness of man was great upon the earth, and that every product of the thoughts of his heart was but evil always. ⁶ And HASHEM reconsidered having made man on earth, and He had heartfelt sadness. ⁷ And HASHEM said, 'I will blot out man whom I created from the face of the ground — from man to beast, to creeping things, and to birds of the sky; for I have reconsidered My having made them.' ⁸ But Noah found grace with HASHEM.

The *Haftarah* for *Bereishis* appears on page 298

פרשת נח

NOAH

Man has infinite capacity to save the world and to destroy it. And he has an equal capacity to perceive the truth and to see right through it.

The generation of the Flood continued man's slide into immorality until God's mercy had reached its limit. It is instructive that the last straw was thievery; as the Sages teach: Even if there is a bushel of sins, it is thievery that leads the condemnations. So man had taken the universe and pushed it over the brink of destruction, but there was one man, Noah, who saved the race and the world. Thanks to his righteousness, humanity survived — proof that no one should ever consider himself too insignificant acting alone to make a difference.

One would expect the survivors of the Flood and their immediate descendants to have learned that immorality is not assured. When the generation that built the Tower of Babel thought that it could do battle with God, it did not need fallible history books to tell them about the Flood. Noah and his children were still alive; eyewitnesses who had lived through man's foolishness and its consequences. But, overcome with delusions of their own power and rationalizing that the Flood had been a natural, coincidental disaster, they built the Tower anyway.

History repeats itself for those who refuse to learn from it.

ט אֵלֶּה תּוֹלְדֹת נֹחַ נֹחַ אִישׁ צַדִּיק תָּמִים הָיָה
בְּדֹרֹתָיו אֶת־הָאֱלֹהִים הִתְהַלֶּךְ־נֹחַ: י וַיּוֹלֶד
נֹחַ שְׁלֹשָׁה בָנִים אֶת־שֵׁם אֶת־חָם וְאֶת־יָפֶת:
יא וַתִּשָּׁחֵת הָאָרֶץ לִפְנֵי הָאֱלֹהִים וַתִּמָּלֵא
הָאָרֶץ חָמָס: יב וַיַּרְא אֱלֹהִים אֶת־הָאָרֶץ וְהִנֵּה
נִשְׁחָתָה כִּי־הִשְׁחִית כָּל־בָּשָׂר אֶת־דַּרְכּוֹ עַל־
הָאָרֶץ: יג וַיֹּאמֶר אֱלֹהִים לְנֹחַ
קֵץ כָּל־בָּשָׂר בָּא לְפָנַי כִּי־מָלְאָה הָאָרֶץ חָמָס
מִפְּנֵיהֶם וְהִנְנִי מַשְׁחִיתָם אֶת־הָאָרֶץ: יד עֲשֵׂה
לְךָ תֵּבַת עֲצֵי־גֹפֶר קִנִּים תַּעֲשֶׂה אֶת־הַתֵּבָה
וְכָפַרְתָּ אֹתָהּ מִבַּיִת וּמִחוּץ בַּכֹּפֶר: טו וְזֶה אֲשֶׁר
תַּעֲשֶׂה אֹתָהּ שְׁלֹשׁ מֵאוֹת אַמָּה אֹרֶךְ הַתֵּבָה
חֲמִשִּׁים אַמָּה רָחְבָּהּ וּשְׁלֹשִׁים אַמָּה קוֹמָתָהּ:
טז צֹהַר ׀ תַּעֲשֶׂה לַתֵּבָה וְאֶל־אַמָּה תְּכַלֶּנָּה
מִלְמַעְלָה וּפֶתַח הַתֵּבָה בְּצִדָּהּ תָּשִׂים תַּחְתִּיִּם
שְׁנִיִּם וּשְׁלִשִׁים תַּעֲשֶׂהָ: יז וַאֲנִי הִנְנִי מֵבִיא
אֶת־הַמַּבּוּל מַיִם עַל־הָאָרֶץ לְשַׁחֵת כָּל־בָּשָׂר
אֲשֶׁר־בּוֹ רוּחַ חַיִּים מִתַּחַת הַשָּׁמָיִם כֹּל
אֲשֶׁר־בָּאָרֶץ יִגְוָע: יח וַהֲקִמֹתִי אֶת־בְּרִיתִי
אִתָּךְ וּבָאתָ אֶל־הַתֵּבָה אַתָּה וּבָנֶיךָ וְאִשְׁתְּךָ
וּנְשֵׁי־בָנֶיךָ אִתָּךְ: יט וּמִכָּל־הָחַי מִכָּל־בָּשָׂר
שְׁנַיִם מִכֹּל תָּבִיא אֶל־הַתֵּבָה לְהַחֲיֹת
אִתָּךְ זָכָר וּנְקֵבָה יִהְיוּ: כ מֵהָעוֹף לְמִינֵהוּ
וּמִן־הַבְּהֵמָה לְמִינָהּ מִכֹּל רֶמֶשׂ הָאֲדָמָה
לְמִינֵהוּ שְׁנַיִם מִכֹּל יָבֹאוּ אֵלֶיךָ לְהַחֲיוֹת:

6/9. Noah. Noah — who re-established the human race after the Flood — was like Adam, in that he, too, was the father of mankind. Therefore, although the Torah has listed him as the last link in the genealogy of his predecessors, it mentions him again, since he and his children were the ancestors of mankind after the Flood (Abarbanel).

נֹחַ אִישׁ צַדִּיק — *Noah was a righteous man.* Since Noah was mentioned to introduce his progeny, Scripture praises him by relating that he was righteous (Rashi). Although the verse began *'these are the offspring of Noah,'* his children are not named until later. Instead it says, *'Noah was a righteous man.'* The Torah records his righteousness as his primary offspring (Kli Yakar).

בְּדֹרֹתָיו — *In his generations.* There are different interpretations of *'in his generations'*: Some Sages maintain that it is in his praise: Noah was righteous even in his corrupt generation; how much more righteous would he have been had he lived in a truly righteous generation! According to others, however, it is critical of him — only *'in his generations,'* i.e., by comparison with his extremely wicked contemporaries, did Noah stand out as a righteous man; but had he lived in the time of Abraham he would have been insignificant (Rashi). Accordingly, the righteous of each generation must be judged in terms of their *own* time (Sefer HaParshiyos).

10. *Shem, Ham, and Japheth.* Japheth was the eldest, but Shem is mentioned first because Scripture enumerates them according to wisdom, not age (Sanhedrin 69b).

11. *Corrupt* — with immorality and idolatry.

Before God. At first they sinned covertly — they were corrupt only *'before God.'* Later they sinned openly — *and the earth had become filled with robbery* — so that their robbery was obvious to all (*Zohar*).

13. The decree is revealed.

14. The Ark. *Rashi* queries: God could have saved Noah in many ways. Why then did God burden him with the task of constructing an Ark? — So that when the curious would see him cutting down lumber and building the Ark for 120 years, they would ask him why. He would answer, 'God is about to bring a Flood on the world because of your sins,' and they would thus be given an opportunity to repent. . . . But Noah's contemporaries paid no attention to him.

15. Even according to the smallest estimate of 18 inches per cubit, the dimensions of the Ark were $450 \times 75 \times 45$ feet = 1,518,750 cubic feet. Each of its three stories had 33,750 sq. feet of floor space for a total of 101,250 sq. ft.

19. There are many huge beasts, such as elephants, and so many species of all sizes that ten such Arks could not contain them along with one year's provisions! It was a miracle that the small Ark could contain so much (*Ramban*).

20. The general directive of the preceding verse is now specified (*Ibn Caspi*).

The animals came of their own accord, and Noah led them past the Ark. The Ark accepted only those which had not been the object of sin, and Noah permitted them to enter (*Rashi; Sanhedrin* 108b).

⁹ These are the offspring of Noah — Noah was a righteous man, perfect in his generations; Noah walked with God. — ¹⁰Noah had begotten three sons: Shem, Ham, and Japheth.

¹¹ Now the earth had become corrupt before God; and the earth had become filled with robbery. ¹² And God saw the earth and behold it was corrupted, for all flesh had corrupted its way upon the earth.

¹³ God said to Noah, 'The end of all flesh has come before Me, for the earth is filled with robbery through them; and behold, I am about to destroy them from the earth. ¹⁴ Make yourself an Ark of gopher wood; make the Ark with compartments, and cover it inside and out with pitch. ¹⁵ This is how you should make it — the length of the Ark: three hundred cubits; its width: fifty cubits, and its height: thirty cubits. ¹⁶ A light shall you make for the Ark, and to a cubit finish it from above. Put the entrance of the Ark in its side; make it with bottom, second, and third decks.

¹⁷ 'And as for Me — Behold I am about to bring the Flood-waters upon the earth to destroy all flesh in which there is a breath of life under the heavens; everything that is in the earth shall expire. ¹⁸But I will establish My covenant with you, and you shall enter the Ark — you, your sons, your wife, and your sons' wives with you. ¹⁹ And from all that lives, of all flesh, two of each shall you bring into the Ark to keep alive with you; they shall be male and female. ²⁰ From the birds according to each kind, and from the animals according to each kind, and from each thing that creeps on the ground according to its kind, two of each shall come to you to keep alive.

כא וְאַתָּה קַח־לְךָ מִכָּל־מַאֲכָל אֲשֶׁר יֵאָכֵל וְאָסַפְתָּ אֵלֶיךָ וְהָיָה לְךָ וְלָהֶם לְאָכְלָה: כב וַיַּעַשׂ נֹחַ כְּכֹל אֲשֶׁר צִוָּה אֹתוֹ אֱלֹהִים כֵּן עָשָׂה: **ז** שני א וַיֹּאמֶר יהוה לְנֹחַ בֹּא־אַתָּה וְכָל־בֵּיתְךָ אֶל־הַתֵּבָה כִּי־אֹתְךָ רָאִיתִי צַדִּיק לְפָנַי בַּדּוֹר הַזֶּה: ב מִכֹּל | הַבְּהֵמָה הַטְּהוֹרָה תִּקַּח־לְךָ שִׁבְעָה שִׁבְעָה אִישׁ וְאִשְׁתּוֹ וּמִן־הַבְּהֵמָה אֲשֶׁר לֹא טְהֹרָה הִוא שְׁנַיִם אִישׁ וְאִשְׁתּוֹ: ג גַּם מֵעוֹף הַשָּׁמַיִם שִׁבְעָה שִׁבְעָה זָכָר וּנְקֵבָה לְחַיּוֹת זֶרַע עַל־פְּנֵי כָל־הָאָרֶץ: ד כִּי לְיָמִים עוֹד שִׁבְעָה אָנֹכִי מַמְטִיר עַל־הָאָרֶץ אַרְבָּעִים יוֹם וְאַרְבָּעִים לָיְלָה וּמָחִיתִי אֶת־כָּל־הַיְקוּם אֲשֶׁר עָשִׂיתִי מֵעַל פְּנֵי הָאֲדָמָה: ה וַיַּעַשׂ נֹחַ כְּכֹל אֲשֶׁר־צִוָּהוּ יהוה: ו וְנֹחַ בֶּן־שֵׁשׁ מֵאוֹת שָׁנָה וְהַמַּבּוּל הָיָה מַיִם עַל־הָאָרֶץ: ז וַיָּבֹא נֹחַ וּבָנָיו וְאִשְׁתּוֹ וּנְשֵׁי־בָנָיו אִתּוֹ אֶל־הַתֵּבָה מִפְּנֵי מֵי הַמַּבּוּל: ח מִן־הַבְּהֵמָה הַטְּהוֹרָה וּמִן־הַבְּהֵמָה אֲשֶׁר אֵינֶנָּה טְהֹרָה וּמִן־הָעוֹף וְכֹל אֲשֶׁר־רֹמֵשׂ עַל־הָאֲדָמָה: ט שְׁנַיִם שְׁנַיִם בָּאוּ אֶל־נֹחַ אֶל־הַתֵּבָה זָכָר וּנְקֵבָה כַּאֲשֶׁר צִוָּה אֱלֹהִים אֶת־נֹחַ: י וַיְהִי לְשִׁבְעַת הַיָּמִים וּמֵי הַמַּבּוּל הָיוּ עַל־הָאָרֶץ: יא בִּשְׁנַת שֵׁשׁ־מֵאוֹת שָׁנָה לְחַיֵּי־נֹחַ בַּחֹדֶשׁ הַשֵּׁנִי בְּשִׁבְעָה־עָשָׂר יוֹם לַחֹדֶשׁ בַּיּוֹם הַזֶּה נִבְקְעוּ כָּל־מַעְיְנֹת תְּהוֹם רַבָּה וַאֲרֻבֹּת הַשָּׁמַיִם נִפְתָּחוּ: יב וַיְהִי הַגֶּשֶׁם עַל־

21. The Midrash records that Noah also stored away vine-shoots and various seeds for future planting after the Flood.

7/1. The final call. With the Flood to begin 'in seven days,' God bids Noah to enter the Ark with his family.

2. The directive is now clarified. Of all 'unclean' animals, two of each species — a male and a female — would *come* to Noah, but of the 'clean' animals he was to *take* seven pairs.

The meaning is: from every animal that the Torah would declare 'clean' [i.e., kosher as food for Israel]. This shows that Noah studied Torah *(Rashi)*.

Seven pairs were taken so he might be able to sacrifice some of them when he left the Ark *(Rashi)*, and also to provide an abundant supply of 'clean' livestock for food in anticipation of God's removal of the prohibition against eating meat [9:3] *(Radak)*.

5. Noah complies.

7. The men and the women entered separately because marital intimacy was forbidden at a time when the whole world was in distress *(Rashi)*.

8. אֲשֶׁר אֵינֶנָּה טְהֹרָה – *of the unclean.* Torah uses this long expression instead of the single word הַטְמֵאָה, *unclean.* This teaches a moral lesson: One should never utter a gross expression with his mouth, for the Torah added letters [in the Hebrew text of our verse] rather than utter a gross expression (*Pesachim* 3a).

9. The *two* mentioned in this verse was the minimum number; however, there were seven pairs of 'clean' animals (*Rashi*).

The people who approached the Ark knew they were doing so *because of the Flood-water* that God had decreed. The beasts were coming because the Spirit was drawing them . . . (*Haamek Davar*).

11. The final entry into the Ark.
In the six hundredth year — in the year 1656 from Creation (*Seder Olam*). The Talmud notes that the waters were scalding hot (*Sanhedrin* 108b).

12. Noting that in verse 17 the narrative mentions 'Flood,' while here it refers to 'rain,' *Rashi* explains that the water began gently because — had the people repented at the last minute — it still would have become a rain of blessing. Only when they refused did it become a Flood.

²¹ 'And as for you, take yourself of every food that is eaten and gather it in to yourself, that it shall be as food for you and for them.' ²² Noah did so; just as God commanded him, so he did.

7 ¹ Then HASHEM said to Noah, 'Come to the Ark, you and all your household, for it is you that I have seen to be righteous before Me in this generation. ² Of every clean animal atake unto you seven pairs, a male with its mate, and of the unclean animals, two, a male with its mate; ³ of the birds of the heavens also, seven pairs, male and female, to keep seed alive upon the face of all the earth. ⁴ For in seven days' time I will send rain upon the earth, forty days and forty nights, and I will blot out all existence that I have made from the face of the ground.' ⁵ And Noah did exactly as HASHEM had commanded him.

⁶ Noah was six hundred years old when the Flood was water upon the earth. ⁷ Noah, with his sons, his wife, and his sons' wives with him, went into the Ark because of the waters of the Flood. ⁸ Of the clean animals, of the unclean animals, of the birds, and of each thing that creeps upon the ground, ⁹ in pairs, they came to Noah into the Ark, male and female, as God had commanded Noah. ¹⁰ And it came to pass on the seventh day that the waters of the Flood were upon the earth.

¹¹ In the six hundredth year of Noah's life, in the second month, on the seventeenth day of the month, on that day all the fountains of the great deep burst forth; and the windows of the heavens were opened. ¹² And the rain was upon

הָאָרֶץ אַרְבָּעִים יוֹם וְאַרְבָּעִים לָיְלָה: יג בְּעֶצֶם הַיּוֹם הַזֶּה בָּא נֹחַ וְשֵׁם־וְחָם וָיֶפֶת בְּנֵי־נֹחַ וְאֵשֶׁת נֹחַ וּשְׁלֹשֶׁת נְשֵׁי־בָנָיו אִתָּם אֶל־הַתֵּבָה: יד הֵמָּה וְכָל־הַחַיָּה לְמִינָהּ וְכָל־הַבְּהֵמָה לְמִינָהּ וְכָל־הָרֶמֶשׂ הָרֹמֵשׂ עַל־הָאָרֶץ לְמִינֵהוּ וְכָל־הָעוֹף לְמִינֵהוּ כֹּל צִפּוֹר כָּל־כָּנָף: טו וַיָּבֹאוּ אֶל־נֹחַ אֶל־הַתֵּבָה שְׁנַיִם שְׁנַיִם מִכָּל־הַבָּשָׂר אֲשֶׁר־בּוֹ רוּחַ חַיִּים: טז וְהַבָּאִים זָכָר וּנְקֵבָה מִכָּל־בָּשָׂר בָּאוּ כַּאֲשֶׁר צִוָּה אֹתוֹ אֱלֹהִים וַיִּסְגֹּר יְהוָה בַּעֲדוֹ: שלישי יז וַיְהִי הַמַּבּוּל אַרְבָּעִים יוֹם עַל־הָאָרֶץ וַיִּרְבּוּ הַמַּיִם וַיִּשְׂאוּ אֶת־הַתֵּבָה וַתָּרָם מֵעַל הָאָרֶץ: יח וַיִּגְבְּרוּ הַמַּיִם וַיִּרְבּוּ מְאֹד עַל־הָאָרֶץ וַתֵּלֶךְ הַתֵּבָה עַל־פְּנֵי הַמָּיִם: יט וְהַמַּיִם גָּבְרוּ מְאֹד מְאֹד עַל־הָאָרֶץ וַיְכֻסּוּ כָּל־הֶהָרִים הַגְּבֹהִים אֲשֶׁר־תַּחַת כָּל־הַשָּׁמָיִם: כ חֲמֵשׁ עֶשְׂרֵה אַמָּה מִלְמַעְלָה גָּבְרוּ הַמָּיִם וַיְכֻסּוּ הֶהָרִים: כא וַיִּגְוַע כָּל־בָּשָׂר ׀ הָרֹמֵשׂ עַל־הָאָרֶץ בָּעוֹף וּבַבְּהֵמָה וּבַחַיָּה וּבְכָל־הַשֶּׁרֶץ הַשֹּׁרֵץ עַל־הָאָרֶץ וְכֹל הָאָדָם: כב כֹּל אֲשֶׁר נִשְׁמַת־רוּחַ חַיִּים בְּאַפָּיו מִכֹּל אֲשֶׁר בֶּחָרָבָה מֵתוּ: כג וַיִּמַח אֶת־כָּל־הַיְקוּם ׀ אֲשֶׁר ׀ עַל־פְּנֵי הָאֲדָמָה מֵאָדָם עַד־בְּהֵמָה עַד־רֶמֶשׂ וְעַד־עוֹף הַשָּׁמַיִם וַיִּמָּחוּ מִן־הָאָרֶץ וַיִּשָּׁאֶר אַךְ־נֹחַ וַאֲשֶׁר אִתּוֹ בַּתֵּבָה: כד וַיִּגְבְּרוּ הַמַּיִם עַל־הָאָרֶץ חֲמִשִּׁים וּמְאַת יוֹם:

14. The verse includes every kind of winged creature — even locusts (Rashi).

15. Here we find man in his loftiest state. The entire world comes to him to save and preserve it (R' Hirsch).

They came in matched pairs — not one species missing — that was the wonder! (Ibn Caspi). . . . All this could not have happened except by a miracle (R' Bachya).

17. The ravages of the Flood.

18. Verse 17 tells us that the waters lifted the Ark; here we are told that as the waters became more violent they tossed it aimlessly about (Radak).

20. Mt. Ararat was the world's highest mountain at the time of the Flood, and the waters rose to 15 cubits above Ararat. The numerous mountains that are now far higher than Ararat came into being as a result of the upheavals of the Flood (Haamek Davar).

21. Even those who climbed to the highest mountain peaks now found nowhere else to flee and they drowned (*Rosh*).

22. The scalding heat of the Flood-waters did not affect the fish because God directed the ravages of the Flood to dry land. The fish did not participate in man's sins, so they were spared (*Maharsha* citing *Zevachim* 113b).

23. The upheaval of those months of intense heat and turmoil caused a great shifting and turning of geological strata and a deep burial of animal remains. Thus the attempt to date the earth and fossils is futile (*Malbim*).

the earth forty days and forty nights.

¹³ On that very day Noah came, with Shem, Ham, and Japheth, Noah's sons with Noah's wife and the three wives of his sons with them into the Ark — ¹⁴ they and every beast after its kind, every cattle after its kind, every creeping thing that creeps on the earth after its kind, and all birds after its kind, and every bird of any kind of wing. ¹⁵ They came to Noah into the Ark; in pairs of all flesh in which there was a breath of life. ¹⁶ Thus they that came, came male and female of all flesh, as God had commanded him. And HASHEM shut it on his behalf.

¹⁷ When the Flood was on the earth forty days, the waters increased and raised the Ark so that it was lifted above the earth. ¹⁸ The waters prevailed and increased greatly upon the earth, and the Ark drifted upon the surface of the waters. ¹⁹ The waters prevailed very much upon the earth, all the high mountains which are under the heavens were covered. ²⁰ Fifteen cubits upward did the waters prevail, and the mountains were covered. ²¹ And all flesh that moves upon the earth expired — among the birds, the cattle, the beasts, and all the things that creeps upon the earth, and all mankind. ²² All in whose nostrils was the breath of the spirit of life, whatever was on dry land, died. ²³ And He blotted out all existence on earth — from man to animals to creeping things and to the bird of the heavens; and they were blotted out from the earth. Only Noah survived, and those with him in the Ark. ²⁴ And the waters prevailed on the earth a hundred and fifty days.

ח**א** וַיִּזְכֹּר אֱלֹהִים אֶת־נֹחַ וְאֵת כָּל־הַחַיָּה וְאֶת־כָּל־הַבְּהֵמָה אֲשֶׁר אִתּוֹ בַּתֵּבָה וַיַּעֲבֵר אֱלֹהִים רוּחַ עַל־הָאָרֶץ וַיָּשֹׁכּוּ הַמָּיִם: **ב** וַיִּסָּכְרוּ מַעְיְנֹת תְּהוֹם וַאֲרֻבֹּת הַשָּׁמָיִם וַיִּכָּלֵא הַגֶּשֶׁם מִן־הַשָּׁמָיִם: **ג** וַיָּשֻׁבוּ הַמַּיִם מֵעַל הָאָרֶץ הָלוֹךְ וָשׁוֹב וַיַּחְסְרוּ הַמַּיִם מִקְצֵה חֲמִשִּׁים וּמְאַת יוֹם: **ד** וַתָּנַח הַתֵּבָה בַּחֹדֶשׁ הַשְּׁבִיעִי בְּשִׁבְעָה־עָשָׂר יוֹם לַחֹדֶשׁ עַל הָרֵי אֲרָרָט: **ה** וְהַמַּיִם הָיוּ הָלוֹךְ וְחָסוֹר עַד הַחֹדֶשׁ הָעֲשִׂירִי בָּעֲשִׂירִי בְּאֶחָד לַחֹדֶשׁ נִרְאוּ רָאשֵׁי הֶהָרִים: **ו** וַיְהִי מִקֵּץ אַרְבָּעִים יוֹם וַיִּפְתַּח נֹחַ אֶת־חַלּוֹן הַתֵּבָה אֲשֶׁר עָשָׂה: **ז** וַיְשַׁלַּח אֶת־הָעֹרֵב וַיֵּצֵא יָצוֹא וָשׁוֹב עַד־יְבֹשֶׁת הַמַּיִם מֵעַל הָאָרֶץ: **ח** וַיְשַׁלַּח אֶת־הַיּוֹנָה מֵאִתּוֹ לִרְאוֹת הֲקַלּוּ הַמַּיִם מֵעַל פְּנֵי הָאֲדָמָה: **ט** וְלֹא־מָצְאָה הַיּוֹנָה מָנוֹחַ לְכַף־רַגְלָהּ וַתָּשָׁב אֵלָיו אֶל־הַתֵּבָה כִּי־מַיִם עַל־פְּנֵי כָל־הָאָרֶץ וַיִּשְׁלַח יָדוֹ וַיִּקָּחֶהָ וַיָּבֵא אֹתָהּ אֵלָיו אֶל־הַתֵּבָה: **י** וַיָּחֶל עוֹד שִׁבְעַת יָמִים אֲחֵרִים וַיֹּסֶף שַׁלַּח אֶת־הַיּוֹנָה מִן־הַתֵּבָה: **יא** וַתָּבֹא אֵלָיו הַיּוֹנָה לְעֵת עֶרֶב וְהִנֵּה עֲלֵה־זַיִת טָרָף בְּפִיהָ וַיֵּדַע נֹחַ כִּי־קַלּוּ הַמַּיִם מֵעַל הָאָרֶץ: **יב** וַיִּיָּחֶל עוֹד שִׁבְעַת יָמִים אֲחֵרִים וַיְשַׁלַּח אֶת־הַיּוֹנָה וְלֹא־יָסְפָה שׁוּב־אֵלָיו עוֹד: **יג** וַיְהִי בְּאַחַת וְשֵׁשׁ־מֵאוֹת שָׁנָה בָּרִאשׁוֹן בְּאֶחָד

8/1. The waters recede. 'Remembered' in this verse implies that He took cognizance of some virtuous act:
— God 'remembered' that Noah cared for the animals for over twelve months in the Ark *(Midrash)* . . .
—He 'remembered' that the cattle had not previously perverted their way, and that they had refrained from mating in the Ark *(Rashi)* . . .
— He noted that Noah was a perfectly righteous man, and His covenant to save him. Concerning the animals, God *remembered* His plan that the earth should continue with the same species as before *(Ramban)*.

The translation of רוּחַ as *spirit* follows *Rashi* and many commentators. *Ramban* and others render *wind*.

4. *Ararat.* The mountain range of Cordeyne *(Midrash; Onkelos; R' Saadiah)*. *Targum Yonasan* identifies this with Armenia.

7. Sending forth the raven.
Ravens feed on carrion of man and beast. Noah reasoned that if the raven would bring some back, he would know that the water had descended enough for the raven to have found some carrion on the ground *(Radak)*.

As a result of the mission, the raven continually flew to and fro until it left the Ark when the earth dried *(Ibn Ezra)*.

8. The dove. It was after seven days that Noah set the dove free: If it would find a resting place it would not return to him *(Rashi)*.

13. The earth dries. *Rashi* notes that the earth's surface had dried, but it was not yet firm enough to walk upon. Thus, Noah waited for God's command to leave the Ark *(Midrash; Radak)*.

8 ¹ God remembered Noah and all the beasts and all the cattle that were with him in the Ark, and God caused a spirit to pass over the earth, and the waters subsided. ² The fountains of the deep and the windows of the heavens were closed, and the rain from heaven was restrained. ³ The waters then receded continuously from upon the earth, and the waters diminished at the end of a hundred and fifty days. ⁴ And the Ark came to rest in the seventh month, on the seventeenth day of the month upon the mountains of Ararat. ⁵ The waters were continuously diminishing until the tenth month. In the tenth month, on the first of the month, the tops of the mountains became visible.

⁶ And it came to pass at the end of forty days, that Noah opened the window of the Ark which he had made. ⁷ He sent out a raven, and it kept going and returning until the waters dried from upon the earth. ⁸ Then he sent out a dove from him to see whether the waters had subsided from the face of the ground. ⁹ But the dove could not find a resting place for the sole of its foot, and it returned to him to the Ark, for water was upon the surface of all the earth. So he put forth his hand, and took it, and brought it to him to the Ark. ¹⁰ He waited again another seven days, and again sent out the dove from the Ark. ¹¹ The dove came back to him in the evening, and behold, an olive-leaf it had plucked with its bill! And Noah knew that the waters had subsided from upon the earth. ¹² Then he waited again another seven days and sent the dove forth; and it did not return to him any more.

¹³ And it came to pass in the six hundred and first year, in the first month, on the first of the

לַחֹדֶשׁ חָרְבוּ הַמַּיִם מֵעַל הָאָרֶץ וַיָּסַר נֹחַ
אֶת־מִכְסֵה הַתֵּבָה וַיַּרְא וְהִנֵּה חָרְבוּ פְּנֵי
הָאֲדָמָה: יד וּבַחֹדֶשׁ הַשֵּׁנִי בְּשִׁבְעָה וְעֶשְׂרִים
יוֹם לַחֹדֶשׁ יָבְשָׁה הָאָרֶץ: רביעי טו וַיְדַבֵּר
אֱלֹהִים אֶל־נֹחַ לֵאמֹר: טז צֵא מִן־הַתֵּבָה
אַתָּה וְאִשְׁתְּךָ וּבָנֶיךָ וּנְשֵׁי־בָנֶיךָ אִתָּךְ: יז כָּל־
הַחַיָּה אֲשֶׁר־אִתְּךָ מִכָּל־בָּשָׂר בָּעוֹף וּבַבְּהֵמָה
וּבְכָל־הָרֶמֶשׂ הָרֹמֵשׂ עַל־הָאָרֶץ °הוֹצֵא אִתָּךְ
וְשָׁרְצוּ בָאָרֶץ וּפָרוּ וְרָבוּ עַל־הָאָרֶץ: יח וַיֵּצֵא־
נֹחַ וּבָנָיו וְאִשְׁתּוֹ וּנְשֵׁי־בָנָיו אִתּוֹ: יט כָּל־הַחַיָּה
כָּל־הָרֶמֶשׂ וְכָל־הָעוֹף כֹּל רוֹמֵשׂ עַל־הָאָרֶץ
לְמִשְׁפְּחֹתֵיהֶם יָצְאוּ מִן־הַתֵּבָה: כ וַיִּבֶן נֹחַ
מִזְבֵּחַ לַיהוה וַיִּקַּח מִכֹּל ׀ הַבְּהֵמָה הַטְּהֹרָה
וּמִכֹּל הָעוֹף הַטָּהוֹר וַיַּעַל עֹלֹת בַּמִּזְבֵּחַ:
כא וַיָּרַח יהוה אֶת־רֵיחַ הַנִּיחֹחַ וַיֹּאמֶר יהוה
אֶל־לִבּוֹ לֹא־אֹסִף לְקַלֵּל עוֹד אֶת־הָאֲדָמָה
בַּעֲבוּר הָאָדָם כִּי יֵצֶר לֵב הָאָדָם רַע מִנְּעֻרָיו
וְלֹא־אֹסִף עוֹד לְהַכּוֹת אֶת־כָּל־חַי כַּאֲשֶׁר
עָשִׂיתִי: כב עֹד כָּל־יְמֵי הָאָרֶץ זֶרַע וְקָצִיר וְקֹר
וָחֹם וְקַיִץ וָחֹרֶף וְיוֹם וָלַיְלָה לֹא יִשְׁבֹּתוּ:
ט א וַיְבָרֶךְ אֱלֹהִים אֶת־נֹחַ וְאֶת־בָּנָיו וַיֹּאמֶר
לָהֶם פְּרוּ וּרְבוּ וּמִלְאוּ אֶת־הָאָרֶץ:
ב וּמוֹרַאֲכֶם וְחִתְּכֶם יִהְיֶה עַל כָּל־חַיַּת
הָאָרֶץ וְעַל כָּל־עוֹף הַשָּׁמָיִם בְּכֹל אֲשֶׁר
תִּרְמֹשׂ הָאֲדָמָה וּבְכָל־דְּגֵי הַיָּם בְּיֶדְכֶם נִתָּנוּ:
° הַיְצֵא ק׳

15. The command to leave the Ark.
The Divine Name *Elohim* is used throughout the narrative because it represents Him as the God of Nature Who created and preserves the natural world (*Haamek Davar*).

17. The *ksiv* (Masoretic spelling) is הוֹצֵא, while the *keri* (Masoretic pronunciation) is הַיְצֵא. *Rashi* explains the duality: הַיְצֵא means *'order them out,'* i.e., tell them to leave on their own, while הוֹצֵא means *'force them out . . . if they refuse to leave.'*

20. Noah brings an offering.
In connection with sacrifices, God is always referred to as HASHEM, the Name signifying the Attribute of Mercy. This proves that offerings are directed toward the Merciful God who desires *life*, not death and suffering. The purpose of the sacrificial service is to bring about a person's closeness and dedication to Godliness. The non-Jewish, blasphemous view of sacrifices as an appeasement of a 'vengeful God of nature' could never be connected with the name HASHEM (*R' Hirsch*).

21. . . . *is evil from his youth.* Man receives the Evil Inclination from birth, before he has the wisdom and maturity to combat it. Thus Mankind in general is undeserving of being wiped out totally because of sin. God will punish them in other ways *(Ramban; Abarbanel).*

22. As long as This World continues to exist, the natural cycle of the seasons will not cease. Apparently, during the Flood it *did* cease.

9/1. Rebuilding a ruined world. The world benefited from God's blessing to Adam until the Generation of the Flood abrogated it with their corruption. When Noah left the Ark, God renewed the blessing of prolific procreation by repeating it to Noah and his sons *(Tanchuma Yashan; Ibn Caspi).*

month, the waters dried from upon the earth; Noah removed the covering of the Ark, and looked — and behold! the surface of the ground had dried. [14] And in the second month, on the twenty-seventh day of the month, the earth was dried out.

[15] God spoke to Noah, saying, [16] 'Go forth from the Ark: you and your wife, your sons, and your sons' wives with you. [17] Every living being that is with you of all flesh, of birds, of animals, and creeping things that creep on earth — order them out with you, and let them teem on the earth and be fruitful and multiply on the earth.' [18] So Noah went forth, and his sons, his wife, and his sons' wives with him. [19] Every living being, every creeping thing, and every bird, everything that moves on earth came out of the Ark by their families.

[20] Then Noah built an altar to HASHEM and took of every clean animal and of every clean bird, and offered burnt offerings on the altar. [21] HASHEM smelled the pleasing aroma, and HASHEM said in His heart: 'I will not continue to curse again the ground because of man, since the imagery of man's heart is evil from his youth; nor will I again continue to smite every living being, as I have done. [22] Continuously, all the days of the earth, seedtime and harvest, cold and heat, summer and winter, day and night, shall not cease.'

9 [1] God blessed Noah and his sons, and He said to them, 'Be fruitful and multiply and fill the land. [2] The fear of you and the dread of you shall be upon every beast of the earth and upon every bird of the heavens, in all that moves on earth and in all the fish of the sea; in your hand they are given.

ג כָּל־רֶ֫מֶשׂ אֲשֶׁר הוּא־חַי לָכֶם יִהְיֶ֖ה לְאָכְלָ֑ה
כְּיֶ֣רֶק עֵ֔שֶׂב נָתַ֥תִּי לָכֶ֖ם אֶת־כֹּֽל: ד אַ֕ךְ־
בָּשָׂ֕ר בְּנַפְשׁ֥וֹ דָמ֖וֹ לֹ֥א תֹאכֵֽלוּ: ה וְאַ֨ךְ אֶת־
דִּמְכֶ֣ם לְנַפְשֹֽׁתֵיכֶם֮ אֶדְרֹשׁ֒ מִיַּ֤ד כָּל־חַיָּה֙
אֶדְרְשֶׁ֔נּוּ וּמִיַּ֣ד הָֽאָדָ֗ם מִיַּד֙ אִ֣ישׁ אָחִ֔יו אֶדְרֹ֖שׁ
אֶת־נֶ֥פֶשׁ הָֽאָדָֽם: ו שֹׁפֵךְ֙ דַּ֣ם הָֽאָדָ֔ם בָּֽאָדָ֖ם
דָּמ֣וֹ יִשָּׁפֵ֑ךְ כִּ֚י בְּצֶ֣לֶם אֱלֹהִ֔ים עָשָׂ֖ה אֶת־
הָֽאָדָֽם: ז וְאַתֶּ֖ם פְּר֣וּ וּרְב֑וּ שִׁרְצ֥וּ בָאָ֖רֶץ וּרְבוּ־
בָֽהּ: חמישי ח וַיֹּ֤אמֶר אֱלֹהִים֙ אֶל־נֹ֔חַ
וְאֶל־בָּנָ֥יו אִתּ֖וֹ לֵאמֹֽר: ט וַאֲנִ֕י הִנְנִ֥י מֵקִ֛ים
אֶת־בְּרִיתִ֖י אִתְּכֶ֑ם וְאֶֽת־זַרְעֲכֶ֖ם אַֽחֲרֵיכֶֽם:
י וְאֵ֣ת כָּל־נֶ֣פֶשׁ הַֽחַיָּה֮ אֲשֶׁ֣ר אִתְּכֶם֒ בָּע֧וֹף
בַּבְּהֵמָ֛ה וּבְכָל־חַיַּ֥ת הָאָ֖רֶץ אִתְּכֶ֑ם מִכֹּל֙ יֹֽצְאֵ֣י
הַתֵּבָ֔ה לְכֹ֖ל חַיַּ֥ת הָאָֽרֶץ: יא וַהֲקִֽמֹתִ֤י אֶת־
בְּרִיתִי֙ אִתְּכֶ֔ם וְלֹֽא־יִכָּרֵ֧ת כָּל־בָּשָׂ֛ר ע֖וֹד מִמֵּ֣י
הַמַּבּ֑וּל וְלֹֽא־יִהְיֶ֥ה ע֛וֹד מַבּ֖וּל לְשַׁחֵ֥ת הָאָֽרֶץ:
יב וַיֹּ֣אמֶר אֱלֹהִ֗ים זֹ֤את אֽוֹת־הַבְּרִית֙ אֲשֶׁר־אֲנִ֣י
נֹתֵ֗ן בֵּינִי֙ וּבֵ֣ינֵיכֶ֔ם וּבֵ֛ין כָּל־נֶ֥פֶשׁ חַיָּ֖ה אֲשֶׁ֣ר
אִתְּכֶ֑ם לְדֹרֹ֖ת עוֹלָֽם: יג אֶת־קַשְׁתִּ֕י נָתַ֖תִּי בֶּֽעָנָ֑ן
וְהָֽיְתָה֙ לְא֣וֹת בְּרִ֔ית בֵּינִ֖י וּבֵ֥ין הָאָֽרֶץ: יד וְהָיָ֕ה
בְּעַֽנְנִ֥י עָנָ֖ן עַל־הָאָ֑רֶץ וְנִרְאֲתָ֥ה הַקֶּ֖שֶׁת בֶּֽעָנָֽן:
טו וְזָכַרְתִּ֣י אֶת־בְּרִיתִ֗י אֲשֶׁ֤ר בֵּינִי֙ וּבֵ֣ינֵיכֶ֔ם וּבֵ֛ין
כָּל־נֶ֥פֶשׁ חַיָּ֖ה בְּכָל־בָּשָׂ֑ר וְלֹֽא־יִֽהְיֶ֨ה ע֤וֹד
הַמַּ֨יִם֙ לְמַבּ֔וּל לְשַׁחֵ֖ת כָּל־בָּשָֽׂר: טז וְהָֽיְתָ֥ה
הַקֶּ֖שֶׁת בֶּֽעָנָ֑ן וּרְאִיתִ֗יהָ לִזְכֹּר֙ בְּרִ֣ית עוֹלָ֔ם בֵּ֣ין
אֱלֹהִ֔ים וּבֵין֙ כָּל־נֶ֣פֶשׁ חַיָּ֔ה בְּכָל־בָּשָׂ֖ר אֲשֶׁ֥ר

3. Permission to eat meat. The animals were saved in an Ark which you toiled to build, and their salvation came about through you. Therefore they are yours to do with as you please — like the green herbs of the field (*B'chor Shor*).

4. But there are limitations. A limb cut from a living animal is prohibited . . .

5. . . . and the spilling of one's own blood, i.e., suicide, is prohibited (*Bava Kamma* 91a; *Rashi*). Also, animals will be held accountable for their deeds against man (*Radak*). Alternatively, this passage refers to a person who turns another over to be killed by wild beasts (*Torah Shleimah* 31,21). Or, according to *Ramban*, God will send wild beasts to avenge bloodshed in cases where there were no witnesses and the human court is powerless to execute judgment.

6. This verse refers to murder.

7. The similar statement made in verse 1 constituted a blessing; here the verse is understood as a command-ment *(Sanhedrin 59b).*

8. The fulfillment of the covenant.

10. This covenant would ex-tend not only to Noah and his descendants, but to every living being.

13. The rainbow as a sign. Rainbows had existed since Creation, but now this natural phenomenon was designated as an eternal symbol of God's covenant never again to destroy humanity by a flood *(Ramban; R' Hirsch).*

³ Every moving thing that lives shall be food for you; as the green herbage I give you everything. ⁴ But flesh; with its soul its blood you shall not eat. ⁵ However, your blood which belongs to your souls I will demand, of every beast will I demand it; but of man, of every man for that of his brother I will demand the soul of man. ⁶ Whoever sheds the blood of man, by man shall his blood be shed; for in the image of God He made man. ⁷ And you, be fruitful and multiply; teem on the earth and multiply on it.'

⁸ And God said to Noah and to his sons with him: ⁹ 'And as for Me, behold I establish My covenant with you and with your offspring after you, ¹⁰ and with every living being that is with you — with the birds, with the cattle, and with every beast of the land with you — of all that departed the Ark, to every beast of the earth. ¹¹ And I will ratify My covenant with you: Never again shall all flesh be cut off by the waters of a flood, and never again shall there be a flood to destroy the earth.'

¹²And God said, 'This is the sign of the covenant that I give between Me and you, and every living being that is with you, to generations forever: ¹³ I have set My bow in the cloud, and it shall be a sign of the covenant between Me and the earth. ¹⁴ And it shall happen, when I place a cloud over the earth, and the bow will be seen in the cloud, ¹⁵ I will remember My covenant between Me and you and every living being among all flesh, and the water shall never again become a flood to destroy all flesh. ¹⁶ And the bow shall be in the cloud, and I will look upon it to remember the everlasting covenant between God and every living being, among all flesh that is

עַל־הָאָ֑רֶץ: יז וַיֹּ֥אמֶר אֱלֹהִ֖ים אֶל־נֹ֑חַ זֹ֤את אֽוֹת־הַבְּרִית֙ אֲשֶׁ֣ר הֲקִמֹ֔תִי בֵּינִ֕י וּבֵ֥ין כָּל־בָּשָׂ֖ר אֲשֶׁ֥ר עַל־הָאָֽרֶץ:

ששי יח וַיִּהְי֣וּ בְנֵי־נֹ֗חַ הַיֹּֽצְאִים֙ מִן־הַתֵּבָ֔ה שֵׁ֥ם וְחָ֖ם וָיָ֑פֶת וְחָ֕ם ה֖וּא אֲבִ֥י כְנָֽעַן: יט שְׁלֹשָׁ֥ה אֵ֖לֶּה בְּנֵי־נֹ֑חַ וּמֵאֵ֖לֶּה נָֽפְצָ֥ה כָל־הָאָֽרֶץ: כ וַיָּ֥חֶל נֹ֖חַ אִ֣ישׁ הָֽאֲדָמָ֑ה וַיִּטַּ֖ע כָּֽרֶם: כא וַיֵּ֥שְׁתְּ מִן־הַיַּ֖יִן וַיִּשְׁכָּ֑ר וַיִּתְגַּ֖ל בְּת֥וֹךְ אָֽהֳלֹֽה: כב וַיַּ֗רְא חָ֚ם אֲבִ֣י כְנַ֔עַן אֵ֖ת עֶרְוַ֣ת אָבִ֑יו וַיַּגֵּ֥ד לִשְׁנֵֽי־אֶחָ֖יו בַּחֽוּץ: כג וַיִּקַּח֩ שֵׁ֨ם וָיֶ֜פֶת אֶת־הַשִּׂמְלָ֗ה וַיָּשִׂ֨ימוּ֙ עַל־שְׁכֶ֣ם שְׁנֵיהֶ֔ם וַיֵּֽלְכוּ֙ אֲחֹ֣רַנִּ֔ית וַיְכַסּ֕וּ אֵ֖ת עֶרְוַ֣ת אֲבִיהֶ֑ם וּפְנֵיהֶם֙ אֲחֹ֣רַנִּ֔ית וְעֶרְוַ֥ת אֲבִיהֶ֖ם לֹ֥א רָאֽוּ: כד וַיִּ֥יקֶץ נֹ֖חַ מִיֵּינ֑וֹ וַיֵּ֕דַע אֵ֛ת אֲשֶׁר־עָ֥שָׂה ל֖וֹ בְּנ֥וֹ הַקָּטָֽן: כה וַיֹּ֖אמֶר אָר֣וּר כְּנָ֑עַן עֶ֥בֶד עֲבָדִ֖ים יִֽהְיֶ֥ה לְאֶחָֽיו: כו וַיֹּ֕אמֶר בָּר֥וּךְ יְהֹוָ֖ה אֱלֹ֣הֵי שֵׁ֑ם וִיהִ֥י כְנַ֖עַן עֶ֥בֶד לָֽמוֹ: כז יַ֤פְתְּ אֱלֹהִים֙ לְיֶ֔פֶת וְיִשְׁכֹּ֖ן בְּאָֽהֳלֵי־שֵׁ֑ם וִיהִ֥י כְנַ֖עַן עֶ֥בֶד לָֽמוֹ: כח וַֽיְחִי־נֹ֖חַ אַחַ֣ר הַמַּבּ֑וּל שְׁלֹ֤שׁ מֵאוֹת֙ שָׁנָ֔ה וַֽחֲמִשִּׁ֖ים שָׁנָֽה: כט וַיִּֽהְי֙וּ כָּל־יְמֵי־נֹ֔חַ תְּשַׁ֤ע מֵאוֹת֙ שָׁנָ֔ה וַֽחֲמִשִּׁ֖ים שָׁנָ֑ה וַיָּמֹֽת:

י א וְאֵ֙לֶּה֙ תּֽוֹלְדֹ֣ת בְּנֵי־נֹ֔חַ שֵׁ֖ם חָ֣ם וָיָ֑פֶת וַיִּוָּֽלְד֥וּ לָהֶ֛ם בָּנִ֖ים אַחַ֥ר הַמַּבּֽוּל: ב בְּנֵ֣י יֶ֔פֶת גֹּ֣מֶר וּמָג֗וֹג וּמָדַ֤י וְיָוָן֙ וְתֻבָ֔ל וּמֶ֖שֶׁךְ וְתִירָֽס: ג וּבְנֵ֖י גֹּ֑מֶר אַשְׁכְּנַ֥ז וְרִיפַ֖ת וְתֹֽגַרְמָֽה: ד וּבְנֵ֥י יָוָ֖ן אֱלִישָׁ֥ה

17. *This is the sign . . .* When you and those like you see it, you must bestir yourselves to rouse people to repent *(Sforno)*.

18. The intoxication and shame of Noah.

19. The Torah stresses in this verse the phenomenon that one righteous and perfect father produced three such radically different sons! *(R' Hirsch)*.

The ancients divided three continents: Asia was taken by Shem; Africa by Ham; and Europe by Japheth *(Abarbanel)*.

23. The verb is in the singular because Shem alone took the initiative in this meritorious deed, then Japheth joined him. Therefore, the descendants of Shem (i.e., Jews) were rewarded with the *mitzvah* of fringed garments [*tzitzis*]; those of Japheth with burial in *Eretz Yisrael* [*Ezek.* 39:11]; those of Ham were eventually *led away by the king of Assyria . . . naked and barefoot* (Midrash; Rashi).

24. Although Ham was not the youngest, he is called *small*, because he was *unfit and despised* (Rashi).

25. Ham sinned and Canaan is cursed! God already blessed Noah and his sons, and there cannot be a curse where a blessing had already been given. Therefore Noah cursed his grandson (Midrash).

28. The death of Noah.

Actually, Noah died later in the narrative, but the Torah does not necessarily record events in chronological sequence. Furthermore, the Torah records a person's death when his significant activity is over.

Noah was born in the year 1056 from Creation. The Flood began in 1656, his

600th year, and he died in 2006, ten years after the Dispersion. Thus, Abraham who was born in 1948 was 58 years old when Noah died *(Seder Olam)*. It follows then that Abraham saw Noah, who in turn saw Lamech, who had seen Adam. Thus from Adam to Abraham there was a word-of-mouth tradition from Creation spanning only four people. Similarly, Moses, who wrote the Torah, saw Kehath [or Amram] who saw Jacob, who saw Abraham. Accordingly, there were not more than seven people who carried the tradition first hand from Adam to Moses *(Abarbanel)*.

10/1. The descendants of Noah. The seventy nations.

The Talmudic tradition that there are seventy primary nations is based upon the ensuing list of Noah's descendants *(R' Bachya)*.

[Some better-known names will be briefly identified here; for a complete commentary, see the full *ArtScroll Bereishis.*]

2. The line of Japheth (14 nations).
Gomer — Germania *(Yoma* 10a); *Targum Yonasan:* Africa.
Magog — Kandia *(Yoma)*; Mongols *(Kesses HaSofer)*.
Madai — Macedonia *(Yoma)*; *Targ. Yonasan:* the Medes.
Javan — Greece; Ionians.
Tiras — Persia *(Rashi)*.

3. Of the seven sons of Japheth (mentioned in v. 2), only the genealogies of Gomer and Javan are continued. The Torah concerns itself with those who developed into heads of new nations.

Ashkenaz — Asia *(Midrash)*; Teutons *(Yossipon)*; Slav *(R' Saadiah)*; later Rabbinic literature identified them with the Germans.

on earth.' [17] And God said to Noah, 'This is the sign of the covenant that I have established between Me and all flesh that is upon the earth.'

[18] The sons of Noah who came out of the Ark were Shem, Ham, and Japheth — Ham being the father of Canaan. [19] These three were the sons of Noah, and from these the whole world was spread out.

[20] Noah, the man of the earth, debased himself and planted a vineyard. [21] He drank of the wine and became drunk, and he uncovered himself within his tent. [22] Ham, the father of Canaan, saw his father's nakedness and told his two brothers outside. [23] And Shem and Japheth took a garment, laid it upon both their shoulders, and they walked backwards, and covered their father's nakedness; their faces were turned away, and they saw not their father's nakedness.

[24] Noah awoke from his wine and realized what his small son had done to him. [25] And he said, 'Cursed is Canaan; a slave of slaves shall he be to his brothers.'

[26] And he said, 'Blessed is HASHEM, the God of Shem; and let Canaan be a slave to them.

[27] 'May God extend Japheth, but he will dwell in the tents of Shem; may Canaan be a slave to them.'

[28] Noah lived after the Flood 350 years. [29] And all the days of Noah were 950 years; and he died.

10 [1] These are the descendants of Shem, Ham, and Japheth, the sons of Noah; sons were born to them after the Flood.

[2] The children of Japheth: Gomer, Magog, Madai, Javan, Tubal, Meshech, and Tiras. [3] The descendants of Gomer: Ashkenaz, Riphath, and Togarmah. [4] The descendants of Javan: Elishah

וְתַרְשִׁישׁ כִּתִּים וְדֹדָנִים: ה מֵאֵלֶּה נִפְרְדוּ אִיֵּי הַגּוֹיִם בְּאַרְצֹתָם אִישׁ לִלְשֹׁנוֹ לְמִשְׁפְּחֹתָם בְּגוֹיֵהֶם: ו וּבְנֵי חָם כּוּשׁ וּמִצְרַיִם וּפוּט וּכְנָעַן: ז וּבְנֵי כוּשׁ סְבָא וַחֲוִילָה וְסַבְתָּה וְרַעְמָה וְסַבְתְּכָא וּבְנֵי רַעְמָה שְׁבָא וּדְדָן: ח וְכוּשׁ יָלַד אֶת־נִמְרֹד הוּא הֵחֵל לִהְיוֹת גִּבֹּר בָּאָרֶץ: ט הוּא־הָיָה גִבֹּר־צַיִד לִפְנֵי יְהוָה עַל־כֵּן יֵאָמַר כְּנִמְרֹד גִּבּוֹר צַיִד לִפְנֵי יְהוָה: י וַתְּהִי רֵאשִׁית מַמְלַכְתּוֹ בָּבֶל וְאֶרֶךְ וְאַכַּד וְכַלְנֵה בְּאֶרֶץ שִׁנְעָר: יא מִן־הָאָרֶץ הַהִוא יָצָא אַשּׁוּר וַיִּבֶן אֶת־נִינְוֵה וְאֶת־רְחֹבֹת עִיר וְאֶת־כָּלַח: יב וְאֶת־רֶסֶן בֵּין נִינְוֵה וּבֵין כָּלַח הִוא הָעִיר הַגְּדֹלָה: יג וּמִצְרַיִם יָלַד אֶת־לוּדִים וְאֶת־עֲנָמִים וְאֶת־לְהָבִים וְאֶת־נַפְתֻּחִים: יד וְאֶת־פַּתְרֻסִים וְאֶת־כַּסְלֻחִים אֲשֶׁר יָצְאוּ מִשָּׁם פְּלִשְׁתִּים וְאֶת־כַּפְתֹּרִים: טו וּכְנַעַן יָלַד אֶת־צִידֹן בְּכֹרוֹ וְאֶת־חֵת: טז וְאֶת־הַיְבוּסִי וְאֶת־הָאֱמֹרִי וְאֵת הַגִּרְגָּשִׁי: יז וְאֶת־הַחִוִּי וְאֶת־הָעַרְקִי וְאֶת־הַסִּינִי: יח וְאֶת־הָאַרְוָדִי וְאֶת־הַצְּמָרִי וְאֶת־הַחֲמָתִי וְאַחַר נָפֹצוּ מִשְׁפְּחוֹת הַכְּנַעֲנִי: יט וַיְהִי גְּבוּל הַכְּנַעֲנִי מִצִּידֹן בֹּאֲכָה גְרָרָה עַד־עַזָּה בֹּאֲכָה סְדֹמָה וַעֲמֹרָה וְאַדְמָה וּצְבֹיִם עַד־לָשַׁע: כ אֵלֶּה בְנֵי־חָם לְמִשְׁפְּחֹתָם לִלְשֹׁנֹתָם בְּאַרְצֹתָם בְּגוֹיֵהֶם: כא וּלְשֵׁם יֻלַּד גַּם־הוּא אֲבִי כָּל־בְּנֵי־עֵבֶר אֲחִי יֶפֶת הַגָּדוֹל: כב בְּנֵי

---

4. Elishah — Ellas [Hellas] (*Midrash*); Italians (*Targ.* to Ezek. 27:7).

Kittim and Dodanim — Cyprus and Rhodes (*Abarbanel*).

5. From these sons of Japheth are descended all those who dwell along the coast, each one in his own land (*R' Hoffman*).

Each according to its language. The reference to different languages refers to the period *after* the Dispersion when God changed their common language [next chapter] and they spoke seventy different tongues (*Radak*).

6. The line of Ham (30 nations).

Cush — Arabia (*Targ. Yonasan*); later identified with Ethiopia, although the varying Biblical descriptions of Cush raise doubts about this.

8. Nimrod. Before Nimrod, there were neither wars nor reigning monarchs. He subjugated the Babylonians until they crowned him [v. 10], after which he went to Assyria and built great cities (*Radak; Ramban*).

9. *A mighty hunter.* This is the literal translation, but *Rashi* and most commentators interpret this figuratively: He ensnared men with his words and incited them to rebel against God. Nimrod was the forerunner of the hypocrite who drapes himself in robes of piety in order to deceive the masses (*R' Hirsch*).

10. Babel. Which is the *city* that, under Nebuchadnezzar, became the center of the Babylonian Empire. It was one of the greatest cities of the ancient world.

11. The translation follows *Rashi*. Ashur [possibly the son of Shem mentioned in v. 22 *(Radak)*] saw that his children were following Nimrod and rebelling against God by building a tower, so he left them *(Rashi)*. According to *Ramban*, the subject of the verse is still Nimrod, and the term אַשּׁוּר means that Nimrod went *to Assyria:* Nimrod expanded his empire to Assyria, whose principal city, *Nineveh*, is mentioned often in Scriptures.

13. The Hamite genealogy, interrupted in v. 7 by the account of Nimrod, continues.

14. *Whence the Philistines came forth.* The Philistines were the illegitimate descendants of both Pathrusim and Casluhim who intermingled with each other adulterously *(Rashi)*.

18. *Afterward . . .* From the above people, there arose other families that were known as *Canaanites (Rashi)*.

21. The line of Shem (26 nations). The line of Shem is mentioned last so the Torah can proceed to recount the history of Abraham and his descendants, who formed the primary nation of mankind.

Who lived on the other side [of the Euphrates], whence came Abraham's ancestors *(Ramban)*.

and Tarshish, the Kittim and the Dodanim. [5] From these the islands of the nations were separated in their lands — each according to its language, by their families, in their nations.

[6] The children of Ham: Cush, Mitzraim, Phut, and Canaan. [7] The children of Cush: Seba, Havilah, Sabtah, Raamah, and Sabteca. The children of Raamah: Sheba and Dedan.

[8] And Cush begot Nimrod. He was the first to be a mighty man on earth. [9] He was a mighty hunter before HASHEM; therefore it is said: 'Like Nimrod a mighty hunter before HASHEM.' [10] The beginning of his kingdom was Babel, Erech, Akkad, and Calneh in the land of Shinar. [11] From that land Ashur went forth and built Nineveh, Rechovoth-Ir, Calah, [12] and Resen between Nineveh and Calah, that is the great city.

[13] And Mitzraim begot Ludim, Anamim, Lehavim, Naphtuhim, [14] Pathrusim, and Casluhim, whence the Philistines came forth, and Caphtorim.

[15] Canaan begot Zidon his first-born, and Heth; [16] and the Jebusite, the Amorite, the Girgashite, [17] the Hivite, the Arkite, the Sinite, [18] the Arvadite, the Zemarite, and the Hamathite. Afterward, the families of the Canaanites branched out. [19] And the Canaanite boundary extended from Zidon going toward Gerar, as far as Gaza; going toward Sodom, Amorah, Admah, and Zeboiim, as far as Lasha. [20] These are the descendants of Ham, by their families, by their languages, in their lands, in their nations.

[21] And to Shem, also to him were born; he was the ancestor of all those who lived on the other side; the brother of Japheth the elder. [22] The sons

שֵׁם עֵילָם וְאַשּׁוּר וְאַרְפַּכְשַׁד וְלוּד וַאֲרָם:
כג וּבְנֵי אֲרָם עוּץ וְחוּל וְגֶתֶר וָמַשׁ:
כד וְאַרְפַּכְשַׁד יָלַד אֶת־שָׁלַח וְשֶׁלַח יָלַד אֶת־
עֵבֶר: כה וּלְעֵבֶר יֻלַּד שְׁנֵי בָנִים שֵׁם הָאֶחָד פֶּלֶג
כִּי בְיָמָיו נִפְלְגָה הָאָרֶץ וְשֵׁם אָחִיו יָקְטָן:
כו וְיָקְטָן יָלַד אֶת־אַלְמוֹדָד וְאֶת־שָׁלֶף וְאֶת־
חֲצַרְמָוֶת וְאֶת־יָרַח: כז וְאֶת־הֲדוֹרָם וְאֶת־
אוּזָל וְאֶת־דִּקְלָה: כח וְאֶת־עוֹבָל וְאֶת־
אֲבִימָאֵל וְאֶת־שְׁבָא: כט וְאֶת־אוֹפִר וְאֶת־
חֲוִילָה וְאֶת־יוֹבָב כָּל־אֵלֶּה בְּנֵי יָקְטָן: ל וַיְהִי
מוֹשָׁבָם מִמֵּשָׁא בֹּאֲכָה סְפָרָה הַר הַקֶּדֶם:
לא אֵלֶּה בְנֵי־שֵׁם לְמִשְׁפְּחֹתָם לִלְשֹׁנֹתָם
בְּאַרְצֹתָם לְגוֹיֵהֶם: לב אֵלֶּה מִשְׁפְּחֹת בְּנֵי־נֹחַ
לְתוֹלְדֹתָם בְּגוֹיֵהֶם וּמֵאֵלֶּה נִפְרְדוּ הַגּוֹיִם
בָּאָרֶץ אַחַר הַמַּבּוּל:

יא שביעי א וַיְהִי כָל־הָאָרֶץ שָׂפָה אֶחָת וּדְבָרִים
אֲחָדִים: ב וַיְהִי בְּנָסְעָם מִקֶּדֶם וַיִּמְצְאוּ בִקְעָה
בְּאֶרֶץ שִׁנְעָר וַיֵּשְׁבוּ שָׁם: ג וַיֹּאמְרוּ אִישׁ
אֶל־רֵעֵהוּ הָבָה נִלְבְּנָה לְבֵנִים וְנִשְׂרְפָה
לִשְׂרֵפָה וַתְּהִי לָהֶם הַלְּבֵנָה לְאָבֶן וְהַחֵמָר הָיָה
לָהֶם לַחֹמֶר: ד וַיֹּאמְרוּ הָבָה נִבְנֶה־לָּנוּ עִיר
וּמִגְדָּל וְרֹאשׁוֹ בַשָּׁמַיִם וְנַעֲשֶׂה־לָּנוּ שֵׁם פֶּן־
נָפוּץ עַל־פְּנֵי כָל־הָאָרֶץ: ה וַיֵּרֶד יהוה לִרְאֹת
אֶת־הָעִיר וְאֶת־הַמִּגְדָּל אֲשֶׁר בָּנוּ בְּנֵי הָאָדָם:
ו וַיֹּאמֶר יהוה הֵן עַם אֶחָד וְשָׂפָה אַחַת לְכֻלָּם
וְזֶה הַחִלָּם לַעֲשׂוֹת וְעַתָּה לֹא־יִבָּצֵר מֵהֶם כֹּל

25. *In his days the earth was divided.* The nations were dispersed from the plain throughout the world. The name Peleg signifies division. The name was prophetic, and was given him prophetically by his father Eber (*Rashi*).

30. *Mesha . . . Sephar.* Mecca and Medina (*R' Saadiah*).

11/1. The Tower of Babel and the Dispersion. *Rambam* in *Moreh Nevuchim* introduces the narrative of the Dispersion and explains that it is one of the fundamental principles of the Torah that the universe had been created *ex nihilo*, and Adam was the forerunner of the human race. Since the human race was later spread over all the earth, of different families, speaking very dissimilar languages, people might come to doubt this origin from one person. Therefore the Torah records the genealogy of the nations, why they were dispersed, and the cause of the formation of their different languages. *Malbim* adds that this is why the sins of that generation are not described at length, since they have no bearing on the reason the narrative is in the Torah.

The year is 1996, 340 years after the Flood. Noah and his children were still alive at the time, and Abraham, 48 years old, had already recognized his creator *(Seder Olam)*.

One language. Hebrew *(Rashi)*.

3. According to the Sages, Nimrod was the primary force behind this rebellion. He planned to build a tower ascending to Heaven and there wage war against Hashem. But though the *Midrashim* perceive sinister and idolatrous motives in this plan, the verses do not reveal the evil motives of the conspirators.

5. Hashem 'descended.' An obvious anthropomorphism. When God wishes to examine the deeds of lowly man, Scripture calls it *descent (Radak)*. Furthermore, the Midrash derives from this that a judge must not condemn the accused until he has investigated the case fully.

6. The plural indicates that God deliberated with His Celestial Court *(Rashi)*. According to others, the plural represents the royal 'We.'

of Shem: Elam, Asshur, Arpachshad, Lud, and Aram. ²³ The sons of Aram: Uz, Hul, Gether, and Mash. ²⁴ Arpachshad begot Shelah, and Shelah begot Eber. ²⁵ And to Eber were born two sons: The name of the first was Peleg, for in his days the earth was divided; and the name of his brother was Joktan. ²⁶ Joktan begot Almodad, Sheleph, Hazarmaveth, Jerah, ²⁷ Hadoram, Uzal, Diklah, ²⁸ Obal, Abimael, Sheba, ²⁹ Ophir, Havilah, and Jobab; all these were the sons of Joktan. ³⁰ Their dwelling place extended from Mesha as far as Sephar, the mountain to the east. ³¹ These are the descendants of Shem according to their families, by their languages, in their lands, by their nations.

³² These are the families of Noah's descendants, according to their generations, by their nations; and from these the nations were separated on the earth after the Flood.

11 ¹ The whole earth was of one language and of common purpose. ² And it came to pass, when they migrated from the east they found a plain in the land of Shinar and settled there. ³ They said to one another, 'Come, let us make bricks and burn them in fire.' And the brick served them as stone, and the bitumen served them as mortar. ⁴ And they said, 'Come, let us build us a city, and a tower with its top in the heavens, and let us make a name for ourselves, lest we be dispersed across the whole earth.'

⁵ HASHEM descended to look at the city and tower which the sons of man built, ⁶ and HASHEM said, 'Behold they are one people with one language for all, and this they begin to do! And now, should it not be withheld from them all

אֲשֶׁר יָזְמוּ לַעֲשׂוֹת: זהָבָה נֵרְדָה וְנָבְלָה שָׁם
שְׂפָתָם אֲשֶׁר לֹא יִשְׁמְעוּ אִישׁ שְׂפַת רֵעֵהוּ:
חוַיָּפֶץ יהוה אֹתָם מִשָּׁם עַל־פְּנֵי כָל־הָאָרֶץ
וַיַּחְדְּלוּ לִבְנֹת הָעִיר: טעַל־כֵּן קָרָא שְׁמָהּ בָּבֶל
כִּי־שָׁם בָּלַל יהוה שְׂפַת כָּל־הָאָרֶץ וּמִשָּׁם
הֱפִיצָם יהוה עַל־פְּנֵי כָּל־הָאָרֶץ:
יאֵלֶּה תּוֹלְדֹת שֵׁם שֵׁם בֶּן־מְאַת שָׁנָה וַיּוֹלֶד
אֶת־אַרְפַּכְשָׁד שְׁנָתַיִם אַחַר הַמַּבּוּל: יאוַיְחִי־
שֵׁם אַחֲרֵי הוֹלִידוֹ אֶת־אַרְפַּכְשָׁד חֲמֵשׁ מֵאוֹת
שָׁנָה וַיּוֹלֶד בָּנִים וּבָנוֹת: יבוְאַרְפַּכְשַׁד
חַי חָמֵשׁ וּשְׁלֹשִׁים שָׁנָה וַיּוֹלֶד אֶת־שָׁלַח:
יגוַיְחִי אַרְפַּכְשַׁד אַחֲרֵי הוֹלִידוֹ אֶת־שֶׁלַח
שָׁלֹשׁ שָׁנִים וְאַרְבַּע מֵאוֹת שָׁנָה וַיּוֹלֶד בָּנִים
וּבָנוֹת: ידוְשֶׁלַח חַי שְׁלֹשִׁים
שָׁנָה וַיּוֹלֶד אֶת־עֵבֶר: טווַיְחִי־שֶׁלַח אַחֲרֵי
הוֹלִידוֹ אֶת־עֵבֶר שָׁלֹשׁ שָׁנִים וְאַרְבַּע מֵאוֹת
שָׁנָה וַיּוֹלֶד בָּנִים וּבָנוֹת: טזוַיְחִי־
עֵבֶר אַרְבַּע וּשְׁלֹשִׁים שָׁנָה וַיּוֹלֶד אֶת־
פָּלֶג: יזוַיְחִי־עֵבֶר אַחֲרֵי הוֹלִידוֹ אֶת־פֶּלֶג
שְׁלֹשִׁים שָׁנָה וְאַרְבַּע מֵאוֹת שָׁנָה וַיּוֹלֶד בָּנִים
וּבָנוֹת: יחוַיְחִי־פֶלֶג שְׁלֹשִׁים שָׁנָה
וַיּוֹלֶד אֶת־רְעוּ: יטוַיְחִי־פֶלֶג אַחֲרֵי הוֹלִידוֹ
אֶת־רְעוּ תֵּשַׁע שָׁנִים וּמָאתַיִם שָׁנָה וַיּוֹלֶד
בָּנִים וּבָנוֹת: כוַיְחִי רְעוּ שְׁתַּיִם
וּשְׁלֹשִׁים שָׁנָה וַיּוֹלֶד אֶת־שְׂרוּג: כאוַיְחִי רְעוּ
אַחֲרֵי הוֹלִידוֹ אֶת־שְׂרוּג שֶׁבַע שָׁנִים וּמָאתַיִם

7-8. The intent is that Hashem would destroy their unity — which underlay the success of their venture (*Akeidas Yitzchak*). *Ramban* notes that this generation attempted to 'mutilate the shoots,' i.e., disrupt the unity between Hashem and His Creation; therefore the punishment of Dispersion [a dispersion of *their* unity] was an appropriate 'measure for measure.'

What they had feared when they said, *'lest we be dispersed* [v. 4] now actually happened (*Rashi*).

9. *Rashi* queries: Whose sin was greater — the generation of the Flood, which did not plan a rebellion against God, or the generation of the Dispersion, which did? The former, who were violent robbers and bore hatred for one another, were utterly destroyed in the Flood, while the latter, who dwelt amicably in brotherly love toward one another, were spared despite their blasphemies! This demonstrates how hateful is strife and how great is peace!

10. Shem to Abraham.

11. The ten generations from Noah to Abraham. "There were ten generations from Noah to Abraham." This demonstrates how long-suffering God was, for all the generations kept on provoking Him until the Patriarch Abraham came and received the reward of them all (*Avos* 5:2).

Chronology of the generations (based upon Seder Olam).

Shem — 1558-2158
Arpachshad — 1658-2096
Shelah — 1693-2126
Eber — 1723-2187
Peleg — 1757-1996
(The Dispersion occurred in the year of his death.)
Reu — 1787-2026
Serug — 1819-2049
Nachor — 1849-1007
Terach — 1878-2083
Abraham — 1948-2123

19. With Peleg, the human life span shortened dramatically. His father lived for 464 years, while he died at only 239.

they propose to do? [7] Come, let us descend and there confuse their language, that they should not understand one another's language.'

[8] And HASHEM dispersed them from there over the face of the whole earth; and they stopped building the city. [9] That is why it was called Babel, because it was there that HASHEM confused the languages of the whole earth, and from there HASHEM scattered them over the face of the whole earth.

[10] These are the descendants of Shem: Shem was 100 years old when he begot Arpachshad, two years after the Flood. [11] And Shem lived five hundred years after begetting Arpachshad, and he begot sons and daughters.

[12] Arpachshad had lived thirty-five years when he begot Shelah. [13] And Arpachshad lived four hundred three years after begetting Shelah; and he begot sons and daughters.

[14] Shelah had lived thirty years when he begot Eber. [15] And Shelah lived four hundred three years after begetting Eber, and begot sons and daughters.

[16] When Eber had lived thirty-four years, he begot Peleg. [17] And Eber lived four hundred thirty years after begetting Peleg, and he begot sons and daughters.

[18] When Peleg had lived thirty years, he begot Reu. [19] And Peleg lived two hundred nine years after begetting Reu, and he begot sons and daughters.

[20]When Reu had lived thirty-two years, he begot Serug. [21] And Reu lived two hundred and seven years after begetting Serug, and he

שָׁנָה וַיּוֹלֶד בָּנִים וּבָנוֹת: כב וַיְחִי
שָׂרוּג שְׁלֹשִׁים שָׁנָה וַיּוֹלֶד אֶת־נָחוֹר: כג וַיְחִי
שָׂרוּג אַחֲרֵי הוֹלִידוֹ אֶת־נָחוֹר מָאתַיִם שָׁנָה
וַיּוֹלֶד בָּנִים וּבָנוֹת: כד וַיְחִי
נָחוֹר תֵּשַׁע וְעֶשְׂרִים שָׁנָה וַיּוֹלֶד אֶת־
תָּרַח: כה וַיְחִי נָחוֹר אַחֲרֵי הוֹלִידוֹ אֶת־תֶּרַח
תְּשַׁע־עֶשְׂרֵה שָׁנָה וּמְאַת שָׁנָה וַיּוֹלֶד בָּנִים
וּבָנוֹת: כו וַיְחִי־תֶרַח שִׁבְעִים שָׁנָה
וַיּוֹלֶד אֶת־אַבְרָם אֶת־נָחוֹר וְאֶת־הָרָן:
כז וְאֵלֶּה תּוֹלְדֹת תֶּרַח תֶּרַח הוֹלִיד אֶת־אַבְרָם
אֶת־נָחוֹר וְאֶת־הָרָן וְהָרָן הוֹלִיד אֶת־לוֹט:
כח וַיָּמָת הָרָן עַל־פְּנֵי תֶּרַח אָבִיו בְּאֶרֶץ
מוֹלַדְתּוֹ בְּאוּר כַּשְׂדִּים: מפטיר כט וַיִּקַּח אַבְרָם
וְנָחוֹר לָהֶם נָשִׁים שֵׁם אֵשֶׁת־אַבְרָם שָׂרָי וְשֵׁם
אֵשֶׁת־נָחוֹר מִלְכָּה בַּת־הָרָן אֲבִי־מִלְכָּה וַאֲבִי
יִסְכָּה: ל וַתְּהִי שָׂרַי עֲקָרָה אֵין לָהּ וָלָד: לא וַיִּקַּח
תֶּרַח אֶת־אַבְרָם בְּנוֹ וְאֶת־לוֹט בֶּן־הָרָן בֶּן־
בְּנוֹ וְאֵת שָׂרַי כַּלָּתוֹ אֵשֶׁת אַבְרָם בְּנוֹ וַיֵּצְאוּ
אִתָּם מֵאוּר כַּשְׂדִּים לָלֶכֶת אַרְצָה כְּנַעַן וַיָּבֹאוּ
עַד־חָרָן וַיֵּשְׁבוּ שָׁם: לב וַיִּהְיוּ יְמֵי־תֶרַח חָמֵשׁ
שָׁנִים וּמָאתַיִם שָׁנָה וַיָּמָת תֶּרַח בְּחָרָן:

The *Haftarah* for *Noah* appears on page 302

26. Birth of Abraham.
At first he was an אַב אֲרָם,
father [i.e., teacher] of Aram,
but ultimately he became a
father to the whole world
[see 17:5] *(Rashi).*

The Talmud [*Bava Basra* 91a]
records that Abraham's
mother was Amthela,
daughter of Karnebo.

27. *Terach . . . Terach.* The
Midrash notes that anyone
whose name is mentioned
twice in close proximity has
a share in the World to
Come. But Terach was an
idolater! The Midrash an-
swers that Terach ultimately
repented and earned a share
in the World to Come!

28. *[And] Haran died in the
presence of Terach his father,* i.e., in his father's lifetime *(Rashi);* his father saw
him die *(Tanchuma).*

Rashi adds that, Midrashically, the phrase signifies
that Haran died מִפְּנֵי, *because of,* Terach. Terach
had complained to Nimrod
that Abraham had smashed
his idols, so Nimrod had
Abraham thrown into a fiery
furnace. Haran could not
decide with whom to side,
and was prepared to join
whomever emerged victori-
ous. When Abraham was
miraculously saved from the
fire, Haran sided with Abraham, whereupon he was
thrown into the furnace.
Since he was willing to defy
Nimrod only because he expected a miracle, he was
unworthy; thus Haran died
in the *fires of Kasdim.*

29. When Haran died, his
brothers married his
daughters to honor the
memory of Haran and to
assuage the grief of Terach
(Imrei Shefer).

Sarai. Her name was later
changed to Sarah [17:15].

Father of Iscah. Iscah was Sarah. She was so called [from the word meaning to *see; gaze*] because she could 'see' the future by holy inspiration, and because everyone *gazed* at her beauty. Also, *Iscah* denotes נְסִיכוּת, *princeliness (Rashi).*

32. *And Terach died in Charan.* In the year 2083; Isaac was 35 years old at the time *(Seder Olam).*

Based on various verses, *Rashi* comments that Terach died more than sixty years after Abraham's departure from Charan. Nevertheless, Terach's death is recorded here to avoid the public implication that Abraham was disrespectful to his father by leaving him in his old age. In another sense, the report of Terach's death is accurate. The Sages teach that even while alive, the wicked are called dead; and the righteous, even when dead, are called alive. Thus the wicked Terach was truly "dead" in the spiritual sense.

Ramban comments that it is common for the Torah to record the father's death before proceeding with the narrative of the son, even though the death occurred many years later.

According to the Masoretic note appearing at the end of the *Sidrah*, there are 153 verses in the *Sidrah* corresponding to the mnemonic בְּצַלְאֵ"ל [=153, *Bezalel* = 'in God's protection' — an allusion to Noah's deliverance in the Ark]; and אָבַ"י יְסָכְּ"ה לוֹ"ט [=153]. The *Haftarah* begins with *Isaiah* 54:1: רָנִּי עֲקָרָה.

begot sons and daughters.

²² When Serug had lived thirty years, he begot Nachor. ²³ And Serug lived two hundred years after begetting Nachor, and he begot sons and daughters. ²⁴ When Nachor had lived twenty-nine years, he begot Terach. ²⁵ And Nachor lived one hundred nineteen years after begetting Terach, and he begot sons and daughters.

²⁶When Terach had lived seventy years, he begot Abram, Nachor, and Haran.

²⁷ Now these are the chronicles of Terach: Terach begot Abram, Nachor, and Haran; and Haran begot Lot. ²⁸ Haran died in the presence of Terach his father, in his native land, in Ur Kasdim. ²⁹ And Abram and Nachor took themselves wives; the name of Abram's wife was Sarai, and the name of Nachor's wife was Milcah, the daughter of Haran, the father of Milcah and the father of Iscah. ³⁰ And Sarai remained barren, she had no child.

³¹ Terach took his son Abram, and Lot the son of Haran, his grandson, and his daughter-in-law Sarai, the wife of Abram his son, and they departed with them from Ur Kasdim to go to the land of Canaan; but when they came as far as Canaan, they settled there.

³² All the days of Terach were two hundred and five years, and Terach died in Charan.

The *Haftarah* for *Noah* appears on page 302

פרשת לך לך

LECH LECHA

With *Lech Lecha*, Creation begins anew, and a new "father" emerges — Abraham — who replaces Adam and Noah as the bearer of God's mission. Indeed, the Sages refer to Abraham as the Chariot of God's Presence, for it was through him that God finally found a home and a resting place on earth, a place where His will was paramount and from which His message would be borne to all of mankind.

The Talmud teaches that the first two thousand years from Creation were an era of תהו, *desolation*; the next two thousand were an era of Torah. When that new era began, Abraham was fifty-two years old. It was four years after the Dispersion and six years before the death of Noah. Abraham had heard about the Deluge from eyewitnesses, from participants, and he had seen the damage that man's stubborn arrogance had wrought. Now he was ready to begin teaching his brethren about the existence and will of God. The Chariot was launched.

The first of Abraham's Ten Tests was God's command that he leave his family and homeland and go as a stranger to the land of Canaan. He and Sarah had their many converts with them, but essentially they were alone. And this is what a Jew must be prepared to be. Abraham was an *Ivri*, from עֵבֶר, *the other side,* meaning that he was from the other side of the River Euphrates. The Sages go further, teaching that Abraham was all alone. He was on one side of a divide and the rest of the world was on the other. This is an isolation that righteous people must be ready to endure. Popularity is pleasant, but it is more important to do right than to curry favor.

יב א וַיֹּאמֶר יהוה אֶל־אַבְרָם לֶךְ־לְךָ מֵאַרְצְךָ
וּמִמּוֹלַדְתְּךָ וּמִבֵּית אָבִיךָ אֶל־הָאָרֶץ אֲשֶׁר
אַרְאֶךָּ: ב וְאֶעֶשְׂךָ לְגוֹי גָּדוֹל וַאֲבָרֶכְךָ וַאֲגַדְּלָה
שְׁמֶךָ וֶהְיֵה בְּרָכָה: ג וַאֲבָרְכָה מְבָרְכֶיךָ
וּמְקַלֶּלְךָ אָאֹר וְנִבְרְכוּ בְךָ כֹּל מִשְׁפְּחֹת
הָאֲדָמָה: ד וַיֵּלֶךְ אַבְרָם כַּאֲשֶׁר דִּבֶּר אֵלָיו יהוה
וַיֵּלֶךְ אִתּוֹ לוֹט וְאַבְרָם בֶּן־חָמֵשׁ שָׁנִים
וְשִׁבְעִים שָׁנָה בְּצֵאתוֹ מֵחָרָן: ה וַיִּקַּח אַבְרָם
אֶת־שָׂרַי אִשְׁתּוֹ וְאֶת־לוֹט בֶּן־אָחִיו וְאֶת־כָּל־
רְכוּשָׁם אֲשֶׁר רָכָשׁוּ וְאֶת־הַנֶּפֶשׁ אֲשֶׁר־עָשׂוּ
בְחָרָן וַיֵּצְאוּ לָלֶכֶת אַרְצָה כְּנַעַן וַיָּבֹאוּ אַרְצָה
כְּנָעַן: ו וַיַּעֲבֹר אַבְרָם בָּאָרֶץ עַד מְקוֹם שְׁכֶם
עַד אֵלוֹן מוֹרֶה וְהַכְּנַעֲנִי אָז בָּאָרֶץ: ז וַיֵּרָא
יהוה אֶל־אַבְרָם וַיֹּאמֶר לְזַרְעֲךָ אֶתֵּן אֶת־
הָאָרֶץ הַזֹּאת וַיִּבֶן שָׁם מִזְבֵּחַ לַיהוה הַנִּרְאֶה
אֵלָיו: ח וַיַּעְתֵּק מִשָּׁם הָהָרָה מִקֶּדֶם לְבֵית־אֵל
וַיֵּט אָהֳלֹה בֵּית־אֵל מִיָּם וְהָעַי מִקֶּדֶם וַיִּבֶן־
שָׁם מִזְבֵּחַ לַיהוה וַיִּקְרָא בְּשֵׁם יהוה: ט וַיִּסַּע
אַבְרָם הָלוֹךְ וְנָסוֹעַ הַנֶּגְבָּה:
י וַיְהִי רָעָב בָּאָרֶץ וַיֵּרֶד אַבְרָם מִצְרַיְמָה לָגוּר
שָׁם כִּי־כָבֵד הָרָעָב בָּאָרֶץ: יא וַיְהִי כַּאֲשֶׁר
הִקְרִיב לָבוֹא מִצְרָיְמָה וַיֹּאמֶר אֶל־שָׂרַי
אִשְׁתּוֹ הִנֵּה־נָא יָדַעְתִּי כִּי אִשָּׁה יְפַת־מַרְאֶה
אָתְּ: יב וְהָיָה כִּי־יִרְאוּ אֹתָךְ הַמִּצְרִים וְאָמְרוּ
אִשְׁתּוֹ זֹאת וְהָרְגוּ אֹתִי וְאֹתָךְ יְחַיּוּ: יג אִמְרִי־

12/1. God's call to Abraham. The command to leave his ancestral home was one of the ten trials of faith with which God tested Abraham, all of which he withstood.

לֶךְ לְךָ — *Get yourself* [literally *go for yourself*]. *Rashi* interprets the seemingly superfluous לְךָ, *for yourself* — 'for your own benefit and for your own good.' And what is this benefit and good? — that *I will make of you a great nation,* for here you will not merit the privilege of having children.

To the land that I will show you. In order to keep him in suspense and thereby make the destination more beloved in his eyes, God did not specify which land. God also wished to reward him for every step he took (*Rashi*).

2. *A blessing.* You will bless whomever you wish (*Rashi*). *Ramban* interprets: You will be the standard of blessing by which people will bless themselves.

4. Lot's father, Haran, had died in the flames of Ur Kasdim [see comm. to 11:28]. The orphaned Lot was raised by his uncle, Abraham, and now accompanied him (*Chizkuni*).

Seventy-five years old. Notwithstanding his natural reluctance to leave his aged father, Terach, Abraham did not hesitate but hurried to do the will of his Creator (*B'chor Shor*).

5. The 'souls' refer to those whom they had converted to faith in Hashem, for Abraham converted the men and Sarah the women. According to the simple meaning, however, it refers to the servants they had acquired (*Rashi*), who agreed unanimously to accompany Abraham on his mission (*Radak*).

6. *Ramban* cites a fundamental principle in understanding the Torah's narrative concerning the Patriarchs: כָּל מַה שֶׁאֵרַע לָאָבוֹת סִימָן לַבָּנִים, 'Whatever happened to the Patriarchs is a portent for the children . . .' The Torah relates at length such incidents as their journeys, digging of wells, etc., because they serve as lessons for the future. Thus, Abraham's stopover in Shechem — in addition to his praying for Jacob's sons who would one day fight against Shechem — was a portent that Shechem would be the first place to be conquered by Jacob's sons [34:25], nearly 300 years before Israel gained full possession of the land. Then he encamped between Bethel and Ai, the latter being the first place conquered by Joshua . . . The story of the Patriarchs is replete with such symbolism.

7. *He built an altar there*, in gratitude for God's promise of children and the possession of the land (*Rashi*).

8. Noting that אָהֳלֹה could be read אָהֳלָהּ, *her tent*, the Midrash comments that Abraham always honored his wife by pitching her tent before his own.

10. Abraham in Egypt. This is the second of Abraham's trials. Immediately after he settled in his new homeland Canaan, God commanded him to leave the land and move to Egypt. This foreshadowed his descendants' descent to Egypt because of a famine . . . (*Ramban*).

11. Abraham became especially sensitive to Sarah's beauty because of the notorious immorality of Egypt. As sojourners, Abraham and Sarah would be at the mercy of the Egyptians, who might lust after her and do away with him (*Abarbanel*).

12 ¹ HASHEM said to Abram, 'Get yourself from your country, from your relatives, and from your father's house to the land that I will show you. ²And I will make of you a great nation; I will bless you, and make your name great, and you shall be a blessing. ³I will bless those who bless you, and him who curses you I will curse; and all the families of the earth shall bless themselves by you.'

⁴ So Abram went as HASHEM had spoken to him, and Lot went with him. Abram was seventy-five years old when he left Charan. ⁵ Abram took his wife Sarai and his nephew Lot, and all their wealth that they had amassed, and the souls they made in Charan; and they embarked for the land of Canaan, and they came to the land of Canaan. ⁶ Abram passed into the land as far as the site of Shechem, until the Plain of Moreh. The Canaanites were then in the land.

⁷ HASHEM appeared to Abram and said, 'To your offspring I will give this land.' So he built an altar there to HASHEM Who appeared to him. ⁸ From there he relocated to the mountain east of Bethel and pitched his tent, with Bethel on the west and Ai on the east; and he built there an altar to HASHEM and invoked HASHEM by Name. ⁹ Then Abram journeyed on, journeying steadily toward the south.

¹⁰ There was a famine in the land, and Abram descended to Egypt to sojourn there, for the famine was severe in the land. ¹¹ And it occurred, as he was about to enter Egypt, he said to his wife Sarai, 'See now, I have known that you are a woman of beautiful appearance. ¹² And it shall occur, when the Egyptians will see you, they will say, "This is his wife!"; then they will kill me, but you they will let live. ¹³ Please say

נָא אֲחֹתִי אָתְּ לְמַעַן יִיטַב־לִי בַעֲבוּרֵךְ וְחָיְתָה נַפְשִׁי בִּגְלָלֵךְ: שני יד וַיְהִי כְּבוֹא אַבְרָם מִצְרָיְמָה וַיִּרְאוּ הַמִּצְרִים אֶת־הָאִשָּׁה כִּי־יָפָה הִוא מְאֹד: טו וַיִּרְאוּ אֹתָהּ שָׂרֵי פַרְעֹה וַיְהַלְלוּ אֹתָהּ אֶל־פַּרְעֹה וַתֻּקַּח הָאִשָּׁה בֵּית פַּרְעֹה: טז וּלְאַבְרָם הֵיטִיב בַּעֲבוּרָהּ וַיְהִי־לוֹ צֹאן־ וּבָקָר וַחֲמֹרִים וַעֲבָדִים וּשְׁפָחֹת וַאֲתֹנֹת וּגְמַלִּים: יז וַיְנַגַּע יהוה | אֶת־פַּרְעֹה נְגָעִים גְּדֹלִים וְאֶת־בֵּיתוֹ עַל־דְּבַר שָׂרַי אֵשֶׁת אַבְרָם: יח וַיִּקְרָא פַרְעֹה לְאַבְרָם וַיֹּאמֶר מַה־זֹּאת עָשִׂיתָ לִּי לָמָּה לֹא־הִגַּדְתָּ לִּי כִּי אִשְׁתְּךָ הִוא: יט לָמָה אָמַרְתָּ אֲחֹתִי הִוא וָאֶקַּח אֹתָהּ לִי לְאִשָּׁה וְעַתָּה הִנֵּה אִשְׁתְּךָ קַח וָלֵךְ: כ וַיְצַו עָלָיו פַּרְעֹה אֲנָשִׁים וַיְשַׁלְּחוּ אֹתוֹ וְאֶת־אִשְׁתּוֹ וְאֶת־כָּל־אֲשֶׁר־לוֹ: יג א וַיַּעַל אַבְרָם מִמִּצְרַיִם הוּא וְאִשְׁתּוֹ וְכָל־אֲשֶׁר־לוֹ וְלוֹט עִמּוֹ הַנֶּגְבָּה: ב וְאַבְרָם כָּבֵד מְאֹד בַּמִּקְנֶה בַּכֶּסֶף וּבַזָּהָב: ג וַיֵּלֶךְ לְמַסָּעָיו מִנֶּגֶב וְעַד־בֵּית־אֵל עַד־ הַמָּקוֹם אֲשֶׁר־הָיָה שָׁם אָהֳלֹה בַּתְּחִלָּה בֵּין בֵּית־אֵל וּבֵין הָעָי: ד אֶל־מְקוֹם הַמִּזְבֵּחַ אֲשֶׁר־ עָשָׂה שָׁם בָּרִאשֹׁנָה וַיִּקְרָא שָׁם אַבְרָם בְּשֵׁם יהוה: שלישי ה וְגַם־לְלוֹט הַהֹלֵךְ אֶת־אַבְרָם הָיָה צֹאן־וּבָקָר וְאֹהָלִים: ו וְלֹא־נָשָׂא אֹתָם הָאָרֶץ לָשֶׁבֶת יַחְדָּו כִּי־הָיָה רְכוּשָׁם רָב וְלֹא יָכְלוּ לָשֶׁבֶת יַחְדָּו: ז וַיְהִי־רִיב בֵּין רֹעֵי מִקְנֵה־

13. *My sister.* Was she then his sister? She was really his niece! [11:29]. But a man often calls his relative 'sister' (*Midrash HaGadol*).

14-15. Events did not go according to Abraham's plan. Sarah's exceptional beauty brought about a different turn of events (*Ran*).

Pharaoh was the royal title of all Egyptian kings, just as Abimelech was the official title of Philistine monarchs.

16. In Egypt Abraham accepted many valuable gifts, but he vehemently refused to accept anything from the king of Sodom [14:23]. In the context of Abraham's claim that Sarah was his sister and that he would allow her to marry a suitable person, had he refused gifts, he would have aroused Pharaoh's suspicions (*Abarbanel; R' Hoffman*).

17. Pharaoh was smitten with a debilitating skin disease that makes cohabitation impossible, thus assuring that Sarah's chastity would be safeguarded (*Rashi; Gur Aryeh*).

18. Although Pharaoh suspected that his affliction was because of Sarah, he was not certain she was Abraham's wife. He made the accusation in order to draw the truth from Abraham.

20. Pharaoh hastens to rid himself of the cause of his Divine affliction, but, not wishing to incur God's further wrath by mistreating Abraham and Sarah, he sends them away in honor, guaranteeing that no evil will befall them . . .

13/1. The Torah uses the verb *went up* when speaking of journeys to the higher elevation of *Eretz Yisrael*. The *Zohar* perceives in the verb an indication that Abraham *ascended spiritually* from the 'lower degrees' of Egypt, thus returning to his former, higher condition.

3. *His journeys.* On the return trip, he lodged in the same places where he stayed on the outward journey. One should not change his lodging unless he has suffered harassment and anguish there. One who does so discredits himself [as he will be considered hard to please or disreputable and he gives the impression that his lodging was unsatisfactory [*Arachin* 16b].

6. Abraham and Lot part ways.

7. Lot's shepherds were dishonest and grazed their flocks on other people's pastures. When Abraham's shepherds rebuked them for this, they responded that the land was Abraham's, and since he was childless, Lot was his heir. However, the Torah specifically negates this contention by emphasizing that the Canaanites and Perizzites were still in the land; Abraham was not yet the legitimate owner (*Rashi*).

that you are my sister, that it may go well with me for your sake, and that I may live on account of you.'

¹⁴ But it occurred, with Abram's coming to Egypt, the Egyptians saw that the woman was very beautiful. ¹⁵ When the officials of Pharaoh's saw her, they lauded her for Pharaoh, and the woman was taken into Pharaoh's house. ¹⁶ And he treated Abram well for her sake, and he acquired sheep, oxen, donkeys, slaves and maidservants, female donkeys, and camels.

¹⁷ But HASHEM afflicted Pharaoh along with his household with severe plagues because of Sarai, the wife of Abram. ¹⁸ Pharaoh summoned Abram and said, 'What is this you have done to me? Why did you not tell me that she is your wife? ¹⁹ Why did you say, "She is my sister," so that I would take her as my wife? Now, here is your wife; take her and go!' ²⁰ So Pharaoh gave men orders concerning him, and they escorted him and his wife and all that was his.

13 ¹ **S**o Abram went up from Egypt, he with his wife and all that was his — and Lot with him — to the south. ² Now Abram was very laden with cattle, silver and gold. ³ He proceeded on his journeys from the south to Bethel to the place where his tent had been formerly, between Bethel and Ai, ⁴ to the site of the altar which he had erected there at first. And there Abram invoked HASHEM by Name.

⁵ Also Lot who went with Abram had flocks, herds, and tents. ⁶ And the land could not support them dwelling together for their possessions were abundant and they were unable to dwell together. ⁷ And there was quarreling between the herdsmen

אַבְרָם וּבֵין רֹעֵי מִקְנֵה־לֹוט וְהַכְּנַעֲנִי וְהַפְּרִזִּי
אָז יֹשֵׁב בָּאָרֶץ: ח וַיֹּאמֶר אַבְרָם אֶל־לֹוט
אַל־נָא תְהִי מְרִיבָה בֵּינִי וּבֵינֶךָ וּבֵין רֹעַי וּבֵין
רֹעֶיךָ כִּי־אֲנָשִׁים אַחִים אֲנָחְנוּ: ט הֲלֹא כָל־
הָאָרֶץ לְפָנֶיךָ הִפָּרֶד נָא מֵעָלָי אִם־הַשְּׂמֹאל
וְאֵימִנָה וְאִם־הַיָּמִין וְאַשְׂמְאִילָה: י וַיִּשָּׂא־לֹוט
אֶת־עֵינָיו וַיַּרְא אֶת־כָּל־כִּכַּר הַיַּרְדֵּן כִּי כֻלָּהּ
מַשְׁקֶה לִפְנֵי | שַׁחֵת יהוה אֶת־סְדֹם וְאֶת־
עֲמֹרָה כְּגַן־יהוה כְּאֶרֶץ מִצְרַיִם בֹּאֲכָה צֹעַר:
יא וַיִּבְחַר־לֹו לֹוט אֵת כָּל־כִּכַּר הַיַּרְדֵּן וַיִּסַּע
לֹוט מִקֶּדֶם וַיִּפָּרְדוּ אִישׁ מֵעַל אָחִיו: יב אַבְרָם
יָשַׁב בְּאֶרֶץ־כְּנָעַן וְלֹוט יָשַׁב בְּעָרֵי הַכִּכָּר
וַיֶּאֱהַל עַד־סְדֹם: יג וְאַנְשֵׁי סְדֹם רָעִים
וְחַטָּאִים לַיהוה מְאֹד: יד וַיהוה אָמַר אֶל־
אַבְרָם אַחֲרֵי הִפָּרֶד־לֹוט מֵעִמֹּו שָׂא־נָא
עֵינֶיךָ וּרְאֵה מִן־הַמָּקֹום אֲשֶׁר־אַתָּה שָׁם
צָפֹנָה וָנֶגְבָּה וָקֵדְמָה וָיָמָּה: טו כִּי אֶת־כָּל־
הָאָרֶץ אֲשֶׁר־אַתָּה רֹאֶה לְךָ אֶתְּנֶנָּה וּלְזַרְעֲךָ
עַד־עֹולָם: טז וְשַׂמְתִּי אֶת־זַרְעֲךָ כַּעֲפַר הָאָרֶץ
אֲשֶׁר | אִם־יוּכַל אִישׁ לִמְנֹות אֶת־עֲפַר הָאָרֶץ
גַּם־זַרְעֲךָ יִמָּנֶה: יז קוּם הִתְהַלֵּךְ בָּאָרֶץ
לְאָרְכָּהּ וּלְרָחְבָּהּ כִּי לְךָ אֶתְּנֶנָּה: יח וַיֶּאֱהַל
אַבְרָם וַיָּבֹא וַיֵּשֶׁב בְּאֵלֹנֵי מַמְרֵא אֲשֶׁר
בְּחֶבְרֹון וַיִּבֶן־שָׁם מִזְבֵּחַ לַיהוה:
יד רביעי א וַיְהִי בִּימֵי אַמְרָפֶל מֶלֶךְ־שִׁנְעָר

10. From his vantage point atop the mountain, Lot inspected the whole area and his gaze rested on the fertile Jordan plain. Our verse indicates that, before God destroyed Sodom, it was as fertile as the Garden of Eden and the well-irrigated land of Egypt.

11. *Lot journeyed* מִקֶּדֶם, *from the east.* In the spiritual sense, by leaving Abraham, Lot separated himself מִקַּדְמוֹנוֹ שֶׁל עוֹלָם [God,] *the Ancient One of the World,* saying: I want neither Abraham nor his God! (*Midrash; Rashi*).

Thus they parted, one from another. This statement is most significant. Though Lot contained the sparks that would produce Ruth, the mother of King David, he *parted from Abram.* In time the rift would become so absolute and irreversible that his male descendants from Ammon and Moab would be prohibited from entering the congregation of Israel [*Deut.* 23:4] (*Pesikta Zutresa*).

13. *The people of Sodom were wicked . . .* but that did not stop Lot from living with them (*Rashi*).

14. The repetition of the promise. After Lot's departure from Abraham, God repeats His promise [12:7], to emphasize that it had been given exclusively to Abraham and his descendants.

16. Just as it is impossible for the dust to be counted, so will it be impossible to count your offspring (*Rashi*). (See *I Kings* 4:20; *Hoshea* 2:1.) *R' Hirsch* notes that this refers not to the Jewish population at any one time, but to the countless total of all the generations of an immortal nation that will flourish throughout history.

17. This is both a promise and a command: A *promise* of God's protection while Abraham would roam freely throughout the land; and a *command* that he walk through the land to symbolize that he was taking possession of the gift (*Ramban*).

14/1. The war of the kings. *Amraphel* is Nimrod, who reigned over Shinar (Babylon), and *Chedorlaomer* is identified in the Midrash as Elam, son of Shem son of Noah.

of Abram's flocks and the herdsmen of Lot's flocks — and the Canaanites and the Perizzites were then dwelling in the land.

⁸ So Abram said to Lot: 'Please let there be no strife between me and you, and between my herdsmen and your herdsmen, for we are kinsmen. ⁹ Is not all the land before you? Please separate from me: If you go left then I will go right, and if you go right then I will go left.'

¹⁰ So Lot raised his eyes and saw the entire plain of the Jordan that it was well watered everywhere — before HASHEM destroyed Sodom and Amorah — like the garden of HASHEM, like the land of Egypt, going toward Zohar. ¹¹ So Lot chose for himself the whole plain of the Jordan, and Lot journeyed from the east, thus they parted, one from another. ¹² Abram remained in the land of Canaan while Lot settled in the cities of the plain and pitched his tents as far as Sodom. ¹³ Now the people of Sodom were wicked and sinful toward HASHEM, exceedingly.

¹⁴ HASHEM said to Abram after Lot had parted from him, 'Raise now your eyes and look out from where you are: northward, southward, eastward and westward. ¹⁵ For all the land that you see, to you will I give it, and to your descendants forever. ¹⁶ I will make your offspring as the dust of the earth so that if one can count the dust of the earth, then your offspring, too, can be counted. ¹⁷ Arise, walk about the land through its length and breadth! For to you will I give it.' ¹⁸ And Abram moved his tent and came to dwell in the plains of Mamre which are in Hebron; and he built there an altar to HASHEM.

14 ¹ And it happened in the days of Amraphel, king of Shinar; Arioch, king of Ellasar;

אַרְיוֹךְ מֶלֶךְ אֶלָּסָר כְּדָרְלָעֹמֶר מֶלֶךְ עֵילָם וְתִדְעָל מֶלֶךְ גּוֹיִם: ב עָשׂוּ מִלְחָמָה אֶת־בֶּרַע מֶלֶךְ סְדֹם וְאֶת־בִּרְשַׁע מֶלֶךְ עֲמֹרָה שִׁנְאָב | מֶלֶךְ אַדְמָה וְשֶׁמְאֵבֶר° מֶלֶךְ °צְבֹיִים וּמֶלֶךְ בֶּלַע הִיא־צֹעַר: ג כָּל־אֵלֶּה חָבְרוּ אֶל־עֵמֶק הַשִּׂדִּים הוּא יָם הַמֶּלַח: ד שְׁתֵּים עֶשְׂרֵה שָׁנָה עָבְדוּ אֶת־כְּדָרְלָעֹמֶר וּשְׁלֹשׁ־עֶשְׂרֵה שָׁנָה מָרָדוּ: ה וּבְאַרְבַּע עֶשְׂרֵה שָׁנָה בָּא כְדָרְלָעֹמֶר וְהַמְּלָכִים אֲשֶׁר אִתּוֹ וַיַּכּוּ אֶת־רְפָאִים בְּעַשְׁתְּרֹת קַרְנַיִם וְאֶת־הַזּוּזִים בְּהָם וְאֵת הָאֵימִים בְּשָׁוֵה קִרְיָתָיִם: ו וְאֶת־הַחֹרִי בְּהַרְרָם שֵׂעִיר עַד אֵיל פָּארָן אֲשֶׁר עַל־הַמִּדְבָּר: ז וַיָּשֻׁבוּ וַיָּבֹאוּ אֶל־עֵין מִשְׁפָּט הִוא קָדֵשׁ וַיַּכּוּ אֶת־כָּל־שְׂדֵה הָעֲמָלֵקִי וְגַם אֶת־הָאֱמֹרִי הַיֹּשֵׁב בְּחַצְצֹן תָּמָר: ח וַיֵּצֵא מֶלֶךְ־סְדֹם וּמֶלֶךְ עֲמֹרָה וּמֶלֶךְ אַדְמָה וּמֶלֶךְ °צְבֹיִים וּמֶלֶךְ בֶּלַע הִוא־צֹעַר וַיַּעַרְכוּ אִתָּם מִלְחָמָה בְּעֵמֶק הַשִּׂדִּים: ט אֵת כְּדָרְלָעֹמֶר מֶלֶךְ עֵילָם וְתִדְעָל מֶלֶךְ גּוֹיִם וְאַמְרָפֶל מֶלֶךְ שִׁנְעָר וְאַרְיוֹךְ מֶלֶךְ אֶלָּסָר אַרְבָּעָה מְלָכִים אֶת־הַחֲמִשָּׁה: י וְעֵמֶק הַשִּׂדִּים בֶּאֱרֹת בֶּאֱרֹת חֵמָר וַיָּנֻסוּ מֶלֶךְ־סְדֹם וַעֲמֹרָה וַיִּפְּלוּ־שָׁמָּה וְהַנִּשְׁאָרִים הֶרָה נָּסוּ: יא וַיִּקְחוּ אֶת־כָּל־רְכֻשׁ סְדֹם וַעֲמֹרָה וְאֶת־כָּל־אָכְלָם וַיֵּלֵכוּ: יב וַיִּקְחוּ אֶת־לוֹט וְאֶת־רְכֻשׁוֹ בֶּן־אֲחִי אַבְרָם וַיֵּלֵכוּ וְהוּא יֹשֵׁב בִּסְדֹם:

° צְבוֹיִם ק׳

5. Chedorlaomer was the leader. Since the five kings revolted against him, he took the initiative, his allies playing a subordinate part (*Rashi*).

Chedorlaomer's forces marched southward, conquering every nation they suspected of complicity in the rebellion, or that they feared would join forces with the five northern kings (*R' Hirsch; Malbim*).

7. Now, the four kings turned back northward to their real goal, still stopping on the way and crushing whatever resistance — real or anticipated — they encountered on the way (*R' Hirsch*).

8. The five rebellious kings took the initiative and attacked the enemy first, before he could invade them (*Haamek Davar*).

10. The five kings were routed by the superior might of the four invading armies. The kings of Sodom and Amorah panicked and fled, falling into the wells. But, as will be explained further, the king of Sodom was miraculously saved.

12. Lot taken captive. The Midrash notes that the invaders took Lot captive because of his relationship to Abraham. They put him in a cage and boasted, 'We have captured Abram's nephew!'

For he was residing in Sodom. For associating with wicked people, he deserved to be captured (*Yafeh To'ar*).

Chedorlaomer, king of Elam, and Tidal, king of Goiim, ² that these made war on Bera, king of Sodom; Birsha, king of Amorah; Shinab, king of Admah; Shemeber, king of Zeboiim; and the king of Bela, which is Zoar. ³ All these had joined at the Valley of Siddim, now the Salt Sea. ⁴ Twelve years they served Chedorlaomer, and they rebelled thirteen years. ⁵ In the fourteenth year, Chedorlaomer and the kings who were with him came and struck the Rephaim at Ashtaroth-Karnaim, the Zuzim in Ham, the Eimim at Shaveh-Kiriataim; ⁶ and the Horites in the mount Seir, as far as Eil Paran which is by the desert. ⁷ Then they turned back and came to Ein Mishpat, which is Kadesh. They struck all the territory of the Amalakites; and also the Amorites who dwell in Hazazon-Tamar.

⁸ And the king of Sodom went forth with the king of Amorah, the king of Admah, the king of Zeboiim and the king of Bela which is Zoar, and engaged them in battle in the Valley of Siddim: ⁹ With Chedorlaomer, king of Elam; Tidal, king of Goiim; Amraphel, king of Shinar; and Arioch, king of Ellasar — four kings against five.

¹⁰ The Valley of Siddom was full of bitumen wells. The kings of Sodom and Amorah fled and fell into them while the rest fled to a mountain. ¹¹ The seized all the wealth of Sodom and Amorah and all their provisions and they departed. ¹² And they captured Lot and his possessions — Abram's nephew — and they left; for he was residing in Sodom.

יג וַיָּבֹא הַפָּלִיט וַיַּגֵּד לְאַבְרָם הָעִבְרִי וְהוּא שֹׁכֵן בְּאֵלֹנֵי מַמְרֵא הָאֱמֹרִי אֲחִי אֶשְׁכֹּל וַאֲחִי עָנֵר וְהֵם בַּעֲלֵי בְרִית־אַבְרָם: יד וַיִּשְׁמַע אַבְרָם כִּי נִשְׁבָּה אָחִיו וַיָּרֶק אֶת־חֲנִיכָיו יְלִידֵי בֵיתוֹ שְׁמֹנָה עָשָׂר וּשְׁלֹשׁ מֵאוֹת וַיִּרְדֹּף עַד־דָּן: טו וַיֵּחָלֵק עֲלֵיהֶם | לַיְלָה הוּא וַעֲבָדָיו וַיַּכֵּם וַיִּרְדְּפֵם עַד־חוֹבָה אֲשֶׁר מִשְּׂמֹאל לְדַמָּשֶׂק: טז וַיָּשֶׁב אֵת כָּל־הָרְכֻשׁ וְגַם אֶת־לוֹט אָחִיו וּרְכֻשׁוֹ הֵשִׁיב וְגַם אֶת־הַנָּשִׁים וְאֶת־הָעָם: יז וַיֵּצֵא מֶלֶךְ־סְדֹם לִקְרָאתוֹ אַחֲרֵי שׁוּבוֹ מֵהַכּוֹת אֶת־כְּדָרְלָעֹמֶר וְאֶת־הַמְּלָכִים אֲשֶׁר אִתּוֹ אֶל־עֵמֶק שָׁוֵה הוּא עֵמֶק הַמֶּלֶךְ: יח וּמַלְכִּי־צֶדֶק מֶלֶךְ שָׁלֵם הוֹצִיא לֶחֶם וָיָיִן וְהוּא כֹהֵן לְאֵל עֶלְיוֹן: יט וַיְבָרֲכֵהוּ וַיֹּאמַר בָּרוּךְ אַבְרָם לְאֵל עֶלְיוֹן קֹנֵה שָׁמַיִם וָאָרֶץ: כ וּבָרוּךְ אֵל עֶלְיוֹן אֲשֶׁר־מִגֵּן צָרֶיךָ בְּיָדֶךָ וַיִּתֶּן־לוֹ מַעֲשֵׂר מִכֹּל: חמישי כא וַיֹּאמֶר מֶלֶךְ־סְדֹם אֶל־אַבְרָם תֶּן־לִי הַנֶּפֶשׁ וְהָרְכֻשׁ קַח־לָךְ: כב וַיֹּאמֶר אַבְרָם אֶל־מֶלֶךְ סְדֹם הֲרִמֹתִי יָדִי אֶל־יהוה אֵל עֶלְיוֹן קֹנֵה שָׁמַיִם וָאָרֶץ: כג אִם־מִחוּט וְעַד שְׂרוֹךְ־נַעַל וְאִם־אֶקַּח מִכָּל־אֲשֶׁר־לָךְ וְלֹא תֹאמַר אֲנִי הֶעֱשַׁרְתִּי אֶת־אַבְרָם: כד בִּלְעָדַי רַק אֲשֶׁר אָכְלוּ הַנְּעָרִים וְחֵלֶק הָאֲנָשִׁים אֲשֶׁר הָלְכוּ אִתִּי עָנֵר אֶשְׁכֹּל וּמַמְרֵא הֵם

13. The 'fugitive' is identified by the Midrash as Og, king of Bashan, the only survivor of the Flood. He is called a fugitive because he had just escaped the battle of the Rephaim [see *Deut.* 3:11].

The Midrash notes that Og's motive was not pure. Og wished to incite Abraham to fight the kings in order to rescue Lot. Confident that Abraham would be killed in the battle, Og thought that he would be free to marry Sarah. For his deed of informing Abraham, Og was rewarded with exceptionally long life; for his wicked motive, Og ultimately fell into the hands of Abraham's descendants (*Rashi*).

Ivri — from the 'other side' [עֵבֶר] of the River [Euphrates] (*Rashi*). — On the 'opposite side' of the rest of Mankind, i.e., he alone served Hashem (*Midrash*). — A descendant of Eber. Only Abraham's descendants are called 'Ivrim' for they alone spoke Hebrew, the language of Eber. Eber's other descendants spoke Aramaic, and are called Arameans (*Radak*).

14. Abraham saves Lot. Abraham armed the disciples he had educated in the service of Hashem. The Sages [*Nedarim* 32a] fault him for using Torah scholars to wage war, and maintain that it was one of the reasons that his descendants were consigned to Egyptian servitude (*Rashi*).

15. Even at night Abraham continued the pursuit. He split up his forces to follow the fugitives as they scattered in various directions (Rashi), and as he forced them to leave the land and return home ignominiously (Ramban).

16. Abraham's triumphant return.

18. Having met Abraham at the Valley of Shaveh, the king of Sodom paid him the honor of accompanying him to the city of Shalem [=Jerusalem] where they were met by Malchizedek, whom the Sages identify as Shem, son of Noah (Ramban).

Bread and wine — as customary on behalf of returning battle-weary soldiers [comp. II Sam. 17:27ff].

A priest of God, the Most High. Unlike the priests of the other nations who served angels, Malchizedek served Hashem (Ramban).

20. A 'blessing' is an acknowledgment that God is the Source of all good (Chinuch #430).

And he [Abram] gave him [Malchizedek] a tenth of everything. He thereby indicated that his descendants would give maaser [tithes] to the Levites (Ramban).

22. Abraham declines the offer. To show devotion to God, Abraham rejects any personal gain from his victory.

23. The general meaning is: Even the most insignificant spoils of my victories will I not retain — thus have I vowed to HASHEM (Ibn Caspi).

I decline all personal gains so that you will not go about boasting that it was you, rather than God, who made me rich (Rashi).

^{13} Then there came the fugitive and told Abram, the Ivri, who dwelt in the plains of Mamre, the Amorite, the brother of Eshkol and Aner, these being Abram's allies. ^{14} And when Abram heard that his kinsman was taken captive, he armed his disciples who had been borne in his house — three hundred and eighteen — and he pursued them as far as Dan. ^{15} And he with his servants deployed against them at night and struck them; he pursued them as far as Chovah which is to the north of Damascus. ^{16} He brought back all the possessions; he also brought back his kinsman, Lot, with his possessions, as well as the women and the people.

^{17} The king of Sodom went out to meet him after his return from defeating Chedorlaomer and the kings that were with him, to the Valley of Shaveh which is the king's valley. ^{18} But Malchizedek, king of Shalem, brought out bread and wine. He was a priest of God, the Most High. ^{19} He blessed him saying: 'Blessed is Abram of God the Most High, Maker of heaven and earth; ^{20} and blessed be God the Most High Who has delivered your foes into your hand'; and he gave him a tenth of everything.

^{21} The king of Sodom said to Abram: 'Give me the people and take the possessions for yourself.'

^{22} Abram said to the king of Sodom: 'I lift up my hand to HASHEM, God Most High, Maker of heaven and earth, ^{23} if so much as a thread to a shoestrap; nor shall I take from anything of yours! So you shall not say, "It is I who made Abram rich." ^{24} Far from me! Only what the young men have eaten, and the share of the men who accompanied me: Aner, Eshkol, and Mamre — they will take their portion.'

טו א אַחַר ׀ הַדְּבָרִים יִקְחוּ חֶלְקָם:
הָאֵלֶּה הָיָה דְבַר־יהוה אֶל־אַבְרָם בַּמַּחֲזֶה
לֵאמֹר אַל־תִּירָא אַבְרָם אָנֹכִי מָגֵן לָךְ
שְׂכָרְךָ הַרְבֵּה מְאֹד: ב וַיֹּאמֶר אַבְרָם אֲדֹנָי
יהוה מַה־תִּתֶּן־לִי וְאָנֹכִי הוֹלֵךְ עֲרִירִי וּבֶן־
מֶשֶׁק בֵּיתִי הוּא דַּמֶּשֶׂק אֱלִיעֶזֶר: ג וַיֹּאמֶר
אַבְרָם הֵן לִי לֹא נָתַתָּה זָרַע וְהִנֵּה בֶן־בֵּיתִי
יוֹרֵשׁ אֹתִי: ד וְהִנֵּה דְבַר־יהוה אֵלָיו לֵאמֹר
לֹא יִירָשְׁךָ זֶה כִּי־אִם אֲשֶׁר יֵצֵא מִמֵּעֶיךָ
הוּא יִירָשֶׁךָ: ה וַיּוֹצֵא אֹתוֹ הַחוּצָה וַיֹּאמֶר
הַבֶּט־נָא הַשָּׁמַיְמָה וּסְפֹר הַכּוֹכָבִים אִם־
תּוּכַל לִסְפֹּר אֹתָם וַיֹּאמֶר לוֹ כֹּה יִהְיֶה זַרְעֶךָ:
ו וְהֶאֱמִן בַּיהוה וַיַּחְשְׁבֶהָ לּוֹ צְדָקָה: ששי
ז וַיֹּאמֶר אֵלָיו אֲנִי יהוה אֲשֶׁר הוֹצֵאתִיךָ
מֵאוּר כַּשְׂדִּים לָתֶת לְךָ אֶת־הָאָרֶץ הַזֹּאת
לְרִשְׁתָּהּ: ח וַיֹּאמַר אֲדֹנָי יהוה בַּמָּה אֵדַע כִּי
אִירָשֶׁנָּה: ט וַיֹּאמֶר אֵלָיו קְחָה לִי עֶגְלָה
מְשֻׁלֶּשֶׁת וְעֵז מְשֻׁלֶּשֶׁת וְאַיִל מְשֻׁלָּשׁ וְתֹר
וְגוֹזָל: י וַיִּקַּח־לוֹ אֶת־כָּל־אֵלֶּה וַיְבַתֵּר אֹתָם
בַּתָּוֶךְ וַיִּתֵּן אִישׁ־בִּתְרוֹ לִקְרַאת רֵעֵהוּ וְאֶת־
הַצִּפֹּר לֹא בָתָר: יא וַיֵּרֶד הָעַיִט עַל־הַפְּגָרִים
וַיַּשֵּׁב אֹתָם אַבְרָם: יב וַיְהִי הַשֶּׁמֶשׁ לָבוֹא
וְתַרְדֵּמָה נָפְלָה עַל־אַבְרָם וְהִנֵּה אֵימָה
חֲשֵׁכָה גְדֹלָה נֹפֶלֶת עָלָיו: יג וַיֹּאמֶר לְאַבְרָם
יָדֹעַ תֵּדַע כִּי־גֵר ׀ יִהְיֶה זַרְעֲךָ בְּאֶרֶץ לֹא

15/1-6. God's reassurance to Abraham. *Fear not, Abram.* Abraham was apprehensive that all his merits had been consumed by the miracle of his victory over the kings. If so, he could not expect Divine assistance in the future, and he might be punished for the men he had slain in the fray (*Rashi*). Moreover, the successors to the defeated kings might collect even greater armies and stage a reprisal attack on him (*Ramban*).

2. Of what avail will Your gifts be to me? Since I am childless, whatever You give me will be inherited by others (*B'chor Shor*).

4. God promised that Abraham would have a son who would be an adult when Abraham died, so that he would not require a guardian nor be susceptible to any servant. In this way *he*, and none other, would be assured of being the heir (*Abarbanel*).

5. As no one can conquer the stars, so will no nation ever succeed in exterminating Israel (*Pesikta Zutresa*).

When Israel does God's Will, we are above all — like the stars; when we disobey His will, we are trampled upon by all — like the dust of the earth [cf. 13:16; 28:14] (*Megillah* 16a).

6. This unswerving faith had been part of Abraham for a long time. Had the meaning been that he *began* to trust from that moment on, the Hebrew would have read וַיַּאֲמֵן בָּהּ׳ (*Ibn Caspi*).

7. The Covenant Between the Parts. This covenant was made when Abraham was seventy years old; thus it *preceded* the prophetic vision of the above verses, which occurred when Abraham was seventy-five years old (*Tosafos, Berachos* 7b).

8. The promise of the land. *My Lord, HASHEM/ELOHIM.* Read as *'Adonai Elohim,'* meaning *'Merciful God'* — Merciful in judgment (*Rashi, Deut.* 3:24).

Why would someone of Abraham's unquestioning faith request a guarantee of God's promise? Abraham was apprehensive that he was not worthy to receive the land and that his descendants might sin and become unworthy to retain it (*Rashi; Mizrachi; Gur Aryeh; Maharzu*).

9. To Abraham's apprehensions, God replies: *'. . . You* and your descendants will merit the land because of the sacrifices you are about to offer, and the Temple services that I will institute as a means of atonement for your children' (*Maharzu*). God's choice of animals alluded to the species from which offerings would be brought in the Temple.

10. Abraham severed the animals into two parts. In the plain sense, the cutting of the animals and passing between the parts constituted the ritual of those who enter a covenant. The smoking furnace and fire were emissaries of the Divine Presence [i.e., as if the *Shechinah* was passing between the parts to symbolize His acceptance of the covenant] (*Rashi*).

The birds, however, he did not cut up, because sacrificial birds are not cut up, as are animals (*Ramban*). Also, since the birds represented Israel [*Song of Songs* 2:14], they were left whole to symbolize that Israel would live forever (*Rashi*).

12. The deep sleep was that which accompanies prophetic manifestations. The fear and darkness represent the difficult times ahead (*Rashi*).

15 ¹ After these events, the word of HASHEM came to Abram in a vision saying, 'Fear not, Abram, I am your shield; your reward is very great.'

²And Abram said, 'My Lord, HASHEM/ELOHIM: What can You give me seeing that I go childless, and the steward of my house is the Damascene Eliezer?'

³ Then Abram said, 'See, to me You have given no offspring; and see, my steward is my heir . . .'

⁴ Suddenly, the word of HASHEM came to him, saying: 'That one will not inherit you. None but him that shall come forth from within you shall be your heir.' ⁵ And He took him outside, and said, 'Gaze, now, toward the Heavens, and count the stars if you are able to count them!' And He said to him, 'So shall your offspring be!' ⁶ And he trusted in HASHEM, and He reckoned it to him as righteousness.

⁷ He said to him, 'I am HASHEM Who brought you out of Ur Kasdim to give you this land as an inheritance.'

⁸ He said, 'My Lord, HASHEM/ELOHIM: Whereby shall I know that I am to inherit it?'

⁹ And He said to him, 'Bring Me three heifers, three goats, three rams, a turtledove and a young dove.' ¹⁰ He brought all these to Him: he cut them in the center, and placed each piece opposite its counterpart. The birds, however, he did not cut up.

¹¹ Birds of prey came down upon the carcasses, and Abram drove them away.

¹² And it happened, as the sun was about to set, a deep sleep fell upon Abram; and behold — a dread! great darkness fell upon him.

¹³ And He said to Abram, 'Know with certainty that your offspring shall be aliens in a land not their

לָהֶם וַעֲבָדוּם וְעִנּוּ אֹתָם אַרְבַּע מֵאוֹת שָׁנָה:
יד וְגַם אֶת־הַגּוֹי אֲשֶׁר יַעֲבֹדוּ דָּן אָנֹכִי וְאַחֲרֵי־
כֵן יֵצְאוּ בִּרְכֻשׁ גָּדוֹל: טו וְאַתָּה תָּבוֹא אֶל־
אֲבֹתֶיךָ בְּשָׁלוֹם תִּקָּבֵר בְּשֵׂיבָה טוֹבָה: טז וְדוֹר
רְבִיעִי יָשׁוּבוּ הֵנָּה כִּי לֹא־שָׁלֵם עֲוֹן הָאֱמֹרִי
עַד־הֵנָּה: יז וַיְהִי הַשֶּׁמֶשׁ בָּאָה וַעֲלָטָה הָיָה
וְהִנֵּה תַנּוּר עָשָׁן וְלַפִּיד אֵשׁ אֲשֶׁר עָבַר בֵּין
הַגְּזָרִים הָאֵלֶּה: יח בַּיּוֹם הַהוּא כָּרַת יהוה אֶת־
אַבְרָם בְּרִית לֵאמֹר לְזַרְעֲךָ נָתַתִּי אֶת־הָאָרֶץ
הַזֹּאת מִנְּהַר מִצְרַיִם עַד־הַנָּהָר הַגָּדֹל נְהַר־
פְּרָת: יט אֶת־הַקֵּינִי וְאֶת־הַקְּנִזִּי וְאֵת הַקַּדְמֹנִי:
כ וְאֶת־הַחִתִּי וְאֶת־הַפְּרִזִּי וְאֶת־הָרְפָאִים:
כא וְאֶת־הָאֱמֹרִי וְאֶת־הַכְּנַעֲנִי וְאֶת־הַגִּרְגָּשִׁי
וְאֶת־הַיְבוּסִי: **טז** א וְשָׂרַי
אֵשֶׁת אַבְרָם לֹא יָלְדָה לוֹ וְלָהּ שִׁפְחָה מִצְרִית
וּשְׁמָהּ הָגָר: ב וַתֹּאמֶר שָׂרַי אֶל־אַבְרָם הִנֵּה־נָא
עֲצָרַנִי יהוה מִלֶּדֶת בֹּא־נָא אֶל־שִׁפְחָתִי
אוּלַי אִבָּנֶה מִמֶּנָּה וַיִּשְׁמַע אַבְרָם לְקוֹל שָׂרָי:
ג וַתִּקַּח שָׂרַי אֵשֶׁת־אַבְרָם אֶת־הָגָר הַמִּצְרִית
שִׁפְחָתָהּ מִקֵּץ עֶשֶׂר שָׁנִים לְשֶׁבֶת אַבְרָם
בְּאֶרֶץ כְּנַעַן וַתִּתֵּן אֹתָהּ לְאַבְרָם אִישָׁהּ
לוֹ לְאִשָּׁה: ד וַיָּבֹא אֶל־הָגָר וַתַּהַר וַתֵּרֶא
כִּי הָרָתָה וַתֵּקַל גְּבִרְתָּהּ בְּעֵינֶיהָ:
ה וַתֹּאמֶר שָׂרַי אֶל־אַבְרָם חֲמָסִי עָלֶיךָ אָנֹכִי
נָתַתִּי שִׁפְחָתִי בְּחֵיקֶךָ וַתֵּרֶא כִּי הָרָתָה
וָאֵקַל בְּעֵינֶיהָ יִשְׁפֹּט יהוה בֵּינִי וּבֵינֶיךָ:

13. **400 years of alien status and exile.** Before his descendants would take possession of the land, Abraham's offspring would be an alien nation. The calculation of the 400 years would begin thirty years after this vision, with the birth of Isaac, because Abraham's descendants were considered aliens. The exile in Egypt lasted for 210 of those years, and the *servitude* and *oppression* took place during that period.

14. . . . So will I also punish the oppressors for the violence they will do the Israelites . . . (*Ramban*).

15. You will be spared from seeing all this trial and tribulation (*Rashi*).

Rashi notes further that though Abraham's father, Terach, was an idolater, the verse still speaks of Abraham 'returning' to him! This proves that Terach repented of his idolatry and returned to God.

16. Until the fourth generation after the exile, the Emorites — representing all the Canaanite nations who lived in *Eretz Yisrael* — will not have accumulated enough sin to deserve expulsion, and God does not punish a nation until its measure is full (*Rashi*).

17. The ratification of the Covenant.

19-21. The following are the ten nations who will one day yield their territory to the descendants of Abraham.

16/1. The birth of Ishmael. Hagar was a daughter of Pharaoh. When he saw the miracles that were wrought on behalf of Sarah he gave Hagar to her, saying, 'Better that she be a servant in their house than a noblewoman in mine' (Midrash; Rashi).

2. Consort with my maidservant. Rachel expressed a similar desire (see 30:3) . . . For in ancient times, the mistress would rear her servant's child and consider it her own (Sechel Tov).

4. Hagar brazenly boasted to the ladies, 'Sarai cannot be as righteous as she seems, for so many years passed without her having children, whereas I conceived immediately!' (Rashi). Now that Hagar had assured Abraham's posterity, she no longer felt subservient to Sarah (Radak).

own, they will serve them, and they will oppress them four hundred years. [14]But also upon the nation which they shall serve, will I execute judgment, and afterwards they shall leave with great possessions. — [15] As for you: you shall go to your ancestors in peace; you shall be buried in a good old age. — [16] And the fourth generation shall return here, for the iniquity of the Emorites shall not yet be full until then.'

[17] So it happened: the sun set, and it was very dark. Behold there was a smoky furnace and a torch of fire which passed between these pieces. [18]On that day HASHEM made a covenant with Abram, saying, 'To your descendants have I given this land, from the river of Egypt to the great river, the Euphrates River: [19] the Kennites, the Kenizzites, and the Kadmonites; [20] the Hittites, the Perizzites and the Rephaim; [21] the Emorites, the Canaanites, the Girgashites and the Jebusites.

16 [1] Now Sarai, Abram's wife, had borne him no children. She had an Egyptian maidservant whose name was Hagar. [2] And Sarai said to Abram, 'See, now, HASHEM has restrained me from bearing. Consort, now, with my maidservant, perhaps I will be built up through her.' And Abram heeded the voice of Sarai.

[3] So Sarai, Abram's wife, took Hagar the Egyptian her maidservant — after Abram lived in the Land of Canaan ten years — and gave her to Abram her husband, to him as a wife. [4]He consorted with Hagar and she conceived; and when she saw that she had conceived, her mistress was lowered in her esteem. [5] So Sarai said to Abram, 'The outrage against me is due to you! It was I who gave my maidservant into your lap, and now that she sees that she has conceived, I became lowered in her esteem. Let HASHEM judge between me and you!'

6. To me she is a wife; I can do nothing. But to you she is a servant; if she mistreated you, do as you please (*Radak; Haamek Davar*).

Sarah's intent was not malicious, but to force Hagar to acknowledge her subordinate position and cease her insulting demeanor. Instead, Hagar fled (*Abarbanel; Sforno*).

8. By addressing her as *maidservant*, the angel reminded her of her subservience to her mistress. She acknowledged this status by referring to Sarah [next verse] as '*my mistress*' (*Chizkuni*).

12. *Wild-ass.* Wild and untamable, taking what he wishes by brutal force. He will be a plunderer, and his descendants will war with everyone.

13. *Could I have seen,* etc. An exclamation of surprise: 'Could I ever have expected to see God's emissaries *even here* in the desert *after seeing* them in Abraham's house where I routinely saw many angels?'

15. Bolstered by this promise, Hagar returned to her mistress, and after a short while she bore Abraham a son.

16. The year was 2034 from Creation.

ו וַיֹּאמֶר אַבְרָם אֶל־שָׂרַי הִנֵּה שִׁפְחָתֵךְ בְּיָדֵךְ עֲשִׂי־לָהּ הַטּוֹב בְּעֵינָיִךְ וַתְּעַנֶּהָ שָׂרַי וַתִּבְרַח מִפָּנֶיהָ: ז וַיִּמְצָאָהּ מַלְאַךְ יְהוָֹה עַל־עֵין הַמַּיִם בַּמִּדְבָּר עַל־הָעַיִן בְּדֶרֶךְ שׁוּר: ח וַיֹּאמַר הָגָר שִׁפְחַת שָׂרַי אֵי־מִזֶּה בָאת וְאָנָה תֵלֵכִי וַתֹּאמֶר מִפְּנֵי שָׂרַי גְּבִרְתִּי אָנֹכִי בֹּרַחַת: ט וַיֹּאמֶר לָהּ מַלְאַךְ יְהוָֹה שׁוּבִי אֶל־גְּבִרְתֵּךְ וְהִתְעַנִּי תַּחַת יָדֶיהָ: י וַיֹּאמֶר לָהּ מַלְאַךְ יְהוָֹה הַרְבָּה אַרְבֶּה אֶת־זַרְעֵךְ וְלֹא יִסָּפֵר מֵרֹב: יא וַיֹּאמֶר לָהּ מַלְאַךְ יְהוָֹה הִנָּךְ הָרָה וְיֹלַדְתְּ בֵּן וְקָרָאת שְׁמוֹ יִשְׁמָעֵאל כִּי־שָׁמַע יְהוָֹה אֶל־עָנְיֵךְ: יב וְהוּא יִהְיֶה פֶּרֶא אָדָם יָדוֹ בַכֹּל וְיַד כֹּל בּוֹ וְעַל־פְּנֵי כָל־אֶחָיו יִשְׁכֹּן: יג וַתִּקְרָא שֵׁם־ יְהוָֹה הַדֹּבֵר אֵלֶיהָ אַתָּה אֵל רֳאִי כִּי אָמְרָה הֲגַם הֲלֹם רָאִיתִי אַחֲרֵי רֹאִי: יד עַל־כֵּן קָרָא לַבְּאֵר בְּאֵר לַחַי רֹאִי הִנֵּה בֵין־קָדֵשׁ וּבֵין בָּרֶד: טו וַתֵּלֶד הָגָר לְאַבְרָם בֵּן וַיִּקְרָא אַבְרָם שֶׁם־בְּנוֹ אֲשֶׁר־יָלְדָה הָגָר יִשְׁמָעֵאל: טז וְאַבְרָם בֶּן־שְׁמֹנִים שָׁנָה וְשֵׁשׁ שָׁנִים בְּלֶדֶת־הָגָר אֶת־יִשְׁמָעֵאל לְאַבְרָם:

יז א וַיְהִי אַבְרָם בֶּן־תִּשְׁעִים שָׁנָה וְתֵשַׁע שָׁנִים וַיֵּרָא יְהוָֹה אֶל־אַבְרָם וַיֹּאמֶר אֵלָיו אֲנִי־אֵל שַׁדַּי הִתְהַלֵּךְ לְפָנַי וֶהְיֵה תָמִים: ב וְאֶתְּנָה בְרִיתִי בֵּינִי וּבֵינֶךָ וְאַרְבֶּה אוֹתְךָ בִּמְאֹד מְאֹד: ג וַיִּפֹּל אַבְרָם עַל־פָּנָיו וַיְדַבֵּר אִתּוֹ אֱלֹהִים

17/1. The covenant of circumcision. The year is 2047 from Creation. Ishmael is 13 years old and Sarah is 89.

Circumcision is one of the ten trials of Abraham. The commandment was given prior to Isaac's birth in order that Isaac's conception take place in holiness and in order to emphasize the miracle that Abraham could have a child even though his organ had been weakened (*Radak*).

El Shaddai. This Name depicts God literally as שַׁדַּי, *Who is sufficient* in granting His mercies, and Who has sufficient power to give (*Rashi* to 43:14).

Walk before Me, i.e., serve Me, by observing the *mitzvah* of circumcision, *and as a result of this, you will become perfect* (*Rashi*).

By removing some of his skin through circumcision — an apparent contradiction to *physical* perfection — man would become *perfect* because this slight diminution of an organ would be the symbol of his covenant with God (*Ibn Ezra*).

'Perfection' implies a condition containing neither superfluity nor deficiency. The Creator created this part of man's body with a redundancy; by removing this defect in his formation, man attains a state of perfection (*R' Saadiah Gaon*).

⁶ Abram said to Sarai, 'Your maidservant is in your hand; do to her as you see fit.' And Sarai dealt harshly with her, so she fled from her.

⁷ An angel of HASHEM found her by the spring of water in the desert, at the spring on the road to Shur. ⁸ And he said, 'Hagar, maidservant of Sarai, where have you come from and where are you going?' And she said, 'I am running away from Sarai my mistress.'

⁹ And an angel of HASHEM said to her, 'Return to your mistress, and submit yourself to her domination.'

¹⁰ And an angel of HASHEM said to her, 'I will greatly increase your offspring, and they will not be counted for abundance.'

¹¹ And an angel of HASHEM said to her, 'Behold you will conceive, and give birth to a son; you shall name him Ishmael, for HASHEM has heard your prayer. ¹² And he shall be a wild-ass of a man: his hand against everyone, and everyone's hand against him; and over all his brothers shall he dwell.'

¹³ And she named HASHEM Who spoke to her 'You are the God of Vision,' for she said, 'Could I have seen even here after having seen?' ¹⁴ Therefore the well was called 'Be'er Lachai Ro'i.' It is between Kadesh and Bered.

¹⁵ Hagar bore Abram a son and Abram named his son, that Hagar bore him, Ishmael. ¹⁶ And Abram was eighty-six years old when Hagar bore Ishmael to Abram.

17 ¹ When Abram was ninety-nine years old, HASHEM appeared to Abram and said to him, 'I am El Shaddai; walk before Me and be perfect. ² I will set My covenant between Me and you, and I will increase you most exceedingly.'

³ Abram fell upon his face, and God spoke with

לֵאמֹר: ד אֲנִי הִנֵּה בְרִיתִי אִתָּךְ וְהָיִיתָ לְאַב
הֲמוֹן גּוֹיִם: ה וְלֹא-יִקָּרֵא עוֹד אֶת-שִׁמְךָ
אַבְרָם וְהָיָה שִׁמְךָ אַבְרָהָם כִּי אַב-הֲמוֹן
גּוֹיִם נְתַתִּיךָ: ו וְהִפְרֵתִי אֹתְךָ בִּמְאֹד מְאֹד
וּנְתַתִּיךָ לְגוֹיִם וּמְלָכִים מִמְּךָ יֵצֵאוּ: שביעי
ז וַהֲקִמֹתִי אֶת-בְּרִיתִי בֵּינִי וּבֵינֶךָ וּבֵין זַרְעֲךָ
אַחֲרֶיךָ לְדֹרֹתָם לִבְרִית עוֹלָם לִהְיוֹת לְךָ
לֵאלֹהִים וּלְזַרְעֲךָ אַחֲרֶיךָ: ח וְנָתַתִּי לְךָ
וּלְזַרְעֲךָ אַחֲרֶיךָ אֵת | אֶרֶץ מְגֻרֶיךָ אֵת
כָּל-אֶרֶץ כְּנַעַן לַאֲחֻזַּת עוֹלָם וְהָיִיתִי לָהֶם
לֵאלֹהִים: ט וַיֹּאמֶר אֱלֹהִים אֶל-אַבְרָהָם
וְאַתָּה אֶת-בְּרִיתִי תִשְׁמֹר אַתָּה וְזַרְעֲךָ אַחֲרֶיךָ
לְדֹרֹתָם: י זֹאת בְּרִיתִי אֲשֶׁר תִּשְׁמְרוּ בֵּינִי
וּבֵינֵיכֶם וּבֵין זַרְעֲךָ אַחֲרֶיךָ הִמּוֹל לָכֶם
כָּל-זָכָר: יא וּנְמַלְתֶּם אֵת בְּשַׂר עָרְלַתְכֶם
וְהָיָה לְאוֹת בְּרִית בֵּינִי וּבֵינֵיכֶם: יב וּבֶן-
שְׁמֹנַת יָמִים יִמּוֹל לָכֶם כָּל-זָכָר לְדֹרֹתֵיכֶם
יְלִיד בָּיִת וּמִקְנַת-כֶּסֶף מִכֹּל בֶּן-נֵכָר אֲשֶׁר
לֹא מִזַּרְעֲךָ הוּא: יג הִמּוֹל | יִמּוֹל יְלִיד בֵּיתְךָ
וּמִקְנַת כַּסְפֶּךָ וְהָיְתָה בְרִיתִי בִּבְשַׂרְכֶם
לִבְרִית עוֹלָם: יד וְעָרֵל | זָכָר אֲשֶׁר לֹא-יִמּוֹל
אֶת-בְּשַׂר עָרְלָתוֹ וְנִכְרְתָה הַנֶּפֶשׁ הַהִוא
מֵעַמֶּיהָ אֶת-בְּרִיתִי הֵפַר: טו וַיֹּאמֶר
אֱלֹהִים אֶל-אַבְרָהָם שָׂרַי אִשְׁתְּךָ לֹא-
תִקְרָא אֶת-שְׁמָהּ שָׂרָי כִּי שָׂרָה שְׁמָהּ:

4. The details of the covenant.
There are two parties to the covenant, and their respective obligations are clearly defined. God's are listed in verses 4-8, and those of Abraham and his descendants are enumerated in verses 9-14.

5. Abram's name is changed to Abraham. The name 'Avraham' is a contraction, depicting his new status as *av hamon* — father of a multitude, whereas *Avram* denoted him in his former status as *av Aram* — father of Aram, his native country. The letter *reish* in his former name was retained after the change even though it was now rendered superfluous, since he no longer belonged only to Aram (*Rashi*).

10. The definition of the covenant.
Every male among you shall be circumcised. This is not the injunction to circumcise — that comes in verse 11 — rather it is a description of what the covenant requires (*Sifsei Chachamim*).

11. This is a positive commandment requiring every father to circumcise his son, and obligating every person to have himself circumcised when he becomes a *bar mitzvah*, if he had not been circumcised previously by his father or the *beis din* (*Radak*).

Circumcision will thus serve as a symbol and sign, just as *tzitzis* and *tefillin* are reminders of Israel's bond and obligation to God (*Radak*).

12. *He that is born in the household,* i.e., from a maidservant; *or purchased with money,* i.e., a slave purchased after he was born (*Rashi*).

14. The penalty for an adult who remains uncircumcised intentionally is כָּרֵת, *excision.* [Excision means that the soul loses its share in the World to Come, and the violator dies childless and prematurely (*Shabbos* 104a; *Rashi*).]

15. The promise to Sarah. Previously, the covenant was solely with Abraham. Now Sarah is called upon as an equal party in this covenant-promise. And just as Abraham's new role was signified by a change of name, so was Sarah's (*R' Hirsch*).

The word *Sarai* means 'my princess'; *Sarah* signifies 'princess — to all the nations of the world.' Prior to the covenant, Sarai's personal majesty made her the princess of Abraham and Aram. Now, however, all limitations were removed from her. She was princess 'par excellence' — to all mankind (*Rashi; Berachos* 13a).

him saying, ⁴'As for Me, this is My covenant with you: you shall be a father of a multitude of nations; ⁵ you shall no longer be called by your name Abram, but your name shall be Abraham, for I have made you the father of a multitude of nations; ⁶ I will make you most exceedingly fruitful, and make nations of you; and kings shall descend from you; ⁷ and I will ratify My covenant between Me and you and between your offspring after you throughout their generations as an everlasting covenant, to be a God to you and to your offspring after you; ⁸ and I will give to you and to your offspring after you the land of your sojourns — the whole of the land of Canaan — as an everlasting possession; and I will be their God.'

⁹ God said to Abraham, 'And as for you, you shall keep My covenant — you and your descendants after you throughout their generations. ¹⁰ This is My covenant which you shall keep between Me and you and your descendants after you: Every male among you shall be circumcised. ¹¹ You shall circumcise the flesh of your surplusage, and that shall be the sign of the covenant between Me and you. ¹² At the age of eight days every male among you shall be circumcised, throughout your generations — he that is born in the household or purchased with money from any stranger who is not of your offspring. ¹³ He that is born in your household or purchased with your money shall surely be circumcised. Thus, My covenant shall be in your flesh for an everlasting covenant. ¹⁴ An uncircumcised male the flesh of whose surplusage shall not be circumcised — such a soul shall be cut off from its people; he has invalidated My covenant.'

¹⁵ And God said to Abraham, 'As for Sarai your wife — do not call her by the name Sarai, for Sarah

טז וּבֵרַכְתִּי אֹתָהּ וְגַם נָתַתִּי מִמֶּנָּה לְךָ בֵּן וּבֵרַכְתִּיהָ וְהָיְתָה לְגוֹיִם מַלְכֵי עַמִּים מִמֶּנָּה יִהְיוּ: יז וַיִּפֹּל אַבְרָהָם עַל־פָּנָיו וַיִּצְחָק וַיֹּאמֶר בְּלִבּוֹ הַלְּבֶן מֵאָה־שָׁנָה יִוָּלֵד וְאִם־שָׂרָה הֲבַת־תִּשְׁעִים שָׁנָה תֵּלֵד: יח וַיֹּאמֶר אַבְרָהָם אֶל־הָאֱלֹהִים לוּ יִשְׁמָעֵאל יִחְיֶה לְפָנֶיךָ: יט וַיֹּאמֶר אֱלֹהִים אֲבָל שָׂרָה אִשְׁתְּךָ יֹלֶדֶת לְךָ בֵּן וְקָרָאתָ אֶת־שְׁמוֹ יִצְחָק וַהֲקִמֹתִי אֶת־בְּרִיתִי אִתּוֹ לִבְרִית עוֹלָם לְזַרְעוֹ אַחֲרָיו: כ וּלְיִשְׁמָעֵאל שְׁמַעְתִּיךָ הִנֵּה | בֵּרַכְתִּי אֹתוֹ וְהִפְרֵיתִי אֹתוֹ וְהִרְבֵּיתִי אֹתוֹ בִּמְאֹד מְאֹד שְׁנֵים־עָשָׂר נְשִׂיאִם יוֹלִיד וּנְתַתִּיו לְגוֹי גָּדוֹל: כא וְאֶת־בְּרִיתִי אָקִים אֶת־יִצְחָק אֲשֶׁר תֵּלֵד לְךָ שָׂרָה לַמּוֹעֵד הַזֶּה בַּשָּׁנָה הָאַחֶרֶת: כב וַיְכַל לְדַבֵּר אִתּוֹ וַיַּעַל אֱלֹהִים מֵעַל אַבְרָהָם: כג וַיִּקַּח אַבְרָהָם אֶת־יִשְׁמָעֵאל בְּנוֹ וְאֵת כָּל־יְלִידֵי בֵיתוֹ וְאֵת כָּל־מִקְנַת כַּסְפּוֹ כָּל־זָכָר בְּאַנְשֵׁי בֵּית אַבְרָהָם וַיָּמָל אֶת־בְּשַׂר עָרְלָתָם בְּעֶצֶם הַיּוֹם הַזֶּה כַּאֲשֶׁר דִּבֶּר אִתּוֹ אֱלֹהִים: מפטיר כד וְאַבְרָהָם בֶּן־תִּשְׁעִים וָתֵשַׁע שָׁנָה בְּהִמֹּלוֹ בְּשַׂר עָרְלָתוֹ: כה וְיִשְׁמָעֵאל בְּנוֹ בֶּן־שְׁלֹשׁ עֶשְׂרֵה שָׁנָה בְּהִמֹּלוֹ אֵת בְּשַׂר עָרְלָתוֹ: כו בְּעֶצֶם הַיּוֹם הַזֶּה נִמּוֹל אַבְרָהָם וְיִשְׁמָעֵאל בְּנוֹ: כז וְכָל־אַנְשֵׁי בֵיתוֹ יְלִיד בָּיִת וּמִקְנַת־כֶּסֶף מֵאֵת בֶּן־נֵכָר נִמֹּלוּ אִתּוֹ:

17. *And [he] laughed.* Jubilantly; as Onkelos renders וַחֲדִי, *and he rejoiced*. In the case of Sarah, however [see 18:12], Onkelos rendered the same verb וַתִּצְחָק as וְחַיְכַת, *she laughed* derisively. Abraham had faith and *rejoiced*, while Sarah *sneered*; hence, God was angry but not with Abraham (Rashi).

18. I am unworthy of so great a reward as to have a son now. It will suffice for me if only Ishmael lived righteously before You . . . (Rashi)

19. *God reaffirms the promise.* The name יִצְחָק, *Isaac*, refers to Abraham's laughter [צְחוֹק] (Rashi).

God specifically declares, here and in v. 21, that the Abrahamitic covenant will be perpetuated *only* through Isaac, and not otherwise (Rashi).

20. 'We see that from the prophecy in this verse, 2337 years elapsed before the Arabs, Ishmael's descendants, became a great nation . . . Throughout this period, Ishmael hoped anxiously, until finally the promise was fulfilled and they dominated the world. We, the descendants of Isaac, for whom the fulfillment of the promises made to us is delayed due to our sins . . . should surely anticipate the fulfillment of God's promises and not despair' (R' Bachya citing R' Chananel).

The *Haftarah* for *Lech Lecha* appears on page 304

24-27. The Torah now proceeds, in its usual custom, to recapitulate the substance of the previous verses, but in more detail and with additional emphasis.

The ages of Abraham and Ishmael are given to show that Abraham, despite his age, and Ishmael, despite his youth, went with vigor to perform the will of God.

According to the Masoretic note appearing at the end of the *sidrah*, there are 126 verses in the *sidrah* numerically corresponding to the mnemonic נִמֹ"לוּ [=126 = *they were circumcised*] and also to מְכְנְדָ"יב [=126.] The allusion of the latter is obscure. *R' David Feinstein* notes that נָדִיב is interpreted in *Chagigah* 3a and *Midrash Shir Hashirim* 7:2 as a reference to Abraham. The meaning of מֵךְ may be derived from *Sotah* 10b, where the word is given two meanings with reference to David: 1) He was humble and self-effacing (from מֵךְ, *poor*); and 2) he was born circumcised (from the word מַכָּה, a *wound*). Either interpretation can be applied to Abraham, who was humble and who circumcised himself. The *Haftarah* begins with *Isaiah* 40:27: לָמֶה תֹאמֵר יַעֲקֹב.

is her name. [16] I will bless her; indeed, I will give you a son through her. I will bless her and she shall give rise to nations; kings of peoples will rise from her.'

[17] And Abraham threw himself upon his face and laughed; and he thought, Shall a child be born to a hundred-year-old man? And Sarah — shall a ninety-year-old woman give birth?' [18] And Abraham said to God, 'O that Ishmael might live before You!' [19] God said, 'Nonetheless, your wife Sarah will bear you a son and you shall name him Isaac; and I will fulfill My covenant with him as an everlasting covenant for his offspring after him. [20] But regarding Ishmael I have heard you: I have blessed him, made him fruitful and will increase him most exceedingly; he will beget twelve princes and I will make him into a great nation. [21] But I will maintain my covenant through Isaac whom Sarah will bear by this time next year.' [22] And when He had finished speaking with him, God ascended from upon Abraham.

[23] Then Abraham took his son Ishmael and all those servants born in his household and all those he had purchased for money — all the male members of Abraham's house — and he circumcised the flesh of their surplusage on that very day as God had spoken with him. [24] Abraham was ninety-nine when he was circumcised on the flesh of his surplusage; [25] And his son Ishmael was thirteen years old when he was circumcised on the flesh of his surplusage. [26] On that very day was Abraham circumcised with Ishmael his son, [27] and all the people of his household, born in his household and purchased for money from a stranger, were circumcised with him.

The *Haftarah* for *Lech Lecha* appears on page 304

פרשת וירא

VAYEIRA

The longing for a child of their own that clouded the successes of Abraham and Sarah is finally rewarded with God's pledge that Sarah would give birth to Isaac. In the midst of Abraham's joy, God informs him — as the 'father of a multitude of nations' — that Sodom and its neighboring cities are about to be destroyed. Sodom has become part of the English language as a term for perversion, but that is not the reason it was condemned. As the Sages teach, Sodom was notorious for its selfishness and cruelty to strangers, a tactic that was intended to safeguard the regions lush prosperity by keeping immigrants away. Abraham is the diametrical opposite. No one knew better than he of the evils of nearby Sodom, but his reaction upon learning of God's decree was to demand justice for the unjust and mercy for the unmerciful.

The birth of Isaac brought mirth and joy to everyone, as a hundred-year-old father and a ninety-year-old mother became youthful again. It was an extension of the creation that began with the emergence of Abraham and Sarah as the Patriarch and Matriarch, who would embody and carry on God's mission for humanity.

This set the stage for the climax of Abraham's ten tests. All his life he had waited for Isaac — *your son, your only one, whom you love* (22:2) — and then he was commanded to offer him upon the altar. Abraham the merciful, Abraham the Patriarch of Israel, Abraham who had prayed for his wife to give birth, Abraham who had preached to the world that God detests human sacrifice, Abraham who had interceded even for Sodom — the same Abraham is commanded to make a human sacrifice of his precious heir. For his willingness to do so, he indeed earned the acknowledgement that he had proven himself to be genuinely God fearing.

יח א וַיֵּרָא אֵלָיו יהוה בְּאֵלֹנֵי מַמְרֵא וְהוּא יֹשֵׁב
פֶּתַח־הָאֹהֶל כְּחֹם הַיּוֹם: ב וַיִּשָּׂא עֵינָיו וַיַּרְא
וְהִנֵּה שְׁלֹשָׁה אֲנָשִׁים נִצָּבִים עָלָיו וַיַּרְא וַיָּרָץ
לִקְרָאתָם מִפֶּתַח הָאֹהֶל וַיִּשְׁתַּחוּ אָרְצָה:
ג וַיֹּאמַר אֲדֹנָי אִם־נָא מָצָאתִי חֵן בְּעֵינֶיךָ
אַל־נָא תַעֲבֹר מֵעַל עַבְדֶּךָ: ד יֻקַּח־נָא מְעַט־
מַיִם וְרַחֲצוּ רַגְלֵיכֶם וְהִשָּׁעֲנוּ תַּחַת הָעֵץ:
ה וְאֶקְחָה פַת־לֶחֶם וְסַעֲדוּ לִבְּכֶם אַחַר תַּעֲבֹרוּ
כִּי־עַל־כֵּן עֲבַרְתֶּם עַל־עַבְדְּכֶם וַיֹּאמְרוּ כֵּן
תַּעֲשֶׂה כַּאֲשֶׁר דִּבַּרְתָּ: ו וַיְמַהֵר אַבְרָהָם
הָאֹהֱלָה אֶל־שָׂרָה וַיֹּאמֶר מַהֲרִי שְׁלֹשׁ סְאִים
קֶמַח סֹלֶת לוּשִׁי וַעֲשִׂי עֻגוֹת: ז וְאֶל־הַבָּקָר רָץ
אַבְרָהָם וַיִּקַּח בֶּן־בָּקָר רַךְ וָטוֹב וַיִּתֵּן אֶל־
הַנַּעַר וַיְמַהֵר לַעֲשׂוֹת אֹתוֹ: ח וַיִּקַּח חֶמְאָה
וְחָלָב וּבֶן־הַבָּקָר אֲשֶׁר עָשָׂה וַיִּתֵּן לִפְנֵיהֶם
וְהוּא עֹמֵד עֲלֵיהֶם תַּחַת הָעֵץ וַיֹּאכֵלוּ:
ט וַיֹּאמְרוּ אֵלָיו אַיֵּה שָׂרָה אִשְׁתֶּךָ וַיֹּאמֶר הִנֵּה
בָאֹהֶל: י וַיֹּאמֶר שׁוֹב אָשׁוּב אֵלֶיךָ כָּעֵת חַיָּה
וְהִנֵּה־בֵן לְשָׂרָה אִשְׁתֶּךָ וְשָׂרָה שֹׁמַעַת פֶּתַח
הָאֹהֶל וְהוּא אַחֲרָיו: יא וְאַבְרָהָם וְשָׂרָה
זְקֵנִים בָּאִים בַּיָּמִים חָדַל לִהְיוֹת לְשָׂרָה אֹרַח
כַּנָּשִׁים: יב וַתִּצְחַק שָׂרָה בְּקִרְבָּהּ לֵאמֹר אַחֲרֵי
בְלֹתִי הָיְתָה־לִּי עֶדְנָה וַאדֹנִי זָקֵן: יג וַיֹּאמֶר
יהוה אֶל־אַבְרָהָם לָמָּה זֶּה צָחֲקָה שָׂרָה
לֵאמֹר הַאַף אֻמְנָם אֵלֵד וַאֲנִי זָקַנְתִּי: יד הֲיִפָּלֵא

1. **Visiting the sick.** It was the third day after Abraham's circumcision and God came and inquired after his welfare (Rashi).

While he was sitting at the entrance of the tent. Abraham was looking for travelers to whom he might offer hospitality (Rashi).

2. Three different angels were sent because each had a different function, and one angel does not [simultaneously] perform two missions. [Michael] informed Abraham of Sarah's conception [v. 14]; [Gabriel] overturned Sodom [19:25]; and Raphael healed Abraham, and later saved Lot. (Midrash)] (Rashi).

3. According to Rashi's second interpretation — which closely follows the majority interpretation of this verse — the word אֲדֹנָי in this passage is sacred, referring to God. Abraham was *taking leave from God,* imploring Him to *pass not away from Your servant,* but wait while he attended to his guests.

'Greater is hospitality to wayfarers than receiving the Divine Presence' [for Abraham, took leave of God to serve his guests] (Shevuos 35b; Shabbos 127a).

4. *And wash your feet.* [Abraham was not yet aware they were angels:] He thought that they were like Arabs who worship the dust of their feet, and he scrupulously avoided bringing the object of idolatry into his house (Rashi).

5. *A morsel of bread.* An understated, modest description of the sumptuous meal about to be served. The Talmud derives from this that 'the righteous say little and do much' (Bava Metzia 87a).

7. *Then Abraham ran. Ramban* emphasizes how this
portrays Abraham's great
desire to show hospitality.
Though he had many ser-
vants eager to serve him,
and he was old and weak
from his circumcision, he
ran *personally* to choose the
animals for the meal.

First, Abraham served the
dairy items for they required
little preparation. Only after
his guests had slaked their
thirst and hunger, did he
bring out the full meal that
consisted of calves' meat
(*Da'as Zekeinim; Malbim*).

**10. The promise of a son is
revealed to Sarah.** *At this
time next year.* It was
Passover, and on the next
Passover, Isaac was born
(*Rashi*).

11. בָּאִים בַּיָּמִים — *Well on
in years.* This describes one
upon whom old age weighs
heavily; one who has 'en-
tered into those days' when
he feels he will soon go the
way of all flesh (*Radak*).

12. Sarah laughs. *And Sarah
laughed at herself* [lit.,
'within herself'], *saying. She
laughed* in disbelief because
she thought that the guest's
statement was simply the
courteous blessing of a human prophet [like that of
Elisha's (see *II Kings* 4:16)]
and not a prophecy from
God. In view of her ad-
vanced age, she thought
that such a miraculous reju-
venation would be as great
a miracle as the resurrection
of the dead, which only God
Himself could accomplish
(*Radak; Sforno*).

13. וַאֲנִי זָקַנְתִּי — *Though I
have aged.* Her actual words
in v. 12 were וַאדֹנִי זָקֵן, *my
husband is old*, but for the
sake of peace between
husband and wife, Scripture
[i.e., God] now changed the
uncomplimentary reference
from her husband to herself
(*Rashi*).

18 ¹ Hashem appeared to him in the plains of
Mamre while he was sitting at the
entrance of the tent in the heat of the day. ² He
lifted his eyes and saw: And behold! three men
were standing over him. He perceived, so he ran
toward them from the entrance of the tent, and
bowed toward the ground. ³ And he said, 'My
Lord, if I find favor in Your eyes, please pass not
away from Your servant.'

⁴'Let some water be brought and wash your feet,
and recline beneath the tree. ⁵ I will fetch a morsel
of bread that you may sustain yourselves, then go
on — inasmuch as you have passed your servant's
way.' They said, 'Do so, just as you have said.'

⁶ So Abraham hastened to the tent to Sarah and
said, 'Hurry! Three se'ahs of meal, fine flour!
Knead and make cakes!' ⁷ Then Abraham ran to the
herd, took a calf, tender and good, and gave it to
the youth who hurried to prepare it. ⁸ He took
cream and milk and the calf which he had
prepared, and placed these before them; he stood
over them beneath the tree and they ate.

⁹ They said to him, 'Where is Sarah your wife?'
And he said, 'In the tent!'

¹⁰ And he said, 'I will surely return to you at this
time next year, and behold Sarah your wife will
have a son.' Now Sarah was listening at the
entrance of the tent which was behind him.

¹¹ Now Abraham and Sarah were old, well on in
years; the manner of women had ceased to be
with Sarah —

¹² And Sarah laughed at herself, saying, 'After I
have withered shall I again have delicate skin? And
my husband is old!'

¹³ Then Hashem said to Abraham, 'Why is it that
Sarah laughed, saying: "Shall I in truth bear a child,
though I have aged?" ¹⁴ — Is anything beyond

מֵיהוָה דָּבָר לַמּוֹעֵד אָשׁוּב אֵלֶיךָ כָּעֵת
חַיָּה וּלְשָׂרָה בֵן: שני טו וַתְּכַחֵשׁ שָׂרָה ׀ לֵאמֹר
לֹא צָחַקְתִּי כִּי ׀ יָרֵאָה וַיֹּאמֶר ׀ לֹא כִּי
צָחָקְתְּ: טז וַיָּקֻמוּ מִשָּׁם הָאֲנָשִׁים וַיַּשְׁקִפוּ עַל־
פְּנֵי סְדֹם וְאַבְרָהָם הֹלֵךְ עִמָּם לְשַׁלְּחָם:
יז וַיהוָה אָמָר הַמְכַסֶּה אֲנִי מֵאַבְרָהָם אֲשֶׁר
אֲנִי עֹשֶׂה: יח וְאַבְרָהָם הָיוֹ יִהְיֶה לְגוֹי גָּדוֹל
וְעָצוּם וְנִבְרְכוּ־בוֹ כֹּל גּוֹיֵי הָאָרֶץ: יט כִּי
יְדַעְתִּיו לְמַעַן אֲשֶׁר יְצַוֶּה אֶת־בָּנָיו וְאֶת־בֵּיתוֹ
אַחֲרָיו וְשָׁמְרוּ דֶּרֶךְ יהוה לַעֲשׂוֹת צְדָקָה
וּמִשְׁפָּט לְמַעַן הָבִיא יהוה עַל־אַבְרָהָם אֵת
אֲשֶׁר־דִּבֶּר עָלָיו: כ וַיֹּאמֶר יהוֹה זַעֲקַת סְדֹם
וַעֲמֹרָה כִּי־רָבָּה וְחַטָּאתָם כִּי כָבְדָה מְאֹד:
כא אֵרֲדָה־נָּא וְאֶרְאֶה הַכְּצַעֲקָתָהּ הַבָּאָה
אֵלַי עָשׂוּ ׀ כָּלָה וְאִם־לֹא אֵדָעָה: כב וַיִּפְנוּ
מִשָּׁם הָאֲנָשִׁים וַיֵּלְכוּ סְדֹמָה וְאַבְרָהָם
עוֹדֶנּוּ עֹמֵד לִפְנֵי יהוָה: כג וַיִּגַּשׁ אַבְרָהָם
וַיֹּאמַר הַאַף תִּסְפֶּה צַדִּיק עִם־רָשָׁע:
כד אוּלַי יֵשׁ חֲמִשִּׁים צַדִּיקִם בְּתוֹךְ הָעִיר
הַאַף תִּסְפֶּה וְלֹא־תִשָּׂא לַמָּקוֹם לְמַעַן
חֲמִשִּׁים הַצַּדִּיקִם אֲשֶׁר בְּקִרְבָּהּ: כה חָלִלָה
לְּךָ מֵעֲשֹׂת ׀ כַּדָּבָר הַזֶּה לְהָמִית צַדִּיק
עִם־רָשָׁע וְהָיָה כַצַּדִּיק כָּרָשָׁע חָלִלָה לָּךְ
הֲשֹׁפֵט כָּל־הָאָרֶץ לֹא יַעֲשֶׂה מִשְׁפָּט:
כו וַיֹּאמֶר יהוֹה אִם־אֶמְצָא בִסְדֹם חֲמִשִּׁים

16. Abraham escorts his guests.

17. Sodom's destruction is revealed. Seeing that Abraham is destined to become a great and mighty nation, future nations will ask, 'How could God have hidden this from him?' or 'How could Abraham have been so callous he failed to pray for his neighbors?' Knowing that he recognizes I love righteousness, Abraham will charge his children to cultivate these virtues. Now, if there is a righteous cause to pardon the Sodomites, he will beseech Me to do so. But if they are completely guilty, he, too, will want their judgment to be carried out (Ramban).

19. The Israelite nation is distinguished in three ways: they are compassionate, bashful, and benevolent. The last is derived from our text: to do charity (Yevamos 79a).

20. Because the outcry of Sodom and Amorah has become great — the outcry of its rebellion against God or the outcry of its violence (Ibn Ezra). Or, according to Ramban: the cry of the oppressed begging for liberation.

21. *And if not, I will know.* If, however, they do not persist in their rebellious ways [but repent (*Onkelos*)], *I will know* what to do: I will punish them, but not destroy them entirely. Cf. a similar thought in *Exod.* 33:5 (*Rashi*).

22. *While Abraham was still standing before* HASHEM. Although the angel who was to destroy Sodom had already reached his destination, Abraham still prayed on the Sodomites' behalf. This follows our Sages' teaching [*Berachos* 10a]: One must not desist from prayer even when a sharp sword is upon his neck (*Sforno*).

23. **Abraham intercedes on behalf of Sodom.** In the following verses Abraham exemplifies his new role as *'father of a multitude of nations'* in its noblest form. Even the wicked inhabitants of Sodom engage his sympathy, and he overflows with sorrow over their impending doom (*Akeidas Yitzchak*).

24. *Fifty righteous people.* Five cities were condemned [see v. 29 and 14:2]. Abraham therefore mentioned fifty — ten righteous people [a quorum; see v. 26], for each city (*Rashi*).

HASHEM?! At the appointed time I will return to you at this time next year, and Sarah will have a son.'

¹⁵ Sarah denied it, saying, 'I did not laugh,' for she was frightened. But he said, 'No, you laughed indeed.'

¹⁶ So the men got up from there, and gazed down toward Sodom, while Abraham walked with them to see them off.

¹⁷ And HASHEM said, 'Shall I conceal from Abraham what I do, ¹⁸ now that Abraham is surely to become a great and mighty nation and all the nations of the earth shall bless themselves by him? ¹⁹ For I have loved him, because he commands his children and his household after him that they keep the way of HASHEM, doing charity and justice, in order that HASHEM might then bring upon Abraham that which He had spoken of him.'

²⁰ So HASHEM said, 'Because the outcry of Sodom and Amorrah has become great, and because their sin has been very grave, ²¹ I will descend and see: If they act in accordance with its outcry — then destruction! And if not, I will know.'

²² — The men had turned from there and went to Sodom, while Abraham was still standing before HASHEM. —

²³ Abraham came forward and said, 'Will You also stamp out the righteous along with the wicked? ²⁴ What if there should be fifty righteous people in the city? Would You still stamp it out rather than spare the place for the sake of the fifty righteous people within it? ²⁵ It would be sacrilege to You to do such a thing, to bring death upon the righteous along with the wicked; letting the righteous and wicked fare alike. It would be sacrilege to You! Shall the Judge of all the earth not do justice?'

²⁶ And HASHEM said, 'If I find in Sodom fifty

צַדִּיקִם בְּתוֹךְ הָעִיר וְנָשָׂאתִי לְכָל־הַמָּקוֹם
בַּעֲבוּרָם: כז וַיַּעַן אַבְרָהָם וַיֹּאמַר הִנֵּה־נָא
הוֹאַלְתִּי לְדַבֵּר אֶל־אֲדֹנָי וְאָנֹכִי עָפָר וָאֵפֶר:
כח אוּלַי יַחְסְרוּן חֲמִשִּׁים הַצַּדִּיקִם חֲמִשָּׁה
הֲתַשְׁחִית בַּחֲמִשָּׁה אֶת־כָּל־הָעִיר וַיֹּאמֶר לֹא
אַשְׁחִית אִם־אֶמְצָא שָׁם אַרְבָּעִים וַחֲמִשָּׁה:
כט וַיֹּסֶף עוֹד לְדַבֵּר אֵלָיו וַיֹּאמַר אוּלַי יִמָּצְאוּן
שָׁם אַרְבָּעִים וַיֹּאמֶר לֹא אֶעֱשֶׂה בַּעֲבוּר
הָאַרְבָּעִים: ל וַיֹּאמֶר אַל־נָא יִחַר לַאדֹנָי
וַאֲדַבֵּרָה אוּלַי יִמָּצְאוּן שָׁם שְׁלֹשִׁים וַיֹּאמֶר
לֹא אֶעֱשֶׂה אִם־אֶמְצָא שָׁם שְׁלֹשִׁים:
לא וַיֹּאמֶר הִנֵּה־נָא הוֹאַלְתִּי לְדַבֵּר אֶל־אֲדֹנָי
אוּלַי יִמָּצְאוּן שָׁם עֶשְׂרִים וַיֹּאמֶר לֹא אַשְׁחִית
בַּעֲבוּר הָעֶשְׂרִים: לב וַיֹּאמֶר אַל־נָא יִחַר
לַאדֹנָי וַאֲדַבְּרָה אַךְ־הַפַּעַם אוּלַי יִמָּצְאוּן
שָׁם עֲשָׂרָה וַיֹּאמֶר לֹא אַשְׁחִית בַּעֲבוּר
הָעֲשָׂרָה: לג וַיֵּלֶךְ יהוה כַּאֲשֶׁר כִּלָּה לְדַבֵּר
אֶל־אַבְרָהָם וְאַבְרָהָם שָׁב לִמְקֹמוֹ: יט שלישי
א וַיָּבֹאוּ שְׁנֵי הַמַּלְאָכִים סְדֹמָה בָּעֶרֶב וְלוֹט
יֹשֵׁב בְּשַׁעַר־סְדֹם וַיַּרְא־לוֹט וַיָּקָם לִקְרָאתָם
וַיִּשְׁתַּחוּ אַפַּיִם אָרְצָה: ב וַיֹּאמֶר הִנֶּה נָּא־
אֲדֹנַי סוּרוּ נָא אֶל־בֵּית עַבְדְּכֶם וְלִינוּ וְרַחֲצוּ
רַגְלֵיכֶם וְהִשְׁכַּמְתֶּם וַהֲלַכְתֶּם לְדַרְכְּכֶם
וַיֹּאמְרוּ לֹּא כִּי בָרְחוֹב נָלִין: ג וַיִּפְצַר־בָּם
מְאֹד וַיָּסֻרוּ אֵלָיו וַיָּבֹאוּ אֶל־בֵּיתוֹ וַיַּעַשׂ לָהֶם

27. God acquiesces to Abraham's petition. Realizing that his first request would be unavailing because the fifty righteous men would not be found in Sodom, but encouraged by his success, Abraham petitions further and begs God's indulgence.

28. *Would You destroy the entire city because of the five?* That is, because of the five who would be lacking from the total of fifty (*Ibn Ezra*). There would still be nine for each city, and You, O righteous One of the Universe, could be added to them, making the required ten for each! (*Midrash; Rashi*).

29. *What if forty would be found there?* Then only four of the cities would be saved. In the following verses he pleaded that thirty should save three cities; or twenty save two; or ten save one (*Rashi*).

33. *HASHEM departed when He had finished speaking to Abraham.* — As soon as the advocate [Abraham] became silent [i.e., had nothing more to say], the Judge departed (*Rashi*).

19/1. **Destruction of Sodom.**

The two angels came. One to destroy Sodom and the other — Raphael, who had healed Abraham (see comm. 18:2) — to save Lot. The third angel, who had made the announcement to Sarah, had departed after concluding his mission (*Rashi*).

2. *Spend the night and wash your feet.* Surely Lot should have *first* washed their feet as did Abraham [18:4], and *then* invited them to spend the night. — However, Lot feared that if the visitors were discovered in his house with clean feet, the Sodomites would accuse him of having harbored them for several days without reporting it, but if their feet were unwashed, it would appear that they had just arrived (*Rashi*).

righteous people in the midst of the city, then I would spare the entire place on their account.'

²⁷ Abraham answered and said, 'Behold, now, I desired to speak to my Lord although I am but dust and ashes. ²⁸ What if the fifty righteous people should lack five? Would You destroy the entire city because of the five?' And He said, 'I will not destroy if I find there forty-five.'

²⁹ He further continued to speak to Him and he said, 'What if forty would be found there?' And He said, 'I will not act on account of the forty.'

³⁰ And he said, 'Let not my Lord be annoyed and I will speak: What if thirty would be found there?' And He said, 'I will not act if I find there thirty.'

³¹ So he said, 'Behold, now, I desired to speak to my Lord: What if twenty would be found there?' And He said, 'I will not destroy on account of the twenty.'

³² So he said, 'Let not my Lord be annoyed and I will speak but this once: What if ten would be found there?' And He said, 'I will not destroy on account of the ten.'

³³ HASHEM departed when He had finished speaking to Abraham, and Abraham returned to his place.

19 ¹ The two angels came to Sodom in the evening and Lot was sitting at the gate of Sodom; now Lot saw and stood up to meet them and he bowed, face to the ground. ² And he said, 'Behold now, my lords; turn about, please, to your servant's house; spend the night and wash your feet, then wake up early and go your way! And they said, 'No, rather we will spend the night in the square.'

³ And he urged them very much so they turned toward him and came to his house. He made a

מִשְׁתֶּה וּמַצּוֹת אָפָה וַיֹּאכֵלוּ: דטֶּרֶם יִשְׁכָּבוּ
וְאַנְשֵׁי הָעִיר אַנְשֵׁי סְדֹם נָסַבּוּ עַל־הַבַּיִת
מִנַּעַר וְעַד־זָקֵן כָּל־הָעָם מִקָּצֶה: הוַיִּקְרְאוּ
אֶל־לוֹט וַיֹּאמְרוּ לוֹ אַיֵּה הָאֲנָשִׁים אֲשֶׁר־בָּאוּ
אֵלֶיךָ הַלָּיְלָה הוֹצִיאֵם אֵלֵינוּ וְנֵדְעָה אֹתָם:
ווַיֵּצֵא אֲלֵהֶם לוֹט הַפֶּתְחָה וְהַדֶּלֶת סָגַר
אַחֲרָיו: זוַיֹּאמַר אַל־נָא אַחַי תָּרֵעוּ: חהִנֵּה־נָא
לִי שְׁתֵּי בָנוֹת אֲשֶׁר לֹא־יָדְעוּ אִישׁ אוֹצִיאָה־
נָּא אֶתְהֶן אֲלֵיכֶם וַעֲשׂוּ לָהֶן כַּטּוֹב בְּעֵינֵיכֶם
רַק לָאֲנָשִׁים הָאֵל אַל־תַּעֲשׂוּ דָבָר כִּי־עַל־כֵּן
בָּאוּ בְּצֵל קֹרָתִי: טוַיֹּאמְרוּ | גֶּשׁ־הָלְאָה
וַיֹּאמְרוּ הָאֶחָד בָּא־לָגוּר וַיִּשְׁפֹּט שָׁפוֹט עַתָּה
נָרַע לְךָ מֵהֶם וַיִּפְצְרוּ בָאִישׁ בְּלוֹט מְאֹד וַיִּגְּשׁוּ
לִשְׁבֹּר הַדָּלֶת: יוַיִּשְׁלְחוּ הָאֲנָשִׁים אֶת־יָדָם
וַיָּבִיאוּ אֶת־לוֹט אֲלֵיהֶם הַבָּיְתָה וְאֶת־הַדֶּלֶת
סָגָרוּ: יאוְאֶת־הָאֲנָשִׁים אֲשֶׁר־פֶּתַח הַבַּיִת הִכּוּ
בַּסַּנְוֵרִים מִקָּטֹן וְעַד־גָּדוֹל וַיִּלְאוּ לִמְצֹא
הַפָּתַח: יבוַיֹּאמְרוּ הָאֲנָשִׁים אֶל־לוֹט עֹד מִי־
לְךָ פֹה חָתָן וּבָנֶיךָ וּבְנֹתֶיךָ וְכֹל אֲשֶׁר־לְךָ
בָּעִיר הוֹצֵא מִן־הַמָּקוֹם: יגכִּי־מַשְׁחִתִים
אֲנַחְנוּ אֶת־הַמָּקוֹם הַזֶּה כִּי־גָדְלָה צַעֲקָתָם
אֶת־פְּנֵי יהוה וַיְשַׁלְּחֵנוּ יהוה לְשַׁחֲתָהּ:
ידוַיֵּצֵא לוֹט וַיְדַבֵּר | אֶל־חֲתָנָיו | לֹקְחֵי בְנֹתָיו
וַיֹּאמֶר קוּמוּ צְּאוּ מִן־הַמָּקוֹם הַזֶּה כִּי־מַשְׁחִית
יהוה אֶת־הָעִיר וַיְהִי כִמְצַחֵק בְּעֵינֵי חֲתָנָיו:

3. *Matzos.* It was [the date that would later become] Passover (*Rashi*).

5. The Sodomites' purpose [in so mistreating strangers] was to prevent the entry of strangers into their land. Because their fertile land was as excellent as *the garden of* HASHEM [13:10], they feared it would attract impoverished fortune seekers. Although the Sodomites were notorious for every kind of wickedness, their fate was sealed because of their persistent selfishness in not helping the poor and needy (*Ramban*).

8. Usually a man will fight to the death for the honor of his wife and daughters, yet this man offers his daughters to be dishonored! Said the Holy One, Blessed is He, to him: 'By your life! It is for *yourself* that you keep them' [for eventually school children will read (v. 36) that Lot's daughters conceived from their father] (*Tanchuma*).

11. How degenerate! Though stricken with blindness, they persisted in their evil plan, seeking the door and vainly trying to enter (*Alshich; Sforno*).

13. Other very wicked nations were not punished as severely as Sodom. Sodom was part of *Eretz Yisrael* which, as God's heritage, could not tolerate such abominations in its midst . . . and it was also God's purpose to make Sodom an example to the Children of Israel who were to inherit it [see *Deut*. 29:17-24] (*Ramban*).

14. *But he seemed like a jester in the eyes of his sons-in-law.* They said to him [with the typical self-assurance of a native Sodomite]: 'Absurd! Organs and cymbals are in the land [i.e., everything in the land is in order, and its inhabitants carefree] and you say that the land is to be overturned!' Grievous is mockery, for the Sodomites were not punished until they mocked Lot (*Midrash; Matnos Kehunah*).

feast for them and baked matzos, and they ate. [4] They had not yet lain down when the townspeople, Sodomites, converged upon the house, both young and old, all the people from every quarter. [5] And they called to Lot and said to him, 'Where are the men who came to you tonight? Bring them out to us that we may know them.' [6] Lot went out to them to the entrance having shut the door behind him, [7] and he said, 'I beg you, my brothers, do not act wickedly. [8] See, now, I have two daughters who have never known a man. I shall bring them out to you and do to them as you please; but to these men do nothing inasmuch as they have come under the shelter of my roof.'

[9] And they said, 'Stand back!' Then they said, 'This fellow came to sojourn and would act as a judge? Now we will treat you worse than them!'' They pressed exceedingly upon the man, upon Lot, and they approached to break the door. [10] The men stretched out their hand and brought Lot into the house with them, and closed the door. [11] And the men who were at the entrance of the house they struck with blindness, both small and great; and they tried vainly to find the entrance. [12] Then the men said to Lot, 'Whom else do you have here — a son-in-law, your sons, or your daughters? All that you have in the city remove from the place, [13] because we are about to destroy this place; for their outcry has become great before HASHEM and HASHEM has therefore sent us to destroy it.'

[14] So Lot went out and spoke to his sons-in-law, [and] the betrothed suitors of his daughters, and he said, 'Get up and leave this place, for HASHEM is about to destroy the city!' But he seemed like a jester in the eyes of his sons-in-law.

טו וּכְמוֹ הַשַּׁחַר עָלָה וַיָּאִיצוּ הַמַּלְאָכִים בְּלוֹט
לֵאמֹר קוּם קַח אֶת־אִשְׁתְּךָ וְאֶת־שְׁתֵּי בְנֹתֶיךָ
הַנִּמְצָאֹת פֶּן־תִּסָּפֶה בַּעֲוֺן הָעִיר: טז וַיִּתְמַהְמָהּ ׀
וַיַּחֲזִקוּ הָאֲנָשִׁים בְּיָדוֹ וּבְיַד־אִשְׁתּוֹ וּבְיַד שְׁתֵּי
בְנֹתָיו בְּחֶמְלַת יְהוָה עָלָיו וַיֹּצִאֻהוּ וַיַּנִּחֻהוּ
מִחוּץ לָעִיר: יז וַיְהִי כְהוֹצִיאָם אֹתָם הַחוּצָה
וַיֹּאמֶר הִמָּלֵט עַל־נַפְשֶׁךָ אַל־תַּבִּיט אַחֲרֶיךָ
וְאַל־תַּעֲמֹד בְּכָל־הַכִּכָּר הָהָרָה הִמָּלֵט פֶּן־
תִּסָּפֶה: יח וַיֹּאמֶר לוֹט אֲלֵהֶם אַל־נָא אֲדֹנָי:
יט הִנֵּה־נָא מָצָא עַבְדְּךָ חֵן בְּעֵינֶיךָ וַתַּגְדֵּל
חַסְדְּךָ אֲשֶׁר עָשִׂיתָ עִמָּדִי לְהַחֲיוֹת אֶת־נַפְשִׁי
וְאָנֹכִי לֹא אוּכַל לְהִמָּלֵט הָהָרָה פֶּן־תִּדְבָּקַנִי
הָרָעָה וָמַתִּי: כ הִנֵּה־נָא הָעִיר הַזֹּאת קְרֹבָה
לָנוּס שָׁמָּה וְהִוא מִצְעָר אִמָּלְטָה נָּא שָׁמָּה
הֲלֹא מִצְעָר הִוא וּתְחִי נַפְשִׁי: רביעי כא וַיֹּאמֶר
אֵלָיו הִנֵּה נָשָׂאתִי פָנֶיךָ גַּם לַדָּבָר הַזֶּה לְבִלְתִּי
הָפְכִּי אֶת־הָעִיר אֲשֶׁר דִּבַּרְתָּ: כב מַהֵר הִמָּלֵט
שָׁמָּה כִּי לֹא אוּכַל לַעֲשׂוֹת דָּבָר עַד־בֹּאֲךָ
שָׁמָּה עַל־כֵּן קָרָא שֵׁם־הָעִיר צוֹעַר: כג הַשֶּׁמֶשׁ
יָצָא עַל־הָאָרֶץ וְלוֹט בָּא צֹעֲרָה: כד וַיהוָה
הִמְטִיר עַל־סְדֹם וְעַל־עֲמֹרָה גָּפְרִית וָאֵשׁ
מֵאֵת יְהוָה מִן־הַשָּׁמָיִם: כה וַיַּהֲפֹךְ אֶת־הֶעָרִים
הָאֵל וְאֵת כָּל־הַכִּכָּר וְאֵת כָּל־יֹשְׁבֵי הֶעָרִים
וְצֶמַח הָאֲדָמָה: כו וַתַּבֵּט אִשְׁתּוֹ מֵאַחֲרָיו וַתְּהִי
נְצִיב מֶלַח: כז וַיַּשְׁכֵּם אַבְרָהָם בַּבֹּקֶר אֶל־

17. *Do not look behind you*. You are as wicked as they are; you are being saved only for Abraham's sake. It is not proper for you to look upon their punishment while you yourself are being spared (*Rashi*).

20. *Rashi* explains *near* as referring to *nearness* in time: קְרוֹבָה יְשִׁיבָתָהּ. It was populated [relatively] recently and so its measure [of sin] is not yet full.

22. *For I cannot do a thing until you arrive there*. The *upheaval* could not begin before Lot's safe arrival in Zoar; the sulphur and fire, however, had begun descending with dawn (*Gur Aryeh*). He therefore named the city Zoar [meaning 'small']. Therefore, i.e., because Lot referred to it all as a *'small'* city [מִצְעָר, v. 20], and because its salvation was due to its being smaller and of lesser iniquity, it came to be called *'Zoar'* — i.e., hamlet. It was originally called *Bela* (*Rashi*).

24. Nothing evil descends directly from heaven: First it descended as beneficent rain; only when it approached earth did it become sulphur and fire (*Tanchuma*). *From HASHEM, out of heaven.* This emphasizes that the *sulphur and fire* were not natural phenomena from the earth, but were Divinely originated visitations *from HASHEM, out of heaven*, without any natural cause (*Sforno*).

26. *Tur* points out that the death of Lot's wife was a necessary precondition to the following episode. Had their mother been alive, Lot's daughters would not have conceived through him.

27. Abraham views the disaster. When Abraham had concluded his pleading for Sodom, God did not tell him what the outcome would be. Therefore, he arose in the morning to see what the final judgment had been (*Da'as Sofrim*).

¹⁵ And just as dawn was breaking, the angels urged Lot on saying: 'Get up — take your wife and your two daughters who are present, lest you be swept away in the punishment of the city!'

¹⁶ Still he lingered — so the men grasped him by his hand, his wife's hand, and the hand of his two daughters in HASHEM's mercy on him; and they took him out and left him outside the city. ¹⁷ And it was as they took them out that one said: 'Flee for your life! Do not look behind you nor stop anywhere in all the plain; flee to the mountain lest you be swept away.'

¹⁸ Lot said to them; 'Please, no! My Lord — See, now, Your servant has found grace in Your eyes and Your kindness was great which you did with me to save my life; but I cannot escape to the mountain lest the evil attach itself to me and I die. ²⁰ Behold, please, this city is near enough to escape there and it is small; I shall flee there. Is it not small? — and I will live.'

²¹ And He replied to him: 'Behold, I have granted you consideration even regarding this, that I not overthrow the city about which you have spoken. ²² Hurry, flee there, for I cannot do a thing until you arrive there.' He therefore named the city Zoar.

²³ The sun rose upon the earth and Lot arrived at Zoar. ²⁴ Now HASHEM had caused to rain upon Sodom and Amorah sulphur and fire; from HASHEM, out of heaven. ²⁵ He overturned these cities and the entire plain; with all the inhabitants of the cities and the vegetation of the soil. ²⁶ His wife peered behind him and she became a pillar of salt.

²⁷ Abraham arose early next morning to the

הַמָּקוֹם אֲשֶׁר־עָמַד שָׁם אֶת־פְּנֵי יְהוָה׃
כח וַיַּשְׁקֵף עַל־פְּנֵי סְדֹם וַעֲמֹרָה וְעַל־כָּל־פְּנֵי
אֶרֶץ הַכִּכָּר וַיַּרְא וְהִנֵּה עָלָה קִיטֹר הָאָרֶץ
כְּקִיטֹר הַכִּבְשָׁן׃ כט וַיְהִי בְּשַׁחֵת אֱלֹהִים אֶת־
עָרֵי הַכִּכָּר וַיִּזְכֹּר אֱלֹהִים אֶת־אַבְרָהָם
וַיְשַׁלַּח אֶת־לוֹט מִתּוֹךְ הַהֲפֵכָה בַּהֲפֹךְ אֶת־
הֶעָרִים אֲשֶׁר־יָשַׁב בָּהֵן לוֹט׃ ל וַיַּעַל לוֹט
מִצּוֹעַר וַיֵּשֶׁב בָּהָר וּשְׁתֵּי בְנֹתָיו עִמּוֹ כִּי יָרֵא
לָשֶׁבֶת בְּצוֹעַר וַיֵּשֶׁב בַּמְּעָרָה הוּא וּשְׁתֵּי
בְנֹתָיו׃ לא וַתֹּאמֶר הַבְּכִירָה אֶל־הַצְּעִירָה
אָבִינוּ זָקֵן וְאִישׁ אֵין בָּאָרֶץ לָבוֹא עָלֵינוּ
כְּדֶרֶךְ כָּל־הָאָרֶץ׃ לב לְכָה נַשְׁקֶה אֶת־אָבִינוּ
יַיִן וְנִשְׁכְּבָה עִמּוֹ וּנְחַיֶּה מֵאָבִינוּ זָרַע׃
לג וַתַּשְׁקֶיןָ אֶת־אֲבִיהֶן יַיִן בַּלַּיְלָה הוּא וַתָּבֹא
הַבְּכִירָה וַתִּשְׁכַּב אֶת־אָבִיהָ וְלֹא־יָדַע
בְּשִׁכְבָהּ וּבְקוּמָהּ׃ לד וַיְהִי מִמָּחֳרָת וַתֹּאמֶר
הַבְּכִירָה אֶל־הַצְּעִירָה הֵן־שָׁכַבְתִּי אֶמֶשׁ
אֶת־אָבִי נַשְׁקֶנּוּ יַיִן גַּם־הַלַּיְלָה וּבֹאִי שִׁכְבִי
עִמּוֹ וּנְחַיֶּה מֵאָבִינוּ זָרַע׃ לה וַתַּשְׁקֶיןָ גַּם
בַּלַּיְלָה הַהוּא אֶת־אֲבִיהֶן יָיִן וַתָּקָם הַצְּעִירָה
וַתִּשְׁכַּב עִמּוֹ וְלֹא־יָדַע בְּשִׁכְבָהּ וּבְקֻמָהּ׃
לו וַתַּהֲרֶיןָ שְׁתֵּי בְנוֹת־לוֹט מֵאֲבִיהֶן׃ לז וַתֵּלֶד
הַבְּכִירָה בֵּן וַתִּקְרָא שְׁמוֹ מוֹאָב הוּא
אֲבִי־מוֹאָב עַד־הַיּוֹם׃ לח וְהַצְּעִירָה גַם־הִוא
יָלְדָה בֵּן וַתִּקְרָא שְׁמוֹ בֶּן־עַמִּי הוּא אֲבִי

29. The summary: In its usual style, the Torah states what had earlier been alluded: Lot had been spared for the sake of his uncle, Abraham (*Ran*).

30. Lot's daughters. Moab and Ammon — the Roots of Jewish Monarchy [see *Overview* to *Ruth*]. Lot's daughters were modest, righteous women whose actions were motivated for the sake of heaven. Therefore, they did not *ask* their father to consort with them. The Torah does not label their actions as incestuous because they sincerely thought there was no other way to insure the propagation of the species. Because their intentions were pure, they merited that Ruth, ancestress of David, and Naamah, queen of Solomon and mother of Rechavam, should descend from them (*R' Bachya*).

31. *Our father is growing old.* — And if not now, when? He may die or become impotent (*Rashi*).

33. In the Torah scroll the word וּבְקוּמָהּ [or of her getting up], referring to the older sister, has a dot over it [a traditional method of drawing attention to a special interpretation] to indicate that though he was not aware בְּשִׁכְבָהּ, of her lying down, he was well aware of וּבְקוּמָהּ, her getting up. Nevertheless, he was not more vigilant on the second night than he was on the first (Rashi; Midrash).

36. Rav Chaninah ben Pazzi observed: Thorns are neither weeded nor sown, yet of their own accord they grow and spring up, whereas how much pain and toil is required before wheat is made to grow (Bereishis Rabbah 45:4). [I.e., Lot's incestuous daughters (= 'thorns') conceived immediately, but how much pain did the Matriarchs endure before they conceived!]

place where he had stood before HASHEM. ²⁸ And he gazed down upon Sodom and Amorrah and the entire surface of the plain; and saw — and behold! the smoke of the earth rose like the smoke of a kiln. ²⁹ And so it was when God destroyed the cities of the plain that God remembered Abraham; so He sent Lot from amidst the upheaval when He overturned the cities in which Lot had lived.

³⁰ Now Lot went up from Zoar and settled on the mountain, his two daughters with him, for he was afraid to remain in Zoar. He dwelt in the cave, he with his two daughters. ³¹ The older one said to the younger, 'Our father is growing old and there is no man to marry us in the usual manner. ³² Come, let us ply our father with wine and lay with him that we may give life to offspring through our father.'

³³ So they plied their father with wine on that night; and the older one came and lay with her father, and he was unaware of her lying down or of her getting up.

³⁴ And it was on the next day that the older one said to the younger, 'Behold, I lay with my father last night; let us ply him with wine tonight as well, and you come lay with him that we may give life to offspring through our father.'

³⁵ So they plied their father with wine that night also. And the younger one got up and lay with him and he was not aware of her lying down and of her getting up.

³⁶ Thus, Lot's two daughters conceived from their father.

³⁷ The older bore a son and named him Moab; he is the ancestors of the Moabites until this day. ³⁸ And the younger one also bore a son and she named him Ben-Ami. He is the ancestor of the

בְּנֵי־עַמּוֹן עַד־הַיּוֹם: ‏ב‏ ‏א‏ וַיִּסַּע מִשָּׁם אַבְרָהָם
אַרְצָה הַנֶּגֶב וַיֵּשֶׁב בֵּין־קָדֵשׁ וּבֵין שׁוּר וַיָּגָר
בִּגְרָר: ‏ב‏ וַיֹּאמֶר אַבְרָהָם אֶל־שָׂרָה אִשְׁתּוֹ
אֲחֹתִי הִוא וַיִּשְׁלַח אֲבִימֶלֶךְ מֶלֶךְ גְּרָר וַיִּקַּח
אֶת־שָׂרָה: ‏ג‏ וַיָּבֹא אֱלֹהִים אֶל־אֲבִימֶלֶךְ
בַּחֲלוֹם הַלָּיְלָה וַיֹּאמֶר לוֹ הִנְּךָ מֵת עַל־
הָאִשָּׁה אֲשֶׁר־לָקַחְתָּ וְהִוא בְּעֻלַת בָּעַל:
‏ד‏ וַאֲבִימֶלֶךְ לֹא קָרַב אֵלֶיהָ וַיֹּאמַר אֲדֹנָי
הֲגוֹי גַּם־צַדִּיק תַּהֲרֹג: ‏ה‏ הֲלֹא הוּא אָמַר־לִי
אֲחֹתִי הִוא וְהִיא־גַם־הִוא אָמְרָה אָחִי הוּא
בְּתָם־לְבָבִי וּבְנִקְיֹן כַּפַּי עָשִׂיתִי זֹאת: ‏ו‏ וַיֹּאמֶר
אֵלָיו הָאֱלֹהִים בַּחֲלֹם גַּם אָנֹכִי יָדַעְתִּי כִּי
בְתָם־לְבָבְךָ עָשִׂיתָ זֹּאת וָאֶחְשֹׂךְ גַּם־אָנֹכִי
אוֹתְךָ מֵחֲטוֹ־לִי עַל־כֵּן לֹא־נְתַתִּיךָ לִנְגֹּעַ
אֵלֶיהָ: ‏ז‏ וְעַתָּה הָשֵׁב אֵשֶׁת־הָאִישׁ כִּי־נָבִיא
הוּא וְיִתְפַּלֵּל בַּעַדְךָ וֶחְיֵה וְאִם־אֵינְךָ מֵשִׁיב
דַּע כִּי־מוֹת תָּמוּת אַתָּה וְכָל־אֲשֶׁר־לָךְ:
‏ח‏ וַיַּשְׁכֵּם אֲבִימֶלֶךְ בַּבֹּקֶר וַיִּקְרָא לְכָל־עֲבָדָיו
וַיְדַבֵּר אֶת־כָּל־הַדְּבָרִים הָאֵלֶּה בְּאָזְנֵיהֶם
וַיִּירְאוּ הָאֲנָשִׁים מְאֹד: ‏ט‏ וַיִּקְרָא אֲבִימֶלֶךְ
לְאַבְרָהָם וַיֹּאמֶר לוֹ מֶה־עָשִׂיתָ לָּנוּ וּמֶה־
חָטָאתִי לָךְ כִּי־הֵבֵאתָ עָלַי וְעַל־מַמְלַכְתִּי
חֲטָאָה גְדֹלָה מַעֲשִׂים אֲשֶׁר לֹא־יֵעָשׂוּ
עָשִׂיתָ עִמָּדִי: ‏י‏ וַיֹּאמֶר אֲבִימֶלֶךְ אֶל־אַבְרָהָם
מָה רָאִיתָ כִּי עָשִׂיתָ אֶת־הַדָּבָר הַזֶּה:

1. Abraham moves to Gerar.

When Abraham perceived that the region had been destroyed and there were no more wayfarers to whom he might extend hospitality, he moved away. Another interpretation: He wished to be far from Lot, who had become notorious because of his intimacy with his daughters (*Rashi*).

Kadesh and Shur were two large cities. Abraham chose this area for it was heavily populated and would thereby provide him the opportunity to spread his belief in God (*Sforno*).

2. Sarah and Abimelech — One of the Ten Trials (see 12:1).

4. *Ramban* notes that 'approach' is a euphemism for intimacy, and Abimelech was punished with impotence for having taken Sarah.

Will You slay a nation even though it is righteous? — Is it Your practice to destroy nations without cause? If so, I must assume that You destroyed the generations of the Flood and of the Dispersion without just cause, just as You now wish to do to me! (*Rashi*; cf. *Rashi* to 18:25: חָלִלָה לָּךְ).

For in comparison with the bestiality of Sodom, Abraham and Sarah were treated hospitably. Even the abduction of Sarah could be seen in a positive light, for Abimelech was doing her the honor of making her his queen (R' Hirsch).

5. גם, too, includes her servants, camel drivers, and donkey drivers. I asked them all and they said, 'He is her brother' (Rashi).

Abimelech felt that if his intentions are good, then he is blameless. Judaism rejects this view. Good intentions do not purify a wrong deed. Its measure is whether it complies with God's will; if it is wrong in His eyes, then good intentions do not give it sanction. Moreover, lack of knowledge is itself sinful, for a person has the obligation to seek instruction. A person in Abimelech's position has the further obligation to set an example of appropriate behavior — is it right that even an unmarried woman must fear the whim of every prince? (R' Hirsch).

6. God is very much aware of Abimelech's good intentions; but it was He who had kept him from the sin of adultery.

7. For he is a prophet and he knows that you did not touch her; therefore, he will pray for you and you will live (Rashi).

10. The early questions were merely rhetorical, and Abimelech required no answer. Now, Abimelech demands to know why Abraham deceived him (Radak).

people of Ammon until this day.

20 ¹ **A**braham journeyed from there to the region of the south and settled between Kadesh and Shur, sojourning in Gerar. ² Abraham said of Sarah his wife, 'She is my sister'; so Abimelech, king of Gerar, sent, and took Sarah. ³ And God came to Abimelech in a dream by night and said to him, 'Behold you are to die because of the woman you have taken; moreover she is a married woman.'

⁴ Now Abimelech had not approached her. So he said, 'O my Lord, will You slay a nation even though it is righteous? ⁵ Did not he himself tell me: "She is my sister"? And she, too, herself said: "He is my brother"! In the innocence of my heart and integrity of my hands have I done this.'

⁶ And God said to him in the dream, 'I, too, knew that it was in the innocence of your heart that you did this, and I, too, prevented you from sinning against Me; that is why I did not permit you to touch her. ⁷ But now, return the man's wife for he is a prophet, and he will pray for you and you will live. But if you do not return her be aware that you shall surely die: you and all that is yours.'

⁸ Abimelech arose early next morning. He summoned all his servants and told them all of these things in their ears, and the people were very frightened. ⁹ Then Abimelech summoned Abraham and said to him, 'What have you done to us? How have I sinned against you that you brought upon me and my kingdom such great sin? Deeds that are not to be done have you done to me!' ¹⁰ And Abimelech said to Abraham, 'What did you see that you did such a thing?'

יא וַיֹּאמֶר אַבְרָהָם כִּי אָמַרְתִּי רַק אֵין־יִרְאַת אֱלֹהִים בַּמָּקוֹם הַזֶּה וַהֲרָגוּנִי עַל־דְּבַר אִשְׁתִּי: יב וְגַם־אָמְנָה אֲחֹתִי בַת־אָבִי הִוא אַךְ לֹא בַת־אִמִּי וַתְּהִי־לִי לְאִשָּׁה: יג וַיְהִי כַּאֲשֶׁר הִתְעוּ אֹתִי אֱלֹהִים מִבֵּית אָבִי וָאֹמַר לָהּ זֶה חַסְדֵּךְ אֲשֶׁר תַּעֲשִׂי עִמָּדִי אֶל כָּל־הַמָּקוֹם אֲשֶׁר נָבוֹא שָׁמָּה אִמְרִי־לִי אָחִי הוּא: יד וַיִּקַּח אֲבִימֶלֶךְ צֹאן וּבָקָר וַעֲבָדִים וּשְׁפָחֹת וַיִּתֵּן לְאַבְרָהָם וַיָּשֶׁב לוֹ אֵת שָׂרָה אִשְׁתּוֹ: טו וַיֹּאמֶר אֲבִימֶלֶךְ הִנֵּה אַרְצִי לְפָנֶיךָ בַּטּוֹב בְּעֵינֶיךָ שֵׁב: טז וּלְשָׂרָה אָמַר הִנֵּה נָתַתִּי אֶלֶף כֶּסֶף לְאָחִיךְ הִנֵּה הוּא־לָךְ כְּסוּת עֵינַיִם לְכֹל אֲשֶׁר אִתָּךְ וְאֵת־כֹּל וְנֹכָחַת: יז וַיִּתְפַּלֵּל אַבְרָהָם אֶל־הָאֱלֹהִים וַיִּרְפָּא אֱלֹהִים אֶת־אֲבִימֶלֶךְ וְאֶת־אִשְׁתּוֹ וְאַמְהֹתָיו וַיֵּלֵדוּ: יח כִּי־עָצֹר עָצַר יהוה בְּעַד כָּל־רֶחֶם לְבֵית אֲבִימֶלֶךְ עַל־דְּבַר שָׂרָה אֵשֶׁת אַבְרָהָם:

כא א וַיהוה פָּקַד אֶת־שָׂרָה כַּאֲשֶׁר אָמָר וַיַּעַשׂ יהוה לְשָׂרָה כַּאֲשֶׁר דִּבֵּר: ב וַתַּהַר וַתֵּלֶד שָׂרָה לְאַבְרָהָם בֵּן לִזְקֻנָיו לַמּוֹעֵד אֲשֶׁר־דִּבֶּר אֹתוֹ אֱלֹהִים: ג וַיִּקְרָא אַבְרָהָם אֶת־שֶׁם־בְּנוֹ הַנּוֹלַד־לוֹ אֲשֶׁר־יָלְדָה־לּוֹ שָׂרָה יִצְחָק: ד וַיָּמָל אַבְרָהָם אֶת־יִצְחָק בְּנוֹ בֶּן־שְׁמֹנַת יָמִים כַּאֲשֶׁר צִוָּה אֹתוֹ אֱלֹהִים: חמישי ה וְאַבְרָהָם בֶּן־מְאַת שָׁנָה

11. As soon as he entered the city, Abraham noted their lack of God-fearing qualities. For when a man enters a town, should he be asked about what he would like to eat or drink, or about the identity of the woman with him: Whether she is his wife or sister? — Since the people of Gerar were concerned only with the identity of Sarah, Abraham immediately perceived that they lacked fear of God, and as such were void of moral restraint (Rashi; Makkos 9b).

12. Having defended his action, Abraham goes on to explain that even *in the literal sense* his claim of being Sarah's brother was not untrue; moreover, he never claimed that Sarah was *not* his wife, but emphasized that she was his sister (*Malbim*). [This demonstrates that even where one is compelled to dissemble, he should remain as close to truth as possible.]

However, one may retort that she was his *brother's daughter* — his niece — and not his *father's* daughter as Abraham claimed; therefore what justification did he have to tell this untruth? — Since "grandchildren are considered as children" she may truly be regarded his sister (*Rashi*).

13. This was Abraham's third justification: Since, at God's command, he had become a wanderer, he resorted to this plan whenever entering a new place; it does not imply low esteem for this particular region (*Malbim*).

14. *And gave them to Abraham*. So that Abraham would be appeased and pray for him (*Rashi*).

15. By inviting Abraham to remain, Abimelech was demonstrating to all that he had not violated her, for a woman with whom the king had been intimate would never be permitted to return to a commoner husband in the king's own land (*Abarbanel*).

16. *Your brother,* i.e., to Abraham, whom you have described as your brother (*Rashi*).
An eye-covering, i.e., a diversion of attention from you; a prevention against people looking contemptuously at you; a vindication.

17. Abraham magnanimously forgives Abimelech and intercedes on his behalf.

21/1. The birth of Isaac.
וַה' פָּקַד אֶת שָׂרָה — HASHEM had remembered Sarah. — *Had* remembered — before He healed Abimelech (*Rashi*).
This section's proximity to the preceding one teaches that כָּל הַמִּתְפַּלֵּל בְּעַד חֲבֵרוֹ וְהוּא צָרִיךְ לְאוֹתוֹ דָּבָר, הוּא נַעֲנֶה תְּחִילָה, 'Whoever prays for mercy on behalf of another when he himself needs that very same thing, he is answered first.' For in the previous section it is said: *Abraham prayed* [for Abimelech] *... and they were relieved . . .* and here it says *and God had [already] remembered Sarah* — even before He healed Abimelech (*Rashi*).

3. *[And] Abraham named.* Abraham complied with God's command [7:19]: *Sarah your wife shall bear you a son and you shall call him Isaac* (*Radak*).
4. *As God had commanded him.* In 7:12 (*Midrash*).

[11] And Abraham said, 'Because I said, "There is but no fear of God in this place and they will slay me because of my wife." [12] Moreover, she is indeed, my sister, my father's daughter, though not my mother's daughter; and she became my wife. [13] And so it was, when God caused me to wander from my father's house, I said to her, "Let this be your kindness which you shall do for me — to whatever place we come, say of me: 'He is my brother.'"

[14] Then Abimelech took sheep, cattle, male and female slaves and gave them to Abraham. And he returned his wife Sarah to him.

[15] And Abimelech said, 'Behold my land is before you: settle wherever you see fit.' [16] And to Sarah he said, 'Behold I have given your brother a thousand pieces of silver. Behold! Let it be for you an eye-covering for all who are with you; and to all you will be vindicated.'

[17] Abraham prayed to God, and God healed Abimelech, his wife, and his maids and they were relieved; [18] for HASHEM had completely restrained every orifice of the household of Abimelech, because of Sarah, the wife of Abraham.

21 [1] HASHEM had remembered Sarah as He had said; and HASHEM did for Sarah as He had spoken. [2] Sarah conceived and bore a son unto Abraham in his old age, at the appointed time of which God had spoken. [3] Abraham named his son who was born to him — whom Sarah had borne him — Isaac.

[4] Abraham circumcised his son Isaac at the age of eight days as God had commanded him. [5] And Abraham was a hundred years old

בְּהִוָּלֶד־לֹו אֵת יִצְחָק בְּנֹו: וַתֹּאמֶר שָׂרָה צְחֹק
עָשָׂה לִי אֱלֹהִים כָּל־הַשֹּׁמֵעַ יִצְחַק־לִי:
ז וַתֹּאמֶר מִי מִלֵּל לְאַבְרָהָם הֵינִיקָה בָנִים שָׂרָה
כִּי־יָלַדְתִּי בֵן לִזְקֻנָיו: ח וַיִּגְדַּל הַיֶּלֶד וַיִּגָּמַל
וַיַּעַשׂ אַבְרָהָם מִשְׁתֶּה גָדֹול בְּיֹום הִגָּמֵל
אֶת־יִצְחָק: ט וַתֵּרֶא שָׂרָה אֶת־בֶּן־הָגָר
הַמִּצְרִית אֲשֶׁר־יָלְדָה לְאַבְרָהָם מְצַחֵק:
י וַתֹּאמֶר לְאַבְרָהָם גָּרֵשׁ הָאָמָה הַזֹּאת וְאֶת־
בְּנָהּ כִּי לֹא יִירַשׁ בֶּן־הָאָמָה הַזֹּאת עִם־בְּנִי
עִם־יִצְחָק: יא וַיֵּרַע הַדָּבָר מְאֹד בְּעֵינֵי אַבְרָהָם
עַל אֹודֹת בְּנֹו: יב וַיֹּאמֶר אֱלֹהִים אֶל־אַבְרָהָם
אַל־יֵרַע בְּעֵינֶיךָ עַל־הַנַּעַר וְעַל־אֲמָתֶךָ כֹּל
אֲשֶׁר תֹּאמַר אֵלֶיךָ שָׂרָה שְׁמַע בְּקֹלָהּ כִּי
בְיִצְחָק יִקָּרֵא לְךָ זָרַע: יג וְגַם אֶת־בֶּן־הָאָמָה
לְגֹוי אֲשִׂימֶנּוּ כִּי זַרְעֲךָ הוּא: יד וַיַּשְׁכֵּם אַבְרָהָם ׀
בַּבֹּקֶר וַיִּקַּח־לֶחֶם וְחֵמַת מַיִם וַיִּתֵּן אֶל־הָגָר
שָׂם עַל־שִׁכְמָהּ וְאֶת־הַיֶּלֶד וַיְשַׁלְּחֶהָ וַתֵּלֶךְ
וַתֵּתַע בְּמִדְבַּר בְּאֵר שָׁבַע: טו וַיִּכְלוּ הַמַּיִם
מִן־הַחֵמֶת וַתַּשְׁלֵךְ אֶת־הַיֶּלֶד תַּחַת אַחַד
הַשִּׂיחִם: טז וַתֵּלֶךְ וַתֵּשֶׁב לָהּ מִנֶּגֶד הַרְחֵק
כִּמְטַחֲוֵי קֶשֶׁת כִּי אָמְרָה אַל־אֶרְאֶה בְּמֹות
הַיָּלֶד וַתֵּשֶׁב מִנֶּגֶד וַתִּשָּׂא אֶת־קֹלָהּ וַתֵּבְךְּ:
יז וַיִּשְׁמַע אֱלֹהִים אֶת־קֹול הַנַּעַר וַיִּקְרָא מַלְאַךְ
אֱלֹהִים ׀ אֶל־הָגָר מִן־הַשָּׁמַיִם וַיֹּאמֶר לָהּ
מַה־לָּךְ הָגָר אַל־תִּירְאִי כִּי־שָׁמַע אֱלֹהִים

6. *Whoever hears will laugh for me.* I.e., rejoice for my sake. The reason for the *universal* joy was that, when Sarah was 'remembered,' many barren women were remembered along with her. Many sick were healed on that day, many prayers were answered along with hers, and there was much joy [שְׂחוֹק, *laughter*] in the world (*Rashi*).

7. This is an exclamatory expression of praise, i.e., *Who but God could have done this?* (*Rashi*).

8. *And was weaned,* from his mother's milk — at the age of twenty-four months (*Rashi*; cf. *Gittin* 75b).

'Weaned' may be understood figuratively: He attained the age of thirteen, i.e., he was weaned from the Evil Inclination for *he grew* to religious majority and personal responsibility for the performance of the *mitzvos.* At that point his Good Inclination became dominant (*Midrash*).

A great feast. It was 'great' because the great men of the generation attended: Shem, Eber, and Abimelech (*Tanchuma; Rashi*).

According to *Tosafos* (*Shabbos* 130a), this feast took place at the child's *circumcision,* the passage being homiletically rendered בְּיוֹם ה'ג מל את בנו, *on the eighth day* [ה'ג, 5 + 3 = 8] *when he circumcised his son.*

9. — *Mocking* [or: *playing; making sport*]. Scripture uses this verb to denote the three cardinal sins of idolatry, adultery, and murder. It denotes *idolatry* with reference to the Golden Calf [*Exod.* 32:6]; *adultery* with reference to Potiphar's wife [39:17]; and in the related root form שׂחק, it refers to *murder* [*II Samuel* 2:14] (*Rashi*).

10. **The expulsion of Ishmael.** The ninth of the Ten Trials (*Pirkei d'Rabbi Eliezer* 30).

11. *Regarding his son,* i.e., because he learned from Ishmael's behavior that he had fallen into evil ways [*Shemos Rabbah* 1]. The *plain meaning* is that Abraham was distressed because Sarah demanded that he drive him away (*Rashi*).

12. [But God comforts Abraham by telling him that Sarah's directive is prophetic and in accordance with His will] . . .

13. Greatness is in store for Ishmael as well . . .

14. Learning that the expulsion of Hagar and Ishmael is God's will, Abraham complies at once . . . *[She] strayed.* According to *Rashi* [once in the desert and away from Abraham's control (*Zohar Chadash Ruth* 82a)], Hagar *strayed* back to the idolatry of her father's house (*Midrash*).

15-16. The Torah emphasizes that she *cast off* the child in utter despair rather than gently place him down, but like all compassionate women she reflects upon her plight and is driven to tears (*Minchah Belulah*).

17. God told her not to fear because Ishmael will be judged according to his present deeds and not according to what he would become in the future. [Comp. *Rosh Hashanah* 16b: A man is judged only for his deeds at the time (of judgment).]
According to *Ramban*, the simple meaning of the verse is: God has heard the prayer of the lad *in the place where he was.* She need not search for water, because he will quench his thirst *in that very place.*

when his son Isaac was born to him. ⁶ Sarah said, 'God has made laughter for me; whoever hears will laugh for me.' ⁷And she said, 'Who is the One Who said to Abraham, "Sarah would nurse children"? For I have borne a son in his old age!'

⁸ The child grew and was weaned. Abraham made a great feast on the day Isaac was weaned. ⁹ Sarah saw the son of Hagar, the Egyptian, whom she had born to Abraham, mocking. ¹⁰ So she said to Abraham, 'Drive out that slavewoman with her son, for the son of that slavewoman shall not inherit with my son, with Isaac!'

¹¹ The matter greatly distressed Abraham regarding his son, ¹² so God said to Abraham, 'Be not distressed over the youth or your slavewoman: Whatever Sarah tells you, heed her voice, since through Isaac will offspring be considered yours. ¹³ But the son of the slavewoman as well will I make into a nation for he is your offspring.'

¹⁴ So Abraham awoke early in the morning, took bread and a skin of water, and gave them to Hagar. He placed them on her shoulder along with the boy, and sent her off. She departed, and strayed in the desert of Beer Sheba.

¹⁵ When the water of the skin was consumed, she cast off the boy beneath one of the trees. ¹⁶ She went and sat herself down at a distance, some bowshots away, for she said, 'Let me not see the death of the child.' And she sat at a distance, lifted her voice, and wept.

¹⁷ God heard the cry of the youth, and an angel of God called to Hagar from heaven and said to her, 'What troubles you, Hagar? Fear not, for God has heeded the cry of the youth in his present

אֶל־ק֣וֹל הַנַּ֔עַר בַּאֲשֶׁ֥ר הוּא־שָֽׁם: יח ק֚וּמִי שְׂאִ֣י
אֶת־הַנַּ֔עַר וְהַחֲזִ֥יקִי אֶת־יָדֵ֖ךְ בּ֑וֹ כִּֽי־לְג֥וֹי גָּד֖וֹל
אֲשִׂימֶֽנּוּ: יט וַיִּפְקַ֤ח אֱלֹהִים֙ אֶת־עֵינֶ֔יהָ וַתֵּ֖רֶא
בְּאֵ֣ר מָ֑יִם וַתֵּ֜לֶךְ וַתְּמַלֵּ֤א אֶת־הַחֵ֙מֶת֙ מַ֔יִם
וַתַּ֖שְׁקְ אֶת־הַנָּֽעַר: כ וַֽיְהִ֧י אֱלֹהִ֛ים אֶת־הַנַּ֖עַר
וַיִּגְדָּ֑ל וַיֵּ֙שֶׁב֙ בַּמִּדְבָּ֔ר וַיְהִ֖י רֹבֶ֥ה קַשָּֽׁת: כא וַיֵּ֖שֶׁב
בְּמִדְבַּ֣ר פָּארָ֑ן וַתִּֽקַּֽח־ל֥וֹ אִמּ֛וֹ אִשָּׁ֖ה מֵאֶ֥רֶץ
מִצְרָֽיִם:

ששי כב וַֽיְהִי֙ בָּעֵ֣ת הַהִ֔וא וַיֹּ֣אמֶר אֲבִימֶ֗לֶךְ וּפִיכֹל֙
שַׂר־צְבָא֔וֹ אֶל־אַבְרָהָ֖ם לֵאמֹ֑ר אֱלֹהִ֣ים עִמְּךָ֔
בְּכֹ֥ל אֲשֶׁר־אַתָּ֖ה עֹשֶֽׂה: כג וְעַתָּ֗ה הִשָּׁ֤בְעָה לִּי֙
בֵֽאלֹהִים֙ הֵ֔נָּה אִם־תִּשְׁקֹ֥ר לִ֖י וּלְנִינִ֣י וּלְנֶכְדִּ֑י
כַּחֶ֜סֶד אֲשֶׁר־עָשִׂ֤יתִי עִמְּךָ֙ תַּעֲשֶׂ֣ה עִמָּדִ֔י וְעִם־
הָאָ֖רֶץ אֲשֶׁר־גַּ֥רְתָּה בָּֽהּ: כד וַיֹּ֙אמֶר֙ אַבְרָהָ֔ם
אָנֹכִ֖י אִשָּׁבֵֽעַ: כה וְהוֹכִ֥חַ אַבְרָהָ֖ם אֶת־אֲבִימֶ֑לֶךְ
עַל־אֹדוֹת֙ בְּאֵ֣ר הַמַּ֔יִם אֲשֶׁ֥ר גָּזְל֖וּ עַבְדֵ֥י
אֲבִימֶֽלֶךְ: כו וַיֹּ֣אמֶר אֲבִימֶ֗לֶךְ לֹ֤א יָדַ֙עְתִּי֙ מִ֣י
עָשָׂ֖ה אֶת־הַדָּבָ֣ר הַזֶּ֑ה וְגַם־אַתָּ֞ה לֹא־הִגַּ֣דְתָּ לִּ֗י
וְגַ֧ם אָנֹכִ֛י לֹ֥א שָׁמַ֖עְתִּי בִּלְתִּ֥י הַיּֽוֹם: כז וַיִּקַּ֤ח
אַבְרָהָם֙ צֹ֣אן וּבָקָ֔ר וַיִּתֵּ֖ן לַאֲבִימֶ֑לֶךְ וַיִּכְרְת֥וּ
שְׁנֵיהֶ֖ם בְּרִֽית: כח וַיַּצֵּ֣ב אַבְרָהָ֗ם אֶת־שֶׁ֛בַע
כִּבְשֹׂ֥ת הַצֹּ֖אן לְבַדְּהֶֽן: כט וַיֹּ֥אמֶר אֲבִימֶ֖לֶךְ
אֶל־אַבְרָהָ֑ם מָ֣ה הֵ֗נָּה שֶׁ֤בַע כְּבָשֹׂת֙ הָאֵ֔לֶּה
אֲשֶׁ֥ר הִצַּ֖בְתָּ לְבַדָּֽנָה: ל וַיֹּ֕אמֶר כִּ֚י אֶת־
שֶׁ֣בַע כְּבָשֹׂ֔ת תִּקַּ֖ח מִיָּדִ֑י בַּעֲבוּר֙ תִּֽהְיֶה־לִּ֣י
לְעֵדָ֔ה כִּ֥י חָפַ֖רְתִּי אֶת־הַבְּאֵ֥ר הַזֹּֽאת: לא עַל־כֵּ֗ן

20. *And he grew up.* The
translation follows the usual
translation of the word. According to *Radak*: *and he
became great,* i.e., with
wealth and prosperity.

21. *He lived in the desert of
Paran.* While there, he married a woman named
Adisha, and ultimately divorced her (*Targum
Yonasan*). [Apparently on
the advice of his father,
whom, according to the
Midrash, she mistreated
when he came to visit.]

**22. The alliance with
Abimelech.** These events
occurred at the time of
Isaac's birth. Knowing all
the miracles that God did
for Abraham, Abimelech
came to seal a covenant
with him (*Rashbam*).

23. Why did Abimelech request that the oath extend
only as far as his grandchildren? — A father's compassion for his descendants
does not extend beyond the
third generation (*Midrash*;
Rashi).

25. Although the peace-lov-
ing Abraham agreed to enter
into the alliance, he seized
the opportunity to state a
grievance regarding a disputed well, for, as the
Midrash notes: 'Reproof
leads to peace.'

Sefer HaYashar and Pirkei d'Rabbi Eliezer elaborate that Abraham's servants had dug a well near Beer Sheba, on the border of Philistia; but Abimelech's servants took the well by force, claiming they were the owners.

26. [Abimelech claims complete ignorance of the incident.]

28. From the gift of sheep and cattle mentioned in the previous verse, Abraham took seven female sheep — שֶׁבַע, seven, corresponding to the שְׁבוּעָה, oath, and set them aside to symbolize the seven/oath significance of their alliance, in commemoration of which they named the place בְּאֵר שֶׁבַע (Radak).

30. Because you are to take these seven ewes from me ... as a token of your acknowledgment of my rights [to the well]. This is similar to the ancient mode of acquisition of property through a symbolic barter effected by removing one's shoe and giving it to the other party [see comm. to Ruth 4:7] (Sforno).

state. [18] Arise, lift up the youth and grasp your hand upon him, for I will make a great nation of him.'

[19] Then God opened her eyes and she perceived a well of water. She went and filled the skin with water and gave the youth to drink.

[20] God was with the youth and he grew up. He dwelt in the desert and became an accomplished archer. [21] He lived in the desert of Paran, and his mother took a wife for him from the land of Egypt.

[22] At that time, Abimelech and Pichol his general said to Abraham, 'God is with you in all that you do. [23] Now swear to me here by God that you will not deal falsely with me nor with my son nor with my grandson. According to the kindness that I have done with you, do with me, and with the land in which you have sojourned.' [24] And Abraham said, 'I will swear.' [25] Then Abraham disputed with Abimelech regarding the well of water that Abimelech's servants had seized. [26] But Abimelech said, 'I do not know who did this thing; furthermore, you have never told me, and moreover I myself have heard nothing of it except for today.'

[27] So Abraham took sheep and cattle and gave them to Abimelech; and the two of them entered into a covenant. [28] Abraham set seven ewes of the flock by themselves, [29] and Abimelech said to Abraham, 'What are these seven ewes which you have set by themselves?'

[30] And he replied, 'Because you are to take these seven ewes from me, that it may serve me as testimony that I dug this well.' [31] Therefore

קָרָא לַמָּקוֹם הַהוּא בְּאֵר שָׁבַע כִּי שָׁם נִשְׁבְּעוּ
שְׁנֵיהֶם: לב וַיִּכְרְתוּ בְרִית בִּבְאֵר שָׁבַע וַיָּקָם
אֲבִימֶלֶךְ וּפִיכֹל שַׂר־צְבָאוֹ וַיָּשֻׁבוּ אֶל־אֶרֶץ
פְּלִשְׁתִּים: לג וַיִּטַּע אֶשֶׁל בִּבְאֵר שָׁבַע וַיִּקְרָא־
שָׁם בְּשֵׁם יְהוָה אֵל עוֹלָם: לד וַיָּגָר אַבְרָהָם
בְּאֶרֶץ פְּלִשְׁתִּים יָמִים רַבִּים:

כב שביעי א וַיְהִי אַחַר הַדְּבָרִים הָאֵלֶּה
וְהָאֱלֹהִים נִסָּה אֶת־אַבְרָהָם וַיֹּאמֶר אֵלָיו
אַבְרָהָם וַיֹּאמֶר הִנֵּנִי: ב וַיֹּאמֶר קַח־נָא אֶת־
בִּנְךָ אֶת־יְחִידְךָ אֲשֶׁר־אָהַבְתָּ אֶת־יִצְחָק
וְלֶךְ־לְךָ אֶל־אֶרֶץ הַמֹּרִיָּה וְהַעֲלֵהוּ שָׁם לְעֹלָה
עַל אַחַד הֶהָרִים אֲשֶׁר אֹמַר אֵלֶיךָ: ג וַיַּשְׁכֵּם
אַבְרָהָם בַּבֹּקֶר וַיַּחֲבֹשׁ אֶת־חֲמֹרוֹ וַיִּקַּח אֶת־
שְׁנֵי נְעָרָיו אִתּוֹ וְאֵת יִצְחָק בְּנוֹ וַיְבַקַּע עֲצֵי
עֹלָה וַיָּקָם וַיֵּלֶךְ אֶל־הַמָּקוֹם אֲשֶׁר־אָמַר־לוֹ
הָאֱלֹהִים: ד בַּיּוֹם הַשְּׁלִישִׁי וַיִּשָּׂא אַבְרָהָם
אֶת־עֵינָיו וַיַּרְא אֶת־הַמָּקוֹם מֵרָחֹק: ה וַיֹּאמֶר
אַבְרָהָם אֶל־נְעָרָיו שְׁבוּ־לָכֶם פֹּה עִם־הַחֲמוֹר
וַאֲנִי וְהַנַּעַר נֵלְכָה עַד־כֹּה וְנִשְׁתַּחֲוֶה וְנָשׁוּבָה
אֲלֵיכֶם: ו וַיִּקַּח אַבְרָהָם אֶת־עֲצֵי הָעֹלָה וַיָּשֶׂם
עַל־יִצְחָק בְּנוֹ וַיִּקַּח בְּיָדוֹ אֶת־הָאֵשׁ וְאֶת־
הַמַּאֲכֶלֶת וַיֵּלְכוּ שְׁנֵיהֶם יַחְדָּו: ז וַיֹּאמֶר יִצְחָק
אֶל־אַבְרָהָם אָבִיו וַיֹּאמֶר אָבִי וַיֹּאמֶר הִנֶּנִּי
בְנִי וַיֹּאמֶר הִנֵּה הָאֵשׁ וְהָעֵצִים וְאַיֵּה הַשֶּׂה
לְעֹלָה: ח וַיֹּאמֶר אַבְרָהָם אֱלֹהִים יִרְאֶה־

31. *Beer Sheba* [lit. *'well of seven,' or 'well of swearing'*].

33. [The Talmudic Sages] Rav and Shmuel differ as to the meaning of *eshel*. Rav understands it to mean that Abraham planted an *orchard*, from which he took fruits to serve to wayfarers, while Shmuel interprets [figuratively] that it was an *inn for lodging* in which he maintained a supply of fruit for wayfarers (*Rashi*). According to the figurative interpretation, אֶשֶׁל is an acrostic of the words אֲכִילָה, *eating*; שְׁתִיָּה, *drinking*; and לְוָיָה, *escorting* — the three basic services a host should provide his guests. (See also *Rashi* to Sotah 10a.)

34. The verse does not read וַיֵּשֶׁב אַבְרָהָם, *and Abraham settled*, usually implying *permanent residence*. Rather the term used is וַיָּגָר, *sojourned*, i.e., as a גֵּר, *alien*. For as *Rashi* points out in his comm. to 15:13, Abraham's years in the land of Philistines after the birth of Isaac were reckoned as part of the 400 years during which his descendants were to be *'strangers in a land not theirs.'*

22/1. The Tenth Trial: The Akeidah.

'This section constitutes the very reason for Israel's existence in God's eyes. It has therefore become part of our daily prayers and accordingly warrants a more penetrating study than other sections' (*Abarbanel*).

According to the accepted chronology, Isaac was thirty-seven at the *Akeidah*. This is derived as follows: Sarah was ninety at his birth, and 127 years at her death. She died when she heard that her son had been taken to be slaughtered (see comm. to 23:2); he was thirty-seven years old then.

Ramban explains the concept of *trial* as follows: Since man has full charge over his own actions, trial refers to the perspective of the person who is being tested. To God who knows all, the outcome is not in doubt, but, He imposes the trial in order to translate into actuality the potential of the person being tested, so that he can be rewarded for the actual *deed*....

2. *Moriah,* i.e., Jerusalem. The Sages explained that it was so named because הוֹרָאָה, *teaching*, went forth from it to the world. *Onkelos* renders: *to the land of Divine Service.* Apparently he takes the word *Moriah* as derived from מוֹר, *myrrh* [nard], one of the spices in the Temple-incense mixture (*Rashi*).

Bring him up there as an offering. God did not say, 'slaughter him,' because He did not intend for Isaac to be slaughtered, but only that he be *brought up* to the mountain and be *prepared* as a burnt-offering. Once Abraham had complied literally and 'brought him up,' God told him to bring him back down [v. 12] (*Rashi*).

3. *And Isaac, his son.* — Making it appear as if he were taking him along only as an afterthought, so as not to arouse questions (*Alshich*).

5. Since Abraham planned to sacrifice Isaac, he should have spoken in the singular and said, 'and *I* will return to you': — He [unwittingly] prophesied that *both* of them would return (*Rashi*).

6. *And the two of them went together,* i.e., in complete harmony. Abraham who knew that he was going to slay his son went with the same alacrity as Isaac who knew nothing of it (*Rashi*).

that place was called Beer Sheba because there the two of them took an oath. [32] Thus, they entered into a covenant at Beer Sheba. Abimelech then arose, with Pichol, his general, and they returned to the land of the Philistines.

[33] He planted an 'eshel' in Beer Sheba, and there he proclaimed the Name of HASHEM, God of the Universe. [34] And Abraham sojourned in the land of the Philistines many years.

22 [1] And it happened after these things that God tested Abraham and said to him, 'Abraham,' and he replied, 'Here I am.'

[2] And He said, 'Please take your son, your only one, whom you love — Isaac — and get yourself to the land of Moriah; bring him up there as an offering upon one of the mountains which I shall indicate to you.'

[3] So Abraham awoke early in the morning and he saddled his donkey; he took his two young men with him and Isaac, his son. He split the wood for the offering, and rose up and went to the place which God had indicated to him.

[4] On the third day, Abraham looked up and perceived the place from afar. [5] And Abraham said to his young men, 'Stay here by yourselves with the donkey, while I and the lad will go yonder; we will worship and we will return to you.'

[6] And Abraham took the wood for the offering, and placed it on Isaac, his son. He took in his hand the fire and the knife, and the two of them went together. [7] Then Isaac spoke to Abraham his father and said, 'Father —'

And he said 'Here I am, my son.'

And he said, 'Here are the fire and the wood, but where is the lamb for the offering?'

[8] And Abraham said, 'God will seek out for

לוֹ הַשֶּׂה לְעֹלָה בְּנִי וַיֵּלְכוּ שְׁנֵיהֶם יַחְדָּו: ט וַיָּבֹאוּ
אֶל־הַמָּקוֹם אֲשֶׁר אָמַר־לוֹ הָאֱלֹהִים וַיִּבֶן שָׁם
אַבְרָהָם אֶת־הַמִּזְבֵּחַ וַיַּעֲרֹךְ אֶת־הָעֵצִים
וַיַּעֲקֹד אֶת־יִצְחָק בְּנוֹ וַיָּשֶׂם אֹתוֹ עַל־הַמִּזְבֵּחַ
מִמַּעַל לָעֵצִים: י וַיִּשְׁלַח אַבְרָהָם אֶת־יָדוֹ וַיִּקַּח
אֶת־הַמַּאֲכֶלֶת לִשְׁחֹט אֶת־בְּנוֹ: יא וַיִּקְרָא אֵלָיו
מַלְאַךְ יהוה מִן־הַשָּׁמַיִם וַיֹּאמֶר אַבְרָהָם |
אַבְרָהָם וַיֹּאמֶר הִנֵּנִי: יב וַיֹּאמֶר אַל־תִּשְׁלַח יָדְךָ
אֶל־הַנַּעַר וְאַל־תַּעַשׂ לוֹ מְאוּמָה כִּי | עַתָּה
יָדַעְתִּי כִּי־יְרֵא אֱלֹהִים אַתָּה וְלֹא חָשַׂכְתָּ
אֶת־בִּנְךָ אֶת־יְחִידְךָ מִמֶּנִּי: יג וַיִּשָּׂא אַבְרָהָם
אֶת־עֵינָיו וַיַּרְא וְהִנֵּה־אַיִל אַחַר נֶאֱחַז בַּסְּבַךְ
בְּקַרְנָיו וַיֵּלֶךְ אַבְרָהָם וַיִּקַּח אֶת־הָאַיִל וַיַּעֲלֵהוּ
לְעֹלָה תַּחַת בְּנוֹ: יד וַיִּקְרָא אַבְרָהָם שֵׁם־
הַמָּקוֹם הַהוּא יהוה | יִרְאֶה אֲשֶׁר יֵאָמֵר הַיּוֹם
בְּהַר יהוה יֵרָאֶה: טו וַיִּקְרָא מַלְאַךְ יהוה
אֶל־אַבְרָהָם שֵׁנִית מִן־הַשָּׁמָיִם: טז וַיֹּאמֶר בִּי
נִשְׁבַּעְתִּי נְאֻם־יהוה כִּי יַעַן אֲשֶׁר עָשִׂיתָ
אֶת־הַדָּבָר הַזֶּה וְלֹא חָשַׂכְתָּ אֶת־בִּנְךָ אֶת־
יְחִידֶךָ: יז כִּי־בָרֵךְ אֲבָרֶכְךָ וְהַרְבָּה אַרְבֶּה
אֶת־זַרְעֲךָ כְּכוֹכְבֵי הַשָּׁמַיִם וְכַחוֹל אֲשֶׁר
עַל־שְׂפַת הַיָּם וְיִרַשׁ זַרְעֲךָ אֵת שַׁעַר אֹיְבָיו:
יח וְהִתְבָּרֲכוּ בְזַרְעֲךָ כֹּל גּוֹיֵי הָאָרֶץ עֵקֶב אֲשֶׁר
שָׁמַעְתָּ בְּקֹלִי: יט וַיָּשָׁב אַבְרָהָם אֶל־נְעָרָיו
וַיָּקֻמוּ וַיֵּלְכוּ יַחְדָּו אֶל־בְּאֵר שָׁבַע וַיֵּשֶׁב
אַבְרָהָם בִּבְאֵר שָׁבַע:

8. God will seek out and select the lamb, but if there is no lamb then *לְעֹלָה בְּנִי, you, my son,* will be the *offering.* Isaac then understood (*Rashi*).

9. Why did Abraham tie him? — Isaac said: 'Father, I am a vigorous young man and you are old. I fear that when I see the slaughtering knife in your hand I will instinctively jerk and possibly injure you. I might also injure myself and thus become unfit for the sacrifice. Or my involuntary movement might make you unable to perform the ritual slaughter properly. Therefore, bind me well so that at the final moment I will not be deficient in filial honor and respect, and thereby not fulfill the commandment properly.' Thereupon, Abraham immediately *bound Isaac, his son.* Could he bind a thirty-seven-year-old man without his consent? (*Midrash*).

11. *Abraham! Abraham! The repetition expresses love* (Rashi).

13. *Afterwards, caught in the thicket by its horns.* אַחַר, *afterwards, i.e., after the preceding events, when the angel had told Abraham not to harm the lad, he looked up and saw a ram caught in the thicket* (Rashi).

14. *HASHEM Yireh* [i.e., 'HASHEM will see']. The original name of the place was *Shalem*, the name given it by Shem, son of Noah — whom the Sages identify with Malchizedek, king of Jerusalem. After the *Akeidah*, Abraham called it *Yireh*. In deference to Shem and Abraham, God synthesized both names and called it *Yerushalayim*.

18. וְהִתְבָּרְכוּ בְזַרְעֶךָ — *Shall bless themselves by your offspring.* — I.e., the nations will pray to God: 'Bless us as You have blessed the offspring of Abraham' (Radak).

Himself the lamb for the offering, my son.' And the two of them went together.

⁹ They arrived at the place which God designated to him. Abraham built the altar there, and arranged the wood; he bound Isaac, his son, and he placed him on the altar atop the wood. ¹⁰ Abraham stretched out his hand, and took the knife to slaughter his son.

¹¹ And an angel of HASHEM called to him from heaven, and said, 'Abraham! Abraham!'

And he said, 'Here I am.'

¹² And he said, 'Do not stretch out your hand against the lad nor do anything to him for now I know that you are a God-fearing man, since you have not withheld your son, your only one, from Me.'

¹³ And Abraham looked up and saw — behold a ram! — afterwards, caught in the thicket by its horns. So Abraham went and took the ram and offered it up as an offering instead of his son. ¹⁴ And Abraham named that site 'HASHEM Yireh,' as it is said this day, on the mountain HASHEM is seen.

¹⁵ The angel of HASHEM called to Abraham a second time from heaven, ¹⁶ and said, 'By Myself I swear, declared HASHEM, that since you have done this thing, and have not withheld your son, your only one, ¹⁷ that I shall surely bless you and greatly increase your offering like the stars of the heavens and like the sand on the seashore; and your offspring shall inherit the gate of its enemy; ¹⁸ and all the nations of the earth shall bless themselves by your offspring, because you have listened to My voice.'

¹⁹ Abraham returned to his young men, and they rose up and went together to Beer Sheba, and Abraham stayed at Beer Sheba.

מפטיר כ וַיְהִי אַחֲרֵי הַדְּבָרִים הָאֵלֶּה וַיֻּגַּד
לְאַבְרָהָם לֵאמֹר הִנֵּה יָלְדָה מִלְכָּה גַם־
הִוא בָּנִים לְנָחוֹר אָחִיךָ: כא אֶת־עוּץ בְּכֹרוֹ
וְאֶת־בּוּז אָחִיו וְאֶת־קְמוּאֵל אֲבִי אֲרָם:
כב וְאֶת־כֶּשֶׂד וְאֶת־חֲזוֹ וְאֶת־פִּלְדָּשׁ וְאֶת־
יִדְלָף וְאֵת בְּתוּאֵל: כג וּבְתוּאֵל יָלַד אֶת־רִבְקָה
שְׁמֹנָה אֵלֶּה יָלְדָה מִלְכָּה לְנָחוֹר אֲחִי אַבְרָהָם:
כד וּפִילַגְשׁוֹ וּשְׁמָהּ רְאוּמָה וַתֵּלֶד גַּם־הִוא
אֶת־טֶבַח וְאֶת־גַּחַם וְאֶת־תַּחַשׁ וְאֶת־מַעֲכָה:

The *Haftarah* for *Vayeira* appears on page 308

20. The birth of Rebecca.
R' Hoffman points out that the birth of Rebecca at this time is another instance of the Divine Providence with which the story of the Patriarchs is replete. Because she was born, Isaac, who was ready to become a 'perfect offering,' did not have to be defiled by marriage to one of the debauched Canaanite women. To accentuate this fact, the Torah did not mention the genealogy of Terach's family previously.

According to the Masoretic note appearing at the end of the *Sidrah*, there are 147 verses in the *Sidrah*, numerically corresponding to the mnemonic אָמְנוֹן [=147; apparently a reference to the profound אֱמוּנָה, *faithfulness*, of Abraham which is the primary theme of this *Sidrah*. This faithfulness reached its zenith when Abraham was confronted by the command to sacrifice the very son in whom his every future promise was to have been fulfilled. Yet his utter אֱמוּנָה, *trust*, in God was such that Abraham complied unhesitatingly.] The *Haftarah* begins with *II Kings* 4:1: וְאִשָּׁה אַחַת.

²⁰ It came to pass after these things, that Abraham was told, saying: Behold, Milcah too has borne children to Nachor, your brother: ²¹ Utz, his firstborn; Buz, his brother; Kemuel, the father of Aram; ²² and Kessed, Hazo, Pildash, Yidlaf, and Bethuel; ²³ And Bethuel begot Rebecca. These eight Milcah bore to Nachor, Abraham's brother. ²⁴ And his concubine whose name was Reumah, also bore children: Tevach, Gaham, Tahash, and Maacah.

The *Haftarah* for *Vayeira* appears on page 308

פרשת חיי שרה

CHAYEI SARAH

The *Sidrah* shows Jewish respect for the dead and concern for the future. It begins with the death of Sarah, and Abraham's intense concern that she be given a proper burial in a place worthy of her greatness. To acquire a burial plot, Abraham negotiates with the transparently greedy Ephron and gladly pays an exorbitant price.

But then, Abraham must look ahead: Isaac had no wife.

To seek a match for Isaac, Abraham looks to his ancestral home, and to choose the suitable girl he sends his trusted disciple and servant, Eliezer. To verify the worthiness of the potential bride, the wise emissary devises an elaborate test. He seeks no miraculous feats or astounding wealth; the future Matriarch of the Jewish people must be sensitive, giving, and unselfish. Rebecca passes the test. Later, after Isaac meets her, he takes her to Sarah's tent, and the spirit of holiness returns to it. It is as if God Himself testifies that 'Sarah' lives anew. Only then is the young Patriarch consoled for the loss of his mother.

Once Isaac and Rebecca are ready to establish their new home, Abraham gives generous gifts to his children by Keturah, and sends them off. Just as Sarah had insisted that Ishmael could not live side by side with Isaac, so Abraham acted on the need to assure that the foundation of the people be built without sediment. The greenhouse of the Jewish people must be free of deleterious influences.

כג א וַיִּהְיוּ חַיֵּי שָׂרָה מֵאָה שָׁנָה וְעֶשְׂרִים שָׁנָה וְשֶׁבַע שָׁנִים שְׁנֵי חַיֵּי שָׂרָה: ב וַתָּמָת שָׂרָה בְּקִרְיַת אַרְבַּע הִוא חֶבְרוֹן בְּאֶרֶץ כְּנָעַן וַיָּבֹא אַבְרָהָם לִסְפֹּד לְשָׂרָה וְלִבְכֹּתָהּ: ג וַיָּקָם אַבְרָהָם מֵעַל פְּנֵי מֵתוֹ וַיְדַבֵּר אֶל־בְּנֵי־חֵת לֵאמֹר: ד גֵּר־וְתוֹשָׁב אָנֹכִי עִמָּכֶם תְּנוּ לִי אֲחֻזַּת־קֶבֶר עִמָּכֶם וְאֶקְבְּרָה מֵתִי מִלְּפָנָי: ה וַיַּעֲנוּ בְנֵי־חֵת אֶת־אַבְרָהָם לֵאמֹר לוֹ: ו שְׁמָעֵנוּ ׀ אֲדֹנִי נְשִׂיא אֱלֹהִים אַתָּה בְּתוֹכֵנוּ בְּמִבְחַר קְבָרֵינוּ קְבֹר אֶת־מֵתֶךָ אִישׁ מִמֶּנּוּ אֶת־קִבְרוֹ לֹא־יִכְלֶה מִמְּךָ מִקְּבֹר מֵתֶךָ: ז וַיָּקָם אַבְרָהָם וַיִּשְׁתַּחוּ לְעַם־הָאָרֶץ לִבְנֵי־חֵת: ח וַיְדַבֵּר אִתָּם לֵאמֹר אִם־יֵשׁ אֶת־נַפְשְׁכֶם לִקְבֹּר אֶת־מֵתִי מִלְּפָנַי שְׁמָעוּנִי וּפִגְעוּ־לִי בְּעֶפְרוֹן בֶּן־צֹחַר: ט וְיִתֶּן־לִי אֶת־מְעָרַת הַמַּכְפֵּלָה אֲשֶׁר־לוֹ אֲשֶׁר בִּקְצֵה שָׂדֵהוּ בְּכֶסֶף מָלֵא יִתְּנֶנָּה לִּי בְּתוֹכְכֶם לַאֲחֻזַּת־קָבֶר: י וְעֶפְרוֹן יֹשֵׁב בְּתוֹךְ בְּנֵי־חֵת וַיַּעַן עֶפְרוֹן הַחִתִּי אֶת־אַבְרָהָם בְּאָזְנֵי בְנֵי־חֵת לְכֹל בָּאֵי שַׁעַר־עִירוֹ לֵאמֹר: יא לֹא־אֲדֹנִי שְׁמָעֵנִי הַשָּׂדֶה נָתַתִּי לָךְ וְהַמְּעָרָה אֲשֶׁר־בּוֹ לְךָ נְתַתִּיהָ לְעֵינֵי בְנֵי־עַמִּי נְתַתִּיהָ לָּךְ קְבֹר מֵתֶךָ: יב וַיִּשְׁתַּחוּ אַבְרָהָם לִפְנֵי עַם־הָאָרֶץ: יג וַיְדַבֵּר אֶל־עֶפְרוֹן בְּאָזְנֵי עַם־הָאָרֶץ לֵאמֹר אַךְ אִם־אַתָּה לוּ שְׁמָעֵנִי נָתַתִּי

23/1. Sarah's life span, and purchase of a burial site.

Sarah's death was mentioned in order to connect it to the purchase of the Cave of Machpelah. Having mentioned her death, the Torah also informs us of the age at which she died (*Rashbam*).

One hundred years, twenty years, and seven years. Rashi explains that the repetiton of *years* teaches that each stage must be interpreted independently [with each term sharing a particular characteristic of its neighboring term]. At a hundred she was like twenty with relation to sin. Just as she was sinless at twenty, having just reached the age of heavenly punishment, so was she still sinless at the age of a hundred. And at twenty she still had the wholesome beauty of a seven-year-old (*Chizkuni*).

2. *Sarah died.* The narrative of her death follows that of the *Akeidah*, because her death was caused by the shock of hearing that her son had almost been slaughtered (*Rashi*).

And Abraham came. From Beer Sheba (*Rashi*) [where he had gone after the *Akeidah*].

וְלִבְכֹּתָהּ, *and to bewail her,* is written with a small כ to indicate that Abraham did not weep *excessively*, for she was old and had led a full life.

3. *The children of Heth.* I.e., Heth was the son of Canaan [10:15]. The Hittites were the leaders of the region, and Abraham gathered them so that his request could be negotiated and approved by the proper authorities.

4. *I am an alien and a resident among you.* I.e., I am a *foreigner* from another land and have *settled* in your midst (*Rashi*).

R' Hirsch explains the connotation: 'As an alien, I have no *right* to your land, but I have lived among you for a long time.'

5-6. The Hittites consider the matter and give Abraham their reply.

7. Abraham acknowledges their response and entreats further.

8. It would have been unseemly for the rich and distinguished Ephron to sell his ancestral inheritance. Abraham, therefore, did not approach him directly and offer an inflated price for the field. Instead, he asked the people of the city to entreat Ephron dignifiedly on his behalf. Abraham asked for it as a "gift," because he would be prepared to pay handsomely for it and still consider it a gift (*Ramban*).

9. *The Cave of Machpelah* [lit., *the cave of the double*]. It was so called because it contained an upper and a lower level; or it was called 'doubled' on account of the זוגות, *couples*, who were [to be] buried there (*Rashi*).

11. *No, my lord.* You need not *purchase* it (*Rashi*).

Abraham was interested only in acquiring the cave itself; he was content that the adjacent field remain Ephron's. Ephron, on the other hand — by way of magnanimity or trickery — offered to give him the field as well as the cave, for it would be unbecoming for Abraham to own the cave as a sepulcher, while the field belonged to another. Abraham rejoiced at Ephron's offer [next verse] and he purchased the entire property for the full price Ephron suggested (*Ramban*).

13. *And [he] spoke to Ephron.* Directly, there being no further need for intermediaries (*Ibn Caspi*).

23 ¹ **S**arah's lifetime was one hundred years, twenty years, and seven years; the years of Sarah's life. ² Sarah died in Kiriath Arba which is Hebron in the land of Canaan. And Abraham came to eulogize Sarah and to bewail her.

³ Abraham rose up from the presence of his dead, and spoke to the children of Heth, saying: ⁴ 'I am an alien and a resident among you. Grant me an estate for a burial site with you, that I may bury my dead from before me.'

⁵ And the children of Heth answered Abraham saying to him: ⁶'Hear us, my lord: You are a prince of God in our midst. In the choicest of our burial places bury your dead. Any of us will not withhold his burial place from burying your dead.'

⁷ Then Abraham rose up and bowed down to the members of the council of the sons of Heth, ⁸ and spoke to them saying: 'If it is truly your will to bury my dead from before me, heed me, and intercede for me with Ephron son of Tzochar. ⁹ That he may grant me the Cave of Machpelah which is his, on the edge of his field — let him grant it to me for its full price! — in your midst as an estate for a burial site.'

¹⁰ Now, Ephron was sitting in the midst of the children of Heth. And Ephron the Hittite responded to Abraham in the hearing of the children of Heth, for all who come to the gate of his town, saying: ¹¹ 'No, my lord; heed me! I have given you the field, and as for the cave that is in it, I have given it to you. In the view of the children of my people have I given it to you; bury your dead.'

¹² So Abraham bowed down before the members of the council, ¹³ and spoke to Ephron in the hearing of the members of the council, saying: 'Rather, if only you would heed me! I give you the

כֶּסֶף הַשָּׂדֶה קַח מִמֶּנִּי וְאֶקְבְּרָה אֶת־מֵתִי
שָׁמָּה: יד וַיַּעַן עֶפְרוֹן אֶת־אַבְרָהָם לֵאמֹר לוֹ:
טו אֲדֹנִי שְׁמָעֵנִי אֶרֶץ אַרְבַּע מֵאֹת שֶׁקֶל־כֶּסֶף
בֵּינִי וּבֵינְךָ מַה־הִוא וְאֶת־מֵתְךָ קְבֹר:
טז וַיִּשְׁמַע אַבְרָהָם אֶל־עֶפְרוֹן וַיִּשְׁקֹל אַבְרָהָם
לְעֶפְרֹן אֶת־הַכֶּסֶף אֲשֶׁר דִּבֶּר בְּאָזְנֵי בְנֵי־חֵת
אַרְבַּע מֵאוֹת שֶׁקֶל כֶּסֶף עֹבֵר לַסֹּחֵר:
שני יז וַיָּקָם ׀ שְׂדֵה עֶפְרוֹן אֲשֶׁר בַּמַּכְפֵּלָה
אֲשֶׁר לִפְנֵי מַמְרֵא הַשָּׂדֶה וְהַמְּעָרָה אֲשֶׁר־
בּוֹ וְכָל־הָעֵץ אֲשֶׁר בַּשָּׂדֶה אֲשֶׁר בְּכָל־
גְּבֻלוֹ סָבִיב: יח לְאַבְרָהָם לְמִקְנָה לְעֵינֵי בְנֵי־
חֵת בְּכֹל בָּאֵי שַׁעַר־עִירוֹ: יט וְאַחֲרֵי־כֵן
קָבַר אַבְרָהָם אֶת־שָׂרָה אִשְׁתּוֹ אֶל־מְעָרַת
שְׂדֵה הַמַּכְפֵּלָה עַל־פְּנֵי מַמְרֵא הִוא
חֶבְרוֹן בְּאֶרֶץ כְּנָעַן: כ וַיָּקָם הַשָּׂדֶה וְהַמְּעָרָה
אֲשֶׁר־בּוֹ לְאַבְרָהָם לַאֲחֻזַּת־קָבֶר מֵאֵת בְּנֵי־
חֵת: כד א וְאַבְרָהָם זָקֵן בָּא
בַּיָּמִים וַיהוָה בֵּרַךְ אֶת־אַבְרָהָם בַּכֹּל: ב וַיֹּאמֶר
אַבְרָהָם אֶל־עַבְדּוֹ זְקַן בֵּיתוֹ הַמֹּשֵׁל בְּכָל־
אֲשֶׁר־לוֹ שִׂים־נָא יָדְךָ תַּחַת יְרֵכִי: ג וְאַשְׁבִּיעֲךָ
בַּיהוה אֱלֹהֵי הַשָּׁמַיִם וֵאלֹהֵי הָאָרֶץ אֲשֶׁר
לֹא־תִקַּח אִשָּׁה לִבְנִי מִבְּנוֹת הַכְּנַעֲנִי אֲשֶׁר
אָנֹכִי יוֹשֵׁב בְּקִרְבּוֹ: ד כִּי אֶל־אַרְצִי וְאֶל־
מוֹלַדְתִּי תֵּלֵךְ וְלָקַחְתָּ אִשָּׁה לִבְנִי לְיִצְחָק:
ה וַיֹּאמֶר אֵלָיו הָעֶבֶד אוּלַי לֹא־תֹאבֶה הָאִשָּׁה

14-15. Ephron names the price . . .
15. *What is it?* I.e., between such friends as we, of what significance is it? (*Rashi*)
16. Abraham consummates the purchase.
Ephron is usually spelled with a ו, i.e., עֶפְרוֹן. In this case it is spelled עֶפְרֹן, defectively. This indicates that Ephron's stature was reduced — because he promised much, but performed not even a little — for in the end he demanded from Abraham large shekels: *centenaria*, as it is said, עֹבֵר לַסֹּחֵר, *negotiable currency* [see below] (*Rashi*).

When the Torah refers to a *shekel*, it generally means a *sela*. Abraham's *shekels*, however, weighed a *centenaria*. Each *centenaria* weighed one hundred *mannah*. A *mannah* is twenty-five *shekels*. Thus, each *centenaria* is worth 2,500 ordinary *shekels* and Abraham paid a total of one million ordinary *shekels* for the cave (*Bava Metzia* 87a; *Rashi*).
17. The Midrashic interpretation of וַיָּקָם is that the property became *elevated* because it passed from the possession of a commoner [Ephron] to that of a king [Abraham].
19. *In the land of Canaan.* This is repeated [see v. 2] to emphasize that burial anywhere in the Land is meritorious (*Haamek Davar*).
24/1. *Well on in years* [lit., *he had entered into the days*]. I.e., one who has 'entered into those days' when he knows he must go the way of all flesh (*Radak*).

His life's work was finished; he had nothing more to strive for, and his concern was for his son who would survive him (*R' Hirsch*).

With everything. With riches, possessions, honor, longevity, and children. The one thing he lacked was to see his son have children to inherit his status and honor (*Ramban*).

2. *The senior servant.* I.e., Eliezer (see 15:2), sixty years previous. Now he is not only the senior servant, but *the elder of his household* (*R' Hoffmann*).

Under my thigh. [*Thigh* is a euphemism for the *membrum virile*; offspring, too, are described as יוֹצְאֵי יְרֵךְ, lit., *coming out of their father's 'thigh'* (46:26; *Exod.* 1:5).] *Rashi* explains that one who takes an oath must place his hand on some sacred object, such as a Torah scroll or *tefillin* [see *Shevuos* 38b]. Because circumcision was the first precept given to Abraham, and through much pain, it was particularly precious to him, and Abraham selected the organ as the object upon which Eliezer should take his oath. [*Targum Yonasan* renders similarly; cf. *Tanchuma*.]

3. Realizing the infirmities of his old age, Abraham feared that he might die before Eliezer's return. Accordingly, the *oath* assured Abraham of unwavering loyalty to his plan, because he knew that Isaac would follow the counsel of Eliezer, *who controlled all that was his* [v. 2] (*Ramban* to v. 1).

From the daughters of the Canaanites. The seed of Canaan was specifically *cursed* [9:25] while Abraham's seed was *blessed* [22:18]. The two could not mingle (*Rashi, Radak*).

5. Eliezer does not doubt that he will find the suitable mate who will consent to marry Isaac, but he is afraid that she might not want to go with him and forsake her family (*R' Hoffmann*).

price of the field, accept it from me, that I may bury my dead there.'

[14] And Ephron replied to Abraham, saying to him: [15] 'My lord, heed me! Land worth four hundred silver shekels — between me and you — what is it? Bury your dead.'

[16] Abraham heeded Ephron, and Abraham weighed out to Ephron the amount which he had mentioned in the hearing of the children of Heth — four hundred silver shekels in negotiable currency. [17] And Ephron's field, which was in Machpelah, facing Mamre — the field and the cave within it and all the trees in the field, within all its surrounding boundaries — passed [18]to Abraham as a purchase in the view of the children of Heth, among all who came to the gate of his town. [19] And afterwards Abraham buried Sarah his wife in the cave of the field of Machpelah facing Mamre, which is Hebron, in the land of Canaan.

[20] Thus, the field with its cave passed to Abraham as an estate for a burial site, from the children of Heth.

24 [1] Now Abraham was old, well on in years, and HASHEM had blessed Abraham with everything. [2] And Abraham said to the senior servant of his household who controlled all that was his: 'Place now your hand under my thigh. [3] And I will have you swear by HASHEM, God of heaven and God of earth, that you not take a wife for my son from the daughters of the Canaanites, among whom I dwell. [4] Rather, to my land and to my kindred shall you go and take a wife for my son — for Isaac.'

[5] The servant said to him: 'Perhaps the woman

לָלֶ֣כֶת אַחֲרַ֔י אֶל־הָאָ֖רֶץ הַזֹּ֑את הֶהָשֵׁ֤ב אָשִׁיב֙
אֶת־בִּנְךָ֔ אֶל־הָאָ֖רֶץ אֲשֶׁר־יָצָ֥אתָ מִשָּֽׁם: ו וַיֹּ֥אמֶר אֵלָ֖יו אַבְרָהָ֑ם הִשָּׁ֣מֶר לְךָ֔ פֶּן־תָּשִׁ֥יב
אֶת־בְּנִ֖י שָֽׁמָּה: ז יְהֹוָ֣ה ׀ אֱלֹהֵ֣י הַשָּׁמַ֗יִם אֲשֶׁ֨ר
לְקָחַ֜נִי מִבֵּ֣ית אָבִי֮ וּמֵאֶ֣רֶץ מֽוֹלַדְתִּי֒ וַֽאֲשֶׁ֨ר
דִּבֶּר־לִ֜י וַֽאֲשֶׁ֤ר נִֽשְׁבַּֽע־לִי֙ לֵאמֹ֔ר לְזַ֨רְעֲךָ֔ אֶתֵּ֖ן
אֶת־הָאָ֣רֶץ הַזֹּ֑את ה֗וּא יִשְׁלַ֤ח מַלְאָכוֹ֙ לְפָנֶ֔יךָ
וְלָֽקַחְתָּ֥ אִשָּׁ֛ה לִבְנִ֖י מִשָּֽׁם: ח וְאִם־לֹ֨א תֹאבֶ֜ה
הָֽאִשָּׁ֗ה לָלֶ֣כֶת אַֽחֲרֶ֔יךָ וְנִקִּ֕יתָ מִשְּׁבֻֽעָתִ֖י זֹ֑את
רַ֣ק אֶת־בְּנִ֔י לֹ֥א תָשֵׁ֖ב שָֽׁמָּה: ט וַיָּ֤שֶׂם הָעֶ֨בֶד֙
אֶת־יָד֔וֹ תַּ֛חַת יֶ֥רֶךְ אַבְרָהָ֖ם אֲדֹנָ֑יו וַיִּשָּׁ֣בַֽע ל֔וֹ
עַל־הַדָּבָ֖ר הַזֶּֽה: שלישי י וַיִּקַּ֣ח הָ֠עֶ֠בֶד עֲשָׂרָ֨ה
גְמַלִּ֜ים מִגְּמַלֵּ֤י אֲדֹנָיו֙ וַיֵּ֔לֶךְ וְכָל־ט֥וּב אֲדֹנָ֖יו
בְּיָד֑וֹ וַיָּ֗קָם וַיֵּ֛לֶךְ אֶל־אֲרַ֥ם נַֽהֲרַ֖יִם אֶל־עִ֥יר
נָחֽוֹר: יא וַיַּבְרֵ֧ךְ הַגְּמַלִּ֛ים מִח֥וּץ לָעִ֖יר אֶל־בְּאֵ֣ר
הַמָּ֑יִם לְעֵ֣ת עֶ֔רֶב לְעֵ֖ת צֵ֥את הַשֹּֽׁאֲבֹֽת:
יב וַיֹּאמַ֓ר ׀ יְהֹוָ֗ה אֱלֹהֵי֙ אֲדֹנִ֣י אַבְרָהָ֔ם הַקְרֵה־
נָ֥א לְפָנַ֖י הַיּ֑וֹם וַֽעֲשֵׂה־חֶ֕סֶד עִ֖ם אֲדֹנִ֥י אַבְרָהָֽם:
יג הִנֵּ֛ה אָֽנֹכִ֥י נִצָּ֖ב עַל־עֵ֣ין הַמָּ֑יִם וּבְנוֹת֙ אַנְשֵׁ֣י
הָעִ֔יר יֹֽצְאֹ֖ת לִשְׁאֹ֥ב מָֽיִם: יד וְהָיָ֣ה הַֽנַּעֲרָ֗ אֲשֶׁ֨ר
אֹמַ֤ר אֵלֶ֨יהָ֙ הַטִּי־נָ֤א כַדֵּךְ֙ וְאֶשְׁתֶּ֔ה וְאָֽמְרָ֣ה
שְׁתֵ֔ה וְגַם־גְּמַלֶּ֖יךָ אַשְׁקֶ֑ה אֹתָ֤הּ הֹכַ֨חְתָּ֙
לְעַבְדְּךָ֣ לְיִצְחָ֔ק וּבָ֣הּ אֵדַ֔ע כִּֽי־עָשִׂ֥יתָ חֶ֖סֶד
עִם־אֲדֹנִֽי: טו וַֽיְהִי־ה֗וּא טֶ֨רֶם֙ כִּלָּ֣ה לְדַבֵּ֔ר וְהִנֵּ֧ה
רִבְקָ֣ה יֹצֵ֗את אֲשֶׁ֤ר יֻלְּדָה֙ לִבְתוּאֵ֣ל בֶּן־מִלְכָּ֔ה

6. Abraham would not let Isaac lose the special sanctity with which he had been invested when he was brought as an עוֹלָה תְּמִימָה, *an offering completely devoted*, to God (*Pesikta Zutresa*); thus he emphasized that Isaac was on no account to leave the land that God had promised to his descendants (*Radak*).

9. Eliezer undertakes the oath.

10. *Aram Naharaim* [lit., *Aram of the two rivers*]. The country was so called because it was situated between two rivers [Euphrates and Tigris] (*Rashi*).

11. Eliezer was not interested in a *wealthy* girl for Isaac. He preferred someone of modest means, the kind who would go to draw water herself, not have servants do it for her (*Malbim*).

12. Eliezer prays for a sign. Eliezer was apprehensive that the girl's family might refuse to let her leave home for a distant marriage. He therefore proposed the following test in order that Abraham's relations would recognize God's hand in the ensuing events, and would consent to allow their daughter to leave home and accompany the man.

13. The criteria are established:
See, I stand here by the spring of water. I.e., away from a home atmosphere, and hence in a better perspective to judge the character of a prospective bride. For here the girl will act freely in accordance with her own innate character, while at home a girl's behavior may reflect the constraint of her family's orders or expectations (*Chizkuni*).

14. *And who replies, "Drink, and I will even water your camels."* I.e., her response will go *beyond* my request, and she will offer all that is needed (*Sforno*).

R' Moshe Feinstein *zt"l* notes that when Rebecca responded to Eliezer's entreaty, she watered the animals without explicitly *offering* to do so. Harav Feinstein explains that Rebecca's kindness was so great that she took it for granted that another's needs should be provided for. That his camels had to be watered was so obvious to her that it was unnecessary for her to announce her intention to do so (*Igros Moshe, Orach Chaim II* responsa 52).

15. So swift was the Divine response to his petition, that while he was still in the midst of his supplication, Providence had already caused Rebecca to leave her house and go to the well.

shall not wish to follow me to this land; shall I take your son back to the land from which you departed?'

⁶ Abraham answered him, 'Beware not to return my son to there. ⁷ HASHEM, God of heaven, Who took me from the house of my father and from the land of my birth; Who spoke concerning me, and Who swore to me saying, "To your offspring will I give this land," He will send His angel before you, and you will take a wife for my son from there. ⁸ But if the woman will not wish to follow you, you shall then be absolved of this oath of mine. However, do not return my son to there.'

⁹ So the servant placed his hand under the thigh of Abraham his master and swore to him regarding this matter. ¹⁰ Then the servant took ten of his master's camels and set out with all the bounty of his master in his hand and made his way to Aram Naharaim to the city of Nachor.

¹¹ He made the camels kneel down outside the city towards a well of water at evening time, the time when women come out to draw. ¹² And he said, 'HASHEM, God of my master Abraham, may You so arrange it for me this day that You do kindness with my master Abraham. ¹³ See, I stand here by the spring of water and the daughters of the townsmen come out to draw. ¹⁴ Let it be that the maiden to whom I shall say, "Please tip over your jug so I may drink," and who replies, "Drink, and I will even water your camels," — her will You have designated for Your servant for Isaac, and may I know through her that You have done kindness with my master.'

¹⁵ And it was before he had finished speaking that suddenly there came out Rebecca — who had been born to Bethuel the son of Milcah

אֵ֣שֶׁת נָח֔וֹר אֲחִ֖י אַבְרָהָ֑ם וְכַדָּ֖הּ עַל־שִׁכְמָֽהּ:
טז וְהַֽנַּעֲרָ֗ טֹבַ֤ת מַרְאֶה֙ מְאֹ֔ד בְּתוּלָ֕ה וְאִ֖ישׁ
לֹ֣א יְדָעָ֑הּ וַתֵּ֣רֶד הָעַ֔יְנָה וַתְּמַלֵּ֥א כַדָּ֖הּ וַתָּֽעַל:
יז וַיָּ֥רׇץ הָעֶ֖בֶד לִקְרָאתָ֑הּ וַיֹּ֕אמֶר הַגְמִיאִ֥ינִי נָ֛א
מְעַט־מַ֖יִם מִכַּדֵּֽךְ: יח וַתֹּ֖אמֶר שְׁתֵ֣ה אֲדֹנִ֑י
וַתְּמַהֵ֗ר וַתֹּ֧רֶד כַּדָּ֛הּ עַל־יָדָ֖הּ וַתַּשְׁקֵֽהוּ:
יט וַתְּכַ֖ל לְהַשְׁקֹת֑וֹ וַתֹּ֗אמֶר גַּ֤ם לִגְמַלֶּ֙יךָ֙
אֶשְׁאָ֔ב עַ֥ד אִם־כִּלּ֖וּ לִשְׁתֹּֽת: כ וַתְּמַהֵ֗ר וַתְּעַ֤ר
כַּדָּהּ֙ אֶל־הַשֹּׁ֔קֶת וַתָּ֥רׇץ ע֛וֹד אֶֽל־הַבְּאֵ֖ר
לִשְׁאֹ֑ב וַתִּשְׁאַ֖ב לְכׇל־גְּמַלָּֽיו: כא וְהָאִ֥ישׁ
מִשְׁתָּאֵ֖ה לָ֑הּ מַחֲרִ֕ישׁ לָדַ֗עַת הַֽהִצְלִ֧יחַ
יְהֹוָ֛ה דַּרְכּ֖וֹ אִם־לֹֽא: כב וַיְהִ֗י כַּאֲשֶׁ֨ר כִּלּ֤וּ
הַגְּמַלִּים֙ לִשְׁתּ֔וֹת וַיִּקַּ֤ח הָאִישׁ֙ נֶ֣זֶם זָהָ֔ב בֶּ֖קַע
מִשְׁקָל֑וֹ וּשְׁנֵ֤י צְמִידִים֙ עַל־יָדֶ֔יהָ עֲשָׂרָ֥ה
זָהָ֖ב מִשְׁקָלָֽם: כג וַיֹּ֙אמֶר֙ בַּת־מִ֣י אַ֔תְּ הַגִּ֥ידִי נָ֖א
לִ֑י הֲיֵ֧שׁ בֵּית־אָבִ֛יךְ מָק֥וֹם לָ֖נוּ לָלִֽין:
כד וַתֹּ֣אמֶר אֵלָ֔יו בַּת־בְּתוּאֵ֖ל אָנֹ֑כִי בֶּן־מִלְכָּ֕ה
אֲשֶׁ֥ר יָלְדָ֖ה לְנָחֽוֹר: כה וַתֹּ֣אמֶר אֵלָ֔יו גַּם־תֶּ֥בֶן
גַּם־מִסְפּ֖וֹא רַ֣ב עִמָּ֑נוּ גַּם־מָק֖וֹם לָלֽוּן:
כו וַיִּקֹּ֣ד הָאִ֔ישׁ וַיִּשְׁתַּ֖חוּ לַֽיהֹוָֽה: רביעי כז וַיֹּ֗אמֶר
בָּר֤וּךְ יְהֹוָה֙ אֱלֹהֵי֙ אֲדֹנִ֣י אַבְרָהָ֔ם אֲשֶׁ֛ר לֹֽא־
עָזַ֥ב חַסְדּ֛וֹ וַאֲמִתּ֖וֹ מֵעִ֣ם אֲדֹנִ֑י אָנֹכִ֗י בַּדֶּ֙רֶךְ֙
נָחַ֣נִי יְהֹוָ֔ה בֵּ֖ית אֲחֵ֥י אֲדֹנִֽי: כח וַתָּ֙רׇץ֙ הַֽנַּעֲרָ֔
וַתַּגֵּ֖ד לְבֵ֣ית אִמָּ֑הּ כַּדְּבָרִ֖ים הָאֵֽלֶּה:

---

16. *Filled her jug and ascended.* Unlike the other girls at the well, who wasted their time in idle chatter, Rebecca did her task quickly and without delay; *she filled her jug and* immediately *ascended* (*Minchah Belulah*).

18. **Rebecca proves equal to the test.**

Rebecca acted in a most exalted manner: She lowered the jug herself to spare him the effort, and וַתַּשְׁקֵהוּ, she actually brought the jug near his mouth, so he would not even have to hold it (*Or HaChaim*).

19. *Kedushas Levi* suggests that her offer to *draw* the water rather than *water* them was an indication of compassion. If she were to give water directly to the camels, how could she choose which to water first? Therefore, she kept pouring water into *the trough* so they could *all drink at once*, and she continued drawing water until they all finished drinking.

And kept running to the well. Rebecca *runs* eagerly when she performs an act of kindness, as did Abraham when he was providing for *his guests* (see 18:7); a further sign of her suitability to join Abraham's household.

I. Levy, in a bracketed comment to R' Hirsch, notes that in their first drink, ten camels would consume at least 140 gallons of water! The task so eagerly undertaken by Rebecca of drawing such large quantities of water for a stranger's camels was indeed not a token gesture.

21. *Astonished at her.* I.e., he was מִשְׁתָּאֵה, *astonished* [over the immediate fulfillment of his prayer which surpassed all his expectations (R' Hirsch)] . . . and was *wondering* about her, i.e., whether she was of his family (*Rashi*).

23. *Da'as Sofrim* notes that, even before receiving an answer about her family, Eliezer asks if he can lodge with them. Apparently he wished to enjoy the hospitality of this generous family, even if it was not related to Abraham.

27. *Blessed be HASHEM, God of my master Abraham.* Abraham was the first to proclaim Him; therefore He is described as *Abraham's God* (*Haamek Davar*).

As for me. Although I am but Abraham's *servant*, far away from him and his land, nevertheless, God has guided me and brought me directly to my destination (*Da'as Sofrim*).

28. *And told her mother's household.* The women had separate houses where they did their work, and a daughter, of course, confides only in her mother (*Rashi*).

the wife of Nachor, brother of Abraham — with her jug upon her shoulder. [16] Now the maiden was very fair to look upon; a virgin whom no man had known. She descended to the spring, filled her jug and ascended.

[17] The servant ran toward her and said, 'Let me sip, if you please, a little water from your jug.' [18] She said, 'Drink, my lord,' and quickly she lowered her jug to her hand and gave him drink. [19] When she finished giving him drink, she said, 'I will draw water even for your camels until they have finished drinking.' [20] So she hurried and emptied her jug into the trough and kept running to the well to draw water; and she drew for all his camels.

[21] The man was astonished at her, reflecting silent to learn whether HASHEM had made his journey successful or not.

[22] And it was, when the camels had finished drinking, the man took a golden nose ring, its weight was a beka, and two bracelets on her arms, then gold shekels was their weight. [23] And he said, 'Whose daughter are you? — pray tell me. Is there room in your father's house for us to spend the night?' [24] She said to him, 'I am the daughter of Bethuel the son of Milcah whom she bore to Nachor.'

[25] And she said to him, 'Even straw and feed is plentiful with us as well as place to lodge.'

[26] So the man bowed low and prostrated himself to HASHEM [27] and said, 'Blessed be HASHEM, God of my master Abraham, who has not withheld His kindness and truth from my master. As for me, HASHEM has guided me on the way to the house of my master's brothers.'

[28] The maiden ran and told her mother's household according to these events.

וּלְרִבְקָה אָח וּשְׁמוֹ לָבָן וַיָּ֥רָץ לָבָ֛ן אֶל־
הָאִ֖ישׁ הַח֑וּצָה אֶל־הָעָֽיִן: ל וַיְהִ֣י | כִּרְאֹ֣ת
אֶת־הַנֶּ֗זֶם וְאֶת־הַצְּמִדִים֙ עַל־יְדֵ֣י אֲחֹת֔וֹ
וּכְשָׁמְע֗וֹ אֶת־דִּבְרֵ֞י רִבְקָ֤ה אֲחֹתוֹ֙ לֵאמֹ֔ר
כֹּֽה־דִבֶּ֥ר אֵלַ֖י הָאִ֑ישׁ וַיָּבֹא֙ אֶל־הָאִ֔ישׁ וְהִנֵּ֛ה
עֹמֵ֥ד עַל־הַגְּמַלִּ֖ים עַל־הָעָֽיִן: לא וַיֹּ֕אמֶר בּ֖וֹא
בְּר֣וּךְ יְהֹוָ֑ה לָ֤מָּה תַעֲמֹד֙ בַּח֔וּץ וְאָנֹכִי֙ פִּנִּ֣יתִי
הַבַּ֔יִת וּמָק֖וֹם לַגְּמַלִּֽים: לב וַיָּבֹ֤א הָאִישׁ֙ הַבַּ֔יְתָה
וַיְפַתַּ֖ח הַגְּמַלִּ֑ים וַיִּתֵּ֨ן תֶּ֤בֶן וּמִסְפּוֹא֙ לַגְּמַלִּ֔ים
וּמַ֙יִם֙ לִרְחֹ֣ץ רַגְלָ֔יו וְרַגְלֵ֥י הָאֲנָשִׁ֖ים אֲשֶׁ֥ר אִתּֽוֹ:
לג וַיּוּשַׂ֤ם °לְפָנָיו֙ לֶאֱכֹ֔ל וַיֹּ֙אמֶר֙ לֹ֣א אֹכַ֔ל עַ֥ד
אִם־דִּבַּ֖רְתִּי דְּבָרָ֑י וַיֹּ֖אמֶר דַּבֵּֽר: לד וַיֹּאמַ֑ר עֶ֥בֶד
אַבְרָהָ֖ם אָנֹֽכִי: לה וַֽיהֹוָ֞ה בֵּרַ֧ךְ אֶת־אֲדֹנִ֛י מְאֹ֖ד
וַיִּגְדָּ֑ל וַיִּתֶּן־ל֞וֹ צֹ֤אן וּבָקָר֙ וְכֶ֣סֶף וְזָהָ֔ב וַעֲבָדִם֙
וּשְׁפָחֹ֔ת וּגְמַלִּ֖ים וַחֲמֹרִֽים: לו וַתֵּ֡לֶד שָׂרָה֩
אֵ֨שֶׁת אֲדֹנִ֥י בֵן֙ לַֽאדֹנִ֔י אַחֲרֵ֖י זִקְנָתָ֑הּ וַיִּתֶּן־ל֖וֹ
אֶת־כָּל־אֲשֶׁר־לֽוֹ: לז וַיַּשְׁבִּעֵ֥נִי אֲדֹנִ֖י לֵאמֹ֑ר
לֹֽא־תִקַּ֤ח אִשָּׁה֙ לִבְנִ֔י מִבְּנוֹת֙ הַֽכְּנַעֲנִ֔י אֲשֶׁ֥ר
אָנֹכִ֖י יֹשֵׁ֥ב בְּאַרְצֽוֹ: לח אִם־לֹ֧א אֶל־בֵּֽית־אָבִ֛י
תֵּלֵ֖ךְ וְאֶל־מִשְׁפַּחְתִּ֑י וְלָקַחְתָּ֥ אִשָּׁ֖ה לִבְנִֽי:
לט וָאֹמַ֖ר אֶל־אֲדֹנִ֑י אֻלַ֛י לֹא־תֵלֵ֥ךְ הָֽאִשָּׁ֖ה
אַֽחֲרָֽי: מ וַיֹּ֖אמֶר אֵלָ֑י יְהֹוָ֞ה אֲשֶׁר־הִתְהַלַּ֣כְתִּי
לְפָנָ֗יו יִשְׁלַ֨ח מַלְאָכ֤וֹ אִתָּךְ֙ וְהִצְלִ֣יחַ דַּרְכֶּ֔ךָ
וְלָקַחְתָּ֤ אִשָּׁה֙ לִבְנִ֔י מִמִּשְׁפַּחְתִּ֖י וּמִבֵּ֥ית אָבִֽי:
מא אָ֤ז תִּנָּקֶה֙ מֵאָ֣לָתִ֔י כִּ֥י תָב֖וֹא אֶל־מִשְׁפַּחְתִּ֑י
°וַיּוּשַׂם ק'

29. **Laban.** From the profound influence Laban exercised in his household it would appear that he was either the *only* son or the oldest (*R' Hoffmann*).

Rashi, following the Midrashic perspective, views Laban's every action in the most sinister light as motivated by greed — thus anticipating the character of Laban as it reveals itself later in his relations with Jacob. *Ramban,* however, interpreting Laban's character strictly on the basis of the simple sense of the Biblical narrative, views him here as *basically* straightforward and honorable.

30. *Upon his hearing his sister Rebecca's words . . .* that the stranger was the servant of Abraham [v. 27], Laban assumed that he surely had gifts for Abraham's family. If Eliezer had given Rebecca such extravagant gifts, Laban could only imagine what lay in store for him!

31. *Come, O blessed of* HASHEM. I.e., blessed with wealth, as I can see (*Radak*).

32. *Unmuzzled the camels.* The camels had been muzzled so that they would not graze in other people's fields (*Rashi; Midrash*).

33. *Until I have spoken my piece.* Eliezer still had a doubt: Perhaps the girl would not consent to follow him to Canaan. He resolved that he would not eat until the matter was settled beyond a doubt (*Rashbam; Tzror HaMor; Malbim*).

34-39. The recapitulation.

Radak emphasizes that Eliezer repeated the whole story in order to convince them that God willed this marriage, thus delicately suggesting that their refusal would not hinder it.

The Torah records Eliezer's entire recapitulation. The Sages exclaimed: יָפָה שִׂיחָתָן שֶׁל עַבְדֵי אֲבוֹת לִפְנֵי הַמָּקוֹם מִתּוֹרָתָן שֶׁל בְּנֵיהֶם, *The ordinary conversation of the Patriarchs' servants is more pleasing before God than even the religious discourses of their children*, for the account of his journey is repeated in the Torah, whereas many important principles are derived only from textual allusions. From Eliezer's subtle changes in recounting the episode, the expositors have perceived great ethical messages revealing his wisdom.

35. With feeling and enthusiasm, Eliezer tells his hosts about Abraham's miracle-filled life. His words are a glorious summary of Abraham's life and accomplishments (*Da'as Sofrim*).

37. I am here only because my master made me take such an oath. There is no shortage of women in my country, but my master rejects them (*Radak; Sforno*).

39. *Rashi* notes that אוּלַי, *perhaps*, is spelled אֻלַי, which could be read as אֵלַי, *to me*. Eliezer was anxious to marry off his own daughter to Isaac, thus the spelling hints that he made this suggestion to Abraham [as if to say I hope that לֹא תֵלֵךְ הָאִשָּׁה אַחֲרָי, *the woman* (I select in Charan) *will not want to follow me*]. But Abraham answered: 'My son is blessed [22:18] and you are accursed [9:25]; the accursed cannot unite with the blessed.'

41. Eliezer did not use Abraham's term שְׁבוּעָה for *oath*, [see v. 8] but substituted the stronger term אָלָה which signifies an *oath reinforced by a curse*, to impress them with the seriousness of Abraham's intention (*Ibn Ezra*).

²⁹ Rebecca had a brother whose name was Laban. Laban ran to the man, outside to the spring. ³⁰For upon seeing the nose ring and bracelets on his sister's arm, and upon his hearing his sister Rebecca's words, saying, 'Thus has the man spoken to me,' he approached the man, who was still standing by the camels by the spring, ³¹ and said, 'Come, O blessed of HASHEM! Why should you stand outside when I have cleared the house, and place for the camels?'

³² So the man entered the house, and unmuzzled the camels. He gave straw and feed for the camels, and water to bathe his feet and the feet of the men who were with him. ³³ Food was set before him, but he said, 'I will not eat until I have spoken my piece.'

And he said, 'Speak.'

³⁴ Then he said, 'A servant of Abraham am I. ³⁵ HASHEM has greatly blessed my master, and he prospered. He has given him sheep, cattle, silver and gold, servants and maidservants, camels and donkeys. ³⁶ Sarah, my master's wife, bore my master a son after she had grown old, and he gave him all that he possesses. ³⁷ And my master made me take an oath saying, "Do not take a wife for my son from the daughters of the Canaanites in whose land I dwell. ³⁸ Unless you go to my father's house and to my family and take a wife for my son." ³⁹ And I said to my master, "Perhaps the woman will not follow me?" ⁴⁰ He replied to me, "HASHEM, before Whom I have walked, will send His angel with you and make your journey successful, and you will take a wife for my son from my family and my father's house. ⁴¹ Then will you be absolved from my oath when you have come to my family;

מב וְאָבֹא הַיּוֹם אֶל־הָעָיִן וָאֹמַר יהוה אֱלֹהֵי אֲדֹנִי אַבְרָהָם אִם־יֶשְׁךָ־נָּא מַצְלִיחַ דַּרְכִּי אֲשֶׁר אָנֹכִי הֹלֵךְ עָלֶיהָ: מג הִנֵּה אָנֹכִי נִצָּב עַל־עֵין הַמָּיִם וְהָיָה הָעַלְמָה הַיֹּצֵאת לִשְׁאֹב וְאָמַרְתִּי אֵלֶיהָ הַשְׁקִינִי־נָא מְעַט־מַיִם מִכַּדֵּךְ: מד וְאָמְרָה אֵלַי גַּם־אַתָּה שְׁתֵה וְגַם לִגְמַלֶּיךָ אֶשְׁאָב הִוא הָאִשָּׁה אֲשֶׁר־הֹכִיחַ יהוה לְבֶן־אֲדֹנִי: מה אֲנִי טֶרֶם אֲכַלֶּה לְדַבֵּר אֶל־לִבִּי וְהִנֵּה רִבְקָה יֹצֵאת וְכַדָּהּ עַל־שִׁכְמָהּ וַתֵּרֶד הָעַיְנָה וַתִּשְׁאָב וָאֹמַר אֵלֶיהָ הַשְׁקִינִי נָא: מו וַתְּמַהֵר וַתּוֹרֶד כַּדָּהּ מֵעָלֶיהָ וַתֹּאמֶר שְׁתֵה וְגַם־גְּמַלֶּיךָ אַשְׁקֶה וָאֵשְׁתְּ וְגַם הַגְּמַלִּים הִשְׁקָתָה: מז וָאֶשְׁאַל אֹתָהּ וָאֹמַר בַּת־מִי אַתְּ וַתֹּאמֶר בַּת־בְּתוּאֵל בֶּן־נָחוֹר אֲשֶׁר יָלְדָה־לּוֹ מִלְכָּה וָאָשִׂם הַנֶּזֶם עַל־אַפָּהּ וְהַצְּמִידִים עַל־יָדֶיהָ: מח וָאֶקֹּד וָאֶשְׁתַּחֲוֶה לַיהוה וָאֲבָרֵךְ אֶת־יהוה אֱלֹהֵי אֲדֹנִי אַבְרָהָם אֲשֶׁר הִנְחַנִי בְּדֶרֶךְ אֱמֶת לָקַחַת אֶת־בַּת־אֲחִי אֲדֹנִי לִבְנוֹ: מט וְעַתָּה אִם־יֶשְׁכֶם עֹשִׂים חֶסֶד וֶאֱמֶת אֶת־אֲדֹנִי הַגִּידוּ לִי וְאִם־לֹא הַגִּידוּ לִי וְאֶפְנֶה עַל־יָמִין אוֹ עַל־שְׂמֹאל: נ וַיַּעַן לָבָן וּבְתוּאֵל וַיֹּאמְרוּ מֵיהוה יָצָא הַדָּבָר לֹא נוּכַל דַּבֵּר אֵלֶיךָ רַע אוֹ־טוֹב: נא הִנֵּה־רִבְקָה לְפָנֶיךָ קַח וָלֵךְ וּתְהִי אִשָּׁה לְבֶן־אֲדֹנֶיךָ כַּאֲשֶׁר דִּבֶּר יהוה:

43. In v. 16 Eliezer used the word נַעֲרָ, *maiden*. Here he tactfully said עַלְמָה which denotes *a young woman in the vigor of her youth,* and carries a more discerning connotation than *maiden*, implying that he was being selective. Furthermore, that such a person would come to the well would be indicative of Divine Providence, since the more distinguished עֲלָמוֹת, *young women,* ordinarily left the menial task of drawing water to others (*Malbim*).

48. *And [I] blessed HASHEM, God of my master Abraham.* Thus Eliezer intimated that she was indeed the woman whom Hashem had designated, and that he is merely seeking their consent to conclude the matter. He further wished to impress this upon them by saying that he *blessed Hashem;* had there been any doubt, such a blessing would have been premature (*Haamek Davar*).

49. חֶסֶד, *kindness*, denotes an action which one is not obligated to do, while אֱמֶת, *truth*, means to *fulfill* the promise of *kindness* (*Ibn Ezra*).

According to *Sforno*: If you will do my master the *kindness* of yielding to his wishes, in sending your daughter so far away, and simultaneously *do truth*, by having *her* true interest in mind . . .

50. The matter stems from Hashem! There is no better evidence of Eliezer's success in having sensitively and discreetly carried out his mission than the response his persuasive eloquence elicits: '*The matter stems from HASHEM!*'

Then Laban and Bethuel answered. Laban was a wicked person and, in his great impudence, he hastened to answer before his father (*Rashi*). *Radak* suggests that Laban ran the household because Bethuel was infirm. Therefore, Laban spoke first.

מַה יָּצָא הַדָּבָר — *The matter stems from HASHEM.* Everything, as you say, has been preordained from Above.

and if they will not give her to you, then, you shall be absolved from my oath."

⁴² 'I came today to the spring and said, "HASHEM God of my master Abraham. If You would graciously make successful the way on which I go — ⁴³ Behold, I am standing by the spring of water. Let it be that the young woman who comes out to draw and to whom I shall say, 'Please give me some water to drink from your jug,' ⁴⁴ and who will answer, 'You may also drink and I will draw water for your camels, too,' — she shall be the woman whom HASHEM has designated for my master's son."

⁴⁵ 'I had not yet finished meditating when suddenly Rebecca came out with a jug on her shoulder, and descended to the spring and drew water. Then I said to her, "Please give me a drink." ⁴⁶ She hurried and lowered her jug from her shoulder and said, "Drink, and I will even water your camels." So I drank and she watered the camels also. ⁴⁷ Then I questioned her and said, "Whose daughter are you?" And she said, "The daughter of Bethuel, son of Nachor, whom Milcah bore to him." And I placed the ring on her nose and the bracelets on her arms. ⁴⁸ Then I bowed and prostrated myself to HASHEM and blessed HASHEM, God of my master Abraham, Who led me on a true path to take the daughter of my master's brother for his son.

⁴⁹ 'And now, if you intend to do kindness and truth with my master, tell me; and if not, tell me, and I will turn to the right or to the left.'

⁵⁰ Then Laban and Bethuel answered, 'The matter stems from HASHEM! We can say to you neither bad nor good. ⁵¹ Here, Rebecca is before you; take her and go, and let her be a wife to your master's son as HASHEM has spoken.'

נב וַיְהִ֗י כַּאֲשֶׁ֤ר שָׁמַע֙ עֶ֣בֶד אַבְרָהָ֔ם אֶת־
דִּבְרֵיהֶ֑ם וַיִּשְׁתַּ֥חוּ אַ֖רְצָה לַיהֹוָֽה: חמישי נג וַיּוֹצֵ֨א
הָעֶ֜בֶד כְּלֵי־כֶ֣סֶף וּכְלֵ֤י זָהָב֙ וּבְגָדִ֔ים וַיִּתֵּ֖ן
לְרִבְקָ֑ה וּמִ֨גְדָּנֹ֔ת נָתַ֥ן לְאָחִ֖יהָ וּלְאִמָּֽהּ:
נד וַיֹּֽאכְל֣וּ וַיִּשְׁתּ֗וּ ה֛וּא וְהָאֲנָשִׁ֥ים אֲשֶׁר־עִמּ֖וֹ
וַיָּלִ֑ינוּ וַיָּק֣וּמוּ בַבֹּ֔קֶר וַיֹּ֖אמֶר שַׁלְּחֻ֥נִי לַֽאדֹנִֽי:
נה וַיֹּ֤אמֶר אָחִ֨יהָ֙ וְאִמָּ֔הּ תֵּשֵׁ֨ב הַנַּֽעֲרָ֥ אִתָּ֛נוּ
יָמִ֖ים א֣וֹ עָשׂ֑וֹר אַחַ֖ר תֵּלֵֽךְ: נו וַיֹּ֤אמֶר אֲלֵהֶם֙
אַל־תְּאַחֲר֣וּ אֹתִ֔י וַֽיהֹוָ֖ה הִצְלִ֣יחַ דַּרְכִּ֑י
שַׁלְּח֕וּנִי וְאֵֽלְכָ֖ה לַֽאדֹנִֽי: נז וַיֹּֽאמְר֖וּ נִקְרָ֣א
לַנַּֽעֲרָ֑ וְנִשְׁאֲלָ֖ה אֶת־פִּֽיהָ: נח וַיִּקְרְא֤וּ לְרִבְקָה֙
וַיֹּֽאמְר֣וּ אֵלֶ֔יהָ הֲתֵֽלְכִ֖י עִם־הָאִ֣ישׁ הַזֶּ֑ה
וַתֹּ֖אמֶר אֵלֵֽךְ: נט וַֽיְשַׁלְּח֛וּ אֶת־רִבְקָ֥ה אֲחֹתָ֖ם
וְאֶת־מֵֽנִקְתָּ֑הּ וְאֶת־עֶ֥בֶד אַבְרָהָ֖ם וְאֶת־אֲנָשָֽׁיו:
ס וַיְבָֽרְכ֤וּ אֶת־רִבְקָה֙ וַיֹּ֣אמְרוּ לָ֔הּ אֲחֹתֵ֕נוּ אַ֖תְּ
הֲיִ֣י לְאַלְפֵ֣י רְבָבָ֑ה וְיִירַ֣שׁ זַרְעֵ֔ךְ אֵ֖ת שַׁ֥עַר
שֹֽׂנְאָֽיו: סא וַתָּ֨קָם רִבְקָ֜ה וְנַֽעֲרֹתֶ֗יהָ וַתִּרְכַּ֨בְנָה֙
עַל־הַגְּמַלִּ֔ים וַתֵּלַ֖כְנָה אַֽחֲרֵ֣י הָאִ֑ישׁ וַיִּקַּ֥ח
הָעֶ֛בֶד אֶת־רִבְקָ֖ה וַיֵּלַֽךְ: סב וְיִצְחָק֙ בָּ֣א מִבּ֔וֹא
בְּאֵ֥ר לַחַ֖י רֹאִ֑י וְה֥וּא יוֹשֵׁ֖ב בְּאֶ֥רֶץ הַנֶּֽגֶב:
סג וַיֵּצֵ֥א יִצְחָ֛ק לָשׂ֥וּחַ בַּשָּׂדֶ֖ה לִפְנ֣וֹת עָ֑רֶב
וַיִּשָּׂ֤א עֵינָיו֙ וַיַּ֔רְא וְהִנֵּ֥ה גְמַלִּ֖ים בָּאִֽים:
סד וַתִּשָּׂ֤א רִבְקָה֙ אֶת־עֵינֶ֔יהָ וַתֵּ֖רֶא אֶת־יִצְחָ֑ק
וַתִּפֹּ֖ל מֵעַ֥ל הַגָּמָֽל: סה וַתֹּ֣אמֶר אֶל־הָעֶ֗בֶד
מִֽי־הָאִ֤ישׁ הַלָּזֶה֙ הַֽהֹלֵ֤ךְ בַּשָּׂדֶה֙ לִקְרָאתֵ֔נוּ

53. וַיִּתֵּ֖ן לְרִבְקָ֑ה — *And gave them to Rebecca.* For the purpose of betrothal [לְשֵׁם קִדּוּשִׁין] to Isaac. The *first presents* at the well were only gifts, since one does not betroth without arranging for consent; that having been done, Eliezer acted as Isaac's agent to betroth her.

55. *Her brother and mother said.* Where was her father? He reconsidered and wished to prevent the marriage; and therefore an angel killed him (*Midrash; Rashi*).

56. Since everything has gone so smoothly and God guided my mission so speedily, it is obvious that He wishes me to return to my master without delay (*Abarbanel*).

57. *And ask her personally.* From this we learn that a woman may be given in marriage only by her consent [*Kiddushin* 11a] (*Rashi*).

59. Whether, as *Rashi* would interpret, they gave permission reluctantly to avoid her threatened defiance, or as *Radak* and *Rambam* interpret, they graciously acquiesced to her wishes, once Rebecca expressed her intention, they no longer hindered her. Immediately, they arranged a procession and blessed her.

And her nurse. For according to the most common Rabbinic chronology, Rebecca was but three years old at the time.

60. *May you come to be thousands of myriads.* May you and your offspring be the recipients of the blessing given to Abraham on Mt. Moriah [22:17]: *I will greatly increase your offspring.* May it be His will that these offspring descend from *you*, as Isaac's wife, and not from another woman (*Rashi*).

61. *[They] proceeded after the man.* Because it is improper for a man to walk behind a woman [lest it lead to impure thoughts] (*Berachos* 61a).

62. Isaac meets his bride. The Torah narrates that Isaac 'happened' to meet them on the road before they entered the city, just as Eliezer's encounter with Rebecca at the well, etc., occurred by what seemed to be 'chance.' In reality it was a result of God's Providential Will (*Radak*).

According to *Rashi*, following the Midrash, Isaac had gone to *Be'er Lachai Ro'i* to bring Hagar back as a wife for Abraham. [This follows the tradition that Keturah (25:1) was Hagar.]

The well of Lachai Ro'i. Isaac went there to pray at the propitious site where Hagar's prayers had once been answered. Even *before* he prayed, his needs were answered, and his bride was already approaching Charan, in the manner of [*Isaiah* 65:24] טֶרֶם יִקְרָאוּ וַאֲנִי אֶעֱנֶה, *before they call I will answer* (*Sforno*).

63. The Talmud (*Berachos* 26b) and Midrash derive from this verse the tradition that Isaac instituted the *Minchah* [afternoon] prayer. That Abraham instituted the *Shacharis* [morning] prayer is derived from 19:27; and that Jacob instituted the *Arvis* [evening] prayer is derived from 28:11.

64. Rebecca realized that Isaac was approaching either to greet them or offer them lodging. As was proper for a woman, she alighted from the camel and stood modestly. [Then, as he was approaching them, she inquired *exactly* who he was, and upon hearing that he was Isaac, she veiled herself (*Ramban*).]

⁵² And it was, when Abraham's servant heard their words, he prostrated himself to the ground unto HASHEM. ⁵³ The servant brought out objects of silver and gold, and garments, and gave them to Rebecca. And delicious fruits he gave to her brother and mother. ⁵⁴ They ate and drank, he and the men who were with him, and they spent the night. When they arose next morning, he said, 'Send me to my master.'

⁵⁵ Her brother and mother said, 'Let the maiden remain with us a year or ten [months]; then she will go.'

⁵⁶ He said to them, 'Do not delay me now that HASHEM has made my journey successful. Send me, and I will go to my master.' ⁵⁷ And they said, 'Let us call the maiden and ask her personally.'

⁵⁸ They called Rebecca and said to her, 'Will you go with this man?'

And she said, 'I will go.'

⁵⁹ So they escorted Rebecca their sister, and her nurse, as well as Abraham's servant and his men. ⁶⁰ They blessed Rebecca and said to her,

'Our sister,

may you come to be thousands of myriads,

and may your offspring inherit

the gate of its foes.'

⁶¹ Then Rebecca arose with her maidens. They rode upon the camels and proceeded after the man. The servant took Rebecca and went.

⁶² Now Isaac came from having gone to the well of Lachai Ro'i, for he dwelt in the south country. ⁶³ Isaac went out to supplicate in the field toward evening and he raised his eyes and saw — Behold! Camels were coming. ⁶⁴ And Rebecca raised her eyes and saw Isaac. She inclined while upon the camel, ⁶⁵ and said to the servant, 'Who is that man walking in the field toward us?'

וַיֹּאמֶר הָעֶבֶד הוּא אֲדֹנִי וַתִּקַּח הַצָּעִיף
וַתִּתְכָּס: סו וַיְסַפֵּר הָעֶבֶד לְיִצְחָק אֵת כָּל־
הַדְּבָרִים אֲשֶׁר עָשָׂה: סז וַיְבִאֶהָ יִצְחָק הָאֹהֱלָה
שָׂרָה אִמּוֹ וַיִּקַּח אֶת־רִבְקָה וַתְּהִי־לוֹ לְאִשָּׁה
וַיֶּאֱהָבֶהָ וַיִּנָּחֵם יִצְחָק אַחֲרֵי אִמּוֹ:

כה א שני וַיֹּסֶף אַבְרָהָם וַיִּקַּח אִשָּׁה וּשְׁמָהּ
קְטוּרָה: ב וַתֵּלֶד לוֹ אֶת־זִמְרָן וְאֶת־יָקְשָׁן
וְאֶת־מְדָן וְאֶת־מִדְיָן וְאֶת־יִשְׁבָּק וְאֶת־שׁוּחַ:
ג וְיָקְשָׁן יָלַד אֶת־שְׁבָא וְאֶת־דְּדָן וּבְנֵי דְדָן הָיוּ
אַשּׁוּרִם וּלְטוּשִׁם וּלְאֻמִּים: ד וּבְנֵי מִדְיָן עֵיפָה
וָעֵפֶר וַחֲנֹךְ וַאֲבִידָע וְאֶלְדָּעָה כָּל־אֵלֶּה בְּנֵי
קְטוּרָה: ה וַיִּתֵּן אַבְרָהָם אֶת־כָּל־אֲשֶׁר־לוֹ
לְיִצְחָק: ו וְלִבְנֵי הַפִּילַגְשִׁים אֲשֶׁר לְאַבְרָהָם
נָתַן אַבְרָהָם מַתָּנֹת וַיְשַׁלְּחֵם מֵעַל יִצְחָק בְּנוֹ
בְּעוֹדֶנּוּ חַי קֵדְמָה אֶל־אֶרֶץ קֶדֶם: ז וְאֵלֶּה יְמֵי
שְׁנֵי־חַיֵּי אַבְרָהָם אֲשֶׁר־חָי מְאַת שָׁנָה
וְשִׁבְעִים שָׁנָה וְחָמֵשׁ שָׁנִים: ח וַיִּגְוַע וַיָּמָת
אַבְרָהָם בְּשֵׂיבָה טוֹבָה זָקֵן וְשָׂבֵעַ וַיֵּאָסֶף
אֶל־עַמָּיו: ט וַיִּקְבְּרוּ אֹתוֹ יִצְחָק וְיִשְׁמָעֵאל
בָּנָיו אֶל־מְעָרַת הַמַּכְפֵּלָה אֶל־שְׂדֵה עֶפְרֹן
בֶּן־צֹחַר הַחִתִּי אֲשֶׁר עַל־פְּנֵי מַמְרֵא: י הַשָּׂדֶה
אֲשֶׁר־קָנָה אַבְרָהָם מֵאֵת בְּנֵי־חֵת שָׁמָּה קֻבַּר
אַבְרָהָם וְשָׂרָה אִשְׁתּוֹ: יא וַיְהִי אַחֲרֵי מוֹת
אַבְרָהָם וַיְבָרֶךְ אֱלֹהִים אֶת־יִצְחָק בְּנוֹ וַיֵּשֶׁב
יִצְחָק עִם־בְּאֵר לַחַי רֹאִי:

67. First he brought her into Sarah's tent. When he observed that her actions were like those of Sarah, he married her (*Malbim*).

As long as Sarah was alive, a lamp burned in her tent from one Sabbath eve to the next, her dough was blessed, and a cloud [signifying the Divine Presence; see *Exodus* 40:34] hung over her tent. When Sarah died, these ceased, but when Rebecca entered the tent they resumed (*Rashi*).

Thus was Isaac consoled after his mother. He found consolation only through his love for his wife. This love was inspired by her righteousness and aptness of deeds, the only criteria upon which the Torah bases the love between husband and wife (*Ramban*).

Keturah is Hagar who received this name because her deeds were as beautiful as incense [*ketores*]; also because she remained chaste from the time she had separated from Abraham (*Midrash; Rashi*).

2. *She bore him.* Although Abraham was by now much older than he was at the birth of Isaac, this is not considered a new miracle. His aged body had already been reinvigorated in order to make possible the birth of Isaac. God merely allowed him to retain that capacity (*Haamek Davar*).

3. The names Sheba and Dedan appear also above (10:7), as the descendants of Raamah son of Cush.

5. *Abraham gave all that he had to Isaac.* Since Isaac was his primary son, Abraham distinguished him from his other children by giving him physical and spiritual possessions (*Malbim*).

6. פִּילַגְשִׁם refers to Hagar/Keturah (*Midrash*).

Who were Abraham's. This attests to the fact that, however hidden, they carried a spark of Abraham in their souls (*Zohar Chadash*).

From the fact that Ishmael participated in Abraham's burial [v. 9], it is apparent that he had not been sent away permanently as were the other concubine-children (*Malbim*).

Eastward, to the east country. Charan in Aram Naharaim and Ur Kasdim, where Abraham's kin lived (*Radak*).

7. The death of Abraham.

Which he lived. I.e., which he had lived *fully;* not one day of his life was wasted.

Abraham lived until his grandson Jacob was fifteen years old. Accordingly, his death took place *after* the events of the coming chapters; but in accordance with the Torah's usual method of narration (as *Ramban* explains in 11:32), it bids farewell, so to speak, to Abraham when there is nothing further of his life that it must recount.

At a hundred he was like seventy and at seventy like five — without sin (*Rashi*).

8. *Abraham expired and died.* The year was 2123 from creation (*Seder Olam*).

At a good old age, mature and content. As God had promised (15:15), the prophesied affliction of his descendants would not begin in his lifetime (*Rashbam*).

9. *His sons Isaac and Ishmael buried him.* Although Ishmael was older, Isaac is mentioned first. We infer from this that Ishmael repented and gave precedence to Isaac (*Rashi*).

11. *That* [lit., *and*] ***God blessed Isaac his son.*** By *bless* is meant that He comforted him in his mourning.

And the servant said, 'He is my master.' She then took the veil and covered herself. ^{66} The servant told Isaac all the things he had done. ^{67} And Isaac brought her into the tent of Sarah his mother. He married Rebecca, she became his wife, and he loved her. And thus was Isaac consoled after his mother.

25 ^{1} **A**braham proceeded and took a wife whose name was Keturah. ^{2} She bore him Zimran, Yakshan, Medan, Midian, Ishbak and Shuah. ^{3} Yakshan begot Sheba and Dedan, and the children of Dedan were Ashurim, Letushim, and Leumim. ^{4} And the children of Midian: Ephah [and] Epher, Chanoch, Abida, and Eldaah. All these were the descendants of Keturah.

^{5} Abraham gave all that he had to Isaac. ^{6} But to the concubine-children who were Abraham's, Abraham gave gifts. Then he sent them away from Isaac his son, while he was still alive — eastward, to the east country.

^{7} Now these are the days of the years of Abraham's life which he lived: a hundred and seventy-five years. ^{8} And Abraham expired and died at a good old age, mature and content, and he was gathered to his people. ^{9} His sons Isaac and Ishmael buried him in the cave of Machpelah, in the field of Ephron the son of Zohar the Hittite, facing Mamre. ^{10} The field that Abraham had bought from the children of Heth — there was Abraham buried, and Sarah his wife. ^{11} And it was after the death of Abraham that God blessed Isaac his son, and Isaac settled near Be'er Lachai R'oi.

שביעי יב וְאֵ֣לֶּה תֹּלְדֹ֛ת יִשְׁמָעֵ֖אל בֶּן־אַבְרָהָ֑ם אֲשֶׁ֨ר יָלְדָ֜ה הָגָ֧ר הַמִּצְרִ֛ית שִׁפְחַ֥ת שָׂרָ֖ה לְאַבְרָהָֽם: יג וְאֵ֗לֶּה שְׁמוֹת֙ בְּנֵ֣י יִשְׁמָעֵ֔אל בִּשְׁמֹתָ֖ם לְתוֹלְדֹתָ֑ם בְּכֹ֤ר יִשְׁמָעֵאל֙ נְבָיֹ֔ת וְקֵדָ֥ר וְאַדְבְּאֵ֖ל וּמִבְשָֽׂם: יד וּמִשְׁמָ֥ע וְדוּמָ֖ה וּמַשָּֽׂא: טו חֲדַ֣ד וְתֵימָ֔א יְט֥וּר נָפִ֖ישׁ וָקֵֽדְמָה: מפטיר טז אֵ֣לֶּה הֵ֞ם בְּנֵ֤י יִשְׁמָעֵאל֙ וְאֵ֣לֶּה שְׁמֹתָ֔ם בְּחַצְרֵיהֶ֖ם וּבְטִ֣ירֹתָ֑ם שְׁנֵים־עָשָׂ֥ר נְשִׂיאִ֖ם לְאֻמֹּתָֽם: יז וְאֵ֗לֶּה שְׁנֵי֙ חַיֵּ֣י יִשְׁמָעֵ֔אל מְאַ֥ת שָׁנָ֛ה וּשְׁלֹשִׁ֥ים שָׁנָ֖ה וְשֶׁ֣בַע שָׁנִ֑ים וַיִּגְוַ֣ע וַיָּ֔מָת וַיֵּאָ֖סֶף אֶל־עַמָּֽיו: יח וַיִּשְׁכְּנ֨וּ מֵֽחֲוִילָ֜ה עַד־שׁ֗וּר אֲשֶׁר֙ עַל־פְּנֵ֣י מִצְרַ֔יִם בֹּאֲכָ֖ה אַשּׁ֑וּרָה עַל־פְּנֵ֥י כָל־אֶחָ֖יו נָפָֽל:

The *Haftarah* for *Chayei Sarah* appears on page 312

12. Ishmael's Genealogy.

In the simple sense, Ishmael's descendants are enumerated in deference to Abraham (*Radak*), [hence the appellation: *Abraham's son,*] and to inform us that the seed of the righteous shall be blessed.

It is emphasized that Abraham regarded him as his son in every sense of the word; it was only in relation to Sarah and her son that Ishmael was considered the son of the maidservant (*Haamek Davar*).

13. *Nebayoth*, the firstborn, and *Kedar*, the second son, are the most important of the Ishmaelite tribes. They are mentioned together in *Isaiah* 60:7. One of Esau's wives was Mahalath, the sister of Nebayoth [28:9].

16. *These are the sons of Ishmael.* As is customary in Scripture, the subject is closed with a general statement summing up the matter; the closing summary also being used as a means of further clarification (*Radak*).

And these are their names by their open cities and by their strongholds [i.e., fortified cities (*Radak*). Whether they took up residence in open cities [denoting, according to *R' Hoffmann*, the circular *encampments* of nomadic tribes] or in *encampments,* they lived in security and honor. All those bearing these tribal names, regardless of where they lived, were descendants of Ishmael (cf. *Radak*).

17. Ishmael's age is given because it assists in calculations with respect to [dating the various events which occurred in the life of] Jacob (*Rashi* [*Yevamos* 64a]).

18. The essential meaning of this passage is the fulfillment of the promise to Hagar in 16:12: *over all his brothers he shall dwell.* As *Rashi* explains there, the blessing meant that Ishmael's descendants would be so numerous that they would have to expand beyond their own borders into those of their brothers.

According to the Masoretic note appearing at the end of the *Sidrah,* there are 105 verses in *Chayei Sarah,* numerically corresponding to the mnemonic יְהוֹיָךְ״ע [= יָהּ יוֹדִיעַ = *Hashem* makes *known*], an allusion to God's having made His will known through Eliezer (24:14). The *Haftarah* begins with *I Kings* 1: וְהַמֶּלֶךְ דָּוִד זָקֵן.

¹² These are the descendants of Ishmael, Abraham's son, whom Hagar the Egyptian, Sarah's maidservant, bore to Abraham. ¹³ These are the names of the sons of Ishmael by their names, in order of their birth: Ishmael's firstborn Nebayoth, Kedar, Adbe'el, and Mivsam, ¹⁴ Mishma, Dumah, and Masa, ¹⁵ Hadad and Sema, Yetur, Nafish, and Kedmah. ¹⁶ These are the sons of Ishmael, and these are their names by their open cities and by their strongholds, twelve chieftains for their nations.

¹⁷ These were the years of Ishmael's life: a hundred and thirty-seven years. He expired and died, and was gathered to his people. ¹⁸ They dwelt from Chavilah to Shur — which is near Egypt — toward Assyria; over all his brothers he dwelt.

The *Haftarah* for *Chayei Sarah* appears on page 312

פרשת תולדות

TOLDOS

Rambam teaches that each of the Patriarchs maintained a yeshivah, in which he taught about the existence of God and His will. Abraham's academy had hundreds if not thousands of students — Isaac had an academy of one. His student was Jacob, whom he trained and appointed to teach others (*Hil. Avodah Zarah* 1:2-3). This gives a clue to the role of Isaac in the history of the Jewish people. On the one hand, he seems the least prominent of the Patriarchs; certainly his life takes up far less space in the Torah than do the lives of Abraham and Jacob. On the other hand, however, Isaac had the task of drawing the line between good and evil, as represented by Jacob and Esau, because the Jewish nation was taking shape, and it could not do so as a mixture of good and evil.

That is why, in contrast to Abraham whose primary characteristic was *chessed*, or kindness, Isaac's was *gevurah,* or strength. It takes strength to differentiate between what is desirable and what is anathema — and then to purge the bad and nurture the good.

Lest one think that Isaac discarded Abraham's way in favor of his own, the Torah stresses at the very beginning of the *Sidrah* that Isaac was the *son of Abraham — Abraham begot Isaac.* In the Jewish scheme of life, kindness and strength must go together; either one without the other is dangerous. Kindness not tempered by strength leads to indulgence and hedonism; strength without kindness leads to selfishness and cruelty.

יט וְאֵ֣לֶּה תּוֹלְדֹ֥ת יִצְחָ֖ק בֶּן־אַבְרָהָ֑ם אַבְרָהָ֖ם
הוֹלִ֥יד אֶת־יִצְחָֽק: כ וַיְהִ֤י יִצְחָק֙ בֶּן־אַרְבָּעִ֣ים
שָׁנָ֔ה בְּקַחְתּ֣וֹ אֶת־רִבְקָ֗ה בַּת־בְּתוּאֵל֙ הָֽאֲרַמִּ֔י
מִפַּדַּ֖ן אֲרָ֑ם אֲח֛וֹת לָבָ֥ן הָאֲרַמִּ֖י ל֥וֹ לְאִשָּֽׁה:
כא וַיֶּעְתַּ֨ר יִצְחָ֤ק לַֽיהֹוָה֙ לְנֹ֣כַח אִשְׁתּ֔וֹ כִּ֥י עֲקָרָ֖ה
הִ֑וא וַיֵּעָ֤תֶר לוֹ֙ יְהֹוָ֔ה וַתַּ֖הַר רִבְקָ֥ה אִשְׁתּֽוֹ:
כב וַיִּתְרֹֽצְצ֤וּ הַבָּנִים֙ בְּקִרְבָּ֔הּ וַתֹּ֣אמֶר אִם־כֵּ֔ן
לָ֥מָּה זֶּ֖ה אָנֹ֑כִי וַתֵּ֖לֶךְ לִדְרֹ֥שׁ אֶת־יְהֹוָֽה:
כג וַיֹּ֨אמֶר יְהֹוָ֜ה לָ֗הּ שְׁנֵ֤י °גוֹיִם֙ בְּבִטְנֵ֔ךְ וּשְׁנֵ֣י
לְאֻמִּ֔ים מִמֵּעַ֖יִךְ יִפָּרֵ֑דוּ וּלְאֹם֙ מִלְאֹ֣ם יֶֽאֱמָ֔ץ
וְרַ֖ב יַעֲבֹ֥ד צָעִֽיר: כד וַיִּמְלְא֥וּ יָמֶ֖יהָ לָלֶ֑דֶת וְהִנֵּ֥ה
תוֹמִ֖ם בְּבִטְנָֽהּ: כה וַיֵּצֵ֤א הָרִאשׁוֹן֙ אַדְמוֹנִ֔י כֻּלּ֖וֹ
כְּאַדֶּ֣רֶת שֵׂעָ֑ר וַיִּקְרְא֥וּ שְׁמ֖וֹ עֵשָֽׂו: כו וְאַֽחֲרֵי־כֵ֞ן
יָצָ֣א אָחִ֗יו וְיָד֤וֹ אֹחֶ֙זֶת֙ בַּעֲקֵ֣ב עֵשָׂ֔ו וַיִּקְרָ֥א שְׁמ֖וֹ
יַעֲקֹ֑ב וְיִצְחָ֛ק בֶּן־שִׁשִּׁ֥ים שָׁנָ֖ה בְּלֶ֥דֶת אֹתָֽם:
כז וַֽיִּגְדְּלוּ֙ הַנְּעָרִ֔ים וַיְהִ֣י עֵשָׂ֗ו אִ֛ישׁ יֹדֵ֥עַ צַ֖יִד
אִ֣ישׁ שָׂדֶ֑ה וְיַעֲקֹב֙ אִ֣ישׁ תָּ֔ם יֹשֵׁ֖ב אֹהָלִֽים:
כח וַיֶּאֱהַ֥ב יִצְחָ֛ק אֶת־עֵשָׂ֖ו כִּי־צַ֣יִד בְּפִ֑יו
וְרִבְקָ֖ה אֹהֶ֥בֶת אֶֽת־יַעֲקֹֽב: כט וַיָּ֥זֶד יַעֲקֹ֖ב נָזִ֑יד
וַיָּבֹ֥א עֵשָׂ֛ו מִן־הַשָּׂדֶ֖ה וְה֥וּא עָיֵֽף: ל וַיֹּ֨אמֶר עֵשָׂ֜ו
אֶֽל־יַעֲקֹ֗ב הַלְעִיטֵ֤נִי נָא֙ מִן־הָאָדֹ֤ם הָאָדֹם֙ הַזֶּ֔ה
כִּ֥י עָיֵ֖ף אָנֹ֑כִי עַל־כֵּ֥ן קָרָֽא־שְׁמ֖וֹ אֱדֽוֹם:
לא וַיֹּ֖אמֶר יַעֲקֹ֑ב מִכְרָ֥ה כַיּ֛וֹם אֶת־בְּכֹֽרָתְךָ֖
לִֽי: לב וַיֹּ֣אמֶר עֵשָׂ֔ו הִנֵּ֛ה אָנֹכִ֥י הוֹלֵ֖ךְ לָמ֑וּת
°גוֹיִם֙ ק'

19. Isaac's genealogy.
The cynics of that generation had been saying that
Sarah must have become
pregnant by Abimelech.
God made Isaac's features
so undeniably similar to
Abraham's that even the
scoffers had to admit that
'it, אַבְרָהָם הוֹלִיד אֶת יִצְחָק,
was indeed *Abraham who
had begotten Isaac!'*
(*Tanchuma; Rashi*).

20. Isaac was 37 years old
at the *Akeidah*, at which
time Rebecca was born. He
waited three years until she
was physically capable of
marriage (*Seder Olam*).

21. Rebecca's barrenness.
Isaac took his barren wife to
pray with her on Mount
Moriah, site of the *Akeidah*
(*Pirkei d'Rabbi Eliezer* 32).

22. Rebecca's pregnancy.
The Rabbis derive וַיִּתְרֹצֲצוּ
from the root רוּץ, *to run:*
When she passed the Torah
academy of Shem and Eber,
Jacob 'ran' and struggled to
come forth; and when she
passed an idolatrous tem-
ple, Esau 'ran' and struggled
to come forth [*Midrash*].

23. The prophecy.
The infants represent two
nations: Israel and Edom;
their struggle in the womb
symbolizes the future rival-
ries between them. In the
end the younger will pre-
vail (*R' Hoffmann*).

HASHEM conveyed it to *her*
and not to Isaac. Never having heard this prophecy, I-
saac could not imagine Esau
to be a sinner (*Chizkuni*).

24-26. The birth.
Esau's ruddiness was a portent that he would shed
blood (*Rashi*).

26. *His hand grasping on to
the heel of Esau.* Portending
that Esau's period of dominion will barely be complete,
before Jacob wrests it from
him (*Rashi*).

27. The personalities emerge.

One who knows hunting. Esau deceived his father by asking such ostensibly sincere questions as how tithes were to be taken from salt and straw [although he knew that these were not subject to tithes] (*Rashi*).

Rashbam interprets it literally as a *cunning hunter.*

But Jacob was a wholesome man. His heart and mouth were consistent with one another (*Rashi*).

28. *For game was in his [Isaac's] mouth,* i.e., Esau supplied Isaac with venison. Midrashically this implies: in *Esau's* mouth; i.e., Esau deceived his father (*Rashi*).

29. Sale of the birthright. Abraham died that day and Jacob cooked a lentil stew to provide his father with the traditional mourner's meal (*Bava Basra* 16b).

Esau came in from the field. The great of all the nations stand in the mourner's row and lament, 'Woe to the world that has lost its leader; woe to the ship that has lost its pilot!' (*Bava Basra* 91b). But Esau goes about his evil business as usual, uninvolved in his family's bereavement.

30. נָא הַלְעִיטֵנִי — *Pour into me, now,* i.e., *stuff me!*

31. Sell your share of our father's inheritance to me *as this day,* i.e., *immediately,* for a sum of money that I shall give you. Then I will give you the food as testimony and ratification of the deal (*Rashbam*).

Your birthright. The sacrificial service was carried out by first-born sons (*Rashi*).

32. *Look, I am going to die.* He rejected the birthright and concerned himself only with what was directly before him (*Pesikta Zutresa*).

[19] **T**hese are the offspring of Isaac, son of Abraham — Abraham begot Isaac. [20] Isaac was forty years old when he took Rebecca, daughter of Bethuel the Aramean from Paddan Aram, sister of Laban the Aramean, as a wife for himself. [21] Isaac entreated HASHEM opposite his wife, because she was barren. HASHEM allowed Himself to be entreated by him, and his wife Rebecca conceived.

[22] The children agitated within her, and she said, 'If so, why am I thus?' And she went to inquire of HASHEM.

[23] And HASHEM said to her: 'Two nations are in your womb; two regimes from your insides shall be separated; the might shall pass from one regime to the other, and the elder shall serve the younger.'

[24] When her term to bear grew full, then behold! there were twins in her womb. [25] The first one emerged red, entirely like a hairy mantle; so they named him Esau. [26] After that his brother emerged with his hand grasping on to the heel of Esau; so he named him Jacob. Isaac was sixty years old when she bore them.

[27] The lads grew up and Esau became one who knows hunting, a man of the field. But Jacob was a wholesome man, abiding in tents. [28] Isaac loved Esau for game was in his mouth; but Rebecca loved Jacob.

[29] Once, Jacob simmered a stew, and Esau came in from the field, exhausted. [30] Esau said to Jacob, 'Pour into me, now, some of that very red stuff for I am exhausted.' (He was therefore named Edom.)

[31] Jacob said, 'Sell, as this day, your birthright to me.'

[32] And Esau said, 'Look, I am going to die so

וְלָמָּה־זֶּה לִי בְּכֹרָה: לג וַיֹּאמֶר יַעֲקֹב הִשָּׁבְעָה לִּי כַּיּוֹם וַיִּשָּׁבַע לוֹ וַיִּמְכֹּר אֶת־בְּכֹרָתוֹ לְיַעֲקֹב: לד וְיַעֲקֹב נָתַן לְעֵשָׂו לֶחֶם וּנְזִיד עֲדָשִׁים וַיֹּאכַל וַיֵּשְׁתְּ וַיָּקָם וַיֵּלַךְ וַיִּבֶז עֵשָׂו אֶת־הַבְּכֹרָה:

כו א וַיְהִי רָעָב בָּאָרֶץ מִלְּבַד הָרָעָב הָרִאשׁוֹן אֲשֶׁר הָיָה בִּימֵי אַבְרָהָם וַיֵּלֶךְ יִצְחָק אֶל־ אֲבִימֶלֶךְ מֶלֶךְ־פְּלִשְׁתִּים גְּרָרָה: ב וַיֵּרָא אֵלָיו יהוה וַיֹּאמֶר אַל־תֵּרֵד מִצְרָיְמָה שְׁכֹן בָּאָרֶץ אֲשֶׁר אֹמַר אֵלֶיךָ: ג גּוּר בָּאָרֶץ הַזֹּאת וְאֶהְיֶה עִמְּךָ וַאֲבָרְכֶךָּ כִּי־לְךָ וּלְזַרְעֲךָ אֶתֵּן אֶת־כָּל־ הָאֲרָצֹת הָאֵל וַהֲקִמֹתִי אֶת־הַשְּׁבֻעָה אֲשֶׁר נִשְׁבַּעְתִּי לְאַבְרָהָם אָבִיךָ: ד וְהִרְבֵּיתִי אֶת־ זַרְעֲךָ כְּכוֹכְבֵי הַשָּׁמַיִם וְנָתַתִּי לְזַרְעֲךָ אֵת כָּל־הָאֲרָצֹת הָאֵל וְהִתְבָּרְכוּ בְזַרְעֲךָ כֹּל גּוֹיֵי הָאָרֶץ: ה עֵקֶב אֲשֶׁר־שָׁמַע אַבְרָהָם בְּקֹלִי וַיִּשְׁמֹר מִשְׁמַרְתִּי מִצְוֺתַי חֻקּוֹתַי וְתוֹרֹתָי: שני ו וַיֵּשֶׁב יִצְחָק בִּגְרָר: ז וַיִּשְׁאֲלוּ אַנְשֵׁי הַמָּקוֹם לְאִשְׁתּוֹ וַיֹּאמֶר אֲחֹתִי הִוא כִּי יָרֵא לֵאמֹר אִשְׁתִּי פֶּן־יַהַרְגֻנִי אַנְשֵׁי הַמָּקוֹם עַל־רִבְקָה כִּי־טוֹבַת מַרְאֶה הִוא: ח וַיְהִי כִּי אָרְכוּ־לוֹ שָׁם הַיָּמִים וַיַּשְׁקֵף אֲבִימֶלֶךְ מֶלֶךְ פְּלִשְׁתִּים בְּעַד הַחַלּוֹן וַיַּרְא וְהִנֵּה יִצְחָק מְצַחֵק אֵת רִבְקָה אִשְׁתּוֹ: ט וַיִּקְרָא אֲבִימֶלֶךְ לְיִצְחָק וַיֹּאמֶר אַךְ הִנֵּה אִשְׁתְּךָ הִוא וְאֵיךְ אָמַרְתָּ אֲחֹתִי הִוא

---

33. This transaction included Esau's right to be buried in the Cave of Machpelah (*Sefer HaYashar*).

34. R' Bachya comments that the food is not identified until after the sale to emphasize the grossness of Esau. For what did he give up his precious birthright? — for a pot of beans!

26/1. Isaac becomes an alien.

There was a famine in the land. Canaan was almost entirely dependent on annual rainfall for its fertility. As seen throughout Scriptures, famine was no infrequent occurrence there.

Isaac followed Abraham's example in going to Egypt [which was irrigated by the Nile] to escape the famine. The shortest route was through Philistia [see *Exodus* 13:17]. While Isaac was there en route to Egypt, God commanded him not to leave *Eretz Yisrael* [v. 2] (*Rashbam*).

2. *'Do not descend to Egypt* for you are an עוֹלָה תְּמִימָה *unblemished offering*, and [residence] outside the Land does not befit you' (*Rashi*).

3. Following *Ramban*, God said: 'I will indicate to you from time to time where to establish residence, *but for the time being*, גּוּר בָּאָרֶץ הַזֹּאת, *stay awhile* [lit., *sojourn*] *in this land*.' Since Philistia is included in the Promised Land, your presence here is not forbidden (*Akeidas Yitzchak*).

4. *All the nations of the earth shall bless themselves by your offspring.* [This is repeated verbatim from 22:18.] Throughout Scripture this phrase means that a man will bless his son by saying, 'May your offspring be like Isaac's!' The source for this idea is 48:20 (*Rashi*).

5. **Do not think** that all these blessings are granted only to induce you not to descend to Egypt. They were already *decreed in Abraham's days because he obeyed*, etc. (*Abarbanel*).

My voice. When I tested him (*Rashi*); he was even prepared to slaughter his only son (*Radak*).

My Ordinances. Rabbinic enactments which serve as barriers against infringement of Biblical prohibitions.

My Commandments. Laws which man's moral sense would have dictated (*Rashi*).

My Decrees. Laws for which reason cannot explain, and which are thus, as it were, *royal decrees* enacted on His subjects (*Rashi*).

And My Torahs [or: *Teachings*]. Both the Written Torah and the Oral Torah, which includes rules and interpretations transmitted to Moses at Sinai (*Rashi*).

The consensus of Rabbinic opinion is that Abraham arrived at a knowledge of the *entire Torah* through Divine Inspiration and observed it voluntarily *(Ramban).*

6. Isaac in Gerar.

7. Because of his covenant with Abraham, Abimelech showed Isaac no malice. It was the *residents* who inquired about the identity of Rebecca (*Ramban*).

'Lest the men of the place kill me.' They would spirit a wife away from her husband and murder him on some pretext (*Ramban to 12:11*).

8. *As his days there lengthened.* He ceased to be careful in concealing his true relationship to Rebecca (*Rashi; Rashbam*).

9. She certainly is not your sister! You 'jested' with her as one jests with a wife, not a sister! (*Radak*).

of what use to me is a birthright?'

³³ Jacob said, 'Swear to me as this day.' He swore to him and sold his birthright to Jacob. ³⁴ Jacob gave Esau bread and lentil stew, and he ate and drank, got up and left. Thus, Esau spurned the birthright.

26 ¹ There was a famine in the land, aside from the first famine that was in the days of Abraham. And Isaac went to Abimelech king of the Philistines, to Gerar.

² HASHEM appeared to him and said, 'Do not descend to Egypt. Dwell in the land that I shall indicate to you. ³ Sojourn in this land and I will be with you and bless you; for to you and your offspring will I give all these lands and establish the oath that I swore to Abraham your father:

⁴ "I will increase your offspring
like the stars of the heavens;
and will give to your offspring all these lands;
and all the nations of the earth
shall bless themselves by your offspring."

⁵ because Abraham obeyed My voice, and safeguarded My Ordinances, My Commandments, My Decrees, and My Torahs.'

⁶ So Isaac settled in Gerar. ⁷ When the men of the place asked about his wife, he said, 'She is my sister,' for he was afraid to say 'my wife' — 'Lest the men of the place kill me because of Rebecca for she is fair to look upon!'

⁸ And it came to pass, as his days there lengthened, that Abimelech king of the Philistines gazed down through the window and saw — behold! Isaac was jesting with his wife Rebecca. ⁹ Abimelech summoned Isaac and said, 'But look! She is your wife! How could you say, "She is my sister?" '

וַיֹּ֙אמֶר֙ אֵלָ֔יו יִצְחָ֔ק כִּ֣י אָמַ֔רְתִּי פֶּן־אָמ֖וּת
עָלֶ֑יהָ: י וַיֹּ֣אמֶר אֲבִימֶ֔לֶךְ מַה־זֹּ֖את עָשִׂ֣יתָ לָּ֑נוּ
כִּ֠מְעַט שָׁכַ֞ב אַחַ֤ד הָעָם֙ אֶת־אִשְׁתֶּ֔ךָ וְהֵבֵאתָ֥
עָלֵ֖ינוּ אָשָֽׁם: יא וַיְצַ֣ו אֲבִימֶ֔לֶךְ אֶת־כָּל־הָעָ֖ם
לֵאמֹ֑ר הַנֹּגֵ֜עַ בָּאִ֥ישׁ הַזֶּ֛ה וּבְאִשְׁתּ֖וֹ מ֥וֹת יוּמָֽת:
יב וַיִּזְרַ֤ע יִצְחָק֙ בָּאָ֣רֶץ הַהִ֔וא וַיִּמְצָ֛א בַּשָּׁנָ֥ה
הַהִ֖וא מֵאָ֣ה שְׁעָרִ֑ים וַיְבָרֲכֵ֖הוּ יְהוָֽה: *שלישי*
יג וַיִּגְדַּ֖ל הָאִ֑ישׁ וַיֵּ֤לֶךְ הָלוֹךְ֙ וְגָדֵ֔ל עַ֥ד כִּֽי־גָדַ֖ל
מְאֹֽד: יד וַֽיְהִי־ל֤וֹ מִקְנֵה־צֹאן֙ וּמִקְנֵ֣ה בָקָ֔ר
וַעֲבֻדָּ֖ה רַבָּ֑ה וַיְקַנְא֥וּ אֹת֖וֹ פְּלִשְׁתִּֽים: טו וְכָל־
הַבְּאֵרֹ֗ת אֲשֶׁ֤ר חָֽפְרוּ֙ עַבְדֵ֣י אָבִ֔יו בִּימֵ֖י אַבְרָהָ֣ם
אָבִ֑יו סִתְּמ֣וּם פְּלִשְׁתִּ֔ים וַיְמַלְא֖וּם עָפָֽר:
טז וַיֹּ֥אמֶר אֲבִימֶ֖לֶךְ אֶל־יִצְחָ֑ק לֵ֥ךְ מֵֽעִמָּ֔נוּ
כִּֽי־עָצַֽמְתָּ־מִמֶּ֖נּוּ מְאֹֽד: יז וַיֵּ֥לֶךְ מִשָּׁ֖ם יִצְחָ֑ק
וַיִּ֥חַן בְּנַֽחַל־גְּרָ֖ר וַיֵּ֥שֶׁב שָֽׁם: יח וַיָּ֨שָׁב יִצְחָ֜ק
וַיַּחְפֹּ֣ר ׀ אֶת־בְּאֵרֹ֣ת הַמַּ֗יִם אֲשֶׁ֤ר חָֽפְרוּ֙ בִּימֵי֙
אַבְרָהָ֣ם אָבִ֔יו וַיְסַתְּמ֥וּם פְּלִשְׁתִּ֖ים אַחֲרֵ֣י מ֣וֹת
אַבְרָהָ֑ם וַיִּקְרָ֤א לָהֶן֙ שֵׁמ֔וֹת כַּשֵּׁמֹ֕ת אֲשֶׁר־קָרָ֥א
לָהֶ֖ן אָבִֽיו: יט וַיַּחְפְּר֥וּ עַבְדֵֽי־יִצְחָ֖ק בַּנָּ֑חַל
וַיִּ֨מְצְאוּ־שָׁ֔ם בְּאֵ֖ר מַ֥יִם חַיִּֽים: כ וַיָּרִ֜יבוּ רֹעֵ֣י
גְרָ֗ר עִם־רֹעֵ֤י יִצְחָק֙ לֵאמֹ֔ר לָ֖נוּ הַמָּ֑יִם וַיִּקְרָ֤א
שֵׁם־הַבְּאֵר֙ עֵ֔שֶׂק כִּ֥י הִֽתְעַשְּׂק֖וּ עִמּֽוֹ: כא וַֽיַּחְפְּרוּ֙
בְּאֵ֣ר אַחֶ֔רֶת וַיָּרִ֖יבוּ גַּם־עָלֶ֑יהָ וַיִּקְרָ֥א
שְׁמָ֖הּ שִׂטְנָֽה: כב וַיַּעְתֵּ֣ק מִשָּׁ֗ם וַיַּחְפֹּר֙ בְּאֵ֣ר
אַחֶ֔רֶת וְלֹ֥א רָב֖וּ עָלֶ֑יהָ וַיִּקְרָ֤א שְׁמָהּ֙ רְחֹב֔וֹת

10. *One of the people has nearly lain with your wife.* According to *Rashi* and most commentators, this was an oblique reference to himself: *one of the people* — the most distinguished one, the king himself.

And as king, I would certainly not be expected first to seek your consent, since it would be an honor for one to give his sister in marriage to the king (*Sforno*).

And you would have brought guilt upon us! As happened when Sarah was taken and death was declared on my entire household [20:7] (*Malbim*).

11. Abimelech realized that no husband of a beautiful woman was safe in his land, and therefore found it necessary to assure Isaac's safety by issuing a *royal decree* on his behalf. What testimony this bears to vindicate Isaac's initial apprehensions when entering this Godless country!

12. Isaac prospers.

A hundredfold. I.e., a hundred times as much as the expected estimate. According to our Rabbis, his estimation was made for the purpose of establishing the quantity due as מַעְשְׂרוֹת, tithes (*Rashi*).

14. *The Philistines envied him.* They envied his tangible wealth, as enumerated above (*Ramban*).

15. *The Philistines stopped up.* They claimed that these wells could become a menace because of marauding troops [i.e., wells might attract robbers; or an invading army could use them as its water supply] (*Rashi*).

It must be emphasized that the Philistines thereby desecrated Abimelech's covenant with Abraham [21:27] (*Midrash HaGadol*).

16. *For you have become much mightier than we.* Though I am king, I do not have in my home as many possessions as you. It is a disgrace to us that you should be wealthier than the king! (*Ramban*).

18. *And he called them the same names.* Isaac's motivation was respect for his father. Thus the Torah teaches a great moral lesson: One should not deviate from his father's way (*R' Bachya*).

19. **The dispute over the wells.** *Isaac's servants dug in the valley.* In search of more water for his abundant herds (*Radak*).

20. *The water is ours!* 'The well is located in the valley and draws from our own water supply, hence, it is ours.' But the Torah testified to the contrary [see v. 19] (*Ramban*).

They quibbled in the exact style that has been used against the Jews in Exile throughout the centuries: 'Yes, you dug the well; the *hole* belongs to you, but the *water* is ours!' (*Hirsch*).

Esek [involvement], i.e., protest (*Rashi*).

21. Once the Philistines saw that they had succeeded in stealing the well by a spurious claim, they continued to steal without any claim at all — just out of sheer enmity (*Haamek Davar*).

Sitnah. I.e., enmity (*Rashi*).

22. *And [he] dug another well.* This time Isaac presided over the digging, or perhaps he even dug the first clod to initiate the venture. It was in his merit that this venture met with no opposition (*Haamek Davar*).

Rechovos [i.e., wide-open spaces]. To make it obvious that this well was not the object of strife (*Radak*).

Isaac said to him, 'Because I was apprehensive that I would be killed because of her.' ¹⁰ Abimelech said, 'What is this that you have done to us? One of the people has nearly lain with your wife, and you would have brought guilt upon us!' ¹¹ Abimelech then warned all the people saying, 'Whoever molests this man or his wife shall surely die.'

¹² Isaac sowed in that land, and in that year he reaped a hundredfold; thus had HASHEM blessed him. ¹³ The man prospered and continually flourished until he was very prosperous. ¹⁴ He had acquired flocks and herds and many enterprises; and the Philistines envied him.

¹⁵ All the wells that his father's servants had dug in the days of Abraham his father, the Philistines stopped up, and filled them with earth.

¹⁶ And Abimelech said to Isaac, 'Go away from us for you have become much mightier that we!'

¹⁷ So Isaac departed from there and encamped in the valley of Gerar. ¹⁸ And Isaac dug anew the wells of water which they had dug in the days of Abraham his father and the Philistines had stopped up after Abraham's death; and he called them the same names that his father had called them.

¹⁹ Isaac's servants dug in the valley and found there a well of fresh water. ²⁰ The herdsmen of Gerar quarreled with Isaac's herdsmen saying, 'The water is ours,' so he named that well Esek because they involved themselves with him. ²¹ Then they dug another well, and they quarreled over that also. So he named it Sitnah. ²² He relocated from there and dug another well. They did not quarrel over it, so he named it Rechovos,

וַיֹּאמֶר כִּי־עַתָּה הִרְחִיב יהוה לָנוּ וּפָרִינוּ
בָאָרֶץ: רביעי כג וַיַּעַל מִשָּׁם בְּאֵר שָׁבַע: כד וַיֵּרָא
אֵלָיו יהוה בַּלַּיְלָה הַהוּא וַיֹּאמֶר אָנֹכִי אֱלֹהֵי
אַבְרָהָם אָבִיךָ אַל־תִּירָא כִּי־אִתְּךָ אָנֹכִי
וּבֵרַכְתִּיךָ וְהִרְבֵּיתִי אֶת־זַרְעֲךָ בַּעֲבוּר אַבְרָהָם
עַבְדִּי: כה וַיִּבֶן שָׁם מִזְבֵּחַ וַיִּקְרָא בְּשֵׁם יהוה
וַיֶּט־שָׁם אָהֳלוֹ וַיִּכְרוּ־שָׁם עַבְדֵי־יִצְחָק בְּאֵר:
כו וַאֲבִימֶלֶךְ הָלַךְ אֵלָיו מִגְּרָר וַאֲחֻזַּת מֵרֵעֵהוּ
וּפִיכֹל שַׂר־צְבָאוֹ: כז וַיֹּאמֶר אֲלֵהֶם יִצְחָק
מַדּוּעַ בָּאתֶם אֵלָי וְאַתֶּם שְׂנֵאתֶם אֹתִי
וַתְּשַׁלְּחוּנִי מֵאִתְּכֶם: כח וַיֹּאמְרוּ רָאוֹ רָאִינוּ
כִּי־הָיָה יהוה | עִמָּךְ וַנֹּאמֶר תְּהִי נָא אָלָה
בֵּינוֹתֵינוּ בֵּינֵינוּ וּבֵינֶךָ וְנִכְרְתָה בְרִית עִמָּךְ:
כט אִם־תַּעֲשֵׂה עִמָּנוּ רָעָה כַּאֲשֶׁר לֹא נְגַעֲנוּךָ
וְכַאֲשֶׁר עָשִׂינוּ עִמְּךָ רַק־טוֹב וַנְּשַׁלֵּחֲךָ
בְּשָׁלוֹם אַתָּה עַתָּה בְּרוּךְ יהוה: חמישי וַיַּעַשׂ
לָהֶם מִשְׁתֶּה וַיֹּאכְלוּ וַיִּשְׁתּוּ: לא וַיַּשְׁכִּימוּ
בַבֹּקֶר וַיִּשָּׁבְעוּ אִישׁ לְאָחִיו וַיְשַׁלְּחֵם יִצְחָק
וַיֵּלְכוּ מֵאִתּוֹ בְּשָׁלוֹם: לב וַיְהִי | בַּיּוֹם הַהוּא
וַיָּבֹאוּ עַבְדֵי יִצְחָק וַיַּגִּדוּ לוֹ עַל־אֹדוֹת הַבְּאֵר
אֲשֶׁר חָפָרוּ וַיֹּאמְרוּ לוֹ מָצָאנוּ מָיִם: לג וַיִּקְרָא
אֹתָהּ שִׁבְעָה עַל־כֵּן שֵׁם־הָעִיר בְּאֵר שֶׁבַע עַד
הַיּוֹם הַזֶּה: לד וַיְהִי עֵשָׂו
בֶּן־אַרְבָּעִים שָׁנָה וַיִּקַּח אִשָּׁה אֶת־יְהוּדִית
בַּת־בְּאֵרִי הַחִתִּי וְאֶת־בָּשְׂמַת בַּת־אֵילֹן

23. Isaac returns to Beer Sheba.

24. *For I am with you.* God's promise of being 'with' the Patriarchs is an affirmation of His Providence in watching over the details of their various activities according to their measure of perfection.

26. Abimelech's visit. The reaffirmation of the treaty.

Targum Yonasan records that: 'When Isaac left Gerar the wells dried up and the trees bore no fruit. They felt that this befell them because they had driven him away, so Abimelech went to Isaac from Gerar . . .'

This group may have included the Philistine herdsmen who had quarreled with Isaac over the wells [vs. 20-21]. Abimelech took them along as a gesture to strengthen the sincerity of his peace overture (*Meshech Chochmah*).

29. *If you dare do evil . . .!* Since oaths are strengthened by a curse, it is as if Abimelech were saying: '*If you do evil to us* — then may God do such and such to you.' In all such cases the Torah shortens the expression, leaving the threatened consequences to the imagination (*Ramban*).

And just as we have done with you only good. We have protected you by warning the people against interfering with you (*Ramban*).

How glaring is their omission of any reference to the herdsmen who quarreled over the wells, or stopped up Abraham's wells! Perhaps in their perverted way, they rationalized, as have anti-Semites through the ages, that their acts of harassment were justifiable.

Rashi and Rashbam render: *Now you, O blessed of HASHEM* — i.e., now you, who are blessed of HASHEM, reciprocate our kindness to you by entering into a treaty with us. As one who is manifestly the blessed of HASHEM, it is in your power to deal graciously with us.

30. Since gentlemen partake of a meal after concluding a transaction, Isaac prepared the feast to consummate the mutual acceptance of the pact (*Radak* and *Tur*).

31. *Early in the morning.* They waited until morning, after they had slept off the effects of the dinner wine, so that no one could claim that the oath was undertaken in anything less than an alert, sober state (*Torah Sheleimah,* 126 note).

32. *'We have found water!'* Without strife or quarreling. Isaac's every effort was successful in *Eretz Yisrael* (*Radak*).

33. According to *Ibn Ezra,* the name *Shibah* — which means *seven* as well as *oath* — commemorates the *seven* ewes which Abraham had given to Abimelech (21:28-31), as well as the oath.

Beer [i.e., the well of] *Sheba.* On account of the בְּאֵר, *well,* which both the father and the son named to commemorate their שְׁבוּעָה, *oath* (*Ramban*).

Until this very day. I.e., the days of Moses [when the Torah was given]. Throughout Scripture, *until this day* means until the time of the scribe who recorded the matter (*Rashbam* to 19:37).

34. Esau marries.

Forty years old. Rashi comments: Esau is compared to a swine which, when it lies down, stretches out its cloven hoofs as if to say, 'See, I am a clean (i.e., kosher) animal.'

saying, 'For now HASHEM has granted us ample space, and we can be fruitful in the land.'

²³ He went up from there to Beer Sheba. ²⁴ HASHEM appeared to him that night and said, "I am the God of your father Abraham. Fear not, for I am with you; I will bless you and increase your offspring because of Abraham my servant.' ²⁵ He built an altar there, invoked HASHEM by Name, and there he pitched his tent; there Isaac's servants began digging a well.

²⁶ Abimelech went to him from Gerar with a group of his friends and Pichol his general. ²⁷ Isaac said to them, 'Why have you come to me? You hate me and drove me away from you!' ²⁸ And they said, 'We have indeed seen that HASHEM has been with you, so we said, "Let the oath between ourselves now be between us and you, and let us make a covenant with you:

²⁹ If you dare do evil to us . . .! Just as we have not molested you, and just as we have done with you only good, and sent you away in peace — Now, you, O blessed of HASHEM!" '

³⁰ He made them a feast and they ate and drank. ³¹ They awoke early in the morning and swore to one another. Then Isaac saw them off and they departed from him in peace.

³² And it was on that very day that Isaac's servants came and told him about the well they had dug, and said to him, 'We have found water!' ³³ And he named it Shibah. Therefore, the name of the city is Beer Sheba until this very day.

³⁴ When Esau was forty years old, he took to wife Judith daughter of Be'eri the Hittite, and Basemath daughter of Elon the Hittite.

הֶחְתִּי: לה וַתִּהְיֶ֖יןָ מֹ֣רַת ר֑וּחַ לְיִצְחָ֖ק
וּלְרִבְקָה: **כז** א וַיְהִי֙ כִּי־זָקֵ֣ן יִצְחָ֔ק
וַתִּכְהֶ֥יןָ עֵינָ֖יו מֵרְאֹ֑ת וַיִּקְרָ֞א אֶת־עֵשָׂ֣ו ׀ בְּנ֣וֹ
הַגָּדֹ֗ל וַיֹּ֤אמֶר אֵלָיו֙ בְּנִ֔י וַיֹּ֥אמֶר אֵלָ֖יו הִנֵּֽנִי:
ב וַיֹּ֕אמֶר הִנֵּה־נָ֖א זָקַ֑נְתִּי לֹ֥א יָדַ֖עְתִּי י֥וֹם מוֹתִֽי:
ג וְעַתָּה֙ שָׂא־נָ֣א כֵלֶ֔יךָ תֶּלְיְךָ֖ וְקַשְׁתֶּ֑ךָ וְצֵא֙
הַשָּׂדֶ֔ה וְצ֥וּדָה לִּ֖י °צידה: ד וַעֲשֵׂה־לִ֨י מַטְעַמִּ֜ים
כַּאֲשֶׁ֥ר אָהַ֛בְתִּי וְהָבִ֥יאָה לִּ֖י וְאֹכֵ֑לָה בַּעֲב֛וּר
תְּבָרֶכְךָ֥ נַפְשִׁ֖י בְּטֶ֥רֶם אָמֽוּת: ה וְרִבְקָ֣ה שֹׁמַ֔עַת
בְּדַבֵּ֣ר יִצְחָ֔ק אֶל־עֵשָׂ֖ו בְּנ֑וֹ וַיֵּ֤לֶךְ עֵשָׂו֙ הַשָּׂדֶ֔ה
לָצ֥וּד צַ֖יִד לְהָבִֽיא: ו וְרִבְקָה֙ אָֽמְרָ֔ה אֶל־יַעֲקֹ֥ב
בְּנָ֖הּ לֵאמֹ֑ר הִנֵּ֤ה שָׁמַ֙עְתִּי֙ אֶת־אָבִ֔יךָ מְדַבֵּ֛ר
אֶל־עֵשָׂ֥ו אָחִ֖יךָ לֵאמֹֽר: ז הָבִ֨יאָה לִּ֥י צַ֛יִד
וַעֲשֵׂה־לִ֥י מַטְעַמִּ֖ים וְאֹכֵ֑לָה וַאֲבָרֶכְכָ֛ה לִפְנֵ֥י
יְהוָ֖ה לִפְנֵ֥י מוֹתִֽי: ח וְעַתָּ֥ה בְנִ֖י שְׁמַ֣ע בְּקֹלִ֑י
לַאֲשֶׁ֥ר אֲנִ֖י מְצַוָּ֥ה אֹתָֽךְ: ט לֶךְ־נָא֙ אֶל־הַצֹּ֔אן
וְקַֽח־לִ֣י מִשָּׁ֗ם שְׁנֵ֛י גְּדָיֵ֥י עִזִּ֖ים טֹבִ֑ים וְאֶעֱשֶׂ֨ה
אֹתָ֧ם מַטְעַמִּ֛ים לְאָבִ֖יךָ כַּאֲשֶׁ֥ר אָהֵֽב: י וְהֵבֵאתָ֥
לְאָבִ֖יךָ וְאָכָ֑ל בַּעֲבֻ֛ר אֲשֶׁ֥ר יְבָרֶכְךָ֖ לִפְנֵ֥י מוֹתֽוֹ:
יא וַיֹּ֣אמֶר יַעֲקֹ֔ב אֶל־רִבְקָ֖ה אִמּ֑וֹ הֵ֣ן עֵשָׂ֤ו אָחִי֙
אִ֣ישׁ שָׂעִ֔ר וְאָנֹכִ֖י אִ֥ישׁ חָלָֽק: יב אוּלַ֤י יְמֻשֵּׁ֙נִי֙
אָבִ֔י וְהָיִ֥יתִי בְעֵינָ֖יו כִּמְתַעְתֵּ֑עַ וְהֵבֵאתִ֥י עָלַ֛י
קְלָלָ֖ה וְלֹ֥א בְרָכָֽה: יג וַתֹּ֤אמֶר לוֹ֙ אִמּ֔וֹ עָלַ֥י
קִלְלָתְךָ֖ בְּנִ֑י אַ֛ךְ שְׁמַ֥ע בְּקֹלִ֖י וְלֵ֥ךְ קַֽח־לִֽי:
°צַ֥יִד ק׳

27/1. Isaac's blessing.

When Isaac had become old. Isaac was 123 years old then. Accordingly, the year was 2171 from Creation (see also chronology in 25:17).

Dimmed from seeing. Rashi offers three reasons for Isaac's failing eyesight.

1 — From the smoke of the incense that Esau's wives offered to their idols. Further, God caused him this blindness to spare him the distress from seeing it further (*Tanchuma*).

2 — When Isaac lay bound on the altar at the *Akeidah*, the ministering angels wept over him. Their tears fell into his eyes and dimmed them.

3 — Providence caused his blindness for the specific reason that Jacob might receive the blessing [and Isaac would not realize whom he was blessing (*Tanchuma*)].

3. Sharpen your knife and slaughter the animal according to the proper ritual, so you do not feed me נְבֵלָה [carrion].

Isaac sent Esau out to the field to hunt, so as to make the task more arduous and therefore the *mitzvah* more meritorious (*Alshich*).

4. *Ramban* comments that Isaac's desire for food before blessing Esau was in order to derive a benefit from him so the blessing would be bestowed wholeheartedly.

5. Rebecca's scheme.

Rebecca did not realize that Jacob would be blessed regardless of whether his father blessed him, and that this was Isaac's intention as well. In her great love for Jacob, she was in turmoil, and this accounts for her subsequent action in advising him to circumvent the truth to receive the blessing from his father (*Radak*).

7. Rebecca added the words לִפְנֵי ה', *in the presence of* HASHEM, to impress upon Jacob the immensity of his father's blessing inasmuch as the prophetic spirit that would descend upon him while he would utter the benedictions (*Radak*).

. . . And as such the blessing would be irrevocable. Accordingly, if Esau was blessed with it, it would remain with his descendants forever and Jacob would never be able to lift his head before him (*Ramban*).

8. Rebecca perceived Jacob's reluctance to participate in this scheme. Thus she emphasized that he was to 'listen to that which *I* — as your mother — command' (*Divrei Yirmiyah*).

10. The stimulus of food bring about physical comfort and 'bribe' the physical senses so they will not deter the soul from uniting with the Source of the Blessing (*Malbim*).

11. 'But,' Jacob asks, 'have you considered the following difficulty?'

12. *Perhaps Father will feel me.* Not suspiciously, but to *affectionately caress me*, and he will discover that I am smooth-skinned. It is noteworthy that Jacob was not afraid that Isaac would recognize his voice. Perhaps they had similar voices [see on v. 22], or Jacob could imitate Esau (*Ramban*).

13. *Your curse be on me.* I.e., I take full responsibility. She had complete confidence in the prophecy that *the elder would serve the younger* [25:23] (*Rashbam*).

'Have no fear that he will curse you. If he does, may it come on me, not you,' this being the way of women to be compassionate and want to suffer for their children (*Yohel Or*) (*Ibn Ezra*).

³⁵ And they were a source of spiritual rebellion to Isaac and to Rebecca.

27 ¹ And it came to pass, when Isaac had become old, and his eyesight dimmed from seeing, that he summoned Esau, his older son, and said to him, 'My son.' And he said to him, 'Here I am.'

² And he said, 'See, now, I have aged; I know not the day of my death. ³ Now sharpen, if you please, your gear — your sword and your bow, and go out to the field and hunt game for me. ⁴ Then make me delicacies such as I love and bring it to me to eat so that I may give you my innermost blessings before I die.'

⁵ Now Rebecca was listening as Isaac spoke to Esau his son. And Esau went to the field to hunt game to bring. ⁶ But Rebecca had said to Jacob her son, saying, 'Behold I heard your father speaking to your brother Esau saying, ⁷ "Bring me some game and make me delicacies to eat, and I will bless you in the presence of HASHEM before my death." ⁸ So now, my son, heed my voice to that which I command you. ⁹ Go now to the flock and fetch me from there two choice young kids of the goats, and I will make of them delicacies for your father, as he loves. ¹⁰ Then bring it to your father and he shall eat, so that he may bless you before his death.'

¹¹ Jacob replied to Rebecca, his mother, 'But my brother Esau is a hairy man and I am a smooth-skinned man. ¹² Perhaps Father will feel me and I shall appear as a mocker; I will thus bring upon myself a curse rather than a blessing.'

¹³ But his mother said to him, 'Your curse be on me, my son. Only heed my voice and go fetch them for me.'

יד וַיֵּ֗לֶךְ וַיִּקַּ֤ח וַיָּבֵא֙ לְאִמּ֔וֹ וַתַּ֤עַשׂ אִמּוֹ֙
מַטְעַמִּ֔ים כַּאֲשֶׁ֖ר אָהֵ֥ב אָבִֽיו: טו וַתִּקַּ֣ח רִבְקָ֡ה
אֶת־בִּגְדֵי֩ עֵשָׂ֨ו בְּנָ֤הּ הַגָּדֹל֙ הַחֲמֻדֹ֔ת אֲשֶׁ֥ר
אִתָּ֖הּ בַּבָּ֑יִת וַתַּלְבֵּ֥שׁ אֶֽת־יַעֲקֹ֖ב בְּנָ֥הּ
הַקָּטָֽן: טז וְאֵ֗ת עֹרֹת֙ גְּדָיֵ֣י הָֽעִזִּ֔ים הִלְבִּ֖ישָׁה
עַל־יָדָ֑יו וְעַ֖ל חֶלְקַ֥ת צַוָּארָֽיו: יז וַתִּתֵּ֧ן אֶת־
הַמַּטְעַמִּ֛ים וְאֶת־הַלֶּ֖חֶם אֲשֶׁ֣ר עָשָׂ֑תָה בְּיַ֖ד
יַעֲקֹ֥ב בְּנָֽהּ: יח וַיָּבֹ֥א אֶל־אָבִ֖יו וַיֹּ֣אמֶר אָבִ֑י
וַיֹּ֣אמֶר הִנֶּ֔נִּי מִ֥י אַתָּ֖ה בְּנִֽי: יט וַיֹּ֨אמֶר יַעֲקֹ֜ב
אֶל־אָבִ֗יו אָֽנֹכִי֙ עֵשָׂ֣ו בְּכֹרֶ֔ךָ עָשִׂ֕יתִי כַּאֲשֶׁ֥ר
דִּבַּ֖רְתָּ אֵלָ֑י קֽוּם־נָ֣א שְׁבָ֗ה וְאָכְלָה֙ מִצֵּידִ֔י
בַּעֲב֖וּר תְּבָרְכַ֥נִּי נַפְשֶֽׁךָ: כ וַיֹּ֤אמֶר יִצְחָק֙
אֶל־בְּנ֔וֹ מַה־זֶּ֛ה מִהַ֥רְתָּ לִמְצֹ֖א בְּנִ֑י וַיֹּ֕אמֶר
כִּ֥י הִקְרָ֛ה יְהוָ֥ה אֱלֹהֶ֖יךָ לְפָנָֽי: כא וַיֹּ֤אמֶר
יִצְחָק֙ אֶֽל־יַעֲקֹ֔ב גְּשָׁה־נָּ֥א וַאֲמֻֽשְׁךָ֖ בְּנִ֑י
הַֽאַתָּ֥ה זֶ֛ה בְּנִ֥י עֵשָׂ֖ו אִם־לֹֽא: כב וַיִּגַּ֧שׁ
יַעֲקֹ֛ב אֶל־יִצְחָ֥ק אָבִ֖יו וַיְמֻשֵּׁ֑הוּ וַיֹּ֗אמֶר
הַקֹּל֙ ק֣וֹל יַעֲקֹ֔ב וְהַיָּדַ֖יִם יְדֵ֥י עֵשָֽׂו: כג וְלֹ֣א
הִכִּיר֗וֹ כִּֽי־הָי֣וּ יָדָ֗יו כִּידֵ֛י עֵשָׂ֥ו אָחִ֖יו
שְׂעִרֹ֑ת וַֽיְבָרְכֵֽהוּ: כד וַיֹּ֕אמֶר אַתָּ֥ה זֶ֖ה בְּנִ֣י עֵשָׂ֑ו
וַיֹּ֖אמֶר אָֽנִי: כה וַיֹּ֗אמֶר הַגִּ֤שָׁה לִּי֙ וְאֹֽכְלָה֙
מִצֵּ֣יד בְּנִ֔י לְמַ֖עַן תְּבָרֶכְךָ֣ נַפְשִׁ֑י וַיַּגֶּשׁ־לוֹ֙ וַיֹּאכַ֔ל
וַיָּ֧בֵא ל֦וֹ יַ֖יִן וַיֵּֽשְׁתְּ: כו וַיֹּ֥אמֶר אֵלָ֖יו יִצְחָ֣ק
אָבִ֑יו גְּשָׁה־נָּ֥א וּשְׁקָה־לִּ֖י בְּנִֽי: כז וַיִּגַּשׁ֙ וַיִּשַּׁק־ל֔וֹ
וַיָּ֛רַח אֶת־רֵ֥יחַ בְּגָדָ֖יו וַֽיְבָרְכֵ֑הוּ וַיֹּ֕אמֶר רְאֵה֙

---

14. Jacob valued the blessings, and should have hurried to bring the delicacies to his father. Therefore, the text here, too, should have said *Jacob ran*, and brought them to his mother. As written, however, the verse indicates clearly that Jacob did not apply himself enthusiastically to this scheme, but reluctantly carried out his mother's request (*HaKsav V'haKaballah*).

15. The disguise.

The precious garments were those that Esau [renowned for his great filial devotion] would wear while he waited upon his father (*Rashbam*).

16. *His arms and the bareness of his neck.* To deceive Isaac into thinking that the smooth-skinned Jacob was the hairy Esau (*Tz'ror HaMor*).

18. Jacob called out 'Father' to test whether his father would recognize his voice. Were Isaac to recognize his voice, Jacob would have abandoned the scheme and act as if he had come to visit (*Alshich*).

19. אָֽנֹכִי עֵשָׂו בְּכֹרֶךָ — *It is I, Esau your first-born.* The commentators take pains to show that Jacob remained as close as possible to the truth during the course of his conversation with Isaac. Some of the interpretations seem very strained in the light of the translation. However, the construction of the Hebrew allows for such interpretation even where the English does not.

Rashi explains: אָֽנֹכִי, *It is I* who bring this to you; עֵשָׂו בְּכֹרֶךָ, *Esau,* (however,) *is your first-born.*

He meant, 'I am who I am; Esau is your first-born,' while others suggest that he said, under his breath, 'I,' and loudly, 'Esau is your first-born' (*Ibn Ezra*).

20. Isaac had specifically asked Esau to take his weapons and *go out to the field* in order to make the task more arduous and hence the *mitzvah* greater [v. 3]. When he saw the quick return, he was apprehensive that 'Esau' had not carried out the mission as bidden.

Following *Malbim*, Isaac understood the reply to mean, 'I had actually planned to hunt far away, but *God arranged it* that game appeared before me near home, where there is usually none to be found.' This 'coincidence' was therefore taken as a sure sign that it was arranged by God — Who obviously did this in Isaac's merit.

21. Isaac's suspicions were aroused since he knew that it was not characteristic of Esau to mention God's name so readily as did the person who now stood before him [verse 20] (*Rashi*).

The Sages comment that Jacob and Esau had similar voices and Isaac could not tell them apart. His statement that the *voice is Jacob's voice* refers to Jacob's *manner of speaking*, inasmuch as Jacob spoke gently and invoked the name of Heaven.

26. Kabbalistically, a kiss brings about the deep spiritual intimacy that Isaac wished to arouse in order to cause the *Shechinah* to alight upon him, preparatory to his giving the blessings (*Alshich; Malbim*).

27. *Rashi*, citing the Midrash, asks: But the pungent smell of washed goatskin is most offensive! — Implicitly this teaches that the fragrance of the Garden of Eden entered the room with him [and it was to *this* fragrance that Isaac referred].

^{14} So he went, fetched, and brought them to his mother, and his mother made delicacies as his father liked. ^{15} Rebecca then took her older son Esau's clean garments which were with her in the house, and clothed Jacob her young son. ^{16} With the skins of the goat-kids she covered his arms and the bareness of his neck. ^{17} She placed the delicacies and the bread which she had prepared into the hand of her son Jacob, ^{18} and he came to his father and said, 'Father,' and he said, 'Here I am. Who are you, my son?'

^{19} Jacob said to his father, 'It is I, Esau your first-born. I have done as you told me. Rise up, please, sit and eat of my game that you may give me your innermost blessing.'

^{20} Isaac said to his son, 'How is it that you found so quickly, my son?' And he said, 'Because HASHEM your God so arranged it for me.'

^{21} And Isaac said to Jacob, 'Come close if you please, so I can feel you, my son. Are you, indeed, my son Esau or not?'

^{22} So Jacob drew close to Isaac his father who felt him and then said, 'The voice is Jacob's voice, but the hands are Esau's hands.' ^{23} But he did not recognize him because his hands were hairy like those of Esau his brother; so he blessed him. ^{24} He said, 'You are, indeed, my son Esau!' And he said, 'I am.'

^{25} He said, 'Serve me and let me eat of my son's game that I may give you my innermost blessing.' So he served him and he ate, and he brought him wine and he drank. ^{26} Then his father Isaac said to him, 'Come close, if you please, and kiss me, my son.' ^{27} So he drew close and kissed him. He smelled the fragrance of his garments and blessed him. He said, 'See,

רֵיחַ בְּנִי כְּרֵיחַ שָׂדֶה אֲשֶׁר בֵּרֲכוֹ יהוה:

ששי כח וְיִתֶּן־לְךָ הָאֱלֹהִים מִטַּל הַשָּׁמַיִם

וּמִשְׁמַנֵּי הָאָרֶץ וְרֹב דָּגָן וְתִירֹשׁ: כט יַעַבְדוּךָ

עַמִּים וְיִשְׁתַּחֲווּ לְךָ לְאֻמִּים הֱוֵה גְבִיר

לְאַחֶיךָ וְיִשְׁתַּחֲווּ לְךָ בְּנֵי אִמֶּךָ אֹרְרֶיךָ אָרוּר

וּמְבָרֲכֶיךָ בָּרוּךְ: ל וַיְהִי כַּאֲשֶׁר כִּלָּה יִצְחָק

לְבָרֵךְ אֶת־יַעֲקֹב וַיְהִי אַךְ יָצֹא יָצָא

יַעֲקֹב מֵאֵת פְּנֵי יִצְחָק אָבִיו וְעֵשָׂו אָחִיו

בָּא מִצֵּידוֹ: לא וַיַּעַשׂ גַּם־הוּא מַטְעַמִּים

וַיָּבֵא לְאָבִיו וַיֹּאמֶר לְאָבִיו יָקֻם אָבִי

וְיֹאכַל מִצֵּיד בְּנוֹ בַּעֲבֻר תְּבָרֲכַנִּי נַפְשֶׁךָ:

לב וַיֹּאמֶר לוֹ יִצְחָק אָבִיו מִי־אָתָּה וַיֹּאמֶר

אֲנִי בִּנְךָ בְכֹרְךָ עֵשָׂו: לג וַיֶּחֱרַד יִצְחָק

חֲרָדָה גְּדֹלָה עַד־מְאֹד וַיֹּאמֶר מִי־אֵפוֹא

הוּא הַצָּד־צַיִד וַיָּבֵא לִי וָאֹכַל מִכֹּל בְּטֶרֶם

תָּבוֹא וָאֲבָרֲכֵהוּ גַּם־בָּרוּךְ יִהְיֶה: לד כִּשְׁמֹעַ

עֵשָׂו אֶת־דִּבְרֵי אָבִיו וַיִּצְעַק צְעָקָה גְּדֹלָה

וּמָרָה עַד־מְאֹד וַיֹּאמֶר לְאָבִיו בָּרֲכֵנִי גַם־

אָנִי אָבִי: לה וַיֹּאמֶר בָּא אָחִיךָ בְּמִרְמָה

וַיִּקַּח בִּרְכָתֶךָ: לו וַיֹּאמֶר הֲכִי קָרָא שְׁמוֹ

יַעֲקֹב וַיַּעְקְבֵנִי זֶה פַעֲמַיִם אֶת־בְּכֹרָתִי לָקָח

וְהִנֵּה עַתָּה לָקַח בִּרְכָתִי וַיֹּאמַר הֲלֹא־

אָצַלְתָּ לִּי בְּרָכָה: לז וַיַּעַן יִצְחָק וַיֹּאמֶר

לְעֵשָׂו הֵן גְּבִיר שַׂמְתִּיו לָךְ וְאֶת־כָּל־אֶחָיו

---

28. *And may [the] God give you.* I.e., may He give you repeatedly (*Rashi*).

The definite article *the God* (הָאֱלֹהִים) accentuates that the reference is to God in His role as *Elohim* — i.e., the Dispenser of Strict Justice, in contrast with the name 'ה, *HASHEM*, which depicts Him in His role as Dispenser of Mercy.

May He give it to you only if you are justifiably worthy of it, but not otherwise. But to Esau he stated unconditionally [v. 39]: *of the fatness of the earth shall be your dwelling* — i.e., whether you deserve it or not (*Rashi*, following *Midrash Tanchuma*).

The above Midrash may seem difficult because Isaac thought that *Esau* was receiving the blessing. We must say that since the blessings were Divinely inspired, these words were placed into Isaac's mouth, although it would be reasonable to assume that he himself was not aware of their full import until he discovered the ruse later.

By virtue *of the dew of the heavens* [i.e., effortlessly, by Divine blessing, not as a result of excessive toil], may the earth yield up its fatness: abundant grain and wine (*Ibn Caspi*).

29. Isaac intended Esau to exercise mastery over Jacob. He intended this for Jacob's benefit because Isaac did not want him to be encumbered by material responsibilities which would hinder his spiritual development. Thus Jacob would have inherited *Eretz Yisrael* and been free to serve God within its holiness, while Esau, upon whom Jacob would be dependent, would rule the land and provide for its inhabitants (*Sforno*).

---

30. Esau returns.

Jacob had scarcely left. As one was on the way out, the other entered (*Rashi*).

32. *Who are you?* Isaac thought that this might be Jacob who, having heard that Esau was to be blessed, also brought delicacies so that he, too, would be blessed (*Ramban*).

33. *Then Isaac trembled in very great perplexity.* When Esau entered the room, Isaac perceived *Gehinnom* open beneath him (*Rashi*).

Indeed, he shall remain blessed. Isaac thus confirmed his blessing. Lest one think that Jacob would not have been blessed had he not engaged in deception, Isaac confirmed it, blessing him now of his own free will (*Midrash; Rashi*).

34. *His father's words.* I.e., Isaac's confirmation of Jacob's blessing (*Malbim*).

35. *With cleverness.* By having disguised himself as a hairy person (*Radak*).

And took your blessing. I.e., it was *your* blessing because it would have been particularly appropriate for you, inasmuch as it concerned material things (*Sforno*).

36. Was he given the name Jacob in prophetic anticipation that he would one day outwit me? (*Rashi*).

Esau had the audacity to lie to his father's face that Jacob had 'taken' his birthright, when in reality Esau himself sold it under oath and flagrantly despised it, as the Torah attests [25:34].

Have you not reserved a blessing for me? Even though you intended to bless me with the *superior* blessing, you certainly did not intend to bestow *everything* on me and leave my brother entirely devoid of your blessing (*Sforno*).

the fragrance of my son is like the fragrance of a field which HASHEM had blessed —

²⁸ And may God give you of the dew of the heavens and of the fatness of the earth, and abundant grain and wine. ²⁹ Peoples will serve you, and regimes will prostrate themselves to you. Be a lord to your kinsmen, and your mother's sons will prostrate themselves to you. Cursed be they who curse you, and blessed be they who bless you.'

³⁰ And it was, when Isaac had finished blessing Jacob, and Jacob had scarcely left from the presence of his father, that Esau his brother came back from his hunt. ³¹ He, too, made delicacies, and brought them to his father. He said to his father, 'Let my father rise and eat of his son's game, so that you may give me your innermost blessing.'

³² His father Isaac said to him, 'Who are you?' And he said, 'I am your firstborn son Esau.'

³³ Then Isaac trembled in very great perplexity, and said, ''Who — where — is the one who hunted game, brought it to me, and I partook of all before you came and I blessed him? Indeed, he shall remain blessed!'

³⁴ When Esau heard his father's words, he cried out an exceedingly great and bitter cry, and said to his father, 'Bless me too, Father!'

³⁵ But he said, 'Your brother came with cleverness and took your blessing.'

³⁶ He said, 'Is it because he was named Jacob that he should outwit me these two times? — He took away my birthright and see, now he took away my blessing!' Then he said, 'Have you not reserved a blessing for me?'

³⁷ Isaac answered, and said to Esau, 'Behold, a lord have I made him over you, and all his kin

נָתַ֣תִּי לוֹ֒ לַעֲבָדִ֗ים וְדָגָ֤ן וְתִירֹשׁ֙ סְמַכְתִּ֔יו
וּלְכָ֣ה אֵפ֔וֹא מָ֥ה אֶֽעֱשֶׂ֖ה בְּנִֽי: לח וַיֹּ֤אמֶר עֵשָׂו֙
אֶל־אָבִ֔יו הַֽבְרָכָ֨ה אַחַ֤ת הִֽוא־לְךָ֙ אָבִ֔י בָּרֲכֵ֥נִי
גַם־אָ֖נִי אָבִ֑י וַיִּשָּׂ֥א עֵשָׂ֛ו קֹל֖וֹ וַיֵּֽבְךְּ: לט וַיַּ֛עַן
יִצְחָ֥ק אָבִ֖יו וַיֹּ֣אמֶר אֵלָ֑יו הִנֵּ֞ה מִשְׁמַנֵּ֤י הָאָ֨רֶץ֙
יִֽהְיֶ֣ה מֽוֹשָׁבֶ֔ךָ וּמִטַּ֥ל הַשָּׁמַ֖יִם מֵעָֽל: מ וְעַל־
חַרְבְּךָ֣ תִֽחְיֶ֔ה וְאֶת־אָחִ֖יךָ תַּֽעֲבֹ֑ד וְהָיָה֙
כַּֽאֲשֶׁ֣ר תָּרִ֔יד וּפָֽרַקְתָּ֥ עֻלּ֖וֹ מֵעַ֥ל צַוָּארֶֽךָ:
מא וַיִּשְׂטֹ֤ם עֵשָׂו֙ אֶֽת־יַעֲקֹ֔ב עַל־הַ֨בְּרָכָ֔ה אֲשֶׁ֥ר
בֵּֽרֲכ֖וֹ אָבִ֑יו וַיֹּ֨אמֶר עֵשָׂ֜ו בְּלִבּ֗וֹ יִקְרְבוּ֙ יְמֵ֣י
אֵ֣בֶל אָבִ֔י וְאַֽהַרְגָ֖ה אֶת־יַעֲקֹ֥ב אָחִֽי: מב וַיֻּגַּ֣ד
לְרִבְקָ֔ה אֶת־דִּבְרֵ֥י עֵשָׂ֖ו בְּנָ֣הּ הַגָּדֹ֑ל וַתִּשְׁלַ֡ח
וַתִּקְרָא֩ לְיַֽעֲקֹ֨ב בְּנָ֜הּ הַקָּטָ֗ן וַתֹּ֤אמֶר אֵלָיו֙ הִנֵּה֙
עֵשָׂ֣ו אָחִ֔יךָ מִתְנַחֵ֥ם לְךָ֖ לְהָרְגֶֽךָ: מג וְעַתָּ֥ה בְנִ֖י
שְׁמַ֣ע בְּקֹלִ֑י וְק֧וּם בְּרַח־לְךָ֛ אֶל־לָבָ֥ן אָחִ֖י
חָרָֽנָה: מד וְיָֽשַׁבְתָּ֥ עִמּ֖וֹ יָמִ֣ים אֲחָדִ֑ים עַ֥ד
אֲשֶׁר־תָּשׁ֖וּב חֲמַ֥ת אָחִֽיךָ: מה עַד־שׁ֨וּב אַף־
אָחִ֜יךָ מִמְּךָ֗ וְשָׁכַח֙ אֵ֣ת אֲשֶׁר־עָשִׂ֣יתָ לּ֔וֹ
וְשָֽׁלַחְתִּ֖י וּלְקַחְתִּ֣יךָ מִשָּׁ֑ם לָמָ֥ה אֶשְׁכַּ֛ל גַּם־
שְׁנֵיכֶ֖ם י֥וֹם אֶחָֽד: מו וַתֹּ֤אמֶר רִבְקָה֙ אֶל־
יִצְחָ֔ק קַ֣צְתִּי בְחַיַּ֔י מִפְּנֵ֖י בְּנ֣וֹת חֵ֑ת אִם־לֹקֵ֣חַ
יַֽ֠עֲקֹב אִשָּׁ֨ה מִבְּנֽוֹת־חֵ֜ת כָּאֵ֗לֶּה מִבְּנ֣וֹת
הָאָ֔רֶץ לָ֥מָּה לִּ֖י חַיִּֽים: כח א וַיִּקְרָ֥א יִצְחָ֛ק
אֶֽל־יַעֲקֹ֖ב וַיְבָ֣רֶךְ אֹת֑וֹ וַיְצַוֵּ֨הוּ֙ וַיֹּ֣אמֶר ל֔וֹ

38. Enable me also to achieve wealth and dominion in this world, independently, and not in the shadow of Jacob. Bless me, as a father blesses *each of* his children with abundance (*Malbim*).

Esau raised his voice and wept. Esau produced but a few tears . . . But see how much peace and tranquility God bestowed upon Esau for those tears! (*Tanchuma*).

For we will remain under Esau's power until we repent and shed tears that can outweigh his (*Zohar*).

39. Esau's blessing.

There is no conflict in the blessing since God's natural blessing is abundant enough for *both* of them. Furthermore, since Jacob was Abraham's heir, he would realize his blessing *in Eretz Yisrael*, while Esau would realize his in another land (*Ramban*).

Many *Chumashim* draw attention to a Masoretic note that this point marks half of the Book of *Bereishis* in number of verses.

40. The implication was not that Esau would be forced to become a brigand and plunderer with his sword, for he was blessed with sustenance from the *fatness of the earth and the dew of the heavens.* Rather, the blessing was that he be victorious in war and survive his battles (*Ramban*).

But your brother you shall serve. This, too, was a blessing: It is better to serve a *brother* than to be in servitude to others (*Radak*).

When Israel shall transgress the Torah, you will have a valid reason to be *aggrieved* over his having taken the blessings; *then you may cast off his yoke from your neck* (*Rashi*).

41. Esau's hatred.
I do not wish to cause my father grief while he is still alive (*Rashi; Ramban*). — Perhaps Esau feared that his father would curse him, and his blessing would then turn into a curse (*Ramban*).

42. Esau's intention was revealed to her by רוּחַ הַקֹּדֶשׁ, *Divine Inspiration* (*Rashi*).

Summoned Jacob. Either out of fear or shame, Jacob had gone into hiding from Esau (*Ramban*).

43. Jacob is advised to flee to Laban.
Although Esau implied that he would not carry out his intention until Isaac died, Rebecca could not be sure when that would happen, so she ordered Jacob not to procrastinate until it would be too late (*Or HaChaim*).

44. Her hope was that things would soon be smoothed over, but in fact, she never saw him again (*Akeidas Yitzchak*).

45. The Midrash notes that Rebecca had innocently hoped to wait until Esau's anger would subside, but she was mistaken. Instead [*Amos* 1:11]: *Edom's . . . anger tore perpetually and he kept his wrath forever.*

She prophesied that they would die on the same day. As stated in *Sotah* 13a, such was indeed the case (*Rashi*).

46. If Jacob takes a wife.
Rather than tell Isaac that she wanted Jacob to leave home because his life was in danger, she used the unsuitability of the Hittite women as a pretext for her decision (*Rashbam*).

28/1. The admonition against marrying a Canaanite; the Abrahamitic blessing is conveyed to Jacob.

And blessed him. The blessing is the one given further in v. 3 (*Radak*).

have I given him as servants. With grain and wine have I supported him, and for you, where . . . what can I do, my son?'

38 And Esau said to his father, 'Have you but one blessing, Father? Bless me too, Father!' And Esau raised his voice and wept.

39 So Isaac his father answered, and said to him:

'Behold, of the fat of the earth shall be your dwelling and of the dew of the heavens from above. **40** By your sword you shall live, but your brother you shall serve. Yet it shall be that when you are aggrieved, you may cast off his yoke from upon your neck.'

41 Now Esau harbored hatred toward Jacob because of the blessing wherewith his father had blessed him. And Esau thought, 'May the days of mourning for my father draw near, then I will kill my brother Jacob.'

42 When Rebecca was told of the words of her older son Esau, she sent for and summoned Jacob her younger son and said to him, 'Behold, your brother Esau is consoling himself regarding you to kill you. **43** So now, my son, heed my voice and arise! Flee to my brother Laban, to Charan, **44** and remain with him a short while until your brother's wrath subsides. **45** — Until your brother's anger against you subsides and he forgets what you have done to him. Then I will send and summon you from there. Why should I be bereaved of both of you on the same day?'

46 Rebecca said to Isaac, 'I am disgusted with my life on account of the daughters of Heth. If Jacob takes a wife of the daughters of Heth like these, of the natives of the land, why need I live?'

28 ¹ So Isaac summoned Jacob and blessed him. He instructed him, saying to him,

לֹא־תִקַּח אִשָּׁה מִבְּנוֹת כְּנָעַן: בקוּם לֵךְ
פַּדֶּנָה אֲרָם בֵּיתָה בְתוּאֵל אֲבִי אִמֶּךְ וְקַח־
לְךָ מִשָּׁם אִשָּׁה מִבְּנוֹת לָבָן אֲחִי אִמֶּךְ: גוְאֵל
שַׁדַּי יְבָרֵךְ אֹתְךָ וְיַפְרְךָ וְיַרְבֶּךָ וְהָיִיתָ לִקְהַל
עַמִּים: דוְיִתֶּן־לְךָ אֶת־בִּרְכַּת אַבְרָהָם לְךָ
וּלְזַרְעֲךָ אִתָּךְ לְרִשְׁתְּךָ אֶת־אֶרֶץ מְגֻרֶיךָ
אֲשֶׁר־נָתַן אֱלֹהִים לְאַבְרָהָם: שביעי הוַיִּשְׁלַח
יִצְחָק אֶת־יַעֲקֹב וַיֵּלֶךְ פַּדֶּנָה אֲרָם אֶל־לָבָן
בֶּן־בְּתוּאֵל הָאֲרַמִּי אֲחִי רִבְקָה אֵם יַעֲקֹב
וְעֵשָׂו: ווַיַּרְא עֵשָׂו כִּי־בֵרַךְ יִצְחָק אֶת־יַעֲקֹב
וְשִׁלַּח אֹתוֹ פַּדֶּנָה אֲרָם לָקַחַת־לוֹ מִשָּׁם
אִשָּׁה בְּבָרְכוֹ אֹתוֹ וַיְצַו עָלָיו לֵאמֹר לֹא־
תִקַּח אִשָּׁה מִבְּנוֹת כְּנָעַן: מפטיר זוַיִּשְׁמַע יַעֲקֹב
אֶל־אָבִיו וְאֶל־אִמּוֹ וַיֵּלֶךְ פַּדֶּנָה אֲרָם: חוַיַּרְא
עֵשָׂו כִּי רָעוֹת בְּנוֹת כְּנָעַן בְּעֵינֵי יִצְחָק אָבִיו:
טוַיֵּלֶךְ עֵשָׂו אֶל־יִשְׁמָעֵאל וַיִּקַּח אֶת־מַחֲלַת ׀
בַּת־יִשְׁמָעֵאל בֶּן־אַבְרָהָם אֲחוֹת נְבָיוֹת עַל־
נָשָׁיו לוֹ לְאִשָּׁה:

The *Haftarah* for *Toldos* appears on page 316

2. In a home where a woman like your mother grew up in spite of the proximity of Laban, you can quite possibly find a worthy wife for yourself (*R' Hirsch*).

4. God blessed Abraham: *I will make of you a great nation; and And all the nations of the earth shall bless themselves by your offspring.* — May all those blessings be said regarding you. May that *great nation* and *blessed seed* issue from you (*Rashi*).

5. No mention is made of Isaac sending wealth along with his son, as would be expected. The Midrash comments that Jacob was robbed at the outset of his journey of whatever possessions he had. [See *Ibn Ezra* there.]

6-9. Esau marries the daughter of Ishmael.

6. In his second blessing to Jacob, Isaac conferred upon him the Abrahamitic gift of *Eretz Yisrael.* Esau calculated that this blessing had been stripped from him because he had wed Canaanite women. Therefore, he now took a daughter of Ishmael in the hope that he might yet regain the Abrahamitic blessing of the land (*Rashbam*).

9. *Rashi* [citing the Sages in *Megillah* 17] notes that the apparently superfluous description *sister of Nebayoth* is added to imply the tradition that Ishmael died after he designated his daughter for Esau. It was *Nebayoth* who actually gave her in marriage to Esau; hence he, too, is mentioned in this connection.

This section justifies the portrait of Esau as a selfish person oblivious to all but his own desires. For twenty-three years he had caused anguish to his parents by the behavior of his Canaanite wives, yet it seems to have dawned on him only now. Instead of divorcing them, however, he merely took another unsuitable wife *in addition* to them. Thus he proved that he had no feeling for the House of Abraham, and Rebecca's assessment of his complete unfitness for the future guidance of that House was fully justified (*R' Hirsch*).

According to the Masoretic note appearing at the end of the *Sidrah,* there are 106 verses in the *Sidrah,* numerically corresponding to the mnemonic עָל"וּ [*they* (i.e., Isaac and Jacob) *ascended* = 106; alluding to the primary themes of the *Sidrah:* the *ascendancy of Isaac* as a result of his experiences in Gerar (see comm. to 26:4,13, and 28), as well as the *ascendancy* of Jacob thanks to the birthright and the blessings]. The *Haftarah* begins with *Malachi* 1:1: מַשָּׂא דְבַר ה׳.

'Do not take a wife from the Canaanite women. ² Arise, go to Paddan Aram to the house of Bethuel your mother's father, and take a wife from there from the daughters of Laban, your mother's brother.

³ 'And may El Shaddai bless you, make you fruitful and make you numerous, and may you be a congregation of peoples.

⁴ 'May He grant you the blessing of Abraham to you and to your offspring with you, that you may possess the land of your sojourns which God gave to Abraham.'

⁵ So Isaac sent away Jacob and he went toward Paddan Aram to Laban the son of Bethuel the Aramean, brother of Rebecca, mother of Jacob and Esau. — When Esau saw that Isaac had blessed Jacob and sent him off to Paddan Aram to take himself a wife from there, charging him as he blessed him, 'You shall not take a wife from among the Canaanite women'; ⁷and that Jacob obeyed his father and mother and went to Paddan Aram. ⁸ Then Esau perceived that the Canaanite women were evil in the eyes of Isaac, his father, ⁹ so Esau went to Ishmael and took Mahalath, the daughter of Ishmael, sister of Nebayoth, in addition to his wives, as a wife for himself.

The *Haftarah* for *Toldos* appears on page 316

פרשת ויצא

VAYEITZEI

The Sages teach that before Jacob went to Charan, where he spent twenty years in a personal exile with the mendacious Laban, he studied for fourteen years in the academy of Shem and Eber, Noah's son and grandson. The contrast between the sacred environment of Isaac and Rebecca is hard to bear, even for a Jacob. One must prepare for it in a rarefied environment of holiness and knowledge of God. What is more, during an exile, especially if it is a gilded one, one must never forget one's roots and ultimate goal. For Jacob, this meant that he could not forget that he was the next Patriarch of Israel, the future father of the *B'nai Yisrael*, the holy nation that still bears his name.

The entire *Sidrah Vayeitzei* is one long paragraph of 145 verses, a very unusual phenomenon. Paragraph breaks in the Torah provide time for reflection on new knowledge or a new situation — but Jacob never made peace with his changed circumstances. He never ceased his concentration on the predicament of being parted from the Holy Land; for to forget that one is in exile is to make peace with the situation.

A superficial reading of Jacob's dealings with Laban would hardly lead one to conclude that Laban was especially wily, and certainly not that he was a charlatan, but the Sages' perception of Laban is one of unrelieved deception and dishonesty. And he is worse than that. In the Haggadah, Laban is described as the one who attempted to perpetrate an evil even greater than Pharoah's against Jacob and his family: *Laban sought to uproot everything*! From this we see the dangers of superficiality. The Torah must be studied in depth, people must be understood in depth, the challenges of everyday life must be analyzed in depth. Laban's smile and unctuous solicitude might deceive many of us, but if it had deceived Jacob, the implications for Jewish history would have been catastrophic. Jacob and his wives remained vigilant; because they did, they could not be uprooted — then or ever.

י וַיֵּצֵא יַעֲקֹב מִבְּאֵר שָׁבַע וַיֵּלֶךְ חָרָנָה: יא וַיִּפְגַּע בַּמָּקוֹם וַיָּלֶן שָׁם כִּי־בָא הַשֶּׁמֶשׁ וַיִּקַּח מֵאַבְנֵי הַמָּקוֹם וַיָּשֶׂם מְרַאֲשֹׁתָיו וַיִּשְׁכַּב בַּמָּקוֹם הַהוּא: יב וַיַּחֲלֹם וְהִנֵּה סֻלָּם מֻצָּב אַרְצָה וְרֹאשׁוֹ מַגִּיעַ הַשָּׁמָיְמָה וְהִנֵּה מַלְאֲכֵי אֱלֹהִים עֹלִים וְיֹרְדִים בּוֹ: יג וְהִנֵּה יְהוָה נִצָּב עָלָיו וַיֹּאמַר אֲנִי יְהוָה אֱלֹהֵי אַבְרָהָם אָבִיךָ וֵאלֹהֵי יִצְחָק הָאָרֶץ אֲשֶׁר אַתָּה שֹׁכֵב עָלֶיהָ לְךָ אֶתְּנֶנָּה וּלְזַרְעֶךָ: יד וְהָיָה זַרְעֲךָ כַּעֲפַר הָאָרֶץ וּפָרַצְתָּ יָמָּה וָקֵדְמָה וְצָפֹנָה וָנֶגְבָּה וְנִבְרְכוּ בְךָ כָּל־מִשְׁפְּחֹת הָאֲדָמָה וּבְזַרְעֶךָ: טו וְהִנֵּה אָנֹכִי עִמָּךְ וּשְׁמַרְתִּיךָ בְּכֹל אֲשֶׁר־תֵּלֵךְ וַהֲשִׁבֹתִיךָ אֶל־הָאֲדָמָה הַזֹּאת כִּי לֹא אֶעֱזָבְךָ עַד אֲשֶׁר אִם־עָשִׂיתִי אֵת אֲשֶׁר־דִּבַּרְתִּי לָךְ: טז וַיִּיקַץ יַעֲקֹב מִשְּׁנָתוֹ וַיֹּאמֶר אָכֵן יֵשׁ יְהוָה בַּמָּקוֹם הַזֶּה וְאָנֹכִי לֹא יָדָעְתִּי: יז וַיִּירָא וַיֹּאמַר מַה־נּוֹרָא הַמָּקוֹם הַזֶּה אֵין זֶה כִּי אִם־בֵּית אֱלֹהִים וְזֶה שַׁעַר הַשָּׁמָיִם: יח וַיַּשְׁכֵּם יַעֲקֹב בַּבֹּקֶר וַיִּקַּח אֶת־הָאֶבֶן אֲשֶׁר־שָׂם מְרַאֲשֹׁתָיו וַיָּשֶׂם אֹתָהּ מַצֵּבָה וַיִּצֹק שֶׁמֶן עַל־רֹאשָׁהּ: יט וַיִּקְרָא אֶת־שֵׁם־הַמָּקוֹם הַהוּא בֵּית־אֵל וְאוּלָם לוּז שֵׁם־הָעִיר לָרִאשֹׁנָה: כ וַיִּדַּר יַעֲקֹב נֶדֶר לֵאמֹר אִם־יִהְיֶה אֱלֹהִים עִמָּדִי וּשְׁמָרַנִי בַּדֶּרֶךְ הַזֶּה אֲשֶׁר אָנֹכִי הוֹלֵךְ וְנָתַן־לִי לֶחֶם לֶאֱכֹל וּבֶגֶד לִלְבֹּשׁ:

28/10. Jacob's flight to Charan. Jacob *departed*. A righteous person's departure from a place leaves a void: As long as he lives in a city, he constitutes its glory, its splendor, and its beauty; when he departs, its glory, splendor, and beauty depart with him.

Jacob did not go *directly* to Charan. Instead, he spent fourteen years in seclusion studying under Eber. He was sixty-three years old when he received his father's blessing and fled; when he finally set off toward Charan he was seventy-seven. This was in the year 2185 from Creation.

11. *The place.* Mt. Moriah. Our Sages interpret the term וַיִּפְגַּע to denote *prayer*. Accordingly, Jacob is credited with instituting עַרְבִית, the Evening Prayer (*Rashi*).

From the stones. Midrashically the Sages render that he took several stones. The stones began quarreling, each one saying, 'Upon *me* shall this righteous man rest his head.' Thereupon God combined them all into one stone. That is why verse 18 reads: *and he took 'the stone'* [singular].

12. The Dream. Dreams mentioned by Scripture are understood to be vehicles of prophecy; otherwise the Torah would not cite them.

The Dream's Symbolism. The vision was a disclosure of the future of the Jewish nation. It alluded to such concepts as the revelation at Sinai, the Four Kingdoms that would subjugate Israel during its exiles, the greatness of *Eretz Yisrael*, the quest for wisdom, Jacob's uniqueness, etc. See Art-Scroll *Bereishis* pp. 1224-7.

14. *As the dust of the earth.* I.e., as *numerous* as the dust of the earth (*Onkelos*).

Sforno connects this phrase with the following one, rendering: Only after your offspring shall have become as degraded *as the dust of the earth* [see *Isaiah* 51:23] *shall they spread out powerfully to the west, east, north, and south.* As the Sages have taught, God's future salvation will come only after Israel has experienced much degradation. [See *Overview* to ArtScroll *Daniel*.]

15. *What I have spoken about you.* 'Do not fear Esau or Laban because I am with you and will not forsake you *until I have completed what I promised regarding you.* I promised Abraham to give this land to his offspring [12:7] and it is only through you — not through Esau — that this promise will be fulfilled.'
(*Ibn Caspi*).

16. Jacob treated his dream as prophecy, for when prophets are shown a vision, they recognize it to be a communication from God.

And I did not know. Had I known, I would not have slept here! (*Midrash; Rashi*).

17. *The abode of God.* This is not an ordinary place, but the Sanctuary of God's Name, a suitable place for prayer (*Targum Yonasan*).

18. *The stone* is singular. The many stones he had collected earlier (v. 11) had coalesced into one stone (*Pirkei d'Rabbi Eliezer*).

19. The word Luz literally means *almond tree*. According to the Midrash, an almond tree concealed the city's entrance, keeping outsiders away [see *Judges* 1:25]. The tree was hollow, and through it one entered a cave which led to the entrance of the city.

[10] Jacob departed from Beer Sheba and went toward Charan. [11] He encountered the place and spent the night there because the sun had set. He took from the stones of the place which he arranged around his head, and lay down in that place. [12] And he dreamt, and behold! A ladder was set earthward and its top reached heavenward. And behold! Angels of God were ascending and descending on it.

[13] And behold! HASHEM was standing over him, and He said, 'I am HASHEM, God of Abraham your father and God of Isaac. The ground upon which you are lying, to you will I give it and to your descendants. [14] Your offspring shall be as the dust of the earth, and you shall spread out powerfully westward, eastward, northward and southward; and all the families of the earth shall bless themselves by you and by your offspring. [15] Behold, I am with you; I will guard you wherever you go, and I will return you to this soil; for I will not forsake you until I have done what I have spoken about you.'

[16] Jacob awoke from his sleep and said, 'Surely HASHEM is present in this place and I did not know!' [17] And he became frightened and said, 'How awesome is this place! This is none other than the abode of God and this is the gate of heavens!' [18] Jacob arose early in the morning and took the stone that he placed around his head and set it up as a pillar; then he poured oil on its top. [19] And he named that place Bethel. However, Luz was the city's name originally.

[20] Then Jacob took a vow, saying, 'If God will be with me, will guard me on this way that I am going; will give me bread to eat and clothes to wear;

כא וְשַׁבְתִּי בְשָׁלוֹם אֶל־בֵּית אָבִי וְהָיָה יהוה לִי
לֵאלֹהִים: כב וְהָאֶבֶן הַזֹּאת אֲשֶׁר־שַׂמְתִּי
מַצֵּבָה יִהְיֶה בֵּית אֱלֹהִים וְכֹל אֲשֶׁר תִּתֶּן־לִי
עַשֵּׂר אֲעַשְּׂרֶנּוּ לָךְ: כט שני א וַיִּשָּׂא יַעֲקֹב רַגְלָיו
וַיֵּלֶךְ אַרְצָה בְנֵי־קֶדֶם: ב וַיַּרְא וְהִנֵּה בְאֵר
בַּשָּׂדֶה וְהִנֵּה־שָׁם שְׁלֹשָׁה עֶדְרֵי־צֹאן רֹבְצִים
עָלֶיהָ כִּי מִן־הַבְּאֵר הַהִוא יַשְׁקוּ הָעֲדָרִים
וְהָאֶבֶן גְּדֹלָה עַל־פִּי הַבְּאֵר: ג וְנֶאֶסְפוּ־שָׁמָּה
כָל־הָעֲדָרִים וְגָלְלוּ אֶת־הָאֶבֶן מֵעַל פִּי הַבְּאֵר
וְהִשְׁקוּ אֶת־הַצֹּאן וְהֵשִׁיבוּ אֶת־הָאֶבֶן עַל־פִּי
הַבְּאֵר לִמְקֹמָהּ: ד וַיֹּאמֶר לָהֶם יַעֲקֹב אַחַי
מֵאַיִן אַתֶּם וַיֹּאמְרוּ מֵחָרָן אֲנָחְנוּ: ה וַיֹּאמֶר
לָהֶם הַיְדַעְתֶּם אֶת־לָבָן בֶּן־נָחוֹר וַיֹּאמְרוּ
יָדָעְנוּ: ו וַיֹּאמֶר לָהֶם הֲשָׁלוֹם לוֹ וַיֹּאמְרוּ שָׁלוֹם
וְהִנֵּה רָחֵל בִּתּוֹ בָּאָה עִם־הַצֹּאן: ז וַיֹּאמֶר הֵן
עוֹד הַיּוֹם גָּדוֹל לֹא־עֵת הֵאָסֵף הַמִּקְנֶה הַשְׁקוּ
הַצֹּאן וּלְכוּ רְעוּ: ח וַיֹּאמְרוּ לֹא נוּכַל עַד אֲשֶׁר
יֵאָסְפוּ כָּל־הָעֲדָרִים וְגָלְלוּ אֶת־הָאֶבֶן מֵעַל פִּי
הַבְּאֵר וְהִשְׁקִינוּ הַצֹּאן: ט עוֹדֶנּוּ מְדַבֵּר עִמָּם
וְרָחֵל ׀ בָּאָה עִם־הַצֹּאן אֲשֶׁר לְאָבִיהָ כִּי רֹעָה
הִוא: י וַיְהִי כַּאֲשֶׁר רָאָה יַעֲקֹב אֶת־רָחֵל בַּת־
לָבָן אֲחִי אִמּוֹ וְאֶת־צֹאן לָבָן אֲחִי אִמּוֹ וַיִּגַּשׁ
יַעֲקֹב וַיָּגֶל אֶת־הָאֶבֶן מֵעַל פִּי הַבְּאֵר וַיַּשְׁקְ
אֶת־צֹאן לָבָן אֲחִי אִמּוֹ: יא וַיִּשַּׁק יַעֲקֹב לְרָחֵל

22. אֲעַשְּׂרֶנּוּ אֲשֶׁר — *I shall repeatedly tithe* [lit., *tithe I shall tithe*] *to You.* This pledge includes a tenth of my children, whom I shall dedicate to Your service. Specifically, this was Levi, who, more than his brothers, was involved in serving God, and to whom Jacob imparted the esoteric teachings and wisdom of the Torah (*Radak*).

[That Jacob actually set aside a tithe from his possessions is mentioned by *Rashi* in 32:33 and *Ibn Ezra* in 35:14.]

29/1. Jacob meets Rachel. *The land of the easterners.* The reference is to Abraham's ancestral home — the regions east of *Eretz Yisrael*; Aram, Ur Kasdim, etc.

2. The Torah narrates this incident at length to illustrate how those who trust in God shall renew their strength [*Isaiah* 40:31]. For though Jacob was weary from his long journey, he was able to roll away the stone unassisted, a task which usually required the combined effort of all the shepherds (*Ramban*).

5. *Laban the son* [i.e., descendant] *of Nachor.* Actually Laban's father was *Bethuel;* he was Nachor's grandson.

6. Realizing that Jacob's curiosity about Laban would involve more details about his personal life than they could supply, they pointed out his daughter, as if to say: *Look, his daughter is coming* — perhaps you should ask her your questions directly! *(Haamek Davar).*

9. *Rachel alone* tended the flocks as there was no other shepherd. Leah did not share this chore, either because the sun might have been harmful to her weak eyes [see v. 17], or because she was older — of marriageable age — and Laban was afraid to let her mix with the shepherds. In the case of Rachel, however, there was no apprehension since she was still too young for the shepherd boys to take an interest in her *(Ramban).*

²¹ and I return in peace to my father's house, and HASHEM will be a God to me — ²² then this stone which I have set up as a pillar shall become a house of God, and whatever You will give me, I shall repeatedly tithe to You.'

29 ¹ So Jacob lifted his feet, and went toward the land of the easterners. ² He looked, and behold — a well in the field! And behold! Three flocks of sheep lay there beside it, for from that well they would water the flocks. Now the stone over the mouth of the well was large. ³ When all the flocks would be assembled there they would roll the stone from the mouth of the well and water the sheep. Then they would put back the stone over the mouth of the well, in its place.

⁴ Jacob said to them, 'My brothers, where are you from?' And they said, 'We are from Charan.' ⁵ He said to them, 'Do you know Laban the son of Nachor?' And they said, 'We know.' ⁶ Then he said, 'Is it well with him?' They answered, 'It is well. And see — his daughter Rachel is coming with the flock!'

⁷ He said, 'Look, it is still broad daylight; it is not yet time to bring the livestock in. Water the sheep and go on grazing.' ⁸ But they said, 'We will be unable to, until all the flocks will have been gathered and they will roll the stone off the mouth of the well. We will then water the sheep.'

⁹ While he was still speaking with them, Rachel had arrived with her father's sheep, for she was a shepherdess. ¹⁰ And it was, when Jacob saw Rachel, daughter of Laban his mother's brother, and the sheep of Laban his mother's brother, Jacob came forward and rolled the stone off the mouth of the well and watered the sheep of Laban his mother's brother. ¹¹ Then Jacob kissed Rachel;

וַיִּשָּׂא אֶת־קֹלוֹ וַיֵּבְךְ: יב וַיַּגֵּד יַעֲקֹב לְרָחֵל כִּי
אֲחִי אָבִיהָ הוּא וְכִי בֶן־רִבְקָה הוּא וַתָּרָץ
וַתַּגֵּד לְאָבִיהָ: יג וַיְהִי כִשְׁמֹעַ לָבָן אֶת־שֵׁמַע ׀
יַעֲקֹב בֶּן־אֲחֹתוֹ וַיָּרָץ לִקְרָאתוֹ וַיְחַבֶּק־לוֹ
וַיְנַשֶּׁק־לוֹ וַיְבִיאֵהוּ אֶל־בֵּיתוֹ וַיְסַפֵּר לְלָבָן
אֵת כָּל־הַדְּבָרִים הָאֵלֶּה: יד וַיֹּאמֶר לוֹ לָבָן
אַךְ עַצְמִי וּבְשָׂרִי אָתָּה וַיֵּשֶׁב עִמּוֹ חֹדֶשׁ
יָמִים: טו וַיֹּאמֶר לָבָן לְיַעֲקֹב הֲכִי־אָחִי
אַתָּה וַעֲבַדְתַּנִי חִנָּם הַגִּידָה לִּי מַה־
מַשְׂכֻּרְתֶּךָ: טז וּלְלָבָן שְׁתֵּי בָנוֹת שֵׁם הַגְּדֹלָה
לֵאָה וְשֵׁם הַקְּטַנָּה רָחֵל: יז וְעֵינֵי לֵאָה רַכּוֹת
וְרָחֵל הָיְתָה יְפַת־תֹּאַר וִיפַת מַרְאֶה: שלישי
יח וַיֶּאֱהַב יַעֲקֹב אֶת־רָחֵל וַיֹּאמֶר אֶעֱבָדְךָ
שֶׁבַע שָׁנִים בְּרָחֵל בִּתְּךָ הַקְּטַנָּה: יט וַיֹּאמֶר
לָבָן טוֹב תִּתִּי אֹתָהּ לָךְ מִתִּתִּי אֹתָהּ לְאִישׁ
אַחֵר שְׁבָה עִמָּדִי: כ וַיַּעֲבֹד יַעֲקֹב בְּרָחֵל
שֶׁבַע שָׁנִים וַיִּהְיוּ בְעֵינָיו כְּיָמִים אֲחָדִים
בְּאַהֲבָתוֹ אֹתָהּ: כא וַיֹּאמֶר יַעֲקֹב אֶל־לָבָן
הָבָה אֶת־אִשְׁתִּי כִּי מָלְאוּ יָמָי וְאָבוֹאָה אֵלֶיהָ:
כב וַיֶּאֱסֹף לָבָן אֶת־כָּל־אַנְשֵׁי הַמָּקוֹם וַיַּעַשׂ
מִשְׁתֶּה: כג וַיְהִי בָעֶרֶב וַיִּקַּח אֶת־לֵאָה בִתּוֹ
וַיָּבֵא אֹתָהּ אֵלָיו וַיָּבֹא אֵלֶיהָ: כד וַיִּתֵּן לָבָן לָהּ
אֶת־זִלְפָּה שִׁפְחָתוֹ לְלֵאָה בִתּוֹ שִׁפְחָה:
כה וַיְהִי בַבֹּקֶר וְהִנֵּה־הִוא לֵאָה וַיֹּאמֶר אֶל־
לָבָן מַה־זֹּאת עָשִׂיתָ לִּי הֲלֹא בְרָחֵל עָבַדְתִּי

11. *And [he] wept.* He wept because he foresaw prophetically that she would not be buried with him [in the Cave of Machpelah]. Another reason he wept was because he had come empty handed. He thought: "Eliezer, who was only my grandfather's *servant,* came for my mother laden with riches, while I come here destitute. Esau's son Eliphaz had taken everything I had' (*Rashi* citing *Midrash*).

12. *Then she ran and told her father.* Her mother was dead and she had no one else to tell but him (*Rashi* following *Midrash*).

13. Laban thought that Jacob must be loaded with money, seeing that a mere household servant [Eliezer] had [years earlier] come with ten richly laden camels [24:10] (*Rashi*).

Seeing that Jacob was empty handed, Laban thought that he might have money hidden on his person. He therefore *embraced* him [to frisk him and discover any hidden treasures] (*Rashi* based on Midrash).

14. Laban invites Jacob to reside with him.

15. Although Jacob had been working without pay, Laban preferred to pay him — and get him to commit himself to continue on the job, rather than risk losing such a capable worker (*R' Hirsch*).

16. Before recording Jacob's response to Laban's inquiry, the Torah interjects these parenthetical verses to inform us that Laban had two daughters, the younger of whom Jacob loved. This digression prepares us for Jacob's response in verse 18, where he requested the younger daughter in marriage (*Rashbam*).

17. *Leah's eyes were tender.* Through constant weeping at the prospect of marrying Esau. People used to say that since Rebecca has two sons and Laban two daughters, the elder daughter would be married to the elder son, while the younger daughter would be married to the younger son (*Rashi*).

Jacob's voluntary separation from his parents. Jacob was away from his parents for a total of thirty-six years, of which he spent fourteen studying in the Academy of Eber. For those years of study, he was not considered negligent for failing to honor his parents. For the other twenty-two years, however, during which he failed to return home — twenty years of service and two years of journeying — the Sages hold that Jacob was derelict. His punishment was that Joseph remained separated from him for a like number of years.

20. The Torah repeats for *Rachel* because Jacob constantly let it be known throughout his service that he was working for *Rachel.* He wanted the bargain to be known to all so Laban could not deny the deal later (*Or HaChaim*).

21. After seven years, Laban said nothing; Jacob was forced to approach Laban to remind him of the arrangement (*Ralbag*).

22. Jacob marries Leah.

25. *And it was, in the morning, that behold it was Leah!* Jacob had given Rachel a prearranged sign [by which he could know who she was]. When Rachel saw that they were about to substitute Leah for her, she confided the sign to her so that she would not be put to shame (*Rashi* from *Megillah* 13b).

and he raised his voice and wept. [12] Jacob told Rachel that he was her father's relative, and that he was Rebecca's son. Then she ran and told her father.

[13] And it was, when Laban heard the news of Jacob his nephew, he ran toward him, embraced him, kissed him, and took him to his house. He recounted to Laban all these events. [14] Then Laban said to him, 'Nevertheless, you are my flesh and blood!' And he stayed with him a month's time.

[15] Then Laban said to Jacob, 'Just because you are my relative should you serve me for nothing? Tell me: What are your wages?'

[16] (Laban had two daughters. The name of the older one was Leah and the name of the younger one was Rachel. [17] Leah's eyes were tender, while Rachel was beautiful of form and beautiful of appearance.)

[18] Jacob loved Rachel, so he said, 'I will work for you seven years, for Rachel your younger daughter.'

[19] Laban said, 'It is better that I give her to you than that I give her to another man. Remain with me.' [20] So Jacob worked seven years for Rachel and they seemed to him a few days because of his love for her.

[21] Jacob said to Laban, 'Deliver my wife for my term is fulfilled, and I will consort with her.'

[22] So Laban gathered all the people of the place and made a feast. [23] And it was in the evening, that he took Leah his daughter and brought her to him. And he consorted with her.

[24] — And Laban gave her Zilpah his maidservant — a maidservant to Leah his daughter.

[25] And it was, in the morning, that behold it was Leah! So he said to Laban, 'What is this you have done to me? Was it not for Rachel that I worked

עִמָּ֔ךְ וְלָ֥מָּה רִמִּיתָֽנִי: כּו וַיֹּ֣אמֶר לָבָ֔ן לֹא־
יֵעָשֶׂ֥ה כֵ֖ן בִּמְקוֹמֵ֑נוּ לָתֵ֥ת הַצְּעִירָ֖ה לִפְנֵ֥י
הַבְּכִירָֽה: כז מַלֵּ֖א שְׁבֻ֣עַ זֹ֑את וְנִתְּנָ֤ה לְךָ֙
גַּם־אֶת־זֹ֗את בַּעֲבֹדָה֙ אֲשֶׁ֣ר תַּעֲבֹ֣ד עִמָּדִ֔י
ע֖וֹד שֶֽׁבַע־שָׁנִ֥ים אֲחֵרֽוֹת: כח וַיַּ֤עַשׂ יַעֲקֹב֙
כֵּ֔ן וַיְמַלֵּ֖א שְׁבֻ֣עַ זֹ֑את וַיִּתֶּן־ל֛וֹ אֶת־רָחֵ֥ל בִּתּ֖וֹ
ל֥וֹ לְאִשָּֽׁה: כט וַיִּתֵּ֤ן לָבָן֙ לְרָחֵ֣ל בִּתּ֔וֹ אֶת־
בִּלְהָ֖ה שִׁפְחָת֑וֹ לָ֖הּ לְשִׁפְחָֽה: ל וַיָּבֹא֙ גַּ֣ם
אֶל־רָחֵ֔ל וַיֶּאֱהַ֥ב גַּֽם־אֶת־רָחֵ֖ל מִלֵּאָ֑ה וַיַּעֲבֹ֣ד
עִמּ֔וֹ ע֖וֹד שֶֽׁבַע־שָׁנִ֥ים אֲחֵרֽוֹת: לא וַיַּ֣רְא
יְהֹוָה֙ כִּֽי־שְׂנוּאָ֣ה לֵאָ֔ה וַיִּפְתַּ֖ח אֶת־רַחְמָ֑הּ
וְרָחֵ֖ל עֲקָרָֽה: לב וַתַּ֤הַר לֵאָה֙ וַתֵּ֣לֶד בֵּ֔ן
וַתִּקְרָ֥א שְׁמ֖וֹ רְאוּבֵ֑ן כִּ֣י אָֽמְרָ֗ה כִּֽי־רָאָ֤ה
יְהֹוָה֙ בְּעָנְיִ֔י כִּ֥י עַתָּ֖ה יֶאֱהָבַ֥נִי אִישִֽׁי: לג וַתַּ֣הַר
ע֗וֹד וַתֵּ֣לֶד בֵּ֔ן וַתֹּ֗אמֶר כִּֽי־שָׁמַ֤ע יְהֹוָה֙
כִּֽי־שְׂנוּאָ֣ה אָנֹ֔כִי וַיִּתֶּן־לִ֖י גַּם־אֶת־זֶ֑ה
וַתִּקְרָ֥א שְׁמ֖וֹ שִׁמְעֽוֹן: לד וַתַּ֣הַר עוֹד֮ וַתֵּ֣לֶד בֵּן֒
וַתֹּ֗אמֶר עַתָּ֤ה הַפַּ֙עַם֙ יִלָּוֶ֤ה אִישִׁי֙ אֵלַ֔י כִּֽי־
יָלַ֥דְתִּי ל֖וֹ שְׁלֹשָׁ֣ה בָנִ֑ים עַל־כֵּ֥ן קָרָֽא־
שְׁמ֖וֹ לֵוִֽי: לה וַתַּ֨הַר ע֜וֹד וַתֵּ֣לֶד בֵּ֗ן וַתֹּ֙אמֶר֙
הַפַּ֙עַם֙ אוֹדֶ֣ה אֶת־יְהֹוָ֔ה עַל־כֵּ֛ן קָרְאָ֥ה שְׁמ֖וֹ
יְהוּדָ֑ה וַתַּעֲמֹ֖ד מִלֶּֽדֶת: ל א וַתֵּ֣רֶא רָחֵ֗ל כִּ֣י
לֹ֤א יָֽלְדָה֙ לְיַעֲקֹ֔ב וַתְּקַנֵּ֥א רָחֵ֖ל בַּאֲחֹתָ֑הּ
וַתֹּ֤אמֶר אֶֽל־יַעֲקֹב֙ הָֽבָה־לִּ֣י בָנִ֔ים וְאִם־אַ֖יִן
מֵתָ֥ה אָנֹֽכִי: ב וַיִּֽחַר־אַ֥ף יַעֲקֹ֖ב בְּרָחֵ֑ל וַיֹּ֕אמֶר

26. Laban justifies his wicked act by shifting responsibility. He portrays himself as having been forced to do so because the community, or some vague influential body, compelled him to act in this way (*Hoffmann*).

27. A new agreement is made for Rachel. *Yet another seven years.* This time it was *Laban*, not Jacob, who set the term. Because Jacob and Rachel were to be married *before* the work would begin, it was to Laban's advantage that there be no ambiguities, so he made sure the terms were clearly agreed upon.

31. The birth of the Tribes.

32. Reuben.

33. Simeon. He was born within the following seven months (*Seder Olam*).

34. Levi. The Matriarchs were prophetesses and knew that Jacob was to beget twelve tribes by four wives. Now that Leah had three children she said, 'Now my husband will have no cause for complaint against me, for I have given him my full share of children' (*Rashi*).

35. Judah. *Therefore she named him Judah* [Hebrew: *Yehudah*]. Which contains the letters referring to Hashem's Name, as well as the root that means 'thankfulness' and 'praise' (*Sforno*).

30/1. Jacob marries Bilhah.

Give me children. I.e., pray on my behalf! (*Ibn Ezra*).

2. *Why do you complain to me.* Am *I* to blame for your condition? Am I in God's place? *He,* not *I, has withheld children from you!* Moreover, *I* am not the barren one — it is from *you* that God withheld children, not from me; I already have children (*Radak; Abarbanel; Malbim*).

for you? Why have you deceived me?'

²⁶ Laban said, 'Such is not done in our place, to give the younger before the elder. ²⁷ Complete the week of this one and we will give you the other one too, for the work which you will perform for me yet another seven years.'

²⁸ So Jacob complied and he completed the week for her. And he gave him Rachel his daughter as his wife for him. ²⁹ And Laban gave Rachel his daughter Bilhah his maidservant — to her as a maidservant. ³⁰ He consorted also with Rachel and loved Rachel even more than Leah. And he worked for him yet another seven years.

³¹ HASHEM saw that Leah was unloved, so He opened her womb. But Rachel remained barren.

³² Leah conceived and bore a son, and she named him Reuben, as she had declared, 'Because HASHEM has discerned my humiliation, for now my husband will love me.'

³³ And she conceived again and bore a son and declared, 'Because HASHEM has heard that I am unloved, He has given me this one also.' And she named his Simeon.

³⁴ Again she conceived, and bore a son and declared, 'This time my husband will become attached to me for I have borne him three sons.' Therefore He named him Levi.

³⁵ She conceived again, and bore a son and declared, 'This time let me gratefully praise HASHEM.' Therefore she named him Judah. Then she stopped giving birth.

30 ¹ Rachel saw that she had not borne children to Jacob, so Rachel became envious of her sister. She said to Jacob, 'Give me children — otherwise I am dead.'

² Jacob's anger flared up at Rachel, and he said,

הֲתַחַת אֱלֹהִים אָנֹכִי אֲשֶׁר־מָנַע מִמֵּךְ פְּרִי־
בָטֶן: ג וַתֹּאמֶר הִנֵּה אֲמָתִי בִלְהָה בֹּא אֵלֶיהָ
וְתֵלֵד עַל־בִּרְכַּי וְאִבָּנֶה גַם־אָנֹכִי מִמֶּנָּה:
ד וַתִּתֶּן־לוֹ אֶת־בִּלְהָה שִׁפְחָתָהּ לְאִשָּׁה וַיָּבֹא
אֵלֶיהָ יַעֲקֹב: ה וַתַּהַר בִּלְהָה וַתֵּלֶד לְיַעֲקֹב בֵּן:
ו וַתֹּאמֶר רָחֵל דָּנַנִּי אֱלֹהִים וְגַם שָׁמַע בְּקֹלִי
וַיִּתֶּן־לִי בֵּן עַל־כֵּן קָרְאָה שְׁמוֹ דָּן: ז וַתַּהַר עוֹד
וַתֵּלֶד בִּלְהָה שִׁפְחַת רָחֵל בֵּן שֵׁנִי לְיַעֲקֹב:
ח וַתֹּאמֶר רָחֵל נַפְתּוּלֵי אֱלֹהִים ׀ נִפְתַּלְתִּי עִם־
אֲחֹתִי גַּם־יָכֹלְתִּי וַתִּקְרָא שְׁמוֹ נַפְתָּלִי: ט וַתֵּרֶא
לֵאָה כִּי עָמְדָה מִלֶּדֶת וַתִּקַּח אֶת־זִלְפָּה
שִׁפְחָתָהּ וַתִּתֵּן אֹתָהּ לְיַעֲקֹב לְאִשָּׁה: י וַתֵּלֶד
זִלְפָּה שִׁפְחַת לֵאָה לְיַעֲקֹב בֵּן: יא וַתֹּאמֶר
לֵאָה בְּגָד וַתִּקְרָא אֶת־שְׁמוֹ גָּד: יב וַתֵּלֶד
זִלְפָּה שִׁפְחַת לֵאָה בֵּן שֵׁנִי לְיַעֲקֹב: יג וַתֹּאמֶר
לֵאָה בְּאָשְׁרִי כִּי אִשְּׁרוּנִי בָּנוֹת וַתִּקְרָא
אֶת־שְׁמוֹ אָשֵׁר: רביעי יד וַיֵּלֶךְ רְאוּבֵן בִּימֵי
קְצִיר־חִטִּים וַיִּמְצָא דוּדָאִים בַּשָּׂדֶה וַיָּבֵא
אֹתָם אֶל־לֵאָה אִמּוֹ וַתֹּאמֶר רָחֵל אֶל־לֵאָה
תְּנִי־נָא לִי מִדּוּדָאֵי בְּנֵךְ: טו וַתֹּאמֶר לָהּ הַמְעַט
קַחְתֵּךְ אֶת־אִישִׁי וְלָקַחַת גַּם אֶת־דּוּדָאֵי
בְּנִי וַתֹּאמֶר רָחֵל לָכֵן יִשְׁכַּב עִמָּךְ הַלַּיְלָה
תַּחַת דּוּדָאֵי בְנֵךְ: טז וַיָּבֹא יַעֲקֹב מִן־
הַשָּׂדֶה בָּעֶרֶב וַתֵּצֵא לֵאָה לִקְרָאתוֹ וַתֹּאמֶר

בָּא גָד ק'

6. Dan.

7. Naftali.

8. *And I have also.* I.e., He has yielded to my importunities (*Rashi*) [by granting me a child through my maidservant].

9. Jacob marries Zilpah.

10. Gad.

12. Asher.

13. This son represents another instance of the good fortune about which the women have been praising me (*Rashbam; Ibn Ezra; Sforno*).

14. The dudaim. The incident of the *dudaim* is one of the most puzzling in the Torah. Of other verses, it is *axiomatic* that human intelligence is capable of only a superficial understanding of God's word; of the verses of the *dudaim*, it is *obvious* beyond doubt that the episode is filled with mysteries of the Torah. Indeed, the Sages and commentators found many teaching in these cryptic verses.

According to *Sforno*, Reuben *deliberately* sought the *dudaim*, which were believed to have fertility-inducing powers (see below). He wanted them for his mother, Leah, because he perceived that she was grieving over the cessation of her childbearing activity [v. 9].

15. [He was my husband before he was yours. Once I was already married to him] you should have never have consented to become my rival-wife (*Sforno*).

Jacob was to have stayed that night with Rachel, but she ceded the privilege to Leah in exchange for the *dudaim*. Because Rachel made light of being with that righteous man, she was not privileged to be buried [i.e., to lie in eternal repose] with him (*Rashi*).

16. The Sages viewed Leah's *going out* unfavorably, as an immodest act. The Midrash gives Leah the uncomplimentary designation of יַצְאָנִית, 'one who is fond of going out.' See *Rashi* to 34:1.

'Am I instead of God Who has withheld from you fruit of the womb?'

[3] She said, 'Here is my maid Bilhah, consort with her that she may bear upon my knees and I too may be built up through her.'

[4] So she gave him Bilhah her maidservant as a wife and Jacob consorted with her. [5] Bilhah conceived and bore Jacob a son. [6] Then Rachel said, 'God has judged me, He has also heard my voice and has given me a son.' She therefore named him Dan.

[7] Bilhah, Rachel's maidservant, conceived again and bore Jacob a second son. [8] And Rachel said, 'Sacred schemes have I maneuvered to equal my sister, and I have also prevailed!' And she named him Naftali.

[9] When Leah saw that she had stopped giving birth she took Zilpah her maidservant and gave her to Jacob as a wife. [10] Zilpah, Leah's maidservant, bore Jacob a son. [11] And Leah declared, 'Good luck has come!' So she named him Gad.

[12] Zilpah, Leah's maidservant, bore a second son to Jacob. [13] Leah declared, 'In my good fortune! For women have deemed me fortunate!' So she named him Asher.

[14] Reuben went out in the days of the wheat harvest. He found dudaim in the field and brought them to Leah his mother. Rachel said to Leah, 'Please give me some of your son's dudaim.'

[15] But she said to her, 'Was your taking my husband insignificant? — And now to take even my son's dudaim!' Rachel said, 'Therefore, he shall lie with you tonight in return for your son's dudaim.'

[16] When Jacob came from the field in the evening, Leah went out to meet him and said,

אֵלַי תָּבֹוא כִּי שָׂכֹר שְׂכַרְתִּיךָ בְּדוּדָאֵי בְּנִי
וַיִּשְׁכַּב עִמָּהּ בַּלַּיְלָה הוּא: יז וַיִּשְׁמַע אֱלֹהִים
אֶל־לֵאָה וַתַּהַר וַתֵּלֶד לְיַעֲקֹב בֵּן חֲמִישִׁי:
יח וַתֹּאמֶר לֵאָה נָתַן אֱלֹהִים שְׂכָרִי אֲשֶׁר־
נָתַתִּי שִׁפְחָתִי לְאִישִׁי וַתִּקְרָא שְׁמוֹ יִשָּׂשכָר:
יט וַתַּהַר עוֹד לֵאָה וַתֵּלֶד בֵּן־שִׁשִּׁי לְיַעֲקֹב:
כ וַתֹּאמֶר לֵאָה זְבָדַנִי אֱלֹהִים ׀ אֹתִי זֶבֶד טוֹב
הַפַּעַם יִזְבְּלֵנִי אִישִׁי כִּי־יָלַדְתִּי לוֹ שִׁשָּׁה בָנִים
וַתִּקְרָא אֶת־שְׁמוֹ זְבֻלוּן: כא וְאַחַר יָלְדָה בַּת
וַתִּקְרָא אֶת־שְׁמָהּ דִּינָה: כב וַיִּזְכֹּר אֱלֹהִים
אֶת־רָחֵל וַיִּשְׁמַע אֵלֶיהָ אֱלֹהִים וַיִּפְתַּח אֶת־
רַחְמָהּ: כג וַתַּהַר וַתֵּלֶד בֵּן וַתֹּאמֶר אָסַף אֱלֹהִים
אֶת־חֶרְפָּתִי: כד וַתִּקְרָא אֶת־שְׁמוֹ יוֹסֵף לֵאמֹר
יֹסֵף יְהוָה לִי בֵּן אַחֵר: כה וַיְהִי כַּאֲשֶׁר יָלְדָה
רָחֵל אֶת־יוֹסֵף וַיֹּאמֶר יַעֲקֹב אֶל־לָבָן שַׁלְּחֵנִי
וְאֵלְכָה אֶל־מְקוֹמִי וּלְאַרְצִי: כו תְּנָה אֶת־נָשַׁי
וְאֶת־יְלָדַי אֲשֶׁר עָבַדְתִּי אֹתְךָ בָּהֵן וְאֵלֵכָה כִּי
אַתָּה יָדַעְתָּ אֶת־עֲבֹדָתִי אֲשֶׁר עֲבַדְתִּיךָ:
כז וַיֹּאמֶר אֵלָיו לָבָן אִם־נָא מָצָאתִי חֵן בְּעֵינֶיךָ
נִחַשְׁתִּי וַיְבָרֲכֵנִי יְהוָה בִּגְלָלֶךָ: חמישי כח וַיֹּאמַר
נָקְבָה שְׂכָרְךָ עָלַי וְאֶתֵּנָה: כט וַיֹּאמֶר אֵלָיו
אַתָּה יָדַעְתָּ אֵת אֲשֶׁר עֲבַדְתִּיךָ וְאֵת אֲשֶׁר־
הָיָה מִקְנְךָ אִתִּי: ל כִּי מְעַט אֲשֶׁר־הָיָה
לְךָ לְפָנַי וַיִּפְרֹץ לָרֹב וַיְבָרֶךְ יְהוָה אֹתְךָ
לְרַגְלִי וְעַתָּה מָתַי אֶעֱשֶׂה גַם־אָנֹכִי לְבֵיתִי:

17. Issachar. *A fifth son.* [I.e., his fifth son *from her*; in total this was his *ninth son.*]

The pronunciation of Yissachar. The double שׂ in Issachar refers to multiple 'rewards' (*sachar*), one of which is Leah's statement *I have clearly 'hired' [sachor secharticha] you with my son's dudaim* (v. 16). Since this has an uncomplimentary connotation, one שׂ is silent and not pronounced. [Thus the name is pronounced *Yissachar* and not *Yissas'char*, as written] (*Daas Zekeinim; Baal HaTurim*).

21. Dinah. *Rashi* [citing *Berachos* 60a] comments that Leah 'passed judgment' (*danah*): '[Jacob is destined to beget twelve tribes. I have already borne six, and each of the handmaids have already borne two, making a total of ten.] If the child I am carrying turns out to be a male, then Rachel will not even be equivalent to one of the handmaids.' She therefore prayed concerning him, and he was changed to a female. [The bracketed addition is from the *Talmud*, ibid.]

22. Rachel conceives; the birth of Joseph. [It was not the *dudaim* that caused Rachel to become pregnant. This verse makes it clear that *God* remembered Rachel; *God hearkened to her prayers;* and it was *He* — alone — Who opened her womb. Children are a gift of God.]

24. She asked for only *one* more son, because she knew prophetically that Jacob would have twelve sons, and eleven of them were already born. The intent, then, of her prayer was: May I be the mother of the son whom Jacob is destined to have (*Rashi*).

25. **Jacob wishes to depart. A new agreement is concluded with Laban.** According to the Midrash, [although Jacob's period of service had ended and he was theoretically free to leave at any time] Jacob waited until Joseph was born. Only after the birth of Joseph, whom Jacob prophetically foresaw to be Esau's conqueror, did Jacob feel he could risk Esau's wrath and safely return home.

27. [Laban is reluctant to part with Jacob who, as he admits, served him well, and in whose merit God had blessed him.]

28. Laban had hoped the pious man would be flattered by this acknowledgment of Heavenly intervention, and declare himself willing to remain without asking for pay. But when Jacob remained silent, Laban realized that he would have to offer an inducement. Accordingly, he asked Jacob to stipulate his terms (*R' Hirsch*).

'It is to me that you must come for I have clearly hired you with my son's dudaim.' So he lay with her that night.

¹⁷ God hearkened to Leah. She conceived and bore Jacob a fifth son. ¹⁸ And Leah declared, 'God has granted me my reward because I gave my maidservant to my husband.' So she named him Issachar.

¹⁹ Then Leah conceived again and bore Jacob a sixth son. ²⁰ Leah said, 'God has endowed me with a good endowment. Now my husband will make his permanent home with me for I have borne him six sons.' So she named him Zebulun. ²¹ Afterwards, she bore a daughter and she named her Dinah.

²² God remembered Rachel. God hearkened to her and He opened her womb. ²³ She conceived and bore a son, and said, 'God has taken away my disgrace.' ²⁴ So she named him Joseph, saying, 'May HASHEM add on for me another son.'

²⁵ And it was, when Rachel had given birth to Joseph, Jacob said to Laban, 'Grant me leave that I may go to my place and to my land. ²⁶ Give me my wives and my children for whom I have served you, and I will go. For you are aware of my service that I labored for you.'

²⁷ But Laban said to him, 'If I have found favor with you! — I have learned by divination that HASHEM has blessed me on account of you.' ²⁸ And he said, 'Specify your wage to me and I will give it.' ²⁹ But he said to him, 'You know how I served you and what your cattle were with me. ³⁰ For the little that you had before I came has expanded substantially as HASHEM has blessed you with my coming. And now, when will I also do something for my own house?'

לא וַיֹּאמֶר מָה אֶתֶּן־לָךְ וַיֹּאמֶר יַעֲקֹב לֹא־
תִתֶּן־לִי מְאוּמָה אִם־תַּעֲשֶׂה־לִּי הַדָּבָר הַזֶּה
אָשׁוּבָה אֶרְעֶה צֹאנְךָ אֶשְׁמֹר: לב אֶעֱבֹר בְּכָל־
צֹאנְךָ הַיּוֹם הָסֵר מִשָּׁם כָּל־שֶׂה ׀ נָקֹד וְטָלוּא
וְכָל־שֶׂה־חוּם בַּכְּשָׂבִים וְטָלוּא וְנָקֹד בָּעִזִּים
וְהָיָה שְׂכָרִי: לג וְעָנְתָה־בִּי צִדְקָתִי בְּיוֹם מָחָר
כִּי־תָבוֹא עַל־שְׂכָרִי לְפָנֶיךָ כֹּל אֲשֶׁר־אֵינֶנּוּ
נָקֹד וְטָלוּא בָּעִזִּים וְחוּם בַּכְּשָׂבִים גָּנוּב הוּא
אִתִּי: לד וַיֹּאמֶר לָבָן הֵן לוּ יְהִי כִדְבָרֶךָ:
לה וַיָּסַר בַּיּוֹם הַהוּא אֶת־הַתְּיָשִׁים הָעֲקֻדִּים
וְהַטְּלֻאִים וְאֵת כָּל־הָעִזִּים הַנְּקֻדּוֹת וְהַטְּלֻאֹת
כֹּל אֲשֶׁר־לָבָן בּוֹ וְכָל־חוּם בַּכְּשָׂבִים וַיִּתֵּן
בְּיַד־בָּנָיו: לו וַיָּשֶׂם דֶּרֶךְ שְׁלֹשֶׁת יָמִים בֵּינוֹ
וּבֵין יַעֲקֹב וְיַעֲקֹב רֹעֶה אֶת־צֹאן לָבָן
הַנּוֹתָרֹת: לז וַיִּקַּח־לוֹ יַעֲקֹב מַקַּל לִבְנֶה לַח
וְלוּז וְעֶרְמוֹן וַיְפַצֵּל בָּהֵן פְּצָלוֹת לְבָנוֹת
מַחְשֹׂף הַלָּבָן אֲשֶׁר עַל־הַמַּקְלוֹת: לח וַיַּצֵּג
אֶת־הַמַּקְלוֹת אֲשֶׁר פִּצֵּל בָּרְהָטִים בְּשִׁקֲתוֹת
הַמָּיִם אֲשֶׁר תָּבֹאןָ הַצֹּאן לִשְׁתּוֹת לְנֹכַח
הַצֹּאן וַיֵּחַמְנָה בְּבֹאָן לִשְׁתּוֹת: לט וַיֶּחֱמוּ הַצֹּאן
אֶל־הַמַּקְלוֹת וַתֵּלַדְןָ הַצֹּאן עֲקֻדִּים נְקֻדִּים
וּטְלֻאִים: מ וְהַכְּשָׂבִים הִפְרִיד יַעֲקֹב וַיִּתֵּן
פְּנֵי הַצֹּאן אֶל־עָקֹד וְכָל־חוּם בְּצֹאן לָבָן
וַיָּשֶׁת לוֹ עֲדָרִים לְבַדּוֹ וְלֹא שָׁתָם עַל־צֹאן
לָבָן: מא וְהָיָה בְּכָל־יַחֵם הַצֹּאן הַמְקֻשָּׁרוֹת

31. [Laban presses further:] מָה אֶתֶּן לָךְ — *What shall I give you* to compensate for what you could expect to earn [if you were to work for yourself] (*Sforno*).

Jacob consents to remain.
[He proceeds to propose an arrangement by which, in the natural order of events, he would gain little:]

Do not give me anything of the flocks you *now* possess; whatever you profited from my past work is yours, because I worked for the right to marry your daughters. My wage for *continuing* to tend your flocks will come from those unnaturally colored animals that will be born *in the future* (*Rashbam*).

32. Jacob's wages.
[Although the commentators differ as to the precise interpretation of *every* detail of the narrative, the arrangement to which Jacob agrees is *basically* as follows: From the flocks in Jacob's care, Laban will remove certain animals of *abnormal color*, leaving the normally colored ones with Jacob. Of the animals to be born from the flocks he was tending, Jacob would be permitted to keep only the *abnormally* colored ones.]

34. [Laban apparently assumed that the pure white and pure black animals left with Jacob would bear only a trifling percentage of miscolored young. Such would have indeed been the case were it not that Jacob — betrayed by Laban's change of terms — adopted special measures as will be explained later.]

35. [In practice, Laban does not allow Jacob to keep the colored animals (see v. 32). Furthermore, the deceitful Laban removes more of the flock than he was entitled to under the original terms.]

36. [As an additional precaution, Laban places a large distance between the flocks he separated and the flocks he left with Jacob.]

37. The peeled rods. Jacob resorts to several devices to outwit his uncle and regain what was rightfully his under the original terms of the arrangement. He places colored rods in front of the flocks at the time they conceived, so that they would bear lambs having the same markings as the rod they were facing. Cf. *Megillah* 13b which justifies Jacob's actions by citing *Psalms* 18:27: *with the trustworthy, act trustingly; and with the crooked, act perversely.*

38. When the female animals would see the rods [in their watering troughs] they would become startled and recoil backwards. At that moment the males would mount them, and they would later give birth to lambs having the same markings as the rod they were facing (*Rashi*).

R' Bachya observes that this concept contains an important lesson. If imagination is a determining factor in the nature of unborn lambs, as this verse describes, then how much more important will it be when sensitive, thinking human beings procreate! Therefore, when husband and wife unite, they must purge their minds of all impure thoughts and every element which is foreign or which concerns third parties. The degree of their moral and spiritual purity will effect the souls of their children (*R' Munk*).

40. Jacob separates the flocks, making the newborn spotted ones lead the monochrome ones, so the latter would be influenced by the leaders and bear similar offspring.

[31] He said, 'What shall I give you?' And Jacob said, 'Do not give me anything. If you will do this thing for me, I will resume pasturing and guarding your flocks: [32] Let me pass through your whole flock today. Remove from there every speckled or spotted sheep, every brownish lamb among the sheep and the spotted or speckled among the goats — that will be my wage. [33] Let my integrity testify for me in the future when it comes before you regarding my wage. Any among the goats that is not speckled or spotted, or among the sheep that is not brownish, may be regarded as stolen if in my possession.'

[34] And Laban said, 'Agreed! If only it would remain as you say.'

[35] So he removed on that very day the ringed and spotted he-goats and all the speckled and spotted goats — every one that contained white, as well as all the brownish ones among the sheep — and he left them in charge of his sons. [36] And he put a distance of three days between himself and Jacob; and Jacob tended Laban's remaining flock.

[37] Jacob then took himself a fresh rod of poplar and hazel and chestnut. He peeled white streaks in them, laying bare the white of the rods. [38] And he set up the rods which he had peeled, in the runnels — in the watering receptacles to which the flocks came to drink — facing the sheep, so they would become stimulated when they came to drink. [39] Then the flocks became stimulated by the rods and the flocks gave birth to ringed ones, speckled ones and spotted ones. [40] Jacob segregated the lambs and he made the sheep face the ringed ones and all the brownish ones among Laban's flocks. He formed separate flocks of his own and did not mingle them with Laban's sheep.

[41] Whenever the early-bearing animals became

וְשָׂם יַעֲקֹב אֶת־הַמַּקְלוֹת לְעֵינֵי הַצֹּאן
בָּרְהָטִים לְיַחֵמֶנָּה בַּמַּקְלוֹת: מב וּבְהַעֲטִיף
הַצֹּאן לֹא יָשִׂים וְהָיָה הָעֲטֻפִים לְלָבָן
וְהַקְּשֻׁרִים לְיַעֲקֹב: מג וַיִּפְרֹץ הָאִישׁ מְאֹד מְאֹד
וַיְהִי־לוֹ צֹאן רַבּוֹת וּשְׁפָחוֹת וַעֲבָדִים וּגְמַלִּים
וַחֲמֹרִים: **לא** א וַיִּשְׁמַע אֶת־דִּבְרֵי בְנֵי־לָבָן
לֵאמֹר לָקַח יַעֲקֹב אֵת כָּל־אֲשֶׁר לְאָבִינוּ
וּמֵאֲשֶׁר לְאָבִינוּ עָשָׂה אֵת כָּל־הַכָּבֹד הַזֶּה:
ב וַיַּרְא יַעֲקֹב אֶת־פְּנֵי לָבָן וְהִנֵּה אֵינֶנּוּ עִמּוֹ
כִּתְמוֹל שִׁלְשׁוֹם: ג וַיֹּאמֶר יהוה אֶל־יַעֲקֹב
שׁוּב אֶל־אֶרֶץ אֲבוֹתֶיךָ וּלְמוֹלַדְתֶּךָ וְאֶהְיֶה
עִמָּךְ: ד וַיִּשְׁלַח יַעֲקֹב וַיִּקְרָא לְרָחֵל וּלְלֵאָה
הַשָּׂדֶה אֶל־צֹאנוֹ: ה וַיֹּאמֶר לָהֶן רֹאֶה אָנֹכִי
אֶת־פְּנֵי אֲבִיכֶן כִּי־אֵינֶנּוּ אֵלַי כִּתְמֹל שִׁלְשֹׁם
וֵאלֹהֵי אָבִי הָיָה עִמָּדִי: ו וְאַתֵּנָה יְדַעְתֶּן כִּי
בְּכָל־כֹּחִי עָבַדְתִּי אֶת־אֲבִיכֶן: ז וַאֲבִיכֶן הֵתֶל
בִּי וְהֶחֱלִף אֶת־מַשְׂכֻּרְתִּי עֲשֶׂרֶת מֹנִים וְלֹא־
נְתָנוֹ אֱלֹהִים לְהָרַע עִמָּדִי: ח אִם־כֹּה יֹאמַר
נְקֻדִּים יִהְיֶה שְׂכָרֶךָ וְיָלְדוּ כָל־הַצֹּאן נְקֻדִּים
וְאִם־כֹּה יֹאמַר עֲקֻדִּים יִהְיֶה שְׂכָרֶךָ וְיָלְדוּ
כָל־הַצֹּאן עֲקֻדִּים: ט וַיַּצֵּל אֱלֹהִים אֶת־מִקְנֵה
אֲבִיכֶם וַיִּתֶּן־לִי: י וַיְהִי בְּעֵת יַחֵם הַצֹּאן
וָאֶשָּׂא עֵינַי וָאֵרֶא בַּחֲלוֹם וְהִנֵּה הָעַתֻּדִים
הָעֹלִים עַל־הַצֹּאן עֲקֻדִּים נְקֻדִּים וּבְרֻדִּים:
יא וַיֹּאמֶר אֵלַי מַלְאַךְ הָאֱלֹהִים בַּחֲלוֹם יַעֲקֹב

41-42. Jacob did not apply these measures indiscriminately. He set up the peeled rods only when the early-bearing sturdier flocks were about to mate, thus securing the hardiest animals for himself.

31/1. Jacob's flight from Charan.

2. The crafty Laban's displeasure is more internalized than that of his brash sons, but he cannot completely *disguise* his frustration. A man's face is the mirror of his feelings (*Akeidas Yitzchak*).

3. Hashem commands Jacob to depart. *Return to the land of your fathers* — your father waits for you; *your 'moledes'* [homiletically: 'she who bore you'] — your mother — waits for you; *and I will be with you* — I, too, am waiting (*Midrash*).

4. Jacob summons his wives and explains his position to them. Jacob knew how difficult it is for people, especially women, to uproot themselves from their home. He therefore consulted with his wives to convince them of the dishonesty of their wicked father, and to impress upon them the necessity of an expedient departure, since only God's protection had prevented Laban from harming him until now (*T'zror HaMor*).

7. *And changed my wage a hundred times* [lit., *ten tens*]. *R' Munk* notes that the Torah specifies only *one* example of Laban's deceit [see 30:35]; however, as *Ramban* emphasizes, there must have been many such instances which the Torah does not enumerate. This is evidenced by Jacob's direct reproach to Laban regarding constant changes of his wage (v. 41), a reproach that Laban did not deny. It is common that the Torah does not supply all details.

10. [Jacob reveals for the first time that he had been shown in a prophetic dream that the birth of parti-colored young was God's compensation of Laban's ill-treatment of him.]

stimulated, Jacob would place the rods in the runnels, in full view of the flock to stimulate them among the rods. ⁴² But when the sheep were late-bearing, he would not emplace. Thus, the late-bearing ones went to Laban and the early-bearing ones to Jacob.

⁴³ The man became exceedingly prosperous and he attained fecund flocks, maidservants and servants, camels and donkeys.

31 ¹ Then he heard the words of Laban's sons saying, 'Jacob has taken all that belonged to our father, and from that which belonged to our father he amassed all this wealth.' ² Jacob also noticed Laban's disposition that behold, it was not toward him as in earlier days. ³ And HASHEM said to Jacob, 'Return to the land of your fathers and to your native land and I will be with you.'

⁴ Jacob sent and summoned Rachel and Leah to the field, to his flock, ⁵ and said to them, 'I have noticed that your father's disposition is not toward me as in earlier days; but the God of my father was with me. ⁶ Now you have known that it was with all my might that I served your father, ⁷ yet your father mocked me and changed my wage a hundred times. But God did not permit him to harm me. ⁸ If he would stipulate: "Spotted ones shall be your wages," then the entire flock bore spotted ones; and if he would stipulate: "Ringed ones shall be your wages," then the entire flock bore ringed ones. ⁹ Thus, God took away your father's livestock, and gave them to me. ¹⁰ It once happened at the mating time of the flock that I raised my eyes and saw in a dream — Behold! The he-goats that mounted the flock were ringed, spotted, and checkered. ¹¹ And an angel of God said to me in the dream, "Jacob!"

וָאֹמַר הִנֵּנִי: יבוַיֹּאמֶר שָׂא־נָא עֵינֶיךָ וּרְאֵה
כָּל־הָעַתֻּדִים הָעֹלִים עַל־הַצֹּאן עֲקֻדִּים נְקֻדִּים
וּבְרֻדִּים כִּי רָאִיתִי אֵת כָּל־אֲשֶׁר לָבָן עֹשֶׂה לָּךְ:
יג אָנֹכִי הָאֵל בֵּית־אֵל אֲשֶׁר מָשַׁחְתָּ שָּׁם מַצֵּבָה
אֲשֶׁר נָדַרְתָּ לִּי שָׁם נֶדֶר עַתָּה קוּם צֵא
מִן־הָאָרֶץ הַזֹּאת וְשׁוּב אֶל־אֶרֶץ מוֹלַדְתֶּךָ:
יד וַתַּעַן רָחֵל וְלֵאָה וַתֹּאמַרְנָה לוֹ הַעוֹד לָנוּ
חֵלֶק וְנַחֲלָה בְּבֵית אָבִינוּ: טו הֲלוֹא נָכְרִיּוֹת
נֶחְשַׁבְנוּ לוֹ כִּי מְכָרָנוּ וַיֹּאכַל גַּם־אָכוֹל
אֶת־כַּסְפֵּנוּ: טז כִּי כָל־הָעֹשֶׁר אֲשֶׁר הִצִּיל
אֱלֹהִים מֵאָבִינוּ לָנוּ הוּא וּלְבָנֵינוּ וְעַתָּה כֹּל
אֲשֶׁר אָמַר אֱלֹהִים אֵלֶיךָ עֲשֵׂה: ששי יז וַיָּקָם
יַעֲקֹב וַיִּשָּׂא אֶת־בָּנָיו וְאֶת־נָשָׁיו עַל־הַגְּמַלִּים:
יח וַיִּנְהַג אֶת־כָּל־מִקְנֵהוּ וְאֶת־כָּל־רְכֻשׁוֹ אֲשֶׁר
רָכָשׁ מִקְנֵה קִנְיָנוֹ אֲשֶׁר רָכַשׁ בְּפַדַּן אֲרָם לָבוֹא
אֶל־יִצְחָק אָבִיו אַרְצָה כְּנָעַן: יט וְלָבָן הָלַךְ לִגְזֹז
אֶת־צֹאנוֹ וַתִּגְנֹב רָחֵל אֶת־הַתְּרָפִים אֲשֶׁר
לְאָבִיהָ: כ וַיִּגְנֹב יַעֲקֹב אֶת־לֵב לָבָן הָאֲרַמִּי
עַל־בְּלִי הִגִּיד לוֹ כִּי בֹרֵחַ הוּא: כא וַיִּבְרַח הוּא
וְכָל־אֲשֶׁר־לוֹ וַיָּקָם וַיַּעֲבֹר אֶת־הַנָּהָר וַיָּשֶׂם
אֶת־פָּנָיו הַר הַגִּלְעָד: כב וַיֻּגַּד לְלָבָן בַּיּוֹם
הַשְּׁלִישִׁי כִּי בָרַח יַעֲקֹב: כג וַיִּקַּח אֶת־אֶחָיו
עִמּוֹ וַיִּרְדֹּף אַחֲרָיו דֶּרֶךְ שִׁבְעַת יָמִים וַיַּדְבֵּק
אֹתוֹ בְּהַר הַגִּלְעָד: כד וַיָּבֹא אֱלֹהִים אֶל־לָבָן
הָאֲרַמִּי בַּחֲלֹם הַלָּיְלָה וַיֹּאמֶר לוֹ הִשָּׁמֶר
לְךָ פֶּן־תְּדַבֵּר עִם־יַעֲקֹב מִטּוֹב עַד־רָע:

13. The angel speaks in the first person, as he is God's emissary (*Radak*).

The God of Bethel. I.e., the God *Who appeared to you* in Bethel [see 28:13] (*Radak; R' Bachya*), and Who promised you My protection, assuring you that I would bring you back to that land (*Malbim*).

14. Rachel and Leah consent. What possible reason can we have for attempting to delay your departure? Have we any hope of inheriting anything of our father's estate together with his sons (*Rashi*)?

17. Jacob's flight.

18. Jacob purposely left in a grand manner — leading his flocks and systematically gathering all his wealth — so as not to arouse the suspicions of Laban's people. Anyone who saw him leaving so openly would assume that he was departing with Laban's full knowledge and consent. Had he gone stealthily, he would have been stamped as a fugitive (*Abarbanel*).

19. *Rachel stole the teraphim that belonged to her father.* To keep him from idol worship (*Rashi*).

Ibn Janach, like Onkelos, defines teraphim as images, idols, but offers no clue to the etymology of the word. Ramban derives it from the root רפה meaning weak [see Exod. 5:17] alluding to the 'weakness' of their prognostications. The Zohar interprets the word as being related to תרף and תורפה, denoting obscenity.

Many consider them to have been a kind of household god, supposed to be the protector of the home, similar to the later Roman Penates. They were consulted as oracles (R' Hirsch).

21. Jacob assumed that God would prevent Laban from learning of his departure. As has often happened in Jewish history, however, God did not act as people wanted Him to. Laban pursued Jacob — but God saved him through other means. God's protection, too, is a common thread in Jewish history (Haamek Davar).

22. Ba'al HaTurim cites a Midrash that the informant was Amalek, a grandson of Esau, who also later informed Pharaoh that Israel had fled [see Exod. 14:5].

24. God's warning to Laban. Before Laban even caught up with Jacob, God had already come to Laban. There are many such verses [which are not in strict chronological sequence, but which parenthetically revert to an earlier incident to supply more detailed information. They are omitted from the original narrative in order not to break the initial continuity of the story] (Ibn Ezra).

And I said, "Here I am." [12] And he said, "Raise your eyes, if you please, and see that all the he-goats mounting the flocks are ringed, spotted, and checkered, for I have seen all that Laban is doing to you. [13] I am the God of Bethel where you anointed a pillar and where you made Me a vow. Now — arise, leave this land and return to your native land." '

[14] Then Rachel and Leah replied and said to him, 'Have we then still a share and an inheritance in our father's house? [15] Are we not considered by him as strangers? For he has sold us and even totally consumed our money! [16] But, all the wealth that God has taken away from our father belongs to us and to our children. So now, whatever God has said to you, do.'

[17] Jacob arose and lifted his children and wives onto the camels. [18] He led away all his livestock and all the wealth which he had amassed — his purchased property which he had amassed in Paddan Aram — to go to his father Isaac, to the land of Canaan.

[19] Laban had gone to shear his sheep, and Rachel stole the teraphim that belonged to her father. [20] Jacob deceived Laban the Aramean by not telling him that he was fleeing. [21] Thus, he fled with all he had and proceeded to cross the river, and he set his direction toward Mount Gilead.

[22] It was told to Laban on the third day that Jacob had fled. [23] So he took his kinsmen with him and pursued him a distance of seven days, catching up with him on Mount Gilead. [24] But God had come to Laban the Aramean in a dream by night and said to him, 'Beware lest you speak with Jacob either good or bad.'

כה וַיַּשֵּׂג לָבָן אֶת־יַעֲקֹב וְיַעֲקֹב תָּקַע אֶת־
אָהֳלוֹ בָּהָר וְלָבָן תָּקַע אֶת־אֶחָיו בְּהַר
הַגִּלְעָד: כו וַיֹּאמֶר לָבָן לְיַעֲקֹב מֶה עָשִׂיתָ
וַתִּגְנֹב אֶת־לְבָבִי וַתְּנַהֵג אֶת־בְּנֹתַי כִּשְׁבֻיוֹת
חָרֶב: כז לָמָּה נַחְבֵּאתָ לִבְרֹחַ וַתִּגְנֹב אֹתִי
וְלֹא־הִגַּדְתָּ לִּי וָאֲשַׁלֵּחֲךָ בְּשִׂמְחָה וּבְשִׁרִים
בְּתֹף וּבְכִנּוֹר: כח וְלֹא נְטַשְׁתַּנִי לְנַשֵּׁק לְבָנַי
וְלִבְנֹתָי עַתָּה הִסְכַּלְתָּ עֲשׂוֹ: כט יֶשׁ־לְאֵל יָדִי
לַעֲשׂוֹת עִמָּכֶם רָע וֵאלֹהֵי אֲבִיכֶם אֶמֶשׁ ׀
אָמַר אֵלַי לֵאמֹר הִשָּׁמֶר לְךָ מִדַּבֵּר עִם־
יַעֲקֹב מִטּוֹב עַד־רָע: ל וְעַתָּה הָלֹךְ הָלַכְתָּ
כִּי־נִכְסֹף נִכְסַפְתָּה לְבֵית אָבִיךָ לָמָּה גָנַבְתָּ
אֶת־אֱלֹהָי: לא וַיַּעַן יַעֲקֹב וַיֹּאמֶר לְלָבָן כִּי
יָרֵאתִי כִּי אָמַרְתִּי פֶּן־תִּגְזֹל אֶת־בְּנוֹתֶיךָ
מֵעִמִּי: לב עִם אֲשֶׁר תִּמְצָא אֶת־אֱלֹהֶיךָ לֹא
יִחְיֶה נֶגֶד אַחֵינוּ הַכֶּר־לְךָ מָה עִמָּדִי וְקַח־
לָךְ וְלֹא־יָדַע יַעֲקֹב כִּי רָחֵל גְּנָבָתַם: לג וַיָּבֹא
לָבָן בְּאֹהֶל־יַעֲקֹב ׀ וּבְאֹהֶל לֵאָה וּבְאֹהֶל
שְׁתֵּי הָאֲמָהֹת וְלֹא מָצָא וַיֵּצֵא מֵאֹהֶל לֵאָה
וַיָּבֹא בְּאֹהֶל רָחֵל: לד וְרָחֵל לָקְחָה אֶת־
הַתְּרָפִים וַתְּשִׂמֵם בְּכַר הַגָּמָל וַתֵּשֶׁב
עֲלֵיהֶם וַיְמַשֵּׁשׁ לָבָן אֶת־כָּל־הָאֹהֶל וְלֹא
מָצָא: לה וַתֹּאמֶר אֶל־אָבִיהָ אַל־יִחַר בְּעֵינֵי
אֲדֹנִי כִּי לוֹא אוּכַל לָקוּם מִפָּנֶיךָ כִּי־דֶרֶךְ
נָשִׁים לִי וַיְחַפֵּשׂ וְלֹא מָצָא אֶת־הַתְּרָפִים:

25. In v. 23 Laban merely reached *close* to him; but now, in the morning, he actually *overtook* him and they met in a face-to-face confrontation (*Lekach Tov*).

26. [Laban reproaches Jacob for having stolen away with his daughters, as if they were captives taken in war.]

Laban portrays himself as the aggrieved father. He mentions his daughters before Jacob's flight or the theft of his *teraphim* (*Haamek Davar*).

30. When the tribal ancestors [i.e., Jacob's sons] heard their grandfather [Laban] saying this, they exclaimed, 'We are ashamed of you, Grandfather, that in your old age you can refer to them as your gods!' (*Midrash*).

32. The Sages in the Midrash perceive this utterance of Jacob to have been an unintentional prognostication for the future. In consequence of this curse, Rachel died on the journey (*Rashi* citing *Midrash*).

Now Jacob did not know that Rachel had stolen them. Thus the Torah testifies that Jacob uttered the imprecation because he suspected that the culprit was an idolatrous servant who had stolen the *teraphim* to worship them in secret. Had Jacob had even the slightest notion that *Rachel* had stolen them, he would: (a) not have denied it so boldly; and (b) never have uttered a curse, since he would not have suspected her of idolatrous motives. He would have been certain that her motive was lofty — to wean her father from idol worship (*Akeidas Yitzchak; Sforno; Alshich*).

34. In display of her utter contempt for Laban's 'gods,' Rachel places the idols beneath her (*Zohar*). [And since 'the way of women' was upon her (v. 35) she knew Laban would not trouble her to rise.]

35. *For the way of women is upon me.* This is a euphemism for menstruation, similar to the expression אֹרַח כַּנָּשִׁים, *the manner of women*, in 18:11 (*Michlol Yofi*).

What kind of excuse was it? Do menstruant women not stand up? Perhaps she meant that her condition had made her feel ill, as is not uncommon for some women (*Ramban*).

²⁵ Laban overtook Jacob. Jacob had pitched his tent on the mountain, while Laban had stationed his kinsmen on Mount Gilead. ²⁶ Laban said to Jacob, 'What have you done that you have deceived me and led my daughters away like captives of the sword? ²⁷ Why have you fled so stealthily, and cheated me? Nor did you tell me — for I would have sent you off with gladness, with songs, with timbrel, and with lyre! ²⁸ And you did not even allow me to kiss my sons and daughters. Now you have acted foolishly. ²⁹ It is in my power to do you all harm. But the God of your father addressed me last night saying, ''Beware of speaking with Jacob either good or bad.'' ³⁰ Now — you have left because you longed greatly for your father's house. But why did you steal my gods?'

³¹ Jacob answered and said to Laban, 'Because I was afraid, for I thought, perhaps you might steal your daughters from me. ³² With whomever you find your gods, he shall not live; in the presence of our kinsmen ascertain for yourself what is with me and take it back.' (Now Jacob did not know that Rachel had stolen them.)

³³ Laban came into Jacob's tent, and into Leah's tent and into the tent of the two maidservants, but he found nothing. When he had left Leah's tent, he came into Rachel's tent. ³⁴ Now Rachel had taken the teraphim, put them into the camel's packsaddle and sat on them. Laban rummaged through the whole tent, and found nothing. ³⁵ She said to her father, 'Let not my lord find it annoying that I cannot rise up before you, for the way of women is upon me.' Thus he searched but did not find the teraphim.

לו וַיִּ֥חַר לְיַעֲקֹ֖ב וַיָּ֣רֶב בְּלָבָ֑ן וַיַּ֤עַן יַעֲקֹב֙ וַיֹּ֣אמֶר
לְלָבָ֔ן מַה־פִּשְׁעִי֙ מַ֣ה חַטָּאתִ֔י כִּ֥י דָלַ֖קְתָּ
אַחֲרָֽי: לז כִּֽי־מִשַּׁ֣שְׁתָּ אֶת־כָּל־כֵּלַ֗י מַה־
מָּצָ֙אתָ֙ מִכֹּ֣ל כְּלֵֽי־בֵיתֶ֔ךָ שִׂ֣ים כֹּ֔ה נֶ֥גֶד אַחַ֖י
וְאַחֶ֑יךָ וְיוֹכִ֖יחוּ בֵּ֥ין שְׁנֵֽינוּ: לח זֶה֩ עֶשְׂרִ֨ים שָׁנָ֤ה
אָנֹכִי֙ עִמָּ֔ךְ רְחֵלֶ֥יךָ וְעִזֶּ֖יךָ לֹ֣א שִׁכֵּ֑לוּ וְאֵילֵ֥י
צֹֽאנְךָ֖ לֹ֥א אָכָֽלְתִּי: לט טְרֵפָה֙ לֹא־הֵבֵ֣אתִי
אֵלֶ֔יךָ אָנֹכִ֣י אֲחַטֶּ֔נָּה מִיָּדִ֖י תְּבַקְשֶׁ֑נָּה גְּנֻֽבְתִ֣י
י֔וֹם וּגְנֻֽבְתִ֖י לָֽיְלָה: מ הָיִ֧יתִי בַיּ֛וֹם אֲכָלַ֥נִי חֹ֖רֶב
וְקֶ֣רַח בַּלָּ֑יְלָה וַתִּדַּ֥ד שְׁנָתִ֖י מֵֽעֵינָֽי: מא זֶה־לִּ֞י
עֶשְׂרִ֣ים שָׁנָה֮ בְּבֵיתֶ֒ךָ֒ עֲבַדְתִּ֜יךָ אַרְבַּֽע־עֶשְׂרֵ֤ה
שָׁנָה֙ בִּשְׁתֵּ֣י בְנֹתֶ֔יךָ וְשֵׁ֥שׁ שָׁנִ֖ים בְּצֹאנֶ֑ךָ
וַתַּֽחֲלֵ֥ף אֶת־מַשְׂכֻּרְתִּ֖י עֲשֶׂ֥רֶת מֹנִֽים: מב לוּלֵ֡י
אֱלֹהֵ֣י אָבִי֩ אֱלֹהֵ֨י אַבְרָהָ֜ם וּפַ֣חַד יִצְחָ֗ק הָ֚יָה
לִ֔י כִּ֥י עַתָּ֖ה רֵיקָ֣ם שִׁלַּחְתָּ֑נִי אֶת־עָנְיִ֞י וְאֶת־
יְגִ֤יעַ כַּפַּי֙ רָאָ֣ה אֱלֹהִ֔ים וַיּ֖וֹכַח אָֽמֶשׁ: שביעי
מג וַיַּ֨עַן לָבָ֜ן וַיֹּ֣אמֶר אֶֽל־יַעֲקֹ֗ב הַבָּנ֨וֹת בְּנֹתַ֜י
וְהַבָּנִ֤ים בָּנַי֙ וְהַצֹּ֣אן צֹאנִ֔י וְכֹ֛ל אֲשֶׁר־אַתָּ֥ה
רֹאֶ֖ה לִי־ה֑וּא וְלִבְנֹתַ֞י מָֽה־אֶֽעֱשֶׂ֤ה לָאֵ֨לֶּה֙
הַיּ֔וֹם א֥וֹ לִבְנֵיהֶ֖ן אֲשֶׁ֥ר יָלָֽדוּ: מד וְעַתָּ֗ה לְכָ֛ה
נִכְרְתָ֥ה בְרִ֖ית אֲנִ֣י וָאָ֑תָּה וְהָיָ֥ה לְעֵ֖ד בֵּינִ֥י
וּבֵינֶֽךָ: מה וַיִּקַּ֥ח יַעֲקֹ֖ב אָ֑בֶן וַיְרִימֶ֖הָ מַצֵּבָֽה:
מו וַיֹּ֨אמֶר יַעֲקֹ֤ב לְאֶחָיו֙ לִקְט֣וּ אֲבָנִ֔ים וַיִּקְח֥וּ
אֲבָנִ֖ים וַיַּֽעֲשׂוּ־גָ֑ל וַיֹּ֥אכְלוּ שָׁ֖ם עַל־הַגָּֽל:

36. The Torah does not record whether or not Laban searched through the belongings of his grandchildren and every servant as well. Perhaps he did; or possibly Laban felt that none but Jacob or his wives — who were Laban's daughters — would have the audacity to enter his tent and steal his 'gods.' Nevertheless when Laban had finished ransacking Jacob's belongings and failed to find what he was searching for, the outraged Patriarch — who had painfully maintained his silence all these years — could contain himself no further.

38. Jacob indignantly justifies himself, by recounting the hardships he endured while in Laban's service. Laban's suspicion that Jacob would steal his gods — or *anything* of his, for that matter — was wholly unjustified, as Jacob proceeds to emphasize (*Haamek Davar*).

41. *I served you fourteen years for your two daughters.* Bitterly, Jacob alludes to Laban's trickery, which caused him to work *fourteen* instead of *seven* years for his wife. He is not more explicit, however, in consideration of Leah's feelings (*Hoffmann*).

And you changed my wage a hundred times. You constantly altered our agreement by changing the terms from spotted to speckled and from ringed to checkered (*Rashi*).

Laban was indeed guilty of this, otherwise Jacob would never have accused him of it to his face. Moreover, were the charge not true, Laban would have denied it vigorously (*Abarbanel*).

42. *God saw my wretchedness and the toil of my hands.* I.e., God perceived that whatever I achieved was by great toil, so He pitied and vindicated me accordingly.

The key factor in God's defense of Jacob was *his wretchedness*. Had not Jacob endured so much suffering, God would have exercised His Attribute of אֶרֶךְ אַפַּיִם, *patient withholding of anger;* Laban would have succeeded and Jacob would have earned even greater reward for the World to Come. But due to Jacob's *wretchedness*, God paid him his wages 'on the day they were due' [*Deut.* 24:15], so to speak, and reprimanded Laban (*Or HaChaim*).

43. Some perceive in Laban's words a claim based on the primitive regional custom that the head of the family was the nominal owner of all that belonged to its members. Unable to answer Jacob's reproaches, Laban invokes this weak claim that entitles him to examine all of Jacob's possessions. He then pretends to be solicitous for the welfare of his daughters and grandchildren, and suggests a pact [see *Hoffman* and *Eisenstein*].

44. Laban proposes a treaty.

46. *To his brethren.* The reference is to *Jacob's sons* who were 'brethren' to him, standing by him in trouble and battle (*Rashi*).

And they ate there on the mound. A meal was part of the ceremony of the covenant, signaling the mutual acceptance of the pact (*Radak* to 26:30; *Rashbam* to 25:31).

³⁶ Then Jacob became angered and he took up his grievance with Laban. Jacob spoke up and said to Laban, 'What is my transgression? What is my sin that you have hotly pursued me? ³⁷ When you rummaged through all my things, what did you find of all your household objects? Set it here before my kinsmen and your kinsmen, and let them decide between the two of us.

³⁸ 'These twenty years I have been with you, your ewes and she-goats never miscarried, nor did I eat rams of your flock. ³⁹ That which was mangled I never brought you — I myself would bear the loss, from me you would exact it, whether it was stolen by day or stolen by night. ⁴⁰ This is how I was: By day scorching heat consumed me, and frost by night; my sleep drifted from my eyes. ⁴¹ This is my twenty years in your household: I served you fourteen years for your two daughters, and six years for your flocks; and you changed my wage a hundred times. ⁴² Had not the God of my father — the God of Abraham and the Dread of Isaac — been with me, you would surely have now sent me away empty handed. God saw my wretchedness and the toil of my hands, so He admonished you last night.'

⁴³ Then Laban spoke up and said to Jacob, 'The daughters are my daughters, the children are my children and the flock is my flock, and all that you see is mine. Yet to my daughters — what could I do to them this day? Or to their children whom they have borne! ⁴⁴ So now, come, let us make a covenant, I and you, and He shall be a witness between me and you.'

⁴⁵ Then Jacob took a stone and raised it up as a monument. ⁴⁶ And Jacob said to his brethren, 'Gather stones!' So they took stones and made a mound, and they ate there on the mound.

מז וַיִּקְרָא־לֹ֥ו לָבָ֖ן יְגַ֣ר שָׂהֲדוּתָ֑א וְיַֽעֲקֹ֔ב קָ֥רָא
לֹ֖ו גַּלְעֵֽד: מח וַיֹּ֣אמֶר לָבָ֗ן הַגַּ֨ל הַזֶּ֥ה עֵ֛ד בֵּינִ֥י
וּבֵֽינְךָ֖ הַיֹּ֑ום עַל־כֵּ֥ן קָֽרָא־שְׁמֹ֖ו גַּלְעֵֽד:
מט וְהַמִּצְפָּה֙ אֲשֶׁ֣ר אָמַ֔ר יִ֥צֶף יְהוָֹ֖ה בֵּינִ֣י וּבֵינֶ֑ךָ
כִּ֥י נִסָּתֵ֖ר אִ֥ישׁ מֵֽרֵעֵֽהוּ: נ אִם־תְּעַנֶּ֣ה אֶת־
בְּנֹתַ֗י וְאִם־תִּקַּ֤ח נָשִׁים֙ עַל־בְּנֹתַ֔י אֵ֥ין אִ֖ישׁ
עִמָּ֑נוּ רְאֵ֕ה אֱלֹהִ֥ים עֵ֖ד בֵּינִ֥י וּבֵינֶֽךָ: נא וַיֹּ֥אמֶר
לָבָ֖ן לְיַֽעֲקֹ֑ב הִנֵּ֣ה ׀ הַגַּ֣ל הַזֶּ֗ה וְהִנֵּה֙ הַמַּצֵּבָ֔ה
אֲשֶׁ֥ר יָרִ֖יתִי בֵּינִ֥י וּבֵינֶֽךָ: נב עֵ֚ד הַגַּ֣ל הַזֶּ֔ה
וְעֵדָ֖ה הַמַּצֵּבָ֑ה אִם־אָ֗נִי לֹֽא־אֶֽעֱבֹ֤ר אֵלֶ֨יךָ֙
אֶת־הַגַּ֣ל הַזֶּ֔ה וְאִם־אַ֠תָּה לֹֽא־תַֽעֲבֹ֨ר אֵלַ֜י
אֶת־הַגַּ֥ל הַזֶּ֛ה וְאֶת־הַמַּצֵּבָ֥ה הַזֹּ֖את לְרָעָֽה:
נג אֱלֹהֵ֨י אַבְרָהָ֜ם וֵֽאלֹהֵ֤י נָחֹור֙ יִשְׁפְּט֣וּ בֵינֵ֔ינוּ
אֱלֹהֵ֖י אֲבִיהֶ֑ם וַיִּשָּׁבַ֣ע יַֽעֲקֹ֔ב בְּפַ֖חַד אָבִ֥יו
יִצְחָֽק: נד וַיִּזְבַּ֨ח יַֽעֲקֹ֥ב זֶ֨בַח֙ בָּהָ֔ר וַיִּקְרָ֥א
לְאֶחָ֖יו לֶֽאֱכָל־לָ֑חֶם וַיֹּ֣אכְלוּ לֶ֔חֶם וַיָּלִ֖ינוּ
בָּהָֽר: לב מפטיר א וַיַּשְׁכֵּ֨ם לָבָ֜ן בַּבֹּ֗קֶר וַיְנַשֵּׁ֤ק
לְבָנָיו֙ וְלִבְנֹותָיו֙ וַיְבָ֣רֶךְ אֶתְהֶ֑ם וַיֵּ֛לֶךְ וַיָּ֥שָׁב
לָבָ֖ן לִמְקֹמֹֽו: ב וְיַֽעֲקֹ֖ב הָלַ֣ךְ לְדַרְכֹּ֑ו וַיִּפְגְּעוּ־בֹ֖ו
מַלְאֲכֵ֥י אֱלֹהִֽים: ג וַיֹּ֤אמֶר יַֽעֲקֹב֙ כַּֽאֲשֶׁ֣ר רָאָ֔ם
מַֽחֲנֵ֥ה אֱלֹהִ֖ים זֶ֑ה וַיִּקְרָ֛א שֵֽׁם־הַמָּקֹ֥ום הַה֖וּא
מַֽחֲנָֽיִם:

The *Haftarah* for *Vayeitzei* appears on page 320

47. He referred to the mound as *Yegar Sahadusa* which means, in Aramaic, 'the mound is a witness' and which, as *Rashi* notes, is the Aramaic equivalent of the Hebrew name Gal-ed. The actual *naming* (קָרָא שְׁמוֹ) came later (next verse).

But Jacob called it Gal-ed [Hebrew for 'the mound is a witness']. Jacob did not abandon the Hebrew language (*Sforno*).

48-50. The first part of the treaty: that Jacob will in no way ill-treat Laban's daughters.

49. *And as for the Mitzpah* [=watchtower]. According to *Rashi*, as explained by *Ramban*, the *watchtower* was a high, conspicuous structure on the mountain; it was *not* the mound or pillar. Thus, our passage is elliptic: It explains that the structure was called *Mitzpah*, *Watchtower*, because . . . (See *Judges* 11:29).

51-53. The second part of the treaty: that neither Laban nor Jacob will pass the mound of stones, thrown up as a landmark, with hostile intentions toward the other.

52. These landmarks will serve as reminders of our pact (*Ibn Caspi*).

53. Laban invoked both the *God of Abraham* [Jacob's grandfather] and the *god of Nachor* [Laban's grandfather], with the explanation that he included the latter because he was also the *god of their* [=Abraham and Nachor's] mutual *father*, Terach (*Sforno*).

וַיִּשָּׁבַע יַעֲקֹב בְּפַחַד אָבִיו יִצְחָק — *And Jacob swore by the Dread of his father Isaac.* I.e., the God whom his father feared (*Targum Yonasan*).

32/1. *And blessed them.* Scripture teaches how effective a blessing can be when it is conferred with total sincerity, for Laban was surely sincere in blessing his own daughters (*Sforno*).

2. *Angels of God.* They were angels who minister in *Eretz Yisrael.* They came to meet him to accompany him to the Holy Land (*Midrash; Rashi*).

3. *This is a Godly camp.* This was meant to assure those with him: 'These are not the troops of Esau or Laban coming to attack us; they are camps of holy angels which God sent to protect us from our enemies' (*Targum Yonasan*).

Machanaim. Lit., *a pair of camps* — the two camps of angels: those who ministered outside the Holy Land who had accompanied him, and those of the Holy Land who now came to meet him (*Tanchuma; Rashi*).

According to the Masoretic note appearing at the end of the *Sidrah,* there are 148 verses in the *Sidrah,* numerically corresponding to the mnemonics י״חֶלְקָ and מְחַנַי״ם, each of which totals 148. The Jewish people are referred to as God's חֶלֶק, *portion,* as in עַמּוֹ 'ה חֵלֶק כִּי, HASHEM'S *portion is His people* [*Deut.* 32:9]. Thus the birth of eleven of the twelve tribes, as described in this *Sidrah,* constitutes the nation that God describes as חֶלְקִי, *My portion.* Additionally, the final word of the *Sidrah* is מְחַנָיִם, *Machanaim,* the name Jacob gave to the place. It also alludes to Jacob's abundant, flourishing growth, a condition which he was to describe in 32:11 as having grown into שְׁנֵי מַחֲנוֹת, *two camps.* The *Haftarah* begins with *Hoshea* 12:13: יַעֲקֹב וַיִּבְרַח.

⁴⁷ Laban called it Yegar Sahadusa, but Jacob called it Gal-ed. ⁴⁸ And Laban declared, 'This mound is a witness between me and you today'; therefore he named it Gal-ed. ⁴⁹ And as for the Mitzpah — because he said, 'May HASHEM keep watch between me and you when we are out of each other's sight. ⁵⁰ If you will ill-treat my daughters or if you will marry wives in addition to my daughters — though no man may be among us — but see! God is a witness between me and you.' ⁵¹ And Laban said to Jacob, 'Here is this mound, and here is the monument which I have cast between me and you. ⁵² This mound shall be witness and the monument shall be witness that I may not cross over to you past this mound, nor may you cross over to me past this mound, with hostile purpose. ⁵³ May the God of Abraham and the god of Nachor judge between us — the god of their father.' And Jacob swore by the Dread of his father Isaac. ⁵⁴ Then Jacob slaughtered an animal on the mountain and summoned his kinsmen to break bread. And they broke bread and spent the night on the mountain.

32 ¹ **A**nd Laban awoke early in the morning; he kissed his sons and his daughters and blessed them. Then Laban went and returned to his place. ² Jacob went on his way, and angels of God encountered him. ³ Jacob said when he saw them, 'This is a Godly camp!' So he named that place Machanaim.

The *Haftarah* for *Vayeitzei* appears on page 320

פרשת וישלח

VAYISHLACH

The Sages teach that every nation has a heavenly power, an angel that guides its destiny on earth. It is a go-between, as it were, between the nation and God. Two nations, however, are unique: Israel and Esau. Israel needs no intermediary; it is God's own people. Esau's angel is of a different order than the others. Just as the nation — Esau, who is Edom, his grandson Amalek, and his descendants the Roman Empire — is the prime force of evil, so its angel is the prime spiritual force of evil, Satan himself.

'Satan descends and seduces man [to sin], then he ascends to anger [God by prosecuting man for his sinfulness], then he receives permission and takes man's life ... Satan, the Evil Inclination, and the Angel of Death are one and the same' (*Bava Basra* 16a). The angel of Esau, therefore, *had* to attack Jacob, because the last and greatest of the Patriarchs symbolized man's struggle to raise himself and the world with him — and Satan exists to impede that effort. Jacob was ready to do battle with the brother who hated him, but there was a deeper aspect to the struggle, the struggle between good and evil that is the basis of man's very existence on earth.

Jacob triumphed, and so earned a new name — Israel — which means that he had defeated an angel. The victory was not Jacob's alone. It was proof that man can be good, that he can rise above his surroundings, surmount adversity, achieve greatness. The Sages teach that Jacob's image is engraved upon God's Throne of Glory; thus he symbolizes man's highest potential. And since we are his children, so his triumph must be our aspiration.

ד וַיִּשְׁלַ֨ח יַעֲקֹ֤ב מַלְאָכִים֙ לְפָנָ֔יו אֶל־עֵשָׂ֖ו אָחִ֑יו אַ֛רְצָה שֵׂעִ֖יר שְׂדֵ֥ה אֱדֽוֹם: ה וַיְצַ֤ו אֹתָם֙ לֵאמֹ֔ר כֹּ֣ה תֹאמְר֔וּן לַֽאדֹנִ֖י לְעֵשָׂ֑ו כֹּ֤ה אָמַר֙ עַבְדְּךָ֣ יַעֲקֹ֔ב עִם־לָבָ֣ן גַּ֔רְתִּי וָאֵחַ֖ר עַד־עָֽתָּה: ו וַֽיְהִי־לִי֙ שׁ֣וֹר וַחֲמ֔וֹר צֹ֖אן וְעֶ֣בֶד וְשִׁפְחָ֑ה וָֽאֶשְׁלְחָה֙ לְהַגִּ֣יד לַֽאדֹנִ֔י לִמְצֹא־חֵ֖ן בְּעֵינֶֽיךָ: ז וַיָּשֻׁ֙בוּ֙ הַמַּלְאָכִ֔ים אֶֽל־יַעֲקֹ֖ב לֵאמֹ֑ר בָּ֤אנוּ אֶל־אָחִ֙יךָ֙ אֶל־עֵשָׂ֔ו וְגַם֙ הֹלֵ֣ךְ לִקְרָֽאתְךָ֔ וְאַרְבַּע־מֵא֥וֹת אִ֖ישׁ עִמּֽוֹ: ח וַיִּירָ֧א יַעֲקֹ֛ב מְאֹ֖ד וַיֵּ֣צֶר ל֑וֹ וַיַּ֣חַץ אֶת־הָעָ֣ם אֲשֶׁר־אִתּ֗וֹ וְאֶת־הַצֹּ֧אן וְאֶת־הַבָּקָ֛ר וְהַגְּמַלִּ֖ים לִשְׁנֵ֥י מַחֲנֽוֹת: ט וַיֹּ֕אמֶר אִם־יָב֥וֹא עֵשָׂ֛ו אֶל־הַמַּחֲנֶ֥ה הָאַחַ֖ת וְהִכָּ֑הוּ וְהָיָ֛ה הַמַּחֲנֶ֥ה הַנִּשְׁאָ֖ר לִפְלֵיטָֽה: י וַיֹּאמֶר֮ יַעֲקֹב֒ אֱלֹהֵי֙ אָבִ֣י אַבְרָהָ֔ם וֵאלֹהֵ֖י אָבִ֣י יִצְחָ֑ק יְהֹוָ֞ה הָאֹמֵ֣ר אֵלַ֗י שׁ֧וּב לְאַרְצְךָ֛ וּלְמוֹלַדְתְּךָ֖ וְאֵיטִ֥יבָה עִמָּֽךְ: יא קָטֹ֜נְתִּי מִכֹּ֤ל הַחֲסָדִים֙ וּמִכָּל־הָ֣אֱמֶ֔ת אֲשֶׁ֥ר עָשִׂ֖יתָ אֶת־עַבְדֶּ֑ךָ כִּ֣י בְמַקְלִ֗י עָבַ֙רְתִּי֙ אֶת־הַיַּרְדֵּ֣ן הַזֶּ֔ה וְעַתָּ֥ה הָיִ֖יתִי לִשְׁנֵ֥י מַחֲנֽוֹת: יב הַצִּילֵ֥נִי נָ֛א מִיַּ֥ד אָחִ֖י מִיַּ֣ד עֵשָׂ֑ו כִּֽי־יָרֵ֤א אָנֹכִי֙ אֹת֔וֹ פֶּן־יָב֣וֹא וְהִכַּ֔נִי אֵ֖ם עַל־בָּנִֽים: יג וְאַתָּ֣ה אָמַ֔רְתָּ הֵיטֵ֥ב אֵיטִ֖יב עִמָּ֑ךְ וְשַׂמְתִּ֤י אֶֽת־זַרְעֲךָ֙ כְּח֣וֹל הַיָּ֔ם אֲשֶׁ֥ר לֹֽא־יִסָּפֵ֖ר מֵרֹֽב: שני יד וַיָּ֥לֶן שָׁ֖ם בַּלַּ֣יְלָה הַה֑וּא וַיִּקַּ֞ח מִן־הַבָּ֧א בְיָד֛וֹ מִנְחָ֖ה לְעֵשָׂ֥ו אָחִֽיו: טו עִזִּ֣ים מָאתַ֗יִם וּתְיָשִׁ֙ים֙ עֶשְׂרִ֔ים רְחֵלִ֥ים מָאתַ֖יִם וְאֵילִ֥ים עֶשְׂרִֽים:

32/4. Jacob dispatches angels to Esau.

This episode is recorded to illustrate how God sent an angel to save His servant from the hand of a stronger enemy. Furthermore, it shows that Jacob did not rely on his own righteousness, but strove mightily, by taking *practical* measures to ensure his safety. Additionally, the story applies to future generations, since everything that happened to Jacob with his brother Esau foreshadows the future experiences of Israel with Esau's descendants [the nations in whose lands we are currently exiled]. Accordingly, we should follow his example by making a threefold preparation in our struggles with Esau's descendants: prayer, gifts [= appeasement], and battle, as shall be noted in the commentary (*Ramban*).

The word מַלְאָכִים may refer equally to *angels* or *human emissaries*. The translation *angels* follows *Rashi*.

אַרְצָה שֵׂעִיר — *To the land of Seir.* The mountainous region from the Dead Sea southward toward the Gulf of Aqaba was the home of Esau and his Edomite descendants (see 14:6).

I have lodged with Laban. The verb גַּרְתִּי, *lodged*, implies staying as a *stranger* [from גֵּר =*alien*].

I have become neither a great prince nor have I achieved status . . . I remained merely an alien. Therefore, you need not hate me for having received Father's blessing [27:29].

The numerical value of גַּרְתִּי equals תרי"ג, 613: *Though I have lodged with Laban,* I have observed the 613 Divine Commandments, and have not learned from his evil ways (*Rashi*).

8. Military preparations.
Jacob divided the camp in such a manner that each camp had some of his men, maidservants, and cattle. His wives and children, however, remained together in the same camp. Jacob's strategy was to station the camp that did not contain his wives and children at the forefront, so that they would serve as a buffer between Esau and Jacob's family (*Abarbanel*).

9. *Then the remaining camp shall survive.* It will survive despite his attack, *because I will fight him.* Accordingly, Jacob prepared himself for three responses to the threat: לְדוֹרוֹן, *for a gift* [i.e., appeasement] — vs. 14-22; לִתְפִלָּה, *for prayer* — v. 10; לְמִלְחָמָה, *for battle* — as our passage [for I will fight him (*Tanchuma*)] (*Rashi*).

10-13. Prayer.

11. *I have been diminished.* My merits have been diminished in the consequence of all the *kindnesses*, which you have already shown me. Therefore I am afraid; perhaps since you promised to me, I have become soiled by sin, and this may cause me to be delivered into Esau's hands (*Rashi*).

The חֲסָדִים, *kindnesses*, are those that God did for him without having first promised them, while אֱמֶת, *truth*, refers to the kindnesses performed in fulfillment of earlier promises.

Jacob proceeds to elaborate on God's kindnesses (*Haamek Davar*).

14. *From that which had come in his hand.* I.e., from that which was in his possession. The most effective gift would be something that came into Jacob's hand from his *own* toil and labor. That was the livestock he now selected.

⁴ Then Jacob sent angels ahead of him to Esau his brother to the land of Seir, the field of Edom. ⁵ He charged them as follows: 'Thus shall you say, "To my lord Esau. So said your servant Jacob: I have lodged with Laban and have lingered until now. ⁶ I have acquired oxen and donkeys, sheep, servants, and maidservants and I am sending to tell my lord to gain favor in your eyes." '

⁷ The angels returned to Jacob, saying, 'We came to your brother, to Esau. Moreover, he is heading toward you, and four hundred men are with him.'

⁸ Jacob became very frightened, and it distressed him. So he divided the people with him, and the flocks, herds, and camels, into two camps. ⁹ For he said, 'If Esau comes to the one camp and strikes it down, then the remaining camp shall survive.' ¹⁰ Then Jacob said, 'God of my father Isaac; HASHEM Who said to me, "Return to your land and to your relatives and I will do good with you" — ¹¹ I have been diminished by all the kindnesses and by all the truth that You have done Your servant. For with my staff I crossed this Jordan and now I have become two camps. ¹² Rescue me, please, from the hand of my brother, from the hand of Esau, for I fear him lest he come and strike me down, mother and children. ¹³ And You had said, "I will surely do good with you and I will make your offspring like the sand of the sea which is too numerous to count." '

¹⁴ He spent the night there, then he took, from that which had come in his hand, a tribute to Esau his brother: ¹⁵ Two hundred she-goats and twenty he-goats; two hundred ewes and twenty rams;

טז גְּמַלִּים מֵינִיקוֹת וּבְנֵיהֶם שְׁלֹשִׁים פָּרוֹת
אַרְבָּעִים וּפָרִים עֲשָׂרָה אֲתֹנֹת עֶשְׂרִים וַעְיָרִם
עֲשָׂרָה: יז וַיִּתֵּן בְּיַד־עֲבָדָיו עֵדֶר עֵדֶר לְבַדּוֹ
וַיֹּאמֶר אֶל־עֲבָדָיו עִבְרוּ לְפָנַי וְרֶוַח תָּשִׂימוּ
בֵּין עֵדֶר וּבֵין עֵדֶר: יח וַיְצַו אֶת־הָרִאשׁוֹן
לֵאמֹר כִּי יִפְגָּשְׁךָ עֵשָׂו אָחִי וּשְׁאֵלְךָ לֵאמֹר
לְמִי־אַתָּה וְאָנָה תֵלֵךְ וּלְמִי אֵלֶּה לְפָנֶיךָ:
יט וְאָמַרְתָּ לְעַבְדְּךָ לְיַעֲקֹב מִנְחָה הִוא שְׁלוּחָה
לַאדֹנִי לְעֵשָׂו וְהִנֵּה גַם־הוּא אַחֲרֵינוּ: כ וַיְצַו גַּם
אֶת־הַשֵּׁנִי גַּם אֶת־הַשְּׁלִישִׁי גַּם אֶת־כָּל־
הַהֹלְכִים אַחֲרֵי הָעֲדָרִים לֵאמֹר כַּדָּבָר הַזֶּה
תְּדַבְּרוּן אֶל־עֵשָׂו בְּמֹצַאֲכֶם אֹתוֹ: כא וַאֲמַרְתֶּם
גַּם הִנֵּה עַבְדְּךָ יַעֲקֹב אַחֲרֵינוּ כִּי־אָמַר
אֲכַפְּרָה פָנָיו בַּמִּנְחָה הַהֹלֶכֶת לְפָנָי וְאַחֲרֵי־
כֵן אֶרְאֶה פָנָיו אוּלַי יִשָּׂא פָנָי: כב וַתַּעֲבֹר
הַמִּנְחָה עַל־פָּנָיו וְהוּא לָן בַּלַּיְלָה־הַהוּא
בַּמַּחֲנֶה: כג וַיָּקָם ׀ בַּלַּיְלָה הוּא וַיִּקַּח אֶת־
שְׁתֵּי נָשָׁיו וְאֶת־שְׁתֵּי שִׁפְחֹתָיו וְאֶת־
אַחַד עָשָׂר יְלָדָיו וַיַּעֲבֹר אֵת מַעֲבַר יַבֹּק:
כד וַיִּקָּחֵם וַיַּעֲבִרֵם אֶת־הַנָּחַל וַיַּעֲבֵר אֶת־
אֲשֶׁר־לוֹ: כה וַיִּוָּתֵר יַעֲקֹב לְבַדּוֹ וַיֵּאָבֵק אִישׁ
עִמּוֹ עַד עֲלוֹת הַשָּׁחַר: כו וַיַּרְא כִּי לֹא יָכֹל
לוֹ וַיִּגַּע בְּכַף־יְרֵכוֹ וַתֵּקַע כַּף־יֶרֶךְ יַעֲקֹב
בְּהֵאָבְקוֹ עִמּוֹ: כז וַיֹּאמֶר שַׁלְּחֵנִי כִּי עָלָה
הַשָּׁחַר וַיֹּאמֶר לֹא אֲשַׁלֵּחֲךָ כִּי אִם־בֵּרַכְתָּנִי:

15-16. Jacob [who as a skilled shepherd was fully familiar with animals' breeding habits (*Ibn Ezra*)] sent sufficient males for the needs of the females (*Rashi*).

17. Jacob wanted each drove to be distinct, so that Esau would take note of the proper proportion of males to females. Thereby he would realize that Jacob planned the tribute to yield him maximum productivity. (*Sforno*).

20. *When you find him.* Following the broader concept that this sequence applies as well to future generations who must defend themselves against Esau's descendants, the implication is: *In this manner shall you speak to Esau whenever you encounter him* (R' Munk).

For he [Jacob] *said, 'I will appease him with the tribute that precedes me.'* Jacob did not actually utter this phrase as part of his instructions to the messengers. Rather, Scripture explains Jacob's motives in sending tribute. The word *said* should accordingly be understood as *said to himself* (*Rashi, Rashbam,* and *Ibn Ezra*).

Ramban maintains that this phrase *did* form part of Jacob's instructions to the emissaries. They were to tell Esau that Jacob had specifically sent them ahead with gifts to 'ransom' him.

23. Jacob moves his encampment.

The river *Jabbok* (today known as Nahr ez-Zerqa, so called because of its blue waters) is a tributary of the Jordan, half way between the Dead Sea and the Sea of Galilee. With its deep banks, the river is a natural boundary. [In modern times, the river's waters have been mostly drained for irrigation.]

25. The struggle with the angel.

Rashi cites the Talmudic interpretation [*Chullin* 91a] that Jacob had forgotten some פַּכִּים קְטַנִּים, *small earthenware pitchers,* and returned to fetch them. From the fact that Jacob risked his life by returning that night for small pitchers, the Sages [ibid.] derive that 'to the righteous, their money is dearer to them than their bodies' — the reason being that they never take anything that is not rightfully theirs.

And a man wrestled with him. The Rabbis explained that this 'man' was the guardian angel of Esau [in the guise of a man] (*Rashi*).

The angel's purpose was to prevent Jacob from fleeing so that he would see God keep His promise that Esau would not harm him (*Rashbam*). *Sforno* comments that God dispatched the angel to pave the way for Jacob's ultimate salvation. The Patriarch would suffer material losses as a result of the struggle, but he would emerge with an even greater victory and blessing.

The angel — representative of the Edomite Empire — will fight with Jacob's descendants, wrestling with them to lead them astray from God's path *until the break of dawn* — the dawn of Israel's salvation — when the long night of exile will finally end (*Lekach Tov*).

26. The angel could not overcome him because Jacob cleaved tenaciously to God (*Sforno*).

He struck the socket of his hip. The angel informed Jacob of the sins of the future leaders of Israel. In his distress, he stopped concentrating on God, thus enabling the angel to hurt him (*Sforno*).

[16] thirty nursing camels with their colts; forty cows and ten bulls; twenty she-donkeys and ten he-donkeys. [17] He put in his servants' charge each drove separately and said to his servants, 'Pass on ahead of me and leave a space between drove and drove.' [18] He instructed the first one as follows, 'When my brother Esau meets you and asks you, saying, "Whose are you, where are you going, and whose are these that are before you?" — [19] You shall say, "Your servant Jacob's. It is a tribute sent to my lord, to Esau, and behold he himself is behind us." '

[20] He similarly instructed the second, also the third, as well as all who followed the droves, saying, 'In this manner shall you speak to Esau when you find him. [21] And you shall say, "Moreover — Behold your servant Jacob is behind us." ' (For he said, 'I will appease him with the tribute that precedes me, and afterwards I will face him; perhaps he will forgive me.') [22] So the tribute passed on before him while he spent that night in the camp.

[23] But he got up that night and took his two wives, his two handmaids and his eleven sons and crossed the ford of the Jabbok. [24] And when he took them and had them cross over the stream, he sent over all his possessions.

[25] Jacob was left alone and a man wrestled with him until the break of dawn. [26] When he perceived that he could not overcome him, he struck the socket of his hip. So Jacob's hip-socket was dislocated as he wrestled with him. [27] And he said, 'Let me go, for dawn has broken.'

And he said, 'I will not let you go unless you bless me.'

כח וַיֹּאמֶר אֵלָיו מַה־שְּׁמֶךָ וַיֹּאמֶר יַעֲקֹב:
כט וַיֹּאמֶר לֹא יַעֲקֹב יֵאָמֵר עוֹד שִׁמְךָ כִּי אִם־יִשְׂרָאֵל כִּי־שָׂרִיתָ עִם־אֱלֹהִים וְעִם־אֲנָשִׁים וַתּוּכָל: ל וַיִּשְׁאַל יַעֲקֹב וַיֹּאמֶר הַגִּידָה־נָּא שְׁמֶךָ וַיֹּאמֶר לָמָּה זֶּה תִּשְׁאַל לִשְׁמִי וַיְבָרֶךְ אֹתוֹ שָׁם: שלישי לא וַיִּקְרָא יַעֲקֹב שֵׁם הַמָּקוֹם פְּנִיאֵל כִּי־רָאִיתִי אֱלֹהִים פָּנִים אֶל־פָּנִים וַתִּנָּצֵל נַפְשִׁי: לב וַיִּזְרַח־לוֹ הַשֶּׁמֶשׁ כַּאֲשֶׁר עָבַר אֶת־פְּנוּאֵל וְהוּא צֹלֵעַ עַל־יְרֵכוֹ: לג עַל־כֵּן לֹא־יֹאכְלוּ בְנֵי־יִשְׂרָאֵל אֶת־גִּיד הַנָּשֶׁה אֲשֶׁר עַל־כַּף הַיָּרֵךְ עַד הַיּוֹם הַזֶּה כִּי נָגַע בְּכַף־יֶרֶךְ יַעֲקֹב בְּגִיד הַנָּשֶׁה: לג א וַיִּשָּׂא יַעֲקֹב עֵינָיו וַיַּרְא וְהִנֵּה עֵשָׂו בָּא וְעִמּוֹ אַרְבַּע מֵאוֹת אִישׁ וַיַּחַץ אֶת־הַיְלָדִים עַל־לֵאָה וְעַל־רָחֵל וְעַל שְׁתֵּי הַשְּׁפָחוֹת: ב וַיָּשֶׂם אֶת־הַשְּׁפָחוֹת וְאֶת־יַלְדֵיהֶן רִאשֹׁנָה וְאֶת־לֵאָה וִילָדֶיהָ אַחֲרֹנִים וְאֶת־רָחֵל וְאֶת־יוֹסֵף אַחֲרֹנִים: ג וְהוּא עָבַר לִפְנֵיהֶם וַיִּשְׁתַּחוּ אַרְצָה שֶׁבַע פְּעָמִים עַד־גִּשְׁתּוֹ עַד־אָחִיו: ד וַיָּרָץ עֵשָׂו לִקְרָאתוֹ וַיְחַבְּקֵהוּ וַיִּפֹּל עַל־צַוָּארָו וַיִּשָּׁקֵהוּ וַיִּבְכּוּ: ה וַיִּשָּׂא אֶת־עֵינָיו וַיַּרְא אֶת־הַנָּשִׁים וְאֶת־הַיְלָדִים וַיֹּאמֶר מִי־אֵלֶּה לָּךְ וַיֹּאמַר הַיְלָדִים אֲשֶׁר־חָנַן אֱלֹהִים אֶת־עַבְדֶּךָ: רביעי ו וַתִּגַּשְׁןָ הַשְּׁפָחוֹת הֵנָּה וְיַלְדֵיהֶן וַתִּשְׁתַּחֲוֶיןָ: ז וַתִּגַּשׁ גַּם־לֵאָה וִילָדֶיהָ

28. Jacob is informed that his name will be changed.

29. I.e., it will no longer be said that your name *Jacob* [יַעֲקֹב, implying *heel*; *deceit,*] suits you and that you attained the blessings by *deceit* [as Esau indeed charged in 27:36] (Rashi).

But Israel [= *prevailing; superiority*]. Instead [it will be said] that you attained the blessings through *prevailing* [שְׂרָרָה] and in an open manner (Rashi). [It was not the *angel* who was *renaming* Jacob; nor was this name-change to be effective immediately. The angel was merely revealing to Jacob what *God Himself* would do later (35:10).]

Thus the name *Yisrael* is explained as a combination of יִשְׂרֶה, *to prevail,* over אֵל, the *Divine,* i.e., the angel. This interpretation of the name's significance is not repeated in 35:10.

30. 'What use could the knowledge of my name be to you? I am powerless except for Hashem. Should you summon me, I would not respond nor can I help you in your distress.' But the angel blessed him for he had been commanded to do so [not because he had independent power] (Ramban; Tur).

31. פְּנִיאֵל — *Peniel* [lit., *face of God*]. In verse 32 the name is given as פְּנוּאֵל, *Penuel.* Both names are identical since the letters א,ה,ו,י are interchangeable (Radak).

For Jacob, the name פְּנִיאֵל has a first-person connotation — פְּנֵי, *my face* (toward) God. But for future generations the place name will signify the imperative: פְּנוּאֵל, *turn to God* (R' Munk).

33. The prohibition of eating the tendon of an animal's thigh.

Two primary tissues are forbidden in the hind-quarter: The inner sinew — the sciatic nerve — near the bone is forbidden by Torah law; the outer sinew — the common peroneal nerve — near the flesh is forbidden by the Sages (Chullin 91a). Every last trace of the nerves must be 'porged,' i.e., removed. Technically, their fat is permitted, but because Jews are scrupulously pious, they treat it as forbidden; accordingly, all the fat covering the sciatic nerve must be removed (ibid. 92b). Additionally, the six nerves which appear like strings must be removed, as well as other veins. The pertinent halachos regarding this prohibition are found in Shulchan Aruch, Yoreh Deah §65.

33/1. The encounter between Jacob and Esau.

2. The more precious and beloved, the farther back they were placed [אַחֲרוֹן אַחֲרוֹן חָבִיב] (Rashi).

4. The preliminaries being over, Jacob confronts Esau, not knowing whether the result will be bloody battle or brotherly reconciliation.

Esau . . . embraced him. Esau's compassion was aroused at the sight of Jacob's numerous prostrations (Rashi from Midrash).

One cannot cry unless he is genuinely moved, for tears flow from the innermost feelings. Esau's kiss accompanied by tears proved that he, too, was a descendant of Abraham (R' Hirsch).

5. Though Esau had asked about the women also, Jacob delicately answered only about the children. Esau understood from his answer that the women were his wives (Ramban).

²⁸ He said to him, 'What is your name?' He replied, 'Jacob.'

²⁹ He said, 'No longer will it be said that your name is Jacob, but Israel, for you have striven with the Divine and with human and have overcome.'

³⁰ Then Jacob inquired, and he said: 'Divulge, if you please, your name.'

And he said, 'Why then do you inquire of my name?' And he blessed him there.

³¹ So Jacob named the place Peniel — 'For I have seen the Divine face to face, yet my life was saved.' ³² The sun rose for him as he passed Penuel and he was limping on his hip. ³³ Therefore the Children of Israel are not to eat the displaced sinew on the hip-socket to this day, because he struck Jacob's hip-socket on the displaced sinew.

33 ¹ Jacob raised his eyes and saw — Behold, Esau was coming, accompanied by four hundred men. So he divided the children among Leah, Rachel and the two handmaids. ² He put the handmaids and their children first, Leah and her children next, and Rachel and Joseph last. ³ Then he himself went on ahead of them and bowed earthward seven times as he approached his brother.

⁴ Esau ran toward him, embraced him, fell upon his neck and kissed him. Then they wept. ⁵ He raised his eyes and saw the women and children, and he asked, 'Who are these to you?'

He answered, 'The children whom God has graciously given your servant.'

⁶ Then the handmaids came forward — they and their children — and they bowed down. ⁷ Leah, too, came forward with her children and

וַיִּשְׁתַּחֲוֻ וְאַחַר נִגַּשׁ יוֹסֵף וְרָחֵל וַיִּשְׁתַּחֲוֻוּ:
ח וַיֹּאמֶר מִי לְךָ כָּל־הַמַּחֲנֶה הַזֶּה אֲשֶׁר
פָּגָשְׁתִּי וַיֹּאמֶר לִמְצֹא־חֵן בְּעֵינֵי אֲדֹנִי:
ט וַיֹּאמֶר עֵשָׂו יֶשׁ־לִי רָב אָחִי יְהִי לְךָ אֲשֶׁר־
לָךְ: י וַיֹּאמֶר יַעֲקֹב אַל־נָא אִם־נָא מָצָאתִי
חֵן בְּעֵינֶיךָ וְלָקַחְתָּ מִנְחָתִי מִיָּדִי כִּי עַל־כֵּן
רָאִיתִי פָנֶיךָ כִּרְאֹת פְּנֵי אֱלֹהִים וַתִּרְצֵנִי:
יא קַח־נָא אֶת־בִּרְכָתִי אֲשֶׁר הֻבָאת לָךְ כִּי־
חַנַּנִי אֱלֹהִים וְכִי יֶשׁ־לִי־כֹל וַיִּפְצַר־בּוֹ וַיִּקָּח:
יב וַיֹּאמֶר נִסְעָה וְנֵלֵכָה וְאֵלְכָה לְנֶגְדֶּךָ:
יג וַיֹּאמֶר אֵלָיו אֲדֹנִי יֹדֵעַ כִּי־הַיְלָדִים רַכִּים
וְהַצֹּאן וְהַבָּקָר עָלוֹת עָלָי וּדְפָקוּם יוֹם אֶחָד
וָמֵתוּ כָּל־הַצֹּאן: יד יַעֲבָר־נָא אֲדֹנִי לִפְנֵי
עַבְדּוֹ וַאֲנִי אֶתְנָהֲלָה לְאִטִּי לְרֶגֶל הַמְּלָאכָה
אֲשֶׁר־לְפָנַי וּלְרֶגֶל הַיְלָדִים עַד אֲשֶׁר־אָבֹא
אֶל־אֲדֹנִי שֵׂעִירָה: טו וַיֹּאמֶר עֵשָׂו אַצִּיגָה־נָּא
עִמְּךָ מִן־הָעָם אֲשֶׁר אִתִּי וַיֹּאמֶר לָמָּה זֶּה
אֶמְצָא־חֵן בְּעֵינֵי אֲדֹנִי: טז וַיָּשָׁב בַּיּוֹם הַהוּא
עֵשָׂו לְדַרְכּוֹ שֵׂעִירָה: יז וְיַעֲקֹב נָסַע סֻכֹּתָה
וַיִּבֶן לוֹ בָּיִת וּלְמִקְנֵהוּ עָשָׂה סֻכֹּת עַל־כֵּן
קָרָא שֵׁם־הַמָּקוֹם סֻכּוֹת: יח וַיָּבֹא
יַעֲקֹב שָׁלֵם עִיר שְׁכֶם אֲשֶׁר בְּאֶרֶץ כְּנַעַן
בְּבֹאוֹ מִפַּדַּן אֲרָם וַיִּחַן אֶת־פְּנֵי הָעִיר:
יט וַיִּקֶן אֶת־חֶלְקַת הַשָּׂדֶה אֲשֶׁר נָטָה־שָׁם

8. Esau now inquires about Jacob's intent in sending the immense tribute.

9. *My brother, let what you have remain yours.* By this statement Esau acquiesced to Jacob's possession of Isaac's blessing (*Rashi*).

11. The translation of בִּרְכָתִי [lit., *my blessing*] as *my gift* follows *Rashi* who explains the term to connote a gift given as a greeting upon seeing someone after a long lapse of time.

12. I [Esau] will do you the favor of slowing down as much as is necessary to keep pace with your slow-moving flocks and family (*Rashi*).

13. *The children are tender.* The oldest, Reuben, was only a little more than twelve years old at the time (*Ibn Ezra*).

Then all the flocks will die. From fatigue (*Rashi*). Jacob's primary concern was for his young children, but delicacy did not permit him to speak of their possible death. 'A covenant is made with the lips' (*Moed Kattan* 18a), and even an unintentional implication, much less an explicit statement, may allude to future events. Such unintended prognostications often become fulfilled as if they were prophecy.

16. Apparently there was a coolness between Jacob and Esau at the parting. It was not accompanied by kissing, as was Jacob's departure from Laban [32:1]. Perceiving this coolness, Jacob gave up any thought of going to Seir to receive more honor from Esau (*Haamek Davar*).

18. Jacob in Shechem.

Jacob arrived intact. Literally, שָׁלֵם means *whole; perfect; unimpaired.* The Torah intimates that he arrived *intact* in body — having been cured of his limp; *intact* financially — lacking nothing, though he had showered a lavish gift upon Esau [for, as *Midrash Tanchuma* notes, God had replenished everything Jacob spent on that gift]; and *intact* in his learning — having forgotten nothing while in Laban's house (*Rashi* from *Shabbos* 33b).

Jacob felt secure only when he reached Shechem because — as the Torah emphasizes — *it was in Eretz Yisrael.* He knew that Esau would not molest him there, either because Isaac was nearby and the inhabitants stood in awe of Isaac and would protect Jacob, or because the merit of *Eretz Yisrael* would protect him. In contrast, during his stay in Succoth, Jacob felt no such security. As the Sages in the Midrash point out, as long as he lived in Succoth, Jacob kept sending extravagant gifts to Esau in Seir, to appease him (*Ramban*).

they bowed down; and afterwards, Joseph and Rachel came forward and bowed down.

⁸ And he asked, 'What did you intend by that whole camp that I met?'

He answered, 'To gain favor in my lord's eyes.'

⁹ Esau said, 'I have plenty. My brother, let what you have remain yours.'

¹⁰ But Jacob said, 'No, I beg of you! If I have after all found favor in your eyes, then accept my tribute from me, inasmuch as I have seen your face, which is like seeing the face of a Divine being, and you were appeased by me. ¹¹ Please accept my gift which was brought to you, inasmuch as I have everything.' He urged him, and he accepted.

¹² And he said, 'Travel on and let us go — I will proceed at your pace.'

¹³ But he said to him, 'My lord knows that the children are tender, and the nursing flocks and herds are upon me; if they will be driven hard for a single day, then all the flocks will die. ¹⁴ Let my lord go ahead of his servant; I will make my way at my slow pace according to the gait of the drove before me and the gait of the children, until I come to my lord at Seir.'

¹⁵ Then Esau said, 'Let me assign to you some of the people who are with me.'

And he said, 'To what purpose? Let me just have favor in my lord's eyes!'

¹⁶ So Esau started back that day on his way toward Seir. ¹⁷ But Jacob journeyed to Succoth and built himself a house, and for his livestock he made shelters; he therefore named the place Succoth.

¹⁸ Jacob arrived intact at the city of Shechem which is in the land of Canaan, upon arriving from Paddan Aram, and he encamped in view of the city. ¹⁹ He bought the parcel of land upon

אֹהֱל֔וֹ מִיַּ֛ד בְּנֵֽי־חֲמ֥וֹר אֲבִ֥י שְׁכֶ֖ם בְּמֵאָ֥ה
קְשִׂיטָֽה: כ וַיַּצֶּב־שָׁ֖ם מִזְבֵּ֑חַ וַיִּקְרָא־ל֔וֹ אֵ֖ל
אֱלֹהֵ֥י יִשְׂרָאֵֽל: **לד** חמישי א וַתֵּצֵ֤א
דִינָה֙ בַּת־לֵאָ֔ה אֲשֶׁ֥ר יָלְדָ֖ה לְיַעֲקֹ֑ב לִרְא֖וֹת
בִּבְנ֥וֹת הָאָֽרֶץ: ב וַיַּ֨רְא אֹתָ֜הּ שְׁכֶ֧ם בֶּן־חֲמ֛וֹר
הַֽחִוִּ֖י נְשִׂ֣יא הָאָ֑רֶץ וַיִּקַּ֥ח אֹתָ֛הּ וַיִּשְׁכַּ֥ב אֹתָ֖הּ
וַיְעַנֶּֽהָ: ג וַתִּדְבַּ֣ק נַפְשׁ֔וֹ בְּדִינָ֖ה בַּֽת־יַעֲקֹ֑ב
וַיֶּֽאֱהַב֙ אֶת־הַֽנַּעֲרָ֔ וַיְדַבֵּ֖ר עַל־לֵ֥ב הַֽנַּעֲרָֽ:
ד וַיֹּ֣אמֶר שְׁכֶ֗ם אֶל־חֲמ֥וֹר אָבִ֖יו לֵאמֹ֑ר קַֽח־לִ֛י
אֶת־הַיַּלְדָּ֥ה הַזֹּ֖את לְאִשָּֽׁה: ה וְיַעֲקֹ֣ב שָׁמַ֗ע כִּ֤י
טִמֵּא֙ אֶת־דִּינָ֣ה בִתּ֔וֹ וּבָנָ֛יו הָי֥וּ אֶת־מִקְנֵ֖הוּ
בַּשָּׂדֶ֑ה וְהֶֽחֱרִ֥שׁ יַעֲקֹ֖ב עַד־בֹּאָֽם: ו וַיֵּצֵ֛א חֲמ֥וֹר
אֲבִֽי־שְׁכֶ֖ם אֶֽל־יַעֲקֹ֑ב לְדַבֵּ֖ר אִתּֽוֹ: ז וּבְנֵ֣י יַעֲקֹ֗ב
בָּ֤אוּ מִן־הַשָּׂדֶה֙ כְּשָׁמְעָ֔ם וַיִּֽתְעַצְּבוּ֙ הָֽאֲנָשִׁ֔ים
וַיִּ֥חַר לָהֶ֖ם מְאֹ֑ד כִּֽי־נְבָלָ֞ה עָשָׂ֣ה בְיִשְׂרָאֵ֗ל
לִשְׁכַּב֙ אֶת־בַּֽת־יַעֲקֹ֔ב וְכֵ֖ן לֹ֥א יֵעָשֶֽׂה:
ח וַיְדַבֵּ֥ר חֲמ֖וֹר אִתָּ֣ם לֵאמֹ֑ר שְׁכֶ֣ם בְּנִ֗י חָֽשְׁקָ֤ה
נַפְשׁוֹ֙ בְּבִתְּכֶ֔ם תְּנ֨וּ נָ֥א אֹתָ֛הּ ל֖וֹ לְאִשָּֽׁה:
ט וְהִֽתְחַתְּנ֖וּ אֹתָ֑נוּ בְּנֹֽתֵיכֶם֙ תִּתְּנוּ־לָ֔נוּ וְאֶת־
בְּנֹתֵ֖ינוּ תִּקְח֥וּ לָכֶֽם: י וְאִתָּ֖נוּ תֵּשֵׁ֑בוּ וְהָאָ֨רֶץ֙
תִּהְיֶ֣ה לִפְנֵיכֶ֔ם שְׁבוּ֙ וּסְחָר֔וּהָ וְהֵֽאָחֲז֖וּ בָּֽהּ:
יא וַיֹּ֤אמֶר שְׁכֶם֙ אֶל־אָבִ֣יהָ וְאֶל־אַחֶ֔יהָ
אֶמְצָא־חֵ֖ן בְּעֵֽינֵיכֶ֑ם וַֽאֲשֶׁ֧ר תֹּֽאמְר֛וּ אֵלַ֖י אֶתֵּֽן:
יב הַרְבּ֨וּ עָלַ֤י מְאֹד֙ מֹ֣הַר וּמַתָּ֔ן וְאֶ֨תְּנָ֔ה כַּֽאֲשֶׁ֥ר
תֹּֽאמְר֖וּ אֵלָ֑י וּתְנוּ־לִ֥י אֶת־הַֽנַּעֲרָ֖ לְאִשָּֽׁה:

19. Jacob wanted to establish an inalienable right to the land by means of purchase (*Ramban*).

The Midrash notes that this became the eventual site of Joseph's sepulcher. It is one of the three places where the Gentiles cannot besmirch Israel by saying, 'You hold stolen property,' since, as our verse tells us, Jacob bought it with uncontested currency.

The altar was not called 'God of Israel' [in the sense that it was regarded as a deity (*Sefer HaZikaron*)]. Rather, Jacob intended that God's praise would be evoked at the mention of the altar's name. 'He Who is *God* — the Holy One, Blessed is He — *is the God* of the person [Jacob] whose name is *Israel*' (*Rashi*).

34/1. Dinah's abduction.

Jacob, who had overcome the terrible trials of the past twenty years, and believed that at last he would find tranquility in *Eretz Yisrael* — as the end of the last chapter indicates — suddenly faces a setback. This people, which is called on to be a nation of priests and God's standard-bearer on earth, had to experience a moral outrage upon its own flesh and blood right from its beginning. It had to undergo this ordeal so that the world could see in its swift and uncompromising reaction the sacred character of its purity. (*R' Munk; R' Hirsch*).

Because Dinah *went out* — in violation of the code of modesty becoming Jacob's daughter — she is called the *daughter of Leah* because Leah, too, was excessively outgoing. With her in mind, they formulated the proverb, 'Like mother like daughter' (*Rashi* from *Midrash* and *Tanchuma*).

2. Was he then a Hivvite? He was an Amorite as noted in 48:22 — Rather, יחו is an adjective meaning *serpentine* in Aramaic. This describes the serpent-like, treacherous manner in which Shechem acted.

3. *He became deeply attached to Dinah, daughter of Jacob,* both because of her great beauty, and because she was the daughter of Jacob, an acknowledged great man (*Radak*).

5. Jacob's family learns of Dinah's violation.

Jacob's suspicions must have been aroused when Dinah did not return home. Jacob might have inquired after her and heard the terrible news that she was being held a prisoner in Shechem's home.

7. *Jacob's sons arrived from the field, when they heard.* Apparently the ugly news reached them in the fields. They arrived at Jacob's tent at about the same time as Chamor, and they did not have the opportunity to consult privately with their father (*Rashbam; Malbim*).

Levush explains that according to *Rashi* the sense of our passage would be: *For he had committed an outrage in Israel* — a nation which had high standards of morality and viewed such dastardly acts with utter contempt, *and furthermore, it was a thing not to be done* — for even the heathen nations had renounced immorality as a consequence of the Flood.

11. Shechem goes into more specific detail regarding his proposal than did his father (*Abarbanel*), and tries to make it more acceptable by offering a huge dowry (*Haamek Davar*).

which he pitched his tent from the children of Chamor, Shechem's father, for one hundred kesitahs. ²⁰ He set up an altar there and proclaimed it 'God is the God of Israel.'

34 ¹ Now Dinah — the daughter of Leah, whom she had borne to Jacob — went out to look over the daughters of the land. ² Shechem, son of Chamor the Hivvite, the prince of the region, saw her; he took her, lay with her, and violated her. ³ He became deeply attached to Dinah, daughter of Jacob; he loved the maiden and appealed to the maiden's emotions. ⁴ So Shechem said to Chamor, his father, as follows, 'Get me this girl for a wife.'

⁵ Now Jacob heard that he had defiled his daughter Dinah, while his sons were with his cattle in the field; so Jacob kept silent until their arrival.

⁶ Chamor, Shechem's father, went out to Jacob to speak to him. ⁷ Jacob's sons arrived from the the field, when they heard. The men were distressed, and were fired deeply with indignation, for he had committed an outrage in Israel by lying with a daughter of Jacob — such a thing may not be done!

⁸ Chamor spoke with them saying, 'My son, Shechem, longs deeply for your daughter — please give her to him as a wife, ⁹ and intermarry with us; give your daughters to us, and take our daughters for yourselves. ¹⁰ And among us you shall dwell; the land will be open before you — settle and trade in it, and acquire property in it.'

¹¹ Then Shechem said to her father and brothers, 'Let me gain favor in your eyes; and whatever you tell me — I will give. ¹² Inflate exceedingly upon me the marriage settlement and gifts and I will give whatever you tell me; only give me the maiden for a wife.'

יג וַיַּעֲנוּ בְנֵי־יַעֲקֹב אֶת־שְׁכֶם וְאֶת־חֲמוֹר אָבִיו בְּמִרְמָה וַיְדַבֵּרוּ אֲשֶׁר טִמֵּא אֵת דִּינָה אֲחֹתָם: יד וַיֹּאמְרוּ אֲלֵיהֶם לֹא נוּכַל לַעֲשׂוֹת הַדָּבָר הַזֶּה לָתֵת אֶת־אֲחֹתֵנוּ לְאִישׁ אֲשֶׁר־לוֹ עָרְלָה כִּי־חֶרְפָּה הִוא לָנוּ: טו אַךְ־בְּזֹאת נֵאוֹת לָכֶם אִם תִּהְיוּ כָמֹנוּ לְהִמֹּל לָכֶם כָּל־זָכָר: טז וְנָתַנּוּ אֶת־בְּנֹתֵינוּ לָכֶם וְאֶת־בְּנֹתֵיכֶם נִקַּח־לָנוּ וְיָשַׁבְנוּ אִתְּכֶם וְהָיִינוּ לְעַם אֶחָד: יז וְאִם־לֹא תִשְׁמְעוּ אֵלֵינוּ לְהִמּוֹל וְלָקַחְנוּ אֶת־בִּתֵּנוּ וְהָלָכְנוּ: יח וַיִּיטְבוּ דִבְרֵיהֶם בְּעֵינֵי חֲמוֹר וּבְעֵינֵי שְׁכֶם בֶּן־חֲמוֹר: יט וְלֹא־אֵחַר הַנַּעַר לַעֲשׂוֹת הַדָּבָר כִּי חָפֵץ בְּבַת־יַעֲקֹב וְהוּא נִכְבָּד מִכֹּל בֵּית אָבִיו: כ וַיָּבֹא חֲמוֹר וּשְׁכֶם בְּנוֹ אֶל־שַׁעַר עִירָם וַיְדַבְּרוּ אֶל־אַנְשֵׁי עִירָם לֵאמֹר: כא הָאֲנָשִׁים הָאֵלֶּה שְׁלֵמִים הֵם אִתָּנוּ וְיֵשְׁבוּ בָאָרֶץ וְיִסְחֲרוּ אֹתָהּ וְהָאָרֶץ הִנֵּה רַחֲבַת־יָדַיִם לִפְנֵיהֶם אֶת־בְּנֹתָם נִקַּח־לָנוּ לְנָשִׁים וְאֶת־בְּנֹתֵינוּ נִתֵּן לָהֶם: כב אַךְ־בְּזֹאת יֵאֹתוּ לָנוּ הָאֲנָשִׁים לָשֶׁבֶת אִתָּנוּ לִהְיוֹת לְעַם אֶחָד בְּהִמּוֹל לָנוּ כָּל־זָכָר כַּאֲשֶׁר הֵם נִמֹּלִים: כג מִקְנֵהֶם וְקִנְיָנָם וְכָל־בְּהֶמְתָּם הֲלוֹא לָנוּ הֵם אַךְ נֵאוֹתָה לָהֶם וְיֵשְׁבוּ אִתָּנוּ: כד וַיִּשְׁמְעוּ אֶל־חֲמוֹר וְאֶל־שְׁכֶם בְּנוֹ כָּל־יֹצְאֵי שַׁעַר עִירוֹ וַיִּמֹּלוּ כָּל־זָכָר כָּל־יֹצְאֵי שַׁעַר עִירוֹ: כה וַיְהִי בַיּוֹם הַשְּׁלִישִׁי בִּהְיוֹתָם

---

13. בְּמִרְמָה — *Cleverly.* I.e., with wisdom (*Rashi,* following the *Midrash* and *Targum*). The Torah thus bears testimony to the fact that Jacob's sons never seriously considered compromising on the fundamental restriction against intermarriage. From the very beginning of the discussions, their response was cleverly calculated to extricate Dinah (*Haamek Davar*).

14. It is beneath their dignity to reply directly to Shechem's monetary offer; first a question of principle must be resolved (*Akeidas Yitzchak*).

Marriage to an uncircumcised man would forever disgrace our family (*Ibn Ezra*).

To us it is a blemish that goes from generation to generation. If one wishes to insult his friend, he would say to him: 'You are uncircumcised,' or: 'You are the son of one who is uncircumcised' (*Rashi*).

15. *By letting every male among you become circumcised. Every male* — so that any difference between our people and yours would disappear, and we can integrate freely.

They chose circumcision as the scheme by which to render them helpless for the massacre in order to inflict injury on the organ that Shechem used to perpetrate his outrage (*Sifsei Kohen*).

17. Jacob's sons avoided any reference to Shechem's vile deed, or even to the fact that Dinah was incarcerated in his house. They merely made it clear that in no way would they permit her to be married to one who is uncircumcised. Should Shechem refuse their proposal, they would *take their daughter* and go (*Akeidas Yitzchak*).

18. The Shechemites accept.

Their proposal seemed good in the view of Chamor. The father was as foolish as the son! (*Lekach Tov*).

19. Although he was *the most respected of all his father's household* [and therefore could have waited and circumcised himself last], nevertheless, the youth lost no time [and made himself the example] . . . so strongly did he desire Jacob's daughter (*Sforno*).

21. Chamor presents the plan in the most glamorous light possible. He tactfully avoids any mention of the *personal* benefit his son sought thereby; the implication is that the town as a *whole* will benefit from this new association, and that Chamor is selflessly interested only in the community's welfare (*R' Hoffmann*).

23. Won't they be ours? This is how it always ended: The Jewish stranger came, toiled, and accumulated wealth which ultimately reverted to his hosts. To induce his people to accept his suggestion, Chamor promised that it would be profitable to them and they would gradually absorb the rich possessions of Jacob's household. Contrast this with the seeming cordiality of Chamor's invitation to Jacob in verse 10! (*Heidenheim*).

24. The stich *all those who depart through the gate of the city* implies that all the residents of the city wanted to flee from the decree of being circumcised against their will. But no male was allowed to leave the city unless he submitted to circumcision: *all the males . . . had to submit to circumcision* (*Chizkuni*).

[13] Jacob's sons answered Shechem and his father Chamor cleverly and they spoke (because he had defiled their sister Dinah). [14] They said to them, 'We cannot do this thing, to give our sister to a man who is uncircumcised, for that would be a disgrace among us. [15] Only on this condition will we acquiesce to you: If you become like us by letting every male among you become circumcised. [16] Then we will give our daughters to you, and take your daughters to ourselves; we will dwell with you, and become a single people. [17] But if you will not listen to us to be circumcised, we will take our daughter and go.'

[18] Their proposal seemed good in the view of Chamor, and in the view of Shechem, Chamor's son. [19] The youth did not delay doing the thing, for he wanted Jacob's daughter. Now he was the most respected of all his father's household.

[20] Chamor — with his son Shechem — went to the gate of their city and spoke to the people of their city, saying, [21] 'These people are peaceable with us; let them settle in the land and trade in it, for see, there is ample room in the land for them! Let us take their daughters for ourselves as wives and give our daughters to them. [22] Only on this condition will the people acquiesce with us to dwell with us to become a single people: that our males become circumcised as they themselves are circumcised. [23] Their livestock, their possessions, and all their animals — won't they be ours? Let us but acquiesce to them and they will settle with us.'

[24] All the people who depart through the gate of his city listened to Chamor and his son Shechem, and all the males — all those who depart through the gate of his city — were circumcised.

[25] And it came to pass on the third day, when

כְּאָבִ֔ים וַיִּקְח֣וּ שְׁנֵֽי־בְנֵֽי־יַ֠עֲקֹב שִׁמְע֨וֹן וְלֵוִ֜י
אֲחֵ֤י דִינָה֙ אִ֣ישׁ חַרְבּ֔וֹ וַיָּבֹ֥אוּ עַל־הָעִ֖יר בֶּ֑טַח
וַיַּֽהַרְג֖וּ כָּל־זָכָֽר: כו וְאֶת־חֲמוֹר֙ וְאֶת־שְׁכֶ֣ם בְּנ֔וֹ
הָֽרְג֖וּ לְפִי־חָ֑רֶב וַיִּקְח֧וּ אֶת־דִּינָ֛ה מִבֵּ֥ית שְׁכֶ֖ם
וַיֵּצֵֽאוּ: כז בְּנֵ֣י יַֽעֲקֹ֗ב בָּ֚אוּ עַל־הַ֣חֲלָלִ֔ים וַיָּבֹ֖זּוּ
הָעִ֑יר אֲשֶׁ֥ר טִמְּא֖וּ אֲחוֹתָֽם: כח אֶת־צֹאנָ֤ם
וְאֶת־בְּקָרָם֙ וְאֶת־חֲמֹ֣רֵיהֶ֔ם וְאֵ֧ת אֲשֶׁר־בָּעִ֛יר
וְאֶת־אֲשֶׁ֥ר בַּשָּׂדֶ֖ה לָקָֽחוּ: כט וְאֶת־כָּל־חֵילָ֣ם
וְאֶת־כָּל־טַפָּ֣ם וְאֶת־נְשֵׁיהֶ֔ם שָׁב֖וּ וַיָּבֹ֑זּוּ וְאֵ֖ת
כָּל־אֲשֶׁ֥ר בַּבָּֽיִת: ל וַיֹּ֨אמֶר יַֽעֲקֹ֜ב אֶל־שִׁמְע֣וֹן
וְאֶל־לֵוִי֮ עֲכַרְתֶּ֣ם אֹתִי֒ לְהַבְאִישֵׁ֨נִי֙ בְּיֹשֵׁ֣ב
הָאָ֔רֶץ בַּֽכְּנַֽעֲנִ֖י וּבַפְּרִזִּ֑י וַֽאֲנִי֙ מְתֵ֣י מִסְפָּ֔ר
וְנֶֽאֶסְפ֤וּ עָלַי֙ וְהִכּ֔וּנִי וְנִשְׁמַדְתִּ֖י אֲנִ֥י וּבֵיתִֽי:
לא וַיֹּֽאמְר֑וּ הַכְזוֹנָ֕ה יַֽעֲשֶׂ֖ה אֶת־אֲחוֹתֵֽנוּ:

לה א וַיֹּ֤אמֶר אֱלֹהִים֙ אֶל־יַֽעֲקֹ֔ב ק֛וּם עֲלֵ֥ה
בֵֽית־אֵ֖ל וְשֶׁב־שָׁ֑ם וַֽעֲשֵׂה־שָׁ֣ם מִזְבֵּ֔חַ לָאֵל֙
הַנִּרְאֶ֣ה אֵלֶ֔יךָ בְּבָ֨רְחֲךָ֔ מִפְּנֵ֖י עֵשָׂ֥ו אָחִֽיךָ:
ב וַיֹּ֤אמֶר יַֽעֲקֹב֙ אֶל־בֵּית֔וֹ וְאֶ֖ל כָּל־אֲשֶׁ֣ר עִמּ֑וֹ
הָסִ֜רוּ אֶת־אֱלֹהֵ֤י הַנֵּכָר֙ אֲשֶׁ֣ר בְּתֹֽכְכֶ֔ם וְהִֽטַּֽהֲר֔וּ
וְהַֽחֲלִ֖יפוּ שִׂמְלֹֽתֵיכֶֽם: ג וְנָק֥וּמָה וְנַֽעֲלֶ֖ה בֵּֽית־
אֵ֑ל וְאֶֽעֱשֶׂה־שָּׁ֣ם מִזְבֵּ֗חַ לָאֵ֞ל הָֽעֹנֶ֤ה אֹתִי֙
בְּי֣וֹם צָֽרָתִ֔י וַיְהִי֙ עִמָּדִ֔י בַּדֶּ֖רֶךְ אֲשֶׁ֥ר הָלָֽכְתִּי:
ד וַיִּתְּנ֣וּ אֶֽל־יַֽעֲקֹ֗ב אֵ֣ת כָּל־אֱלֹהֵ֤י הַנֵּכָר֙ אֲשֶׁ֣ר
בְּיָדָ֔ם וְאֶת־הַנְּזָמִ֖ים אֲשֶׁ֣ר בְּאָזְנֵיהֶ֑ם וַיִּטְמֹ֤ן
אֹתָם֙ יַֽעֲקֹ֔ב תַּ֚חַת הָֽאֵלָ֔ה אֲשֶׁ֖ר עִם־שְׁכֶֽם:

25. Simeon and Levi decimate Shechem.

They waited until the third day since it took until then to circumcise all the males; by the third day, *all* of them were circumcised and in pain. Furthermore, the verse does not necessarily mean *physical* pain, but *grief* and *regret* over having submitted to the circumcision (*Daas Zekeinim; Chizkuni*).

Each [man] took his sword. The Midrash notes that Levi was thirteen years old at the time. Thus, as *Lekach Tov* points out, it is implied in this Midrashic comment that whenever the Torah uses the term אִישׁ, *man*, it refers to a male over thirteen years old. [Cf. *Rashi* to *Nazir* 29b s.v. ורבי יוסי.]

They killed every male. Simeon and Levi acted only after they heard of the insincere and devious manner in which Chamor and Shechem reported their proposal to the people of Shechem [v. 23]. The duplicity made it clear that their circumcision was not sincere (*Chizkuni*).

27. The verb *defiled* is in the plural. Thereby the Torah bears testimony that *all* the Shechemites were collectively guilty for Shechem's atrocity by allowing it to go unchecked, and by their subsequent insincerity.

30. By their rash violence, Simeon and Levi disturbed Jacob's composure and placed him in a potentially untenable position should the Canaanites choose to attack (*Rashi*).

You have discomposed me. The family's reputation and honor had been crystal clear, but you have besmirched it (*R' Hirsch*).

31. *Should he treat our sister like a harlot?* Should he then have been permitted, unchecked and unpunished, to treat our sister like a harlot, like a loose woman who has no avenger? (*Radak*). We, as her brothers, had the obligation to defend her honor (*Sforno*).

As the episode draws to a close, the brothers make a point of saying that Dinah remained 'fully' worthy of being their sister.

Jacob does not agree with his sons' contention that their extreme violence was justified, but he maintains his silence, stifling his outrage. Only on his deathbed does he curse their anger [49:6] (*R' Hoffman*).

35/1. Jacob journeys to Bethel.

Nearly twenty-two years earlier, Jacob had vowed that Bethel would be the site of *God's house* [28:22]. The command that he now return there was to imply that he must fulfill the vow without delay; because he had not done so sooner, he had been punished by the abduction of Dinah (*Rashi; Radak*).

2. *R' Hirsch* notes that Jacob's order was similar to that given by Moses before the Revelation at Sinai: *he sanctified the people and they washed their garments* [*Exodus* 19:14]. For Jacob's family, the ascent to Bethel where God had revealed Himself to the Patriarch had the same significance as the assembly at Mount Sinai for his descendants.

4. *And Jacob buried them underneath the terebinth near Shechem.* In a location which will neither be tilled nor sown (*Ramban*), so that others should not come upon them and be led astray (*Radak*).

they were in pain, that two of Jacob's sons, Simeon and Levi, Dinah's brothers, each took his sword and they came upon the city confidently. They killed every male, ²⁶ And Chamor and Shechem his son they killed at the point of the sword. Then they took Dinah from Shechem's house and left.

²⁷ The sons of Jacob came upon the slain, and they plundered the city which had defiled their sister. ²⁸ Their flocks, their herds, their donkeys, whatever was in the town and whatever was in the field, they took. ²⁹ All their wealth, all their children and wives they took captive and they plundered, as well as everything in the house.

³⁰ Jacob said to Simeon and to Levi, 'You have discomposed me, making me odious among the inhabitants of the land, the Canaanites and Perizzites. I am few in number and should they band together and attack me, I will be annihilated — I and my household.'

³¹ And they said, 'Should he treat our sister like a harlot?'

35 ¹ **G**od said to Jacob, 'Arise — go up to Bethel and remain there, and make an altar there to God Who appeared to you when you fled from Esau your brother.' ² So Jacob said to his household and to all those who were with him, 'Discard the alien gods that are in your midst; cleanse yourselves and change your clothes. ³ Then come, let us go up to Bethel; I will make there an altar to God Who answered me in my time of distress, and was with me on the road that I have traveled.' ⁴ So they gave to Jacob all the alien gods that were in their possession, as well as the rings that were in their ears, and Jacob buried them underneath the terebinth near Shechem.

ה וַיִּסָּעוּ וַיְהִי ׀ חִתַּת אֱלֹהִים עַל־הֶעָרִים אֲשֶׁר סְבִיבֹתֵיהֶם וְלֹא רָדְפוּ אַחֲרֵי בְּנֵי יַעֲקֹב: ו וַיָּבֹא יַעֲקֹב לוּזָה אֲשֶׁר בְּאֶרֶץ כְּנַעַן הִוא בֵּית־אֵל הוּא וְכָל־הָעָם אֲשֶׁר־עִמּוֹ: ז וַיִּבֶן שָׁם מִזְבֵּחַ וַיִּקְרָא לַמָּקוֹם אֵל בֵּית־אֵל כִּי שָׁם נִגְלוּ אֵלָיו הָאֱלֹהִים בְּבָרְחוֹ מִפְּנֵי אָחִיו: ח וַתָּמָת דְּבֹרָה מֵינֶקֶת רִבְקָה וַתִּקָּבֵר מִתַּחַת לְבֵית־אֵל תַּחַת הָאַלּוֹן וַיִּקְרָא שְׁמוֹ אַלּוֹן בָּכוּת:

ט וַיֵּרָא אֱלֹהִים אֶל־יַעֲקֹב עוֹד בְּבֹאוֹ מִפַּדַּן אֲרָם וַיְבָרֶךְ אֹתוֹ: י וַיֹּאמֶר־לוֹ אֱלֹהִים שִׁמְךָ יַעֲקֹב לֹא־יִקָּרֵא שִׁמְךָ עוֹד יַעֲקֹב כִּי אִם־יִשְׂרָאֵל יִהְיֶה שְׁמֶךָ וַיִּקְרָא אֶת־שְׁמוֹ יִשְׂרָאֵל: יא וַיֹּאמֶר לוֹ אֱלֹהִים אֲנִי אֵל שַׁדַּי פְּרֵה וּרְבֵה גּוֹי וּקְהַל גּוֹיִם יִהְיֶה מִמֶּךָּ וּמְלָכִים מֵחֲלָצֶיךָ יֵצֵאוּ: ששי יב וְאֶת־הָאָרֶץ אֲשֶׁר נָתַתִּי לְאַבְרָהָם וּלְיִצְחָק לְךָ אֶתְּנֶנָּה וּלְזַרְעֲךָ אַחֲרֶיךָ אֶתֵּן אֶת־הָאָרֶץ: יג וַיַּעַל מֵעָלָיו אֱלֹהִים בַּמָּקוֹם אֲשֶׁר־דִּבֶּר אִתּוֹ: יד וַיַּצֵּב יַעֲקֹב מַצֵּבָה בַּמָּקוֹם אֲשֶׁר־דִּבֶּר אִתּוֹ מַצֶּבֶת אָבֶן וַיַּסֵּךְ עָלֶיהָ נֶסֶךְ וַיִּצֹק עָלֶיהָ שָׁמֶן: טו וַיִּקְרָא יַעֲקֹב אֶת־שֵׁם הַמָּקוֹם אֲשֶׁר דִּבֶּר אִתּוֹ שָׁם אֱלֹהִים בֵּית־אֵל: טז וַיִּסְעוּ מִבֵּית אֵל וַיְהִי־עוֹד כִּבְרַת־הָאָרֶץ לָבוֹא אֶפְרָתָה וַתֵּלֶד רָחֵל וַתְּקַשׁ בְּלִדְתָּהּ: יז וַיְהִי בְהַקְשֹׁתָהּ בְּלִדְתָּהּ וַתֹּאמֶר לָהּ הַמְיַלֶּדֶת

5. The Canaanites' fear to attack was a hidden miracle [because it could be attributed to the great natural strength of Jacob and his sons]. However, the Torah did not describe it in detail, referring to it only by allusion in 48:22 and with the passing reference here (*Ramban*).

7. Jacob had already given it the name *Bethel* in 28:19. He now added the name *El* — an act that had a significance similar to his naming of the altar in Shechem as *El Elohei Yisrael* 33:20 [i.e., to commemorate the fact that God wrought miracles for him there] (*Radak*).

8. The death of Rebecca and Deborah. *Rashi* and *Ramban* discuss the Midrashic tradition that this verse alludes also to Rebecca's death, as implied by the name *Alon Bachuth,* Oak of Weeping, which the Midrash perceives to mean *double weeping* [interpreting the word בָּכוּת as if it were the plural — בְּכֻיּוֹת] — one for Rebecca, and the other for Deborah.

Rebecca's death was not mentioned explicitly because people would have cursed her as the one who gave birth to the wicked Esau (*Rashi*).

9. *And God appeared to Jacob again when he came from Paddan Aram.* This appearance occurred *after* the weeping had ceased, since the *Shechinah* does not reside where there is sadness (*Sforno*).

And He blessed him. With the blessing of consolation given to mourners [upon Rebecca's death] (*Rashi*).

10. Jacob is formally named Israel.

You shall no longer be called only [or: primarily] Jacob (*Ibn Ezra*).

Israel is a name which signifies prince and chief.

The name Jacob continued to be used in matters pertaining to the physical and mundane, while Israel was used in matters reflecting the spiritual role of the Patriarch and his descendants (*R' Bachya*).

11. God ratifies the earlier blessings.

I am sufficient [שַׁדַּי = שֶׁאֲנִי דַּי] to bless, for the blessings are Mine (*Rashi*).

12. As part of this pledge of abundant progeny, God reiterates the promise of the land, since the nation of Israel is associated with the land (*Malbim*).

13. *God ascended from upon him.* It was not merely a vision or dream, but the *Shechinah* [if one can so perceive It] actually rested upon Jacob. (*Ramban*).

In the place where He had spoken with him, when he had left home for Charan. At this very site, God now appeared to him again and then ascended (*Sforno*).

14. Jacob fulfills his vow.

16. The birth of Benjamin and death of Rachel.

The Sages observe that a woman's account is examined in heaven when she is in labor, for we have learned in *Mishnah Shabbos* 2:6 that for three transgressions do women die in childbirth. Our mother Rachel was not guilty of any of these three, nevertheless, because Jacob said, 'With whomever you find your gods, he shall not live' (31:32), she was punished, and her judgment was not carried out until she was in childbirth. Thus people say, 'When the ox is fallen, the knife is sharpened' (*Midrash Lekach Tov*).

⁵ They set out, and there fell a Godly terror on the cities which were around them, so that they did not pursue Jacob's sons.

⁶ Thus Jacob came to Luz in the land of Canaan — which is Bethel — he, and all the people who were with him. ⁷ And he built an altar there and named the place El Bethel, for it was there that God had been revealed to him during his flight from his brother.

⁸ Deborah, the wet-nurse of Rebecca, died, and she was buried below Bethel, below the plateau; and he named it Alon Bachuth.

⁹ **A**nd God appeared to Jacob again when he came from Paddan Aram, and He blessed him.

¹⁰ Then God said to him, 'Your name is Jacob. You shall not always be named Jacob, but Israel shall be your name.' Thus He named him Israel. ¹¹ And God said to him, 'I am El Shaddai. Be fruitful and multiply; a nation and a congregation of nations shall descend from you, and kings shall issue from your loins. ¹² The land that I gave to Abraham and to Isaac, I will give to you; and to your offspring after you I will give the land.' ¹³ Then God ascended from upon him in the place where He had spoken with him.

¹⁴ Jacob had set up a pillar at the place where God had spoken with him — a pillar of stone — and he poured a libation upon it, and poured oil upon it. ¹⁵ Then Jacob named the place where God had spoken with him Bethel.

¹⁶ They journeyed from Bethel and there was still a stretch of land to go to Ephrath, when Rachel went into labor and had difficulty in her childbirth. ¹⁷ And it was when her labor was at its most difficult, that the midwife said to her,

אַל־תִּירְאִי כִּי־גַם־זֶה לָךְ בֵּן: יח וַיְהִי בְּצֵאת
נַפְשָׁהּ כִּי מֵתָה וַתִּקְרָא שְׁמוֹ בֶּן־אוֹנִי וְאָבִיו
קָרָא־לוֹ בִנְיָמִין: יט וַתָּמָת רָחֵל וַתִּקָּבֵר בְּדֶרֶךְ
אֶפְרָתָה הִוא בֵּית לָחֶם: כ וַיַּצֵּב יַעֲקֹב מַצֵּבָה
עַל־קְבֻרָתָהּ הִוא מַצֶּבֶת קְבֻרַת־רָחֵל עַד־
הַיּוֹם: כא וַיִּסַּע יִשְׂרָאֵל וַיֵּט אָהֳלֹה מֵהָלְאָה
לְמִגְדַּל־עֵדֶר: כב וַיְהִי בִּשְׁכֹּן יִשְׂרָאֵל בָּאָרֶץ
הַהִוא וַיֵּלֶךְ רְאוּבֵן וַיִּשְׁכַּב אֶת־בִּלְהָה פִּילֶגֶשׁ
אָבִיו וַיִּשְׁמַע יִשְׂרָאֵל

וַיִּהְיוּ בְנֵי־יַעֲקֹב שְׁנֵים עָשָׂר: כג בְּנֵי לֵאָה בְּכוֹר
יַעֲקֹב רְאוּבֵן וְשִׁמְעוֹן וְלֵוִי וִיהוּדָה וְיִשָּׂשכָר
וּזְבֻלוּן: כד בְּנֵי רָחֵל יוֹסֵף וּבִנְיָמִן: כה וּבְנֵי בִלְהָה
שִׁפְחַת רָחֵל דָּן וְנַפְתָּלִי: כו וּבְנֵי זִלְפָּה שִׁפְחַת
לֵאָה גָּד וְאָשֵׁר אֵלֶּה בְּנֵי יַעֲקֹב אֲשֶׁר יֻלַּד־לוֹ
בְּפַדַּן אֲרָם: כז וַיָּבֹא יַעֲקֹב אֶל־יִצְחָק אָבִיו
מַמְרֵא קִרְיַת הָאַרְבַּע הִוא חֶבְרוֹן אֲשֶׁר־גָּר־
שָׁם אַבְרָהָם וְיִצְחָק: כח וַיִּהְיוּ יְמֵי יִצְחָק מְאַת
שָׁנָה וּשְׁמֹנִים שָׁנָה: כט וַיִּגְוַע יִצְחָק וַיָּמָת וַיֵּאָסֶף
אֶל־עַמָּיו זָקֵן וּשְׂבַע יָמִים וַיִּקְבְּרוּ אֹתוֹ עֵשָׂו
וְיַעֲקֹב בָּנָיו:

לו א וְאֵלֶּה תֹּלְדוֹת עֵשָׂו הוּא אֱדוֹם: ב עֵשָׂו לָקַח
אֶת־נָשָׁיו מִבְּנוֹת כְּנָעַן אֶת־עָדָה בַּת־אֵילוֹן
הַחִתִּי וְאֶת־אָהֳלִיבָמָה בַּת־עֲנָה בַּת־צִבְעוֹן
הַחִוִּי: ג וְאֶת־בָּשְׂמַת בַּת־יִשְׁמָעֵאל אֲחוֹת
נְבָיוֹת: ד וַתֵּלֶד עָדָה לְעֵשָׂו אֶת־אֱלִיפָז וּבָשְׂמַת

18. *Ben Oni.* Son of my mourning [as if to say: His birth caused my death] (*Ibn Ezra; Ramban*).

Benjamin. Rashi offers two interpretations: (a) The name means יָמִין בֶּן, *son of the right,* that is, *son of the south* [i.e., if someone faces the east, the south is to his right]. This name commemorates that of all Jacob's children only Benjamin was born in Canaan which lay *south* of Paddan Aram. (b) The word יָמִים, *days,* can be spelled יָמִין. Thus, Jacob named him 'son of my days' as if to say that he was born in his father's advanced years.

Ramban concludes that Rachel, near death, called him *Ben Oni,* meaning 'son of my mourning.' Jacob wished to preserve the *form* of the name given by the child's mother, but wished to give it an optimistic connotation. So, reinterpreting *Oni* to mean 'strength,' he named the child *Benyamin* [lit., *son of the right*], i.e., 'son of power' or 'son of strength,' since the right hand is a symbol of strength and success.

19. According to *Seder Olam* there was a tradition that Rachel was born on the day Jacob received his father's blessings. He was sixty-three then, and was ninety-nine when he entered the land [see footnote end of v. 8]. Therefore Rachel was thirty-six years old when she died.

Jacob chose this site instead of bringing her the short distance to Bethlehem, because he foresaw that his descendants would pass that way on the road to exile. He buried Rachel there so she should pray for them as it is said [*Jeremiah 31:14*]: *Rachel weeping for her children* (*Midrash*).

22. Reuben's incident with Bilhah.

After Rachel's death, Jacob established his primary residence in the tent of Bilhah, Rachel's maidservant. To defend his mother's honor, Reuben took the liberty of moving Jacob's bed to Leah's tent. This is all that actually transpired, as explained by the Talmud; nevertheless Scripture describes it in stark terms as if Reuben had sinned grievously. This is in line with the dictum that even minor transgressions of great people are judged with the utmost gravity, because their conduct is measured by infinitely higher standards than ours. This concept is explained at length in the *Overview* to the ArtScroll *Ruth*.

23. That the birthright was taken from Reuben and given to Joseph [see *I Chron.* 5:1] was only with respect to Joseph's being counted as two tribes [just as a firstborn son receives a double share of his father's property] (*Rashi*).

27. Jacob reunites with his father.

Jacob resided with Isaac until his death, twenty-one years later.

28. The death of Isaac.

The Torah does not follow a chronological order in recording Isaac's death here. The sale of Joseph actually *preceded* Isaac's death by twelve years (*Rashi*).

36/1. The chronicles of Esau.

4. There are traditions that Eliphaz, Esau's firstborn, was the most deserving of his children. *Rashi* [29:11] notes that 'he had been raised on Isaac's knee, and did not obey his father's command to kill Jacob.'

'Have no fear, for this one, too, is a son for you.' ¹⁸ And it came to pass, as her soul was departing — for she died — that she named him Ben Oni, but his father called him Benjamin. ¹⁹ Thus Rachel died, and was buried on the road to Ephrath, which is Bethlehem. ²⁰ Jacob set up a monument over her grave; it is the monument of Rachel's grave until today.

²¹ Israel journeyed on, and he pitched his tent beyond Migdal Eder. ²² And it came to pass, while Israel dwelt in that land, that Reuben went and lay with Bilhah, his father's concubine, and Israel heard.

The sons of Jacob were twelve. ²³ The sons of Leah: Jacob's firstborn, Reuben; Simeon; Levi; Judah; Issachar; and Zebulun. ²⁴ The sons of Rachel: Joseph and Benjamin. ²⁵ The sons of Bilhah, maidservant of Rachel: Dan and Naftali. ²⁶ And the sons of Zilpah, maidservant of Leah: Gad and Asher. — These are the sons of Jacob, who were born to him in Paddan Aram.

²⁷ Jacob came to Isaac his father, at Mamre, Kiriath Arba; that is Hebron where Abraham and Isaac sojourned. ²⁸ Isaac's days were one hundred and eighty years. ²⁹ And Isaac expired and died, and he was gathered to his people, old and fulfilled of days. His sons, Esau and Jacob, buried him.

36 ¹ And these are the genealogies of Esau who is Edom. ² Esau had taken his wives from among the Canaanite women: Adah, daughter of Elon the Hittite; Oholibamah, daughter of Anah, daughter of Zibeon the Hivvite; ³ and Basemath, daughter of Ishmael, sister of Nebayoth.

⁴ Adah bore to Esau Eliphaz; Basemath bore

יָלְדָה אֶת־רְעוּאֵל: הוְאָהֳלִיבָמָה יָלְדָה אֶת־
יְעִישׁ וְאֶת־יַעְלָם וְאֶת־קֹרַח אֵלֶּה בְּנֵי עֵשָׂו
אֲשֶׁר יֻלְּדוּ־לוֹ בְּאֶרֶץ כְּנָעַן: ווַיִּקַּח עֵשָׂו
אֶת־נָשָׁיו וְאֶת־בָּנָיו וְאֶת־בְּנֹתָיו וְאֶת־כָּל־
נַפְשׁוֹת בֵּיתוֹ וְאֶת־מִקְנֵהוּ וְאֶת־כָּל־בְּהֶמְתּוֹ
וְאֵת כָּל־קִנְיָנוֹ אֲשֶׁר רָכַשׁ בְּאֶרֶץ כְּנַעַן וַיֵּלֶךְ
אֶל־אֶרֶץ מִפְּנֵי יַעֲקֹב אָחִיו: זכִּי־הָיָה רְכוּשָׁם
רָב מִשֶּׁבֶת יַחְדָּו וְלֹא יָכְלָה אֶרֶץ מְגוּרֵיהֶם
לָשֵׂאת אֹתָם מִפְּנֵי מִקְנֵיהֶם: חוַיֵּשֶׁב עֵשָׂו בְּהַר
שֵׂעִיר עֵשָׂו הוּא אֱדוֹם: טוְאֵלֶּה תֹּלְדוֹת עֵשָׂו
אֲבִי אֱדוֹם בְּהַר שֵׂעִיר: יאֵלֶּה שְׁמוֹת בְּנֵי־עֵשָׂו
אֱלִיפַז בֶּן־עָדָה אֵשֶׁת עֵשָׂו רְעוּאֵל בֶּן־בָּשְׂמַת
אֵשֶׁת עֵשָׂו: יאוַיִּהְיוּ בְּנֵי אֱלִיפָז תֵּימָן אוֹמָר צְפוֹ
וְגַעְתָּם וּקְנַז: יבוְתִמְנַע ׀ הָיְתָה פִילֶגֶשׁ לֶאֱלִיפַז
בֶּן־עֵשָׂו וַתֵּלֶד לֶאֱלִיפַז אֶת־עֲמָלֵק אֵלֶּה בְּנֵי
עָדָה אֵשֶׁת עֵשָׂו: יגוְאֵלֶּה בְּנֵי רְעוּאֵל נַחַת
וָזֶרַח שַׁמָּה וּמִזָּה אֵלֶּה הָיוּ בְּנֵי בָשְׂמַת אֵשֶׁת
עֵשָׂו: ידוְאֵלֶּה הָיוּ בְּנֵי אָהֳלִיבָמָה בַת־עֲנָה
בַת־צִבְעוֹן אֵשֶׁת עֵשָׂו וַתֵּלֶד לְעֵשָׂו אֶת־יְעִישׁ
וְאֶת־יַעְלָם וְאֶת־קֹרַח: טואֵלֶּה אַלּוּפֵי בְנֵי־
עֵשָׂו בְּנֵי אֱלִיפַז בְּכוֹר עֵשָׂו אַלּוּף תֵּימָן אַלּוּף
אוֹמָר אַלּוּף צְפוֹ אַלּוּף קְנַז: טזאַלּוּף־קֹרַח
אַלּוּף גַּעְתָּם אַלּוּף עֲמָלֵק אֵלֶּה אַלּוּפֵי אֱלִיפַז
בְּאֶרֶץ אֱדוֹם אֵלֶּה בְּנֵי עָדָה: יזוְאֵלֶּה בְּנֵי
רְעוּאֵל בֶּן־עֵשָׂו אַלּוּף נַחַת אַלּוּף זֶרַח אַלּוּף

יְעוּשׁ ק׳

---

5. This Korach was later [v. 16] included among the chiefs of *Eliphaz* [son of *Adah*, while here he is listed as a son of Esau through *Oholibamah*!]. This alludes to the fact that Korach was really the illegitimate child of Eliphaz, Esau's son, through an adulterous union with Oholibamah, his father's wife (*Rashi* from *Midrash*).

Esau's sons who were born to him in the land of Canaan. In the following verses, by contrast, we shall be told of the descendants who were born to him later in the land of Seir (*R' Hoffmann*).

6. Esau separates himself from Jacob.

To a land, [an unspecified land;] to wherever he found a suitable spot to dwell (*Rashi*). Ultimately, as we see in the next verse, he settled in Mount Seir.

Since Jacob had purchased the birthright, he was Isaac's heir, so *he* remained in the ancestral land, while Esau sought another country (*Rashbam*).

8. *Esau settled on Mount Seir.* He successfully captured the fortified mountain from the original inhabitants, the Horites, descendants of Seir. Esau gained the territory by Divine sanction, as it is written [*Deut.* 2:5]: *because I have given Mount Seir to Esau for a possession.*

Esau who is Edom. Until this point, only Esau *himself* was called Edom, but when he established himself in Seir [next verse] and had grandchildren there, his offspring became the *nation* named Edom. In the next verse, therefore, he is called *ancestor of Edom* (*Haamek Davar*).

This is stated [although the women of Esau's other sons are not mentioned (Ramban)] to emphasize that Abraham was held in such esteem that people were eager to attach themselves to his descendants. As we see in v. 22, Timna was a descendant of chiefs; she was the sister of Lotan who was one of the chiefs of Seir [Lotan was a son of Seir himself (v. 20)], a Horite who lived there from ancient times. Yet she was so anxious to marry a descendant of Abraham that she said to Eliphaz: 'If I am unworthy to become your wife, let me at least be your concubine!' (Rashi).

Ramban suggests that Timna is mentioned as Amalek's mother to draw attention to the fact that Amalek — as the child of a concubine — was of lowly birth, not a true heir of Esau, and did not dwell with the other offspring of Esau on Mount Seir. Only the sons of the true wives were called Esau's seed, not those of the concubines. In this, Esau followed the practice of his grandfather, Abraham (see 21:10).

Reuel; [5] and Oholibamah bore Jeush, Jalam, and Korach. These are Esau's sons who were born to him in the land of Canaan.

[6] Esau took his wives, his sons, his daughters, and all the members of his household — his livestock and all his animals, and all the wealth he had acquired in the land of Canaan — and went to a land because of his brother Jacob. [7] For their wealth was too abundant for them to dwell together, and the land of their sojourns could not support them because of their livestock. [8] So Esau settled on Mount Seir; Esau who is Edom.

[9] And these are the progeny of Esau, ancestor of Edom, on Mount Seir. [10] These are the names of Esau's sons: Eliphaz, son of Adah, Esau's wife; Reuel, son of Basemath, Esau's wife.

[11] The sons of Eliphaz were: Teman; Omar; Zepho; Gatam; and Kenaz. [12] And Timna was a concubine of Eliphaz, son of Esau, and she bore Amalek to Eliphaz. — These are the children of Adah, Esau's wife.

[13] And these are the sons of Reuel: Nahath; Zerah; Shammah; and Mizah. — These are the children of Basemath, Esau's wife.

[14] And these were the sons of Oholibamah, daughter of Anah, daughter of Zibeon, Esau's wife: She bore to Esau Jeush, Jalam, and Korach.

[15] These are the chiefs of the children of Esau. The descendants of Esau's firstborn Eliphaz: Chief Teman, Chief Omar, Chief Zepho, Chief Kenaz. [16] Chief Korach, Chief Gatam, and Chief Amalek; these are the chiefs of Eliphaz in the land of Edom — These are the descendants of Adah.

[17] And these are the descendants of Reuel, Esau's son: Chief Nahath, Chief Zerah, Chief

שַׁמָּה אַלּוּף מִזָּה אֵלֶּה אַלּוּפֵי רְעוּאֵל`
בְּאֶרֶץ אֱדוֹם אֵלֶּה בְּנֵי בָשְׂמַת אֵשֶׁת עֵשָׂו:
יח וְאֵלֶּה בְּנֵי אָהֳלִיבָמָה` אֵשֶׁת עֵשָׂו אַלּוּף
יְעוּשׁ אַלּוּף יַעְלָם אַלּוּף קֹרַח אֵלֶּה
אַלּוּפֵי אָהֳלִיבָמָה בַּת־עֲנָה אֵשֶׁת עֵשָׂו:
יט אֵלֶּה בְנֵי־עֵשָׂו וְאֵלֶּה אַלּוּפֵיהֶם הוּא
אֱדוֹם: שביעי כ אֵלֶּה
בְנֵי־שֵׂעִיר` הַחֹרִי יֹשְׁבֵי הָאָרֶץ לוֹטָן
וְשׁוֹבָל וְצִבְעוֹן וַעֲנָה: כא וְדִשׁוֹן וְאֵצֶר וְדִישָׁן
אֵלֶּה אַלּוּפֵי הַחֹרִי בְּנֵי שֵׂעִיר בְּאֶרֶץ
אֱדוֹם: כב וַיִּהְיוּ בְנֵי־לוֹטָן חֹרִי וְהֵימָם
וַאֲחוֹת לוֹטָן תִּמְנָע: כג וְאֵלֶּה` בְּנֵי שׁוֹבָל
עַלְוָן וּמָנַחַת וְעֵיבָל שְׁפוֹ וְאוֹנָם: כד וְאֵלֶּה
בְנֵי־צִבְעוֹן וְאַיָּה וַעֲנָה הוּא עֲנָה אֲשֶׁר
מָצָא אֶת־הַיֵּמִם` בַּמִּדְבָּר בִּרְעֹתוֹ אֶת־
הַחֲמֹרִים לְצִבְעוֹן אָבִיו: כה וְאֵלֶּה בְנֵי־עֲנָה
דִשֹׁן וְאָהֳלִיבָמָה בַּת־עֲנָה: כו וְאֵלֶּה בְּנֵי
דִישָׁן חֶמְדָּן וְאֶשְׁבָּן וְיִתְרָן וּכְרָן:
כז אֵלֶּה בְּנֵי־אֵצֶר בִּלְהָן וְזַעֲוָן וַעֲקָן:
כח אֵלֶּה בְנֵי־דִישָׁן עוּץ וַאֲרָן: כט אֵלֶּה אַלּוּפֵי
הַחֹרִי אַלּוּף לוֹטָן אַלּוּף שׁוֹבָל אַלּוּף צִבְעוֹן
אַלּוּף עֲנָה: ל אַלּוּף דִּשֹׁן אַלּוּף אֵצֶר אַלּוּף
דִּישָׁן אֵלֶּה אַלּוּפֵי הַחֹרִי לְאַלֻּפֵיהֶם בְּאֶרֶץ
שֵׂעִיר:

19. In this genealogy lay the roots of Edom, which evolved into Rome, the perpetual enemy of Israel (*Lekach Tov*).

20. The Seirite genealogy.

The Seirites, an ancient, populous nation, were the original inhabitants of the land of Seir [see 14:16]. The children of Esau supplanted them by a miraculous event, for God gave it to Esau's descendants as a heritage, just as He gave the other portions of the land to Israel. [See *Deut.* 2:5; *Ramban* to *Deut.* 2:10; and also comm. above, end of v. 2.]

Who were settled in the land. The Torah mentions this to emphasize that God is the Master of the Land, and He bequeaths the earth to whomever He desires. The Seirites were *the original inhabitants of Seir*, and yet God caused them to surrender it to the descendants of Esau, for such was His will (*Radak*).

24. *The same.* He is the Anah mentioned above in verse 20. There is an apparent contradiction between the two verses: there he appears as Zibeon's *brother* [the putative son of Seir], while here he is called Zibeon's *son!* This teaches that Zibeon committed incest with his own mother and fathered Anah (*Rashi*).

Who discovered the mules in the desert while he was pasturing the sheep for Zibeon, his father. I.e., he crossbred a donkey with a mare and the result was a mule. Being himself illegitimate, he introduced a 'tainted' animal [i.e., born of a heterogeneous breeding] into the world [thus intimating that 'evil begets evil'] (*Rashi; Midrash; Pesachim 54a*).

29. The Horite chiefs.

Shammah, and Chief Mizah; these are the chiefs of Reuel in the land of Edom. — These are the descendants of Basemath, Esau's wife.

¹⁸ And these are the descendants of Oholibamah, Esau's wife: Chief Jeush, Chief Jalam, and Chief Korach. — These are the chiefs of Oholibamah, daughter of Anah, Esau's wife. ¹⁹ These are the children of Esau, and these are their chiefs; he is Edom.

²⁰ These are the sons of Seir, the Horites, who were settled in the land: Lotan; Shobal; Zibeon; and Anah. ²¹ Dishon; Etzer; and Dishan. — These are the chiefs of the Horites, the descendants of Seir in the land of Edom.

²² The sons of Lotan were: Chori and Hemam; Lotan's sister was Timna.

²³ These are the sons of Shobal: Alvan; Manachath; Ebal; Shepho; and Onam.

²⁴ These are the sons of Zibeon: Ayah and Anah — the same Anah who discovered the mules in the desert while he was pasturing the sheep for Zibeon, his father.

²⁵ These are the children of Anah: Dishon and Oholibamah daughter of Anah.

²⁶ These are the sons of Dishan: Chemdan; Eshban; Yisran; and Keran.

²⁷ These are the sons of Etzer: Bilhan; Zaavan; and Akan.

²⁸ These are the sons of Dishan: Utz and Aran.

²⁹ These are the chiefs of the Horites: Chief Lotan; Chief Shobal; Chief Zibeon; Chief Anah; ³⁰ Chief Dishon; Chief Etzer; and Chief Dishan. — These are the chiefs of the Horites, chief by chief, in the land of Seir.

לא וְאֵ֣לֶּה הַמְּלָכִ֗ים אֲשֶׁ֤ר מָֽלְכוּ֙ בְּאֶ֣רֶץ אֱד֔וֹם לִפְנֵ֥י מְלָךְ־מֶ֖לֶךְ לִבְנֵ֣י יִשְׂרָאֵ֑ל: לב וַיִּמְלֹ֣ךְ בֶּֽאֱד֔וֹם בֶּ֖לַע בֶּן־בְּע֑וֹר וְשֵׁ֥ם עִיר֖וֹ דִּנְהָֽבָה: לג וַיָּ֖מָת בָּ֑לַע וַיִּמְלֹ֣ךְ תַּחְתָּ֔יו יוֹבָ֥ב בֶּן־זֶ֖רַח מִבָּצְרָֽה: לד וַיָּ֖מָת יוֹבָ֑ב וַיִּמְלֹ֣ךְ תַּחְתָּ֔יו חֻשָׁ֖ם מֵאֶ֥רֶץ הַתֵּֽימָנִֽי: לה וַיָּ֣מָת חֻשָׁ֗ם וַיִּמְלֹ֣ךְ תַּחְתָּ֡יו הֲדַ֣ד בֶּן־בְּדַ֗ד הַמַּכֶּ֤ה אֶת־מִדְיָן֙ בִּשְׂדֵ֣ה מוֹאָ֔ב וְשֵׁ֥ם עִיר֖וֹ עֲוִֽית: לו וַיָּ֖מָת הֲדָ֑ד וַיִּמְלֹ֣ךְ תַּחְתָּ֔יו שַׂמְלָ֖ה מִמַּשְׂרֵקָֽה: לז וַיָּ֖מָת שַׂמְלָ֑ה וַיִּמְלֹ֣ךְ תַּחְתָּ֔יו שָׁא֖וּל מֵרְחֹב֥וֹת הַנָּהָֽר: לח וַיָּ֖מָת שָׁא֑וּל וַיִּמְלֹ֣ךְ תַּחְתָּ֔יו בַּ֥עַל חָנָ֖ן בֶּן־עַכְבּֽוֹר: לט וַיָּ֡מָת בַּ֣עַל חָנָן֮ בֶּן־עַכְבּוֹר֒ וַיִּמְלֹ֣ךְ תַּחְתָּ֗יו הֲדַ֔ר וְשֵׁ֥ם עִיר֖וֹ פָּ֑עוּ וְשֵׁ֨ם אִשְׁתּ֤וֹ מְהֵֽיטַבְאֵל֙ בַּת־מַטְרֵ֔ד בַּ֖ת מֵ֥י זָהָֽב: מפטיר מ וְ֠אֵ֠לֶּה שְׁמ֞וֹת אַלּוּפֵ֤י עֵשָׂו֙ לְמִשְׁפְּחֹתָ֔ם לִמְקֹֽמֹתָ֖ם בִּשְׁמֹתָ֑ם אַלּ֥וּף תִּמְנָ֛ע אַלּ֥וּף עַלְוָ֖ה אַלּ֥וּף יְתֵֽת: מא אַלּ֧וּף אָֽהֳלִֽיבָמָ֛ה אַלּ֥וּף אֵלָ֖ה אַלּ֥וּף פִּינֹֽן: מב אַלּ֥וּף קְנַ֛ז אַלּ֥וּף תֵּימָ֖ן אַלּ֥וּף מִבְצָֽר: מג אַלּ֥וּף מַגְדִּיאֵ֖ל אַלּ֣וּף עִירָ֑ם אֵ֣לֶּה ׀ אַלּוּפֵ֣י אֱד֗וֹם לְמֹֽשְׁבֹתָם֙ בְּאֶ֣רֶץ אֲחֻזָּתָ֔ם ה֥וּא עֵשָׂ֖ו אֲבִ֥י אֱדֽוֹם:

The *Haftarah* for *Vayishlach* appears on page 324

31. The Edomite kings.

Before a king reigned over the Children of Israel. The chapter lists eight Edomite kings who reigned before the first Jewish king. *Ibn Ezra* cites two interpretations of the period under discussion: a) The eight Edomite kings reigned up to the time of Moses. If so, this passage is a historical rendering of events that occurred before the Torah was given. b) The passage is prophetic, giving the names of eight Edomite kings who were destined to reign in *future* years, prior to Saul, the first Jewish king.

35. When Midian attacked Moab, this Edomite king came to Moab's aid and defeated Midian. From this we learn that Midian and Moab were enemies, but in the time of Balaam they made peace in order to combine against Israel (*Rashi*).

40-41. **The chiefs following the Edomite monarchy.**

The phrases *by their regions, by their names* indicate a change in the manner of naming the chiefs. The earlier group of kings [v. 15ff] used their own names. After Hadad's death and the end of the Edomite monarchy, the kingship ceased and the ensuing leaders were known as 'chieftains' of their respective regions. This new procedure is evident from *I Chronicles 1:51: And Hadad (= Hadar) died and the chiefs of Edom were: the chief of Timna, etc. (Rashi).*

43. הוּא עֵשָׂו אֲבִי אֱדוֹם — *That is Esau, father of Edom.* This is Esau [who remained] in his wickedness from beginning to end [he never repented (*Torah Temimah*)] (*Megillah* 11a).

According to the Masoretic note appearing at the end of the *Sidrah*, there are 154 verses in the *Sidrah* numerically corresponding to the mnemonic קֶלִיט'ה [related to מִקְלָט, *refuge, asylum*]. This alludes to the theme of our *Sidrah* which, as expressed by *Ramban* in his introduction to 32:4, is to teach us how to survive in Exile among Esau's descendants. The *Haftarah* begins with *Obadiah* 1:1: חֲזוֹן עוֹבַדְיָה.

³¹ Now these are the kings who reigned in the land of Edom before a king reigned over the Children of Israel: ³² Bela, son of Beor, reigned in Edom, and the name of his city was Dinhabah. ³³ And Bela died, and Jobab son of Zerah, from Bozrah, succeeded him as king. ³⁴ And Jobab died and Husham, of the land of the Temanites, succeeded him as king. ³⁵ And Husham died, and Hadad son of Bedad, who defeated the Midianites in the field of Moab, succeeded him as king, and the name of his city was Avith. ³⁶ And Hadad died, and Samlah of Masrekah succeeded him as king. ³⁷ Samlah died, and Saul of Rechovos Nahar succeeded him as king. ³⁸ And Saul died, and Baal Hanan, son of Achbor, succeeded him as king. ³⁹ Baal Hanan, son of Achbor, died, and Hadar succeeded him as king. The name of his city was Pau and his wife's name was Mehetabel, daughter of Matred, daughter of Me-zahab.

⁴⁰ Now these are the names of the chiefs of Esau, by their families, by their regions, by their names: The chief of Timna; the chief of Alvah; the chief of Jetheth. ⁴¹ the chief of Oholibamah; the chief of Elah; the chief of Pinon; ⁴² the chief of Kenaz; the chief of Teman; the chief of Mivtzar; ⁴³ the chief of Magdiel and the chief of Iram.

These are the chiefs of Edom by their settlements, in the land of their possession. — That is Esau, father of Edom.

The *Haftarah* for *Vayishlach* appears on page 324

פרשת וישב

VAYEISHEV

The destiny of Jacob's family begins to unfold in *Vayeishev*. The Patriarch has finally arrived home and he looks forward to living out his remaining decades in tranquility. But God had other ideas. The time had come to propare the way for the foreordained Egyptian exile and the nation-building that would lead to Sinai and the Promised Land, and the vehicle would be Joseph.

It began with Joseph's dreams. As his brothers correctly perceived, the dreams indicated that he would reign, but not, as they suspected, that he craved power. It was God Who had assigned that he be the leader of the family, a position he earned by his personal greatness. The brothers were convinced that he represented a danger to the family and its destiny and they had not only the right but the duty to stifle his plans forever. Again, as with Jacob's dream of tranquility, man proposes and God disposes.

The hand of Heaven was at work. They thought they would kill him, and a dead man cannot reign. They made him a slave, and a slave can never be king. But God thought otherwise. Joseph *would* be king. Wherever he went, he ruled. As a slave of Potiphar, he was placed in charge of the household; as a disgraced prisoner, he was placed in charge of the prison; as a despised Hebrew, he was called to interpret Pharaoh's dreams and then placed in charge of the entire country; and, finally, his entire family bowed to him. Indeed, what had become of his dreams!

Jacob grieves while Joseph prepares the way for him to come to Egypt. Judah goes to shear his sheep, and unwittingly becomes the forebear of the Davidic dynasty.

In this *Sidrah*, we see God weaving the future, with and around an unsuspecting man.

לז א וַיֵּשֶׁב יַעֲקֹב בְּאֶרֶץ מְגוּרֵי אָבִיו בְּאֶרֶץ כְּנָעַן: ב אֵלֶּה ׀ תֹּלְדוֹת יַעֲקֹב יוֹסֵף בֶּן־שְׁבַע־עֶשְׂרֵה שָׁנָה הָיָה רֹעֶה אֶת־אֶחָיו בַּצֹּאן וְהוּא נַעַר אֶת־בְּנֵי בִלְהָה וְאֶת־בְּנֵי זִלְפָּה נְשֵׁי אָבִיו וַיָּבֵא יוֹסֵף אֶת־דִּבָּתָם רָעָה אֶל־אֲבִיהֶם: ג וְיִשְׂרָאֵל אָהַב אֶת־יוֹסֵף מִכָּל־בָּנָיו כִּי־בֶן־זְקֻנִים הוּא לוֹ וְעָשָׂה לוֹ כְּתֹנֶת פַּסִּים: ד וַיִּרְאוּ אֶחָיו כִּי־אֹתוֹ אָהַב אֲבִיהֶם מִכָּל־אֶחָיו וַיִּשְׂנְאוּ אֹתוֹ וְלֹא יָכְלוּ דַּבְּרוֹ לְשָׁלֹם: ה וַיַּחֲלֹם יוֹסֵף חֲלוֹם וַיַּגֵּד לְאֶחָיו וַיּוֹסִפוּ עוֹד שְׂנֹא אֹתוֹ: ו וַיֹּאמֶר אֲלֵיהֶם שִׁמְעוּ־נָא הַחֲלוֹם הַזֶּה אֲשֶׁר חָלָמְתִּי: ז וְהִנֵּה אֲנַחְנוּ מְאַלְּמִים אֲלֻמִּים בְּתוֹךְ הַשָּׂדֶה וְהִנֵּה קָמָה אֲלֻמָּתִי וְגַם־נִצָּבָה וְהִנֵּה תְסֻבֶּינָה אֲלֻמֹּתֵיכֶם וַתִּשְׁתַּחֲוֶיןָ לַאֲלֻמָּתִי: ח וַיֹּאמְרוּ לוֹ אֶחָיו הֲמָלֹךְ תִּמְלֹךְ עָלֵינוּ אִם־מָשׁוֹל תִּמְשֹׁל בָּנוּ וַיּוֹסִפוּ עוֹד שְׂנֹא אֹתוֹ עַל־חֲלֹמֹתָיו וְעַל־דְּבָרָיו: ט וַיַּחֲלֹם עוֹד חֲלוֹם אַחֵר וַיְסַפֵּר אֹתוֹ לְאֶחָיו וַיֹּאמֶר הִנֵּה חָלַמְתִּי חֲלוֹם עוֹד וְהִנֵּה הַשֶּׁמֶשׁ וְהַיָּרֵחַ וְאַחַד עָשָׂר כּוֹכָבִים מִשְׁתַּחֲוִים לִי: י וַיְסַפֵּר אֶל־אָבִיו וְאֶל־אֶחָיו וַיִּגְעַר־בּוֹ אָבִיו וַיֹּאמֶר לוֹ מָה הַחֲלוֹם הַזֶּה אֲשֶׁר חָלָמְתָּ הֲבוֹא נָבוֹא אֲנִי וְאִמְּךָ וְאַחֶיךָ לְהִשְׁתַּחֲוֺת לְךָ אָרְצָה: יא וַיְקַנְאוּ־בוֹ אֶחָיו וְאָבִיו שָׁמַר אֶת־הַדָּבָר: שני יב וַיֵּלְכוּ אֶחָיו לִרְעוֹת אֶת־צֹאן

The Midrash perceives our passage to connote how Jacob, after his lifelong struggles, wished finally לֵישֵׁב בְּשַׁלְוָה, *to settle down in tranquility,* but the anguish of the Joseph affair sprang upon him. For when the righteous look forward to tranquility, the Holy One, Blessed is He, says, 'Are the righteous not satisfied with what awaits them in the World to Come that they expect to live at ease in This World too?' (*Rashi*).

2. *Joseph, at the age of seventeen.* From this chronological detail we can calculate that Jacob was 108 at the time, since he was ninety-one when Joseph was born. Isaac, who was sixty at the time of Jacob's birth, was then 168 years old. He lived for twelve years after the sale. This incident occurred nine years after Jacob was reunited with his father. Following the traditional dating, Leah died at about this time (see *Seder Olam* 2).

נַעַר, *a youth,* implies that he *acted* like an adolescent — dressing his hair and adorning his eyes to look handsome (*Rashi*).

3. The Torah now details for us the additional cause for the brothers' hatred of Joseph: jealousy over Jacob's obvious favoritism for him (*Radak*).

A child of his old age. For he was born to him in his old age (*Rashi*). Alternatively, he was a *wise* son to him [following the Talmudic dictum that זָקֵן means זֶה שֶׁקָּנָה חָכְמָה, *one who acquired wisdom*]. Whatever Jacob learned in the Academy of Shem and Eber during his fourteen years there he transmitted to Joseph (*Rashi* quoting *Onkelos*).

A fine woolen tunic. The translation follows *Rashi*: A garment of *fine wool.*

It was a long-sleeved embroidered tunic, made of variously colored strips of fine wool (*Yafeh Toar*).

5. Joseph's dream.

Dreams mentioned in Scripture are generally understood to be vehicles of prophecy. To be sure, Joseph's dreams, and those of Pharaoh and his officials, contain revelations of future events which can originate only from a transcendent Source. All these dreams were prognostications and fulfilled according to their interpretations.

7. The symbolism of the 'sheaves' intimated to Joseph that they would come to bow down to him because of grain. That they *gathered around* indicated that they would surround him like subjects around a king (*Ramban*).

9. Joseph's second dream: *The bowing heavenly spheres.*

The message of this dream — although employing a different metaphor — is essentially the same as that of the first. A dream repeated indicates that certainty of the fulfillment, as we find 41:32.

10. 'Your mother [Rachel] is long dead [so your dream cannot be fulfilled]!' Jacob did not realize that the 'moon' referred to Bilhah who had reared him.

Although Jacob *did* take the dreams seriously, he spoke strongly against Joseph to remove the jealousy and resentment of the brothers. By intimating that just as the dream was absurd with respect to *Rachel*, he attempted to reassure them that it had no validity with regard to *them* (*Rashi*).

37 ¹ Jacob settled in the land where his father had sojourned, in the land of Canaan. ²These are the chronicles of Jacob — Joseph, at the age of seventeen, was a shepherd with his brothers by the sheep, but he was a youth with the sons of Bilhah and the sons of Zilpah, his father's wives. And Joseph would bring evil reports about them to their father. ³ Now Israel loved Joseph more than all his sons since he was a child of his old age, and he made him a fine woolen tunic. ⁴ His brothers saw that it was he whom their father loved most of all his brothers so they hated him; and they could not speak to him peaceably.

⁵Joseph dreamt a dream which he told to his brothers, and they hated him even more. ⁶He said to them, 'Hear, if you please, this dream which I dreamt: ⁷ Behold — we were binding sheaves in the middle of the field when, behold! — my sheaf arose and remained standing; then behold! — your sheaves gathered around and bowed down to my sheaf.'

⁸ His brothers answered, 'Would you then reign over us? Would you then dominate us?' And they hated him even more — because of his dreams and because of his talk.

⁹ He dreamt another dream, and related it to his brothers. And he said, 'Look, I dreamt another dream: Behold! the sun, the moon, and eleven stars were bowing down to me.'

¹⁰ And he related it to his father and to his brothers. His father scolded him, and said to him, 'What is this dream that you have dreamt! Are we to come — I and your mother and your brothers — to bow down to you to the ground?' ¹¹ So his brothers were jealous of him, but his father kept the matter in mind.

¹² Now, his brothers went to pasture their

אֲבִיהֶם בִּשְׁכֶם: יג וַיֹּאמֶר יִשְׂרָאֵל אֶל־יוֹסֵף
הֲלוֹא אַחֶיךָ רֹעִים בִּשְׁכֶם לְכָה וְאֶשְׁלָחֲךָ
אֲלֵיהֶם וַיֹּאמֶר לוֹ הִנֵּנִי: יד וַיֹּאמֶר לוֹ לֶךְ־נָא
רְאֵה אֶת־שְׁלוֹם אַחֶיךָ וְאֶת־שְׁלוֹם הַצֹּאן
וַהֲשִׁבֵנִי דָּבָר וַיִּשְׁלָחֵהוּ מֵעֵמֶק חֶבְרוֹן וַיָּבֹא
שְׁכֶמָה: טו וַיִּמְצָאֵהוּ אִישׁ וְהִנֵּה תֹעֶה בַּשָּׂדֶה
וַיִּשְׁאָלֵהוּ הָאִישׁ לֵאמֹר מַה־תְּבַקֵּשׁ: טז וַיֹּאמֶר
אֶת־אַחַי אָנֹכִי מְבַקֵּשׁ הַגִּידָה־נָּא לִי אֵיפֹה
הֵם רֹעִים: יז וַיֹּאמֶר הָאִישׁ נָסְעוּ מִזֶּה כִּי
שָׁמַעְתִּי אֹמְרִים נֵלְכָה דֹּתָיְנָה וַיֵּלֶךְ יוֹסֵף אַחַר
אֶחָיו וַיִּמְצָאֵם בְּדֹתָן: יח וַיִּרְאוּ אֹתוֹ מֵרָחֹק
וּבְטֶרֶם יִקְרַב אֲלֵיהֶם וַיִּתְנַכְּלוּ אֹתוֹ לַהֲמִיתוֹ:
יט וַיֹּאמְרוּ אִישׁ אֶל־אָחִיו הִנֵּה בַּעַל הַחֲלֹמוֹת
הַלָּזֶה בָּא: כ וְעַתָּה | לְכוּ וְנַהַרְגֵהוּ וְנַשְׁלִכֵהוּ
בְּאַחַד הַבֹּרוֹת וְאָמַרְנוּ חַיָּה רָעָה אֲכָלָתְהוּ
וְנִרְאֶה מַה־יִּהְיוּ חֲלֹמֹתָיו: כא וַיִּשְׁמַע רְאוּבֵן
וַיַּצִּלֵהוּ מִיָּדָם וַיֹּאמֶר לֹא נַכֶּנּוּ נָפֶשׁ: כב וַיֹּאמֶר
אֲלֵהֶם | רְאוּבֵן אַל־תִּשְׁפְּכוּ־דָם הַשְׁלִיכוּ
אֹתוֹ אֶל־הַבּוֹר הַזֶּה אֲשֶׁר בַּמִּדְבָּר וְיָד אַל־
תִּשְׁלְחוּ־בוֹ לְמַעַן הַצִּיל אֹתוֹ מִיָּדָם
לַהֲשִׁיבוֹ אֶל־אָבִיו: שלישי כג וַיְהִי כַּאֲשֶׁר־בָּא
יוֹסֵף אֶל־אֶחָיו וַיַּפְשִׁיטוּ אֶת־יוֹסֵף אֶת־
כֻּתָּנְתּוֹ אֶת־כְּתֹנֶת הַפַּסִּים אֲשֶׁר עָלָיו:
כד וַיִּקָּחֻהוּ וַיַּשְׁלִכוּ אֹתוֹ הַבֹּרָה וְהַבּוֹר רֵק אֵין
בּוֹ מָיִם: כה וַיֵּשְׁבוּ לֶאֱכָל־לֶחֶם וַיִּשְׂאוּ עֵינֵיהֶם

12. The sale of Joseph.
We are not dealing with a
band of robbers and mur-
derers who would lightly
murder for the sake of a
coat. Why, then, did the
brothers sell Joseph? *Sforno*
notes that when the brothers examined their deeds to
find why God had punished
them (42:21), they found no
cause for remorse in the
sale of Joseph. They con-
demned themselves only for
hard-heartedly ignoring his
pleas for mercy. Clearly
they considered the act to
have been harsh but not
wrong. Accordingly, we
must be alert for hints that
could help explain the affair
(R' Hirsch).

14. מֵעֵמֶק חֶבְרוֹן, *from the
depth of Hebron.* But He-
bron is situated on a *mountain!* [Rather, the term מֵעֵמֶק
חֶבְרוֹן, *from the 'valley' of
Hebron,* is to be understood
figuratively: Jacob's decision
to send Joseph to what appeared to be his doom was
in fulfillment of עֵצָה עֲמוּקָה,
the profound [lit., *deep*] de-
sign which had been confided to Abraham — who is
here called חֶבְרוֹן, a contraction of the words חָבֵר נָאֶה,
pleasant companion of God
— who was buried in He-
bron. Events beginning with
Joseph's trip would begin
the fulfillment of God's
prophecy to Abraham
[15:13]: *Your offspring shall
be aliens in a land not their
own* (Midrash; Rashi; Targum Yonasan).

15. This 'man' was the angel Gabriel, in the likeness
of a man (*Targum Yonasan*).

17. They are no longer in
this pasture and it is point-
less to search for them in
this vicinity and further
(*Sforno*).

Dothan, still known as Tel Dothan, is about fifteen miles north of Shechem. It was known for its broad plains, and its very fine pasturage. The gully of Dothan was a main artery in the trade-route connecting Syria to Egypt via the Sharon Valley (R' Hoffmann).

18. The brothers plot to kill Joseph.

21. Reuben reacts.

Reuben was the most injured by Joseph inasmuch as Joseph was to assume some of Reuben's rights as firstborn [see 35:22 and I Chron. 5:1]; nevertheless, he opposed his brothers. He could not protect Joseph openly so he used the subterfuge of suggesting a 'cleaner' way of killing their brother, in the hope that he would be able to save him (Daas Sofrim).

Joseph did not say, 'Do not shed *his* blood' — rather, they should not shed *any* blood, they should not stoop to the crime of murder. He wanted to sound dispassionate, and not appear to have any special love for Joseph (Ramban).

22. *Intending to rescue him* [Joseph] *from their hand, to return him to his father.* The Divine Spirit [i.e., Scripture (Rashbam)] thus bears witness that Reuben wished only to rescue him, by returning later and pulling him out. As the eldest son, he knew he would be held responsible (Rashi).

24. *The pit was empty; no water was in it.* If the pit was empty, isn't it obvious that *no water was in it?* The redundancy implies that there was no *water* in it — but there *were* serpents and scorpions in it (Rashi Shabbos 22a).

father's flock in Shechem. [13] And Israel said to Joseph, 'Your brothers are pasturing in Shechem, are they not? Come, I will send you to them.' He said to him: 'I am ready.' [14] And he said to him, 'Go now, look into the welfare of your brothers and the welfare of the flock, and bring me back word.' So he sent him from the depth of Hebron, and he arrived at Shechem.

[15] A man discovered him, and behold — he was blundering in the field. The man asked him, saying, 'What do you seek?' [16] And he said, 'My brothers do I seek. Tell me, please, where they are pasturing.' [17] The man said: 'They have journeyed on from here for I heard them saying, "Let us go to Dothan."' So Joseph went after his brothers and found them at Dothan.

[18] They saw him from afar. And before he got near them they conspired against him to kill him. [19] And they said to one another 'Look! That dreamer is coming! [20] So now, come and let us kill him, and throw him into one of the pits; and we will say, "A wild beast devoured him." Then we shall see what will become of his dreams.'

[21] Reuben heard, and he rescued him from their hand. He said, 'We will not strike him mortally!' [22] And Reuben said to them: 'Shed no blood! Throw him into this pit in the wilderness, but lay no hand on him!' — intending to rescue him from their hand, to return him to his father.

[23] And so it was, when Joseph came to his brothers they stripped Joseph of his tunic, the fine woolen tunic which he had on. [24] Then they took him, and cast him into the pit. The pit was empty; no water was in it.

[25] They sat to eat food. Raising their eyes

וַיִּרְאוּ וְהִנֵּה אֹרְחַת יִשְׁמְעֵאלִים בָּאָה מִגִּלְעָד
וּגְמַלֵּיהֶם נֹשְׂאִים נְכֹאת וּצְרִי וָלֹט הוֹלְכִים
לְהוֹרִיד מִצְרָיְמָה: כו וַיֹּאמֶר יְהוּדָה אֶל־אֶחָיו
מַה־בֶּצַע כִּי נַהֲרֹג אֶת־אָחִינוּ וְכִסִּינוּ אֶת־
דָּמוֹ: כז לְכוּ וְנִמְכְּרֶנּוּ לַיִּשְׁמְעֵאלִים וְיָדֵנוּ אַל־
תְּהִי־בוֹ כִּי־אָחִינוּ בְשָׂרֵנוּ הוּא וַיִּשְׁמְעוּ
אֶחָיו: כח וַיַּעַבְרוּ אֲנָשִׁים מִדְיָנִים סֹחֲרִים
וַיִּמְשְׁכוּ וַיַּעֲלוּ אֶת־יוֹסֵף מִן־הַבּוֹר וַיִּמְכְּרוּ
אֶת־יוֹסֵף לַיִּשְׁמְעֵאלִים בְּעֶשְׂרִים כָּסֶף וַיָּבִיאוּ
אֶת־יוֹסֵף מִצְרָיְמָה: כט וַיָּשָׁב רְאוּבֵן אֶל־
הַבּוֹר וְהִנֵּה אֵין־יוֹסֵף בַּבּוֹר וַיִּקְרַע אֶת־
בְּגָדָיו: ל וַיָּשָׁב אֶל־אֶחָיו וַיֹּאמַר הַיֶּלֶד אֵינֶנּוּ
וַאֲנִי אָנָה אֲנִי־בָא: לא וַיִּקְחוּ אֶת־כְּתֹנֶת יוֹסֵף
וַיִּשְׁחֲטוּ שְׂעִיר עִזִּים וַיִּטְבְּלוּ אֶת־הַכֻּתֹּנֶת
בַּדָּם: לב וַיְשַׁלְּחוּ אֶת־כְּתֹנֶת הַפַּסִּים וַיָּבִיאוּ
אֶל־אֲבִיהֶם וַיֹּאמְרוּ זֹאת מָצָאנוּ הַכֶּר־נָא
הַכְּתֹנֶת בִּנְךָ הִוא אִם־לֹא: לג וַיַּכִּירָהּ וַיֹּאמֶר
כְּתֹנֶת בְּנִי חַיָּה רָעָה אֲכָלָתְהוּ טָרֹף טֹרַף
יוֹסֵף: לד וַיִּקְרַע יַעֲקֹב שִׂמְלֹתָיו וַיָּשֶׂם שַׂק
בְּמָתְנָיו וַיִּתְאַבֵּל עַל־בְּנוֹ יָמִים רַבִּים:
לה וַיָּקֻמוּ כָל־בָּנָיו וְכָל־בְּנֹתָיו לְנַחֲמוֹ וַיְמָאֵן
לְהִתְנַחֵם וַיֹּאמֶר כִּי־אֵרֵד אֶל־בְּנִי אָבֵל
שְׁאֹלָה וַיֵּבְךְּ אֹתוֹ אָבִיו: לו וְהַמְּדָנִים מָכְרוּ
אֹתוֹ אֶל־מִצְרָיִם לְפוֹטִיפַר סְרִיס פַּרְעֹה שַׂר
הַטַּבָּחִים:

25. Though God is long-suffering, He eventually exacts punishment. 'You sold your brother, then sat down to eat,' the Holy One, Blessed is He, said of the Tribal Ancestors. 'There will yet come a time that your descendants will be sold in the midst of a feast!' And so it was many centuries later in Shushan when the king and Haman sat down to drink [*Esther* 3:15], that the extermination of the Jews was plotted (*Midrash Tehillim* 10).

27. *Come let us sell him to the Ishmaelites.* They are traveling to a distant country; the matter will never be discovered (*Ramban* v. 25).

28. *Midianite men, traders, passed by.* Previously, only an *Ishmaelite* caravan was mentioned; this was another caravan. The Torah thus indicates that he was sold several times (*Rashi*).

The solemn ban against divulging what had occurred.

The brothers proclaimed a חֵרֶם, *solemn ban*, forbidding anyone from divulging to Jacob what had occurred. According to *Sefer Chassidim*, ed. *Mekitzei Nirdamim* §1562, Joseph too was adjured by this dreaded oath. He was prohibited from attempting to return to Jacob, or even notifying him by word of mouth or letter of his whereabouts without their consent. This accounts for Joseph's failure to contact Jacob throughout his twenty-two-year period in Egypt. Joseph was bound by the oath, because when a qualified quorum of ten invokes a solemn ban, the entire community becomes bound by it.

The Sages in *Yerushalmi Shekalim* 2:3 remark that because they sold Rachel's firstborn for twenty *dinarim* [one *shekel* = four *dinarim*] of silver, therefore we redeem our firstborn sons for twenty *dinarim* of silver [=five *shekalim*] as an atonement for our ancestors' misdeed (*R' Bachya*).

29. Reuben discovers Joseph's absence.

Reuben was not present at Joseph's sale, it having been his turn to attend Jacob. Alternatively, he was not present at the sale because he was occupied with acts of penitence [for the incident with Bilhah; see 35:22] (*Rashi* from *Midrash*).

31. The brothers' alibi.

34. *Jacob rent his garments because of mourning; and placed sackcloth on his loins* as an act of penitence. For, as *Mahari Weil* writes in his *Responsa:* If one dispatched an emissary to a dangerous area and that emissary is killed, the sender must undertake acts of penitence (*Malbim*).

35. There had never been a case of a child's death in the house of the Patriarchs because the race of the righteous is blessed. This is why Jacob mourned for his son so long and refused to allow himself to be comforted. In addition to his great love for Joseph he considered this to be a severe punishment intended for him (*Ramban* to 38:7).

36. The end of the chapter emphasizes that Joseph was sold several times. And so the brothers completely lost track of him. They probably shared the feeling that Joseph was not gone forever. Therefore, they could bear Jacob's suffering because they were convinced that eventually his suffering would give way to the joy of finding his lost son. But for the moment, the Patriarchal family was plunged into despair (*R' Munk*).

they **saw, behold! — a caravan of Ishmaelites was coming from Gilead, their camels bearing spicery, balsam, and lotus — on their way to bring them down to Egypt.** [26] **Judah said to his brothers, 'What gain will there be if we kill our brother and cover up his blood?** [27] **Come let us sell him to the Ishmaelites — but let our hand not be upon him, for he is our brother, our own flesh.' His brothers agreed.**

[28] **Midianite men, traders, passed by. They drew Joseph up and lifted him out of the pit and sold Joseph to the Ishmaelites for twenty pieces of silver. Then they brought Joseph to Egypt.**

[29] **Reuben returned to the pit — and behold, Joseph was not in the pit! So he rent his garments.** [30] **Returning to his brothers he said, 'The boy is gone! And I — where can I go?'**

[31] **They took Joseph's tunic, slaughtered a goatling, and dipped the tunic in the blood.** [32] **They dispatched the fine woolen tunic and they brought it to their father, and said, 'We found this. Identify, if you please: Is it your son's tunic or not?'** [33] **He recognized it and he said, 'My son's tunic! A savage beast devoured him! Joseph has surely been torn to bits!'** [34] **Then Jacob rent his garments and placed sackcloth on his loins. He mourned for his son many days.** [35] **All his sons and all his daughters arose to comfort him, but he refused to comfort himself, and said: 'For I will go down to the grave mourning for my son.' And his father bewailed him.**

[36] **Now the Medanites had sold him to Egypt, for Potiphar, a courtier of Pharaoh, the Chamberlain of the Butchers.**

לח א רביעי וַיְהִי בָּעֵת הַהִוא וַיֵּרֶד יְהוּדָה
מֵאֵת אֶחָיו וַיֵּט עַד־אִישׁ עֲדֻלָּמִי וּשְׁמוֹ
חִירָה: ב וַיַּרְא־שָׁם יְהוּדָה בַּת־אִישׁ כְּנַעֲנִי
וּשְׁמוֹ שׁוּעַ וַיִּקָּחֶהָ וַיָּבֹא אֵלֶיהָ: ג וַתַּהַר וַתֵּלֶד
בֵּן וַיִּקְרָא אֶת־שְׁמוֹ עֵר: ד וַתַּהַר עוֹד וַתֵּלֶד
בֵּן וַתִּקְרָא אֶת־שְׁמוֹ אוֹנָן: ה וַתֹּסֶף עוֹד וַתֵּלֶד
בֵּן וַתִּקְרָא אֶת־שְׁמוֹ שֵׁלָה וְהָיָה בִכְזִיב
בְּלִדְתָּהּ אֹתוֹ: ו וַיִּקַּח יְהוּדָה אִשָּׁה לְעֵר
בְּכוֹרוֹ וּשְׁמָהּ תָּמָר: ז וַיְהִי עֵר בְּכוֹר יְהוּדָה
רַע בְּעֵינֵי יְהוָה וַיְמִתֵהוּ יְהוָה: ח וַיֹּאמֶר
יְהוּדָה לְאוֹנָן בֹּא אֶל־אֵשֶׁת אָחִיךָ וְיַבֵּם
אֹתָהּ וְהָקֵם זֶרַע לְאָחִיךָ: ט וַיֵּדַע אוֹנָן כִּי לֹא
לּוֹ יִהְיֶה הַזָּרַע וְהָיָה אִם־בָּא אֶל־אֵשֶׁת אָחִיו
וְשִׁחֵת אַרְצָה לְבִלְתִּי נְתָן־זֶרַע לְאָחִיו:
י וַיֵּרַע בְּעֵינֵי יְהוָה אֲשֶׁר עָשָׂה וַיָּמֶת גַּם־אֹתוֹ:
יא וַיֹּאמֶר יְהוּדָה לְתָמָר כַּלָּתוֹ שְׁבִי אַלְמָנָה
בֵית־אָבִיךְ עַד־יִגְדַּל שֵׁלָה בְנִי כִּי אָמַר
פֶּן־יָמוּת גַּם־הוּא כְּאֶחָיו וַתֵּלֶךְ תָּמָר וַתֵּשֶׁב
בֵּית אָבִיהָ: יב וַיִּרְבּוּ הַיָּמִים וַתָּמָת בַּת־שׁוּעַ
אֵשֶׁת־יְהוּדָה וַיִּנָּחֶם יְהוּדָה וַיַּעַל עַל־גֹּזְזֵי
צֹאנוֹ הוּא וְחִירָה רֵעֵהוּ הָעֲדֻלָּמִי תִּמְנָתָה:
יג וַיֻּגַּד לְתָמָר לֵאמֹר הִנֵּה חָמִיךְ עֹלֶה
תִמְנָתָה לָגֹז צֹאנוֹ: יד וַתָּסַר בִּגְדֵי אַלְמְנוּתָהּ
מֵעָלֶיהָ וַתְּכַס בַּצָּעִיף וַתִּתְעַלָּף וַתֵּשֶׁב
בְּפֶתַח עֵינַיִם אֲשֶׁר עַל־דֶּרֶךְ תִּמְנָתָה כִּי

38/1. Judah and Tamar: The roots of the Messiah and the Israelite monarchy.

Judah 'went down' in the sense that his brothers *deposed* him from his position of leadership. This narrative interrupts the story of Joseph to teach how Judah was lowered in esteem by his brothers as a result of the incident with Joseph. For when they saw their father's intense grief, they blamed Judah for it and deposed him. 'You told us to sell him,' they complained. 'Had you advised us to send him back to Father, we would have listened!' (*Rashi* from *Midrash*).

And turned away. From his brothers and became the partner of a certain Adullamite man (*Rashi*).

3. Er. This name, in the literal sense, means *Awaken!* (*Ramban*).

4. Onan. Judah had named the firstborn son, and his wife named their second child. The word אוֹנָן has the connotation of *complaining* and *sorrow*.

6. Er marries Tamar.
Er was very young when he married, for all the events related in this chapter transpired in the twenty-two years between the sale of Joseph and Jacob's descent to Egypt (*Seder Olam*).

7. Er dies.
Rashi explains that Er's sin was the same as Onan's [see v. 9] — he wasted his semen. This is deduced from the statement [v. 10] that God *caused him* [Onan] *to die also*, the word *also* implying *for the same reason* [as Er]. Why did Er destroy his semen? Tamar was exceedingly beautiful, and he did not want her beauty to be marred by pregnancy. [Cf. *Oznaim LaTorah*.]

8. This is a reference to יבום [*yibum*], *levirate marriage*, the details of which are given in *Deut.* 25:5ff. Briefly, when a man died without offspring, Torah law obliged his brother to marry the widow, and the son of this union was considered the spiritual son of the deceased. One who refused to perform *yibum* was considered to be derelict in his duty to the deceased brother. The widow was to loosen his shoe from his foot, spit in front of him, and say, 'So shall be done to the man who does not build up his brother's house.' In earlier times, this obligation could be carried out by other relatives as well, as Judah did later in the narrative.

11. Judah rebuffs Tamar.

12. That Judah's wife and sons died young is perceived in *Sotah* 13a as punishment for Judah's complicity in the sale of Joseph. He *began* a good deed of telling his brothers not to kill Joseph, but neglected to follow through. One who abandons a good deed without completing it, the Sages teach, will eventually bury his wife and children, as happened to Judah.

14. Tamar disguises herself. She intends to force Judah himself to perform the levirate duty.

For . . . she had not been given to him as a wife. This explains why Tamar did such an undignified thing. She was determined to have children from Judah. [Since it could not be through Shelah, she had no alternative but that it be from Judah himself (*Gur Aryeh*)] (*Rashi*).

38 ¹ It was at that time that Judah went down from his brothers and turned away towards an Adullamite man whose name was Hirah. ² There Judah saw the daughter of a prominent merchant whose name was Shua. He married her and consorted with her. ³ She conceived and bore a son and he named him Er. ⁴ She conceived again and bore a son and she named him Onan. ⁵ And yet again and she bore a son; and named him Shelah; and it was in Chezib when she bore him.

⁶ Judah took a wife for Er his firstborn. Her name was Tamar. ⁷ But Er, Judah's firstborn, was evil in the eyes of HASHEM, and HASHEM caused him to die. ⁸ Then Judah said to Onan. 'Consort with your brother's wife and enter into levirate marriage with her, and establish offspring for your brother.'

⁹ But Onan knew that the seed would not be his. So it was, whenever he would consort with his brother's wife, he would let it go to waste on the ground so as not to provide offspring for his brother. ¹⁰ What he did was evil in the eyes of HASHEM, and He caused him to die also.

¹¹ Then Judah said to Tamar, his daughter-in-law, 'Remain a widow in your father's house until my son Shelah grows up' — for he thought, 'Lest he also die like his brothers.' — So Tamar went and lived in her father's house.

¹² Many days passed and Shua's daughter, the wife of Judah, died. When Judah was consoled, he went up to oversee his sheepshearers — he and his Adullamite friend, Hirah — to Timnah.

¹³ And Tamar was told as follows, 'Behold, your father-in-law is coming up to Timnah for the sheepshearing.' ¹⁴ So she removed her widow's garb from upon her, covered herself with a veil, and wrapped herself up. She then sat by the crossroad which is on the road toward Timnah, for

רָאֲתָה כִּי־גָדַל שֵׁלָה וְהִוא לֹא־נִתְּנָה לוֹ
לְאִשָּׁה: טו וַיִּרְאֶהָ יְהוּדָה וַיַּחְשְׁבֶהָ לְזוֹנָה כִּי
כִסְּתָה פָּנֶיהָ: טז וַיֵּט אֵלֶיהָ אֶל־הַדֶּרֶךְ וַיֹּאמֶר
הָבָה־נָּא אָבוֹא אֵלַיִךְ כִּי לֹא יָדַע כִּי כַלָּתוֹ הִוא
וַתֹּאמֶר מַה־תִּתֶּן־לִי כִּי תָבוֹא אֵלָי: יז וַיֹּאמֶר
אָנֹכִי אֲשַׁלַּח גְּדִי־עִזִּים מִן־הַצֹּאן וַתֹּאמֶר
אִם־תִּתֵּן עֵרָבוֹן עַד שָׁלְחֶךָ: יח וַיֹּאמֶר מָה
הָעֵרָבוֹן אֲשֶׁר אֶתֶּן־לָךְ וַתֹּאמֶר חֹתָמְךָ
וּפְתִילֶךָ וּמַטְּךָ אֲשֶׁר בְּיָדֶךָ וַיִּתֶּן־לָהּ וַיָּבֹא
אֵלֶיהָ וַתַּהַר לוֹ: יט וַתָּקָם וַתֵּלֶךְ וַתָּסַר צְעִיפָהּ
מֵעָלֶיהָ וַתִּלְבַּשׁ בִּגְדֵי אַלְמְנוּתָהּ: כ וַיִּשְׁלַח
יְהוּדָה אֶת־גְּדִי הָעִזִּים בְּיַד רֵעֵהוּ הָעֲדֻלָּמִי
לָקַחַת הָעֵרָבוֹן מִיַּד הָאִשָּׁה וְלֹא מְצָאָהּ:
כא וַיִּשְׁאַל אֶת־אַנְשֵׁי מְקֹמָהּ לֵאמֹר אַיֵּה
הַקְּדֵשָׁה הִוא בָעֵינַיִם עַל־הַדָּרֶךְ וַיֹּאמְרוּ
לֹא־הָיְתָה בָזֶה קְדֵשָׁה: כב וַיָּשָׁב אֶל־יְהוּדָה
וַיֹּאמֶר לֹא מְצָאתִיהָ וְגַם אַנְשֵׁי הַמָּקוֹם אָמְרוּ
לֹא־הָיְתָה בָזֶה קְדֵשָׁה: כג וַיֹּאמֶר יְהוּדָה
תִּקַּח־לָהּ פֶּן נִהְיֶה לָבוּז הִנֵּה שָׁלַחְתִּי הַגְּדִי
הַזֶּה וְאַתָּה לֹא מְצָאתָהּ: כד וַיְהִי ׀ כְּמִשְׁלֹשׁ
חֳדָשִׁים וַיֻּגַּד לִיהוּדָה לֵאמֹר זָנְתָה תָּמָר
כַּלָּתֶךָ וְגַם הִנֵּה הָרָה לִזְנוּנִים וַיֹּאמֶר
יְהוּדָה הוֹצִיאוּהָ וְתִשָּׂרֵף: כה הִוא מוּצֵאת
וְהִיא שָׁלְחָה אֶל־חָמִיהָ לֵאמֹר לְאִישׁ אֲשֶׁר־

16. The moral perspective of Judah's action.

Judah's action must be viewed in the moral perspective of ancient times when harlotry was not yet forbidden. All morality depends on the Torah. Had the Torah not forbidden certain foods, we would be able to enjoy them guiltlessly. The same is true of harlotry; before the Torah was given it was simply not prohibited. (See *Rambam Ishus* 1:4.) That the Patriarchs — and presumably their families — observed the Torah before it was given is not a contradiction. They observed it *voluntarily* and Judah was not obligated to go beyond what was absolutely *required* of him. [Cf. the case of Jacob marrying two sisters which later Torah law absolutely forbade.]

17. Tamar needed something she could use later as proof of her intention. Therefore she consented to consort with Judah only on condition that he leave her a pledge (*Sforno*).

18. So great was the passion burning within him [as a result of the Providential intervention (*Abarbanel*)] that Judah gave these three valuable items as a pledge for a single goat (*Ibn Ezra*).

19. *Bereishis Rabbasi* records a difference of opinion regarding why the Adullamite's name is not recorded here. According to one view, his anonymity was preserved in deference to his selflessness in performing this shameful mission out of love and friendship for the righteous Judah. According to another view, his name is omitted as a token of rebuke, because he undertook to participate in this disgraceful affair.

23. *Lest we become a laughingstock* — for having pledged things as valuable as a signet, wrap, and staff for such a trifle *(Ibn Ezra)*.

24. *Judah is informed of Tamar's 'trespass.'*

Tamar boasted about her pregnancy. The Midrash records that she would go to the bathhouse and say: 'Prophets and Redeemers will descend from me!'

And moreover, she has conceived by harlotry. This is proven by the fact that she is pregnant *(Rashbam)*.

Let her be burned! Because Tamar was the daughter of Shem who was a priest, they sentenced her to be burnt *(Rashi* citing Midrash).

Judah condemned her to this punishment because he was a great chief, and his daughter-in-law's harlotry was an affront to his status, just as a priest's daughter who committed harlotry is condemned for having 'thereby profaned her father.' This judgment would not have been meted out to a commoner *(Ramban)*.

25. Tamar did not shame Judah publicly by naming him as the father. She reasoned: 'If he admits it voluntarily, well and good; if not, let them burn me, but let me not publicly disgrace him.' Thus the Sages taught [*Sotah* 10b]: 'One should let himself be thrown into a fiery furnace rather than expose his neighbor to public shame' *(Rashi)*.

With the expression הַכֶּר נָא [*identify, if you please: Is it your son's tunic or not?* (37:32)], Judah had caused his father untold anguish. God repaid him 'measure for measure.' Tamar now made her accusation with that same expression, and its impact registered solidly upon Judah *(Sotah* 10b).

she saw that Shelah had grown, and she had not been given to him as a wife.

¹⁵ When Judah saw her, he thought her to be a harlot since she had covered her face. ¹⁶ So he detoured to her by the road and said, 'Come, if you please, let me consort with you,' for he did not know that she was his daughter-in-law. And she said, 'What will you give me if you consort with me?'

¹⁷ He replied, 'I will send you a kid of the goats from the flock.'

And she said, 'Provided you leave a pledge until you send it.'

¹⁸ And he said, 'What pledge shall I give you?'

She replied, 'Your signet, your wrap, and your staff that is in your hand.' And he gave them to her. He consorted with her and she conceived by him.

¹⁹ Then she arose, left, and removed her veil from upon her. She put on her widow's garb.

²⁰ Judah sent the kid of the goats through his friend the Adullamite to retrieve the pledge from the woman. But he did not find her. ²¹ He inquired of the people of her place, 'Where is the prostitute, the one at the crossroads by the road?' And they said, 'There was no prostitute here.'
²² So he returned to Judah and said, 'I did not find her; even the local men said, "There was no prostitute here." ' ²³ So Judah said, 'Let her keep them, lest we become a laughingstock. I really sent her this kid, but you could not find her.'

²⁴ About three months passed, and Judah was told, 'Your daughter-in-law has committed harlotry, and moreover, she has conceived by harlotry.' Judah said, 'Take her out and let her be burned!'

²⁵ As she was taken out, she sent word to her father-in-law, as follows, 'By the man to whom

אֵלֶּה לּוֹ אָנֹכִי הָרָה וַתֹּאמֶר הַכֶּר־נָא
לְמִי הַחֹתֶמֶת וְהַפְּתִילִים וְהַמַּטֶּה הָאֵלֶּה:
כו וַיַּכֵּר יְהוּדָה וַיֹּאמֶר צָדְקָה מִמֶּנִּי
כִּי־עַל־כֵּן לֹא־נְתַתִּיהָ לְשֵׁלָה בְנִי וְלֹא־יָסַף
עוֹד לְדַעְתָּהּ: כז וַיְהִי בְּעֵת לִדְתָּהּ וְהִנֵּה
תְאוֹמִים בְּבִטְנָהּ: כח וַיְהִי בְלִדְתָּהּ וַיִּתֶּן־יָד
וַתִּקַּח הַמְיַלֶּדֶת וַתִּקְשֹׁר עַל־יָדוֹ שָׁנִי לֵאמֹר
זֶה יָצָא רִאשֹׁנָה: כט וַיְהִי | כְּמֵשִׁיב יָדוֹ וְהִנֵּה
יָצָא אָחִיו וַתֹּאמֶר מַה־פָּרַצְתָּ עָלֶיךָ
פָּרֶץ וַיִּקְרָא שְׁמוֹ פָּרֶץ: ל וְאַחַר יָצָא
אָחִיו אֲשֶׁר עַל־יָדוֹ הַשָּׁנִי וַיִּקְרָא שְׁמוֹ
זָרַח: **לט** חמישי א וְיוֹסֵף
הוּרַד מִצְרָיְמָה וַיִּקְנֵהוּ פּוֹטִיפַר סְרִיס פַּרְעֹה
שַׂר הַטַּבָּחִים אִישׁ מִצְרִי מִיַּד הַיִּשְׁמְעֵאלִים
אֲשֶׁר הוֹרִדֻהוּ שָׁמָּה: ב וַיְהִי יהוה אֶת־יוֹסֵף
וַיְהִי אִישׁ מַצְלִיחַ וַיְהִי בְּבֵית אֲדֹנָיו הַמִּצְרִי:
ג וַיַּרְא אֲדֹנָיו כִּי יהוה אִתּוֹ וְכֹל אֲשֶׁר־
הוּא עֹשֶׂה יהוה מַצְלִיחַ בְּיָדוֹ: ד וַיִּמְצָא
יוֹסֵף חֵן בְּעֵינָיו וַיְשָׁרֶת אֹתוֹ וַיַּפְקִדֵהוּ עַל־
בֵּיתוֹ וְכָל־יֶשׁ־לוֹ נָתַן בְּיָדוֹ: ה וַיְהִי מֵאָז
הִפְקִיד אֹתוֹ בְּבֵיתוֹ וְעַל כָּל־אֲשֶׁר יֶשׁ־לוֹ
וַיְבָרֶךְ יהוה אֶת־בֵּית הַמִּצְרִי בִּגְלַל יוֹסֵף
וַיְהִי בִּרְכַּת יהוה בְּכָל־אֲשֶׁר יֶשׁ־לוֹ בַּבַּיִת

26. 'She is more righteous than I!'

צָדְקָה מִמֶּנִּי — *She is right; it is from me.* The translation follows *Rashi* who renders: צָדְקָה, *she is right* in what she said: מִמֶּנִּי, *it is from me.* Alternatively, *Rashi* cites the Sages that a *bas kol* [Heavenly voice] came forth and said מִמֶּנִּי, i.e., 'From Me and My agency did these events unfold!'

27. Tamar bears twins.

28. *Took a crimson thread and tied it.* In order to identify him as the firstborn (*Sforno*).

29. Peretz.

This was part of the Divine plan. Zerach desired to emerge first but God declared: Messiah is destined to descend from Peretz; is it right, then, that Zerach should emerge first? Let Zerach return to his mother's womb, and Peretz shall be born first! (*Aggadas Bereishis*).

Judah named the child *Peretz* [meaning *strength* (*Rashi*) or *breaking forth* (*Ramban*)] because of what the midwife had said (*Radak*).

30. Zerach — *Brightness.* Alluding to the brightness of the crimson thread (*Rashi*).

39/1. Joseph in Egypt.

The Torah returns to the narrative that it had interrupted with the Judah/Tamar interlude. As noted in 38:1, Judah's degradation had been interpolated because his role in the sale of Joseph had caused the brothers to demote him from his leadership status. Furthermore, the close proximity of the narratives of Tamar and Potiphar's wife indicates that both women had pure motives [both of them desiring to found a family in

Israel]. Potiphar's wife had foreseen by astrological signs that she was destined to be the ancestress of children by Joseph — but she did not know whether *she* or her daughter would have the children. [According to tradition, Joseph married her daughter. See *Rashi* to 41:45] (*Rashi*).

Prelude to Exile.

Joseph's descent into Egypt was the prelude to the Egyptian exile foretold to Abraham at the Covenant Between the Parts [15:13]. *Joseph had been brought down to Egypt* has the deeper implication that Joseph *brought down* [הוֹרִיד] his father and the tribal ancestors to Egypt (*Tanchuma Yashan*). That is, God engineered Joseph's descent to Egypt in order to implement His decree that Jacob would be exiled, but to spare him the harshness of a *forced descent*.

Thus, Joseph's descent to Egypt was Divinely orchestrated so Jacob and his sons would come in an honorable way. According to *Hadar Zekeinim*, the Divine Presence, as it were, descended with Joseph.

Although Joseph was questioned about his origin, he admitted only that he was an *Ivri* [Hebrew]. He kept the oath of secrecy against attempting to return to his father or revealing his identity (*Midrash HaGadol*) [see note to 37:28; *Ramban* to 42:9].

4. Perceiving that Joseph was Divinely assisted, Potiphar took a special liking to him. First he made him his personal attendant, and afterwards appointed him over the household.

these belong I am with child.' And she said, 'Identify, if you please, whose are this seal, this wrap, and this staff.'

²⁶ Judah recognized; and he said, 'She is right; it is from me, inasmuch as I did not give her to Shelah my son.' And he was not intimate with her anymore.

²⁷ And it came to pass at the time she gave birth that behold! There were twins in her womb. ²⁸ And it happened that as she gave birth, one put out a hand; the midwife took a crimson thread and tied it on his hand saying, 'This one emerged first!' ²⁹ And it was, as he drew back his hand, that behold! his brother emerged. And she said, 'With what strength you asserted yourself!' And he named him Peretz. ³⁰ Afterwards his brother on whose hand was the crimson thread came out. And he named him Zerach.

39 ¹ And Joseph had been brought down to Egypt. Potiphar, a courtier of Pharaoh, the Chamberlain of the Butchers, a prominent Egyptian, purchased him from the Ishmaelites who had brought him down there. ²HASHEM was with Joseph, and he became a successful man; he remained in the house of his Egyptian master. ³ His master perceived that HASHEM was with him, and whatever he did HASHEM made succeed through him. ⁴ Joseph found favor in his eyes, and he attended him. He appointed him over his household, and whatever he had he placed in his custody.

⁵ And it happened, that from the time he appointed him in his house and over whatever he had, HASHEM blessed the Egyptian's house on Joseph's account, so that HASHEM's blessing was in whatever he owned, in the house and

וּבַשָּׂדֶה: וַיַּעֲזֹב כָּל־אֲשֶׁר־לוֹ בְּיַד־יוֹסֵף וְלֹא־
יָדַע אִתּוֹ מְאוּמָה כִּי אִם־הַלֶּחֶם אֲשֶׁר־הוּא
אוֹכֵל וַיְהִי יוֹסֵף יְפֵה־תֹאַר וִיפֵה מַרְאֶה: ששי
ז וַיְהִי אַחַר הַדְּבָרִים הָאֵלֶּה וַתִּשָּׂא אֵשֶׁת־
אֲדֹנָיו אֶת־עֵינֶיהָ אֶל־יוֹסֵף וַתֹּאמֶר שִׁכְבָה
עִמִּי: ח וַיְמָאֵן | וַיֹּאמֶר אֶל־אֵשֶׁת אֲדֹנָיו הֵן
אֲדֹנִי לֹא־יָדַע אִתִּי מַה־בַּבָּיִת וְכֹל אֲשֶׁר־יֶשׁ־
לוֹ נָתַן בְּיָדִי: ט אֵינֶנּוּ גָדוֹל בַּבַּיִת הַזֶּה מִמֶּנִּי
וְלֹא־חָשַׂךְ מִמֶּנִּי מְאוּמָה כִּי אִם־אוֹתָךְ בַּאֲשֶׁר
אַתְּ־אִשְׁתּוֹ וְאֵיךְ אֶעֱשֶׂה הָרָעָה הַגְּדֹלָה הַזֹּאת
וְחָטָאתִי לֵאלֹהִים: י וַיְהִי כְּדַבְּרָהּ אֶל־יוֹסֵף יוֹם
| יוֹם וְלֹא־שָׁמַע אֵלֶיהָ לִשְׁכַּב אֶצְלָהּ לִהְיוֹת
עִמָּהּ: יא וַיְהִי כְּהַיּוֹם הַזֶּה וַיָּבֹא הַבַּיְתָה לַעֲשׂוֹת
מְלַאכְתּוֹ וְאֵין אִישׁ מֵאַנְשֵׁי הַבַּיִת שָׁם בַּבָּיִת:
יב וַתִּתְפְּשֵׂהוּ בְּבִגְדוֹ לֵאמֹר שִׁכְבָה עִמִּי וַיַּעֲזֹב
בִּגְדוֹ בְּיָדָהּ וַיָּנָס וַיֵּצֵא הַחוּצָה: יג וַיְהִי כִּרְאוֹתָהּ
כִּי־עָזַב בִּגְדוֹ בְּיָדָהּ וַיָּנָס הַחוּצָה: יד וַתִּקְרָא
לְאַנְשֵׁי בֵיתָהּ וַתֹּאמֶר לָהֶם לֵאמֹר רְאוּ הֵבִיא
לָנוּ אִישׁ עִבְרִי לְצַחֶק בָּנוּ בָּא אֵלַי לִשְׁכַּב עִמִּי
וָאֶקְרָא בְּקוֹל גָּדוֹל: טו וַיְהִי כְשָׁמְעוֹ כִּי־
הֲרִימֹתִי קוֹלִי וָאֶקְרָא וַיַּעֲזֹב בִּגְדוֹ אֶצְלִי וַיָּנָס
וַיֵּצֵא הַחוּצָה: טז וַתַּנַּח בִּגְדוֹ אֶצְלָהּ עַד־בּוֹא
אֲדֹנָיו אֶל־בֵּיתוֹ: יז וַתְּדַבֵּר אֵלָיו כַּדְּבָרִים
הָאֵלֶּה לֵאמֹר בָּא־אֵלַי הָעֶבֶד הָעִבְרִי אֲשֶׁר־
הֵבֵאתָ לָּנוּ לְצַחֶק בִּי: יח וַיְהִי כַּהֲרִימִי קוֹלִי

6. *Except for the bread he ate*. This is a delicate expression; *bread* here refers to his wife (*Rashi*). The sense is that Potiphar unquestionably entrusted to Joseph everything except for his own wife.

7. **Joseph repels the unwelcome advances of Potiphar's wife.**

8. וַיְמָאֵן — *But he adamantly refused*. The adverb *adamantly* is suggested by the staccato and emphatic cantillation by which this word is punctuated: the *shalsheles*, followed by the *psik*, both of which set off the word and enhance the absoluteness of its implication. It indicates that Joseph's refusal was constant, categorical, and definitive. Joseph repulsed her with absolute firmness.

9. Joseph presses further with the human aspect of his refusal. How can he be such an ingrate to the master who trusted him?

I will have sinned against God! Apart from wronging your husband, I would also be sinning against God (*Mizrachi*).

10. She tried to entice him in every way possible: with words; by varying her dress; by threats of imprisonment, humiliation and physical harm; by offering him huge sums of money (*Yoma* 35b).

11. וַיְהִי כְּהַיּוֹם הַזֶּה — *Then there was an opportune day* [lit., *and it was like this day*]. This translation follows *Rashi* (from *Sotah* 36b and *Tanchuma*). It was an important day — a festival when they all went to their temple. She, however, pleaded illness and stayed home, for she reasoned: I will never have such an opportunity to seduce Joseph כְּהַיּוֹם הַזֶּה, *as this day*.

12. Joseph resisted temptation when his father's countenance appeared through the window and admonished him that if he consorted with an adulteress, his name would later be omitted from the High Priest's breastplate (*Sotah* 36b).

13. Joseph is slandered.

When Potiphar's wife saw that he had left his garment and fled, she was afraid that he might expose her to the household or to her husband. Anticipating this, she hurried to them first and made a scene, accusing him of having removed his garment to violate her, 'but when he saw that I screamed he fled in confusion' (*Ramban*).

14. We see from 43:32 the Egyptians abhorred the Hebrews and would not even eat with them. The Hebrews were given only field work and were never brought into the house. Therefore, Potiphar's wife charged that for her husband to have brought a Hebrew slave into the house and appointed him to a position of trust was an affront to them. 'No wonder he took advantage of it and saw fit to exploit his position and trifle with our sensibilities!' (*Ramban*).

17. To her husband, Potiphar's wife elaborates upon her vindictive slander.

in the field. ⁶ He left all that he had in Joseph's custody and with him present he concerned himself with nothing except for the bread he ate. Now Joseph was handsome of form and handsome of appearance.

⁷ After these things, his master's wife cast her eyes upon Joseph and she said, 'Lie with me.' ⁸ But he adamantly refused. He said to his master's wife, 'Look — with me here, my master concerns himself about nothing in the house, and whatever he has he placed in my custody. ⁹ There is no one greater in this house than I, and he has denied me nothing but you, since you are his wife. How then can I perpetrate this great evil? I will have sinned against God!'

¹⁰ And so it was — just as she coaxed Joseph day after day, so he would not listen to her to lie beside her, to be with her. ¹¹ Then there was an opportune day when he entered the house to do his work — no man of the household staff being there in the house — ¹² that she caught hold of him by his garment, saying, 'Lie with me!' But he left his garment in her hand, and he fled, going outside.

¹³ When she saw that he had left his garment in her hand and fled outside, ¹⁴ she called out to the men of her household and said to them as follows, 'Look! He brought us a Hebrew man to sport with us! He came to lie with me but I called out with a loud scream. ¹⁵ And when he heard that I raised my voice and screamed, he left his garment beside me, fled, and went outside!'

¹⁶ She kept his garment beside her until his master came home. ¹⁷ Then she told him a similar account saying, 'The Hebrew slave whom you brought to us came to me to sport with me. ¹⁸ But it happened that when I raised my voice

וָאֶקְרָ֖א וַיַּעֲזֹ֥ב בִּגְד֛וֹ אֶצְלִ֖י וַיָּ֥נָס הַחֽוּצָה: יט וַיְהִ֡י
כִשְׁמֹ֣עַ אֲדֹנָיו֩ אֶת־דִּבְרֵ֨י אִשְׁתּ֜וֹ אֲשֶׁ֨ר דִּבְּרָ֤ה
אֵלָיו֙ לֵאמֹ֔ר כַּדְּבָרִ֣ים הָאֵ֔לֶּה עָ֥שָׂה לִ֖י עַבְדֶּ֑ךָ
וַיִּ֣חַר אַפּֽוֹ: כ וַיִּקַּח֩ אֲדֹנֵ֨י יוֹסֵ֜ף אֹת֗וֹ וַיִּתְּנֵ֨הוּ֙
אֶל־בֵּ֣ית הַסֹּ֔הַר מְק֕וֹם אֲשֶׁר־°אֲסוּרֵ֥י הַמֶּ֖לֶךְ
אֲסוּרִ֑ים וַֽיְהִי־שָׁ֖ם בְּבֵ֥ית הַסֹּֽהַר: כא וַיְהִ֤י יְהֹוָה֙
אֶת־יוֹסֵ֔ף וַיֵּ֥ט אֵלָ֖יו חָ֑סֶד וַיִּתֵּ֣ן חִנּ֔וֹ בְּעֵינֵ֖י שַׂ֥ר
בֵּית־הַסֹּֽהַר: כב וַיִּתֵּ֞ן שַׂ֤ר בֵּֽית־הַסֹּ֨הַר֙ בְּיַד־יוֹסֵ֔ף
אֵ֚ת כָּל־הָ֣אֲסִירִ֔ם אֲשֶׁ֖ר בְּבֵ֣ית הַסֹּ֑הַר וְאֵ֨ת
כָּל־אֲשֶׁ֤ר עֹשִׂים֙ שָׁ֔ם ה֖וּא הָיָ֥ה עֹשֶֽׂה: כג אֵ֣ין |
שַׂ֣ר בֵּית־הַסֹּ֗הַר רֹאֶ֤ה אֶֽת־כָּל־מְא֨וּמָה֙ בְּיָד֔וֹ
בַּאֲשֶׁ֥ר יְהֹוָ֖ה אִתּ֑וֹ וַֽאֲשֶׁר־ה֥וּא עֹשֶׂ֖ה יְהֹוָ֥ה
מַצְלִֽיחַ:
מ א וַיְהִ֗י אַחַר֙ הַדְּבָרִ֣ים הָאֵ֔לֶּה חָֽטְא֛וּ
מַשְׁקֵ֥ה מֶֽלֶךְ־מִצְרַ֖יִם וְהָאֹפֶ֑ה לַאֲדֹנֵיהֶ֖ם
לְמֶ֥לֶךְ מִצְרָֽיִם: ב וַיִּקְצֹ֣ף פַּרְעֹ֔ה עַ֖ל שְׁנֵ֣י
סָרִיסָ֑יו עַ֚ל שַׂ֣ר הַמַּשְׁקִ֔ים וְעַ֖ל שַׂ֥ר הָאוֹפִֽים:
ג וַיִּתֵּ֨ן אֹתָ֜ם בְּמִשְׁמַ֗ר בֵּ֛ית שַׂ֥ר הַטַּבָּחִ֖ים
אֶל־בֵּ֣ית הַסֹּ֑הַר מְק֕וֹם אֲשֶׁ֥ר יוֹסֵ֖ף אָס֥וּר שָֽׁם:
ד וַ֠יִּפְקֹ֠ד שַׂ֣ר הַטַּבָּחִ֧ים אֶת־יוֹסֵ֛ף אִתָּ֖ם
וַיְשָׁ֣רֶת אֹתָ֑ם וַיִּהְי֥וּ יָמִ֖ים בְּמִשְׁמָֽר: ה וַיַּֽחַלְמוּ֩
חֲל֨וֹם שְׁנֵיהֶ֜ם אִ֤ישׁ חֲלֹמוֹ֙ בְּלַ֣יְלָה אֶחָ֔ד אִ֖ישׁ
כְּפִתְר֣וֹן חֲלֹמ֑וֹ הַמַּשְׁקֶ֣ה וְהָאֹפֶ֗ה אֲשֶׁר֙ לְמֶ֣לֶךְ
מִצְרַ֔יִם אֲשֶׁ֥ר אֲסוּרִ֖ים בְּבֵ֥ית הַסֹּֽהַר: ו וַיָּבֹ֧א
אֲלֵיהֶ֛ם יוֹסֵ֖ף בַּבֹּ֑קֶר וַיַּ֣רְא אֹתָ֔ם וְהִנָּ֖ם זֹֽעֲפִֽים:
°אֲסִירֵ֥י ק׳

20. Joseph was imprisoned for twelve years: one year for each of the ten brothers about whom he had brought evil reports [37:2] — plus two more in punishment for placing his trust in the Chamberlain of the Cupbearers, instead of in God alone (*Seder Olam; Tanchuma*).

23. The warden of the prison never demanded an accounting of Joseph nor did he guard him. He realized that Joseph was innocent, that Hashem was with him, and that Hashem made him succeed in everything he undertook (*Targum Yonasan*).

40/1. Joseph interprets dreams in prison.

Because Potiphar's accursed wife had made Joseph the subject of general gossip, God now arranged for a new scandal: He brought about the offenses of these men [prominent officials of the royal palace] so that people's attention should be diverted to them and away from Joseph. God's other purpose, in causing the officials' offenses and imprisonment, was to make them the instruments of Joseph's relief and ultimate elevation to a high position (*Rashi*).

That the cupbearer of the king of Egypt and the baker transgressed. In the case of one, a fly was found in his goblet of wine, while in the case of the other, a pebble was discovered in his bread (*Rashi* from *Midrash*).

The cupbearer's offense was less serious than that of the baker, since a fly could have fallen in at any time, and presumably was not in the goblet when the cupbearer originally prepared and served it. That is why the cupbearer was restored to his position (v. 21). The baker, however, was guilty of negligence since a pebble must have been in the dough or oven all along (*Mizrachi; Gur Aryeh*. See *Gittin* 6b for an analogy).

Furthermore, the presence of a pebble was a more serious offense since it could have choked Pharaoh, whereas a dead fly, while repulsive, is harmless (*Radak*).

4. Joseph's long period of incarceration with political prisoners was part of the Divine scheme. It gave him the opportunity to gain their trust and learn about the intimate workings of government (*Abarbanel*).

5. The dreams of the chamberlains.

Each one according to the interpretation of his dream. As *Ibn Ezra* and *Radak* interpret, each dream contained an accurate vision of the future, verifying that it was a true dream — not the kind which one fantasizes as the result of anxiety and of which only a part is fulfilled. Cf. *Rashbam*: Each dreamed a dream worthy of interpretation; they were significant and not mere fantasies.

and screamed, he left his garment beside me, and ran outside.'

[19] And it was, when his master heard his wife's words which she spoke to him, saying, 'Your slave did things like these to me,' and his anger flared up. [20] Then Joseph's master took him and placed him in the prison — the place where the king's prisoners were confined. And he remained there in prison.

[21] HASHEM was with Joseph, and He endowed him with charisma; He made the prison warden view him favorably. [22] The prison warden placed all inmates of the prison in Joseph's custody, and everything that was done there, he would accomplish. [23] The prison warden did not scrutinize anything that was in his charge inasmuch as HASHEM was with him. And whatever he did HASHEM made successful.

40 [1] **A**nd it happened after these things that the cupbearer of the king of Egypt and the baker transgressed against their master, against the king of Egypt. [2] Pharaoh was enraged at his two courtiers, the Chamberlain of the Cupbearers and the Chamberlain of the Bakers. [3] And he placed them in the ward of the house of the Chamberlain of the Butchers, into the prison, the place where Joseph was confined. [4]The Chamberlain of the Butchers appointed Joseph to be with them, and he attended them and they remained in the ward for a period of days.

[5] The two of them dreamt a dream, each one had his dream on the same night, each one according to the interpretation of his dream — the cupbearer and the baker of the king of Egypt who were confined in the prison.

[6] Joseph came to them in the morning. He saw them — Behold! they were aggrieved.

וַיִּשְׁאַ֗ל אֶת־סְרִיסֵ֤י פַרְעֹה֙ אֲשֶׁ֣ר אִתּ֣וֹ ז
בְמִשְׁמַ֖ר בֵּ֣ית אֲדֹנָ֑יו לֵאמֹ֕ר מַדּ֛וּעַ פְּנֵיכֶ֥ם
רָעִ֖ים הַיּֽוֹם: וַיֹּאמְר֣וּ אֵלָ֗יו חֲל֤וֹם חָלַ֙מְנוּ֙ ח
וּפֹתֵ֖ר אֵ֣ין אֹת֑וֹ וַיֹּ֨אמֶר אֲלֵהֶ֜ם יוֹסֵ֗ף הֲל֤וֹא
לֵֽאלֹהִים֙ פִּתְרֹנִ֔ים סַפְּרוּ־נָ֖א לִֽי: וַיְסַפֵּ֧ר ט
שַׂר־הַמַּשְׁקִ֛ים אֶת־חֲלֹמ֖וֹ לְיוֹסֵ֑ף וַיֹּ֣אמֶר ל֔וֹ
בַּֽחֲלוֹמִ֕י וְהִנֵּה־גֶ֖פֶן לְפָנָֽי: וּבַגֶּ֖פֶן שְׁלֹשָׁ֣ה י
שָֽׂרִיגִ֑ם וְהִ֤וא כְפֹרַ֙חַת֙ עָֽלְתָ֣ה נִצָּ֔הּ הִבְשִׁ֥ילוּ
אַשְׁכְּלֹתֶ֖יהָ עֲנָבִֽים: וְכ֥וֹס פַּרְעֹ֖ה בְּיָדִ֑י יא
וָֽאֶקַּ֣ח אֶת־הָֽעֲנָבִ֗ים וָֽאֶשְׁחַ֤ט אֹתָם֙ אֶל־כּ֣וֹס
פַּרְעֹ֔ה וָֽאֶתֵּ֥ן אֶת־הַכּ֖וֹס עַל־כַּ֥ף פַּרְעֹֽה:
וַיֹּ֧אמֶר ל֣וֹ יוֹסֵ֗ף זֶ֣ה פִּתְרֹנ֑וֹ שְׁלֹ֙שֶׁת֙ הַשָּׂ֣רִגִ֔ים יב
שְׁלֹ֥שֶׁת יָמִ֖ים הֵֽם: בְּע֣וֹד ׀ שְׁלֹ֣שֶׁת יָמִ֗ים יג
יִשָּׂ֤א פַרְעֹה֙ אֶת־רֹאשֶׁ֔ךָ וַֽהֲשִֽׁיבְךָ֖ עַל־כַּנֶּ֑ךָ
וְנָֽתַתָּ֤ כוֹס־פַּרְעֹה֙ בְּיָד֔וֹ כַּמִּשְׁפָּ֖ט הָֽרִאשׁ֔וֹן
אֲשֶׁ֥ר הָיִ֖יתָ מַשְׁקֵֽהוּ: כִּ֣י אִם־זְכַרְתַּ֤נִי אִתְּךָ֙ יד
כַּֽאֲשֶׁר֙ יִ֣יטַב לָ֔ךְ וְעָשִֽׂיתָ־נָּ֥א עִמָּדִ֖י חָ֑סֶד
וְהִזְכַּרְתַּ֙נִי֙ אֶל־פַּרְעֹ֔ה וְהֽוֹצֵאתַ֖נִי מִן־הַבַּ֥יִת
הַזֶּֽה: כִּֽי־גֻנֹּ֣ב גֻּנַּ֔בְתִּי מֵאֶ֖רֶץ הָֽעִבְרִ֑ים וְגַם־ טו
פֹּ֛ה לֹֽא־עָשִׂ֥יתִי מְא֖וּמָה כִּֽי־שָׂמ֥וּ אֹתִ֖י בַּבּֽוֹר:
וַיַּ֥רְא שַׂר־הָֽאֹפִ֖ים כִּ֣י ט֣וֹב פָּתָ֑ר וַיֹּ֙אמֶר֙ טז
אֶל־יוֹסֵ֔ף אַף־אֲנִי֙ בַּֽחֲלוֹמִ֔י וְהִנֵּ֗ה שְׁלֹשָׁ֛ה סַלֵּ֥י
חֹרִ֖י עַל־רֹאשִֽׁי: וּבַסַּ֣ל הָֽעֶלְי֗וֹן מִכֹּ֛ל מַֽאֲכַ֥ל יז
פַּרְעֹ֖ה מַֽעֲשֵׂ֣ה אֹפֶ֑ה וְהָע֗וֹף אֹכֵ֥ל אֹתָ֛ם מִן־
הַסַּ֖ל מֵעַ֥ל רֹאשִֽׁי: וַיַּ֤עַן יוֹסֵף֙ וַיֹּ֣אמֶר זֶ֣ה יח

8. *But there is no interpreter for it.* I.e., no one can explain the prophetic portents of the dream. Apparently they had sent for interpreters, or perhaps there were people with them in prison, but none could interpret it. Or the implication of their remark could be: 'No one in the world could, in our opinion, interpret these dreams, so difficult are they' (*Ramban*).

Just as God sends the dream, so He grants man the wisdom to interpret it; otherwise, the dream would have been in vain. Therefore *relate it to me* — perhaps God will give me the wisdom to interpret it (*Radak*).

10. There are usually many more than three tendrils on a vine. Accordingly Joseph perceived a special significance in this number (*Daas Sofrim*)

12. The interpretation.

Abarbanel emphasizes that Joseph successfully interpreted the dream only because of God's inspiration.

13. *Pharaoh will lift up your head.* The idiom *lift up your head* means *to count* [cf. *Exod.* 30:12]. The sense here is that when Pharaoh will assemble his other servants to wait upon him during the meal, *he will count you among them* (*Rashi*).

14. Joseph asks the cupbearer to intercede on his behalf.

Your rise to prominence in accordance with my interpretation will be so astounding that you will merely need mention me to Pharaoh in order to free me from prison, for he will certainly listen to you (*Rashbam*).

Because Joseph placed his trust in the Chamberlain of the Cupbearers instead of in God Himself, he was punished by having his prison sentence increased by two years (*Seder Olam; Tanchuma; Shemos Rabbah*).

15. 'Do not think you would be committing an injustice by praising me and being instrumental in securing my release from jail, for I am not a slave by birth. I am really innocent and should not have been here in the first place!' (*Rashbam; Ramban*).

It is noteworthy that is the very first time throughout all Joseph's trials that he breaks his silence and protests his innocence.

When Joseph came to Potiphar's house he apparently told them he was a Hebrew [39:14]. The territory around Hebron, where they resided, was referred to as the land of the *Ivrim*, not because the Canaanites acknowledged it as theirs, but because of the prominence achieved by the descendants of Abraham, who was acknowledged by the inhabitants as a *prince of god* [23:6] (*Ramban*).

16. The baker's dream.

17. Not only did birds eat Pharaoh's food, they had the impudence to eat it right off the basket on the baker's head, and he was powerless to stop them! No bird would have the temerity to do that to a living person! (*R' Hirsch*).

⁷ And he asked Pharaoh's courtiers who were with him in the ward of his master's house, saying, 'Why do you appear downcast today?' ⁸ And they said to him, 'We dreamt a dream, but there is no interpreter for it.' So Joseph said to them, 'Do not interpretations belong to God? Relate it to me, if you please.'

⁹ Then the Chamberlain of the Cupbearers recounted his dream to Joseph and said to him, 'In my dream — Behold! there was a grapevine in front of me! ¹⁰ On the grapevine were three tendrils. And it was as though it budded — its blossoms bloomed and its clusters ripened into grapes. ¹¹ And Pharaoh's cup was in my hand and I took the grapes, pressed them into Pharaoh's cup, and I placed the cup on Pharaoh's palm.'

¹² Joseph said to him, 'This is its interpretation: The three tendrils are three days. ¹³ In another three days Pharaoh will lift up your head and will restore you to your post, and you will place Pharaoh's cup in his hand as was the former practice when you were his cupbearer. ¹⁴ If only you would think of me with yourself when he benefits you, and you will do me a kindness, if you please, and mention me to Pharaoh, then you would get me out of this building. ¹⁵ For indeed I was kidnaped from the land of the Hebrews, and even here I have done nothing for them to have put me in the pit.'

¹⁶ The Chamberlain of the Bakers saw that he had interpreted well. He said to Joseph, 'I, too! In my dream — Behold! three wicker baskets were on my head. ¹⁷ And in the uppermost basket were all kinds of Pharaoh's food — baker's handiwork — and the birds were eating them from the basket above my head.'

¹⁸ Joseph responded and said, 'This is its

פְּתְרֹנ֑וֹ שְׁלֹ֣שֶׁת הַסַּלִּ֔ים שְׁלֹ֥שֶׁת יָמִ֖ים הֵֽם: יט בְּע֣וֹד ׀ שְׁלֹ֣שֶׁת יָמִ֗ים יִשָּׂ֨א פַרְעֹ֤ה אֶת־רֹֽאשְׁךָ֙ מֵֽעָלֶ֔יךָ וְתָלָ֥ה אֽוֹתְךָ֖ עַל־עֵ֑ץ וְאָכַ֨ל הָע֛וֹף אֶת־בְּשָׂרְךָ֖ מֵֽעָלֶֽיךָ: מפטיר כ וַיְהִ֣י ׀ בַּיּ֣וֹם הַשְּׁלִישִׁ֗י י֚וֹם הֻלֶּ֣דֶת אֶת־פַּרְעֹ֔ה וַיַּ֥עַשׂ מִשְׁתֶּ֖ה לְכָל־עֲבָדָ֑יו וַיִּשָּׂ֞א אֶת־רֹ֣אשׁ ׀ שַׂ֣ר הַמַּשְׁקִ֗ים וְאֶת־רֹ֛אשׁ שַׂ֥ר הָֽאֹפִ֖ים בְּת֥וֹךְ עֲבָדָֽיו: כא וַיָּ֛שֶׁב אֶת־שַׂ֥ר הַמַּשְׁקִ֖ים עַל־מַשְׁקֵ֑הוּ וַיִּתֵּ֥ן הַכּ֖וֹס עַל־כַּ֥ף פַּרְעֹֽה: כב וְאֵ֛ת שַׂ֥ר הָֽאֹפִ֖ים תָּלָ֑ה כַּֽאֲשֶׁ֥ר פָּתַ֛ר לָהֶ֖ם יוֹסֵֽף: כג וְלֹֽא־זָכַ֧ר שַֽׂר־הַמַּשְׁקִ֛ים אֶת־יוֹסֵ֖ף וַיִּשְׁכָּחֵֽהוּ:

The *Haftarah* for *Vayeishev* appears on page 328.
When *Vayeishev* is read during Chanukah, the regular
Haftarah is omitted. The *Haftarah* for the Sabbath of
Chanukah appears on page 344.

---

19. יִשָּׂא פַרְעֹה אֶת רֹאשְׁךָ מֵעָלֶיךָ — *Pharaoh will lift your head from you.* This term יִשָּׂא רֹאשׁ, *lift off the head,* is used here in the literal sense meaning: *he will behead you.*

Pharaoh's birthday. According to *Rashi,* it was literally his birthday. *R' Bachya,* following *Radak,* interprets that on that day a son was born to Pharaoh. As crown prince, the baby was named Pharaoh because he would eventually ascend to the throne. To celebrate the event, the king made a great feast.

23. *The Chamberlain of the Cupbearers did not remember Joseph* on the day he was freed; *and he forgot him* in the future (*Rashi*).

The Midrash perceives another intent of this verse: True, the Chamberlain of the Cupbearers forgot Joseph, but the Holy One, Blessed is He, did not, as the events in the next *Sidrah* will graphically portray.

According to the Masoretic note appearing at the end of the *Sidrah,* there are 112 verses in *Vayeishev*, numerically corresponding to the mnemonic יָבֵק. The root of the word is בקק, *emptying out.* The allusion is that this *Sidrah* contains the beginning of the process which was to culminate in Israel's first exile, the process by which Jacob and his family were *emptied out* of their native land and forced to spend 210 years in Egypt. The *Haftarah* begins with *Amos* 2:6: כֹּה אָמַר ה'.

interpretation: The three baskets are three days. [19] In three days Pharaoh will lift your head from you and hang you on a tree. Birds will eat your flesh from you.'

[20] And it was on the third day, Pharaoh's birthday, that he made a feast for all his servants and he counted the Chamberlain of the Cupbearers and the Chamberlain of the Bakers among his servants. [21] He restored the Chamberlain of the Cupbearers to his cupbearing and he placed the cup on Pharaoh's palm. [22] But the Chamberlain of the Bakers he hung just as Joseph had interpreted to them.

[23] Yet the Chamberlain of the Cupbearers did not remember Joseph, and he forgot him.

The *Haftarah* for *Vayeishev* appears on page 328.
When *Vayeishev* is read during Chanukah, the regular *Haftarah*
is omitted. The *Haftarah* for the Sabbath of Chanukah
appears on page 344.

פרשת מקץ

MIKEITZ

The time has come for Joseph's dreams — the prophetic dreams — to come true, so God's Providence molds history. Again, dreams. Pharaoh dreams and he is troubled. He senses that they are a message about events too portentous to ignore. Reluctantly, his wine steward tells him about the disgraced Hebrew slave who is rotting in Potiphar's dungeon. It is Rosh Hashanah, and judgment is handed down from on high that Joseph's fortunes shall turn. He interprets the dreams and becomes viceroy of the world's leading power.

Seven years of prosperity and then begin seven years of famine — and only Egypt has an abundance of food, thanks to the wisdom and firmness of Joseph. Finally, the event he had awaited: His brothers come to purchase food, and Joseph's terrible ordeal begins. Joseph knew that the dreams that caused his brothers to hate him were in reality prophecies, and it was his duty to make the prophecies come true. To do so, he had to conceal his identity from them, just as he had to conceal from his beloved father for twenty-two years that he was alive.

One of the episodes in the ordeal through which he put his brothers reveals their caliber. When Joseph told them that he would hold one of them hostage, they said to one another, 'Indeed we are guilty concerning our brother inasmuch as we saw his heartfelt anguish when he pleaded with us and we paid no heed. That is why this distress has come upon us.' They had not sold Joseph frivolously, and they did not feel that they had acted in violation of the *Halachah* as they understood it. But they had been cold to his anguish and deaf to his pleas. For that they deserved their present suffering. The fathers of the Jewish people do not attribute suffering to 'fate' or 'coincidence.' Nor do they they blame others. They seek shortcomings in themselves, and pinpoint their guilt in a lack of compassion.

מא א וַיְהִי מִקֵּץ שְׁנָתַיִם יָמִים וּפַרְעֹה חֹלֵם
וְהִנֵּה עֹמֵד עַל־הַיְאֹר: ב וְהִנֵּה מִן־הַיְאֹר
עֹלֹת שֶׁבַע פָּרוֹת יְפוֹת מַרְאֶה וּבְרִיאֹת בָּשָׂר
וַתִּרְעֶינָה בָּאָחוּ: ג וְהִנֵּה שֶׁבַע פָּרוֹת אֲחֵרוֹת
עֹלוֹת אַחֲרֵיהֶן מִן־הַיְאֹר רָעוֹת מַרְאֶה
וְדַקּוֹת בָּשָׂר וַתַּעֲמֹדְנָה אֵצֶל הַפָּרוֹת עַל־
שְׂפַת הַיְאֹר: ד וַתֹּאכַלְנָה הַפָּרוֹת רָעוֹת
הַמַּרְאֶה וְדַקֹּת הַבָּשָׂר אֵת שֶׁבַע הַפָּרוֹת יְפֹת
הַמַּרְאֶה וְהַבְּרִיאֹת וַיִּיקַץ פַּרְעֹה: ה וַיִּישָׁן
וַיַּחֲלֹם שֵׁנִית וְהִנֵּה ׀ שֶׁבַע שִׁבֳּלִים עֹלוֹת
בְּקָנֶה אֶחָד בְּרִיאוֹת וְטֹבוֹת: ו וְהִנֵּה שֶׁבַע
שִׁבֳּלִים דַּקּוֹת וּשְׁדוּפֹת קָדִים צֹמְחוֹת
אַחֲרֵיהֶן: ז וַתִּבְלַעְנָה הַשִּׁבֳּלִים הַדַּקּוֹת אֵת
שֶׁבַע הַשִּׁבֳּלִים הַבְּרִיאוֹת וְהַמְּלֵאוֹת וַיִּיקַץ
פַּרְעֹה וְהִנֵּה חֲלוֹם: ח וַיְהִי בַבֹּקֶר וַתִּפָּעֶם
רוּחוֹ וַיִּשְׁלַח וַיִּקְרָא אֶת־כָּל־חַרְטֻמֵּי מִצְרַיִם
וְאֶת־כָּל־חֲכָמֶיהָ וַיְסַפֵּר פַּרְעֹה לָהֶם אֶת־
חֲלֹמוֹ וְאֵין־פּוֹתֵר אוֹתָם לְפַרְעֹה: ט וַיְדַבֵּר
שַׂר הַמַּשְׁקִים אֶת־פַּרְעֹה לֵאמֹר אֶת־חֲטָאַי
אֲנִי מַזְכִּיר הַיּוֹם: י פַּרְעֹה קָצַף עַל־עֲבָדָיו
וַיִּתֵּן אֹתִי בְּמִשְׁמַר בֵּית שַׂר הַטַּבָּחִים אֹתִי
וְאֵת שַׂר הָאֹפִים: יא וַנַּחַלְמָה חֲלוֹם בְּלַיְלָה
אֶחָד אֲנִי וָהוּא אִישׁ כְּפִתְרוֹן חֲלֹמוֹ חָלָמְנוּ:
יב וְשָׁם אִתָּנוּ נַעַר עִבְרִי עֶבֶד לְשַׂר הַטַּבָּחִים
וַנְּסַפֶּר־לוֹ וַיִּפְתָּר־לָנוּ אֵת חֲלֹמֹתֵינוּ

41/1. Pharaoh's dream.

Two years to the day after
the release of the Chamberlain of the Cupbearers — a
total of twelve years since
Joseph was imprisoned. At
this point, Joseph was almost thirty years old, Jacob
120, and Isaac 180. Isaac
died about this time.

The River, i.e., the Nile. The
Nile was venerated as god
of Egypt. Midrashically,
therefore, Pharaoh's position *'over'* the Nile suggests
that he haughtily imagined
himself superior to his god.

2. The symbolism is clear:
Since famine and abundance
in Egypt depend on the
overflow of the Nile, Pharaoh saw the cows — which
symbolize plowing [since
oxen are usually harnessed
for this purpose] — coming
up from the river (*Ramban*).

That the cows were *beautiful* alludes to years of plenty
when people look favorably
upon one another (*Rashi*).

3. *Seven other cows.* Symbolic of another season of
plowing (*Ralbag*).

Emerged after them out of
the River. Thus intimating
that famine would follow on
the heels of the plenty
(*Haamek Davar*).

4. *The ugly, gaunt cows*
then ate up the seven beautiful, robust cows. This symbolized that all the joy of
the years of plenty would be
forgotten during the famine
(*Rashi*).

5. The passage does not
read *and he dreamt* עוֹד,
more, but *he dreamt* שֵׁנִית, *a
second time*, to intimate
that it was essentially a single dream which was being
repeated (*Kli Yakar*).

Grain is a symbol of harvest
(*Ramban v.* 2); that one
stalk had seven ears indicated abundance
(*Rashbam*).

6. *Thin and scorched by the east wind.* This intimated that any attempt to harvest [symbolized, as noted, by the ears of grain], would be unsuccessful. All the new crops would be *scorched* by the east wind (*Ramban*).

8. The term חַרְטֻמִּים has the general connotation of *magician* or *soothsayer.* The translation *necromancer* follows *Rashi.*

There *were* interpreters, but no one who could interpret it satisfactorily *for Pharaoh.* [They offered interpretations applicable to him as an *individual,* but not as a *Pharaoh;* they failed to realize that the dream of a king must have implications for the nation as a whole] (*Rashi*).

9. The Chamberlain of the Cupbearers 'remembers' Joseph.

Seeing Pharaoh's anguished state, the chamberlain realized that he was putting himself in great danger by withholding his knowledge of someone who could interpret Pharaoh's dream correctly (*Midrash*).

Even though I will have to recall my sins to make this revelation, I will do it for the sake of your majesty — to tell you of my personal knowledge of an interpreter (*Radak; Ibn Ezra*).

12. Cursed are the wicked because even their favors are incomplete! The chamberlain recalled Joseph in the most disparaging terms. He called him נַעַר, *a youth* — ignorant and unfit for distinction; עִבְרִי, a *Hebrew* — a foreigner who does not even understand our language; עֶבֶד, a *slave* — and it is written in the laws of Egypt that a slave can neither be ruler nor wear the robes of a noble (*Rashi*).

41 ¹ It happened at the end of two years to the day: Pharaoh was dreaming that behold! he was standing over the River, ² when behold! out of the River there emerged seven cows, beautiful, and robust, and they were grazing in the marshland. ³ Then behold! seven other cows emerged after them out of the River — ugly and gaunt; and they stood next to the cows on the bank of the River. ⁴ The ugly, gaunt cows then ate up the seven beautiful, robust cows. And Pharaoh awoke. ⁵ He fell asleep and dreamt a second time, and behold! seven ears of grain were sprouting on a single stalk — healthy and good. ⁶And suddenly! seven ears, thin and scorched by the east wind, were growing after them. ⁷ Then the seven thin ears swallowed up the seven healthy and full ears. Pharaoh awoke and behold! it had been a dream.

⁸ And it was in the morning: His spirit was agitated so he sent and summoned all the necromancers of Egypt and all its wise men. Pharaoh related his dream to them but none could interpret them for Pharaoh.

⁹ Then the Chamberlain of the Cupbearers spoke up before Pharaoh, 'My transgressions do I mention today. ¹⁰ Pharaoh had once become incensed at his servants and placed me in the ward of the house of the Chamberlain of the Butchers — me and the Chamberlain of the Bakers. ¹¹ We dreamt a dream on the same night, I and he; each of us dreamt according to the interpretation of his dream. ¹² And there, with us, was a Hebrew youth, a slave of the Chamberlain of the Butchers. We related it to him, and he interpreted our dreams for us;

אִישׁ כַּחֲלֹמוֹ פָּתָר: יג וַיְהִי כַּאֲשֶׁר פָּתַר־לָנוּ כֵּן הָיָה אֹתִי הֵשִׁיב עַל־כַּנִּי וְאֹתוֹ תָלָה: יד וַיִּשְׁלַח פַּרְעֹה וַיִּקְרָא אֶת־יוֹסֵף וַיְרִיצֻהוּ מִן־הַבּוֹר וַיְגַלַּח וַיְחַלֵּף שִׂמְלֹתָיו וַיָּבֹא אֶל־פַּרְעֹה: שני טו וַיֹּאמֶר פַּרְעֹה אֶל־יוֹסֵף חֲלוֹם חָלַמְתִּי וּפֹתֵר אֵין אֹתוֹ וַאֲנִי שָׁמַעְתִּי עָלֶיךָ לֵאמֹר תִּשְׁמַע חֲלוֹם לִפְתֹּר אֹתוֹ: טז וַיַּעַן יוֹסֵף אֶת־פַּרְעֹה לֵאמֹר בִּלְעָדָי אֱלֹהִים יַעֲנֶה אֶת־שְׁלוֹם פַּרְעֹה: יז וַיְדַבֵּר פַּרְעֹה אֶל־יוֹסֵף בַּחֲלֹמִי הִנְנִי עֹמֵד עַל־שְׂפַת הַיְאֹר: יח וְהִנֵּה מִן־הַיְאֹר עֹלֹת שֶׁבַע פָּרוֹת בְּרִיאוֹת בָּשָׂר וִיפֹת תֹּאַר וַתִּרְעֶינָה בָּאָחוּ: יט וְהִנֵּה שֶׁבַע פָּרוֹת אֲחֵרוֹת עֹלוֹת אַחֲרֵיהֶן דַּלּוֹת וְרָעוֹת תֹּאַר מְאֹד וְרַקּוֹת בָּשָׂר לֹא־רָאִיתִי כָהֵנָּה בְּכָל־אֶרֶץ מִצְרַיִם לָרֹעַ: כ וַתֹּאכַלְנָה הַפָּרוֹת הָרַקּוֹת וְהָרָעוֹת אֵת שֶׁבַע הַפָּרוֹת הָרִאשֹׁנוֹת הַבְּרִיאֹת: כא וַתָּבֹאנָה אֶל־קִרְבֶּנָה וְלֹא נוֹדַע כִּי־בָאוּ אֶל־קִרְבֶּנָה וּמַרְאֵיהֶן רַע כַּאֲשֶׁר בַּתְּחִלָּה וָאִיקָץ: כב וָאֵרֶא בַּחֲלֹמִי וְהִנֵּה שֶׁבַע שִׁבֳּלִים עֹלֹת בְּקָנֶה אֶחָד מְלֵאֹת וְטֹבוֹת: כג וְהִנֵּה שֶׁבַע שִׁבֳּלִים צְנֻמוֹת דַּקּוֹת שְׁדֻפוֹת קָדִים צֹמְחוֹת אַחֲרֵיהֶם: כד וַתִּבְלַעְןָ הַשִּׁבֳּלִים הַדַּקֹּת אֵת שֶׁבַע הַשִּׁבֳּלִים הַטֹּבוֹת וָאֹמַר אֶל־הַחַרְטֻמִּים וְאֵין מַגִּיד לִי: כה וַיֹּאמֶר יוֹסֵף אֶל־פַּרְעֹה חֲלוֹם פַּרְעֹה אֶחָד הוּא אֵת אֲשֶׁר הָאֱלֹהִים עֹשֶׂה

14. According to the traditional chronology [see *Rosh Hashanah* 10b], Joseph was released from prison on Rosh Hashanah in the year 2230 from Creation.

In *Torah Anthology*, R' Aryeh Kaplan [note 21] calculates accordingly that 'the king of Egypt in the time of Joseph was most probably Amenhotep I of the eighteenth dynasty who ruled 1545-1525 B.C.E.' [2217-2237 from Creation].

He was rushed — in the manner of every case of Divine salvation which comes hastily and unexpectedly. Similarly, the coming of the Messiah will be sudden and hasty [see *Malachi* 3:1] (*Sforno*).

19-21. *R' Hirsch* infers from Pharaoh's elaborate description of the bad cows that they made a far stronger impression on him than did the good ones. Pharaoh stresses bad qualities in order to emphasize the impression they made on him.

19. In repeating the dream, Pharaoh fails to mention that the emaciated cows emerged מִן הַיְאֹר, *from the River* (see v. 3). Since Egypt considered the Nile a god, Pharaoh avoided the connotation that something ugly and auguring misfortune could emanate from the gods (*Kli Yakar; Akeidah; Bereishis Rabbasi*).

24. Pharaoh did not mention that he had summoned the *wise men* as well. He was not surprised that the wise men — who rely on logic — could not fathom the inner symbolisms of his dream. He was dismayed, rather, that the necromancers — who could use *'magic'* to decipher the dream — were also unable to interpret it (*Haamek Davar*).

25. *The dream of Pharaoh is a single one.* The dreams complement each other: They are two components of a cogent whole. The cows represent plowing, and the ears of grain represent reaping (*Abarbanel*).

he interpreted for each in accordance with his dream. [13] And it was that just as he interpreted for us so did it happen: me he restored to my post and him he hanged.'

[14] So Pharaoh sent and summoned Joseph, and he was rushed from the dungeon. He shaved and changed his clothes, and he came to Pharaoh. [15] And Pharaoh said to Joseph, 'I dreamt a dream, but no one can interpret it. Now I heard it said of you that you comprehend a dream to interpret it.'

[16] Joseph answered Pharaoh saying, 'That is beyond me. It is God Who will respond with Pharaoh's welfare.'

[17] Then Pharaoh said to Joseph, 'In my dream, behold! I was standing upon the bank of the River. [18] And behold, out of the River there emerged seven cows, robust and handsome, and they were grazing in the marshland. [19] Suddenly, seven other cows emerged after them — scrawny and of very inferior form and of emaciated flesh; I have never seen inferiority like theirs in all the land of Egypt. [20] And the emaciated and inferior cows ate up the first seven healthy cows. [21] Thus they came inside them. But it was not apparent that they had come inside them, for their appearance remained as inferior as at first. Then I awoke. [22] I then saw in my dream: Behold! seven ears of grain were sprouting on a single stalk — full and good. [23] And suddenly! seven ears of grain, withered, thin and scorched by the east wind were growing after them. [24] Then the thin ears of grain swallowed up the seven good ears. I said this to the necromancers, but no one could explain it to me.'

[25] Joseph said to Pharaoh, 'The dream of Pharaoh is a single one. What God is about to do,

הִגִּיד לְפַרְעֹה: כּוֹ שֶׁבַע פָּרֹת הַטֹּבֹת שֶׁבַע שָׁנִים
הֵנָּה וְשֶׁבַע הַשִּׁבֳּלִים הַטֹּבֹת שֶׁבַע שָׁנִים הֵנָּה
חֲלוֹם אֶחָד הוּא: כּז וְשֶׁבַע הַפָּרוֹת הָרַקּוֹת
וְהָרָעֹת הָעֹלֹת אַחֲרֵיהֶן שֶׁבַע שָׁנִים הֵנָּה
וְשֶׁבַע הַשִּׁבֳּלִים הָרֵקוֹת שְׁדֻפוֹת הַקָּדִים יִהְיוּ
שֶׁבַע שְׁנֵי רָעָב: כּח הוּא הַדָּבָר אֲשֶׁר דִּבַּרְתִּי
אֶל־פַּרְעֹה אֲשֶׁר הָאֱלֹהִים עֹשֶׂה הֶרְאָה אֶת־
פַּרְעֹה: כּט הִנֵּה שֶׁבַע שָׁנִים בָּאוֹת שָׂבָע גָּדוֹל
בְּכָל־אֶרֶץ מִצְרָיִם: ל וְקָמוּ שֶׁבַע שְׁנֵי רָעָב
אַחֲרֵיהֶן וְנִשְׁכַּח כָּל־הַשָּׂבָע בְּאֶרֶץ מִצְרָיִם
וְכִלָּה הָרָעָב אֶת־הָאָרֶץ: לא וְלֹא־יִוָּדַע הַשָּׂבָע
בָּאָרֶץ מִפְּנֵי הָרָעָב הַהוּא אַחֲרֵי־כֵן כִּי־כָבֵד
הוּא מְאֹד: לב וְעַל הִשָּׁנוֹת הַחֲלוֹם אֶל־פַּרְעֹה
פַּעֲמָיִם כִּי־נָכוֹן הַדָּבָר מֵעִם הָאֱלֹהִים וּמְמַהֵר
הָאֱלֹהִים לַעֲשֹׂתוֹ: לג וְעַתָּה יֵרֶא פַרְעֹה אִישׁ
נָבוֹן וְחָכָם וִישִׁיתֵהוּ עַל־אֶרֶץ מִצְרָיִם:
לד יַעֲשֶׂה פַרְעֹה וְיַפְקֵד פְּקִדִים עַל־הָאָרֶץ
וְחִמֵּשׁ אֶת־אֶרֶץ מִצְרַיִם בְּשֶׁבַע שְׁנֵי הַשָּׂבָע:
לה וְיִקְבְּצוּ אֶת־כָּל־אֹכֶל הַשָּׁנִים הַטֹּבֹת
הַבָּאֹת הָאֵלֶּה וְיִצְבְּרוּ־בָר תַּחַת יַד־פַּרְעֹה
אֹכֶל בֶּעָרִים וְשָׁמָרוּ: לו וְהָיָה הָאֹכֶל לְפִקָּדוֹן
לָאָרֶץ לְשֶׁבַע שְׁנֵי הָרָעָב אֲשֶׁר תִּהְיֶיןָ בְּאֶרֶץ
מִצְרָיִם וְלֹא־תִכָּרֵת הָאָרֶץ בָּרָעָב: לז וַיִּיטַב
הַדָּבָר בְּעֵינֵי פַרְעֹה וּבְעֵינֵי כָּל־עֲבָדָיו:
לח וַיֹּאמֶר פַּרְעֹה אֶל־עֲבָדָיו הֲנִמְצָא כָזֶה אִישׁ

26. *The seven good cows are seven years, and the good ears are seven years.* I.e., they represent the *same* seven years, not a total of fourteen. The dream was repeated to indicate that the matter has been set in motion and is about to happen, as Joseph expressly told Pharaoh in v. 32 (*Rashi*).

29. Having outlined the dream's general interpretation, Joseph now proceeds to interpret it in detail.

This passage implies that the *abundance* was only *in the land of Egypt*, whereas no such limitation is made regarding the *famine*. That the famine would extend to other lands may be indicated by Pharaoh's vision that the good cows remained in the reed grass near the river *in Egypt* [v. 2], whereas the inferior cows wandered away, implying that the famine would spread beyond the borders of Egypt (*Ramban v. 2*).

30. The 'ravaging' refers to areas [even in Egypt] which will lack the foresight or ability to prepare against the famine — they will be utterly consumed. This was symbolized in the dream by the inferior stalks which were devoid of kernels (*Haamek Davar*).

33. Joseph's plan.

Joseph must have viewed as providential the sudden and dramatic manner in which he was brought before Pharaoh. He still had faith in the fulfillment of his adolescent dreams [37:5-9] and felt that the long-awaited turning-point in his destiny had finally arrived. If so, he had to utilize this unique opportunity. He did so by offering his unsolicited counsel. His advice was so relevant and wise that Pharaoh was enormously impressed (*R' Munk*).

34. The translation of חֹמֵשׁ derives from the Hebrew word חָמֵשׁ, *five*, and the verse means that Pharaoh should buy a *fifth* of the land of Egypt during the seven years of abundance.

Along similar lines, *Rashbam* and *Radak* observe that this was a proposal that Pharaoh double the usual one-tenth tax on grain, and have his overseers collect a *fifth* of all the produce for the royal granary during that period.

35. *And let them gather all the food of those approaching good years.* As a levy from the landowners. These were exacted from them even against their will (*Rashbam*).

As culled from the commentators, this passage is telling us that the regional overseers should store up the winnowed and sifted fine grain; grain that could be stored without rotting, and this should be placed directly under Pharaoh's own 'hand' — i.e., under his personal control and stored in his granaries (*Rashi*). Every city is to have its own royal granaries. This will save transport costs and will reassure the citizens that their food is not being taken for the benefit of others (*Tur; Ralbag; R' Bachya*).

37. The interpretation is well received.

38. Joseph is appointed viceroy of Egypt.

Pharaoh realized that only Joseph could properly implement and administer the master plan for national salvation. Therefore, he sought means to make an exception to the law that a slave could not be appointed to the aristocracy.

He has told to Pharaoh: ²⁶ The seven good cows are seven years, and the good ears are seven years. it is one dream. ²⁷ Now, the seven emaciated and bad cows who emerged after them are seven years as are the seven emaciated ears scorched by the east wind. There shall be seven years of famine. ²⁸ It is the matter that I have spoken to Pharaoh: What God is about to do He has shown to Pharaoh.

²⁹ 'Behold! seven years are coming — a great abundance throughout all the land of Egypt. ³⁰ Then seven years of famine will arise after them; and all the abundance in the land of Egypt will be forgotten. The famine will ravage the land. ³¹ And the abundance will be unknown in the land in the face of the subsequent famine — for it will be terribly severe. ³² As for the repetition of the dream to Pharaoh twice, it is because the matter stands ready before God and God is hastening to accomplish it.

³³ 'Now let Pharaoh seek out a discerning and wise man and set him over the land of Egypt. ³⁴ Let Pharaoh proceed and let him appoint overseers on the land, and he shall prepare the land of Egypt during the seven years of abundance. ³⁵ And let them gather all the food of those approaching good years; let them amass fine grain under Pharaoh's authority for food in the cities, and safeguard it. ³⁶ The food will be a reserve for the land against the seven years of famine which will befall the land of Egypt, so that the land will not perish in the famine.'

³⁷ The matter appeared good to Pharaoh and to all his servants. ³⁸ Pharaoh said to his servants, 'Could we find another like him — a man

כָּזֶ֔ה אִ֕ישׁ אֲשֶׁ֛ר ר֥וּחַ אֱלֹהִ֖ים בּֽוֹ: שלישי
לט וַיֹּ֤אמֶר פַּרְעֹה֙ אֶל־יוֹסֵ֔ף אַחֲרֵ֨י הוֹדִ֤יעַ
אֱלֹהִים֙ אֽוֹתְךָ֙ אֶת־כָּל־זֹ֔את אֵין־נָב֥וֹן וְחָכָ֖ם
כָּמֽוֹךָ: מ אַתָּה֙ תִּהְיֶ֣ה עַל־בֵּיתִ֔י וְעַל־פִּ֖יךָ יִשַּׁ֣ק
כָּל־עַמִּ֑י רַ֥ק הַכִּסֵּ֖א אֶגְדַּ֥ל מִמֶּֽךָּ: מא וַיֹּ֥אמֶר
פַּרְעֹ֖ה אֶל־יוֹסֵ֑ף רְאֵה֙ נָתַ֣תִּי אֹֽתְךָ֔ עַ֖ל כָּל־
אֶ֥רֶץ מִצְרָֽיִם: מב וַיָּ֨סַר פַּרְעֹ֤ה אֶת־טַבַּעְתּוֹ֙
מֵעַ֣ל יָד֔וֹ וַיִּתֵּ֥ן אֹתָ֖הּ עַל־יַ֣ד יוֹסֵ֑ף וַיַּלְבֵּ֤שׁ אֹתוֹ֙
בִּגְדֵי־שֵׁ֔שׁ וַיָּ֛שֶׂם רְבִ֥ד הַזָּהָ֖ב עַל־צַוָּארֽוֹ:
מג וַיַּרְכֵּ֣ב אֹת֗וֹ בְּמִרְכֶּ֤בֶת הַמִּשְׁנֶה֙ אֲשֶׁר־ל֔וֹ
וַיִּקְרְא֥וּ לְפָנָ֖יו אַבְרֵ֑ךְ וְנָת֣וֹן אֹת֔וֹ עַ֖ל כָּל־אֶ֥רֶץ
מִצְרָֽיִם: מד וַיֹּ֧אמֶר פַּרְעֹ֛ה אֶל־יוֹסֵ֖ף אֲנִ֣י פַרְעֹ֑ה
וּבִלְעָדֶ֗יךָ לֹֽא־יָרִ֨ים אִ֧ישׁ אֶת־יָד֛וֹ וְאֶת־רַגְל֖וֹ
בְּכָל־אֶ֥רֶץ מִצְרָֽיִם: מה וַיִּקְרָ֨א פַרְעֹ֥ה שֵׁם־יוֹסֵף֮
צָֽפְנַ֣ת פַּעְנֵחַ֒ וַיִּתֶּן־ל֣וֹ אֶת־אָֽסְנַ֗ת בַּת־פּ֥וֹטִי
פֶ֛רַע כֹּהֵ֥ן אֹ֖ן לְאִשָּׁ֑ה וַיֵּצֵ֥א יוֹסֵ֖ף עַל־אֶ֥רֶץ
מִצְרָֽיִם: מו וְיוֹסֵף֙ בֶּן־שְׁלֹשִׁ֣ים שָׁנָ֔ה בְּעָמְד֕וֹ
לִפְנֵ֖י פַּרְעֹ֣ה מֶֽלֶךְ־מִצְרָ֑יִם וַיֵּצֵ֤א יוֹסֵף֙ מִלִּפְנֵ֣י
פַרְעֹ֔ה וַיַּֽעֲבֹ֖ר בְּכָל־אֶ֥רֶץ מִצְרָֽיִם: מז וַתַּ֣עַשׂ
הָאָ֔רֶץ בְּשֶׁ֖בַע שְׁנֵ֣י הַשָּׂבָ֑ע לִקְמָצִֽים: מח וַיִּקְבֹּ֞ץ
אֶת־כָּל־אֹ֣כֶל ׀ שֶׁ֣בַע שָׁנִ֗ים אֲשֶׁ֤ר הָיוּ֙ בְּאֶ֣רֶץ
מִצְרַ֔יִם וַיִּתֶּן־אֹ֖כֶל בֶּֽעָרִ֑ים אֹ֧כֶל שְׂדֵֽה־הָעִ֛יר
אֲשֶׁ֥ר סְבִֽיבֹתֶ֖יהָ נָתַ֥ן בְּתוֹכָֽהּ: מט וַיִּצְבֹּ֨ר יוֹסֵ֥ף
בָּ֛ר כְּח֥וֹל הַיָּ֖ם הַרְבֵּ֣ה מְאֹ֑ד עַ֛ד כִּֽי־חָדַ֥ל לִסְפֹּ֖ר
כִּי־אֵ֥ין מִסְפָּֽר: נ וּלְיוֹסֵ֤ף יֻלַּד֙ שְׁנֵ֣י בָנִ֔ים בְּטֶ֣רֶם

39. After his courtiers acknowledged that Joseph was indeed endowed with God-given talents, Pharaoh turned to Joseph and addressed him directly (*Akeidah; Abarbanel*).

42. *Ramban* explains that the king's ring contained his royal seal [cf. *Esther* 8:8]. The ring symbolized that Joseph would henceforth be the leader of the entire government and would have the authority to seal decrees, as he desired.

43. *And they proclaimed before him: 'Avrech'!* I.e., as he rode on the chariot, the servants called out before him 'Avrech'! (*Rashi*).

Avrech is a composite of two words: אַב, *father,* [i.e., counselor; mentor] to the *rech,* which means king in Aramaic (*Rashi; Onkelos*).

Av (father) or *ab,* though *rach* (tender) in years (*Midrash*).

44. אֲנִי פַרְעֹה — *I am Pharaoh.* I.e., as king, I have the authority to issue decrees for my kingdom and therefore I decree that : *Without you no one may lift,* etc. Alternatively: *I remain the king, but without your permission no one shall lift,* etc. It is similar in meaning to [v. 40]: *Only by the throne shall I outrank you,* but Pharaoh reiterated it as he gave Joseph the ring (*Rashi*).

45. Appointees to a high position were customarily assigned a name commensurate with their new eminence (*Rashbam*).

Tzafnas Pane'ach. Rashi and Rashbam interpret: מְפָרֵשׁ הַצְּפוּנוֹת, *'he who explains what is hidden.' There is no other example of the word Pane'ach in Scripture.*

Poti Phera, Chief of On, is identical with Potiphar [see above 37:36].

46. The knowledge of Joseph's age at this juncture points to the hand of Providence. Were it not for his God-given wisdom and grace, one so young could never have risen to the highest position in a great land (*Abarbanel*).

47. The seven years of abundance. Joseph's plan is implemented.

48-49. The execution of the plan outlined in verses 35-36.

49. *R' David Feinstein* explains that such a policy of accumulation generally has a goal of gathering a predetermined minimum amount. Once that goal has been reached, it is no longer necessary to be as scrupulous in counting future accumulations. This, then, is the intent of our verse: The stores of grain became so huge that it was no longer necessary to keep count; there would surely be more than enough for every conceivable exigency.

50. Joseph's children: Manasseh and Ephraim.

To be the only Jew in Egypt, and to be married to the daughter of an idolatrous priest, yet to raise children who remain the model after whom Jewish parents bless their children — *may God make you like Ephraim and Manasseh* (48:20) — is no small privilege.

in whom is the spirit of God?'

³⁹ Then Pharaoh said to Joseph, 'Since God has informed you of all this, there can be no one so discerning and wise as you. ⁴⁰ You shall be in charge of my palace and by your command shall all my people be sustained. Only by the throne shall I outrank you.'

⁴¹ Then Pharaoh said to Joseph, 'See — I have placed you in charge of all the land of Egypt.' ⁴² And Pharaoh removed his ring from his hand and put it on Joseph's hand. He then had him dressed in garments of fine linen and he placed the gold chain upon his neck. ⁴³ He also had him ride in his second royal chariot and they proclaimed before him: 'Avrech!' Thus, he placed him in charge of all the land of Egypt.

⁴⁴ Pharaoh said to Joseph, 'I am Pharaoh. And without you no man may lift up his hand or foot in all the land of Egypt.' ⁴⁵ Pharaoh named Joseph Tzafnas Pane'ach, and he gave him Asenath daughter of Poti Phera, Chief of On, for a wife. Thus Joseph emerged in charge of the land of Egypt. ⁴⁶ Now Joseph was thirty years old when he stood before Pharaoh king of Egypt. Joseph left Pharaoh's presence and he passed through the entire land of Egypt.

⁴⁷ The earth produced during the seven years of abundance by the handfuls. ⁴⁸ He gathered all food of the seven years that came to pass in Egypt, and he placed food in the cities — the food of the field around each city he placed within it. ⁴⁹ Joseph amassed grain like the sand of the sea in great abundance until he ceased taking stock, for there was no number.

⁵⁰ Now to Joseph were born two sons — before

תָּב֗וֹא שְׁנַ֣ת הָרָעָב֒ אֲשֶׁ֣ר יָֽלְדָה־לּוֹ֙ אָֽסְנַ֔ת
בַּת־פּ֥וֹטִי פֶ֖רַע כֹּהֵ֣ן אֽוֹן: נא וַיִּקְרָ֥א יוֹסֵ֛ף
אֶת־שֵׁ֥ם הַבְּכ֖וֹר מְנַשֶּׁ֑ה כִּֽי־נַשַּׁ֤נִי אֱלֹהִים֙
אֶת־כָּל־עֲמָלִ֔י וְאֵ֖ת כָּל־בֵּ֥ית אָבִֽי: נב וְאֵ֗ת שֵׁ֤ם
הַשֵּׁנִי֙ קָרָ֣א אֶפְרָ֑יִם כִּֽי־הִפְרַ֥נִי אֱלֹהִ֖ים בְּאֶ֥רֶץ
עָנְיִֽי: רביעי נג וַתִּכְלֶ֕ינָה שֶׁ֖בַע שְׁנֵ֣י הַשָּׂבָ֑ע אֲשֶׁ֥ר
הָיָ֖ה בְּאֶ֥רֶץ מִצְרָֽיִם: נד וַתְּחִלֶּ֜ינָה שֶׁ֤בַע שְׁנֵ֤י
הָֽרָעָב֙ לָב֔וֹא כַּֽאֲשֶׁ֖ר אָמַ֣ר יוֹסֵ֑ף וַיְהִ֤י רָעָב֙
בְּכָל־הָ֣אֲרָצ֔וֹת וּבְכָל־אֶ֥רֶץ מִצְרַ֖יִם הָ֥יָה לָֽחֶם:
נה וַתִּרְעַב֙ כָּל־אֶ֣רֶץ מִצְרַ֔יִם וַיִּצְעַ֥ק הָעָ֛ם אֶל־
פַּרְעֹ֖ה לַלָּ֑חֶם וַיֹּ֨אמֶר פַּרְעֹ֤ה לְכָל־מִצְרַ֨יִם֙ לְכ֣וּ
אֶל־יוֹסֵ֔ף אֲשֶׁר־יֹאמַ֥ר לָכֶ֖ם תַּֽעֲשֽׂוּ: נו וְהָֽרָעָ֣ב
הָיָ֔ה עַ֖ל כָּל־פְּנֵ֣י הָאָ֑רֶץ וַיִּפְתַּ֨ח יוֹסֵ֜ף אֶֽת־כָּל־
אֲשֶׁ֤ר בָּהֶם֙ וַיִּשְׁבֹּ֣ר לְמִצְרַ֔יִם וַיֶּֽחֱזַ֥ק הָֽרָעָ֖ב
בְּאֶ֥רֶץ מִצְרָֽיִם: נז וְכָל־הָאָ֨רֶץ֙ בָּ֣אוּ מִצְרַ֔יְמָה
לִשְׁבֹּ֖ר אֶל־יוֹסֵ֑ף כִּֽי־חָזַ֥ק הָֽרָעָ֖ב בְּכָל־הָאָֽרֶץ:
מב א וַיַּ֣רְא יַֽעֲקֹ֔ב כִּ֥י יֶשׁ־שֶׁ֖בֶר בְּמִצְרָ֑יִם וַיֹּ֤אמֶר
יַֽעֲקֹב֙ לְבָנָ֔יו לָ֥מָּה תִּתְרָאֽוּ: ב וַיֹּ֕אמֶר הִנֵּ֣ה
שָׁמַ֔עְתִּי כִּ֥י יֶשׁ־שֶׁ֖בֶר בְּמִצְרָ֑יִם רְדוּ־שָׁ֨מָּה֙
וְשִׁבְרוּ־לָ֣נוּ מִשָּׁ֔ם וְנִֽחְיֶ֖ה וְלֹ֥א נָמֽוּת: ג וַיֵּֽרְד֥וּ
אֲחֵֽי־יוֹסֵ֖ף עֲשָׂרָ֑ה לִשְׁבֹּ֥ר בָּ֖ר מִמִּצְרָֽיִם:
ד וְאֶת־בִּנְיָמִין֙ אֲחִ֣י יוֹסֵ֔ף לֹֽא־שָׁלַ֥ח יַֽעֲקֹ֖ב
אֶת־אֶחָ֑יו כִּ֣י אָמַ֔ר פֶּן־יִקְרָאֶ֖נּוּ אָסֽוֹן: ה וַיָּבֹ֨אוּ֙
בְּנֵ֣י יִשְׂרָאֵ֔ל לִשְׁבֹּ֖ר בְּת֣וֹךְ הַבָּאִ֑ים כִּֽי־הָיָ֥ה
הָֽרָעָ֖ב בְּאֶ֥רֶץ כְּנָֽעַן: ו וְיוֹסֵ֗ף ה֚וּא הַשַּׁלִּ֣יט עַל־

51. *Manasseh.* [Hebrew: *Menasheh.*] Lit., He Who causes to forget (R' Shmuel ben Chofni Gaon).

For he said, 'God has made me forget [Hebrew: *nashah,* in assonance with *Menasheh*] *all my hardship'* [lit., *toil*].

Thus, in effect, Manasseh's name was an acknowledgement that God had given Joseph the fortitude to comply with the solemn oath [see 37:28] against contacting Jacob, and to allow Providence to take its course. For although Joseph was obligated by the *mitzvah* of honoring his father to contact him, nevertheless the Will of God as evidenced by the prophetic dream inspired him to subordinate his own wishes to those of his Creator, and God replaced Joseph's constant thoughts of his father with other thoughts.

52. *Ephraim* [i.e, fruitful, from the Hebrew *pri*].

For he said, God has made me fruitful [Hebrew: *hifrani* from פְּרִי, *fruit*, in assonance with *Ephraim*].

53. The onset of the famine.

55. *When all the land of Egypt hungered.* For all the stored grain rotted except that which Joseph had stored up.

Joseph demands that the Egyptians be circumcised.

'Go to Joseph. Whatever he tells you, do.' [Pharaoh had to give them this firm order because] Joseph demanded them to [first] be circumcised [or else he would not provide them with grain] (*Rashi*; bracketed additions are from *Tanchuma*).

Joseph, in his prophetic wisdom, was preparing for the eventual descent of his brothers to Egypt. He knew that gentiles mock Jews because they are circumcised. By making the Egyptians circumcise themselves, he made it impossible for them to ridicule the circumcised Jews (*Yafeh Toar*).

42/1. The brothers in Eygpt.

It is now the second year of the famine (*Seder Olam*). Although his family still has provisions, Jacob is concerned and dispatches his sons to Egypt.

Why do you make yourselves conspicuous? [Lit., seen.] Why do you show yourselves as having plenty [to eat]? Such behavior will bring the envy and ill will on the part of the families of Ishmael and Esau (*Taanis* 10b; *Rashi*).

Do not travel with food in your hands lest you cause ill feelings. And do not all enter [Egypt] through one gate for fear of the evil eye [for someone might feel envy that one man should be blessed with ten such sons] (*Midrash*).

2. Jacob did not use the verb לְכוּ, *go*, but רְדוּ [*go down*], thereby alluding to the 210 years that they would be enslaved in Egypt. [The numerical value of the word רְדוּ is 210: ר = 200; ד = 4; וּ = 6] (*Rashi*).

4. It was destined from Above that Benjamin — who had not participated in the sale of Joseph — not accompany them so that he would be spared their tribulations in Egypt. Although he suffered with them when he joined them on their second trip, he was compensated for this by having the intense joy of meeting Joseph (*Oznaim LaTorah*).

the year of famine was to set in — whom Asenath daughter of Poti Phera, Chief of On, bore to him. ⁵¹ Joseph named the firstborn Manasseh for, 'God has made me forget all my hardship and all my father's household.' ⁵² And the second son he named Ephraim for, 'God has made me fruitful in the land of my suffering.'

⁵³ The seven years of abundance that came to pass in the land of Egypt ended. ⁵⁴ And the seven years of famine began approaching just as Joseph had said. There was famine in all the lands, but in all the land of Egypt there was bread.

⁵⁵ When all the land of Egypt hungered, the people cried out to Pharaoh for bread. So Pharaoh said to all of Egypt, 'Go to Joseph. Whatever he tells you, do.' ⁵⁶ When the famine spread over all the face of the earth, Joseph opened all the containers and sold provisions to Egypt. And the famine became severe in the land of Egypt. ⁵⁷ All the earth came to Egypt unto Joseph to buy provisions, for the famine had become severe in all the earth.

42. ¹ Jacob perceived that there were provisions in Egypt. So Jacob said to his sons, 'Why do you make yourselves conspicuous?' ² And he said, 'Behold, I have heard that there are provisions in Egypt. Go down there and purchase for us from there, that we may live and not die.' ³ So Joseph's brothers — ten of them — went down to buy grain from Egypt. ⁴ But Benjamin, Joseph's brother, Jacob did not send along with his brothers, for he said, 'Lest disaster befall him.' ⁵ So the sons of Israel come to buy provisions among the arrivals, for the famine prevailed in the land of Canaan.

⁶ Now Joseph, he was the viceroy over the

הָאָ֗רֶץ ה֤וּא הַמַּשְׁבִּיר֙ לְכָל־עַ֣ם הָאָ֔רֶץ וַיָּבֹ֙אוּ֙
אֲחֵ֣י יוֹסֵ֔ף וַיִּשְׁתַּחֲווּ־ל֥וֹ אַפַּ֖יִם אָֽרְצָה: ז וַיַּ֥רְא
יוֹסֵ֖ף אֶת־אֶחָ֑יו וַיַּכִּרֵ֑ם וַיִּתְנַכֵּ֤ר אֲלֵיהֶם֙ וַיְדַבֵּ֨ר
אִתָּ֜ם קָשׁ֗וֹת וַיֹּ֤אמֶר אֲלֵהֶם֙ מֵאַ֣יִן בָּאתֶ֔ם
וַיֹּ֣אמְר֔וּ מֵאֶ֥רֶץ כְּנַ֖עַן לִשְׁבָּר־אֹֽכֶל: ח וַיַּכֵּ֥ר יוֹסֵ֖ף
אֶת־אֶחָ֑יו וְהֵ֖ם לֹ֥א הִכִּרֻֽהוּ: ט וַיִּזְכֹּ֣ר יוֹסֵ֔ף אֵ֚ת
הַחֲלֹמ֔וֹת אֲשֶׁ֥ר חָלַ֖ם לָהֶ֑ם וַיֹּ֤אמֶר אֲלֵהֶם֙
מְרַגְּלִ֣ים אַתֶּ֔ם לִרְא֛וֹת אֶת־עֶרְוַ֥ת הָאָ֖רֶץ
בָּאתֶֽם: י וַיֹּאמְר֥וּ אֵלָ֖יו לֹ֣א אֲדֹנִ֑י וַעֲבָדֶ֥יךָ בָּ֖אוּ
לִשְׁבָּר־אֹֽכֶל: יא כֻּלָּ֕נוּ בְּנֵ֥י אִישׁ־אֶחָ֖ד נָ֑חְנוּ
כֵּנִ֣ים אֲנַ֔חְנוּ לֹא־הָי֥וּ עֲבָדֶ֖יךָ מְרַגְּלִֽים:
יב וַיֹּ֖אמֶר אֲלֵהֶ֑ם לֹ֕א כִּֽי־עֶרְוַ֥ת הָאָ֖רֶץ בָּאתֶ֥ם
לִרְאֽוֹת: יג וַיֹּאמְר֗וּ שְׁנֵ֣ים עָשָׂר֩ עֲבָדֶ֨יךָ אַחִ֣ים ׀
אֲנַ֜חְנוּ בְּנֵ֧י אִישׁ־אֶחָ֛ד בְּאֶ֥רֶץ כְּנַ֖עַן וְהִנֵּ֨ה
הַקָּטֹ֤ן אֶת־אָבִ֙ינוּ֙ הַיּ֔וֹם וְהָאֶחָ֖ד אֵינֶֽנּוּ:
יד וַיֹּ֥אמֶר אֲלֵהֶ֖ם יוֹסֵ֑ף ה֗וּא אֲשֶׁ֤ר דִּבַּ֙רְתִּי֙
אֲלֵכֶ֣ם לֵאמֹ֔ר מְרַגְּלִ֖ים אַתֶּֽם: טו בְּזֹ֖את תִּבָּחֵ֑נוּ
חֵ֣י פַרְעֹ֔ה אִם־תֵּצְא֣וּ מִזֶּ֔ה כִּ֧י אִם־בְּב֛וֹא
אֲחִיכֶ֥ם הַקָּטֹ֖ן הֵֽנָּה: טז שִׁלְח֨וּ מִכֶּ֣ם אֶחָד֮ וְיִקַּ֣ח
אֶת־אֲחִיכֶם֒ וְאַתֶּם֙ הֵאָ֣סְר֔וּ וְיִבָּֽחֲנוּ֙ דִּבְרֵיכֶ֔ם
הַֽאֱמֶ֖ת אִתְּכֶ֑ם וְאִם־לֹ֕א חֵ֣י פַרְעֹ֔ה כִּ֥י מְרַגְּלִ֖ים
אַתֶּֽם: יז וַיֶּאֱסֹ֥ף אֹתָ֛ם אֶל־מִשְׁמָ֖ר שְׁלֹ֥שֶׁת
יָמִֽים: יח וַיֹּ֨אמֶר אֲלֵהֶ֤ם יוֹסֵף֙ בַּיּ֣וֹם הַשְּׁלִישִׁ֔י
זֹ֥את עֲשׂ֖וּ וִֽחְי֑וּ אֶת־הָאֱלֹהִ֖ים אֲנִ֥י יָרֵֽא:
חמישי יט אִם־כֵּנִ֣ים אַתֶּ֔ם אֲחִיכֶ֣ם אֶחָ֔ד יֵאָסֵ֖ר

7. Joseph recognizes his brothers.

8. They did not recognize him was because he was bearded but when they had last seen him [twenty-two years earlier when he was seventeen] he had no beard [Kesubos 27b] (Rashi).

9. Since Benjamin was absent at this first meeting, Joseph arranged a scheme to bring him to Egypt so the first dream could be fulfilled. Only then could he reveal his true identity and bid them to summon Jacob so the second dream could be fulfilled (Ramban).

Ramban emphasizes that were it not for such considerations, Joseph would have been guilty of a serious sin in inflicting anxiety on Jacob, first by sending his brothers home without Simeon and then by demanding that Benjamin be brought to him. He would surely have identified himself immediately and spared his father pain and worry. Similarly, the anxiety Joseph later inflicted upon them by hiding the goblet in Benjamin's sack was for the sole purpose of testing their love for Benjamin before allowing him to travel with them.

11. All of us — sons of one man are we. The Divine Spirit was enkindled within them and they unwittingly included Joseph in their statement by saying are we — including him; all of us are the sons of one father (Midrash; Rashi).

12. 'It cannot be as you say. If you are brothers traveling together, you should have entered the country together and not by ten different gates. Therefore, since you entered by different gates, you must be involved in some conspiracy' (Rashi; Ramban).

13. *We, your servants, are twelve brothers.* According to *R' Avraham ben HaRambam,* citing his grandfather, R' Maimon, their response did not counter the spying charge, but was in answer to another, unrecorded question Joseph must have asked about their family. Such additional dialogue is alluded to by the brothers in their recapitulation of their adventures to Jacob, later in 43:7. In usual Scriptural style, the Torah did not elaborate on the dialogue.

14. Joseph pretends to find their protests of innocence unconvincing, and reemphasizes his firm belief in their guilt. As the supreme viceroy of Egypt, he does not have to justify his accusations rationally; it suffices that such is his whim.

15. If your statement regarding a youngest brother can be verified, I will believe everything else you said as well (*B'chor Shor*).

By Pharaoh's life. Lit., *the life of Pharaoh,* i.e., if Pharaoh shall live. This was a formula for a kind of oath, as if to say, 'I swear by Pharaoh's life' (*Gur Aryeh*). Whenever Joseph swore falsely [as he did now when his oath was not intended seriously for he *did* release them before they brought their youngest brother to Egypt (see *v.* 19)], he swore by Pharaoh's life (*Rashi*).

18. Realizing that none of them would volunteer to fetch Benjamin, Joseph makes a different proposal.

I fear God. And accordingly, I will not keep *all* of you imprisoned while your families are starving. I will release *most* of you to bring provisions home while I detain only one of you as a hostage (*Radak; Ramban; Sforno*).

land, he was the provider to all the populace. Joseph's brothers came and they bowed to him, faces to the ground.

^{7} Joseph saw his brothers and he recognized them but he acted like a stranger toward them and spoke with them harshly. He asked them, 'From where do you come?' And they said, 'From the land of Canaan to buy food.' ^{8} Thus, Joseph recognized his brothers but they did not recognize him.

^{9} Joseph recalled the dreams that he dreamed about them, so he said to them, 'You are spies! To see nakedness of the land have you come!'

^{10} They answered him, 'Not so, my lord. But your servants have come to buy food. ^{11} All of us — sons of one man are we. We are truthful people; your servants have never seen spies.'

^{12} And he said to them, 'No! But to see the land in its nakedness you have come.'

^{13} And they replied, 'We, your servants, are twelve brothers, the sons of one man in the land of Canaan. The youngest is now with our father and one is gone.'

^{14} But Joseph said to them, 'It is just as I have declared to you: "You are spies!" ^{15} By this shall you be tested: By Pharaoh's life you will not leave here unless your youngest brother comes here. ^{16} Send one of you, and let him fetch your brother while you shall remain imprisoned, so that your words may be tested whether truth is with you. But if not, by Pharaoh's life — surely you are spies!' ^{17} Then he herded them into a ward for three days.

^{18} Joseph said to them on the third day, 'Do this and live; I fear God: ^{19} If you are truthful people, let one of your brothers be imprisoned

בְּבֵית מִשְׁמַרְכֶם וְאַתֶּם לְכוּ הָבִיאוּ שֶׁבֶר
רַעֲבוֹן בָּתֵּיכֶם: כ וְאֶת־אֲחִיכֶם הַקָּטֹן תָּבִיאוּ
אֵלַי וְיֵאָמְנוּ דִבְרֵיכֶם וְלֹא תָמוּתוּ וַיַּעֲשׂוּ־כֵן:
כא וַיֹּאמְרוּ אִישׁ אֶל־אָחִיו אֲבָל אֲשֵׁמִים ׀
אֲנַחְנוּ עַל־אָחִינוּ אֲשֶׁר רָאִינוּ צָרַת נַפְשׁוֹ
בְּהִתְחַנְנוֹ אֵלֵינוּ וְלֹא שָׁמָעְנוּ עַל־כֵּן בָּאָה
אֵלֵינוּ הַצָּרָה הַזֹּאת: כב וַיַּעַן רְאוּבֵן אֹתָם
לֵאמֹר הֲלוֹא אָמַרְתִּי אֲלֵיכֶם ׀ לֵאמֹר אַל־
תֶּחֶטְאוּ בַיֶּלֶד וְלֹא שְׁמַעְתֶּם וְגַם־דָּמוֹ הִנֵּה
נִדְרָשׁ: כג וְהֵם לֹא יָדְעוּ כִּי שֹׁמֵעַ יוֹסֵף כִּי
הַמֵּלִיץ בֵּינֹתָם: כד וַיִּסֹּב מֵעֲלֵיהֶם וַיֵּבְךְּ וַיָּשָׁב
אֲלֵהֶם וַיְדַבֵּר אֲלֵהֶם וַיִּקַּח מֵאִתָּם אֶת־שִׁמְעוֹן
וַיֶּאֱסֹר אֹתוֹ לְעֵינֵיהֶם: כה וַיְצַו יוֹסֵף וַיְמַלְאוּ
אֶת־כְּלֵיהֶם בָּר וּלְהָשִׁיב כַּסְפֵּיהֶם אִישׁ אֶל־
שַׂקּוֹ וְלָתֵת לָהֶם צֵדָה לַדָּרֶךְ וַיַּעַשׂ לָהֶם כֵּן:
כו וַיִּשְׂאוּ אֶת־שִׁבְרָם עַל־חֲמֹרֵיהֶם וַיֵּלְכוּ
מִשָּׁם: כז וַיִּפְתַּח הָאֶחָד אֶת־שַׂקּוֹ לָתֵת מִסְפּוֹא
לַחֲמֹרוֹ בַּמָּלוֹן וַיַּרְא אֶת־כַּסְפּוֹ וְהִנֵּה־הוּא
בְּפִי אַמְתַּחְתּוֹ: כח וַיֹּאמֶר אֶל־אֶחָיו הוּשַׁב
כַּסְפִּי וְגַם הִנֵּה בְאַמְתַּחְתִּי וַיֵּצֵא לִבָּם וַיֶּחֶרְדוּ
אִישׁ אֶל־אָחִיו לֵאמֹר מַה־זֹּאת עָשָׂה אֱלֹהִים
לָנוּ: כט וַיָּבֹאוּ אֶל־יַעֲקֹב אֲבִיהֶם אַרְצָה
כְּנָעַן וַיַּגִּידוּ לוֹ אֵת כָּל־הַקֹּרֹת אֹתָם לֵאמֹר:
ל דִּבֶּר הָאִישׁ אֲדֹנֵי הָאָרֶץ אִתָּנוּ קָשׁוֹת וַיִּתֵּן
אֹתָנוּ כִּמְרַגְּלִים אֶת־הָאָרֶץ: לא וַנֹּאמֶר אֵלָיו

21. The brothers become introspective and recognize their lot as a Divine punishment for their cruel treatment of Joseph. 'Happy are the righteous,' declares *Midrash HaGadol*, 'who submit to retribution with joy and declare the Almighty just in whatever way He acts.'

When he pleaded with us and we paid no heed. They regarded this callousness toward Joseph's entreaties as deserving even greater punishment than the actual sale. That he implored them is not related in the story of the sale [ch. 37], since it is obvious that he must have invoked every possible plea to save himself from death (*Ramban*).

23. They had spoken to Joseph through an interpreter, so they assumed that he did not understand Hebrew. [Now the interpreter had left — for it is obvious that they would not have spoken these incriminating words had he still been present (*Radak; Mizrachi*).] According to the *Midrash*, the interpreter was Manasseh, Joseph's firstborn son (*Rashi*).

24. Why did Joseph choose Simeon as a hostage? He had thrown Joseph into the pit and said to Levi, *Look! That dreamer is coming* [37:19]. Alternatively, he wished to separate Simeon from Levi lest the two of them conspire to kill him (*Rashi*).

27. *The one of them.* Levi. Now that he was separated from his companion Simeon, he was *the one* (*Rashi*).

According to *Abarbanel* and *Malbim*, Joseph ordered that the money of all the brothers be placed near the *bottom* of their packs, but that Levi's be near the top. He wanted Levi to be the first to discover the money and be distressed even during the journey. The reason was that Levi was the most guilty for the sale [and this would provide him atonement, measure for measure].

28. His fright was greatest when he recognized the money as *his own* so that he was vulnerable to a personal accusation. This was part of Joseph's scheme. He wanted the brothers to realize how fully they were in his power and that he could do as he pleased with them (*R' Hirsch*).

What is this that God has done to us — by letting us be suspected? For the money was returned only to furnish a pretext for a plot against us (*Rashi*).

29. Their report to their father.

The following is exactly how the brothers related their experiences to Jacob. A comparison of the following *verbatim* recapitulation with the narrative above, however, will show how they concealed certain things, to minimize the gravity of their dilemma (*Akeidah; Ralbag*).

in your place of confinement while the rest of you go and bring provisions for the hunger of your households. ²⁰ Then bring your youngest brother to me so your words will be verified and you will not die.' And they consented.

²¹ They then said to one another, 'Indeed we are guilty concerning our brother inasmuch as we saw his heartfelt anguish when he pleaded with us and we paid no heed. That is why this distress has come upon us.'

²² Reuben retorted to them as follows, 'Did I not say to you in effect, "Do not sin against the boy," but you would not listen! And his blood as well — see! it is being avenged.' ²³ Now they did not know that Joseph understood, for an interpreter was between them.

²⁴ He turned away from them and wept. He returned to them and spoke to them; he took Simeon from them and imprisoned him before their eyes. ²⁵ Joseph commanded that they fill their vessels with grain, and to return each one's money to his sack and to give them provisions for the journey. And so he did for them. ²⁶ Then they loaded their purchase onto their donkeys and departed from there.

²⁷ When the one of them opened the sack to give feed to his donkey at the inn, he saw his money right there in the mouth of his sack. ²⁸ So he said to his brothers, 'My money has been returned and look! it, too, is in my sack!' Their hearts sank and they turned trembling one to another, saying, 'What is this that God has done to us?'

²⁹ They came to Jacob their father in the land of Canaan and they told him of all their experiences as follows: ³⁰ 'The man, the lord of the land, spoke harshly to us and considered us as if we were spying out the land. ³¹ But we said to him,

כֵּנִים אֲנַחְנוּ לֹא הָיִינוּ מְרַגְּלִים: לב שְׁנֵים־עָשָׂר
אֲנַחְנוּ אַחִים בְּנֵי אָבִינוּ הָאֶחָד אֵינֶנּוּ וְהַקָּטֹן
הַיּוֹם אֶת־אָבִינוּ בְּאֶרֶץ כְּנָעַן: לג וַיֹּאמֶר אֵלֵינוּ
הָאִישׁ אֲדֹנֵי הָאָרֶץ בְּזֹאת אֵדַע כִּי כֵנִים אַתֶּם
אֲחִיכֶם הָאֶחָד הַנִּיחוּ אִתִּי וְאֶת־רַעֲבוֹן
בָּתֵּיכֶם קְחוּ וָלֵכוּ: לד וְהָבִיאוּ אֶת־אֲחִיכֶם
הַקָּטֹן אֵלַי וְאֵדְעָה כִּי לֹא מְרַגְּלִים אַתֶּם כִּי
כֵנִים אַתֶּם אֶת־אֲחִיכֶם אֶתֵּן לָכֶם וְאֶת־
הָאָרֶץ תִּסְחָרוּ: לה וַיְהִי הֵם מְרִיקִים שַׂקֵּיהֶם
וְהִנֵּה־אִישׁ צְרוֹר־כַּסְפּוֹ בְּשַׂקּוֹ וַיִּרְאוּ אֶת־
צְרֹרוֹת כַּסְפֵּיהֶם הֵמָּה וַאֲבִיהֶם וַיִּירָאוּ:
לו וַיֹּאמֶר אֲלֵהֶם יַעֲקֹב אֲבִיהֶם אֹתִי שִׁכַּלְתֶּם
יוֹסֵף אֵינֶנּוּ וְשִׁמְעוֹן אֵינֶנּוּ וְאֶת־בִּנְיָמִן תִּקָּחוּ
עָלַי הָיוּ כֻלָּנָה: לז וַיֹּאמֶר רְאוּבֵן אֶל־אָבִיו
לֵאמֹר אֶת־שְׁנֵי בָנַי תָּמִית אִם־לֹא אֲבִיאֶנּוּ
אֵלֶיךָ תְּנָה אֹתוֹ עַל־יָדִי וַאֲנִי אֲשִׁיבֶנּוּ אֵלֶיךָ:
לח וַיֹּאמֶר לֹא־יֵרֵד בְּנִי עִמָּכֶם כִּי־אָחִיו מֵת
וְהוּא לְבַדּוֹ נִשְׁאָר וּקְרָאָהוּ אָסוֹן בַּדֶּרֶךְ אֲשֶׁר
תֵּלְכוּ־בָהּ וְהוֹרַדְתֶּם אֶת־שֵׂיבָתִי בְּיָגוֹן
שְׁאוֹלָה: מג א וְהָרָעָב כָּבֵד בָּאָרֶץ: ב וַיְהִי
כַּאֲשֶׁר כִּלּוּ לֶאֱכֹל אֶת־הַשֶּׁבֶר אֲשֶׁר הֵבִיאוּ
מִמִּצְרָיִם וַיֹּאמֶר אֲלֵיהֶם אֲבִיהֶם שֻׁבוּ
שִׁבְרוּ־לָנוּ מְעַט־אֹכֶל: ג וַיֹּאמֶר אֵלָיו יְהוּדָה
לֵאמֹר הָעֵד הֵעִד בָּנוּ הָאִישׁ לֵאמֹר לֹא־
תִרְאוּ פָנַי בִּלְתִּי אֲחִיכֶם אִתְּכֶם: ד אִם־יֶשְׁךָ

35. They were terrified. They knew that the money in *all* their sacks could not possibly be an oversight. It was obvious that a plot was being implemented against them (*Alshich*).

36. Upon me has it all befallen. I.e., all of these disasters (*Ibn Ezra*).

Your grief, as brothers, cannot compare with mine as a father! (*Akeidah*).

According to *Malbim*, the meaning is different: The blame for all of their misfortune is upon me. I caused Joseph's death by sending him into danger, and I will be similarly held accountable for Simeon's and Benjamin's deaths, for allowing them to go to a place of danger, and I dread the punishment in store for me because of this.

37. Reuben's proposal.

You may slay my two sons. Reuben spoke figuratively, in the sense of obligating himself under the penalty of a *curse* (*Ramban*).

38. 'He is a fool, this eldest son of mine,' Jacob declared. 'He suggests that I should kill his sons. Are not his sons also my sons?' (*Rashi*).

The reasons Jacob gave for refusing Reuben's offer were sincere, quite valid, and equally applicable to Judah's. Nevertheless Jacob acceded to Judah's request because he had more confidence in him, and because the timing of his offer was propitious (*Ramban*).

Then you will have brought down my hoariness [lit., white hair; metaphorically old age] in sorrow to the grave. I will never cease mourning. Benjamin is Rachel's only survivor; while he is with me, I find consolation for the loss of his mother and brother; if he should die, it would seem to me as though the three of them died on the same day (see *Rashi* 44:29).

43/1. The brothers return to Egypt.

The famine was severe in the land. It grew more severe (*Ralbag*). In this context, the *land* refers to the land *par excellence* — *Eretz Yisrael* (*Akeidah*).

2. Judah had advised his brothers to wait until the household ran out of food — for then Jacob would be more disposed to let Benjamin go (*Rashi; Ramban* 42:37).

3. Judah quoted the Egyptian viceroy in stronger terms than the brothers had used earlier (42:24). They had minimized their predicament in order to spare Jacob and give him less reason to oppose Benjamin's return with them. Now, that only extreme urgency would make Jacob consent, the situation demanded unabashed candor.

''We are truthful men: we have never been spies! ³² We are twelve brothers, sons of our father. One is gone and the youngest is now with our father in the land of Canaan.'' ³³ Then the man, the lord of the land, said to us, ''By this I will ascertain whether you are truthful people: One of your brothers leave with me, and what is needed for the hunger of your households take and go. ³⁴ And bring your youngest brother to me so I will know that you are not spies, but truthful people. I will restore your brother to you and you will be free to circulate about the land.'' '

³⁵ Then, as they were emptying their sacks, behold! every man's bundle of money was in his sack. When they and their father saw their bundles of money, they were terrified. ³⁶ Their father Jacob said to them, 'I am the one whom you bereaved! Joseph is gone, Simeon is gone, and now you would take away Benjamin? Upon me has it all befallen!'

³⁷ Then Reuben said to his father as follows, 'You may slay my two sons if I fail to bring him back to you. Put him in my care and I will return him to you.'

³⁸ But he said, 'My son shall not go down with you, for his brother is dead and he alone is left. Should disaster befall him on the journey which you shall take, then you will have brought down my hoariness in sorrow to the grave.'

43 ¹ The famine was severe in the land. ² When they had finished eating the provisions which they had brought from Egypt their father said to them, 'Go back, buy us some food.' ³ But Judah said to him as follows, 'The man sternly warned us saying, ''You dare not see my face unless your brother is with you.'' ⁴ If you are ready

מְשַׁלֵּחַ אֶת־אָחִינוּ אִתָּנוּ נֵרְדָה וְנִשְׁבְּרָה לְךָ
אֹכֶל: ה וְאִם־אֵינְךָ מְשַׁלֵּחַ לֹא נֵרֵד כִּי־הָאִישׁ
אָמַר אֵלֵינוּ לֹא־תִרְאוּ פָנַי בִּלְתִּי אֲחִיכֶם
אִתְּכֶם: ו וַיֹּאמֶר יִשְׂרָאֵל לָמָה הֲרֵעֹתֶם לִי
לְהַגִּיד לָאִישׁ הַעוֹד לָכֶם אָח: ז וַיֹּאמְרוּ שָׁאוֹל
שָׁאַל־הָאִישׁ לָנוּ וּלְמוֹלַדְתֵּנוּ לֵאמֹר הַעוֹד
אֲבִיכֶם חַי הֲיֵשׁ לָכֶם אָח וַנַּגֶּד־לוֹ עַל־פִּי
הַדְּבָרִים הָאֵלֶּה הֲיָדוֹעַ נֵדַע כִּי יֹאמַר הוֹרִידוּ
אֶת־אֲחִיכֶם: ח וַיֹּאמֶר יְהוּדָה אֶל־יִשְׂרָאֵל
אָבִיו שִׁלְחָה הַנַּעַר אִתִּי וְנָקוּמָה וְנֵלֵכָה וְנִחְיֶה
וְלֹא נָמוּת גַּם־אֲנַחְנוּ גַם־אַתָּה גַּם־טַפֵּנוּ:
ט אָנֹכִי אֶעֶרְבֶנּוּ מִיָּדִי תְּבַקְשֶׁנּוּ אִם־לֹא
הֲבִיאֹתִיו אֵלֶיךָ וְהִצַּגְתִּיו לְפָנֶיךָ וְחָטָאתִי לְךָ
כָּל־הַיָּמִים: י כִּי לוּלֵא הִתְמַהְמָהְנוּ כִּי־עַתָּה
שַׁבְנוּ זֶה פַעֲמָיִם: יא וַיֹּאמֶר אֲלֵהֶם יִשְׂרָאֵל
אֲבִיהֶם אִם־כֵּן | אֵפוֹא זֹאת עֲשׂוּ קְחוּ מִזִּמְרַת
הָאָרֶץ בִּכְלֵיכֶם וְהוֹרִידוּ לָאִישׁ מִנְחָה מְעַט
צֳרִי וּמְעַט דְּבַשׁ נְכֹאת וָלֹט בָּטְנִים וּשְׁקֵדִים:
יב וְכֶסֶף מִשְׁנֶה קְחוּ בְיֶדְכֶם וְאֶת־הַכֶּסֶף
הַמּוּשָׁב בְּפִי אַמְתְּחֹתֵיכֶם תָּשִׁיבוּ בְיֶדְכֶם
אוּלַי מִשְׁגֶּה הוּא: יג וְאֶת־אֲחִיכֶם קָחוּ וְקוּמוּ
שׁוּבוּ אֶל־הָאִישׁ: יד וְאֵל שַׁדַּי יִתֵּן לָכֶם רַחֲמִים
לִפְנֵי הָאִישׁ וְשִׁלַּח לָכֶם אֶת־אֲחִיכֶם אַחֵר
וְאֶת־בִּנְיָמִין וַאֲנִי כַּאֲשֶׁר שָׁכֹלְתִּי שָׁכָלְתִּי:
טו וַיִּקְחוּ הָאֲנָשִׁים אֶת־הַמִּנְחָה הַזֹּאת

6. As noted, Israel is the name used to depict Jacob in his spiritual role as Patriarch of the Jewish nation. In this case, he is referred to as Israel, because he offered them a teaching for future generations. Whenever Jews are forced to appear before hostile rulers, they should not offer more information than the question requires (*Haamek Davar*).

7. As a group, they defended themselves against Jacob's charge that they had loose tongues (*Akeidah*).

8. Judah's proposal.

10. *We could have by now returned twice.* I.e., we could have been there and back twice by this time (*Ralbag*). We would long since have returned with Simeon, and you would not have had all this anxiety (*Rashi*).

11. Jacob acquiesces.

Why was Judah's offer more acceptable than Reuben's? In addition to the reasons recorded above, there might be another possibility: When Jacob said, 'Upon *me* has it all befallen' (42:36), he implied, as mentioned by the commentators, that only a father could realize the magnitude of the loss of two of his children. Only Judah who had been bereaved of two children 38:7,10) could appreciate his father's grief. Therefore, when *he* accepted responsibility for Benjamin's welfare, Jacob acquiesced.

And bring it down to the man as a tribute. A gift to the fabulously wealthy 'civilized' ruler of Egypt must emphasize quality, not quantity. Some of the items listed here were identical to those brought by Ishmaelite caravans to Egypt [37:25]. Apparently, they were not readily available in Egypt (cf. *Sforno; Chizkuni*).

12. *Double the money.* Take twice as much money as you had on your first trip; perhaps the price of grain has risen (*Rashi*). Or perhaps he wanted them to buy a double ration to spare themselves the difficulty of an early return to Egypt for more provisions (*R' Abraham ben HaRambam*).

Return in your hands — literally. Do not leave it in your sacks, nor wait until you are asked for it, but *carry it in your hands* to demonstrate immediately on your return that you are honest men and intend to return any money not rightfully yours (*Alshich*).

Perhaps it was an oversight. Jacob reasoned that the officials may have put the payments on top of the sacks to help them identify the owners of the sacks, and then, due to the confusion, forgotten to take the money when delivering the filled sacks to the customers (*Rashbam; Radak*).

13. The verb *take* is in plural. Although it was only to Judah that he entrusted Benjamin, Jacob addressed *all* his sons, so they should feel a sense of collective responsibility (*Sechel Tov*).

14. 'Now, that you have the money, the gift, and your brother Benjamin' (*Midrash*), Jacob said, 'you lack nothing but prayer. I will pray for you' (*Rashi*).

And as for me — [in contrast with you] — until you return, I will be in constant suspense, not knowing if I am to be even more bereaved than I already have been. As I consider myself bereft of Joseph and of Simeon, so I will now feel bereft of Benjamin [a feeling I will continue to have until you return safely] (*Rashi*).

to send our brother with us we will go down and buy you food. [5] But if you do not send, we will not go down for the man said to us, "You dare not see my face unless your brother is with you." '

[6] Then Israel said, 'Why did you treat me so ill by telling the man that you had another brother?'

[7] And they said, 'The man persistently asked about us and our relatives, saying, "Is your father still alive? Have you a brother?" and we responded to him according to these words. Could we possibly have known that he would say, "Bring your brother down"?'

[8] Then Judah said to Israel his father, 'Send the lad with me, and let us arise and go, so we will live and not die, we as well as you as well as our children. [9] — I will personally guarantee him; of my own hand you can demand him. If I do not bring him back to you and stand him before you, then I will have sinned to you for all time. — [10] For had we not delayed we could have by now returned twice.'

[11] Israel their father said to them, 'If it must be so, then do this: Take of the land's glory in your baggage and bring it down to the man as a tribute — a bit of balsam, a bit of honey, wax, lotus, pistachios and almonds. [12] And take with you double the money, and the money that was returned in the mouth of your sacks return in your hands; perhaps it was an oversight. [13] Take your brother, too, and arise, return to the man. [14] And may El Shaddai grant you mercy before the man that he may release to you your other brother as well as Benjamin. And as for me, as I have been bereaved, so I am bereaved.'

[15] So the men took this tribute and they

וּמִשְׁנֶה־כֶּסֶף לָקְחוּ בְיָדָם וְאֶת־בִּנְיָמֵן וַיָּקֻמוּ וַיֵּרְדֵוּ מִצְרַ֫יִם וַיַּעַמְדוּ לִפְנֵי יוֹסֵף: ששי טז וַיַּ֫רְא יוֹסֵף אִתָּם אֶת־בִּנְיָמִין וַיֹּאמֶר לַאֲשֶׁר עַל־ בֵּיתוֹ הָבֵא אֶת־הָאֲנָשִׁים הַבָּ֫יְתָה וּטְבֹ֫חַ טֶ֫בַח וְהָכֵן כִּי אִתִּי יֹאכְלוּ הָאֲנָשִׁים בַּצָּהֳרָ֫יִם: יז וַיַּ֫עַשׂ הָאִישׁ כַּאֲשֶׁר אָמַר יוֹסֵף וַיָּבֵא הָאִישׁ אֶת־ הָאֲנָשִׁים בֵּ֫יתָה יוֹסֵף: יח וַיִּירְאוּ הָאֲנָשִׁים כִּי הוּבְאוּ בֵּית יוֹסֵף וַיֹּאמְרוּ עַל־דְּבַר הַכֶּ֫סֶף הַשָּׁב בְּאַמְתְּחֹתֵ֫ינוּ בַּתְּחִלָּה אֲנַ֫חְנוּ מוּבָאִים לְהִתְגֹּלֵל עָלֵ֫ינוּ וּלְהִתְנַפֵּל עָלֵ֫ינוּ וְלָקַ֫חַת אֹתָ֫נוּ לַעֲבָדִים וְאֶת־חֲמֹרֵ֫ינוּ: יט וַיִּגְּשׁוּ אֶל־הָאִישׁ אֲשֶׁר עַל־בֵּית יוֹסֵף וַיְדַבְּרוּ אֵלָיו פֶּ֫תַח הַבָּ֫יִת: כ וַיֹּאמְרוּ בִּי אֲדֹנִי יָרֹד יָרַ֫דְנוּ בַּתְּחִלָּה לִשְׁבָּר־ אֹ֫כֶל: כא וַיְהִי כִּי־בָ֫אנוּ אֶל־הַמָּלוֹן וַנִּפְתְּחָה אֶת־אַמְתְּחֹתֵ֫ינוּ וְהִנֵּה כֶֽסֶף־אִישׁ בְּפִי אַמְתַּחְתּוֹ כַּסְפֵּ֫נוּ בְּמִשְׁקָלוֹ וַנָּ֫שֶׁב אֹתוֹ בְּיָדֵ֫נוּ: כב וְכֶ֫סֶף אַחֵר הוֹרַ֫דְנוּ בְיָדֵ֫נוּ לִשְׁבָּר־אֹ֫כֶל לֹא יָדַ֫עְנוּ מִי־שָׂם כַּסְפֵּ֫נוּ בְּאַמְתְּחֹתֵ֫ינוּ: כג וַיֹּ֫אמֶר שָׁלוֹם לָכֶם אַל־תִּירָ֫אוּ אֱלֹֽהֵיכֶם וֵאלֹהֵי אֲבִיכֶם נָתַן לָכֶם מַטְמוֹן בְּאַמְתְּחֹתֵיכֶם כַּסְפְּכֶם בָּא אֵלָי וַיּוֹצֵא אֲלֵהֶם אֶת־שִׁמְעוֹן: כד וַיָּבֵא הָאִישׁ אֶת־הָאֲנָשִׁים בֵּ֫יתָה יוֹסֵף וַיִּתֶּן־מַ֫יִם וַיִּרְחֲצוּ רַגְלֵיהֶם וַיִּתֵּן מִסְפּוֹא לַחֲמֹרֵיהֶם: כה וַיָּכִ֫ינוּ אֶת־הַמִּנְחָה עַד־בּוֹא יוֹסֵף בַּצָּהֳרָ֫יִם כִּי שָׁמְעוּ כִּי־שָׁם יֹ֫אכְלוּ לָֽחֶם:

16. Joseph sees Benjamin and tests his brothers' sincerity.

That Joseph was deeply moved by the sight of Benjamin is clear from the next several verses. Nevertheless, he still refrained from revealing his identity because he still had vital questions: Had the brothers lost their jealousy of Rachel's children? How would they react when he showed favoritism to Benjamin? What would they do when he announced his intention to detain Benjamin — who 'stole' the goblet — as a slave? Had they kidnapped Benjamin from Jacob? (*Akeidah; R' Hirsch*).

The one in charge of his house. His son, Manasseh (*Midrash*).

Have meat slaughtered, and prepare it. According to the Sages in *Chullin* 91a, the expression וּטְבֹ֫חַ טֶ֫בַח implies that Manasseh was to expose the slaughter-incision [to show the brothers that the meat had been slaughtered according to *halachah*. Although the Torah had not yet been given, Jacob's sons observed the commandments according to the tradition of their forefathers (*Rashi* there).]

18. The brothers feared that whereas Joseph would be deterred from harming them publicly, in the privacy of Joseph's home, an act of injustice could be committed against them with impunity (*Akeidah*).

Along with our donkeys. They feared the consequences of their donkeys' loss: 'He will rob even our donkeys with our sacks; we will not be able to send grain home and our families will die of hunger!' (*Ramban*).

21. *At the inn.* Suggesting: There was no way we could return the money then without putting our lives in jeopardy, because the viceroy had warned us not to come to Egypt again without our youngest brother (*HaKsav V'HaKabbalah*).

23. **The steward reassures them.**

It was not to charge you with a crime that I brought you here, but as guests to dine with my master (*Abarbanel; Malbim*).

Your payment had reached me. The money you found was a Divine blessing; *your money*, however, was duly received by me — have no fears about that! (*Radak*).

25. *They had heard.* From the steward and from the members of the household who were preparing the meal. *Bread* is a general term for *food* (*Radak*).

took double money in their hand, as well as Benjamin. They set out and went down to Egypt and stood before Joseph.

[16] Joseph saw Benjamin with them. He said to the one in charge of his house, 'Bring the men into the house; have meat slaughtered, and prepare it, for it is with me that these men will dine at noon.' [17] The man did as Joseph said, and the man brought the men to Joseph's house. [18] But the men became frightened when they were brought to Joseph's house, and they said, 'Because of the money replaced in our sacks originally are we being brought so that a charge can be fabricated against us, that it crash down on us, and that we be taken as slaves along with our donkeys.' [19] They approached the man who was in charge of Joseph's house and spoke to him at the entrance of the house. [20] And they said, ''If you please, my lord: We had indeed come down originally to buy food. [21] But it happened, when we arrived at the inn, that behold! each one's money was in the mouth of his sack; it was our own money in full; so we have brought it back in our hand. [22] We have also brought other money down in our hand to buy food. We do not know who put our money in our sacks.'

[23] He replied, 'All is peaceful with you; fear not. Your God and the God of your father must have put a treasure in your sacks. Your payment had reached me.' And he brought Simeon out to them.

[24] Then the man brought the men into Joseph's house. He provided water and they washed their feet, and he gave feed to their donkeys. [25] They prepared the tribute for when Joseph would come at noon, for they had heard that they were to dine there.

כו וַיָּבֹא יוֹסֵף הַבַּ֫יְתָה וַיָּבִ֩יאוּ ל֨וֹ אֶת־הַמִּנְחָ֤ה
אֲשֶׁר־בְּיָדָ֖ם הַבָּ֑יְתָה וַיִּשְׁתַּֽחֲווּ־ל֖וֹ אָֽרְצָה: כז וַיִּשְׁאַ֤ל לָהֶם֙ לְשָׁל֔וֹם וַיֹּ֗אמֶר הֲשָׁל֛וֹם
אֲבִיכֶ֥ם הַזָּקֵ֖ן אֲשֶׁ֣ר אֲמַרְתֶּ֑ם הַעוֹדֶ֖נּוּ חָֽי: כח וַיֹּֽאמְר֗וּ שָׁל֛וֹם לְעַבְדְּךָ֥ לְאָבִ֖ינוּ עוֹדֶ֣נּוּ חָ֑י
וַיִּקְּד֖וּ וַיִּֽשְׁתַּֽחֲוֽוּ: כט וַיִּשָּׂ֤א עֵינָיו֙ וַיַּ֣רְא אֶת־
בִּנְיָמִ֣ין אָחִיו֮ בֶּן־אִמּוֹ֒ וַיֹּ֗אמֶר הֲזֶה֙ אֲחִיכֶ֣ם
הַקָּטֹ֔ן אֲשֶׁ֥ר אֲמַרְתֶּ֖ם אֵלָ֑י וַיֹּאמַ֕ר אֱלֹהִ֥ים
יָחְנְךָ֖ בְּנִֽי: שביעי ל וַיְמַהֵ֣ר יוֹסֵ֗ף כִּֽי־נִכְמְר֤וּ
רַֽחֲמָיו֙ אֶל־אָחִ֔יו וַיְבַקֵּ֖שׁ לִבְכּ֑וֹת וַיָּבֹ֥א
הַחַ֖דְרָה וַיֵּ֥בְךְּ שָֽׁמָּה: לא וַיִּרְחַ֥ץ פָּנָ֖יו וַיֵּצֵ֑א
וַיִּ֨תְאַפַּ֔ק וַיֹּ֖אמֶר שִׂ֥ימוּ לָֽחֶם: לב וַיָּשִׂ֥ימוּ ל֣וֹ
לְבַדּ֗וֹ וְלָהֶם֙ לְבַדָּ֔ם וְלַמִּצְרִ֛ים הָאֹֽכְלִ֥ים אִתּ֖וֹ
לְבַדָּ֑ם כִּי֩ לֹ֨א יֽוּכְל֜וּן הַמִּצְרִ֗ים לֶֽאֱכֹ֤ל אֶת־
הָֽעִבְרִים֙ לֶ֔חֶם כִּֽי־תֽוֹעֵבָ֥ה הִ֖וא לְמִצְרָֽיִם: לג וַיֵּֽשְׁב֣וּ לְפָנָ֔יו הַבְּכֹר֙ כִּבְכֹ֣רָת֔וֹ וְהַצָּעִ֖יר
כִּצְעִֽרָת֑וֹ וַיִּתְמְה֥וּ הָֽאֲנָשִׁ֖ים אִ֥ישׁ אֶל־רֵעֵֽהוּ: לד וַיִּשָּׂ֨א מַשְׂאֹ֜ת מֵאֵ֣ת פָּנָיו֮ אֲלֵהֶם֒ וַתֵּ֜רֶב
מַשְׂאַ֧ת בִּנְיָמִ֛ן מִמַּשְׂאֹ֥ת כֻּלָּ֖ם חָמֵ֣שׁ יָד֑וֹת
וַיִּשְׁתּ֥וּ וַיִּשְׁכְּר֖וּ עִמּֽוֹ: מד א וַיְצַ֞ו אֶת־אֲשֶׁ֣ר
עַל־בֵּיתוֹ֮ לֵאמֹר֒ מַלֵּ֞א אֶת־אַמְתְּחֹ֤ת
הָֽאֲנָשִׁים֙ אֹ֔כֶל כַּֽאֲשֶׁ֥ר יֽוּכְל֖וּן שְׂאֵ֑ת וְשִׂ֥ים
כֶּֽסֶף־אִ֖ישׁ בְּפִ֥י אַמְתַּחְתּֽוֹ: ב וְאֶת־גְּבִיעִ֞י
גְבִ֣יעַ הַכֶּ֗סֶף תָּשִׂים֙ בְּפִי֙ אַמְתַּ֣חַת הַקָּטֹ֔ן וְאֵ֖ת
כֶּ֣סֶף שִׁבְר֑וֹ וַיַּ֕עַשׂ כִּדְבַ֥ר יוֹסֵ֖ף אֲשֶׁ֥ר דִּבֵּֽר:

26. This is the first time all
Joseph's brothers — including Benjamin — bowed
down to him. This is per-
ceived by many commenta-
tors as the fulfillment of
Joseph's first dream [37:7].

27. הַעוֹדֶ֖נּוּ חָֽי — *Does he
still live?* The sequence of
Joseph's questions seems
strange; first he asked about
Jacob's health and *then*
whether he was still alive. *R'
Hirsch* comments that this
order reveals Joseph's anxiety about his father. He
asked after his father's welfare as would be expected
— but then he had a fright-
ening thought: Perhaps my
father has died in the in-
terim! Quickly he adds, 'He
is still alive, is he not?'

Other commentators re-
solve the sequence of the
questions by suggesting that
the second question does
not mean: Is he still *alive*?
but, is he still *vigorous*? Cf.
this sense of the word in
Joshua 5:8 and *Rashi* to
Psalms 58:10. Thus, Joseph
first inquired after Jacob's
general welfare, then after
the state of his health.

30. Joseph became so emotional because he could still
not reveal his true identity
to Benjamin, and because
he knew that he would in-
flict further suffering on him
in the matter of the goblet
[ch. 44] (*Haamek Davar*).

31. The meal with Joseph.

They served him separately.
In deference to his royal
rank (*B'chor Shor; Radak*);
furthermore, since Egyptians
and Hebrews did not, as
noted further in this verse,
dine together, Joseph did
not dine with his brothers,
nor did he and his brothers
dine together with the Egyptians (*Sforno*).

It was a loathsome thing to the Egyptians to eat together with the Hebrews [and other foreigners] (Rashi).

34. Chizkuni explains why the brothers, who observed the laws of the Torah before it was given, were permitted to drink the wine of non-Jews. The prohibition against such wine falls under two categories: יֵין נָסֶךְ, wine used for idolatry, and סְתָם יֵינָם, their ordinary wine. The first category is forbidden by the Torah, and the brothers would have avoided drinking it. The second category, ordinary wine, was prohibited only by the Sages. Since it was a Rabbinic prohibition, the brothers were not required to observe it, prior to its enactment.

44/1. The final test. Benjamin is accused of thievery.

The brothers' attitude toward the privileged treatment afforded Benjamin convinced Joseph that they were no longer spiteful, but not all his doubts had been resolved. Would they be ready to fight and sacrifice for the sake of a child of Rachel? To test them, he arranged for Benjamin to be arrested for theft (Ramban).

With as much food as they can carry. More than their money's worth (Ramban).

This placing of each man's money in his sack was to be done with the brothers' knowledge, ostensibly in reparation for Joseph's earlier harsh treatment. The official who filled the grain sacks would close and seal them; therefore the brothers did not open their sacks and discover the silver goblet that had been slipped into Benjamin's sack (Ramban).

²⁶ When Joseph came home they brought the tribute that was in their hands to him into the house, and they prostrated themselves to him toward the ground. ²⁷ He inquired after their welfare, and he said, 'Is your aged father of whom you spoke at peace? Does he still live?'

²⁸ They replied, 'Your servant our father is at peace; he still lives.' And they bowed and prostrated themselves.

²⁹ Then he lifted up his eyes and saw his brother Benjamin, his mother's son, so he said, 'Is this your "little" brother of whom you spoke to me?' And he said, 'God be gracious to you, my son.'

³⁰ Then Joseph rushed because his compassion for his brother had been stirred and he wanted to weep. So he went into the room and wept there. ³¹ He washed his face and went out, fortified himself and said, 'Serve food.' ³² They served him separately and them separately and the Egyptians who ate with him separately, for the Egyptians could not bear to eat food with the Hebrews, it being loathsome to Egypt. ³³ They were seated before him, the firstborn according to his seniority and the youngest according to his youth. The men looked at one another in astonishment.

³⁴ He had portions that had been set before him served to them, and Benjamin's portion was five times as much as the portion of any of them. They drank and became intoxicated with him.

44 ¹ Then he instructed the one in charge of his house saying, 'Fill the men's sacks with as much food as they can carry and put each man's money in the mouth of his sack. ² And my goblet — my silver goblet — place in the mouth of the youngest one's sack along with the money of his purchase.' And he followed Joseph's word exactly.

ג הַבֹּקֶר אֹור וְהָאֲנָשִׁים שֻׁלְּחוּ הֵמָּה
וַחֲמֹרֵיהֶם: ד הֵם יָצְאוּ אֶת־הָעִיר לֹא
הִרְחִיקוּ וְיֹוסֵף אָמַר לַאֲשֶׁר עַל־בֵּיתֹו קוּם
רְדֹף אַחֲרֵי הָאֲנָשִׁים וְהִשַּׂגְתָּם וְאָמַרְתָּ
אֲלֵהֶם לָמָּה שִׁלַּמְתֶּם רָעָה תַּחַת טֹובָה:
ה הֲלֹוא זֶה אֲשֶׁר יִשְׁתֶּה אֲדֹנִי בֹּו וְהוּא נַחֵשׁ
יְנַחֵשׁ בֹּו הֲרֵעֹתֶם אֲשֶׁר עֲשִׂיתֶם: ו וַיַּשִּׂגֵם
וַיְדַבֵּר אֲלֵהֶם אֶת־הַדְּבָרִים הָאֵלֶּה: ז וַיֹּאמְרוּ
אֵלָיו לָמָּה יְדַבֵּר אֲדֹנִי כַּדְּבָרִים הָאֵלֶּה
חָלִילָה לַעֲבָדֶיךָ מֵעֲשֹׂות כַּדָּבָר הַזֶּה: ח הֵן
כֶּסֶף אֲשֶׁר מָצָאנוּ בְּפִי אַמְתְּחֹתֵינוּ הֱשִׁיבֹנוּ
אֵלֶיךָ מֵאֶרֶץ כְּנָעַן וְאֵיךְ נִגְנֹב מִבֵּית אֲדֹנֶיךָ
כֶּסֶף אֹו זָהָב: ט אֲשֶׁר יִמָּצֵא אִתֹּו מֵעֲבָדֶיךָ
וָמֵת וְגַם־אֲנַחְנוּ נִהְיֶה לַאדֹנִי לַעֲבָדִים:
י וַיֹּאמֶר גַּם־עַתָּה כְדִבְרֵיכֶם כֶּן־הוּא אֲשֶׁר
יִמָּצֵא אִתֹּו יִהְיֶה־לִּי עָבֶד וְאַתֶּם תִּהְיוּ נְקִיִּם:
יא וַיְמַהֲרוּ וַיֹּורִדוּ אִישׁ אֶת־אַמְתַּחְתֹּו אָרְצָה
וַיִּפְתְּחוּ אִישׁ אַמְתַּחְתֹּו: יב וַיְחַפֵּשׂ בַּגָּדֹול
הֵחֵל וּבַקָּטֹן כִּלָּה וַיִּמָּצֵא הַגָּבִיעַ בְּאַמְתַּחַת
בִּנְיָמִן: יג וַיִּקְרְעוּ שִׂמְלֹתָם וַיַּעֲמֹס אִישׁ
עַל־חֲמֹרֹו וַיָּשֻׁבוּ הָעִירָה: מפטיר יד וַיָּבֹא
יְהוּדָה וְאֶחָיו בֵּיתָה יֹוסֵף וְהוּא עֹודֶנּוּ שָׁם
וַיִּפְּלוּ לְפָנָיו אָרְצָה: טו וַיֹּאמֶר לָהֶם יֹוסֵף
מָה־הַמַּעֲשֶׂה הַזֶּה אֲשֶׁר עֲשִׂיתֶם הֲלֹוא
יְדַעְתֶּם כִּי־נַחֵשׁ יְנַחֵשׁ אִישׁ אֲשֶׁר כָּמֹנִי:

4. *Get up, chase after the men.* While the fear of the city is still upon them (*Tanchuma*).

Before directly accusing them of stealing the goblet, he accused them of ingratitude, a charge sometimes worse than theft. The assumption was that these words of reproof would crush their courage and put them on the defensive. 'My master invited you to a feast, gave you food and drink at no cost — and you went ahead and rewarded him by stealing his personal utensil!' (*Sechel Tov*).

5. הֲלֹוא זֶה אֲשֶׁר יִשְׁתֶּה אֲדֹנִי בֹּו — *It is the one from which my master drinks.* Someone who would dare steal the royal cup from which a monarch drinks demonstrates disdain for royalty — any bribe or ransom is inadequate to pardon him (*Ramban*).

And he regularly divines with it. There was a certain art of divination by which one foretold events by the surface motion of wine in a special cup (*Eisenstein*). All such forms of soothsaying were prohibited by Torah law [cf. *Deut.* 18:10].

8. Their argument, known in Talmudic literature as *kal vachomer*, (a fortiori, deduction from 'minor to major') was based on simple logic: If they proved their honesty by coming all the way back from Canaan to return money that they had not even taken, how could they now be accused of having stolen?

9. Although the brothers vehemently denied the charge, they went even further. So certain were they that none of them was guilty, they agreed to accept an unusually harsh punishment if the cup was found among them.

10. The steward agrees, but not to their exaggerated proposal.

Although you suggest that your offer to become slaves is merely voluntary, you are wrong since there is a suspicion against all of you; you should be arrested until the matter is clarified. Nevertheless, *as per your words* — that you are innocent of the theft and unaware that it even happened — *so shall it be.* I will free all but the culprit (*Ramban*).

You will be free to return home. This too was a test to see whether they would willingly leave Benjamin behind (*Haamek Davar*).

11. This was further demonstration of their eagerness to exonerate themselves as quickly as possible. They did not wait for him to open their sacks; each one opened his own and offered to be searched first (*Bereishis Rabbasi*).

13. Their distress was magnified by the fact that it happened to be Benjamin, and they agonized over the potentially fatal grief it would cause Jacob when he learned of it (*Ralbag; Abarbanel*).

14. They were directed to go to Joseph's house to spare them the shame of appearing before other Egyptians (*Midrash HaGadol*).

They fell to the ground before him, in obeisance. According to *Tanchuma,* it was now that Joseph's dream of the eleven bowing stars [37:9] was fulfilled.

15. With affected indignation, Joseph reproaches them for what they have done.

---

[3] The day dawned and the men were sent off, they and their donkeys. [4] They had left the city, had not gone far, when Joseph said to his steward, 'Get up, chase after the men. When you overtake them, you are to say to them, "Why do you repay evil for good? [5] It is the one from which my master drinks, and he regularly divines with it. You have behaved badly in what you have done!" '

[6] He overtook them and spoke those words to them. [7] And they said to him, 'Why does my lord say such things? It would be sacrilegious for your servants to do such a thing! [8] Here, look: The money that we found in the mouth of our sacks we brought back to you from the land of Canaan. How then could we have stolen from your master's house any silver or gold? [9] Anyone among your servants with whom it is found shall die, and we also will become slaves to my lord.'

[10] He replied, 'Although what you say now is also correct, nevertheless, with whomever it is found shall be my slave, but the rest of you shall be exonerated.'

[11] Hurriedly, each one lowered his sack to the ground and each one opened his sack. [12] He searched; he began with the oldest and ended with the youngest. And the goblet was found in Benjamin's sack. [13] They rent their garments. Each one reloaded his donkey and they returned to the city.

[14] When Judah arrived with his brothers to Joseph's house, he was still there. They fell to the ground before him. [15] Joseph said to them, 'What is this deed that you have perpetrated? Do you not realize that a man like me practices divination!'

טז וַיֹּ֣אמֶר יְהוּדָ֗ה מַה־נֹּאמַר֙ לַֽאדֹנִ֔י מַה־נְּדַבֵּ֖ר וּמַה־נִּצְטַדָּ֑ק הָֽאֱלֹהִ֗ים מָצָא֙ אֶת־עֲוֺ֣ן עֲבָדֶ֔יךָ הִנֶּ֤נּוּ עֲבָדִים֙ לַֽאדֹנִ֔י גַּם־אֲנַ֕חְנוּ גַּ֛ם אֲשֶׁר־נִמְצָ֥א הַגָּבִ֖יעַ בְּיָדֽוֹ: יז וַיֹּ֕אמֶר חָלִ֣ילָה לִּ֔י מֵֽעֲשׂ֖וֹת זֹ֑את הָאִ֡ישׁ אֲשֶׁר֩ נִמְצָ֨א הַגָּבִ֜יעַ בְּיָד֗וֹ ה֚וּא יִֽהְיֶה־לִּ֣י עָ֔בֶד וְאַתֶּ֕ם עֲל֥וּ לְשָׁל֖וֹם אֶל־אֲבִיכֶֽם:

The *Haftarah* for *Mikeitz* appears on page 330. When *Mikeitz* is read during Chanukah, the regular *Haftarah* is omitted. The *Haftarah* for the (first) Sabbath of Chanukah appears on page 336; for the second Sabbath of Chanukah, see page 348.

16. Judah speaks on their behalf and attempts no excuse, for the facts seem to allow none (*Abarbanel*).

What can we say to my lord in our defense? *How can we speak* to my father to whom I assured Benjamin's safety? *And how can we justify ourselves* before the Divine Presence? (*Tanchuma Yashan*).

'We know we committed no wrong in this matter. Rather it emanates from God, Who caused all of this to befall us because He wishes to seize this opportunity to punish us for an earlier sin. It is as if the previous misdeed had lain in abeyance, but now it is *uncovered* — *found*, as it were — to be dealt with. "The Creditor has found an opportunity to collect His debt" ' (*Rashi* from *Midrash*).

17. Joseph presses his advantage. In order to make them realize more keenly their precarious position, he declares that he will retain only Benjamin.

It now became apparent to Judah that this was not a Divine punishment for their former sins or else *all* of them would have been enslaved. It was either the viceroy's capriciousness, or the result of some sin of Benjamin. Therefore, from this point on, Judah began exercising his responsibility to do whatever he could for Benjamin (*Haamek Davar*).

According to the Masoretic note appearing at the end of the *Sidrah*, there are 146 verses in the *Sidrah*, numerically corresponding to the mnemonics וִֽיחִזְקִיָּ"ה, [*Yechizkiyahu*], אֲמַצְיָ"ה [*Amatzyah*], יִֽהְיֶה לִּי עָבֶ"ד, [*he shall be My slave*]. The *Sidrah* contains 2,025 letters. The *Haftarah* begins with *I Kings* 3:15: וַיִּקַ֥ץ שְׁלֹמֹֽה.

The names *Yechizkiyahu* and *Amatzyah* are the same as the mnemonics used for the *Sidrah Bereishis*, implying that the two portions have common themes. *Bereishis*, the portion of Creation, proclaims God's all-powerful majesty; as Creator of the universe, only He sustains it and determines it course, whatever pretensions man may have to the contrary. In *Sidrah Mikeitz*, we find Pharaoh considering himself a god and Egypt worshipping the Nile as its deity. Through the devices of abundance and famine, God displays beyond doubt that only *His* is the power. Pharaoh and his people are forced to acknowledge that they are subservient to Joseph whose distinction is that whatever his position — slave or viceroy — he remains but a servant of God: *He shall be My slave.*

Only in this *sidra*h is a mnemonic provided for the number of *words*, in this case 2025. This alludes to Chanukah, which falls in the week of *Sidrah Mikeitz*. On Chanukah, we light a new נֵר, *lamp*, for each of the eight nights. The numerical value of נֵר is 250; accordingly, the eight lights of Chanukah give a total of 2000. Chanukah begins on the *twenty-fifth* of Kislev. Thus, 2025 is an allusion to the lights and the date of Chanukah *(Torah Temimah)*.

The theme of Chanukah is especially appropriate to *Mikeitz*. We commemorate even the first day's burning, even though the oil in the jug enough to burn for a day without miraculous intervention. By doing so we testify to our belief, that even the seemingly 'natural' process of burning oil is in essence a miracle because it is a manifestation of God's will.

¹⁶ So Judah said, 'What can we say to my lord? How can we speak? And how can we justify ourselves? God has uncovered the sin of your servants. Here we are: We are ready to be slaves to my lord — both we and the one in whose hand the goblet was found.'

¹⁷ But he replied, 'It would be sacrilegious for me to do this. The man in whose possession the goblet was found, only he shall be my slave, and as for you — go up in peace to your father.'

The *Haftarah* for *Mikeitz* appears on page 330. When *Mikeitz* is read during Chanukah, the regular *Haftarah* is omitted. The *Haftarah* for the (first) Sabbath of Chanukah appears on page 336; for the second Sabbath of Chanukah, see page 348.

פרשת ויגש

VAYIGASH

Judah confronts the Egyptian viceroy, Joseph reveals himself and Jacob comes to Egypt — these are the dramatic highlights of *Vayigash*. The Sages and commentators have seen Joseph's revelation to his brothers as an episode packed with eternal lessons. His brothers had been racked by questions and doubts ever since they had descended to Egypt and become the butt of the strange viceroy's anger and suspicion. Clearly he was God's tool — because there was no blind coincidence in the world view of those supremely righteous people — but why was God doing this to them? And what did their dilemma portend for the destiny of the Jewish nation? Had the Divine promises to Jacob been annulled due to the family's sins — and if so, where had they fallen short?

And then Joseph said, 'I am Joseph. Does my father still live?' Suddenly everything fell into perspective for the brothers. So it will be at the End of Days. The curtain will be withdrawn from history, and its mysteries will have been deciphered.

It was the dreaded time when Jacob had to go down to Egypt, in fulfillment of the old prophecy to Abraham, that his offspring would be exiles and slaves in a harsh, foreign land. Jacob feared the consequences of such an exile. *He* would survive with his Jewishness intact, and so would his children — of that he was sure. But what would happen to future generations of Israel? This was a fear that future Jewish parents would have throughout history. God assured Jacob, '*I shall descend with you to Egypt,* and I shall surely also bring you up . . .' God joins us in exile, and He does not forsake us. This assurance has comforted Jewry throughout its long and often traumatic history.

יח וַיִּגַּ֨שׁ אֵלָ֜יו יְהוּדָ֗ה וַיֹּאמֶר֮ בִּ֣י אֲדֹנִי֒ יְדַבֶּר־נָ֨א
עַבְדְּךָ֤ דָבָר֙ בְּאׇזְנֵ֣י אֲדֹנִ֔י וְאַל־יִ֥חַר אַפְּךָ֖
בְּעַבְדֶּ֑ךָ כִּ֥י כָמ֖וֹךָ כְּפַרְעֹֽה: יט אֲדֹנִ֣י שָׁאַ֔ל
אֶת־עֲבָדָ֖יו לֵאמֹ֑ר הֲיֵשׁ־לָכֶ֥ם אָ֖ב אוֹ־אָֽח:
כ וַנֹּ֨אמֶר֙ אֶל־אֲדֹנִ֔י יֶשׁ־לָ֨נוּ֙ אָ֣ב זָקֵ֔ן וְיֶ֥לֶד זְקֻנִ֖ים
קָטָ֑ן וְאָחִ֣יו מֵ֗ת וַיִּוָּתֵ֨ר ה֤וּא לְבַדּוֹ֙ לְאִמּ֔וֹ וְאָבִ֖יו
אֲהֵבֽוֹ: כא וַתֹּ֨אמֶר֙ אֶל־עֲבָדֶ֔יךָ הֽוֹרִדֻ֖הוּ אֵלָ֑י
וְאָשִׂ֥ימָה עֵינִ֖י עָלָֽיו: כב וַנֹּ֨אמֶר֙ אֶל־אֲדֹנִ֔י לֹא־
יוּכַ֥ל הַנַּ֖עַר לַעֲזֹ֣ב אֶת־אָבִ֑יו וְעָזַ֥ב אֶת־אָבִ֖יו
וָמֵֽת: כג וַתֹּ֨אמֶר֙ אֶל־עֲבָדֶ֔יךָ אִם־לֹ֥א יֵרֵ֛ד
אֲחִיכֶ֥ם הַקָּטֹ֖ן אִתְּכֶ֑ם לֹ֥א תֹסִפ֖וּן לִרְא֥וֹת פָּנָֽי:
כד וַֽיְהִי֙ כִּ֣י עָלִ֔ינוּ אֶֽל־עַבְדְּךָ֖ אָבִ֑י וַנַּ֨גֶּד־ל֔וֹ אֵ֖ת
דִּבְרֵ֥י אֲדֹנִֽי: כה וַיֹּ֖אמֶר אָבִ֑ינוּ שֻׁ֖בוּ שִׁבְרוּ־לָ֥נוּ
מְעַט־אֹֽכֶל: כו וַנֹּ֕אמֶר לֹ֥א נוּכַ֖ל לָרֶ֑דֶת אִם־יֵ֩שׁ
אָחִ֨ינוּ הַקָּטֹ֤ן אִתָּ֙נוּ֙ וְיָרַ֔דְנוּ כִּי־לֹ֣א נוּכַ֗ל
לִרְאוֹת֙ פְּנֵ֣י הָאִ֔ישׁ וְאָחִ֥ינוּ הַקָּטֹ֖ן אֵינֶ֥נּוּ אִתָּֽנוּ:
כז וַיֹּ֛אמֶר עַבְדְּךָ֥ אָבִ֖י אֵלֵ֑ינוּ אַתֶּ֣ם יְדַעְתֶּ֔ם כִּ֥י
שְׁנַ֖יִם יָֽלְדָה־לִּ֥י אִשְׁתִּֽי: כח וַיֵּצֵ֤א הָֽאֶחָד֙ מֵֽאִתִּ֔י
וָאֹמַ֕ר אַ֖ךְ טָרֹ֣ף טֹרָ֑ף וְלֹ֥א רְאִיתִ֖יו עַד־הֵֽנָּה:
כט וּלְקַחְתֶּ֧ם גַּם־אֶת־זֶ֛ה מֵעִ֥ם פָּנַ֖י וְקָרָ֣הוּ אָס֑וֹן
וְהֽוֹרַדְתֶּ֧ם אֶת־שֵׂיבָתִ֛י בְּרָעָ֖ה שְׁאֹֽלָה: ל וְעַתָּ֗ה
כְּבֹאִי֙ אֶל־עַבְדְּךָ֣ אָבִ֔י וְהַנַּ֖עַר אֵינֶ֣נּוּ אִתָּ֑נוּ
וְנַפְשׁ֖וֹ קְשׁוּרָ֥ה בְנַפְשֽׁוֹ: שני לא וְהָיָ֗ה כִּרְאוֹת֛וֹ
כִּי־אֵ֥ין הַנַּ֖עַר וָמֵ֑ת וְהוֹרִ֨ידוּ עֲבָדֶ֜יךָ אֶת־שֵׂיבַ֩ת

44/18. Judah intercedes. As we learned in the conclusion of the last *Sidrah*, Benjamin had been caught with the viceroy's goblet, and Joseph ruled that Benjamin would have to remain in Egypt as a slave while the other brothers would return to their father. All the brothers were dumbfounded, but only Judah risked his life to intercede. His speech was eloquent, controlled, yet emotional; respectful, yet firm and daring. He petitioned without humiliating himself. He could not protest the fairness of the verdict, because the goblet *was* found in Benjamin's sack! Instead he offered himself as a slave — not knowing that he was speaking to the very brother whom he had once sold as a slave to Egypt . . .

For you are like Pharaoh. That is, I consider you as important as the king. The Midrash interprets the inner connotation of the phrase to imply: You will be smitten with leprosy for detaining Benjamin, just as Pharaoh was smitten for detaining my great-grandmother, Sarah, for only one night [above 12:17].

19. Judah's appeal was designed to evoke Joseph's compassion as a self-proclaimed God-fearing man [42:18]. Accordingly, at great personal risk, he presented an emotional argument, that was impelled by his pledge to, and love of, his father: If only one of us must remain as a slave let it be me, so that our aged and anxious father may again see his beloved youngest son. I, who guaranteed Benjamin's safety, could not return home without him, 'lest I witness the ill fate that would overtake my father.'

22. *For should he leave his father [then] he will die.* Jacob reasoned: 'It may have been decreed that the sons of Rachel should perish on the road. I sent Joseph on a journey and he did not return; the same might happen to Benjamin if I sent him, for their mother, too, died on the road' (*Midrash HaChafetz*).

27. The following passage was not recorded in the original account of the dialogue, in keeping with the rule that the Torah is brief in one place and expansive in another, reserving details for wherever they would be more pertinent.

31. The question arises: Benjamin had ten children at home; why didn't Judah mention the grief that Benjamin's *children* would experience at their father's absence?

R' Menachem Mendel of Kotzk used this as an example of how parents have more compassion for their children's misfortunes than the children for the parents.

¹⁸ Then Judah approached him and said: 'If you please, my lord, may your servant speak a word in my lord's ears and let not your anger flare up at your servant — for you are like Pharaoh. ¹⁹ My lord had asked his servants as follows: "Have you a father or brother?" ²⁰ 'And we said to my lord, "We have an old father and a young child of his old age; his brother is dead, he alone is left of his mother, and his father loves him." ²¹ 'Then you said to his servants, "Bring him down to me, and I will set my eye on him." ²² 'We said to my lord, "The youth cannot leave his father, for should he leave his father he will die." ²³ 'But you said to your servants, "If your youngest brother does not come down with you, you will not see my face again!" ²⁴ 'And it was, when we went up to your servant my father we told him my lord's words. ²⁵ And our father said, "Go back buy us some food." ²⁶ We said, "We cannot go down. Only if our youngest brother is with us, then we will go down, for we cannot see the man's face if our youngest brother is not with us." ²⁷ 'Then your servant my father said to us, "You know that my wife bore me two [sons]. ²⁸ One has left me and I presumed: Alas, he has surely been torn to pieces ! for I have not seen him since. ²⁹ So should you take this one, too, from my presence, and disaster befall him, then you will have brought down my hoariness in evil to the grave." ³⁰ 'And now, if I come to your servant my father and the youth is not with us — since his soul is so bound up with his soul! — ³¹ it will happen that when he sees the youth is missing he will die, and your servants will have brought down the hoari-

עַבְדְּךָ אָבִינוּ בְּיָגוֹן שְׁאֹלָה: לֹג כִּי עַבְדְּךָ עָרַב
אֶת־הַנַּעַר מֵעִם אָבִי לֵאמֹר אִם־לֹא אֲבִיאֶנּוּ
אֵלֶיךָ וְחָטָאתִי לְאָבִי כָּל־הַיָּמִים: לֹג וְעַתָּה
יֵשֶׁב־נָא עַבְדְּךָ תַּחַת הַנַּעַר עֶבֶד לַאדֹנִי
וְהַנַּעַר יַעַל עִם־אֶחָיו: לֹד כִּי־אֵיךְ אֶעֱלֶה
אֶל־אָבִי וְהַנַּעַר אֵינֶנּוּ אִתִּי פֶּן אֶרְאֶה בָרָע
אֲשֶׁר יִמְצָא אֶת־אָבִי: מה א וְלֹא־יָכֹל יוֹסֵף
לְהִתְאַפֵּק לְכֹל הַנִּצָּבִים עָלָיו וַיִּקְרָא הוֹצִיאוּ
כָל־אִישׁ מֵעָלָי וְלֹא־עָמַד אִישׁ אִתּוֹ
בְּהִתְוַדַּע יוֹסֵף אֶל־אֶחָיו: ב וַיִּתֵּן אֶת־קֹלוֹ
בִּבְכִי וַיִּשְׁמְעוּ מִצְרַיִם וַיִּשְׁמַע בֵּית פַּרְעֹה:
ג וַיֹּאמֶר יוֹסֵף אֶל־אֶחָיו אֲנִי יוֹסֵף הַעוֹד אָבִי
חָי וְלֹא־יָכְלוּ אֶחָיו לַעֲנוֹת אֹתוֹ כִּי נִבְהֲלוּ
מִפָּנָיו: ד וַיֹּאמֶר יוֹסֵף אֶל־אֶחָיו גְּשׁוּ־נָא אֵלַי
וַיִּגָּשׁוּ וַיֹּאמֶר אֲנִי יוֹסֵף אֲחִיכֶם אֲשֶׁר־
מְכַרְתֶּם אֹתִי מִצְרָיְמָה: ה וְעַתָּה אַל־תֵּעָצְבוּ
וְאַל־יִחַר בְּעֵינֵיכֶם כִּי־מְכַרְתֶּם אֹתִי הֵנָּה כִּי
לְמִחְיָה שְׁלָחַנִי אֱלֹהִים לִפְנֵיכֶם: ו כִּי־זֶה
שְׁנָתַיִם הָרָעָב בְּקֶרֶב הָאָרֶץ וְעוֹד חָמֵשׁ
שָׁנִים אֲשֶׁר אֵין־חָרִישׁ וְקָצִיר: ז וַיִּשְׁלָחַנִי
אֱלֹהִים לִפְנֵיכֶם לָשׂוּם לָכֶם שְׁאֵרִית
בָּאָרֶץ וּלְהַחֲיוֹת לָכֶם לִפְלֵיטָה גְּדֹלָה: שלישי
ח וְעַתָּה לֹא־אַתֶּם שְׁלַחְתֶּם אֹתִי הֵנָּה כִּי
הָאֱלֹהִים וַיְשִׂימֵנִי לְאָב לְפַרְעֹה וּלְאָדוֹן

32. Judah proceeds to explain why of all the brothers only he has taken the initiative to plead Benjamin's cause . . .

45/1. Joseph identifies himself. With Judah's selfless offer of himself as a substitute for Benjamin, Joseph finally had the irrefutable proof of the change in his brothers' old attitude, as exemplified by their filial devotion to Jacob, their love for Benjamin, and their sincere contrition for their crime against Joseph himself. It was to ascertain this that he subjected them to all these tribulations to begin with. Moreover, his brothers had had their share of the expiatory humiliation they deserved. Joseph felt, therefore, that the time of reconciliation had at last arrived (Akeidah; Abarbanel; R' Hirsch; R' Munk).

3. 'I am Joseph! Does my father still live?'

5. God, not you, sent me here. His purpose was to implant me here to preserve life; therefore you need not be distressed. You were only His instrument for accomplishing this goal. All of us were destined to descend to Egypt in fulfillment of God's decree that Abraham's descendants would be aliens in a foreign land [15:13]. Normally we should have gone to Egypt in iron fetters [in the manner of all enslaved exiles], but the Holy One, Blessed is He, chose to orchestrate events so that Father and the rest of you would be spared the harshness of a *forced descent* into hostile conditions. Instead, he sent me here to prepare the way and provide for you so you could follow in honor (gathered from *Tanchuma; Lekach Tov*).

ness of your servant our father, in sorrow to the grave. ³² 'For your servant took responsibility for the youth from my father saying, "If I do not bring him back to you then I will be sinning to my father for all time." ³³ 'Now, therefore, please let your servant remain instead of the youth as a servant to my lord, and let the youth go up with his brothers. ³⁴ For how can I go up to my father if the youth is not with me lest I see the evil that would befall my father!'

45 ¹ Now Joseph could not restrain himself in the presence of all who attended him, so he called out, 'Make everyone withdraw from me!' Thus no one remained with him when Joseph made himself known to his brothers. ² He cried uncontrollably. Egypt heard, and Pharaoh's household heard.

³ And Joseph said to his brothers, 'I am Joseph. Does my father still live?' But his brothers could not answer him because they felt disconcerted before him.

⁴ Then Joseph said to his brothers, 'Come close to me, if you please,' and they came close. And he said, 'I am Joseph your brother — it is me, whom you sold into Egypt. ⁵ And now, be not distressed, nor reproach yourselves for having sold me here, for it was to be a provider that God sent me ahead of you. ⁶ For this has been two of the hunger years in the midst of the land, and there are yet five years in which there shall be neither plowing nor harvest. ⁷ Thus God has sent me ahead of you to insure your survival in the land and to sustain you for a momentous deliverance. ⁸ And now: It was not you who sent me here, but God. He has made me father to Pharaoh, master

לְכָל־בֵּית֖וֹ וּמֹשֵׁ֕ל בְּכָל־אֶ֥רֶץ מִצְרָֽיִם: ט מַהֲרוּ֮
וַעֲל֣וּ אֶל־אָבִי֒ וַאֲמַרְתֶּ֣ם אֵלָ֗יו כֹּ֤ה אָמַר֙ בִּנְךָ֣
יוֹסֵ֔ף שָׂמַ֧נִי אֱלֹהִ֛ים לְאָד֖וֹן לְכָל־מִצְרָ֑יִם רְדָ֥ה
אֵלַ֖י אַֽל־תַּעֲמֹֽד: י וְיָשַׁבְתָּ֣ בְאֶֽרֶץ־גֹּ֗שֶׁן וְהָיִ֣יתָ
קָר֣וֹב אֵלַ֔י אַתָּה֙ וּבָנֶ֣יךָ וּבְנֵ֣י בָנֶ֔יךָ וְצֹאנְךָ֥ וּבְקָרְךָ֖
וְכָל־אֲשֶׁר־לָֽךְ: יא וְכִלְכַּלְתִּ֤י אֹֽתְךָ֙ שָׁ֔ם כִּי־ע֛וֹד
חָמֵ֥שׁ שָׁנִ֖ים רָעָ֑ב פֶּן־תִּוָּרֵ֛שׁ אַתָּ֥ה וּבֵֽיתְךָ֖
וְכָל־אֲשֶׁר־לָֽךְ: יב וְהִנֵּ֤ה עֵֽינֵיכֶם֙ רֹא֔וֹת וְעֵינֵ֖י
אָחִ֣י בִנְיָמִ֑ין כִּי־פִ֖י הַֽמְדַבֵּ֥ר אֲלֵיכֶֽם: יג וְהִגַּדְתֶּ֣ם
לְאָבִ֗י אֶת־כָּל־כְּבוֹדִי֙ בְּמִצְרַ֔יִם וְאֵ֖ת כָּל־אֲשֶׁ֣ר
רְאִיתֶ֑ם וּמִֽהַרְתֶּ֛ם וְהֽוֹרַדְתֶּ֥ם אֶת־אָבִ֖י הֵֽנָּה:
יד וַיִּפֹּ֛ל עַל־צַוְּארֵ֥י בִנְיָמִֽן־אָחִ֖יו וַיֵּ֑בְךְּ וּבִ֨נְיָמִ֔ן
בָּכָ֖ה עַל־צַוָּארָֽיו: טו וַיְנַשֵּׁ֥ק לְכָל־אֶחָ֖יו וַיֵּ֣בְךְּ
עֲלֵיהֶ֑ם וְאַֽחֲרֵי כֵ֔ן דִּבְּר֥וּ אֶחָ֖יו אִתּֽוֹ: טז וְהַקֹּ֣ל
נִשְׁמַ֗ע בֵּ֤ית פַּרְעֹה֙ לֵאמֹ֔ר בָּ֖אוּ אֲחֵ֣י יוֹסֵ֑ף וַיִּיטַב֙
בְּעֵינֵ֣י פַרְעֹ֔ה וּבְעֵינֵ֖י עֲבָדָֽיו: יז וַיֹּ֤אמֶר פַּרְעֹה֙
אֶל־יוֹסֵ֔ף אֱמֹ֥ר אֶל־אַחֶ֖יךָ זֹ֣את עֲשׂ֑וּ טַֽעֲנוּ֙
אֶת־בְּעִ֣ירְכֶ֔ם וּלְכוּ־בֹ֖אוּ אַ֥רְצָה כְּנָֽעַן: יח וּקְח֧וּ
אֶת־אֲבִיכֶ֛ם וְאֶת־בָּתֵּיכֶ֖ם וּבֹ֣אוּ אֵלָ֑י וְאֶתְּנָ֣ה
לָכֶ֗ם אֶת־טוּב֙ אֶ֣רֶץ מִצְרַ֔יִם וְאִכְל֖וּ אֶת־חֵ֥לֶב
הָאָֽרֶץ: רביעי יט וְאַתָּ֣ה צֻוֵּ֔יתָה זֹ֣את עֲשׂ֑וּ קְחֽוּ־
לָכֶם֩ מֵאֶ֨רֶץ מִצְרַ֜יִם עֲגָל֗וֹת לְטַפְּכֶם֙ וְלִנְשֵׁיכֶ֔ם
וּנְשָׂאתֶ֥ם אֶת־אֲבִיכֶ֖ם וּבָאתֶֽם: כ וְעֵ֣ינְכֶ֔ם אַל־
תָּחֹ֖ס עַל־כְּלֵיכֶ֑ם כִּי־ט֛וּב כָּל־אֶ֥רֶץ מִצְרַ֖יִם
לָכֶ֥ם הֽוּא: כא וַיַּֽעֲשׂוּ־כֵן֙ בְּנֵ֣י יִשְׂרָאֵ֔ל וַיִּתֵּ֨ן לָהֶ֤ם

9. *And say to him.* By your informing Father of my whereabouts, you will annul the solemn ban you imposed against telling him, which has prevented me from contacting him until now.

10. Goshen was a fertile region in northeast Egypt, east of the Nile delta. The Israelites lived there throughout their stay in Egypt, their primary residence being in Rameses, its major city. Goshen contained Egypt's most fertile soil and in 47:6 it is described as *the best of the land.*

Joseph purposely assigned this region to his family to keep them segregated from the mainstream of Egypt's idolatrous, immoral life, and to allow them to freely pursue their shepherding, which was hateful to the Egyptians.

12. The brothers had been standing dumbfounded before him all this time; Joseph was apprehensive that they still might be doubtful about his true identity, so he proceeds to reassure them again that he is really Joseph.

14. *Then he fell upon his brother Benjamin's neck* [lit., *necks*] *and wept.* The implication of the plural is that he wept on both sides of his neck (*Chizkuni*). Midrashically, Joseph wept for the two Temples, which would be in Benjamin's territory and would be destroyed (*Rashi*).

And Benjamin wept upon his neck. He wept for the Tabernacle of Shiloh, which was destined to be in Joseph's territory and would be destroyed by the Philistines (*Rashi*).

16. Pharaoh echoes Joseph's invitation and orders that wagons be sent for Jacob and his family.

19. Joseph's integrity and honesty were such that Pharaoh knew Joseph would never abuse his high office for personal advantage [especially in this case, since the export of wagons from Egypt was prohibited]; thus he might not send his father anything. Therefore Pharaoh specifically *commanded* him to do the following (*Ramban*).

of his entire household, and ruler throughout the entire land of Egypt. ⁹ Hurry — go up to my father and say to him, "So said your son Joseph: 'God has made me master of all Egypt. Come down to me please; do not delay. ¹⁰ You will reside in the land of Goshen and you will be near to me — you, your sons, your grandchildren, your flock and herd and all that is yours. ¹¹ And I will provide for you there — for there will be five more years of famine — so you do not become destitute, you, your household, and all that is yours.' "

¹² 'Behold! Your eyes see as do the eyes of my brother Benjamin that it is my mouth that is speaking to you. ¹³ Therefore, tell my father of all my glory in Egypt and all that you saw. But you must hurry, and bring my father down here.'

¹⁴ Then he fell upon his brother Benjamin's neck and wept; and Benjamin wept upon his neck. ¹⁵ He then kissed all his brothers and wept upon them, and afterwards his brothers conversed with him.

¹⁶ The news was heard in Pharaoh's palace saying, 'Joseph's brothers have come!' And it pleased Pharaoh and his servants. ¹⁷ Pharaoh said to Joseph, 'Say to your brothers, "Do this: Load up your animals and go directly to the land of Canaan. ¹⁸ Bring your father and your households and come to me. I will give you the best of the land of Egypt and you will eat the fat of the land." ¹⁹ And you are commanded [to say]: "Do this: Take yourselves from the land of Egypt wagons for your small children and for your wives; transport your father and come. ²⁰ And do not be concerned with your belongings for the best of all the land of Egypt shall be yours." '

²¹ The sons of Israel consented, and Joseph gave them wagons by Pharaoh's word. He also

יוֹסֵף עֲגָלוֹת עַל־פִּי פַרְעֹה וַיִּתֵּן לָהֶם צֵדָה
לַדָּרֶךְ: כב לְכֻלָּם נָתַן לָאִישׁ חֲלִפוֹת שְׂמָלֹת
וּלְבִנְיָמִן נָתַן שְׁלֹשׁ מֵאוֹת כֶּסֶף וְחָמֵשׁ חֲלִפֹת
שְׂמָלֹת: כג וּלְאָבִיו שָׁלַח כְּזֹאת עֲשָׂרָה חֲמֹרִים
נֹשְׂאִים מִטּוּב מִצְרָיִם וְעֶשֶׂר אֲתֹנֹת נֹשְׂאֹת בָּר
וָלֶחֶם וּמָזוֹן לְאָבִיו לַדָּרֶךְ: כד וַיְשַׁלַּח אֶת־
אֶחָיו וַיֵּלֵכוּ וַיֹּאמֶר אֲלֵהֶם אַל־תִּרְגְּזוּ בַּדָּרֶךְ:
כה וַיַּעֲלוּ מִמִּצְרָיִם וַיָּבֹאוּ אֶרֶץ כְּנַעַן אֶל־יַעֲקֹב
אֲבִיהֶם: כו וַיַּגִּדוּ לוֹ לֵאמֹר עוֹד יוֹסֵף חַי
וְכִי־הוּא מֹשֵׁל בְּכָל־אֶרֶץ מִצְרָיִם וַיָּפָג לִבּוֹ כִּי
לֹא־הֶאֱמִין לָהֶם: כז וַיְדַבְּרוּ אֵלָיו אֵת כָּל־
דִּבְרֵי יוֹסֵף אֲשֶׁר דִּבֶּר אֲלֵהֶם וַיַּרְא אֶת־
הָעֲגָלוֹת אֲשֶׁר־שָׁלַח יוֹסֵף לָשֵׂאת אֹתוֹ
וַתְּחִי רוּחַ יַעֲקֹב אֲבִיהֶם: חמישי כח וַיֹּאמֶר
יִשְׂרָאֵל רַב עוֹד־יוֹסֵף בְּנִי חָי אֵלְכָה וְאֶרְאֶנּוּ
בְּטֶרֶם אָמוּת: **מו** א וַיִּסַּע יִשְׂרָאֵל וְכָל־
אֲשֶׁר־לוֹ וַיָּבֹא בְּאֵרָה שָּׁבַע וַיִּזְבַּח זְבָחִים
לֵאלֹהֵי אָבִיו יִצְחָק: ב וַיֹּאמֶר אֱלֹהִים ׀
לְיִשְׂרָאֵל בְּמַרְאֹת הַלַּיְלָה וַיֹּאמֶר יַעֲקֹב ׀
יַעֲקֹב וַיֹּאמֶר הִנֵּנִי: ג וַיֹּאמֶר אָנֹכִי הָאֵל אֱלֹהֵי
אָבִיךָ אַל־תִּירָא מֵרְדָה מִצְרַיְמָה כִּי־לְגוֹי
גָּדוֹל אֲשִׂימְךָ שָׁם: ד אָנֹכִי אֵרֵד עִמְּךָ מִצְרַיְמָה
וְאָנֹכִי אַעַלְךָ גַם־עָלֹה וְיוֹסֵף יָשִׁית יָדוֹ
עַל־עֵינֶיךָ: ה וַיָּקָם יַעֲקֹב מִבְּאֵר שָׁבַע
וַיִּשְׂאוּ בְנֵי־יִשְׂרָאֵל אֶת־יַעֲקֹב אֲבִיהֶם וְאֶת־

24. *'Do not become agitated on the way.'* Rashi offers three interpretations of our passage: a) Do not become involved in halachic discussion lest the road become 'angry' at you [a figurative expression, meaning: lest you become so engrossed that you lose your way]; b) do not be annoyed by the journey lest you travel too quickly or travel into the night before stopping to rest; c) according to the 'plain' sense of the passage, however, Joseph feared that the brothers would quarrel with each other and engage in mutual recrimination over who was responsible for selling him. He therefore cautioned them against quarreling on the way.

26. *For he could not believe them.* This is the fate of a liar: He is disbelieved even when he tells the truth! Jacob had believed them when they came and showed him Joseph's bloodstained tunic, indicating that a wild beast had devoured him; but now he did not believe them even though they were telling the truth (*Avos d'Rabbi Nosson*).

27. The sign of the eglah arufah. To convince their disbelieving father that Joseph had sent these messages, they presented further evidence. To prove to Jacob that he was indeed the viceroy of Egypt, Joseph had directed his brothers to say that when he had left Jacob, they had been studying the topic of *eglah arufah* [the calf whose neck was broken in expiation of an unsolved murder (see *Deut.* 21:1-9)]. The word עֲגָלוֹת, *wagons,* can also be translated *calves,* thus alluding to the topic. Therefore it is written [further in this verse], *And he saw the agalos that Joseph had sent,* and it does not say . . . that Pharaoh had sent (*Rashi*).

Then the spirit of their father Jacob was revived. I.e., he believed the joyous news, and the prophetic spirit, which had left him during his grief, rested upon him again in his joy (*Rashi*).

46/1. Jacob undertakes the journey to Joseph.

R' Shlomo Ashtruc in *Midrashei HaTorah* writes that without doubt Jacob was aware of the vision at the Covenant Between the Parts that Abraham's descendants would be aliens and slaves in a strange land, and he was fearful that the literal exile and servitude would begin with him. He prayed to the *God of his father Isaac,* because Isaac had been spared the travails of physical exile and slavery, even though the four hundred years of alien status commenced with his birth. Jacob prayed for the same dispensation. Accordingly he offered these sacrifices imploring God to spare him these travails just as He had spared Isaac. God granted his prayer, as we shall learn below.

2. God appears to Jacob in a nocturnal prophetic revelation and grants him permission to migrate to Egypt.

gave them provisions for the journey. ²² To each of them he gave changes of clothing; but to Benjamin he gave three hundred pieces of silver and five changes of clothing. ²³ And to his father he sent the following: ten he-donkeys laden with the best of Egypt and ten she-donkeys laden with grain, bread, and food for his father for the journey. ²⁴ And he sent off his brothers, and they went. He said to them, 'Do not become agitated on the way.'

²⁵ They went up from Egypt and came to the land of Canaan to Jacob their father. ²⁶ And they told him, saying, 'Joseph is still alive,' also that he was ruler over all the land of Egypt. But his heart rejected it for he could not believe them. ²⁷ However, when they related to him all the words that Joseph had spoken to them, and he saw the wagons that Joseph had sent to transport him, then the spirit of their father Jacob was revived.

²⁸ And Israel said, 'How great! My son Joseph still lives! I must go and see him before I die.'

46 ¹ So Israel set out with all that he had and he came to Beer Sheba. He slaughtered sacrifices to the God of his father Isaac.

² God spoke to Israel in night visions and He said, 'Jacob, Jacob,' and he said, 'Here I am.'

³ And He said, 'I am the God — God of your father. Have no fear of descending to Egypt, for I shall establish you as a great nation there. ⁴ I shall descend with you to Egypt, and I shall also surely bring you up; and Joseph shall place his hand on your eyes.'

⁵ So Jacob arose from Beer Sheba. The sons of Israel transported Jacob their father, as well as

טַפָּם֙ וְאֶת־נְשֵׁיהֶ֔ם בָּעֲגָל֕וֹת אֲשֶׁר־שָׁלַ֥ח
פַּרְעֹ֖ה לָשֵׂ֥את אֹתֽוֹ: ו וַיִּקְח֣וּ אֶת־מִקְנֵיהֶ֗ם
וְאֶת־רְכוּשָׁם֙ אֲשֶׁ֤ר רָֽכְשׁוּ֙ בְּאֶ֣רֶץ כְּנַ֔עַן וַיָּבֹ֖אוּ
מִצְרָ֑יְמָה יַֽעֲקֹ֖ב וְכָל־זַרְע֥וֹ אִתּֽוֹ: ז בָּנָ֞יו וּבְנֵ֤י
בָנָיו֙ אִתּ֔וֹ בְּנֹתָ֥יו וּבְנ֖וֹת בָּנָ֑יו וְכָל־זַרְע֖וֹ הֵבִ֥יא
אִתּ֖וֹ מִצְרָֽיְמָה: ח וְאֵ֨לֶּה שְׁמ֜וֹת
בְּנֵֽי־יִשְׂרָאֵ֛ל הַבָּאִ֥ים מִצְרַ֖יְמָה יַֽעֲקֹ֣ב וּבָנָ֑יו
בְּכֹ֥ר יַֽעֲקֹ֖ב רְאוּבֵֽן: ט וּבְנֵ֖י רְאוּבֵ֑ן חֲנ֥וֹךְ וּפַלּ֖וּא
וְחֶצְרֹ֥ן וְכַרְמִֽי: י וּבְנֵ֣י שִׁמְע֗וֹן יְמוּאֵ֧ל וְיָמִ֛ין
וְאֹ֥הַד וְיָכִ֖ין וְצֹ֑חַר וְשָׁא֖וּל בֶּן־הַֽכְּנַעֲנִֽית:
יא וּבְנֵ֣י לֵוִ֔י גֵּֽרְשׁ֕וֹן קְהָ֖ת וּמְרָרִֽי: יב וּבְנֵ֣י יְהוּדָ֗ה
עֵ֧ר וְאוֹנָ֛ן וְשֵׁלָ֖ה וָפֶ֣רֶץ וָזָ֑רַח וַיָּ֨מָת עֵ֤ר וְאוֹנָן֙
בְּאֶ֣רֶץ כְּנַ֔עַן וַיִּֽהְי֥וּ בְנֵי־פֶ֖רֶץ חֶצְרֹ֥ן וְחָמֽוּל:
יג וּבְנֵ֣י יִשָּׂשכָ֑ר תּוֹלָ֥ע וּפֻוָּ֖ה וְי֥וֹב וְשִׁמְרֹֽן: יד וּבְנֵ֣י
זְבֻל֑וּן סֶ֥רֶד וְאֵל֖וֹן וְיַחְלְאֵֽל: טו אֵ֣לֶּה ׀ בְּנֵ֣י לֵאָ֗ה
אֲשֶׁ֨ר יָֽלְדָ֤ה לְיַֽעֲקֹב֙ בְּפַדַּ֣ן אֲרָ֔ם וְאֵ֖ת דִּינָ֣ה בִתּ֑וֹ
כָּל־נֶ֧פֶשׁ בָּנָ֛יו וּבְנוֹתָ֖יו שְׁלשִׁ֥ים וְשָׁלֹֽשׁ: טז וּבְנֵ֣י
גָ֗ד צִפְי֤וֹן וְחַגִּי֙ שׁוּנִ֣י וְאֶצְבֹּ֔ן עֵרִ֥י וַֽאֲרוֹדִ֖י
וְאַרְאֵלִֽי: יז וּבְנֵ֣י אָשֵׁ֗ר יִמְנָ֧ה וְיִשְׁוָ֛ה וְיִשְׁוִ֥י
וּבְרִיעָ֖ה וְשֶׂ֣רַח אֲחֹתָ֑ם וּבְנֵ֣י בְרִיעָ֔ה חֶ֖בֶר
וּמַלְכִּיאֵֽל: יח אֵ֚לֶּה בְּנֵ֣י זִלְפָּ֔ה אֲשֶׁר־נָתַ֥ן לָבָ֖ן
לְלֵאָ֣ה בִתּ֑וֹ וַתֵּ֧לֶד אֶת־אֵ֛לֶּה לְיַֽעֲקֹ֖ב שֵׁ֥שׁ
עֶשְׂרֵ֖ה נָֽפֶשׁ: יט בְּנֵ֤י רָחֵל֙ אֵ֣שֶׁת יַֽעֲקֹ֔ב
יוֹסֵ֖ף וּבִנְיָמִֽן: כ וַיִּוָּלֵ֣ד לְיוֹסֵף֮ בְּאֶ֣רֶץ מִצְרַ֒יִם֒

---

7. The Torah characteristically proceeds to specify who are included in the general designation offspring.

9. Reuben's sons.

10. Simeon's sons.

Son of the Canaanite woman. In the most literal sense, this verse is tacit proof that, of all the brothers, only Simeon married a woman of Canaanite descent. The Torah therefore singles him out for taking a Canaanite wife. [The Canaanites were an accursed nation, and one must recall Abraham's intense efforts to assure that Isaac would not marry a Canaanite woman (see 24:3), and Isaac's similar charge to Jacob (28:1)] (*Ibn Ezra*).

According to predominant Rabbinic view, 'Canaanitess' refers to Dinah. Saul was actually the son of Dinah who is here called a Canaanitess because she had been ravished by the Canaanite Shechem. When her brothers killed Shechem, Dinah refused to accompany them until Simeon agreed to marry her, which he did (*Rashi*; *Midrash*).

12. Judah's sons.

13. Issachar's sons.

15. The birth of Yocheved; the unnamed descendant. A detailed count, however, yields only thirty-two! The thirty-third one is Yocheved who was born as they entered the gateway between the walls, on the way into the city.

their small children and wives, in the wagons which Pharaoh had sent to transport him. ⁶ They took their livestock and their wealth which they had amassed in the land of Canaan and they came to Egypt — Jacob and all his offspring with him. ⁷ His sons and grandsons with him, his daughters and granddaughters and all his offspring he brought with him to Egypt.

⁸ Now these are the names of the children of Israel who were coming to Egypt — Jacob and his children: Jacob's first-born, Reuben.

⁹ Reuben's sons: Chanoch, Pallu, Chetzron and Carmi.

¹⁰ Simeon's sons: Yemuel, Yamin, Ohad, Yachin, Tzochar, and Saul, son of the Canaanite woman.

¹¹ Levi's sons: Gershon, Kehas, and Merari.

¹² Judah's sons: Er, Onan, Shelah, Peretz and Zerach; but Er and Onan had died in the land of Canaan — and Peretz's sons were Chetzron and Chamul.

¹³ Issachar's sons: Tola, Puvah, Yov and Shimron.

¹⁴ Zebulun's sons: Sered, Elon and Yachl'el. ¹⁵ These are the sons of Leah whom she bore to Jacob in Paddan Aram, in addition to Dinah his daughter. All the persons — his sons and daughters — numbered thirty-three.

¹⁶ Gad's sons: Tziphion, Chaggi, Shuni, Etzbon, Eri, Arodi, and Areli.

¹⁷ Asher's sons: Yimnah, Yishvah, Yishvi, Beriah, and their sister Serach; Beriah's sons, Cheber and Malkiel. ¹⁸ These were the descendants of Zilpah whom Laban had given to Leah his daughter. These she bore to Jacob: sixteen persons.

¹⁹ The sons of Rachel, Jacob's wife: Joseph and Benjamin.

²⁰ To Joseph were born in the land of Egypt —

אֲשֶׁר יָלְדָה־לּוֹ אָסְנַת בַּת־פּֽוֹטִי פֶרַע כֹּהֵן אֹן
אֶת־מְנַשֶּׁה וְאֶת־אֶפְרָֽיִם: כא וּבְנֵי בִנְיָמִן בֶּלַע
וָבֶכֶר וְאַשְׁבֵּל גֵּרָא וְנַעֲמָן אֵחִי וָרֹאשׁ מֻפִּים
וְחֻפִּים וָאָֽרְדְּ: כב אֵלֶּה בְּנֵי רָחֵל אֲשֶׁר יֻלַּד
לְיַעֲקֹב כָּל־נֶפֶשׁ אַרְבָּעָה עָשָֽׂר: כג וּבְנֵי־דָן
חֻשִֽׁים: כד וּבְנֵי נַפְתָּלִי יַחְצְאֵל וְגוּנִי וְיֵצֶר
וְשִׁלֵּֽם: כה אֵלֶּה בְּנֵי בִלְהָה אֲשֶׁר־נָתַן לָבָן
לְרָחֵל בִּתּוֹ וַתֵּלֶד אֶת־אֵלֶּה לְיַעֲקֹב כָּל־נֶפֶשׁ
שִׁבְעָֽה: כו כָּל־הַ֠נֶּפֶשׁ הַבָּאָה לְיַעֲקֹב מִצְרַיְמָה
יֹצְאֵי יְרֵכוֹ מִלְּבַד נְשֵׁי בְנֵי־יַעֲקֹב כָּל־נֶפֶשׁ
שִׁשִּׁים וָשֵֽׁשׁ: כז וּבְנֵי יוֹסֵף אֲשֶׁר־יֻלַּד־לוֹ
בְמִצְרַיִם נֶפֶשׁ שְׁנָיִם כָּל־הַנֶּפֶשׁ לְבֵית־יַעֲקֹב
הַבָּאָה מִצְרַיְמָה שִׁבְעִֽים: ששי כח וְאֶת־
יְהוּדָה שָׁלַח לְפָנָיו אֶל־יוֹסֵף לְהוֹרֹת לְפָנָיו
גֹּשְׁנָה וַיָּבֹאוּ אַרְצָה גֹּֽשֶׁן: כט וַיֶּאְסֹר יוֹסֵף
מֶרְכַּבְתּוֹ וַיַּעַל לִקְרַאת־יִשְׂרָאֵל אָבִיו גֹּשְׁנָה
וַיֵּרָא אֵלָיו וַיִּפֹּל עַל־צַוָּארָיו וַיֵּבְךְּ עַל־צַוָּארָיו
עֽוֹד: ל וַיֹּאמֶר יִשְׂרָאֵל אֶל־יוֹסֵף אָמוּתָה
הַפָּעַם אַחֲרֵי רְאוֹתִי אֶת־פָּנֶיךָ כִּי עוֹדְךָ חָֽי:
לא וַיֹּאמֶר יוֹסֵף אֶל־אֶחָיו וְאֶל־בֵּית אָבִיו
אֶעֱלֶה וְאַגִּידָה לְפַרְעֹה וְאֹמְרָה אֵלָיו אַחַי
וּבֵית־אָבִי אֲשֶׁר בְּאֶרֶץ־כְּנַעַן בָּאוּ אֵלָֽי:
לב וְהָאֲנָשִׁים רֹעֵי צֹאן כִּי־אַנְשֵׁי מִקְנֶה הָיוּ
וְצֹאנָם וּבְקָרָם וְכָל־אֲשֶׁר לָהֶם הֵבִֽיאוּ:
לג וְהָיָה כִּי־יִקְרָא לָכֶם פַּרְעֹה וְאָמַר מַה־

26. The totals. That is, all the persons who set out on the journey from Canaan to Egypt numbered 66, excluding Joseph and his sons, who were awaiting them in Egypt. [Leah's listed descendants: 32; Zilpah's: 16; Rachel's: 11; Bilhah's: 7 = 66.]

27. The 70 descendants. Sixty-six are enumerated, Yocheved was born en route and Joseph and his two sons were in Egypt.

Other views of who completed the total number of 70:

• The Patriarch Jacob himself is counted among the group as the expression *Jacob and his children* in v. 8 implies [see *Ibn Ezra* v. 15].

• The Divine Presence was the seventieth, for God joined their group, as it were, in fulfillment of His promise to Jacob [in v. 4]: *I shall descend with you.*

• Furthermore, *Rosh* at the end of *Pesachim* asserts that in the simple sense, no one is 'missing,' since it is common for the Torah to round off a number when just one unit is missing (e.g., 69 to 70).

28. *To prepare ahead of him.* I.e., in advance of his arrival (*Rashi*) in Goshen. To prepare a place for him [Jacob] and show him how to settle there (*Rashi*).

Rashi cites an alternate interpretation from the Midrash, which understands לְהוֹרֹת in its other sense of *to teach*: 'To establish for him a House of Study [בֵּית הַתַּלְמוּד] from which teaching [הוֹרָאָה] could go forth.'

29. *[He] fell on his neck, and he wept on his neck excessively.* Joseph wept greatly and continuously. Jacob, however, did not fall upon Joseph's neck, nor did he kiss him, for, as the Sages say, Jacob was reciting the *Shema* at that moment (*Rashi*).

Ramban maintains that, in the literal sense, the subject of the verb *wept* is not Joseph but Jacob, the antecedent of the preceding pronoun אֵלָיו, *to him.* Accordingly he interprets: *And he* [Jacob] *fell on* [Joseph's] *neck and he* [Jacob] *wept* . . . *Ramban* sums up his interpretation: 'It is quite well known whose tears are more present, the aged parent who finds his long-lost son alive after having despaired and mourned for him, or the young son who rules?'

31. *Joseph ensures his family's settlement in Goshen.*

Chiddushei HaRim remarks that Joseph was establishing a pattern for his successors to follow in every generation: Do not seek the grace of gentile rulers; neither emulate their ways nor mingle with them socially. Joseph knew that shepherds were detested by Egypt, yet he openly told Pharaoh that his brothers were shepherds in order to separate them from the Egyptians and in order that they should be settled in a separate region.

whom Asenath daughter of Poti Phera Chief of On bore to him — Manasseh and Ephraim.

²¹ Benjamin's sons: Bela, Becher, Ashbel, Gera, Naaman, Echi, Rosh, Mupim, Chupim, and Ard. ²² These were the descendants of Rachel who were born to Jacob, fourteen persons in all.

²³ Dan's sons: Chushim.

²⁴ Naftali's sons: Yahz'el, Guni, Yezer and Shilem. ²⁵ These were the descendants of Bilhah whom Laban had given to Rachel his daughter. She bore these to Jacob: seven persons in all.

²⁶ All the persons coming with Jacob to Egypt — his own descendants aside from the wives of Jacob's sons — sixty-six persons in all.

²⁷ And Joseph's sons who were born to him in Egypt numbered two persons. All the persons of Jacob's household who came to Egypt [totaled] seventy.

²⁸ He sent Judah ahead of him to Joseph to prepare ahead of him in Goshen. And they arrived in the region of Goshen.

²⁹ Joseph harnessed his chariot and went up to meet Israel his father in Goshen. He appeared before him, fell on his neck, and he wept on his neck excessively. ³⁰ Then Israel said to Joseph, 'Now I can die, after my having seen your face, because you are still alive.'

³¹ And Joseph said to his brothers and to his brothers' household, 'I will go up and tell Pharaoh, and I will say to him, "My brothers and my father's household who were in the land of Canaan have come to me. ³² The men are shepherds, for they have been cattlemen. Their sheep and cattle — and everything they own — they have brought." ³³ And it shall be, when Pharaoh summons you, and says, "What is

מַעֲשֵׂיכֶם: לד וַאֲמַרְתֶּם אַנְשֵׁי מִקְנֶה הָיוּ
עֲבָדֶ֫יךָ מִנְּעוּרֵ֫ינוּ וְעַד־עַ֫תָּה גַּם־אֲנַ֫חְנוּ
גַּם־אֲבֹתֵ֫ינוּ בַּעֲבוּר תֵּשְׁבוּ בְּאֶ֫רֶץ גֹּ֫שֶׁן כִּי־
תוֹעֲבַת מִצְרַ֫יִם כָּל־רֹ֫עֵה צֹאן: **מז** א וַיָּבֹ֫א
יוֹסֵף֙ וַיַּגֵּ֣ד לְפַרְעֹ֔ה וַיֹּ֕אמֶר אָבִ֣י וְאַחַ֗י וְצֹאנָ֤ם
וּבְקָרָם֙ וְכָל־אֲשֶׁ֣ר לָהֶ֔ם בָּ֖אוּ מֵאֶ֣רֶץ כְּנָ֑עַן
וְהִנָּ֖ם בְּאֶ֥רֶץ גֹּֽשֶׁן: ב וּמִקְצֵ֣ה אֶחָ֔יו לָקַ֖ח
חֲמִשָּׁ֣ה אֲנָשִׁ֑ים וַיַּצִּגֵ֖ם לִפְנֵ֥י פַרְעֹֽה: ג וַיֹּ֧אמֶר
פַּרְעֹ֛ה אֶל־אֶחָ֖יו מַה־מַּעֲשֵׂיכֶ֑ם וַיֹּאמְר֣וּ אֶל־
פַּרְעֹ֗ה רֹעֵ֥ה צֹאן֙ עֲבָדֶ֔יךָ גַּם־אֲנַ֖חְנוּ גַּם־
אֲבוֹתֵֽינוּ: ד וַיֹּאמְר֣וּ אֶל־פַּרְעֹ֗ה לָג֣וּר בָּאָ֘רֶץ֒
בָּ֒אנוּ כִּי־אֵ֣ין מִרְעֶ֗ה לַצֹּאן֙ אֲשֶׁ֣ר לַעֲבָדֶ֔יךָ
כִּי־כָבֵ֥ד הָרָעָ֖ב בְּאֶ֣רֶץ כְּנָ֑עַן וְעַתָּ֛ה יֵֽשְׁבוּ־
נָ֥א עֲבָדֶ֖יךָ בְּאֶ֥רֶץ גֹּֽשֶׁן: ה וַיֹּ֣אמֶר פַּרְעֹ֔ה
אֶל־יוֹסֵ֖ף לֵאמֹ֑ר אָבִ֥יךָ וְאַחֶ֖יךָ בָּ֥אוּ אֵלֶֽיךָ:
ו אֶ֤רֶץ מִצְרַ֙יִם֙ לְפָנֶ֣יךָ הִ֔וא בְּמֵיטַ֣ב הָאָ֗רֶץ
הוֹשֵׁ֥ב אֶת־אָבִ֖יךָ וְאֶת־אַחֶ֑יךָ יֵשְׁבוּ֙ בְּאֶ֣רֶץ
גֹּ֔שֶׁן וְאִם־יָדַ֗עְתָּ וְיֶשׁ־בָּם֙ אַנְשֵׁי־חַ֔יִל וְשַׂמְתָּ֛ם
שָׂרֵ֥י מִקְנֶ֖ה עַל־אֲשֶׁר־לִֽי: ז וַיָּבֵ֤א יוֹסֵף֙ אֶת־
יַעֲקֹ֣ב אָבִ֔יו וַיַּֽעֲמִדֵ֖הוּ לִפְנֵ֣י פַרְעֹ֑ה וַיְבָ֥רֶךְ
יַעֲקֹ֖ב אֶת־פַּרְעֹֽה: ח וַיֹּ֥אמֶר פַּרְעֹ֖ה אֶל־
יַעֲקֹ֑ב כַּמָּ֕ה יְמֵ֖י שְׁנֵ֥י חַיֶּֽיךָ: ט וַיֹּ֤אמֶר יַעֲקֹב֙
אֶל־פַּרְעֹ֔ה יְמֵי֙ שְׁנֵ֣י מְגוּרַ֔י שְׁלֹשִׁ֥ים וּמְאַ֖ת
שָׁנָ֑ה מְעַ֣ט וְרָעִ֗ים הָיוּ֙ יְמֵי֙ שְׁנֵ֣י חַיַּ֔י וְלֹ֣א הִשִּׂ֗יגוּ
אֶת־יְמֵי֙ שְׁנֵי֙ חַיֵּ֣י אֲבֹתַ֔י בִּימֵ֖י מְגוּרֵיהֶֽם:

47/1. וַיָּבֹא יוֹסֵף וַיַּגֵּד לְפַרְעֹה
— *Then Joseph came and told Pharaoh.* It does not say *he went up* to Pharaoh's private, upper-level chamber [see 46:31], for Providence arranged for Joseph to find Pharaoh below with his officials (*Haamek Davar*).

2. *He took five men.* From the weakest of them — from those who did not *look* robust; because if Pharaoh had seen powerful men, he would have enlisted them as soldiers (*Rashi*).

Joseph wanted Pharaoh to see for himself, from their words and general demeanor, that they were suitable only for shepherding (*Sforno*).

7. Joseph presents Jacob to Pharaoh. *And presented* [lit., *stood*] *him to Pharaoh.* From the *Mesorah* [traditional spelling as found in Torah Scrolls], according to which וַיַּעֲמִדֵהוּ is spelled 'defectively' [without the י after the מ], *Baal HaTurim* infers that Jacob's standing here was 'defective.' He was extremely old and Joseph had to support him.

9. The days that I have lived as a רֵג, *stranger, alien,* have totaled 130 years, for I have been a stranger in other people's lands all my life *(Rashi).*

And they have not attained the life spans of my forefathers in the days of their sojourns.

And they have not attained — in happiness *(Rashi).*

My life is not comparable to the lives of my fathers. They lived *more,* in the sense that every day of their existence was *living,* and they were able to carry out their missions under cheerful conditions. — Jacob was modestly assessing the qualitative paucity of his life *(R' Hirsch).*

your occupation?'' ³⁴ Then you are to say, ''Your servants have been cattlemen from our youth till now, both we and our forefathers,'' so that you may be able to stay on the region of Goshen, since all shepherds are abhorrent to Egyptians.'

47 ¹ Then Joseph came and told Pharaoh, and he said, 'My father and my brothers, their sheep, their cattle, and everything they own, have arrived from the land of Canaan and they are now in the region of Goshen.' ² From the least of his brothers he took five men and presented them to Pharaoh. ³ Pharaoh said to his brothers, 'What is your occupation?' They answered Pharaoh, 'Your servants are shepherds — we as well as our forefathers.' ⁴ And they said to Pharaoh, 'We have come to sojourn in this land, since there is no grazing for your servants' sheep, for the famine is severe in the land of Canaan. Now, if you please, allow your servants to dwell in the region of Goshen.'

⁵ And Pharaoh said to Joseph as follows, 'Your father and your brothers have come to you. ⁶ The land of Egypt is before you — in the best part of the land settle your father and your brothers. Let them settle in the region of Goshen, and if you know that there are capable men among them, appoint them as chamberlains over the livestock that belongs to me.'

⁷ Then Joseph brought Jacob, his father, and presented him to Pharaoh, and Jacob blessed Pharaoh. ⁸ Pharaoh said to Jacob, 'How many years have you lived?' ⁹ Jacob answered Pharaoh, 'The years of my sojourns have been a hundred and thirty years. Few and bad have been the years of my life, and they have not attained the life spans of my forefathers in the days of their sojourns.'

יַוַיְבָ֧רֶךְ יַעֲקֹ֛ב אֶת־פַּרְעֹ֑ה וַיֵּצֵ֖א מִלִּפְנֵ֥י פַרְעֹֽה: שביעי יאוַיּוֹשֵׁ֣ב יוֹסֵף֮ אֶת־אָבִ֣יו וְאֶת־אֶחָיו֒ וַיִּתֵּ֨ן לָהֶ֤ם אֲחֻזָּה֙ בְּאֶ֣רֶץ מִצְרַ֔יִם בְּמֵיטַ֥ב הָאָ֖רֶץ בְּאֶ֣רֶץ רַעְמְסֵ֑ס כַּאֲשֶׁ֖ר צִוָּ֥ה פַרְעֹֽה: יבוַיְכַלְכֵּ֤ל יוֹסֵ֨ף אֶת־אָבִ֤יו וְאֶת־אֶחָיו֙ וְאֵ֖ת כָּל־בֵּ֣ית אָבִ֑יו לֶ֖חֶם לְפִ֥י הַטָּֽף: יגוְלֶ֤חֶם אֵין֙ בְּכָל־הָאָ֔רֶץ כִּֽי־כָבֵ֥ד הָרָעָ֖ב מְאֹ֑ד וַתֵּ֜לַהּ אֶ֤רֶץ מִצְרַ֨יִם֙ וְאֶ֣רֶץ כְּנַ֔עַן מִפְּנֵ֖י הָרָעָֽב: ידוַיְלַקֵּ֣ט יוֹסֵ֗ף אֶת־כָּל־הַכֶּ֨סֶף֙ הַנִּמְצָ֤א בְאֶֽרֶץ־מִצְרַ֨יִם֙ וּבְאֶ֣רֶץ כְּנַ֔עַן בַּשֶּׁ֖בֶר אֲשֶׁר־הֵ֣ם שֹׁבְרִ֑ים וַיָּבֵ֥א יוֹסֵ֛ף אֶת־הַכֶּ֖סֶף בֵּ֥יתָה פַרְעֹֽה: טווַיִּתֹּ֣ם הַכֶּ֗סֶף מֵאֶ֤רֶץ מִצְרַ֨יִם֙ וּמֵאֶ֣רֶץ כְּנַ֔עַן וַיָּבֹ֩אוּ֩ כָל־מִצְרַ֨יִם אֶל־יוֹסֵ֤ף לֵאמֹר֙ הָֽבָה־לָּ֣נוּ לֶ֔חֶם וְלָ֥מָּה נָמ֛וּת נֶגְדֶּ֖ךָ כִּ֥י אָפֵ֥ס כָּֽסֶף: טזוַיֹּ֤אמֶר יוֹסֵף֙ הָב֣וּ מִקְנֵיכֶ֔ם וְאֶתְּנָ֥ה לָכֶ֖ם בְּמִקְנֵיכֶ֑ם אִם־אָפֵ֖ס כָּֽסֶף: יזוַיָּבִ֣יאוּ אֶת־מִקְנֵיהֶם֮ אֶל־יוֹסֵף֒ וַיִּתֵּ֣ן לָהֶם֩ יוֹסֵ֨ף לֶ֜חֶם בַּסּוּסִ֗ים וּבְמִקְנֵ֤ה הַצֹּאן֙ וּבְמִקְנֵ֣ה הַבָּקָ֔ר וּבַחֲמֹרִ֑ים וַיְנַהֲלֵ֤ם בַּלֶּ֨חֶם֙ בְּכָל־מִקְנֵהֶ֔ם בַּשָּׁנָ֖ה הַהִֽוא: יחוַתִּתֹּם֮ הַשָּׁנָ֣ה הַהִוא֒ וַיָּבֹ֨אוּ אֵלָ֜יו בַּשָּׁנָ֣ה הַשֵּׁנִ֗ית וַיֹּ֤אמְרוּ לוֹ֙ לֹֽא־נְכַחֵ֣ד מֵֽאֲדֹנִ֔י כִּ֚י אִם־תַּ֣ם הַכֶּ֔סֶף וּמִקְנֵ֥ה הַבְּהֵמָ֖ה אֶל־אֲדֹנִ֑י לֹ֤א נִשְׁאַר֙ לִפְנֵ֣י אֲדֹנִ֔י בִּלְתִּ֥י אִם־גְּוִיָּתֵ֖נוּ וְאַדְמָתֵֽנוּ: יטלָ֧מָּה נָמ֣וּת לְעֵינֶ֗יךָ גַּם־אֲנַ֨חְנוּ֙ גַּם־אַדְמָתֵ֔נוּ קְנֵֽה־אֹתָ֥נוּ וְאֶת־אַדְמָתֵ֖נוּ בַּלָּ֑חֶם וְנִֽהְיֶ֞ה אֲנַ֤חְנוּ וְאַדְמָתֵ֨נוּ֙

10. As a result of Jacob's blessing, the famine came to an end after only two years, instead of the seven years foretold by Joseph (*Midrash*).

13. Joseph's agrarian policy. According to *Rashi*, the following narrative occurred before Jacob arrived in Egypt. The Torah now resumes its narrative of the famine.

15. All the money was not used up at the same time. Obviously the poor used up their money before the rich. Our passage speaks of the time when even the money of the rich was depleted (*Tur*).

16. Joseph's proposal to barter livestock for food. This was all part of Joseph's master plan — to impoverish the Egyptians and make them totally dependent upon the king. His argument was: 'To give you bread is not within my authority. However, if it is indeed as you say, that your money is used up, then bring me your cattle and I will give you food in exchange. If you still have livestock, you have no right to ask for charity.'

18. In the next year. The second year of the famine. Although Joseph had said to his brothers [45:6]: *And there are yet five years in which there shall be neither plowing nor harvest,* as soon as Jacob came to Egypt a blessing came with him; they began to sow, and the famine came to an end [see v. 10 above]. This is derived from *Tosefta Sotah* 10:9.

10 Then Jacob blessed Pharaoh, and left Pharaoh's presence.

11 So Joseph settled his father and his brothers and he gave them a possession in the land of Egypt in the best part of the land, in the region of Rameses, as Pharaoh had commanded. 12 Joseph sustained his father and his brothers and all of his father's household with food according to the children.

13 Now there was no bread in all the earth for the famine was very severe. The land of Egypt and the land of Canaan became weary from hunger. 14 Joseph gathered all the money that was to be found in the land of Egypt and in the land of Canaan through the provisions which they were purchasing, and Joseph brought the money into Pharaoh's palace. 15 And when the money was exhausted from the land of Egypt and from the land of Canaan, all the Egyptians came to Joseph, saying, 'Give us bread; why should we die in your presence? — for the money is gone!' 16 And Joseph said, 'Bring your livestock and I will provide for you in return for your livestock if the money is gone.' 17 So they brought their livestock to Joseph, and Joseph gave them bread in return for the horses, for the flocks of sheep, for the herds of cattle, and for the donkeys; thus he provided them with bread for all their livestock during that year.

18 And when that year ended, they came to him in the next year and said to him, 'We will not withhold from my lord that with the money and flocks of cattle having been exhausted to my lord, nothing is left before my lord but our bodies and our land. 19 Why should we die before your eyes, both we and our land? Acquire us and our land for bread; and we — with our land — will become

עֲבָדִים לְפַרְעֹה וְתֶן־זֶרַע וְנִחְיֶה וְלֹא נָמוּת
וְהָאֲדָמָה לֹא תֵשָׁם: כּ וַיִּקֶן יוֹסֵף אֶת־כָּל־
אַדְמַת מִצְרַיִם לְפַרְעֹה כִּי־מָכְרוּ מִצְרַיִם אִישׁ
שָׂדֵהוּ כִּי־חָזַק עֲלֵהֶם הָרָעָב וַתְּהִי הָאָרֶץ
לְפַרְעֹה: כא וְאֶת־הָעָם הֶעֱבִיר אֹתוֹ לֶעָרִים
מִקְצֵה גְבוּל־מִצְרַיִם וְעַד־קָצֵהוּ: כב רַק אַדְמַת
הַכֹּהֲנִים לֹא קָנָה כִּי חֹק לַכֹּהֲנִים מֵאֵת פַּרְעֹה
וְאָכְלוּ אֶת־חֻקָּם אֲשֶׁר נָתַן לָהֶם פַּרְעֹה
עַל־כֵּן לֹא מָכְרוּ אֶת־אַדְמָתָם: כג וַיֹּאמֶר יוֹסֵף
אֶל־הָעָם הֵן קָנִיתִי אֶתְכֶם הַיּוֹם וְאֶת־
אַדְמַתְכֶם לְפַרְעֹה הֵא־לָכֶם זֶרַע וּזְרַעְתֶּם
אֶת־הָאֲדָמָה: כד וְהָיָה בַּתְּבוּאֹת וּנְתַתֶּם
חֲמִישִׁית לְפַרְעֹה וְאַרְבַּע הַיָּדֹת יִהְיֶה לָכֶם
לְזֶרַע הַשָּׂדֶה וּלְאָכְלְכֶם וְלַאֲשֶׁר בְּבָתֵּיכֶם
וְלֶאֱכֹל לְטַפְּכֶם: מפטיר כה וַיֹּאמְרוּ הֶחֱיִתָנוּ
נִמְצָא־חֵן בְּעֵינֵי אֲדֹנִי וְהָיִינוּ עֲבָדִים לְפַרְעֹה:
כו וַיָּשֶׂם אֹתָהּ יוֹסֵף לְחֹק עַד־הַיּוֹם הַזֶּה
עַל־אַדְמַת מִצְרַיִם לְפַרְעֹה לַחֹמֶשׁ רַק אַדְמַת
הַכֹּהֲנִים לְבַדָּם לֹא הָיְתָה לְפַרְעֹה: כז וַיֵּשֶׁב
יִשְׂרָאֵל בְּאֶרֶץ מִצְרַיִם בְּאֶרֶץ גֹּשֶׁן וַיֵּאָחֲזוּ בָהּ
וַיִּפְרוּ וַיִּרְבּוּ מְאֹד:

The *Haftarah* for *Vayigash* appears on page 332

---

20. According to *Haamek Davar*, the reason Joseph did not make them slaves was for the welfare of the state. He wanted them to remain self-supporting and not become wards of the state. As *Malbim* emphasizes, a ruler must always feel responsible for the sustenance of his subjects; and it would have been wrong for him to have made them slaves in return for bread.

21. וְאֶת הָעָם הֶעֱבִיר אֹתוֹ לֶעָרִים — *[And] as for the nation, he resettled it by cities* [i.e., from city to city]. That is, Joseph transferred the population from one city to the other to establish the monarchy's undisputed ownership of the land, and to demonstrate that individuals no longer had claim to any property they formerly owned. He was concerned that, if he let them remain in their former homes, each would cling tenaciously to his former property, and he wanted it absolutely apparent that anyone's association with a certain piece of state property was exclusively at the king's pleasure (*Rashi; Radak; Chizkuni; Meshech Chochmah*).

22. *Only the land of the priests he did not buy,* for the reason that the verse proceeds to tell us.

Joseph's true rationale for granting this dispensation to the idolatrous priests is discussed in the comm. to the end of v. 26 below.

23. *Joseph demands a fifth of all produce for the king.*

The following is the sharecropping arrangement as it would apply in the future, when their planting — from Joseph's seed and on state property — would yield produce.

24. *A fifth to Pharaoh.* Under our arrangement, it would have been proper for the king, who is now lord of the land, to take *four* fifths of the harvest and leave only the remaining fifth for you. However, I will deal generously with you: *You will take the portion due to the owner of the land — four fifths — and Pharaoh will receive only the portion due to the tenant — one fifth.* The one restriction will be that you must remain to work the fields and cannot leave them (*Ramban*).

26. Joseph prophetically established a precedent that would later benefit Israel. By giving a privileged status to the clergy, Joseph made it possible for the tribe of Levi — who were the 'clerics' in Israel — to be exempt from the servitude to which the Egyptians later subjected the other tribes (*R' Yaakov Kaminetzky*).

27. According to the Masoretic note appearing at the end of the *Sidrah,* there are 106 verses in *Vayigash,* numerically corresponding to the mnemonic יְהַלֵּל אֵ"ל, literally *praised be God.* This refers to the praises due God for having spared Joseph and reuniting Jacob's family. It further alludes to the praise due to God for orchestrating the events that led to the Egyptian bondage. For just as the Jew is obligated to praise God for the goodness He bestows, so must we praise Him for that which appears evil. The *Haftarah* begins with *Ezekiel* 37:15: וְאַתָּה בֶן אָדָם קַח לְךָ עֵץ.

serfs to Pharaoh; and provide seed so that we may live and not die, and the land will not become desolate.'

²⁰ Thus Joseph acquired all the land of Egypt for Pharaoh, for every Egyptian sold his field because the famine had overwhelmed them. And the land became Pharaoh's. ²¹ As for the nation, he resettled it by cities, from one end of Egypt's borders to the other. ²² Only the land of the priests he did not buy, since the priests had a stipend from Pharaoh, and they lived off their stipend that Pharaoh had given them, therefore they did not sell their land.

²³ Joseph said to the people, 'Look — I have acquired you this day with your land for Pharaoh; here is seed for you — sow the land. ²⁴ At the ingathering of the harvests you will give a fifth to Pharaoh; the [other] four parts shall remain yours — as seed for the field, food for yourselves and for those in your household, and to feed your little ones.'

²⁵ And they said, 'You have saved our lives; may we find favor in your eyes, my lord, and we will be serfs to Pharaoh.'

²⁶ So Joseph imposed it as a statute till this day regarding the land of Egypt: It was Pharaoh's for the fifth; only the priests' land alone did not become Pharaoh's.

²⁷ Thus Israel settled in the land of Egypt in the region of Goshen; they acquired property in it and they were fruitful and multiplied greatly.

The *Haftarah* for *Vayigash* appears on page 332

פרשת ויחי

VAYECHI

In *Ramban's* view, *Genesis* is the Book of Creation, not because it is the story of the creation of heaven and earth — that takes up only one chapter — but because it is the story of the creation of the Jewish nation. That story began with Abraham, who was an individual, and ended with the death of Jacob, when his offspring had gone beyond the stage of being a family and had achieved nationhood.

Before his death, the Patriarch set forth the road map of that nation. First he assigned the privilege of firstborn to Joseph, giving his two sons, Manasseh and Ephraim, the status of separate tribes. In doing so, he placed the junior son Ephraim first, because he was outstanding in Torah study, and that would always be the primary Jewish value.

As he lay on his death bed, Jacob summoned all his children and blessed them, each according to his own unique characteristic, and according to the role he would be called upon to play in the development of the Jewish people. The nation is like a wheel and the tribes its spokes. All the spokes are necessary for the wheel's strength and proper functioning, and each emanates from the same center, but each has its own place. So, too, the tribes. Their goal and core is the same: service of God in consonance with His Torah, but each has its own unique mission: Judah's is royalty; Levi's is priesthood; Issachar's is Torah study; Zevulun's is commerce in support of Torah scholars; and so on. But in diversity there must be unity for the sake of the common goal, and when there is, there is strength.

כח וַיְחִי יַעֲקֹב בְּאֶרֶץ מִצְרַיִם שְׁבַע עֶשְׂרֵה
שָׁנָה וַיְהִי יְמֵי־יַעֲקֹב שְׁנֵי חַיָּיו שֶׁבַע שָׁנִים
וְאַרְבָּעִים וּמְאַת שָׁנָה: כט וַיִּקְרְבוּ יְמֵי־
יִשְׂרָאֵל לָמוּת וַיִּקְרָא ׀ לִבְנוֹ לְיוֹסֵף וַיֹּאמֶר
לוֹ אִם־נָא מָצָאתִי חֵן בְּעֵינֶיךָ שִׂים־נָא יָדְךָ
תַּחַת יְרֵכִי וְעָשִׂיתָ עִמָּדִי חֶסֶד וֶאֱמֶת
אַל־נָא תִקְבְּרֵנִי בְּמִצְרָיִם: ל וְשָׁכַבְתִּי עִם־
אֲבֹתַי וּנְשָׂאתַנִי מִמִּצְרַיִם וּקְבַרְתַּנִי
בִּקְבֻרָתָם וַיֹּאמַר אָנֹכִי אֶעֱשֶׂה כִדְבָרֶךָ:
לא וַיֹּאמֶר הִשָּׁבְעָה לִי וַיִּשָּׁבַע לוֹ וַיִּשְׁתַּחוּ
יִשְׂרָאֵל עַל־רֹאשׁ הַמִּטָּה:

מח א וַיְהִי אַחֲרֵי הַדְּבָרִים הָאֵלֶּה וַיֹּאמֶר
לְיוֹסֵף הִנֵּה אָבִיךָ חֹלֶה וַיִּקַּח אֶת־שְׁנֵי בָנָיו
עִמּוֹ אֶת־מְנַשֶּׁה וְאֶת־אֶפְרָיִם: ב וַיַּגֵּד
לְיַעֲקֹב וַיֹּאמֶר הִנֵּה בִּנְךָ יוֹסֵף בָּא
אֵלֶיךָ וַיִּתְחַזֵּק יִשְׂרָאֵל וַיֵּשֶׁב עַל־הַמִּטָּה:
ג וַיֹּאמֶר יַעֲקֹב אֶל־יוֹסֵף אֵל שַׁדַּי נִרְאָה־
אֵלַי בְּלוּז בְּאֶרֶץ כְּנָעַן וַיְבָרֶךְ אֹתִי: ד וַיֹּאמֶר
אֵלַי הִנְנִי מַפְרְךָ וְהִרְבִּיתִךָ וּנְתַתִּיךָ לִקְהַל
עַמִּים וְנָתַתִּי אֶת־הָאָרֶץ הַזֹּאת לְזַרְעֲךָ
אַחֲרֶיךָ אֲחֻזַּת עוֹלָם: ה וְעַתָּה שְׁנֵי־
בָנֶיךָ הַנּוֹלָדִים לְךָ בְּאֶרֶץ מִצְרַיִם עַד־בֹּאִי
אֵלֶיךָ מִצְרַיְמָה לִי־הֵם אֶפְרַיִם וּמְנַשֶּׁה
כִּרְאוּבֵן וְשִׁמְעוֹן יִהְיוּ־לִי: ו וּמוֹלַדְתְּךָ
אֲשֶׁר־הוֹלַדְתָּ אַחֲרֵיהֶם לְךָ יִהְיוּ עַל שֵׁם

The 'closed' section. *Vayechi* is
unique in that it follows the preceding *parashah* with only a one-
letter division between them, although the general rule calls for at
least a nine-letter space. *Rashi*,
therefore, calls it סתומה, *closed*:
This *sidrah* includes Jacob's death,
and as soon as he died, the hearts
of the children of Israel were
"closed" due to the suffering and
despair of the impending bondage. The spiritual bondage began
to materialize immediately after
Jacob's death, even though the
actual travails of *enslavement* did
not commence until the death of
all his sons (*Tur*). Another reason:
Jacob wanted to tell his children
the time of the 'End' [i.e., the
Messianic age when Israel's exiles
would finally end], but his
prophetic vision was 'closed' [i.e.,
concealed] from him (*Rashi* from
Midrash and *Zohar*).

28. At God's command, Jacob did
not return to Canaan after seeing
Joseph, but remained in Egypt for
the last seventeen years of his life
(*Abarbanel*).

29. According to *Rashi*, Jacob insisted on not being buried in
Egypt for several reasons: a) He
knew that the soil of Egypt would
one day be plagued with כִּנִּים,
vermin [*Exod*. 8:12], which would
swarm beneath his body; b) those
who are buried outside of *Eretz
Yisrael* will not come to life at the
Resurrection until they roll
through the earth to *Eretz Yisrael*;
c) to prevent the Egyptians from
making his tomb a shrine of idol
worship.

31. Then Israel *prostrated himself*
[to Joseph]. As the proverb says,
תַּעֲלָה בְּעִדָּנֵיהּ סְגִיד לֵיהּ, 'When the
fox has his hour, bow down to
him' (*Rashi*).

48/1. Jacob's illness.

After Joseph returned from
Goshen, Jacob became ill. When
Joseph was informed, he brought
his two sons so that Jacob would
bless them (*Ramban* 47:29).

3. The birthright is transferred to Joseph.

Jacob formally makes Ephraim and Manasseh equal to any of his other sons — in effect adopting them as his own — thereby transferring to Joseph a double portion of the inheritance.

4. God informed me that there will yet descend from me a *nation and a congregation of nations* (35:11), meaning that I will have additional progeny besides the eleven sons I had at that time. *Nation* alluded to Benjamin [who was born after the promise was made]. *A congregation of nations* intimated that two more *besides* Benjamin would descend from me to become nations. Since no more sons were born to me, I assume that one of my sons was intended to branch out into two tribes. That blessing I now confer upon you (*Rashi* from *Pesikta*).

7. *But as for me — when I came from Paddan* . . . [How this statement fits in the context of the chapter is unclear. *Rashi* connects it with Jacob's earlier request that Joseph inter him in Canaan: In fairness, how could Jacob ask to be taken for burial to the Cave of Machpelah when he did not do the same for Rachel, who died on the way home from Paddan? Apparently Jacob sensed that Joseph harbored resentment about this, and he seized this opportunity to explain his action:]

Even though she died but a short distance from Bethlehem, I buried her by the roadside at the command of God (*Rashi*).

Know that it was by the command of God that I buried her there, so that she might be of help to her children, when Nebuzaradan, the chief general of Nebuchadnezzar, king of Babylon (see *II Kings* 25:8ff), would lead Israel into captivity after the destruction of the First Temple. For we find that when the Jews were passing along that road, Rachel ascended over her grave, and wept, beseeching mercy upon them [see *Jeremiah* 31:14ff].

28 Jacob lived in the land of Egypt seventeen years. And the days of Jacob — the years of his life — were one hundred and forty-seven years. ²⁹The time approached for Israel to die, so he called for his son, for Joseph and said to him, 'Please — if I have found favor in your eyes, please place your hand under my thigh and do kindness and truth with me — please do not bury me in Egypt. ³⁰ For I will lie down with my fathers and you shall transport me out of Egypt and bury me in their sepulcher.' He said, 'I personally will do as you have said.' ³¹ He replied, 'Swear to me,' and he swore to him. Then Israel prostrated himself towards the head of the bed.

48 ¹ And it came to pass after these things that someone said to Joseph, 'Behold! your father is ill.' So he took his two sons, Ephraim and Manasseh, with him.

² Jacob was told, 'Behold your son Joseph has come to you.' So Israel exerted himself and sat up on the bed. ³ Jacob said to Joseph, 'El Shaddai had appeared to me in Luz in the land of Canaan and He blessed me. ⁴ He said to me "Behold: I will make you fruitful and numerous; I will make you a congregation of nations, and I will give this land to your offspring after you as a permanent possession." ⁵ And now, your two sons who were born to you in Egypt before my coming to you in Egypt shall be mine; Ephraim and Manasseh shall be mine like Reuben and Simeon. ⁶But progeny born to you after them shall be yours; they will be included under the name

אֲחֵיהֶ֖ם יִקָּרְא֑וּ בְּנַחֲלָתָֽם: ז וַאֲנִ֣י ׀ בְּבֹאִ֣י
מִפַּדָּ֗ן מֵ֩תָה֩ עָלַ֨י רָחֵ֜ל בְּאֶ֤רֶץ כְּנַ֙עַן֙ בַּדֶּ֔רֶךְ
בְּע֥וֹד כִּבְרַת־אֶ֖רֶץ לָבֹ֣א אֶפְרָ֑תָה וָאֶקְבְּרֶ֤הָ
שָּׁם֙ בְּדֶ֣רֶךְ אֶפְרָ֔ת הִ֖וא בֵּ֥ית לָֽחֶם: ח וַיַּ֥רְא
יִשְׂרָאֵ֖ל אֶת־בְּנֵ֣י יוֹסֵ֑ף וַיֹּ֖אמֶר מִי־אֵֽלֶּה:
ט וַיֹּ֤אמֶר יוֹסֵף֙ אֶל־אָבִ֔יו בָּנַ֣י הֵ֔ם אֲשֶׁר־
נָֽתַן־לִ֥י אֱלֹהִ֖ים בָּזֶ֑ה וַיֹּאמַ֕ר קָֽחֶם־נָ֥א אֵלַ֖י
וַאֲבָֽרֲכֵֽם: שני וְעֵינֵ֤י יִשְׂרָאֵל֙ כָּֽבְד֣וּ מִזֹּ֔קֶן
לֹ֥א יוּכַ֖ל לִרְא֑וֹת וַיַּגֵּ֤שׁ אֹתָם֙ אֵלָ֔יו וַיִּשַּׁ֥ק
לָהֶ֖ם וַיְחַבֵּ֥ק לָהֶֽם: יא וַיֹּ֤אמֶר יִשְׂרָאֵל֙ אֶל־
יוֹסֵ֔ף רְאֹ֥ה פָנֶ֖יךָ לֹ֣א פִלָּ֑לְתִּי וְהִנֵּ֨ה הֶרְאָ֥ה
אֹתִ֛י אֱלֹהִ֖ים גַּ֥ם אֶת־זַרְעֶֽךָ: יב וַיּוֹצֵ֥א יוֹסֵ֛ף
אֹתָ֖ם מֵעִ֣ם בִּרְכָּ֑יו וַיִּשְׁתַּ֥חוּ לְאַפָּ֖יו אָֽרְצָה:
יג וַיִּקַּ֣ח יוֹסֵף֮ אֶת־שְׁנֵיהֶם֒ אֶת־אֶפְרַ֤יִם
בִּֽימִינוֹ֙ מִשְּׂמֹ֣אל יִשְׂרָאֵ֔ל וְאֶת־מְנַשֶּׁ֥ה
בִשְׂמֹאל֖וֹ מִימִ֣ין יִשְׂרָאֵ֑ל וַיַּגֵּ֖שׁ אֵלָֽיו:
יד וַיִּשְׁלַח֩ יִשְׂרָאֵ֨ל אֶת־יְמִינ֜וֹ וַיָּ֣שֶׁת עַל־
רֹ֣אשׁ אֶפְרַ֗יִם וְה֣וּא הַצָּעִ֔יר וְאֶת־שְׂמֹאל֖וֹ
עַל־רֹ֣אשׁ מְנַשֶּׁ֑ה שִׂכֵּל֙ אֶת־יָדָ֔יו כִּ֥י מְנַשֶּׁ֖ה
הַבְּכֽוֹר: טו וַיְבָ֥רֶךְ אֶת־יוֹסֵ֖ף וַיֹּאמַ֑ר
הָֽאֱלֹהִ֡ים אֲשֶׁר֩ הִתְהַלְּכ֨וּ אֲבֹתַ֤י לְפָנָיו֙
אַבְרָהָ֣ם וְיִצְחָ֔ק הָֽאֱלֹהִים֙ הָֽרֹעֶ֣ה אֹתִ֔י
מֵֽעוֹדִ֖י עַד־הַיּ֥וֹם הַזֶּֽה: טז הַמַּלְאָךְ֩ הַגֹּאֵ֨ל
אֹתִ֜י מִכָּל־רָ֗ע יְבָרֵךְ֮ אֶת־הַנְּעָרִים֒ וְיִקָּרֵ֤א
בָהֶם֙ שְׁמִ֔י וְשֵׁ֥ם אֲבֹתַ֖י אַבְרָהָ֣ם וְיִצְחָ֑ק

8. *Rashi,* following the Midrash, explains that Jacob wished to bless the children, but the Divine Spirit departed from him because Jacob *saw* [prophetically] that wicked kings would descend from Joseph's sons — Jeroboam and Ahab from Ephraim, and Jehu and his sons from Manasseh. He therefore said to Joseph, '*Who are these?*' meaning: Where did these sons, who are apparently unworthy of a blessing, come from?

9. Joseph responded with an assurance that the children were begotten from a marriage of holiness, and worthy of being blessed (notwithstanding the fact that they — not unlike the other brothers — would be the ancestors of certain wicked descendants).

13. Jacob blesses Ephraim and Manasseh.

Traditionally one blesses another by laying one's hand on the person's head. The right hand has spiritual primacy and is the preferred one for the performance of *mitzvos.*

Since Ephraim was the younger, Joseph positioned him on his own right side, facing Jacob's left hand (*Rashi*). However, as R' David Feinstein observes, by positioning Ephraim with his right hand, Joseph, in effect, was unwittingly affirming Ephraim's supremacy.

14. Jacob extended his right hand diagonally toward Ephraim, who was on his left side (*Akeidah*).

כִּי מְנַשֶּׁה הַבְּכוֹר — *For Manasseh was the firstborn.* That Jacob had to resort to this skillful crossing of his hands instead of extending his hands straight ahead was *because* Manasseh was the firstborn, but Jacob did not wish to bless him with the right hand (*Rashi*).

15. By blessing Joseph's children, Jacob was, in effect, blessing Joseph.

16. This is the essence of the prayer that began with the previous verse: May You, O God, grant Your 'emissary' — the angel whom You always dispatched to redeem me from all evil — the mission to bless the lads, etc. The prayer-blessing in this verse was certainly not addressed to the angel himself, who clearly has no power to act except as an agent of the Holy One, to Whom Jacob referred in the previous verse. The syntax of this translation follows *R' Avraham ben HaRambam* and avoids many difficulties encountered by other translations.

May they act so righteously that all will couple their names not only with mine, but with my illustrious forebears as well (*R' David Feinstein*).

of their brothers with regard to their inheritance. [7] But as for me — when I came from Paddan, Rachel died on me in the land of Canaan on the road, while there was still a stretch of land to go to Ephrath; and I buried her there on the road to Ephrath, which is Bethlehem.'

[8] Then Israel saw Joseph's sons and he said, 'Who are these?' [9] And Joseph said to his father, 'They are my sons whom God has given me here.' He said, 'Bring them to me, if you please, and I will bless them.'

[10] Now Israel's eyes were heavy with age; he could not see. So he brought them near him and he kissed them and hugged them. [11] Israel said to Joseph, 'I dared not accept the thought that I would see your face, and here God has shown me even your offspring!'

[12] Joseph then removed them from his knees and he prostrated himself with his face toward the ground.

[13] Joseph took the two of them — Ephraim with his right hand, to Israel's left, and Manasseh with his left hand, to Israel's right — and he drew close to him. [14] But Israel extended his right hand and laid it on Ephraim's head though he was the younger and his left hand on Manasseh's head. He maneuvered his hands, for Manasseh was the firstborn. [15] And he blessed Joseph saying, 'O God before Whom my forefathers Abraham and Isaac walked — God Who shepherds me from my inception until this day: [16] May the angel who redeems me from all evil bless the lads, and may my name be declared upon them, and the names of my forefathers Abraham and Isaac, and may they

וַיִּדְגּ֥וּ לָרֹ֖ב בְּקֶ֥רֶב הָאָֽרֶץ: שלישי יז וַיַּ֣רְא יוֹסֵ֗ף

כִּי־יָשִׁ֨ית אָבִ֤יו יַד־יְמִינ֙וֹ עַל־רֹ֣אשׁ אֶפְרַ֔יִם

וַיֵּ֖רַע בְּעֵינָ֑יו וַיִּתְמֹ֣ךְ יַד־אָבִ֗יו לְהָסִ֥יר אֹתָ֛הּ

מֵעַ֥ל רֹאשׁ־אֶפְרַ֖יִם עַל־רֹ֥אשׁ מְנַשֶּֽׁה:

יח וַיֹּ֧אמֶר יוֹסֵ֛ף אֶל־אָבִ֖יו לֹא־כֵ֣ן אָבִ֑י כִּי־

זֶ֣ה הַבְּכֹ֔ר שִׂ֥ים יְמִֽינְךָ֖ עַל־רֹאשֽׁוֹ: יט וַיְמָאֵ֣ן

אָבִ֗יו וַיֹּ֨אמֶר֙ יָדַ֤עְתִּי בְנִי֙ יָדַ֔עְתִּי גַּם־ה֥וּא

יִֽהְיֶה־לְּעָ֖ם וְגַם־ה֣וּא יִגְדָּ֑ל וְאוּלָ֗ם אָחִ֤יו

הַקָּטֹן֙ יִגְדַּ֣ל מִמֶּ֔נּוּ וְזַרְע֖וֹ יִהְיֶ֥ה מְלֹֽא־הַגּוֹיִֽם:

כ וַיְבָ֨רֲכֵ֜ם בַּיּ֣וֹם הַהוּא֮ לֵאמוֹר֒ בְּךָ֗ יְבָרֵ֤ךְ

יִשְׂרָאֵל֙ לֵאמֹ֔ר יְשִֽׂמְךָ֣ אֱלֹהִ֔ים כְּאֶפְרַ֖יִם

וְכִמְנַשֶּׁ֑ה וַיָּ֥שֶׂם אֶת־אֶפְרַ֖יִם לִפְנֵ֥י מְנַשֶּֽׁה:

כא וַיֹּ֤אמֶר יִשְׂרָאֵל֙ אֶל־יוֹסֵ֔ף הִנֵּ֥ה אָנֹכִ֖י מֵ֑ת

וְהָיָ֤ה אֱלֹהִים֙ עִמָּכֶ֔ם וְהֵשִׁ֣יב אֶתְכֶ֔ם אֶל־

אֶ֖רֶץ אֲבֹתֵיכֶֽם: כב וַֽאֲנִ֞י נָתַ֧תִּי לְךָ֛ שְׁכֶ֥ם

אַחַ֖ד עַל־אַחֶ֑יךָ אֲשֶׁ֤ר לָקַ֨חְתִּי֙ מִיַּ֣ד הָֽאֱמֹרִ֔י

בְּחַרְבִּ֖י וּבְקַשְׁתִּֽי:

מט רביעי א וַיִּקְרָ֥א יַֽעֲקֹ֖ב אֶל־בָּנָ֑יו וַיֹּ֗אמֶר

הֵאָֽסְפוּ֙ וְאַגִּ֣ידָה לָכֶ֔ם אֵ֛ת אֲשֶׁר־יִקְרָ֥א

אֶתְכֶ֖ם בְּאַֽחֲרִ֥ית הַיָּמִֽים: ב הִקָּֽבְצ֥וּ וְשִׁמְע֖וּ

בְּנֵ֣י יַֽעֲקֹ֑ב וְשִׁמְע֖וּ אֶל־יִשְׂרָאֵ֥ל אֲבִיכֶֽם:

ג רְאוּבֵן֙ בְּכֹ֣רִי אַ֔תָּה כֹּחִ֖י וְרֵאשִׁ֣ית אוֹנִ֑י

יֶ֥תֶר שְׂאֵ֖ת וְיֶ֥תֶר עָֽז: ד פַּ֤חַז כַּמַּ֨יִם֙ אַל־

תּוֹתַ֔ר כִּ֥י עָלִ֖יתָ מִשְׁכְּבֵ֣י אָבִ֑יךָ אָ֥ז חִלַּ֖לְתָּ

יְצוּעִ֥י עָלָֽה:

---

19 *I know, my son, I know.* That he is the firstborn (*Rashi*).

20. *So he blessed them that day.* It may be inferred from *Rashi* that the term *that day* refers to the day, whenever it is, that Jewish parents would wish to bless their children. Whenever such days arrive, they will use the text of Jacob's blessing. *Targum Yonasan* explains the reference as alluding to the day when a newborn child is circumcised, and Sephardic communities pronounce Jacob's blessing on such occasions. On the eve of the Sabbath many fathers bless their sons with the formula: *May God make you like Ephraim and Manasseh.* [They bless their daughters by saying, '*May God make you like Sarah, Rebecca, Rachel, and Leah.*']

21. Having blessed Joseph's sons and made them two tribes, Jacob once again turns to Joseph and informs him that his descendants will be heir to an additional portion of *Eretz Yisrael,* which Jacob now bequeathed to him (*Ramban; Akeidah; Haamek Davar*).

22. Since you are undertaking responsibility for my burial, I have bequeathed to you an inheritance for *your* burial — Shechem. [Cf. *Joshua* 24:32.] *Shechem* means literally the city of Shechem as your own portion beyond that of your brothers (*Rashi*).

Alternately, *Rashi* offers another meaning of *shechem: portion. I have given you one portion more than your brothers* — this refers to the *birthright.* Thus Joseph's children would receive two portions of *Eretz Yisrael.*

From the hand of the Emorite. When Simeon and Levi slew the inhabitants of Shechem, all the surrounding nations gathered together against them, and Jacob took up arms to do battle with them (*Rashi*).

49/1. Jacob blesses his children.

Blessings occupy a prominent place throughout the Torah and particularly in the book of *Genesis*. That the righteous can confer a blessing is a privilege conferred by God and He provides the metaphysical force that makes the blessing efficacious . . . At this moment in Egypt, Jacob's progeny were embarking on the historic task of constituting an independent nation. Before he died, the Patriarch wished to confer upon them the Divine blessing for success in this undertaking of universal importance (*R' Munk*).

In the End of Days. I.e., in the Messianic era (*Ramban* and almost all commentators).

3. Reuben.

Jacob rebuked his older sons, and, by extension, the younger ones felt rebuked as well.

Reuben, you are my firstborn. Jacob begins by recounting what Reuben should have achieved as firstborn, then he explains why Reuben lost those privileges.

4. Because of the פַּחַז, *impetuosity*, with which you rushed to vent your anger [in the incident with Bilhah], a hasty recklessness *like that of fast-flowing waters —* therefore אַל תּוֹתַר, *you cannot be foremost,* you do not deserve to partake of the abundant superiorities that were designated for you (*Rashi*).

Targum Yonasan [following the Midrash] interpretively comments: But because you sinned, my son, the birthright is given to Joseph, the kingship to Judah, and the priesthood to Levi. The former is clearly stated in *I Chronicles* 5:1: *But since he* [Reuben] *desecrated his father's couch, his birthright was given to the sons of Joseph the son of Israel.*

Because you mounted your father's bed. See 35:22.

proliferate abundantly like fish within the land.'

[17] Joseph saw that his father was placing his right hand on Ephraim's head and it displeased him; so he supported his father's hand to remove it from Ephraim's head to Manasseh's. [18] And Joseph said to his father, 'Not so, Father, for this is the firstborn; place your right hand on his head.'

[19] But his father refused, saying, 'I know, my son, I know; he too will become a people, and he too will become great; yet his younger brother shall become greater than he, and his offspring['s fame] will fill the nations.' [20] So he blessed them that day, saying, 'By you shall Israel invoke blessing, saying, "May God make you like Ephraim and like Manasseh" ' — thus he put Ephraim before Manasseh.

[21] Then Israel said to Joseph, 'Behold I am about to die; God will be with you and will bring you back to the land of your fathers. [22] And as for me, I have given you Shechem — one portion more than your brothers, which I took from the hand of the Emorite with my sword and with my bow.'

49 [1] **T**hen Jacob called for his sons and said, 'Assemble yourselves and I will tell you what will befall you in the End of Days. [2] Gather yourselves and listen, O sons of Jacob and listen to Israel your father.

[3] 'Reuben, you are my firstborn, my strength and my initial vigor, foremost in rank and foremost in power. [4] Water-like impetuosity — you cannot be foremost, because you mounted your father's bed; then you desecrated Him Who ascended my couch.

ה שִׁמְעוֹן וְלֵוִי אַחִים כְּלֵי חָמָס
מְכֵרֹתֵיהֶם: ו בְּסֹדָם אַל־תָּבֹא נַפְשִׁי
בִּקְהָלָם אַל־תֵּחַד כְּבֹדִי כִּי בְאַפָּם הָרְגוּ
אִישׁ וּבִרְצֹנָם עִקְּרוּ־שׁוֹר: ז אָרוּר אַפָּם כִּי
עָז וְעֶבְרָתָם כִּי קָשָׁתָה אֲחַלְּקֵם בְּיַעֲקֹב
וַאֲפִיצֵם בְּיִשְׂרָאֵל:
ח יְהוּדָה אַתָּה יוֹדוּךָ אַחֶיךָ יָדְךָ בְּעֹרֶף
אֹיְבֶיךָ יִשְׁתַּחֲווּ לְךָ בְּנֵי אָבִיךָ: ט גּוּר
אַרְיֵה יְהוּדָה מִטֶּרֶף בְּנִי עָלִיתָ כָּרַע
רָבַץ כְּאַרְיֵה וּכְלָבִיא מִי יְקִימֶנּוּ: י לֹא־
יָסוּר שֵׁבֶט מִיהוּדָה וּמְחֹקֵק מִבֵּין
רַגְלָיו עַד כִּי־יָבֹא שִׁילֹה וְלוֹ יִקְּהַת
עַמִּים: יא אֹסְרִי לַגֶּפֶן עִירֹה וְלַשֹּׂרֵקָה בְּנִי
אֲתֹנוֹ כִּבֵּס בַּיַּיִן לְבֻשׁוֹ וּבְדַם־עֲנָבִים
סוּתֹה: יב חַכְלִילִי עֵינַיִם מִיָּיִן וּלְבֶן־שִׁנַּיִם
מֵחָלָב:
יג זְבוּלֻן לְחוֹף יַמִּים יִשְׁכֹּן וְהוּא לְחוֹף
אֳנִיֹּת וְיַרְכָתוֹ עַל־צִידֹן:
יד יִשָּׂשכָר חֲמֹר גָּרֶם רֹבֵץ בֵּין
הַמִּשְׁפְּתָיִם: טו וַיַּרְא מְנֻחָה כִּי טוֹב
וְאֶת־הָאָרֶץ כִּי נָעֵמָה וַיֵּט שִׁכְמוֹ לִסְבֹּל
וַיְהִי לְמַס־עֹבֵד: טז יְהִי־דָן יָדִין
עַמּוֹ כְּאַחַד שִׁבְטֵי יִשְׂרָאֵל: יז יְהִי־דָן

---

5. Simeon and Levi.
Having explained why Reuben forfeited the prerogatives of the birthright, Jacob now explains why Simeon and Levi, the next oldest, were also unworthy of kingship. Men of the sword are unworthy of being 'the king who by justice establishes the land' [Proverbs 29:4] (Sforno; Abarbanel; Malbim).

Their weaponry is a stolen craft. Your wielding of מְכֵרֹת, *weaponry,* as illustrated by your participation in murderous plots, is not a Jewish trait (Rashi from Midrash).

6. *They maimed an ox.* I.e., they sought to disable Joseph who is figuratively likened to an ox; see Deut. 33:17 (Rashi).

7. *Rashi* explains: Even when Jacob was chastising them he did not curse *them,* but their rage.

8. Judah.
When Judah heard Jacob's rebuke he began drawing back, afraid that Jacob might chastise him over the the affair of Tamar. So Jacob called him soothingly, 'Judah — *you* [the 'you' is emphatic] are not like them. *You,* your brothers shall acknowledge!' (Midrash; Rashi).

One does not say, 'I am a Reubenite or a Simeonite,' but 'I am a Yehudi' [Judahite; Jew] (Midrash).

9. *From the prey, my son, you elevated yourself.* Following *Rashi:* Jacob had suspected Judah of responsibility for Joseph's murder, a deed he described with the word טָרָף, *tearing apart.* Thus, *Rashi* perceives our passage to say: *You, my son, had risen above the act of 'tearing',* of which I had suspected you; to the contrary, you were instrumental in *sparing* him.

10. *Until Shiloh arrives.* The general Rabbinic consensus is that this phrase refers to the coming of the Messiah. This constitutes the primary Torah source for the belief that the Messiah will come.

11. Though Jacob could not reveal the 'End' to his sons, he did provide them with tiny glimpses of the Messianic era (Abarbanel).

Judah's district will be productive, and flow with wine like a fountain. A single vine will produce as many grapes as a donkey can carry (*Rashi*; *Rashbam*).

13. Zebulun.

Having given a glimpse of the Messianic era and of Judah as a fitting leader of the future House of Israel, the Patriarch turns to his other children. He bestows his blessings upon each according to his particular role in the harmony of the twelve tribes (*Abarbanel*).

Zebulun precedes Issachar.

Although Issachar was older, Jacob gave Zebulun precedence, because [as *Rashi* notes] Issachar's Torah-learning was made possible by Zebulun, who engaged in commerce and supported Issachar (*Tanchuma;* cf. *Ibn Ezra*).

14. Issachar.

Although the simile of *strong-boned donkey* and the references to *land* seem to allude to *agricultural* pursuit — a view indeed expressed by one Sage in the Midrash and followed by several commentators — *Rashi* favors the traditional Rabbinic interpretation that this reflects Issachar's *spiritual* role as *bearer of the yoke of Torah* and cultivator of the spiritual treasures of the people.

He rests between the boundaries. The Torah Sages toil day and night in their studies and know no *formal* rest, but are spiritually tranquil (*Shaarei Aharon*).

16. Dan.

Dan was the oldest son of Bilhah, Rachel's maidservant (*Abarbanel*).

Dan will avenge [lit., *judge*].The prophetic allusion is to Dan's descendant, Samson [one of the Judges of Israel, who single-handedly fought the Philistines (*Judges* 13:24 — 16:31)] (*Rashi*).

17. *Dan will be a serpent on the highway.* Following *Rashi* and *Ramban*, the words apply to Samson whose single-handed battle tactics corresponded closely to Jacob's description.

⁵ 'Simeon and Levi are comrades, their weaponry is a stolen craft. ⁶ Into their conspiracy, may my soul not enter! With their congregation, do not join, O my honor! For in their anger they murdered people and at their whim they maimed an ox. ⁷ Accursed is their rage for it is fierce, and their wrath for it was harsh; I will separate them within Jacob, and I will disperse them in Israel.

⁸ 'Judah — you, your brothers shall acknowledge; your hand will be at your enemies' nape. Your father's sons will prostrate themselves before you.

⁹ 'A lion cub is Judah; from the prey, my son, you elevated yourself. He crouches, lies down like a lion, and like an awesome lion, who dares rouse him? ¹⁰ The scepter shall not depart from Judah nor a scholar from among his descendants until Shiloh arrives and his will be an assemblage of nations. ¹¹ He will tie his donkey to the vine; to the vine branch his donkey's foal. He will launder his garments in wine and his robe in the blood of grapes. ¹² Red eyed from wine, and white toothed from milk.

¹³ 'Zebulun shall settle by the seashore. He shall be at the ship's harbor, and his last border will reach Zidon.

¹⁴ 'Issachar is a strong-boned donkey; he rests between the boundaries. ¹⁵ He saw tranquility that it was good, and the land that it was pleasant, yet he bent his shoulder to bear and he became an indentured laborer.

¹⁶ 'Dan will avenge his people, the tribes of Israel will be united as one. ¹⁷ Dan will be

נָחָשׁ עֲלֵי־דֶרֶךְ שְׁפִיפֹן עֲלֵי־אֹרַח הַנֹּשֵׁךְ
עִקְּבֵי־סוּס וַיִּפֹּל רֹכְבוֹ אָחוֹר: יח לִישׁוּעָתְךָ
קִוִּיתִי יהוה: חמישי יט גָּד גְּדוּד
יְגוּדֶנּוּ וְהוּא יָגֻד עָקֵב: כ מֵאָשֵׁר
שְׁמֵנָה לַחְמוֹ וְהוּא יִתֵּן מַעֲדַנֵּי־
מֶלֶךְ: כא נַפְתָּלִי אַיָּלָה
שְׁלֻחָה הַנֹּתֵן אִמְרֵי־שָׁפֶר: כב בֵּן
פֹּרָת יוֹסֵף בֵּן פֹּרָת עֲלֵי־עָיִן בָּנוֹת
צָעֲדָה עֲלֵי־שׁוּר: כג וַיְמָרֲרֻהוּ וָרֹבּוּ
וַיִּשְׂטְמֻהוּ בַּעֲלֵי חִצִּים: כד וַתֵּשֶׁב בְּאֵיתָן
קַשְׁתּוֹ וַיָּפֹזּוּ זְרֹעֵי יָדָיו מִידֵי אֲבִיר
יַעֲקֹב מִשָּׁם רֹעֶה אֶבֶן יִשְׂרָאֵל: כה מֵאֵל
אָבִיךָ וְיַעְזְרֶךָּ וְאֵת שַׁדַּי וִיבָרֲכֶךָּ בִּרְכֹת
שָׁמַיִם מֵעָל בִּרְכֹת תְּהוֹם רֹבֶצֶת תָּחַת
בִּרְכֹת שָׁדַיִם וָרָחַם: כו בִּרְכֹת אָבִיךָ
גָּבְרוּ עַל־בִּרְכֹת הוֹרַי עַד־תַּאֲוַת גִּבְעֹת
עוֹלָם תִּהְיֶיןָ לְרֹאשׁ יוֹסֵף וּלְקָדְקֹד נְזִיר
אֶחָיו:
שׁשׁי כז בִּנְיָמִין זְאֵב יִטְרָף בַּבֹּקֶר יֹאכַל
עַד וְלָעֶרֶב יְחַלֵּק שָׁלָל: כח כָּל־
אֵלֶּה שִׁבְטֵי יִשְׂרָאֵל שְׁנֵים עָשָׂר
וְזֹאת אֲשֶׁר־דִּבֶּר לָהֶם אֲבִיהֶם וַיְבָרֶךְ
אוֹתָם אִישׁ אֲשֶׁר כְּבִרְכָתוֹ בֵּרַךְ אֹתָם:

---

18. *For Your salvation do I long, HASHEM!* Jacob was intimating that Samson would utter a heartfelt plea to God for salvation (Rashi).

19. Gad.

Although Gad's territory was on the east of Jordan, they nobly sent armed troops across the Jordan to assist their brothers in waging war, and remained until the Land was conquered (Rashi; Midrash).

And after the conquest, Gad will return safely *in its tracks,* i.e., by the same roads and paths upon which they had initially traveled — and not one of the troops will be missing (Rashi).

20. Asher.

Asher's land will be so rich in olive groves that it will flow with oil like a fountain (Rashi).

And he will provide kingly delicacies. His rich produce will be worthy of royal tables and will be sought by kings (Radak).

21. Naftali.

Having blessed Zilpah's son, Jacob now reverts to bless Bilhah's younger son, and thus conclude the sons of the maidservants.

Naftali is a hind let loose. Rashi offers three Midrashic interpretations: 1. In Naftali's *territory,* the crops will ripen swiftly, like a hind let loose to run free. 2. This alludes to the war against Sisera [during the time of Deborah the prophetess (Judges 4ff)]. The valiant warriors of Naftali were nimble as hinds, and played a leading role in this battle. 3. It refers to the Talmudic tradition that on the day Jacob was buried, the swift Naftali ran with proof that Jacob, not Esau, was entitled to be buried in the Cave of Machpelah.

22. Joseph.

Climbed heights to gaze. Egyptian girls climbed atop the wall to catch a glimpse of Joseph's beauty when he passed by (Rashi).

23. According to *Rashi* (as understood by the commentators), this verse is linked with the next verse: Joseph rose to prominence despite the hatred he suffered.

They embittered him and became antagonists. Joseph's brothers, Potiphar and his wife all dealt bitterly with Joseph (*Rashi*).

24. But, by the grace of God, he rose to prominence . . .

But his bow was firmly emplaced. [Notwithstanding the above,] Joseph's power [as regent of Egypt] was firmly established. *His bow* alludes to *his power* (*Rashi*).

From the hands of the Mighty Power of Jacob. The above happened to Joseph thanks to the Holy One, Blessed is He, who is the 'Mighty One' of Jacob (*Rashi*).

He shepherded the stone of Israel. Joseph became *the shepherd* who provided sustenance for Jacob, *the stone of Israel.* The word *stone* denotes kingship, the primary personage of the nation (*Rashi*).

26. To the endless bounds of the world's hills. I.e., the blessings I received were unlimited, figuratively expanding to the furthest hills in the world.

The exile from his brothers, i.e., Joseph, who was separated from his family (*Onkelos*).

27. Benjamin.

Benjamin's descendants — likened to a wolf — were mighty, fearless warriors, as depicted in the affair of the Concubine at Gibeah [*Judges* chs. 19-20] (*Radak*).

In the morning he will devour prey. This refers to Saul who rose as Israel's champion during the 'morning' of national existence — when Israel began to flourish and shine (*Rashi* from *Tanchuma*).

In the evening he will distribute spoils. Even in the dark *evening* of its history, when Israel will have been exiled to Babylon, Benjamin *will divide the spoils,* of victory. This is an allusion to Mordechai and Esther, of the tribe of Benjamin, who divided the spoils of Haman [see *Esther* 8:7] (*Rashi*).

28. He blessed each according to his appropriate blessing. I.e., the unique blessing destined to befall him. The future would prove the prophetic veracity of his benedictions (*Ramban* to 41:12).

a serpent on the highway, a viper by the path that bites a horse's heels so its rider falls backward. ^{18} For Your salvation do I long, HASHEM!

^{19} 'Gad will recruit a regiment and it will retreat in its tracks.

^{20} 'From Asher — his bread will have richness, and he will provide kingly delicacies.

^{21} 'Naftali is a hind let loose who delivers beautiful sayings.

^{22} 'A charming son is Joseph, a charming son to the eye; each of the girls climbed heights to gaze. ^{23} They embittered him and became antagonists; the arrow-tongued men hated him. ^{24} But his bow was firmly emplaced and his arms were gilded, From the hands of the Mighty Power of Jacob — from there, he shepherded the stone of Israel. ^{25} [That was] from the God of your father and He will help you, and with Shaddai — and He will bless you [with] blessings of heaven from above, blessings of the deep crouching below, blessings of the bosom and womb. ^{26} The blessings of your father surpassed the blessings of my fathers, to the endless bounds of the world's hills. Let them be upon Joseph's head and upon the head of the exile from his brothers.

^{27} 'Benjamin is a predatory wolf; in the morning he will devour prey and in the evening he will distribute spoils.'

^{28} All these are the tribes of Israel — twelve — and this is what their father spoke to them when he blessed them. He blessed each according to his appropriate blessing.

כט וַיְצַו אוֹתָם וַיֹּאמֶר אֲלֵהֶם אֲנִי נֶאֱסָף
אֶל-עַמִּי קִבְרוּ אֹתִי אֶל-אֲבֹתָי אֶל-
הַמְּעָרָה אֲשֶׁר בִּשְׂדֵה עֶפְרוֹן הַחִתִּי:
ל בַּמְּעָרָה אֲשֶׁר בִּשְׂדֵה הַמַּכְפֵּלָה אֲשֶׁר-
עַל-פְּנֵי מַמְרֵא בְּאֶרֶץ כְּנָעַן אֲשֶׁר קָנָה
אַבְרָהָם אֶת-הַשָּׂדֶה מֵאֵת עֶפְרֹן הַחִתִּי
לַאֲחֻזַּת-קָבֶר: לא שָׁמָּה קָבְרוּ אֶת-אַבְרָהָם
וְאֵת שָׂרָה אִשְׁתּוֹ שָׁמָּה קָבְרוּ אֶת-יִצְחָק
וְאֵת רִבְקָה אִשְׁתּוֹ וְשָׁמָּה קָבַרְתִּי אֶת-
לֵאָה: לב מִקְנֵה הַשָּׂדֶה וְהַמְּעָרָה אֲשֶׁר-בּוֹ
מֵאֵת בְּנֵי-חֵת: לג וַיְכַל יַעֲקֹב לְצַוֺּת אֶת-
בָּנָיו וַיֶּאֱסֹף רַגְלָיו אֶל-הַמִּטָּה וַיִּגְוַע וַיֵּאָסֶף
אֶל-עַמָּיו: נ א וַיִּפֹּל יוֹסֵף עַל-פְּנֵי אָבִיו
וַיֵּבְךְּ עָלָיו וַיִּשַּׁק-לוֹ: ב וַיְצַו יוֹסֵף אֶת-עֲבָדָיו
אֶת-הָרֹפְאִים לַחֲנֹט אֶת-אָבִיו וַיַּחַנְטוּ
הָרֹפְאִים אֶת-יִשְׂרָאֵל: ג וַיִּמְלְאוּ-לוֹ
אַרְבָּעִים יוֹם כִּי כֵּן יִמְלְאוּ יְמֵי הַחֲנֻטִים
וַיִּבְכּוּ אֹתוֹ מִצְרַיִם שִׁבְעִים יוֹם: ד וַיַּעַבְרוּ
יְמֵי בְכִיתוֹ וַיְדַבֵּר יוֹסֵף אֶל-בֵּית פַּרְעֹה
לֵאמֹר אִם-נָא מָצָאתִי חֵן בְּעֵינֵיכֶם דַּבְּרוּ-
נָא בְּאָזְנֵי פַרְעֹה לֵאמֹר: ה אָבִי הִשְׁבִּיעַנִי
לֵאמֹר הִנֵּה אָנֹכִי מֵת בְּקִבְרִי אֲשֶׁר כָּרִיתִי
לִי בְּאֶרֶץ כְּנַעַן שָׁמָּה תִּקְבְּרֵנִי וְעַתָּה
אֶעֱלֶה-נָּא וְאֶקְבְּרָה אֶת-אָבִי וְאָשׁוּבָה:
ו וַיֹּאמֶר פַּרְעֹה עֲלֵה וּקְבֹר אֶת-אָבִיךְ

29. Jacob's final command.

Bury me with my fathers. So that not only my soul, but my body, too, will be with them (*Malbim*).

30. Jacob goes into great detail about the burial site. Seventeen years had elapsed since the family had left the land of Canaan, so he was very specific in informing his sons about its location and his rights to the property.

31. *And there I buried Leah.* This is the first and only reference in the Torah to Leah's death. The Torah records only those events God deemed necessary for us to know; apparently the time and circumstances of Leah's death did not fit into this category.

According to *Seder Olam*, Leah died at 45, at the time Joseph was sold. This occurred twelve years before Isaac died.

That Isaac was still alive when Jacob buried Leah would explain why Esau did not try to stop Jacob from burying her in the cave. As long as either of his parents was alive, Esau would not defy Isaac's wishes regarding the cave. Esau dared show his true colors only at Jacob's burial (*R' David Feinstein*).

33. Jacob dies.

When Jacob finished instructing his sons. He is likened to one about to embark on a journey and instructs his family how to act in his absence (*Pesikta; Malbim*).

Until this point Jacob had been sitting up on the bed with his feet on the floor. He now raised his feet and lay down (*Ibn Ezra; Rashbam*).

He expired and was gathered to his people. This expression refers to quick death without prolonged sickness or pain; the death enjoyed by the righteous. According to some, it comes unexpectedly, even while one is very alert. According to others, it refers to a state of unconsciousness preceding death, hence, the term וַיִּגְוַע, *expired*, lit., *shriveled* (like something deflated), which colloquially has the connotation of 'he breathed his last.'

Jacob lives on.

In recording the passing of Abraham (25:8) and Isaac (35:29), the Torah adds the word וַיָּמָת, *and he died*. However, the term 'death' *per se* is not mentioned here. Our Rabbis [*Taanis* 5b] said, 'Jacob our father is not dead' (*Rashi*).

Most later commentators perceive the above statement to imply that Jacob lives spiritually through his legacy to the Children of Israel.

50/1. *Joseph fell upon his father's face.* Haamek Davar suggests that Joseph is mentioned because he was nearest to Jacob at the last moment of his life, listening to his final whispered instructions, in which Jacob presumably revealed to him certain Divine secrets not known to his brothers. Because he was privy to such prophetic information while Jacob experienced a final surge of the Divine Presence, Joseph could allude to signs of redemption when he later addressed his brothers [v. 25].

2. Joseph's purpose in embalming Jacob.

Joseph's purpose was only to preserve his father's body from putrefaction during the long journey to the sepulcher at Machpelah.

3. *And Egypt bewailed him for seventy days.* Forty for embalming plus thirty for weeping. [The Egyptians bewailed Jacob so intensely] because they had been blessed on his account: with his arrival the famine had ceased, and the Nile was blessed (*Rashi*).

4. According to many commentators, this need for permission demonstrated that certain subtle forms of the Egyptian bondage had begun to take effect. With Jacob's death, Joseph's prominence was somewhat diminished.

5. Joseph was careful to stress that his father had insisted on an oath. This emphasized that in addition to filial *duty*, an *oath* was involved, which he was obligated to fulfill. This was indeed the determining factor in Pharaoh's grant of permission. See v. 6 (*Abarbanel; Malbim; Akeidah*).

[29] Then he instructed them; and he said to them, 'I am about to be gathered to my people. Bury me with my fathers in the cave that is in the field of Ephron the Hittite. [30] In the cave that is in the field of Machpelah, which faces Mamre, in the land of Canaan, which Abraham bought with the field from Ephron the Hittite as an estate for a burial site. [31] There they buried Abraham and Sarah his wife; there they buried Isaac and Rebecca his wife; and there I buried Leah. [32] Purchase of the field and the cave within it was from the sons of Heth.'

[33] When Jacob finished instructing his sons, he drew his feet into the bed. He expired and was gathered to his people.

50 [1] Then Joseph fell upon his father's face. He wept over him and kissed him. [2] Joseph ordered his servants, the physicians, to embalm his father; so the physicians embalmed Israel.

[3] Its forty-day term was completed, for such is the term of the embalmed; and Egypt bewailed him for seventy days. [4] When his bewailing period passed, Joseph spoke to Pharaoh's household saying, 'If you please — if I have found favor in your eyes, speak now in the ears of Pharaoh as follows. [5] My father had adjured me, saying, "Behold, I am about to die. In my grave, which I have hewn for myself in the land of Canaan — there you are to bury me." Now, I will go up if you please, and bury my father; then I will return.' [6] And Pharaoh said, 'Go up and bury your father

כַּאֲשֶׁר הִשְׁבִּיעֶךָ: ז וַיַּעַל יוֹסֵף לִקְבֹּר אֶת־
אָבִיו וַיַּעֲלוּ אִתּוֹ כָּל־עַבְדֵי פַרְעֹה זִקְנֵי
בֵיתוֹ וְכֹל זִקְנֵי אֶרֶץ־מִצְרָיִם: ח וְכֹל בֵּית
יוֹסֵף וְאֶחָיו וּבֵית אָבִיו רַק טַפָּם וְצֹאנָם
וּבְקָרָם עָזְבוּ בְּאֶרֶץ גֹּשֶׁן: ט וַיַּעַל עִמּוֹ
גַּם־רֶכֶב גַּם־פָּרָשִׁים וַיְהִי הַמַּחֲנֶה כָּבֵד
מְאֹד: י וַיָּבֹאוּ עַד־גֹּרֶן הָאָטָד אֲשֶׁר בְּעֵבֶר
הַיַּרְדֵּן וַיִּסְפְּדוּ־שָׁם מִסְפֵּד גָּדוֹל וְכָבֵד
מְאֹד וַיַּעַשׂ לְאָבִיו אֵבֶל שִׁבְעַת יָמִים:
יא וַיַּרְא יוֹשֵׁב הָאָרֶץ הַכְּנַעֲנִי אֶת־הָאֵבֶל
בְּגֹרֶן הָאָטָד וַיֹּאמְרוּ אֵבֶל־כָּבֵד זֶה
לְמִצְרָיִם עַל־כֵּן קָרָא שְׁמָהּ אָבֵל מִצְרַיִם
אֲשֶׁר בְּעֵבֶר הַיַּרְדֵּן: יב וַיַּעֲשׂוּ בָנָיו לוֹ כֵּן
כַּאֲשֶׁר צִוָּם: יג וַיִּשְׂאוּ אֹתוֹ בָנָיו אַרְצָה
כְּנַעַן וַיִּקְבְּרוּ אֹתוֹ בִּמְעָרַת שְׂדֵה
הַמַּכְפֵּלָה אֲשֶׁר קָנָה אַבְרָהָם אֶת־הַשָּׂדֶה
לַאֲחֻזַּת־קֶבֶר מֵאֵת עֶפְרֹן הַחִתִּי עַל־פְּנֵי
מַמְרֵא: יד וַיָּשָׁב יוֹסֵף מִצְרַיְמָה הוּא
וְאֶחָיו וְכָל־הָעֹלִים אִתּוֹ לִקְבֹּר אֶת־אָבִיו
אַחֲרֵי קָבְרוֹ אֶת־אָבִיו: טו וַיִּרְאוּ אֲחֵי־
יוֹסֵף כִּי־מֵת אֲבִיהֶם וַיֹּאמְרוּ לוּ יִשְׂטְמֵנוּ
יוֹסֵף וְהָשֵׁב יָשִׁיב לָנוּ אֵת כָּל־הָרָעָה
אֲשֶׁר גָּמַלְנוּ אֹתוֹ: טז וַיְצַוּוּ אֶל־יוֹסֵף
לֵאמֹר אָבִיךָ צִוָּה לִפְנֵי מוֹתוֹ לֵאמֹר:

7. The burial procession.

So Joseph went up to bury his father. Although he was the greatest man of his time, he still personally attended to his father's burial. In reward for this — measure for measure — Moses, the greatest of all, personally attended to Joseph's remains (*Sotah* 9b).

8. Some commentators maintain that the brothers wanted to take along everyone — including their children and belongings — but Pharaoh would not permit it. Thus, subtle aspects of the Egyptian bondage began with Jacob's death. Because of this, Joseph found it necessary to reassure his brothers [v. 24 below] that God would surely remember them and bring them out of Egypt when the time came (*Malbim*).

9. *Chariots and horsemen.* According to the Midrash, these were not part of the mourning cortege, but were for battle [in the event Esau would dispute the right to bury Jacob in the Cave of Machpelah].

And the camp was very imposing. Besides the literal meaning, this might also allude to a *celestial camp* [of angels] who came to guard Jacob in death as they had in life (*R' Bachya*).

11. *'This is a grievous mourning for Egypt.'* The Canaanites realized why the Egyptians were mourning even more intensely now than they had previously. As the party neared Jacob's burial place and saw how even the Canaanite kings paid tribute to Jacob by putting their crowns on his coffin, the Egyptians felt the full impact of their great loss. Then they lamented that they could not have the privilege of burying Jacob in their own country, where his presence, even in death, would be a lasting source of merit for them. It was a *grievous mourning for Egypt,* since they perceived how greatly Jacob's absence would affect *Egypt,* for a righteous person's presence brings benefit, even after his death [see *Sotah* 36a].

Therefore it was named Avel Mitzraim. The local populace was so impressed by the unprecedented national mourning of the great Egyptian state that their ruler chose this place-name to memorialize a foreign nation's love and respect for a Jewish Patriarch (*R' Munk*).

13. *His sons carried him to the land of Canaan.* His *sons*, not his grandsons. For Jacob had commanded them: My bier should not be carried by an Egyptian or by one of your sons, because they are children of Canaanite women. You yourselves shall carry it (*Rashi*).

The death of Esau at the Cave of Machpelah.

In *Sotah* 13a we learn that Esau protested the burial, claiming Jacob had used his share for Leah's burial, and the remaining grave was therefore Esau's. He protested that he had sold Jacob only the double share of the firstborn, but not his burial rights. Since the sons' documentary proof was in Egypt, they sent the fleet-footed Naftali to run and fetch it. Among those present was Chushim son of Dan, who was deaf. When he learned what was happening, he shouted: 'Is my grandfather to lie there in disgrace until Naftali returns from Egypt?' With that he took a club and struck Esau on the head so hard that his eyes fell out and rolled to Jacob's feet. Jacob [who according to the Talmud 'did not die'] opened his eyes and smiled.

15. *Joseph's brothers fear his retribution.*

During Jacob's lifetime, they used to dine at Joseph's table and he would receive them with open arms out of deference to his father. After Jacob's death, however, he ceased to invite them (*Rashi* from *Midrash*).

16. *Your father gave orders before his death.* They altered the facts for the sake of peace. Jacob had never given such a command since he did not suspect Joseph of seeking vengeance (*Rashi*).

as he adjured you.'

⁷ So Joseph went up to bury his father, and with him went up all of Pharaoh's servants, the elders of his household, all the elders of the land of Egypt, ⁸ and all of Jacob's household — his brothers, and his father's household; only their little ones, their sheep, and their cattle did they leave in the land of Goshen. ⁹ And he brought up with him both chariots and horsemen; and the camp was very imposing.

¹⁰ They came to Goren HaAtad, which is across the Jordan, and there they held a very great and imposing eulogy. And he observed a seven-day mourning period for his father. ¹¹ When the Canaanite inhabitants of the land saw the mourning in Goren HaAtad, they said, 'This is a grievous mourning for Egypt.' Therefore it was named Avel Mitzraim, which is across the Jordan.

¹² His sons did for him as he had instructed them. ¹³ His sons carried him to the land of Canaan and they buried him in the cave of the Machpelah field, the field that Abraham had bought as a burial estate from Ephron the Hittite, facing Mamre.

¹⁴ Joseph returned to Egypt — he and his brothers, and all who had gone up with him to bury his father — after he buried his father.

¹⁵ Joseph's brothers perceived that their father was dead, and they said, 'Perhaps Joseph will nurse hatred against us and then he will surely repay us all the evil that we did him.' ¹⁶ So they instructed that Joseph be told, 'Your father gave orders before his death, saying:

יז כֹּה־תֹאמְרוּ לְיוֹסֵף אָנָּא שָׂא נָא פֶּשַׁע
אַחֶיךָ וְחַטָּאתָם כִּי־רָעָה גְמָלוּךָ וְעַתָּה
שָׂא נָא לְפֶשַׁע עַבְדֵי אֱלֹהֵי אָבִיךָ
וַיֵּבְךְּ יוֹסֵף בְּדַבְּרָם אֵלָיו: יח וַיֵּלְכוּ גַּם־
אֶחָיו וַיִּפְּלוּ לְפָנָיו וַיֹּאמְרוּ הִנֶּנּוּ לְךָ
לַעֲבָדִים: יט וַיֹּאמֶר אֲלֵהֶם יוֹסֵף אַל־
תִּירָאוּ כִּי הֲתַחַת אֱלֹהִים אָנִי: כ וְאַתֶּם
חֲשַׁבְתֶּם עָלַי רָעָה אֱלֹהִים חֲשָׁבָהּ
לְטֹבָה לְמַעַן עֲשֹׂה כַּיּוֹם הַזֶּה לְהַחֲיֹת
עַם־רָב: שביעי כא וְעַתָּה אַל־תִּירָאוּ אָנֹכִי
אֲכַלְכֵּל אֶתְכֶם וְאֶת־טַפְּכֶם וַיְנַחֵם אוֹתָם
וַיְדַבֵּר עַל־לִבָּם: כב וַיֵּשֶׁב יוֹסֵף בְּמִצְרַיִם
הוּא וּבֵית אָבִיו וַיְחִי יוֹסֵף מֵאָה וָעֶשֶׂר
שָׁנִים: מפטיר כג וַיַּרְא יוֹסֵף לְאֶפְרַיִם בְּנֵי
שִׁלֵּשִׁים גַּם בְּנֵי מָכִיר בֶּן־מְנַשֶּׁה יֻלְּדוּ
עַל־בִּרְכֵּי יוֹסֵף: כד וַיֹּאמֶר יוֹסֵף אֶל־אֶחָיו
אָנֹכִי מֵת וֵאלֹהִים פָּקֹד יִפְקֹד אֶתְכֶם
וְהֶעֱלָה אֶתְכֶם מִן־הָאָרֶץ הַזֹּאת אֶל־
הָאָרֶץ אֲשֶׁר נִשְׁבַּע לְאַבְרָהָם לְיִצְחָק
וּלְיַעֲקֹב: כה וַיַּשְׁבַּע יוֹסֵף אֶת־בְּנֵי יִשְׂרָאֵל
לֵאמֹר פָּקֹד יִפְקֹד אֱלֹהִים אֶתְכֶם
וְהַעֲלִתֶם אֶת־עַצְמֹתַי מִזֶּה: כו וַיָּמָת יוֹסֵף
בֶּן־מֵאָה וָעֶשֶׂר שָׁנִים וַיַּחַנְטוּ אֹתוֹ וַיִּישֶׂם
בָּאָרוֹן בְּמִצְרָיִם:

The *Haftarah* for *Vayechi* appears on page 334

17. As soon as they mentioned his father, he wept out of sheer love, and his compassion was aroused. However, we find it nowhere specifically mentioned that Joseph formally *forgave* them. Their sin was eventually atoned for with the death of the Ten Martyrs centuries later (*R' Bachya*).

18. The emissaries returned to the brothers and reported that Joseph did not answer them but merely wept. *B'chor Shor* writes that the brothers took this as a sign that Joseph bore them no malice and they felt it was safe to go to him and fling themselves down before him in obeisance and gratitude.

19. Joseph reassures them.

For am I instead of God? Have I the power to harm you even if I wanted to? You all devised harm for me yet you did not succeed because God turned it to good; how then could I *alone* without God's consent harm you all? Therefore: fear not (*Rashi*).

21. *I will sustain you* — during the duration of the renewed famine. For according to *Tosefta Sotah*, after Jacob died, the famine — which had ceased with Jacob's arrival in the second year of the hunger — resumed [and lasted for another five years to complete the foretold total of seven years].

22. Joseph in Egypt.

The narrative now reverts to Joseph and sums up his life after his father's demise (*Abarbanel*).

And Joseph lived one hundred and ten years. Since Joseph ascended to rulership at the age of 30 [see 41:46], he ruled for a total of 80 years — longer than anyone before him, and rarely duplicated (*Abarbanel; Malbim*).

23. Although Joseph died before any of his brothers, he lived to see Ephraim's children, grandchildren, and great-grandchildren.

24. Joseph imparts signs of the Redemption to his brothers and adjures them to bury his remains in Eretz Yisrael.

I am about to die. This teaches that he gathered them all at the time of his death and charged them, as a father charges his children (Sechel Tov).

The year was 2309; fifty-four years since Jacob's death in 2255.

The words "Pakod Yifkod" identify the Redeemer.

During the last moments of his life, Jacob had imparted to Joseph some secret signs of the future redemption from Egypt, which Joseph now transmitted to his brothers. The words in our verse, although not recorded above in Jacob's name, were a direct quotation from Jacob.

In *Exodus* 3:16, the words פָּקֹד פָּקַדְתִּי, *I have indeed remembered*, were pivotal in the acceptance by the Israelites of Moses' announcement of the impending redemption.

God promised Moses: *'They will listen to you.'* Rashi explains: As soon as you address them with the words פָּקֹד פָּקַדְתִּי, *I have indeed remembered you*, they will know that these are the words that will herald the redemption.

25. Joseph had them vow that they would administer the oath from generation to generation [לֵאמֹר לְדוֹרוֹת] until it could be fulfilled.

By using the term *my bones* instead of *my body* it was clear that Joseph — unlike his father — was not requesting that they bury him in *Eretz Yisrael* immediately after his death.

26. The death of Joseph.

. . . The presence in Egypt of Joseph's coffin symbolized that his spirit would remain with his children during the hardships awaiting them *in Egypt*. On this note of moral comfort, *Genesis* comes to an end . . . The end of the Patriarchal epoch is not a conclusion, but a beginning. The nucleus of the future "nation of Priests" has been created and firmly established. Though a period of suffering and trial is about to begin, the nation will emerge from it with its spiritual strength formed to endure for all time (R' Munk).

---

[293]   BEREISHIS/GENESIS

---

17 "Thus shall you say to Joseph: 'O please, kindly forgive the spiteful deed of your brothers and their sin for they have done you evil'; "so now, please forgive the spiteful deed of the servants of your father's God." ' And Joseph wept when they spoke to him.

¹⁸ His brothers themselves also went and flung themselves before him and said, 'We are ready to be your slaves.' ¹⁹ But Joseph said to them, 'Fear not, for am I instead of God? ²⁰ Although you intended me harm, God intended it for good: in order to accomplish — it is as clear as this day — that a vast people be kept alive. ²¹ So now, fear not — I will sustain you and your little ones.' Thus he comforted them and appealed to their emotions.

²² Joseph dwelt in Egypt — he and his father's household — and Joseph lived one hundred and ten years.

²³ Joseph saw three generations through Ephraim; even the sons of Machir son of Manasseh were raised on Joseph's knees.

²⁴ Joseph said to his brothers, 'I am about to die, but God will surely remember you and bring you up out of this land to the land which He promised on oath to Abraham, to Isaac, and to Jacob.' ²⁵ Then Joseph adjured the children of Israel saying 'When God will indeed remember you, then you must bring my bones up out of here.'

²⁶ Joseph died at the age of one hundred and ten years; they embalmed him and he was placed in a coffin in Egypt.

The *Haftarah* for *Vayechi* appears on page 334

חֲזַק חֲזַק וְנִתְחַזֵּק

According to the Masoretic note appearing at the end of the *Sidrah*, there are 85 verses in the *Sidrah*, numerically corresponding to the mnemonic פֶּ"ה אֶל פֶּ"ה [literally *'mouth to mouth'* (each word פֶּה equals 85)]. This alludes to the theme of our *Sidrah*, in which Jacob spoke to his children, relating to them the blessings that would form the core of their mission for all time. In the mnemonic of our *Sidrah*, *HaRav David Feinstein*, who interprets these Masoretic notes, finds support for his contention that they are meant not only as convenient memory devices but to encapsulate the message of the *Sidrah*. If nothing were intended except a reminder that there are 85 verses, it would have been sufficient to use only the word פֶּה, *mouth,* or פֹּה, *here* — but this would tell us nothing about the *Sidrah* itself; therefore it was expanded to פֶּה אֶל פֶּה, *mouth to mouth.*

The Book of *Bereishis* contains 1,534 verses. The mnemonic is אָ"ך ל"ד [the א with a dot over it =1,000; the final ך = 500; ל = 30; ד = 4]; the phrase וְעַל חַרְבְּךָ תִחְיֶה, *and by your sword you shall live* [27:40], marks the midpoint of the Book; it contains 12 *parshiyos* [weekly portions], the mnemonic begins זֶ"ה שְׁמִי לְעֹלָם [*Exod.* 3:15]: *This is My name forever/for concealment;* Its *Sidros* [smaller Masoretic divisions according to the Triennial cycle once in use in *Eretz Yisrael*] number 43, the mnemonic being: גַּ"ם בָּרוּךְ יִהְיֶה [27:33]: *He too, shall be blessed;* Its chapters number 50, the mnemonic being: ה' חָנֵּנוּ לְ"ךָ קִוִּינוּ [*Isaiah* 33:2]: *O HASHEM, be gracious to us, in You we have hoped;* The total number of פְּתוּחוֹת, traditional 'open' line divisions between Masoretic chapters in Torah Scrolls, is 43; while the סְתוּמוֹת, 'closed' smaller-spaced divisions, number 48, totaling 91 chapters. The mnemonic is צֵ"א אַתָּה וְכָל הָעָם אֲשֶׁר בְּרַגְלֶיךָ [*Exod.* 11:8]: *Go out, you and all the people who follow you.*

ההפטרות

THE HAFTARAHS

ברכה קודם ההפטרה

בָּרוּךְ אַתָּה יהוה אֱלֹהֵינוּ מֶלֶךְ הָעוֹלָם, אֲשֶׁר בָּחַר בִּנְבִיאִים טוֹבִים, וְרָצָה בְדִבְרֵיהֶם הַנֶּאֱמָרִים בֶּאֱמֶת, בָּרוּךְ אַתָּה יהוה, הַבּוֹחֵר בַּתּוֹרָה וּבְמֹשֶׁה עַבְדּוֹ, וּבְיִשְׂרָאֵל עַמּוֹ, וּבִנְבִיאֵי הָאֱמֶת וָצֶדֶק: (.אָמֵן —Cong.)

ברכות לאחר ההפטרה

בָּרוּךְ אַתָּה יהוה אֱלֹהֵינוּ מֶלֶךְ הָעוֹלָם, צוּר כָּל הָעוֹלָמִים, צַדִּיק בְּכָל הַדּוֹרוֹת, הָאֵל הַנֶּאֱמָן הָאוֹמֵר וְעוֹשֶׂה, הַמְדַבֵּר וּמְקַיֵּם, שֶׁכָּל דְּבָרָיו אֱמֶת וָצֶדֶק. נֶאֱמָן אַתָּה הוּא יהוה אֱלֹהֵינוּ, וְנֶאֱמָנִים דְּבָרֶיךָ, וְדָבָר אֶחָד מִדְּבָרֶיךָ אָחוֹר לֹא יָשׁוּב רֵיקָם, כִּי אֵל מֶלֶךְ נֶאֱמָן (וְרַחֲמָן) אָתָּה. בָּרוּךְ אַתָּה יהוה, הָאֵל הַנֶּאֱמָן בְּכָל דְּבָרָיו. (.אָמֵן —Cong.)

רַחֵם עַל צִיּוֹן כִּי הִיא בֵּית חַיֵּינוּ, וְלַעֲלוּבַת נֶפֶשׁ תּוֹשִׁיעַ בִּמְהֵרָה בְיָמֵינוּ. בָּרוּךְ אַתָּה יהוה, מְשַׂמֵּחַ צִיּוֹן בְּבָנֶיהָ. (.אָמֵן —Cong.)

שַׂמְּחֵנוּ יהוה אֱלֹהֵינוּ בְּאֵלִיָּהוּ הַנָּבִיא עַבְדֶּךָ, וּבְמַלְכוּת בֵּית דָּוִד מְשִׁיחֶךָ, בִּמְהֵרָה יָבֹא וְיָגֵל לִבֵּנוּ, עַל כִּסְאוֹ לֹא יֵשֵׁב זָר וְלֹא יִנְחֲלוּ עוֹד אֲחֵרִים אֶת כְּבוֹדוֹ, כִּי בְשֵׁם קָדְשְׁךָ נִשְׁבַּעְתָּ לּוֹ, שֶׁלֹּא יִכְבֶּה נֵרוֹ לְעוֹלָם וָעֶד. בָּרוּךְ אַתָּה יהוה, מָגֵן דָּוִד. (.אָמֵן —Cong.)

עַל הַתּוֹרָה, וְעַל הָעֲבוֹדָה, וְעַל הַנְּבִיאִים, וְעַל יוֹם הַשַּׁבָּת הַזֶּה שֶׁנָּתַתָּ לָּנוּ יהוה אֱלֹהֵינוּ, לִקְדֻשָּׁה וְלִמְנוּחָה, לְכָבוֹד וּלְתִפְאָרֶת. עַל הַכֹּל יהוה אֱלֹהֵינוּ, אֲנַחְנוּ מוֹדִים לָךְ, וּמְבָרְכִים אוֹתָךְ, יִתְבָּרַךְ שִׁמְךָ בְּפִי כָּל חַי תָּמִיד לְעוֹלָם וָעֶד. בָּרוּךְ אַתָּה יהוה, מְקַדֵּשׁ הַשַּׁבָּת. (.אָמֵן —Cong.)

BLESSING BEFORE THE HAFTARAH

בָּרוּךְ Blessed are You, HASHEM, our God, King of the universe, Who
has chosen good prophets and was pleased with their words that
were uttered with truth. Blessed are You, HASHEM, Who chooses the
Torah; Moses, His servant; Israel, His nation; and the prophets of truth
and righteousness. (Cong.— Amen.)

BLESSINGS AFTER THE HAFTARAH

בָּרוּךְ Blessed are You, HASHEM, King of the universe, Rock of all
eternities, Righteous in all generations, the trustworthy God,
Who says and does, Who speaks and fulfills, all of Whose words
are true and righteous. Trustworthy are You, HASHEM, our God,
and trustworthy are Your words, not one of Your words is turned back
to its origin unfulfilled, for You are God, trustworthy (and compassionate) King. Blessed are You, HASHEM, the God Who is trustworthy in all
His words. (Cong.— Amen.)

רַחֵם Have mercy on Zion for it is the source of our life; to the one who
is deeply humiliated bring salvation speedily, in our days.
Blessed are You, HASHEM, Who gladdens Zion through her children. (Cong.— Amen.)

שַׂמְּחֵנוּ Gladden us, HASHEM, our God, with Elijah the prophet, Your
servant, and with the kingdom of the House of David, Your
anointed, may he come speedily and cause our heart to exult. On his
throne let no stranger sit nor let others continue to inherit his honor, for
by Your holy Name You swore to him that his heir will not be
extinguished forever and ever. Blessed are You, HASHEM, Shield of
David. (Cong.— Amen.)

עַל הַתּוֹרָה For the Torah reading, for the prayer service, for the
reading from the Prophets for this Sabbath day that You,
HASHEM, our God, have given us for holiness and contentment, for glory
and splendor — for all this, HASHEM, our God, we gratefully thank You
and bless You. May Your Name be blessed by the mouth of all the
living, always, for all eternity. Blessed are You, HASHEM, Who sanctifies
[the Sabbath,] Israel and the festival seasons. (Cong.— Amen.)

הפטרת בראשית

ישעיה מב:ה - מג:י

ה כֹּה־אָמַ֨ר הָאֵ֣ל ׀ יהוה בּוֹרֵ֤א הַשָּׁמַ֙יִם֙ וְנ֣וֹטֵיהֶ֔ם רֹקַ֥ע הָאָ֖רֶץ וְצֶאֱצָאֶ֑יהָ נֹתֵ֤ן נְשָׁמָה֙ לָעָ֣ם עָלֶ֔יהָ וְר֖וּחַ לַהֹלְכִ֥ים בָּֽהּ׃ ו אֲנִ֧י יהוה קְרָאתִ֥יךָֽ בְצֶ֖דֶק וְאַחְזֵ֣ק בְּיָדֶ֑ךָ וְאֶצָּרְךָ֗ וְאֶתֶּנְךָ֛ לִבְרִ֥ית עָ֖ם לְא֥וֹר גּוֹיִֽם׃ ז לִפְקֹ֙חַ עֵינַ֣יִם עִוְר֑וֹת לְהוֹצִ֤יא מִמַּסְגֵּר֙ אַסִּ֔יר מִבֵּ֥ית כֶּ֖לֶא יֹ֥שְׁבֵי חֹֽשֶׁךְ׃ ח אֲנִ֥י יהוה ה֖וּא שְׁמִ֑י וּכְבוֹדִי֙ לְאַחֵ֣ר לֹֽא־אֶתֵּ֔ן וּתְהִלָּתִ֖י לַפְּסִילִֽים׃ ט הָרִֽאשֹׁנ֖וֹת הִנֵּה־בָ֑אוּ וַחֲדָשׁוֹת֙ אֲנִ֣י מַגִּ֔יד בְּטֶ֥רֶם תִּצְמַ֖חְנָה אַשְׁמִ֥יעַ אֶתְכֶֽם׃ י שִׁ֤ירוּ לַֽיהוה֙ שִׁ֣יר חָדָ֔שׁ תְּהִלָּת֖וֹ מִקְצֵ֣ה הָאָ֑רֶץ יֽוֹרְדֵ֤י הַיָּם֙ וּמְלֹא֔וֹ אִיִּ֖ים וְיֹֽשְׁבֵיהֶֽם׃ יא יִשְׂא֤וּ מִדְבָּר֙ וְעָרָ֔יו חֲצֵרִ֖ים תֵּשֵׁ֣ב קֵדָ֑ר יָרֹ֙נּוּ֙ יֹ֣שְׁבֵי סֶ֔לַע מֵרֹ֥אשׁ הָרִ֖ים יִצְוָֽחוּ׃ יב יָשִׂ֥ימוּ לַֽיהוה כָּב֑וֹד וּתְהִלָּת֖וֹ בָּֽאִיִּ֥ים יַגִּֽידוּ׃ יג יהוה כַּגִּבּ֣וֹר יֵצֵ֔א כְּאִ֥ישׁ מִלְחָמ֖וֹת יָעִ֣יר קִנְאָ֑ה יָרִ֙יעַ֙ אַף־יַצְרִ֔יחַ עַל־אֹיְבָ֖יו יִתְגַּבָּֽר׃ יד הֶחֱשֵׁ֙יתִי֙ מֵֽעוֹלָ֔ם אַחֲרִ֖ישׁ אֶתְאַפָּ֑ק כַּיּֽוֹלֵדָ֣ה אֶפְעֶ֔ה אֶשֹּׁ֥ם וְאֶשְׁאַ֖ף יָֽחַד׃ טו אַחֲרִ֤יב הָרִים֙ וּגְבָע֔וֹת וְכָל־עֶשְׂבָּ֖ם אוֹבִ֑ישׁ וְשַׂמְתִּ֤י נְהָרוֹת֙ לָֽאִיִּ֔ים וַאֲגַמִּ֖ים אוֹבִֽישׁ׃ טז וְהוֹלַכְתִּ֣י עִוְרִ֗ים בְּדֶ֙רֶךְ֙ לֹ֣א יָדָ֔עוּ בִּנְתִיב֥וֹת לֹֽא־יָדְע֖וּ אַדְרִיכֵ֑ם אָשִׂים֩ מַחְשָׁ֨ךְ לִפְנֵיהֶ֜ם לָא֗וֹר וּמַֽעֲקַשִּׁים֙ לְמִישׁ֔וֹר אֵ֚לֶּה הַדְּבָרִ֔ים עֲשִׂיתִ֖ם וְלֹ֥א עֲזַבְתִּֽים׃ יז נָסֹ֤גוּ אָחוֹר֙ יֵבֹ֣שׁוּ בֹ֔שֶׁת הַבֹּטְחִ֖ים בַּפָּ֑סֶל הָאֹמְרִ֥ים לְמַסֵּכָ֖ה אַתֶּ֥ם אֱלֹהֵֽינוּ׃ יח הַחֵרְשִׁ֖ים שְׁמָ֑עוּ וְהַעִוְרִ֖ים הַבִּ֥יטוּ לִרְאֽוֹת׃ יט מִ֤י עִוֵּר֙ כִּ֣י אִם־עַבְדִּ֔י וְחֵרֵ֖שׁ כְּמַלְאָכִ֣י אֶשְׁלָ֑ח מִ֤י עִוֵּר֙ כִּמְשֻׁלָּ֔ם וְעִוֵּ֖ר כְּעֶ֥בֶד יהוה׃ כ רָאִ֥ית [רָא֖וֹת קרי] רַבּ֖וֹת וְלֹ֣א תִשְׁמֹ֑ר פָּק֥וֹחַ אָזְנַ֖יִם וְלֹ֥א יִשְׁמָֽע׃ כא יהוה חָפֵ֖ץ לְמַ֣עַן צִדְק֑וֹ יַגְדִּ֥יל תּוֹרָ֖ה וְיַאְדִּֽיר׃

Sefardim and the community of Frankfurt am Main
conclude the *Haftarah* here.

The *Sidrah* began with the story of Creation and the august role of man in bringing God's goal to fruition; of his downfall and God's mercy in allowing him a new life in which he could redeem himself. The *Haftarah*'s theme is similar.

Creation is not a phenomenon that took place in primeval times and then was left to proceed of its own inertia. The first verse of the *Haftarah* speaks of Creation in the present tense, because God must renew it constantly; otherwise the universe would cease to exist. So He does. His purpose is for Israel to guide mankind to His service: *to bring the people to the covenant, to be a light to the nations*; to help them remove the impediments that prevent their eyes and ears from seeing and hearing the truth.

HAFTARAS BEREISHIS

Isaiah 42:5 - 43:10

But Israel falters. It sins, and God allows it to be plundered as a result of its failure. The downfall is not permanent, however. God may look from afar, but He remains vigilant and seeks the opportunity to restore Israel to its eminence. No one seems to care, to see, but God always keeps His original purpose in mind, and only Israel is equal to it. Is there any other nation that can bear witness to God's greatness, His mercy, and the fulfillment of His prophecies? Can the nations or their gods match Israel's loyalty, despite its frequent lapses?

Ultimately, Israel knows, and because it does it will be redeemed and be the instrument for the triumph of the spirit.

⁵ So said the God, HASHEM, Who creates the heavens and stretches them forth, spreads out the earth and what grows from it, gives a soul to the people upon it, and a spirit to those who walk on it:

⁶ I am HASHEM; in righteousness have I called you and taken hold of your hand; I have protected you and appointed you to bring the people to the covenant, to be a light for the nations; ⁷ to bring sight to blinded eyes, to remove a prisoner from confinement, dwellers in darkness from a dungeon.

⁸ I am HASHEM; that is My Name, and I shall not surrender My glory to another nor My praise to the graven idols. ⁹ Behold! the early prophecies have come about; now I relate new ones, before they sprout I shall let you hear [them].

¹⁰ Sing to HASHEM a new song, His praise from the end of the earth, those who go down to the sea and those that fill it, the islands and their inhabitants. ¹¹ Let the desert and its cities raise their voice, the open places where Kedar dwells, let those who dwell on bedrock sing out, from mountain summits shout. ¹² Let them render glory to HASHEM and declare His glory in the islands. ¹³ HASHEM shall go forth like a warrior, like a man of wars He shall arouse His resentment, He shall shout triumphantly, even roar, He shall overpower His enemies.

¹⁴ I have long kept silent, been quiet, restrained Myself — I will cry out like a woman giving birth; I will both lay waste and swallow up. ¹⁵ I will desolate mountains and hills and wither all their herbage, I will turn rivers into islands and dry up marshes. ¹⁶ I will lead the blind on a way they did not know, on paths they did not know will I have them walk; I will turn darkness to light before them and make the rutted places straight — these things shall I have done and not neglected them. ¹⁷ Those who trust in graven idols will be driven back and deeply shamed, those who say to molten idols, 'You are our gods.'

¹⁸ O you deaf ones, listen; and you blind ones, gaze to see! ¹⁹ Who is blind but My servant, or as deaf as My agent whom I dispatch; who is blind as the perfect one and blind as the servant of HASHEM? ²⁰ Seeing much but heeding not, opening ears but hearing not. ²¹ HASHEM desires for the sake of its righteousness that the Torah be made great and glorious.

Sefardim and the community of Frankfurt am Main conclude the *Haftarah* here.

כב וְהוּא עַם־בָּזוּז וְשָׁסוּי הָפֵחַ בַּחוּרִים כֻּלָּם וּבְבָתֵּי כְלָאִים הָחְבָּאוּ הָיוּ לָבַז וְאֵין מַצִּיל מְשִׁסָּה וְאֵין־אֹמֵר הָשַׁב: כג מִי בָכֶם יַאֲזִין זֹאת יַקְשֵׁב וְיִשְׁמַע לְאָחוֹר: כד מִי־נָתַן לִמְשׁוֹסָה [לִמְשִׁסָּה קרי] יַעֲקֹב וְיִשְׂרָאֵל לְבֹזְזִים הֲלוֹא יהוה זוּ חָטָאנוּ לוֹ וְלֹא־אָבוּ בִדְרָכָיו הָלוֹךְ וְלֹא שָׁמְעוּ בְּתוֹרָתוֹ: כה וַיִּשְׁפֹּךְ עָלָיו חֵמָה אַפּוֹ וֶעֱזוּז מִלְחָמָה וַתְּלַהֲטֵהוּ מִסָּבִיב וְלֹא יָדָע וַתִּבְעַר־בּוֹ וְלֹא־יָשִׂים עַל־לֵב: מג א וְעַתָּה כֹּה־אָמַר יהוה בֹּרַאֲךָ יַעֲקֹב וְיֹצֶרְךָ יִשְׂרָאֵל אַל־תִּירָא כִּי גְאַלְתִּיךָ קָרָאתִי בְשִׁמְךָ לִי־אָתָּה: ב כִּי־תַעֲבֹר בַּמַּיִם אִתְּךָ אָנִי וּבַנְּהָרוֹת לֹא יִשְׁטְפוּךָ כִּי־תֵלֵךְ בְּמוֹ־אֵשׁ לֹא תִכָּוֶה וְלֶהָבָה לֹא תִבְעַר־בָּךְ: ג כִּי אֲנִי יהוה אֱלֹהֶיךָ קְדוֹשׁ יִשְׂרָאֵל מוֹשִׁיעֶךָ נָתַתִּי כָפְרְךָ מִצְרַיִם כּוּשׁ וּסְבָא תַּחְתֶּיךָ: ד מֵאֲשֶׁר יָקַרְתָּ בְעֵינַי נִכְבַּדְתָּ וַאֲנִי אֲהַבְתִּיךָ וְאֶתֵּן אָדָם תַּחְתֶּיךָ וּלְאֻמִּים תַּחַת נַפְשֶׁךָ: ה אַל־תִּירָא כִּי אִתְּךָ־אָנִי מִמִּזְרָח אָבִיא זַרְעֶךָ וּמִמַּעֲרָב אֲקַבְּצֶךָּ: ו אֹמַר לַצָּפוֹן תֵּנִי וּלְתֵימָן אַל־תִּכְלָאִי הָבִיאִי בָנַי מֵרָחוֹק וּבְנוֹתַי מִקְצֵה הָאָרֶץ: ז כֹּל הַנִּקְרָא בִשְׁמִי וְלִכְבוֹדִי בְּרָאתִיו יְצַרְתִּיו אַף־עֲשִׂיתִיו: ח הוֹצִיא עַם־עִוֵּר וְעֵינַיִם יֵשׁ וְחֵרְשִׁים וְאָזְנַיִם לָמוֹ: ט כָּל־הַגּוֹיִם נִקְבְּצוּ יַחְדָּו וְיֵאָסְפוּ לְאֻמִּים מִי בָהֶם יַגִּיד זֹאת וְרִאשֹׁנוֹת יַשְׁמִיעֻנוּ יִתְּנוּ עֵדֵיהֶם וְיִצְדָּקוּ וְיִשְׁמְעוּ וְיֹאמְרוּ אֱמֶת: י אַתֶּם עֵדַי נְאֻם־יהוה וְעַבְדִּי אֲשֶׁר בָּחָרְתִּי לְמַעַן תֵּדְעוּ וְתַאֲמִינוּ לִי וְתָבִינוּ כִּי־אֲנִי הוּא לְפָנַי לֹא־נוֹצַר אֵל וְאַחֲרַי לֹא יִהְיֶה:

²² But it is a looted, downtrodden people, all of them trapped in holes, and hidden away in prisons; they are looted without rescuer, downtrodden with no one saying, 'Give back!' ²³ Who among you will give ear to this, who will hearken to hear what will happen later? ²⁴ Who delivered Jacob to plunder and Israel to looters, was it not HASHEM — the One against Whom we sinned and in Whose ways they refused to walk and Whose Torah we would not heed? ²⁵ So He poured His fiery wrath upon it and the power of war, and He set it on fire all around — but he would not know; it burned within him — but he did not take it to heart.

43. ¹ And now, so says HASHEM, your Creator, O Jacob; the One Who fashioned you, O Israel: Fear not, for I have redeemed you, I have called you by name, for you are Mine. ² When you pass through water, I am with you; and through rivers, they will not flood you; when you walk through fire, you will not be burned; and a flame will not kindle among you. ³ For I am HASHEM your God, the Holy One of Israel, your Savior; I gave Egypt as your ransom, and Cush and Seba instead of you.

⁴ Because you were worthy in My eyes you were honored and I loved you, so I gave a person instead of you and regimes instead of your soul. ⁵ Fear not, for I am with you; from the east will I bring your offspring and from the west will I gather you. ⁶ I shall say to the north, 'Give back,' and to the south, 'Do not withhold, bring My sons from afar and My daughters from the end of the earth'; ⁷ everyone who is called by My Name and whom I have created for My glory, whom I have fashioned, even perfected; ⁸ to remove the people that was blind though it has eyes, and deaf though they have ears.

⁹ Were all the nations gathered together and all the regimes assembled — who among them could have declared this, could have let us hear the early prophecies? Let them bring their witnesses and they will be vindicated; else let them hear and they will say, 'It is true.'

¹⁰ You are My witnesses, the words of HASHEM, and My servant, whom I have chosen, so that you will know and believe in Me, and understand that I am He; before Me nothing was created by a god and after Me it shall not be!

הפטרת נח

ישעיה נד:א-נה:ו

נד א רָנִּי עֲקָרָה לֹא יָלָדָה פִּצְחִי רִנָּה וְצַהֲלִי
לֹא־חָלָה כִּי־רַבִּים בְּנֵי־שׁוֹמֵמָה מִבְּנֵי בְעוּלָה אָמַר
יְהֹוָה: ב הַרְחִיבִי ׀ מְקוֹם אָהֳלֵךְ וִירִיעוֹת מִשְׁכְּנוֹתַיִךְ
יַטּוּ אַל־תַּחְשֹׂכִי הַאֲרִיכִי מֵיתָרַיִךְ וִיתֵדֹתַיִךְ חַזֵּקִי:
ג כִּי־יָמִין וּשְׂמֹאול תִּפְרֹצִי וְזַרְעֵךְ גּוֹיִם יִירָשׁ וְעָרִים
נְשַׁמּוֹת יוֹשִׁיבוּ: ד אַל־תִּירְאִי כִּי־לֹא תֵבוֹשִׁי וְאַל־
תִּכָּלְמִי כִּי לֹא תַחְפִּירִי כִּי בֹשֶׁת עֲלוּמַיִךְ תִּשְׁכָּחִי
וְחֶרְפַּת אַלְמְנוּתַיִךְ לֹא תִזְכְּרִי־עוֹד: ה כִּי בֹעֲלַיִךְ
עֹשַׂיִךְ יְהֹוָה צְבָאוֹת שְׁמוֹ וְגֹאֲלֵךְ קְדוֹשׁ יִשְׂרָאֵל
אֱלֹהֵי כָל־הָאָרֶץ יִקָּרֵא: ו כִּי־כְאִשָּׁה עֲזוּבָה
וַעֲצוּבַת רוּחַ קְרָאָךְ יְהֹוָה וְאֵשֶׁת נְעוּרִים כִּי תִמָּאֵס
אָמַר אֱלֹהָיִךְ: ז בְּרֶגַע קָטֹן עֲזַבְתִּיךְ וּבְרַחֲמִים
גְּדֹלִים אֲקַבְּצֵךְ: ח בְּשֶׁצֶף קֶצֶף הִסְתַּרְתִּי פָנַי רֶגַע
מִמֵּךְ וּבְחֶסֶד עוֹלָם רִחַמְתִּיךְ אָמַר גֹּאֲלֵךְ יְהֹוָה:
ט כִּי־מֵי נֹחַ זֹאת לִי אֲשֶׁר נִשְׁבַּעְתִּי מֵעֲבֹר מֵי־נֹחַ
עוֹד עַל־הָאָרֶץ כֵּן נִשְׁבַּעְתִּי מִקְּצֹף עָלַיִךְ וּמִגְּעָר־
בָּךְ: י כִּי הֶהָרִים יָמוּשׁוּ וְהַגְּבָעוֹת תְּמוּטֶינָה וְחַסְדִּי
מֵאִתֵּךְ לֹא־יָמוּשׁ וּבְרִית שְׁלוֹמִי לֹא תָמוּט אָמַר
מְרַחֲמֵךְ יְהֹוָה:

Sefardim conclude the *Haftarah* here.

יא עֲנִיָּה סֹעֲרָה לֹא נֻחָמָה הִנֵּה אָנֹכִי מַרְבִּיץ בַּפּוּךְ
אֲבָנַיִךְ וִיסַדְתִּיךְ בַּסַּפִּירִים: יב וְשַׂמְתִּי כַּדְכֹד
שִׁמְשֹׁתַיִךְ וּשְׁעָרַיִךְ לְאַבְנֵי אֶקְדָּח וְכָל־גְּבוּלֵךְ
לְאַבְנֵי־חֵפֶץ: יג וְכָל־בָּנַיִךְ לִמּוּדֵי יְהֹוָה וְרַב שְׁלוֹם
בָּנָיִךְ: יד בִּצְדָקָה תִּכּוֹנָנִי רַחֲקִי מֵעֹשֶׁק כִּי־לֹא
תִירָאִי וּמִמְּחִתָּה כִּי לֹא־תִקְרַב אֵלָיִךְ: טו הֵן
גּוֹר יָגוּר אֶפֶס מֵאוֹתִי מִי־גָר אִתָּךְ עָלַיִךְ יִפּוֹל:

Man has infinite capacity to save the world and to destroy it. And he has an equal capacity to perceive the truth and to see right through it.

The generation of the Flood continued man's slide into immorality until God's mercy had reached its limit. It is instructive that the last straw was thievery; as the Sages teach: Even if there is a bushel of sins, it is thievery that leads the condemnations. So man had taken the universe and pushed it over the brink of destruction, but there was one man, Noah, who saved the race and the world. Thanks to his righteousness, humanity survived — proof that no one should ever consider himself too insignificant acting alone to make a difference.

One would expect the survivors of the Flood and their immediate descendants to have learned that immortality is not assured. When the generation that built the Tower of Babel thought that it could do battle with God, it did not need fallible history books to tell them about the Flood. Noah and his children were still alive; eyewitnesses who had lived through man's foolishness and its consequences. But, overcome with delusions of their own power and rationalizing that the Flood had been a natural, coincidental disaster, they built the Tower anyway.

History repeats itself for those who refuse to learn from it.

HAFTARAS NOACH
Isaiah 54:1-55:6

54 ¹ Sing out, O barren one, who has not given birth, break out into glad song and be jubilant, you who had no labor pains, for the children of the desolate [Jerusalem] outnumber the children of the inhabited [city], said HASHEM. ² Broaden the place of your tent and stretch out the curtains of your dwellings, stint not; lengthen your cords and strengthen your pegs. ³ For rightward and leftward you shall spread out mightily, your offspring will inherit nations, and they will inhabit desolate cities. ⁴ Fear not, for you will not be shamed, do not feel humiliated for you will not be mortified; for you will forget the shame of your youth, and the mortification of your widowhood you will remember no more. ⁵ For your Master is your Maker — HASHEM, Master of Legions is His Name; your Redeemer is the Holy One of Israel — God of all the world shall He be called. ⁶ For like a wife who had been forsaken and melancholy will HASHEM have recalled you, and like a wife of one's youth who had become despised — so said your God. ⁷ For but a brief moment have I forsaken you, and with abundant mercy shall I gather you in. ⁸ With a slight wrath have I concealed My face from you for a moment, but with eternal kindness shall I show you mercy, says your Redeemer, HASHEM.

⁹ For like the waters of Noah shall this be to Me: as I have sworn that the waters of Noah shall not again pass over the earth, so have I sworn not to be wrathful with you or rebuke you. ¹⁰ For the mountains may be moved and the hills may falter, but My kindness shall not be removed from you and My covenant of peace shall not falter, says the One Who shows you mercy, HASHEM.

Sefardim conclude the Haftarah here.

¹¹ O afflicted, storm-tossed, unconsoled one, behold! I shall lay your floor stones upon pearls and make your foundation of sapphires. ¹² I shall make your windows of rubies and your gates of garnets, and your entire boundary of precious stones. ¹³ All your children will be students of HASHEM, and your children will have abundant peace. ¹⁴ Establish yourself through righteousness, distance yourself from oppression for you need not fear it, and from panic for it will not come near you. ¹⁵ One need fear indeed if he is not with Me; whoever aggressively opposes you will fall because of you.

טז הֵן [הִנֵּה קרי] אָנֹכִי בָּרָאתִי חָרָשׁ נֹפֵחַ בְּאֵשׁ פֶּחָם וּמוֹצִיא כְלִי לְמַעֲשֵׂהוּ וְאָנֹכִי בָּרָאתִי מַשְׁחִית לְחַבֵּל: יז כָּל־כְּלִי יוּצַר עָלַיִךְ לֹא יִצְלָח וְכָל־לָשׁוֹן תָּקוּם־אִתָּךְ לַמִּשְׁפָּט תַּרְשִׁיעִי זֹאת נַחֲלַת עַבְדֵי יְהוָה וְצִדְקָתָם מֵאִתִּי נְאֻם־יְהוָה: **נה** א הוֹי כָּל־ צָמֵא לְכוּ לַמַּיִם וַאֲשֶׁר אֵין־לוֹ כָּסֶף לְכוּ שִׁבְרוּ וֶאֱכֹלוּ וּלְכוּ שִׁבְרוּ בְּלוֹא־כֶסֶף וּבְלוֹא מְחִיר יַיִן וְחָלָב: ב לָמָּה תִשְׁקְלוּ־כֶסֶף בְּלוֹא־לֶחֶם וִיגִיעֲכֶם בְּלוֹא לְשָׂבְעָה שִׁמְעוּ שָׁמוֹעַ אֵלַי וְאִכְלוּ־טוֹב וְתִתְעַנַּג בַּדֶּשֶׁן נַפְשְׁכֶם: ג הַטּוּ אָזְנְכֶם וּלְכוּ אֵלַי שִׁמְעוּ וּתְחִי נַפְשְׁכֶם וְאֶכְרְתָה לָכֶם בְּרִית עוֹלָם חַסְדֵי דָוִד הַנֶּאֱמָנִים: ד הֵן עֵד לְאוּמִּים נְתַתִּיו נָגִיד וּמְצַוֵּה לְאֻמִּים: ה הֵן גּוֹי לֹא־תֵדַע תִּקְרָא וְגוֹי לֹא־יְדָעוּךָ אֵלֶיךָ יָרוּצוּ לְמַעַן יְהוָה אֱלֹהֶיךָ וְלִקְדוֹשׁ יִשְׂרָאֵל כִּי פֵאֲרָךְ:

הפטרת לך לך

ישעיה מ:כז - מא:טז

כז לָמָּה תֹאמַר יַעֲקֹב וּתְדַבֵּר יִשְׂרָאֵל נִסְתְּרָה דַרְכִּי מֵיהוָה וּמֵאֱלֹהַי מִשְׁפָּטִי יַעֲבוֹר: כח הֲלוֹא יָדַעְתָּ אִם־לֹא שָׁמַעְתָּ אֱלֹהֵי עוֹלָם | יְהוָה בּוֹרֵא קְצוֹת הָאָרֶץ לֹא יִיעַף וְלֹא יִיגָע אֵין חֵקֶר לִתְבוּנָתוֹ: כט נֹתֵן לַיָּעֵף כֹּחַ וּלְאֵין אוֹנִים עָצְמָה יַרְבֶּה: ל וְיִעֲפוּ נְעָרִים וְיִגָעוּ וּבַחוּרִים כָּשׁוֹל יִכָּשֵׁלוּ: לא וְקוֹיֵ יְהוָה יַחֲלִיפוּ כֹחַ יַעֲלוּ אֵבֶר כַּנְּשָׁרִים יָרוּצוּ וְלֹא יִיגָעוּ יֵלְכוּ וְלֹא יִיעָפוּ: **מא** א הַחֲרִישׁוּ אֵלַי אִיִּים וּלְאֻמִּים יַחֲלִיפוּ כֹחַ יִגְּשׁוּ אָז יְדַבֵּרוּ יַחְדָּו לַמִּשְׁפָּט נִקְרָבָה: ב מִי הֵעִיר מִמִּזְרָח צֶדֶק יִקְרָאֵהוּ לְרַגְלוֹ יִתֵּן לְפָנָיו גּוֹיִם וּמְלָכִים יַרְדְּ יִתֵּן כֶּעָפָר חַרְבּוֹ כְּקַשׁ נִדָּף קַשְׁתּוֹ:

Abraham was summoned by God and given the mission of bringing His will to fruition and His message to the nations. The *Haftarah* builds upon this theme, and encourages Israel to maintain its optimistic spirit even in the face of its own failure and exile, and stubborn resistance on the part of the nations.

'God gives strength to the weary ...' Isaiah proclaims; those who trust Him will find new strength and ultimately prevail. Rather than focus on the shortcomings of people — Jews and Gentiles — we should look to the obvious manifestations of God's sovereignty and recognize that, despite what transitory events may sometimes indicate, the only intelligent course is to serve God.

¹⁶ Behold! I have created the smith who blows on a charcoal flame and withdraws a tool for his labor, and I have created the destroyer to ruin. ¹⁷ Any weapon sharpened against you shall not succeed, and any tongue that shall rise against you in judgment you shall condemn; this is the heritage of the servant of HASHEM, and their righteousness is from Me, the words of HASHEM.

55. ¹ Ho, all who are thirsty, go to the water, even one who has no money; go buy and eat, go and buy without money, and without barter wine and milk. ² Why do you weigh out money for that which is not bread and [fruit of] your toil for that which does not satisfy? Listen well to Me and eat what is good, and let your soul delight in abundance. ³ Incline your ear and come to Me, listen and your soul will rejuvenate; I shall seal an eternal covenant with you, the enduring kindnesses [promised] David. ⁴ Behold! I have appointed him a witness to the peoples, a prince and a commander to the peoples. ⁵ Behold! a nation that you did not know you will call, and a nation that knew you not will run to you, for the sake of HASHEM, your God, the Holy One of Israel, for He has glorified you!

But what do unthinking people do in the face of these manifestations? They persist in their idol worship, exhort their comrades to be firm in their misdirection, and tell the artisans to use their glue and nails to fashion stronger idols!

Let Israel ignore them. Instead let it have faith in God's assurances that good will triumph. Israel may seem weak and helpless as a worm, but it will triumph in the end and defeat those who now seem invincible.

HAFTARAS LECH LECHA
Isaiah 40:27-41:16

²⁷ Why do you say, O Jacob, and declare, O Israel: My way is hidden from HASHEM, and my cause has been passed over by my God. ²⁸ Could you not have known even if you did not hear, that an eternal God is HASHEM, Creator of the ends of the earth, that He neither wearies nor tires, that His discernment is beyond investigation? ²⁹ He gives strength to the weary, and for the powerless, He gives abundant might. ³⁰ Youths may weary and tire and young men may constantly falter. ³¹ But those whose hope is in HASHEM will have renewed strength, they will grow wings like eagles; they will run and not grow tired, walk and not grow weary.

41. ¹ Listen silently to me, O islands, and let the regimes renew strength; let them approach, then let them speak — together we will come near for judgment. ² Who aroused [Abraham] from the east, who would proclaim His righteousness at every footstep? Let Him place nations before him, and may he dominate kings, may his sword make [victims] like dust, and his bow like shredded straw.

ג יִרְדְּפֵם יַעֲבֹור שָׁלֹום אֹרַח בְּרַגְלָיו לֹא יָבֹוא:
ד מִי־פָעַל וְעָשָׂה קֹרֵא הַדֹּרֹות מֵרֹאשׁ אֲנִי יהוֹה
רִאשֹׁון וְאֶת־אַחֲרֹנִים אֲנִי־הוּא: ה רָאוּ אִיִּים
וְיִירָאוּ קְצֹות הָאָרֶץ יֶחֱרָדוּ קָרְבוּ וַיֶּאֱתָיוּן: ו אִישׁ
אֶת־רֵעֵהוּ יַעֲזֹרוּ וּלְאָחִיו יֹאמַר חֲזָק: ז וַיְחַזֵּק
חָרָשׁ אֶת־צֹרֵף מַחֲלִיק פַּטִּישׁ אֶת־הֹולֶם פָּעַם
אֹמֵר לַדֶּבֶק טֹוב הוּא וַיְחַזְּקֵהוּ בְמַסְמְרִים לֹא
יִמֹּוט: ח וְאַתָּה יִשְׂרָאֵל עַבְדִּי יַעֲקֹב אֲשֶׁר בְּחַרְתִּיךָ
זֶרַע אַבְרָהָם אֹהֲבִי: ט אֲשֶׁר הֶחֱזַקְתִּיךָ מִקְצֹות
הָאָרֶץ וּמֵאֲצִילֶיהָ קְרָאתִיךָ וָאֹמַר לְךָ עַבְדִּי־אַתָּה
בְּחַרְתִּיךָ וְלֹא מְאַסְתִּיךָ: י אַל־תִּירָא כִּי עִמְּךָ־אָנִי
אַל־תִּשְׁתָּע כִּי־אֲנִי אֱלֹהֶיךָ אִמַּצְתִּיךָ אַף־עֲזַרְתִּיךָ
אַף־תְּמַכְתִּיךָ בִּימִין צִדְקִי: יא הֵן יֵבֹשׁוּ וְיִכָּלְמוּ כֹּל
הַנֶּחֱרִים בָּךְ יִהְיוּ כְאַיִן וְיֹאבְדוּ אַנְשֵׁי רִיבֶךָ:
יב תְּבַקְשֵׁם וְלֹא תִמְצָאֵם אַנְשֵׁי מַצֻּתֶךָ יִהְיוּ כְאַיִן
וּכְאֶפֶס אַנְשֵׁי מִלְחַמְתֶּךָ: יג כִּי אֲנִי יהוָה אֱלֹהֶיךָ
מַחֲזִיק יְמִינֶךָ הָאֹמֵר לְךָ אַל־תִּירָא אֲנִי עֲזַרְתִּיךָ:
יד אַל־תִּירְאִי תֹּולַעַת יַעֲקֹב מְתֵי יִשְׂרָאֵל אֲנִי
עֲזַרְתִּיךְ נְאֻם־יהוָה וְגֹאֲלֵךְ קְדֹושׁ יִשְׂרָאֵל: טו הִנֵּה
שַׂמְתִּיךְ לְמֹורַג חָרוּץ חָדָשׁ בַּעַל פִּיפִיֹּות תָּדוּשׁ
הָרִים וְתָדֹק וּגְבָעֹות כַּמֹּץ תָּשִׂים: טז תִּזְרֵם וְרוּחַ
תִּשָּׂאֵם וּסְעָרָה תָּפִיץ אֹתָם וְאַתָּה תָּגִיל בַּיהוָה
בִּקְדֹושׁ יִשְׂרָאֵל תִּתְהַלָּל:

³ Let him pursue them and pass on safely, on a path that his feet have never trodden.

⁴ Who wrought and accomplished it? He Who called the generations from the beginning — I am HASHEM the first, and with the last ones, I will be the same.

⁵ The islands saw and feared, the ends of the earth shuddered, they approached and came — ⁶ but a man would help his fellow [worship idols], and to his brother he would say, 'Be strong.' ⁷ The carpenter encourages the goldsmith, the finishing hammerer [encourages] the one who pounds from the start; he would say of the glue that it is good, strengthen it with nails that it not falter.

⁸ But you, Israel, My servant, Jacob, whom I have chosen, offspring of Abraham, who loved me: ⁹ whom I have grasped from the ends of the earth, I have summoned you from its leaders, and I have said to you, 'You are My servant, I have chosen you and not despised you.'

¹⁰ Fear not for I am with you, do not go astray for I am your God; I have strengthened you, even helped you, even supported you with the right hand of My righteousness.

¹¹ Behold! all who are angry with you shall be shamed and humiliated; those who contend with you shall be like nothing and shall perish. ¹² You shall seek them but not find them, the men who struggle with you; they shall be like utter nothingness, the men who battle with you. ¹³ For I, HASHEM, your God, grasp your right hand, the One who tells you: 'Fear not, for I help you.'

¹⁴ Fear not, O worm, Jacob, O people of Israel, for I [I shall be] your help — the words of HASHEM — Redeemer, the Holy One of Israel. ¹⁵ Behold! I have made you a new, sharp threshing tool with many blades; you shall thresh mountains and grind them small, and make the hills like chaff. ¹⁶ You shall winnow them and the wind will carry them off, the storm will scatter them — but you will rejoice in HASHEM, in the Holy One of Israel will you glory!

הפטרת וירא

מלכים ב: ד:א-לז

ד א וְאִשָּׁה אַחַת מִנְּשֵׁי בְנֵי־הַנְּבִיאִים צָעֲקָה אֶל־
אֱלִישָׁע לֵאמֹר עַבְדְּךָ אִישִׁי מֵת וְאַתָּה יָדַעְתָּ כִּי
עַבְדְּךָ הָיָה יָרֵא אֶת־יְהֹוָה וְהַנֹּשֶׁה בָּא לָקַחַת
אֶת־שְׁנֵי יְלָדַי לוֹ לַעֲבָדִים: ב וַיֹּאמֶר אֵלֶיהָ אֱלִישָׁע
מָה אֶעֱשֶׂה־לָּךְ הַגִּידִי לִי מַה־יֶּשׁ־לָכְי [לָךְ קרי] בַּבָּיִת
וַתֹּאמֶר אֵין לְשִׁפְחָתְךָ כֹל בַּבַּיִת כִּי אִם־אָסוּךְ שָׁמֶן:
ג וַיֹּאמֶר לְכִי שַׁאֲלִי־לָךְ כֵּלִים מִן־הַחוּץ מֵאֵת כָּל־
שכניכי [שְׁכֵנָיִךְ קרי] כֵּלִים רֵקִים אַל־תַּמְעִיטִי:
ד וּבָאת וְסָגַרְתְּ הַדֶּלֶת בַּעֲדֵךְ וּבְעַד־בָּנַיִךְ וְיָצַקְתְּ עַל
כָּל־הַכֵּלִים הָאֵלֶּה וְהַמָּלֵא תַּסִּיעִי: ה וַתֵּלֶךְ מֵאִתּוֹ
וַתִּסְגֹּר הַדֶּלֶת בַּעֲדָהּ וּבְעַד בָּנֶיהָ הֵם מַגִּשִׁים אֵלֶיהָ
וְהִיא מיצקת [מוֹצָקֶת קרי]: ו וַיְהִי | כִּמְלֹאת הַכֵּלִים
וַתֹּאמֶר אֶל־בְּנָהּ הַגִּישָׁה אֵלַי עוֹד כֶּלִי וַיֹּאמֶר אֵלֶיהָ
אֵין עוֹד כֶּלִי וַיַּעֲמֹד הַשָּׁמֶן: ז וַתָּבֹא וַתַּגֵּד לְאִישׁ
הָאֱלֹהִים וַיֹּאמֶר לְכִי מִכְרִי אֶת־הַשֶּׁמֶן וְשַׁלְּמִי
אֶת־נשיכי [נִשְׁיֵךְ קרי] וְאַתְּ בניכי [וּבָנַיִךְ קרי] תִּחְיִי
בַּנּוֹתָר: ח וַיְהִי הַיּוֹם וַיַּעֲבֹר אֱלִישָׁע אֶל־שׁוּנֵם וְשָׁם
אִשָּׁה גְדוֹלָה וַתַּחֲזֶק־בּוֹ לֶאֱכָל־לָחֶם וַיְהִי מִדֵּי עָבְרוֹ
יָסֻר שָׁמָּה לֶאֱכָל־לָחֶם: ט וַתֹּאמֶר אֶל־אִישָׁהּ
הִנֵּה־נָא יָדַעְתִּי כִּי אִישׁ אֱלֹהִים קָדוֹשׁ הוּא עֹבֵר
עָלֵינוּ תָּמִיד: י נַעֲשֶׂה־נָּא עֲלִיַּת־קִיר קְטַנָּה וְנָשִׂים לוֹ
שָׁם מִטָּה וְשֻׁלְחָן וְכִסֵּא וּמְנוֹרָה וְהָיָה בְּבֹאוֹ אֵלֵינוּ
יָסוּר שָׁמָּה: יא וַיְהִי הַיּוֹם וַיָּבֹא שָׁמָּה וַיָּסַר אֶל־
הָעֲלִיָּה וַיִּשְׁכַּב־שָׁמָּה: יב וַיֹּאמֶר אֶל־גֵּיחֲזִי נַעֲרוֹ
קְרָא לַשּׁוּנַמִּית הַזֹּאת וַיִּקְרָא־לָהּ וַתַּעֲמֹד לְפָנָיו:
יג וַיֹּאמֶר לוֹ אֱמָר־נָא אֵלֶיהָ הִנֵּה חָרַדְתְּ | אֵלֵינוּ
אֶת־כָּל־הַחֲרָדָה הַזֹּאת מֶה לַעֲשׂוֹת לָךְ הֲיֵשׁ
לְדַבֶּר־לָךְ אֶל־הַמֶּלֶךְ אוֹ אֶל־שַׂר הַצָּבָא וַתֹּאמֶר

Elisha, like Abraham, embodied the nobility of Judaism for his generation, and, as it does of Abraham, Scripture expresses Elisha's greatness by setting forth his compassion for others. The *Haftarah* cites two such episodes: The first involves a destitute widow who has no one to help her, and the second involves a wealthy, influential woman who needs no favors from anyone.

It may be that the case of the widow was chosen because her plight seemed to be like that of a visitor to Sodom, so unconcerned did her neighbors seem to be. According to the Sages, she was the widow of the prophet Obadiah, who risked his life and spent his fortune to support and shelter hundreds of prophets from the sword of Ahab and Jezebel. Yet when his widow was confronted with a creditor who was about to seize her children as slaves in payment for the debts, she had nowhere to turn, but to Elisha. Where was Abraham's legacy of mercy? But in the kingdom of the Ten Tribes, where that legacy had apparently been squandered, Elisha was still there to listen, empathize, and help.

The second episode involves the Shunemite woman who had everything — but no children. Elisha shows his gratitude by blessing her with a son, as God blessed Sarah with a son.

When the child died suddenly, Elisha revived him by placing himself upon the lifeless little body, and injecting his own life, as it were, into the prostrate body. This has become an eternal lesson for those who wish to teach and inspire Jewish children — to breathe life into them. A teacher must give himself over to his charges if he hopes to succeed.

HAFTARAS VAYEIRA

II Kings 4:1-37

4 ¹ A certain woman from among the wives of the disciples of the prophets cried out to Elisha, saying: 'Your servant, my husband, has died and you know that your servant was God fearing — now the creditor has come to take my two children to be his slaves.'

² Elisha said to her: 'What can I do for you? — tell me what you have in the house.'

She answered: 'Your maidservant has nothing in the house except for a jug of oil.'

³ He said, 'Go borrow vessels from the outside — from all your neighbors — empty vessels, do not be sparing. ⁴ Then go in and shut the door behind yourself and behind your children; pour into all these vessels and remove each full one.'

⁵ She left him and shut the door behind herself and behind her children. They brought her and she poured. ⁶ When all the vessels were full she said to her son, ' Bring me another vessel.'

He said to her, 'There is not another vessel,' and the oil stopped.

⁷ She came and told the man of God. He said, 'Go sell the oil and pay your creditors, and you and your children will live on the remainder.'

⁸ It happened one day that Elisha traveled to Shunem. An outstanding woman was there and she importuned him to eat a meal; so it was that whenever he passed by, he would turn there to eat a meal. ⁹ She said to her husband, 'Behold! — I now know that the man of God who passes by us regularly is holy. ¹⁰ Let us now make a small walled attic and place there for him a bed, a table, a chair, and a lamp, so whenever he comes to us, he can turn there.'

¹¹ It happened one day that he came there, and turned to the attic and lay down there. ¹² He said to Gechazi his attendant: 'Call this Shunemite woman.' ¹³ He called her and she stood before him. He said to him: 'Say to her now, "Behold! — you have shown us this great solicitude; what can be done for you? Can something be said on your behalf to the king or the army commander?" ' She said:

בְּתוֹךְ עַמִּי אָנֹכִי יֹשָׁבֶת: יד וַיֹּאמֶר וּמֶה לַעֲשׂוֹת לָהּ
וַיֹּאמֶר גֵּיחֲזִי אֲבָל בֵּן אֵין־לָהּ וְאִישָׁהּ זָקֵן: טו וַיֹּאמֶר
קְרָא־לָהּ וַיִּקְרָא־לָהּ וַתַּעֲמֹד בַּפָּתַח: טז וַיֹּאמֶר
לַמּוֹעֵד הַזֶּה כָּעֵת חַיָּה אתי [אַתְּ קרי] חֹבֶקֶת בֵּן
וַתֹּאמֶר אַל־אֲדֹנִי אִישׁ הָאֱלֹהִים אַל־תְּכַזֵּב
בְּשִׁפְחָתֶךָ: יז וַתַּהַר הָאִשָּׁה וַתֵּלֶד בֵּן לַמּוֹעֵד הַזֶּה
כָּעֵת חַיָּה אֲשֶׁר־דִּבֶּר אֵלֶיהָ אֱלִישָׁע: יח וַיִּגְדַּל הַיָּלֶד
וַיְהִי הַיּוֹם וַיֵּצֵא אֶל־אָבִיו אֶל־הַקֹּצְרִים: יט וַיֹּאמֶר
אֶל־אָבִיו רֹאשִׁי ׀ רֹאשִׁי וַיֹּאמֶר אֶל־הַנַּעַר שָׂאֵהוּ
אֶל־אִמּוֹ: כ וַיִּשָּׂאֵהוּ וַיְבִיאֵהוּ אֶל־אִמּוֹ וַיֵּשֶׁב עַל־
בִּרְכֶּיהָ עַד־הַצׇּהֳרַיִם וַיָּמֹת: כא וַתַּעַל וַתַּשְׁכִּבֵהוּ עַל־
מִטַּת אִישׁ הָאֱלֹהִים וַתִּסְגֹּר בַּעֲדוֹ וַתֵּצֵא: כב וַתִּקְרָא
אֶל־אִישָׁהּ וַתֹּאמֶר שִׁלְחָה נָא לִי אֶחָד מִן־הַנְּעָרִים
וְאַחַת הָאֲתֹנוֹת וְאָרוּצָה עַד־אִישׁ הָאֱלֹהִים
וְאָשׁוּבָה: כג וַיֹּאמֶר מַדּוּעַ אתי הלכתי [אַתְּ הֹלֶכֶת
קרי] אֵלָיו הַיּוֹם לֹא־חֹדֶשׁ וְלֹא שַׁבָּת וַתֹּאמֶר שָׁלוֹם:

Sefardim and the community of Frankfurt am Main
conclude the *Haftarah* here.

כד וַתַּחֲבֹשׁ הָאָתוֹן וַתֹּאמֶר אֶל־נַעֲרָהּ נְהַג וָלֵךְ אַל־
תַּעֲצׇר־לִי לִרְכֹּב כִּי אִם־אָמַרְתִּי לָךְ: כה וַתֵּלֶךְ וַתָּבֹא
אֶל־אִישׁ הָאֱלֹהִים אֶל־הַר הַכַּרְמֶל וַיְהִי כִּרְאוֹת
אִישׁ־הָאֱלֹהִים אֹתָהּ מִנֶּגֶד וַיֹּאמֶר אֶל־גֵּיחֲזִי נַעֲרוֹ
הִנֵּה הַשּׁוּנַמִּית הַלָּז: כו עַתָּה רוּץ־נָא לִקְרָאתָהּ
וֶאֱמׇר־לָהּ הֲשָׁלוֹם לָךְ הֲשָׁלוֹם לְאִישֵׁךְ הֲשָׁלוֹם
לַיָּלֶד וַתֹּאמֶר שָׁלוֹם: כז וַתָּבֹא אֶל־אִישׁ הָאֱלֹהִים
אֶל־הָהָר וַתַּחֲזֵק בְּרַגְלָיו וַיִּגַּשׁ גֵּיחֲזִי לְהׇדְפָהּ
וַיֹּאמֶר אִישׁ הָאֱלֹהִים הַרְפֵּה־לָהּ כִּי־נַפְשָׁהּ מָרָה־לָהּ
וַיהֹוָה הֶעְלִים מִמֶּנִּי וְלֹא הִגִּיד לִי: כח וַתֹּאמֶר
הֲשָׁאַלְתִּי בֵן מֵאֵת אֲדֹנִי הֲלֹא אָמַרְתִּי לֹא תַשְׁלֶה
אֹתִי: כט וַיֹּאמֶר לְגֵיחֲזִי חֲגֹר מׇתְנֶיךָ וְקַח מִשְׁעַנְתִּי
בְיָדְךָ וָלֵךְ כִּי־תִמְצָא אִישׁ לֹא תְבָרְכֶנּוּ וְכִי־

' I dwell among my people.'

[14] So he said, 'What can be done for her?' Gechazi said, 'But she has no son, and her husband is old.'

[15] He said, 'Call her,' so he called her and she stood in the doorway. [16] He said, 'At this season next year you will be embracing a son.' She said, 'No, my master, O man of God, do not deceive your maidservant!'

[17] The woman conceived and bore a son at that season the next year, of which Elisha had spoken to her.

[18] The child grew up, and it happened one day that he went out to his father to the reapers. [19] He said to his father, 'My head! My head!' His father said to the attendant, 'Carry him to his mother.' [20] He carried him and brought him to his mother. He sat on her lap until noon, and died. [21] She went up and laid him on the bed of the man of God, shut the door upon him and left.

[22] She called to her husband and said, 'Please send me one of the attendants and one of the asses so that I can hurry to the man of God and return.'

[23] He said, 'Why are you going to him today? It is not a New Moon or a Sabbath!' She said, 'All is well.'

Sefardim and the community of Frankfurt am Main
conclude the Haftarah here.

[24] She saddled the ass and said to her attendant, 'Drive and go, and do not impede me from riding unless I tell you.' [25] She went and came to the man of God at Mount Carmel. When the man of God saw her from afar, he said to Gechazi, his attendant, 'Behold! — it is that Shunemite woman. [26] Now, please run toward her and say to her, "Is it well with you, is it well with your husband, is it well with the child?" ' And she said, 'All is well.'

[27] She came to the man of God at the mountain and grasped his legs. Gechazi approached to push her off, but the man of God said, 'Leave her for her soul is embittered, but HASHEM has hidden it from me and not told me.'

[28] She said, ' Did I request a son of my master? Did I not say, "Do not mislead me?" '

[29] He said to Gechazi, 'Gird your loins — take my staff in your hand and go. If you meet a man, do not greet him, and

יְבָרֶכְךָ אִישׁ לֹא תַעֲנֶנּוּ וְשַׂמְתָּ מִשְׁעַנְתִּי עַל־פְּנֵי
הַנָּעַר: ל וַתֹּאמֶר אֵם הַנַּעַר חַי־יהוה וְחֵי־נַפְשְׁךָ
אִם־אֶעֶזְבֶךָ וַיָּקָם וַיֵּלֶךְ אַחֲרֶיהָ: לא וְגֵחֲזִי עָבַר
לִפְנֵיהֶם וַיָּשֶׂם אֶת־הַמִּשְׁעֶנֶת עַל־פְּנֵי הַנַּעַר וְאֵין
קוֹל וְאֵין קָשֶׁב וַיָּשָׁב לִקְרָאתוֹ וַיַּגֶּד־לוֹ לֵאמֹר לֹא
הֵקִיץ הַנָּעַר: לב וַיָּבֹא אֱלִישָׁע הַבָּיְתָה וְהִנֵּה הַנַּעַר
מֵת מֻשְׁכָּב עַל־מִטָּתוֹ: לג וַיָּבֹא וַיִּסְגֹּר הַדֶּלֶת בְּעַד
שְׁנֵיהֶם וַיִּתְפַּלֵּל אֶל־יהוה: לד וַיַּעַל וַיִּשְׁכַּב עַל־הַיֶּלֶד
וַיָּשֶׂם פִּיו עַל־פִּיו וְעֵינָיו עַל־עֵינָיו וְכַפָּיו עַל־כַּפָּו
וַיִּגְהַר עָלָיו וַיָּחָם בְּשַׂר הַיָּלֶד: לה וַיָּשָׁב וַיֵּלֶךְ בַּבַּיִת
אַחַת הֵנָּה וְאַחַת הֵנָּה וַיַּעַל וַיִּגְהַר עָלָיו וַיְזוֹרֵר הַנַּעַר
עַד־שֶׁבַע פְּעָמִים וַיִּפְקַח הַנַּעַר אֶת־עֵינָיו: לו וַיִּקְרָא
אֶל־גֵּחֲזִי וַיֹּאמֶר קְרָא אֶל־הַשֻּׁנַמִּית הַזֹּאת וַיִּקְרָאֶהָ
וַתָּבֹא אֵלָיו וַיֹּאמֶר שְׂאִי בְנֵךְ: לז וַתָּבֹא וַתִּפֹּל
עַל־רַגְלָיו וַתִּשְׁתַּחוּ אָרְצָה וַתִּשָּׂא אֶת־בְּנָהּ וַתֵּצֵא:

הפטרת חיי שרה

מלכים א׳ א:א-לא

א וְהַמֶּלֶךְ דָּוִד זָקֵן בָּא בַּיָּמִים וַיְכַסֻּהוּ בַּבְּגָדִים וְלֹא
יִחַם לוֹ: ב וַיֹּאמְרוּ לוֹ עֲבָדָיו יְבַקְשׁוּ לַאדֹנִי הַמֶּלֶךְ
נַעֲרָה בְתוּלָה וְעָמְדָה לִפְנֵי הַמֶּלֶךְ וּתְהִי־לוֹ סֹכֶנֶת
וְשָׁכְבָה בְחֵיקֶךָ וְחַם לַאדֹנִי הַמֶּלֶךְ: ג וַיְבַקְשׁוּ נַעֲרָה
יָפָה בְּכֹל גְּבוּל יִשְׂרָאֵל וַיִּמְצְאוּ אֶת־אֲבִישַׁג
הַשּׁוּנַמִּית וַיָּבִאוּ אֹתָהּ לַמֶּלֶךְ: ד וְהַנַּעֲרָה יָפָה
עַד־מְאֹד וַתְּהִי לַמֶּלֶךְ סֹכֶנֶת וַתְּשָׁרְתֵהוּ וְהַמֶּלֶךְ לֹא
יְדָעָהּ: ה וַאֲדֹנִיָּה בֶן־חַגִּית מִתְנַשֵּׂא לֵאמֹר אֲנִי
אֶמְלֹךְ וַיַּעַשׂ לוֹ רֶכֶב וּפָרָשִׁים וַחֲמִשִּׁים אִישׁ רָצִים
לְפָנָיו: ו וְלֹא־עֲצָבוֹ אָבִיו מִיָּמָיו לֵאמֹר מַדּוּעַ כָּכָה
עָשִׂיתָ וְגַם־הוּא טוֹב־תֹּאַר מְאֹד וְאֹתוֹ יָלְדָה אַחֲרֵי
אַבְשָׁלוֹם: ז וַיִּהְיוּ דְבָרָיו עִם יוֹאָב בֶּן־צְרוּיָה וְעִם

Like that of the *Sidrah*, the theme of the *Haftarah* deals with succession. Abraham needed to find a mother for the Jewish people, and David had to select the new head of the dynasty that would lead Israel and the world to God's appointed destiny. But there the similarity ends.

Isaac and Eliezer were devoted to the desires of Abraham, because they knew that he, in turn, represented only the will of God. As the Sages teach, when one nullifies his will before God's, God will nullify the will of others before his will (*Avos* 2:4). Abraham's will was paramount, because those nearest him knew that he spoke for God.

if a man greets you do not respond to him. Place my staff upon the lad's face.'

³⁰ The lad's mother said, 'As HASHEM lives and as you live, I will not leave you!' So he stood up and followed her.

³¹ Gechazi went before them and placed the staff on the lad's face, but there was no sound and nothing was heard. He returned toward him and told him, saying, 'The lad has not revived.'

³² Elisha came to the house and behold! — the lad was dead, laid out on his bed. ³³ He entered and shut the door behind them both, and prayed to HASHEM. ³⁴ Then he went up and lay upon the lad, and placed his mouth upon his mouth, his eyes upon his eyes, his palms upon his palms, and prostrated himself upon him, and he warmed the flesh of the lad. ³⁵ He withdrew and walked about the house, once this way and once that way, then he went up and prostrated himself upon him; the lad sneezed seven times. The lad opened his eyes.

³⁶ He called Gechazi and said, 'Call this Shunemite woman.' He called her and she came to him; he said, 'Pick up your son!' ³⁷ She came and fell at his feet and bowed down to the ground; she picked up her son and left.

But as a nation grows and prospers, there are new challenges. When there is wealth, power, and influence, there are people who crave position. The great King David, as he lay old, weak, and unaware, became the victim of a cabal. Prince Adonijah, the senior son, handsome, and well connected, tried to seize the throne. Pushed aside would be Solomon, the wise and devoted son whom David had designated. Can one imagine how the history of Israel would have been harmed if the king had been the imperious prince to whom monarchy meant lavish feasting amid fawning courtiers, instead of the wisest of men, whose legacy was the Temple, and the Books of Proverbs, Song of Songs, and Ecclesiastes?

HAFTARAS CHAYEI SARAH
I Kings 1:1-31

1 ¹ King David was old, advanced in years; they covered him with garments, but he did not become warm. ² His servants said to him, 'Let there be sought for my lord, the king, a virgin girl, who will stand before the king and be his attendant; she will lie in your bosom and my lord the king will be warmed.' ³ They sought a beautiful girl throughout the boundary of Israel, and they found Abishag the Shunamitess and brought her to the king.

⁴ The girl was exceedingly beautiful, and she became the king's attendant and she served him, but the king was not intimate with her.

⁵ Adonijah son of Haggith exalted himself, saying, 'I shall reign!' He provided himself with a chariot and riders, and fifty men running before him. ⁶ All his life the king had never saddened him by saying, 'Why do you do this?' Moreover, he was very handsome and he was born after Absalom.

⁷ He held discussions with Joab son of Zaruyah and with

אֶבְיָתָר הַכֹּהֵן וַיַּעְזְרוּ אַחֲרֵי אֲדֹנִיָּה: ח וְצָדוֹק הַכֹּהֵן
וּבְנָיָהוּ בֶן־יְהוֹיָדָע וְנָתָן הַנָּבִיא וְשִׁמְעִי וְרֵעִי
וְהַגִּבּוֹרִים אֲשֶׁר לְדָוִד לֹא הָיוּ עִם־אֲדֹנִיָּהוּ: ט וַיִּזְבַּח
אֲדֹנִיָּהוּ צֹאן וּבָקָר וּמְרִיא עִם אֶבֶן הַזֹּחֶלֶת אֲשֶׁר־
אֵצֶל עֵין רֹגֵל וַיִּקְרָא אֶת־כָּל־אֶחָיו בְּנֵי הַמֶּלֶךְ
וּלְכָל־אַנְשֵׁי יְהוּדָה עַבְדֵי הַמֶּלֶךְ: י וְאֶת־נָתָן הַנָּבִיא
וּבְנָיָהוּ וְאֶת־הַגִּבּוֹרִים וְאֶת־שְׁלֹמֹה אָחִיו לֹא קָרָא:
יא וַיֹּאמֶר נָתָן אֶל־בַּת־שֶׁבַע אֵם־שְׁלֹמֹה לֵאמֹר
הֲלוֹא שָׁמַעַתְּ כִּי מָלַךְ אֲדֹנִיָּהוּ בֶן־חַגִּית וַאֲדֹנֵינוּ דָוִד
לֹא יָדָע: יב וְעַתָּה לְכִי אִיעָצֵךְ נָא עֵצָה וּמַלְּטִי אֶת־
נַפְשֵׁךְ וְאֶת־נֶפֶשׁ בְּנֵךְ שְׁלֹמֹה: יג לְכִי וּבֹאִי ׀ אֶל־
הַמֶּלֶךְ דָּוִד וְאָמַרְתְּ אֵלָיו הֲלֹא־אַתָּה אֲדֹנִי הַמֶּלֶךְ
נִשְׁבַּעְתָּ לַאֲמָתְךָ לֵאמֹר כִּי־שְׁלֹמֹה בְנֵךְ יִמְלֹךְ אַחֲרַי
וְהוּא יֵשֵׁב עַל־כִּסְאִי וּמַדּוּעַ מָלַךְ אֲדֹנִיָּהוּ: יד הִנֵּה
עוֹדָךְ מְדַבֶּרֶת שָׁם עִם־הַמֶּלֶךְ וַאֲנִי אָבוֹא אַחֲרַיִךְ
וּמִלֵּאתִי אֶת־דְּבָרָיִךְ: טו וַתָּבֹא בַת־שֶׁבַע אֶל־הַמֶּלֶךְ
הַחַדְרָה וְהַמֶּלֶךְ זָקֵן מְאֹד וַאֲבִישַׁג הַשּׁוּנַמִּית מְשָׁרַת
אֶת־הַמֶּלֶךְ: טז וַתִּקֹּד בַּת־שֶׁבַע וַתִּשְׁתַּחוּ לַמֶּלֶךְ
וַיֹּאמֶר הַמֶּלֶךְ מַה־לָּךְ: יז וַתֹּאמֶר לוֹ אֲדֹנִי אַתָּה
נִשְׁבַּעְתָּ בַּיהוה אֱלֹהֶיךָ לַאֲמָתֶךָ כִּי־שְׁלֹמֹה בְנֵךְ
יִמְלֹךְ אַחֲרָי וְהוּא יֵשֵׁב עַל־כִּסְאִי: יח וְעַתָּה הִנֵּה
אֲדֹנִיָּה מָלָךְ וְעַתָּה אֲדֹנִי הַמֶּלֶךְ לֹא יָדָעְתָּ: יט וַיִּזְבַּח
שׁוֹר וּמְרִיא־וְצֹאן לָרֹב וַיִּקְרָא לְכָל־בְּנֵי הַמֶּלֶךְ
וּלְאֶבְיָתָר הַכֹּהֵן וּלְיֹאָב שַׂר הַצָּבָא וְלִשְׁלֹמֹה עַבְדְּךָ
לֹא קָרָא: כ וְאַתָּה אֲדֹנִי הַמֶּלֶךְ עֵינֵי כָל־יִשְׂרָאֵל
עָלֶיךָ לְהַגִּיד לָהֶם מִי יֵשֵׁב עַל־כִּסֵּא אֲדֹנִי־הַמֶּלֶךְ
אַחֲרָיו: כא וְהָיָה כִּשְׁכַב אֲדֹנִי־הַמֶּלֶךְ עִם־אֲבֹתָיו
וְהָיִיתִי אֲנִי וּבְנִי שְׁלֹמֹה חַטָּאִים: כב וְהִנֵּה עוֹדֶנָּה
מְדַבֶּרֶת עִם־הַמֶּלֶךְ וְנָתָן הַנָּבִיא בָּא: כג וַיַּגִּידוּ לַמֶּלֶךְ
לֵאמֹר הִנֵּה נָתָן הַנָּבִיא וַיָּבֹא לִפְנֵי הַמֶּלֶךְ וַיִּשְׁתַּחוּ
לַמֶּלֶךְ עַל־אַפָּיו אָרְצָה: כד וַיֹּאמֶר נָתָן אֲדֹנִי הַמֶּלֶךְ

But the Guardian of Israel neither slumbers nor sleeps. Nathan and Bathsheba bring the planned travesty to David's sickbed, and the elderly king arouses his greatness once more. He promises them that his pledge remains in effect and that Solomon *will* reign. It is indicative of the inherent goodness of the nation that it was not necessary for the *Haftarah* to include the outcome. Adonijah and his cabal were an aberration that represented only their own small group. Solomon became king.

Abiathar the Kohen; they supported and followed Adonijah.

⁸ But Zaddok the Kohen, Benaiahu son of Jehoiada, Nathan the prophet, Shim'i, Re'i, and David's mighty men were not with Adonijah.

⁹ Adonijah slaughtered sheep, bulls, and fatted cattle at the Zoheleth stone that was near Ein-Rogel, and he invited all of his brothers, the sons of the king; and all the men of Judah, the king's servants. ¹⁰ But Nathan the prophet, Benaiahu, the mighty men, and his brother Solomon he did not invite.

¹¹ Nathan said to Bathsheba, Solomon's mother, as follows, 'Have you not heard that Adonijah son of Haggith has reigned? — and our lord David does not know. ¹² So come, I will counsel you now; save your life and the life of your son Solomon. ¹³ Go and come to King David and say to him: "My lord, the king, have you not sworn to your maidservant saying: 'Your son Solomon will reign after me and he will sit on my throne?' Why has Adonijah reigned?"

¹⁴ 'Behold! — while you are still speaking there with the king I will come in after you and supplement your words.'

¹⁵ Bathsheba came to the king in the chamber. The king was very old and Abishag the Shunamitess served the king. ¹⁶ Bathsheba bowed and prostrated herself to the king; and the king said, 'What concerns you?'

¹⁷ She said to him, 'My lord, you swore to your maidservant by HASHEM, your God, that "Shlomo, your son, will reign after me, and he will sit on my throne." ¹⁸ But now, behold! — Adonijah reigns — and my lord, the king, does not know! ¹⁹ He has slaughtered bulls, fatted cattle and sheep in abundance, and invited all the king's sons, as well as Abiathar the Kohen and Joab the general of the army — but he has not invited your servant Solomon. ²⁰ And you, my lord, the king, the eyes of all Israel are upon you, to tell them who will sit on the throne of my lord, the king, after him. ²¹ It will happen that when my lord, the king, sleeps with his ancestors, I and my son Solomon will be missing.'

²² Behold! — she was still speaking with the king when Nathan the prophet arrived. ²³ They told the king saying, 'Behold — Nathan the prophet!' He came before the king and prostrated himself to the king with his face to the ground. ²⁴ Nathan said, 'My lord, the king,

אַתָּה אָמַרְתָּ אֲדֹנִיָּהוּ יִמְלֹךְ אַחֲרָי וְהוּא יֵשֵׁב
עַל־כִּסְאִי: כה כִּי ׀ יָרַד הַיּוֹם וַיִּזְבַּח שׁוֹר וּמְרִיא־
וְצֹאן לָרֹב וַיִּקְרָא לְכָל־בְּנֵי הַמֶּלֶךְ וּלְשָׂרֵי הַצָּבָא
וּלְאֶבְיָתָר הַכֹּהֵן וְהִנָּם אֹכְלִים וְשֹׁתִים לְפָנָיו וַיֹּאמְרוּ
יְחִי הַמֶּלֶךְ אֲדֹנִיָּהוּ: כו וְלִי אֲנִי־עַבְדֶּךָ וּלְצָדֹק הַכֹּהֵן
וְלִבְנָיָהוּ בֶן־יְהוֹיָדָע וְלִשְׁלֹמֹה עַבְדְּךָ לֹא קָרָא: כז אִם
מֵאֵת אֲדֹנִי הַמֶּלֶךְ נִהְיָה הַדָּבָר הַזֶּה וְלֹא הוֹדַעְתָּ
אֶת־עבדיך [עַבְדְּךָ קרי] מִי יֵשֵׁב עַל־כִּסֵּא אֲדֹנִי־
הַמֶּלֶךְ אַחֲרָיו: כח וַיַּעַן הַמֶּלֶךְ דָּוִד וַיֹּאמֶר קִרְאוּ־לִי
לְבַת־שָׁבַע וַתָּבֹא לִפְנֵי הַמֶּלֶךְ וַתַּעֲמֹד לִפְנֵי הַמֶּלֶךְ:
כט וַיִּשָּׁבַע הַמֶּלֶךְ וַיֹּאמַר חַי־יְהוָה אֲשֶׁר־פָּדָה אֶת־
נַפְשִׁי מִכָּל־צָרָה: ל כִּי כַּאֲשֶׁר נִשְׁבַּעְתִּי לָךְ בַּיהוָה
אֱלֹהֵי יִשְׂרָאֵל לֵאמֹר כִּי־שְׁלֹמֹה בְנֵךְ יִמְלֹךְ אַחֲרַי
וְהוּא יֵשֵׁב עַל־כִּסְאִי תַּחְתָּי כִּי כֵּן אֶעֱשֶׂה הַיּוֹם הַזֶּה:
לא וַתִּקֹּד בַּת־שֶׁבַע אַפַּיִם אֶרֶץ וַתִּשְׁתַּחוּ לַמֶּלֶךְ
וַתֹּאמֶר יְחִי אֲדֹנִי הַמֶּלֶךְ דָּוִד לְעֹלָם:

הפטרת תולדות
מלאכי א:א–ב:ז

א א מַשָּׂא דְבַר־יְהוָה אֶל־יִשְׂרָאֵל בְּיַד מַלְאָכִי:
ב אָהַבְתִּי אֶתְכֶם אָמַר יְהוָה וַאֲמַרְתֶּם בַּמָּה אֲהַבְתָּנוּ
הֲלוֹא־אָח עֵשָׂו לְיַעֲקֹב נְאֻם־יְהוָה וָאֹהַב אֶת־יַעֲקֹב:
ג וְאֶת־עֵשָׂו שָׂנֵאתִי וָאָשִׂים אֶת־הָרָיו שְׁמָמָה וְאֶת־
נַחֲלָתוֹ לְתַנּוֹת מִדְבָּר: ד כִּי־תֹאמַר אֱדוֹם רֻשַּׁשְׁנוּ
וְנָשׁוּב וְנִבְנֶה חֳרָבוֹת כֹּה אָמַר יְהוָה צְבָאוֹת הֵמָּה
יִבְנוּ וַאֲנִי אֶהֱרוֹס וְקָרְאוּ לָהֶם גְּבוּל רִשְׁעָה וְהָעָם
אֲשֶׁר־זָעַם יְהוָה עַד־עוֹלָם: ה וְעֵינֵיכֶם תִּרְאֶינָה
וְאַתֶּם תֹּאמְרוּ יִגְדַּל יְהוָה מֵעַל לִגְבוּל יִשְׂרָאֵל: ו בֵּן
יְכַבֵּד אָב וְעֶבֶד אֲדֹנָיו וְאִם־אָב אָנִי אַיֵּה כְבוֹדִי
וְאִם־אֲדוֹנִים אָנִי אַיֵּה מוֹרָאִי אָמַר ׀ יְהוָה צְבָאוֹת

The *Sidrah* depicts perhaps the major turning point in the spiritual history of the world — the choice of Jacob over Esau to receive the Torah and bear the Patriarchal legacy. But the choice was not automatic. Esau was the firstborn and, however one understands Isaac's motives, he wished to confer the blessings upon Esau. Only God's will, as set in motion by Rebecca, secured the blessings for Jacob.

have you said, "Adonijah will reign after me and he will sit on my throne?" [25] For he has gone down today and slaughtered bulls, fatted cattle, and sheep in abundance, and he has invited all the king's sons, the generals of the army, and Abiathar the Kohen, and they are eating and drinking before him — and they said, "Long live King Adonijah." [26] But me — I, who am your servant — Zaddok the Kohen, Benaiahu son of Jehoiada, and your servant Solomon he did not invite. [27] If this matter came from my lord, the king, would you not have informed your servant who should sit on the throne of my lord, the king, after him?'

[28] King David answered and said, 'Call Bathsheba to me.' She came before the king and stood before the king. [29] The king swore and said, 'As HASHEM lives, Who has redeemed my life from every travail — [30] as I have sworn to you by HASHEM, the God of Israel, saying, "Solomon your son will reign after me and he will sit on my throne in my place," so shall I fulfill this very day.'

[31] Bathsheba bowed with her face to the ground and prostrated herself to the king; and she said, 'May my lord, King David, live forever!'

HAFTARAS TOLDOS
Malachi 1:1-2:7

The *Haftarah* says at the outset that God's choice of Jacob was a sign of God's love for Jacob and His hatred for Esau. Because of this hatred, the prophet states that Edom, the nation that stems from Esau, will not prosper; that it is doomed to destruction, as indeed the evil that is incarnate in Edom will untimately be destroyed. It will take time. The Roman Empire that brought about the current exile and most of the powers that have persecuted Israel during its long, long duration are regarded by the Rabbinic tradition as descendants — spiritual, if not direct — of Edom. Like most prophecies we do not know when this one will be fulfilled; we know only that it will.

1 [1] The prophetic burden of the word of HASHEM, through Malachi. [2] 'I loved you,' said HASHEM, and you said, 'How have You loved us?' Was not Esau a brother of Jacob — the words of HASHEM — yet I loved Jacob. [3] But I hated Esau and I made his mountains a desolation, and his heritage for the desert serpents. [4] Though Edom said, 'We have become destitute, but we shall return and rebuild the ruins'; so said HASHEM, Master of Legions, 'They may build, but I shall tear down; they shall call them, "the boundary of wickedness, and the people who infuriated HASHEM to eternity." [5] Your eyes shall see and you shall say, "HASHEM is great beyond the boundary of Israel." '

[6] 'A son will honor his father and a slave his master; if I am a Father, where is My honor, and if I am a Master where is My reverence?' says HASHEM, Master of Legions,

לָכֶ֤ם הַכֹּֽהֲנִים֙ בּוֹזֵ֣י שְׁמִ֔י וַאֲמַרְתֶּ֕ם בַּמֶּ֥ה בָזִ֖ינוּ אֶת־
שְׁמֶֽךָ: ז מַגִּישִׁ֤ים עַֽל־מִזְבְּחִי֙ לֶ֣חֶם מְגֹאָ֔ל וַאֲמַרְתֶּ֖ם
בַּמֶּ֣ה גֵֽאַלְנ֑וּךָ בֶּֽאֱמׇרְכֶ֔ם שֻׁלְחַ֥ן יְהֹוָ֖ה נִבְזֶ֥ה הֽוּא:
ח וְכִֽי־תַגִּשׁ֨וּן עִוֵּ֤ר לִזְבֹּ֙חַ֙ אֵ֣ין רָ֔ע וְכִ֥י תַגִּ֛ישׁוּ פִּסֵּ֥חַ
וְחֹלֶ֖ה אֵ֣ין רָ֑ע הַקְרִיבֵ֨הוּ נָ֜א לְפֶחָתֶ֗ךָ הֲיִרְצְךָ֙ א֣וֹ
הֲיִשָּׂ֣א פָנֶ֔יךָ אָמַ֖ר יְהֹוָ֥ה צְבָאֽוֹת: ט וְעַתָּ֛ה חַלּוּ־נָ֥א
פְנֵי־אֵ֖ל וִֽיחׇנֵּ֑נוּ מִיֶּדְכֶם֙ הָ֣יְתָה זֹּ֔את הֲיִשָּׂ֤א מִכֶּם֙ פָּנִ֔ים
אָמַ֖ר יְהֹוָ֥ה צְבָאֽוֹת: י מִ֤י גַם־בָּכֶם֙ וְיִסְגֹּ֣ר דְּלָתַ֔יִם
וְלֹֽא־תָאִ֥ירוּ מִזְבְּחִ֖י חִנָּ֑ם אֵֽין־לִ֨י חֵ֜פֶץ בָּכֶ֗ם אָמַר֙
יְהֹוָ֣ה צְבָא֔וֹת וּמִנְחָ֖ה לֹֽא־אֶרְצֶ֥ה מִיֶּדְכֶֽם: יא כִּ֣י
מִמִּזְרַח־שֶׁ֜מֶשׁ וְעַד־מְבוֹא֗וֹ גָּד֤וֹל שְׁמִי֙ בַּגּוֹיִ֔ם וּבְכׇל־
מָק֗וֹם מֻקְטָ֥ר מֻגָּ֛שׁ לִשְׁמִ֖י וּמִנְחָ֣ה טְהוֹרָ֑ה כִּֽי־גָד֤וֹל
שְׁמִי֙ בַּגּוֹיִ֔ם אָמַ֖ר יְהֹוָ֥ה צְבָאֽוֹת: יב וְאַתֶּ֖ם מְחַלְּלִ֣ים
אוֹת֑וֹ בֶּאֱמׇרְכֶ֗ם שֻׁלְחַ֤ן אֲדֹנָי֙ מְגֹאָ֣ל ה֔וּא וְנִיב֖וֹ נִבְזֶ֥ה
אׇכְלֽוֹ: יג וַאֲמַרְתֶּם֩ הִנֵּ֨ה מַתְּלָאָ֜ה וְהִפַּחְתֶּ֣ם אוֹת֗וֹ
אָמַר֙ יְהֹוָ֣ה צְבָא֔וֹת וַהֲבֵאתֶ֣ם גָּז֗וּל וְאֶת־הַפִּסֵּ֙חַ֙
וְאֶת־הַ֣חוֹלֶ֔ה וַהֲבֵאתֶ֖ם אֶת־הַמִּנְחָ֑ה הַאֶרְצֶ֥ה אוֹתָ֛הּ
מִיֶּדְכֶ֖ם אָמַ֥ר יְהֹוָֽה: יד וְאָר֣וּר נוֹכֵ֗ל וְיֵ֤שׁ בְּעֶדְרוֹ֙ זָכָ֔ר
וְנֹדֵ֛ר וְזֹבֵ֥חַ מׇשְׁחָ֖ת לַֽאדֹנָ֑י כִּי֩ מֶ֨לֶךְ גָּד֜וֹל אָ֗נִי אָמַר֙
יְהֹוָ֣ה צְבָא֔וֹת וּשְׁמִ֖י נוֹרָ֥א בַגּוֹיִֽם: ב א וְעַתָּ֗ה אֲלֵיכֶ֛ם
הַמִּצְוָ֥ה הַזֹּ֖את הַכֹּֽהֲנִֽים: ב אִם־לֹ֣א תִשְׁמְע֡וּ וְאִם־לֹא֩
תָשִׂ֨ימוּ עַל־לֵ֜ב לָתֵ֧ת כָּב֣וֹד לִשְׁמִ֗י אָמַר֙ יְהֹוָ֣ה צְבָא֔וֹת
וְשִׁלַּחְתִּ֤י בָכֶם֙ אֶת־הַמְּאֵרָ֔ה וְאָרוֹתִ֖י אֶת־בִּרְכֽוֹתֵיכֶ֑ם
וְגַם֙ אָר֔וֹתִיהָ כִּ֥י אֵינְכֶ֖ם שָׂמִ֥ים עַל־לֵֽב: ג הִנְנִ֨י
גֹעֵ֤ר לָכֶם֙ אֶת־הַזֶּ֔רַע וְזֵרִ֤יתִי פֶ֙רֶשׁ֙ עַל־פְּנֵיכֶ֔ם
פֶּ֖רֶשׁ חַגֵּיכֶ֑ם וְנָשָׂ֥א אֶתְכֶ֖ם אֵלָֽיו: ד וִֽידַעְתֶּ֕ם כִּ֚י
שִׁלַּ֣חְתִּי אֲלֵיכֶ֔ם אֵ֖ת הַמִּצְוָ֣ה הַזֹּ֑את לִהְי֤וֹת בְּרִיתִי֙
אֶת־לֵוִ֔י אָמַ֖ר יְהֹוָ֥ה צְבָאֽוֹת: ה בְּרִיתִ֣י ׀ הָיְתָ֣ה אִתּ֗וֹ
הַֽחַיִּים֙ וְהַ֨שָּׁל֔וֹם וָאֶתְּנֵֽם־ל֥וֹ מוֹרָ֖א וַיִּֽירָאֵ֑נִי וּמִפְּנֵ֥י
שְׁמִ֖י נִחַ֥ת הֽוּא: ו תּוֹרַ֣ת אֱמֶ֗ת הָיְתָה֙ בְּפִ֔יהוּ וְעַוְלָ֖ה
לֹא־נִמְצָ֣א בִשְׂפָתָ֑יו בְּשָׁל֤וֹם וּבְמִישׁוֹר֙ הָלַ֣ךְ אִתִּ֔י

But this is not enough. Israel cannot achieve its destiny merely because of Esau's downfall. A chosen people must deserve its chosenness. Thus the prophet chastises Israel severely for the hypocrisy of those who think that they, encouraged and abetted by their priests, can turn their service of God into an insincere practice. How dare they offer their old, crippled, and ill animals as offerings to God, while retaining the best for themselves? Would they dare do the same for their human rulers?

In closing, the prophet exhorts the *Kohanim* to live up to their calling. They must be the teachers and models. Only if they live up to their responsibility can they pull the people up with them. The same remonstrance applies to all leaders — they have the duty to teach and lead by example.

to you, 'O Kohanim who scorn My Name — yet you say, "How have we scorned You?" [7] You bring abominable bread upon My Altar, and you say, "How have we scorned You?" — by your saying, "The table of HASHEM is scorned." [8] And when you bring a blind animal to slaughter, is it not evil? When you bring a lame or sick animal, is it not evil? Offer it if you please to your governor — will he show you favor or will he turn his countenance toward you?' says HASHEM, Master of Legions. [9] And now, if you please, beg HASHEM to be gracious to us — this is your doing — will He turn His countenance to any of you? says HASHEM, Master of Legions.

[10] 'If there were only someone among you who would lock the doors so that you could not kindle upon My Altar in vain! I have no desire for you,' says HASHEM, Master of Legions, 'and I will not accept a meal-offering from your hand. [11] For from the rising of the sun to its setting, My Name is great among the nations and everywhere is brought up in smoke and brought for My Name's sake, and it is a pure meal-offering, for My Name is great among the nations,' says HASHEM, Master of Legions. [12] 'But you desecrate it by your saying, "The table of my Lord is abominable" and by his statement that "His food is scornful." [13] You say, "Behold! — it is so burdensome!" and you sadden Him,' says HASHEM, Master of Legions, 'and you bring stolen, lame, and sick animals and bring one for an offering, shall I accept it from your hand?' says HASHEM. [14] Accursed is the charlatan who has a male in his flock but pledges and slaughters an inferior one to the Lord, for I am a great King,' says HASHEM, Master of Legions, 'and My Name is awesome among the nations.'

2. [1] 'And now, this commandment is upon you, O Kohanim. [2] If you will not listen and if you will not take to heart to render honor to My Name,' says HASHEM, Master of Legions, 'I shall send the curse among you and curse your blessings — indeed, I have already cursed them, because you do not take to heart. [3] Behold! — I will rebuke the seed because of you, and scatter dung upon your faces, the dung of your festival offerings; [the sin] will carry you to this.

[4] 'Know that I have sent this commandment to you so that My covenant would be with Levi, says HASHEM, Master of Legions. [5] 'My covenant of life and peace was with him, I gave them to him for the sake of fear with which he feared Me, for he shuddered before My Name. [6] The teaching of truth was in his mouth and no injustice was found on his lips; he walked with Me in peace and fairness,

וְרַבִּים הֵשִׁיב מֵעָוֹן: ז כִּי־שִׂפְתֵי כֹהֵן יִשְׁמְרוּ־דַעַת
וְתוֹרָה יְבַקְשׁוּ מִפִּיהוּ כִּי מַלְאַךְ יהוה־צְבָאוֹת הוּא:

הפטרת ויצא

הושע יא:ז-יד:י

Sefardim begin the Haftarah here.

The Sages teach that Hosea, the prophet of this *Haftarah*, was one of the greatest of the prophets. A contemporary of Isaiah, he too cried out vainly against the rapidly deteriorating Kingdom of Samaria, the Ten Tribes of Israel. Hosea remonstrates with the people, and contrasts God's mercies of the past with Israel's failure to recognize that everything they have is due to God's kindness. And it is a kindness that remains strong, despite Israel's shortcomings. God says poignantly that He will never desert Ephraim, the wayward leader of the Ten Tribes, despite His justifiable wrath. Like a spurned but still merciful Father, God confesses that He will not make a permanent end of Ephraim, because He has pledged that Israel will remain His people and because Israel, innately good as it is, will eventually heed God's call to repent and resume its mission. When God will *roar like a lion* that the End has come, even Ephraim's children will come rushing from the west to declare their renewed allegiance to Him.

The prophet contrasts the rebelliousness of Ephraim with the loyalty of Judah, but declares that Judah, too, will falter. And when that time comes, Judah will be punished as well. It will be a sad outcome for the people who descended from a Patriarch who defeated Esau's angel, as described in the *Sidrah*, but God's justice must be served. Thus Judah will join Ephraim in an exile that will recall the origins of the nation in Egypt.

ז וְעַמִּי תְלוּאִים לִמְשׁוּבָתִי וְאֶל־עַל יִקְרָאֻהוּ יַחַד
לֹא יְרוֹמֵם: ח אֵיךְ אֶתֶּנְךָ אֶפְרַיִם אֲמַגֶּנְךָ יִשְׂרָאֵל
אֵיךְ אֶתֶּנְךָ כְאַדְמָה אֲשִׂימְךָ כִּצְבֹאיִם נֶהְפַּךְ עָלַי לִבִּי
יַחַד נִכְמְרוּ נִחוּמָי: ט לֹא אֶעֱשֶׂה חֲרוֹן אַפִּי לֹא
אָשׁוּב לְשַׁחֵת אֶפְרָיִם כִּי אֵל אָנֹכִי וְלֹא־אִישׁ
בְּקִרְבְּךָ קָדוֹשׁ וְלֹא אָבוֹא בְּעִיר: י אַחֲרֵי יהוה יֵלְכוּ
כְּאַרְיֵה יִשְׁאָג כִּי־הוּא יִשְׁאַג וְיֶחֶרְדוּ בָנִים מִיָּם:
יא יֶחֶרְדוּ כְצִפּוֹר מִמִּצְרַיִם וּכְיוֹנָה מֵאֶרֶץ אַשּׁוּר
וְהוֹשַׁבְתִּים עַל־בָּתֵּיהֶם נְאֻם־יהוה: יב סְבָבֻנִי
בְכַחַשׁ אֶפְרַיִם וּבְמִרְמָה בֵּית יִשְׂרָאֵל וִיהוּדָה עֹד רָד
עִם־אֵל וְעִם־קְדוֹשִׁים נֶאֱמָן: ב אֶפְרַיִם רֹעֶה רוּחַ
וְרֹדֵף קָדִים כָּל־הַיּוֹם כָּזָב וָשֹׁד יַרְבֶּה וּבְרִית
עִם־אַשּׁוּר יִכְרֹתוּ וְשֶׁמֶן לְמִצְרַיִם יוּבָל: ג וְרִיב
לַיהוה עִם־יְהוּדָה וְלִפְקֹד עַל־יַעֲקֹב כִּדְרָכָיו
כְּמַעֲלָלָיו יָשִׁיב לוֹ: ד בַּבֶּטֶן עָקַב אֶת־אָחִיו וּבְאוֹנוֹ
שָׂרָה אֶת־אֱלֹהִים: ה וַיָּשַׂר אֶל־מַלְאָךְ וַיֻּכָל בָּכָה
וַיִּתְחַנֶּן־לוֹ בֵּית־אֵל יִמְצָאֶנּוּ וְשָׁם יְדַבֵּר עִמָּנוּ:
ו וַיהוה אֱלֹהֵי הַצְּבָאוֹת יהוה זִכְרוֹ: ז וְאַתָּה בֵּאלֹהֶיךָ
תָשׁוּב חֶסֶד וּמִשְׁפָּט שְׁמֹר וְקַוֵּה אֶל־אֱלֹהֶיךָ תָּמִיד:
ח כְּנַעַן בְּיָדוֹ מֹאזְנֵי מִרְמָה לַעֲשֹׁק אָהֵב: ט וַיֹּאמֶר
אֶפְרַיִם אַךְ עָשַׁרְתִּי מָצָאתִי אוֹן לִי כָּל־יְגִיעַי לֹא
יִמְצְאוּ־לִי עָוֹן אֲשֶׁר־חֵטְא: י וְאָנֹכִי יהוה אֱלֹהֶיךָ
מֵאֶרֶץ מִצְרָיִם עֹד אוֹשִׁיבְךָ בָאֳהָלִים כִּימֵי מוֹעֵד:
יא וְדִבַּרְתִּי עַל־הַנְּבִיאִים וְאָנֹכִי חָזוֹן הִרְבֵּיתִי וּבְיַד

and he turned many away from sin. [7] For the lips of a Kohen should safeguard knowledge, and they should seek teaching from his mouth, for he is an agent of HASHEM, Master of Legions.'

HAFTARAS VAYEITZEI
Hosea 11:7-14:10
Sefardim begin the Haftarah here.

[7] My people is unsure about returning to Me; it is summoned to the Most High One, but it does not rise in unity. [8] How can I give you over, O Ephraim, hand you over, O Israel, how can I make you like Admah, make you like Zevoim? My heart is transformed within Me, My regrets were stirred up all at once. [9] I will not carry out My burning wrath, I will not return to destroy Ephraim; for I am God and not a man, the Holy One within you, and I will not come to [a different] city. [10] They will follow HASHEM [when He calls] like a roaring lion, for when He roars the children will hasten from the west. [11] They will hasten like a bird from Egypt and like a dove from the land of Assyria; and I shall return them to their homes, the words of HASHEM.

12. [1] Ephraim surrounded Me with lies and the House of Israel with deceit; but Judah enforces the mastery of God, and is faithful to the Holy One. [2] Ephraim feeds on wind and pursues the east wind, all day long he multiplies lies and violence; and he seals a covenant with Assyria and delivers oil to Egypt. [3] HASHEM will have a grievance against Judah, will recall upon Jacob according to his ways, will requite him according to his deeds. [4] In the womb he held his brother's heel, and in his prime he became an angel's master. [5] He mastered an angel and triumphed, [the angel] wept and entreated him: 'In Bethel He will find us and there He will speak with us.' [6] HASHEM is the God of Legions, His remembrance is HASHEM. [7] And you should find tranquility in God, observe kindness and justice and place hope in your God constantly. [8] [You are like] a trader with false scales in his hand, who loves to defraud. [9] Ephraim claims, 'Surely I am grown wealthy, I have succeeded because of my power; in all of my accomplishments they will not find in me any iniquity that is a sin.' [10] But I HASHEM am your God since the land of Egypt, I shall settle you in tents again as in times of yore. [11] I spoke to the prophets and I multiplied visions, and through the

That prophet continues his rebuke of the Kingdom of the Ten Tribes, led by its leading tribe, Ephraim, had come to think that it was invincible, by means of its wealth and power. It had forgotten its humble origins: that Jacob had once been a humble shepherd who had been reduced to tending sheep in order to earn the right to his bride, and that Ephraim had achieved its eminence as a leading tribe only because it *spoke harshly* against Solomon's successor, Rehoboam, who abused his holy calling. Thus it should have been clear to Ephraim that protection and success are gifts of God, and are not acquired by strength, guile, or coincidence.

But Ephraim sinned through arrogance and idolatry, and thereby was condemned to defeat, exile, and death. God does not forget sins; He binds them up and stores them away, as it were, to punish the perpetrators when His wisdom decrees that they are no longer entitled to Divine forbearance. Israel's sins are all the more serious because the nation ignored its infinite debt to God. Had He not brought them forth from Egypt and made them a nation?

Nevertheless, God does not abandon Israel. The prophets ghastly warning of retribution concludes with a loving call to repentance. It is the same passage which begins the *Haftarah* of *Shabbos Shuvah*, the Sabbath of the Ten Days of Repentance. True, Israel, as

הַנְּבִיאִים אֲדַמֶּה: יב אִם־גִּלְעָד אָוֶן אַךְ־שָׁוְא הָיוּ
בַּגִּלְגָּל שְׁוָרִים זִבֵּחוּ גַּם מִזְבְּחוֹתָם כְּגַלִּים עַל תַּלְמֵי
שָׂדָי:

Ashkenazim begin the *Haftarah* here.

יג וַיִּבְרַח יַעֲקֹב שְׂדֵה אֲרָם וַיַּעֲבֹד יִשְׂרָאֵל בְּאִשָּׁה
וּבְאִשָּׁה שָׁמָר: יד וּבְנָבִיא הֶעֱלָה יְהֹוָה אֶת־יִשְׂרָאֵל
מִמִּצְרָיִם וּבְנָבִיא נִשְׁמָר: טו הִכְעִיס אֶפְרַיִם
תַּמְרוּרִים וְדָמָיו עָלָיו יִטּוֹשׁ וְחֶרְפָּתוֹ יָשִׁיב לוֹ אֲדֹנָיו:
יג א כְּדַבֵּר אֶפְרַיִם רְתֵת נָשָׂא הוּא בְּיִשְׂרָאֵל וַיֶּאְשַׁם
בַּבַּעַל וַיָּמֹת: ב וְעַתָּה ׀ יוֹסִפוּ לַחֲטֹא וַיַּעֲשׂוּ לָהֶם
מַסֵּכָה מִכַּסְפָּם כִּתְבוּנָם עֲצַבִּים מַעֲשֵׂה חָרָשִׁים
כֻּלֹּה לָהֶם הֵם אֹמְרִים זֹבְחֵי אָדָם עֲגָלִים יִשָּׁקוּן:
ג לָכֵן יִהְיוּ כַּעֲנַן־בֹּקֶר וְכַטַּל מַשְׁכִּים הֹלֵךְ כְּמֹץ
יְסֹעֵר מִגֹּרֶן וּכְעָשָׁן מֵאֲרֻבָּה: ד וְאָנֹכִי יְהֹוָה אֱלֹהֶיךָ
מֵאֶרֶץ מִצְרָיִם וֵאלֹהִים זוּלָתִי לֹא תֵדָע וּמוֹשִׁיעַ אַיִן
בִּלְתִּי: ה אֲנִי יְדַעְתִּיךָ בַּמִּדְבָּר בְּאֶרֶץ תַּלְאֻבוֹת:

Sefardim conclude the *Haftarah* here.

ו כְּמַרְעִיתָם וַיִּשְׂבָּעוּ שָׂבְעוּ וַיָּרָם לִבָּם עַל־כֵּן
שְׁכֵחוּנִי: ז וָאֱהִי לָהֶם כְּמוֹ־שָׁחַל כְּנָמֵר עַל־דֶּרֶךְ
אָשׁוּר: ח אֶפְגְּשֵׁם כְּדֹב שַׁכּוּל וְאֶקְרַע סְגוֹר לִבָּם
וְאֹכְלֵם שָׁם כְּלָבִיא חַיַּת הַשָּׂדֶה תְּבַקְּעֵם: ט שִׁחֶתְךָ
יִשְׂרָאֵל כִּי־בִי בְעֶזְרֶךָ: י אֱהִי מַלְכְּךָ אֵפוֹא וְיוֹשִׁיעֲךָ
בְּכָל־עָרֶיךָ וְשֹׁפְטֶיךָ אֲשֶׁר אָמַרְתָּ תְּנָה־לִּי מֶלֶךְ
וְשָׂרִים: יא אֶתֶּן־לְךָ מֶלֶךְ בְּאַפִּי וְאֶקַּח בְּעֶבְרָתִי:
יב צָרוּר עֲוֹן אֶפְרָיִם צְפוּנָה חַטָּאתוֹ: יג חֶבְלֵי יוֹלֵדָה
יָבֹאוּ לוֹ הוּא־בֵן לֹא חָכָם כִּי־עֵת לֹא־יַעֲמֹד
בְּמִשְׁבַּר בָּנִים: יד מִיַּד שְׁאוֹל אֶפְדֵּם מִמָּוֶת אֶגְאָלֵם
אֱהִי דְבָרֶיךָ מָוֶת אֱהִי קָטָבְךָ שְׁאוֹל נֹחַם יִסָּתֵר
מֵעֵינָי: טו כִּי הוּא בֵּין אַחִים יַפְרִיא יָבוֹא קָדִים

symbolized by Ephraim, has sinned grievously, but its essence remains good and pure. It is not hopelessly evil; it has *stumbled* into sin. The potential for repentance always remains, and God is always ready to accept it and forgive.

prophets I spoke metaphors. [12] If travail befalls Gilead, surely it is because they were false — in Gilgal they sacrificed oxen, their altars as well were like stony heaps on the furrows of the fields.

Ashkenazim begin the *Haftarah* here.

[13] Jacob fled to the field of Aram; Israel labored for a wife, and for a wife he tended [sheep]. [14] Through a prophet HASHEM brought up Israel from Egypt, and through a prophet it was tended. [15] Ephraim provoked with bitter sins; his bloodshed will spread upon him, and his Lord will bring his disgrace back to him.

13. [1] When Ephraim spoke harshly, he was uplifted in Israel; but when he sinned with the Baal, he died. [2] And now they continue to sin, and they made themselves molten idols from their silver, idols in those images, entirely the work of artisans; of them they say, 'To kiss the calves is like offering a human.' [3] Therefore they shall be like the morning cloud and like the early dew that passes on, like chaff storming away from the threshing floor and smoke out the skylight.

[4] I am HASHEM, your God, since the land of Egypt and you did not know a god other than Me, and there is no Savior other than Me. [5] I knew you in the wilderness, in a thirsty land.

Sefardim conclude the *Haftarah* here.

[6] When they came to their pasture they were satiated, they were satiated and became haughty, that is why they forgot Me. [7] So I became toward them like a lion, I lurk like a leopard on the way. [8] I shall strike at them like a bear bereft, and tear at their closed heart; I shall devour them like a young lion, split them like a beast of the field. [9] You corrupted yourself, O Israel, for your help is only through Me. [10] — I shall be [eternal] but where is your king who is to save you in all your cities, and your judges of whom you said, 'Give me a king and leaders.'? [11] I gave you a king in My anger and took him away in My wrath.

[12] Ephraim's iniquity is bound up; his sin is stored away. [13] Labor pains shall come upon him; he is an unwise son, for the time shall come when he cannot withstand the birthstool of children. [14] From the power of the grave I would save them, from death I would redeem them — but I will speak with you of death, I will cut you off to the grave; comfort will be hidden from My eyes. [15] For he was to be the fruitful one among brothers — but the east wind,

רֽוּחַ יְהֹוָה מִמִּדְבָּר עֹלֶה וְיֵבֹ֣שׁ מְקוֹרוֹ וְיֶחֱרַ֣ב מַעְיָנ֗וֹ
הוּא יִשְׁסֶ֣ה אוֹצָ֔ר כָּל־כְּלִ֖י חֶמְדָּֽה: **יד** א תֶּאְשַׁם֙
שֹֽׁמְר֔וֹן כִּ֥י מָרְתָ֖ה בֵּֽאלֹהֶ֑יהָ בַּחֶ֣רֶב יִפֹּ֔לוּ עֹלְלֵיהֶ֣ם
יְרֻטָּ֔שׁוּ וְהָרִיּוֹתָ֖יו יְבֻקָּֽעוּ: ב שׁוּבָה֙ יִשְׂרָאֵ֔ל עַ֖ד יְהֹוָ֣ה
אֱלֹהֶ֑יךָ כִּ֥י כָשַׁ֖לְתָּ בַּֽעֲוֺנֶֽךָ: ג קְח֤וּ עִמָּכֶם֙ דְּבָרִ֔ים
וְשׁ֖וּבוּ אֶל־יְהֹוָ֑ה אִמְר֣וּ אֵלָ֗יו כָּל־תִּשָּׂ֤א עָוֺן֙ וְקַח־ט֔וֹב
וּֽנְשַׁלְּמָ֥ה פָרִ֖ים שְׂפָתֵֽינוּ: ד אַשּׁ֣וּר | לֹ֣א יֽוֹשִׁיעֵ֗נוּ
עַל־סוּס֙ לֹ֣א נִרְכָּ֔ב וְלֹֽא־נֹ֧אמַר ע֛וֹד אֱלֹהֵ֖ינוּ לְמַֽעֲשֵׂ֣ה
יָדֵ֑ינוּ אֲשֶׁר־בְּךָ֖ יְרֻחַ֥ם יָתֽוֹם: ה אֶרְפָּא֙ מְשׁ֣וּבָתָ֔ם
אֹֽהֲבֵ֖ם נְדָבָ֑ה כִּ֛י שָׁ֥ב אַפִּ֖י מִמֶּֽנּוּ: ו אֶֽהְיֶ֤ה כַטַּל֙
לְיִשְׂרָאֵ֔ל יִפְרַ֖ח כַּשּֽׁוֹשַׁנָּ֑ה וְיַ֥ךְ שָֽׁרָשָׁ֖יו כַּלְּבָנֽוֹן: ז יֵֽלְכוּ֙
יֹֽנְקוֹתָ֔יו וִיהִ֥י כַזַּ֖יִת הוֹד֑וֹ וְרֵ֥יחַֽ ל֖וֹ כַּלְּבָנֽוֹן: ח יָשֻׁ֨בוּ֙
יֹֽשְׁבֵ֣י בְצִלּ֔וֹ יְחַיּ֥וּ דָגָ֖ן וְיִפְרְח֣וּ כַגָּ֑פֶן זִכְר֖וֹ כְּיֵ֥ין לְבָנֽוֹן:
ט אֶפְרַ֕יִם מַה־לִּ֥י ע֖וֹד לָֽעֲצַבִּ֑ים אֲנִ֧י עָנִ֣יתִי וַֽאֲשׁוּרֶ֗נּוּ
אֲנִי֙ כִּבְר֣וֹשׁ רַֽעֲנָ֔ן מִמֶּ֖נִּי פֶּרְיְךָ֥ נִמְצָֽא: י מִ֤י חָכָם֙ וְיָ֣בֵֽן
אֵ֔לֶּה נָב֖וֹן וְיֵֽדָעֵ֑ם כִּֽי־יְשָׁרִ֞ים דַּרְכֵ֣י יְהֹוָ֗ה וְצַדִּקִים֙
יֵ֣לְכוּ בָ֔ם וּפֹֽשְׁעִ֖ים יִכָּ֥שְׁלוּ בָֽם:

הפטרת וישלח

עובדיה א:א–כא

א א חֲז֖וֹן עֹֽבַדְיָ֑ה כֹּֽה־אָמַ֩ר אֲדֹנָ֨י יֱהֹוִ֜ה* לֶֽאֱד֗וֹם
שְׁמוּעָ֨ה שָׁמַ֜עְנוּ מֵאֵ֣ת יְהֹוָ֗ה וְצִיר֙ בַּגּוֹיִ֣ם שֻׁלָּ֔ח
ק֛וּמוּ וְנָק֥וּמָה עָלֶ֖יהָ לַמִּלְחָמָֽה: ב הִנֵּ֥ה קָטֹ֛ן נְתַתִּ֖יךָ
בַּגּוֹיִ֑ם בָּז֥וּי אַתָּ֖ה מְאֹֽד: ג זְד֤וֹן לִבְּךָ֙ הִשִּׁיאֶ֔ךָ שֹֽׁכְנִ֥י
בְחַגְוֵי־סֶ֖לַע מְר֣וֹם שִׁבְתּ֑וֹ אֹמֵ֣ר בְּלִבּ֔וֹ מִ֥י יֽוֹרִדֵ֖נִי
אָֽרֶץ: ד אִם־תַּגְבִּ֣יהַּ כַּנֶּ֔שֶׁר וְאִם־בֵּ֥ין כּֽוֹכָבִ֖ים
שִׂ֣ים קִנֶּ֑ךָ מִשָּׁ֥ם אֽוֹרִֽידְךָ֖ נְאֻם־יְהֹוָֽה: ה אִם־
גַּנָּבִ֤ים בָּֽאוּ־לְךָ֙ אִם־שׁ֣וֹדְדֵי לַ֔יְלָה אֵ֣יךְ נִדְמֵ֔יתָה
הֲל֥וֹא יִגְנְב֖וּ דַּיָּ֑ם אִם־בֹּֽצְרִים֙ בָּ֣אוּ לָ֔ךְ הֲל֖וֹא יַשְׁאִ֥ירוּ

*Although the Divine Name יהוה is pronounced as if it were spelled אֲדֹנָי,
when it is vowelized יֱהֹוִה it is pronounced as if it were spelled אֱלֹהִים.

The Book of *Obadiah,* the
shortest in all of Scripture,
is read in its entirety as the
Haftarah of the *Sidrah* that
deals with the climactic encounter between Jacob and
Esau, and the subject of the
Book is God's wrath against
Edom, the descendants of
Esau. The Sages teach that,
of all the prophets, this vision was left for Obadiah
for two reasons: (a) He was
a descendant of an Edomite
proselyte (*Yalkut, Job* 897;
Zohar); and, (b) Obadiah
was the antithesis of Esau.
Esau lived among two righteous people, Isaac and Rebecca, yet he did not learn
from them. Obadiah, on the
other hand, was a courtier
of two of the wickedest
people in the annals of our

HASHEM's wind, will come up from the desert, his spring will be dried and his wellspring made arid, it will plunder the treasury of every desirable vessel.

14. ¹ Samaria will be desolate because she rebelled against her God; they will fall by the sword, their babes will be smashed to bits, and its pregnant women torn asunder. ² Return, O Israel, to HASHEM, your God, for you have stumbled through your iniquity. ³ Take words with you and return to HASHEM; say to Him: 'Forgive every sin and accept goodness, and let our lips substitute for bulls. ⁴ Assyria cannot help us, we will not ride steeds, nor will we ever again call our handiwork "our god" — only in You will the orphan find compassion.'

⁵ I shall heal their rebelliousness, I shall love them willingly, for My wrath will be withdrawn from them. ⁶ I shall be like the dew to Israel, it will blossom like a rose and strike its roots like [the forest of] Lebanon. ⁷ Its tender branches will spread, and its glory will be like an olive tree; its aroma will be like the Lebanon. ⁸ Tranquil will be those who sit in its shade, they will refresh themselves like grain and blossom like the grapevine, their reputation will be like the wine of Lebanon.

⁹ When Ephraim says, 'What more need have I for idols?', I will respond and look to him. I am like an ever-fresh cypress, from Me shall your fruit be found.

¹⁰ Whoever is wise will understand these, a discerning person will know them, for the ways of HASHEM are fair — the righteous will walk on them, but sinners will stumble on them.

HAFTARAS VAYISHLACH
Obadiah 1:1-21

people, King Ahab and Queen Jezebel, yet he remained righteous. Moreover, at a time when his king and queen murdered nearly all of the prophets of God, Obadiah risked his life to shelter and feed a hundred surviving prophets.

The *Haftarah* follows Edom through various periods of its history, culminating in its eventual defeat and final downfall in Messianic times. Edom began as a small and insignificant kingdom to the south of *Eretz Yisrael*, that, like a jackal, despoiled Israel in the wake of the triumphs of others. It enjoyed the

1 ¹ A vision of Obadiah. So said my Lord HASHEM/ELOHIM about Edom: We have heard tidings from HASHEM and among the nations an envoy has been sent, 'Arise! Let us rise up against her to do battle!'' ² Behold! I have made you small among the nations, you are exceedingly despised. ³ Your wanton heart has seduced you, you who dwells in the cleft of the rock, whose habitation is high, who says in his heart, 'Who can bring me down to earth!' ⁴ Though you ascend as high as an eagle and place your nest among the stars — from there I will bring you down! — the words of HASHEM.

⁵ If thieves had come upon you, or robbers in the night — how utterly you are cut off! — they would have stolen their fill; if cutters of grapes had come upon you, they would have

travails and suffering of its 'cousin,' instead of feeling compassion. Then, in a vision of the future, Obadiah turns to the Roman Empire and its barbaric treatment of the Jews under its control. True to Isaac's blessing, Rome lived by the sword, and its sword drank thirstily of Jewish blood.

עֲלָלוֹת: ו אֵיךְ נֶחְפְּשׂוּ עֵשָׂו נִבְעוּ מַצְפֻּנָיו: ז עַד־הַגְּבוּל שִׁלְּחוּךָ כֹּל אַנְשֵׁי בְרִיתֶךָ הִשִּׁיאוּךָ יָכְלוּ לְךָ אַנְשֵׁי שְׁלֹמֶךָ לַחְמְךָ יָשִׂימוּ מָזוֹר תַּחְתֶּיךָ אֵין תְּבוּנָה בּוֹ: ח הֲלוֹא בַּיּוֹם הַהוּא נְאֻם יְהוָה וְהַאֲבַדְתִּי חֲכָמִים מֵאֱדוֹם וּתְבוּנָה מֵהַר עֵשָׂו: ט וְחַתּוּ גִבּוֹרֶיךָ תֵּימָן לְמַעַן יִכָּרֶת־אִישׁ מֵהַר עֵשָׂו מִקָּטֶל: י מֵחֲמַס אָחִיךָ יַעֲקֹב תְּכַסְּךָ בוּשָׁה וְנִכְרַתָּ לְעוֹלָם: יא בְּיוֹם עֲמָדְךָ מִנֶּגֶד בְּיוֹם שְׁבוֹת זָרִים חֵילוֹ וְנָכְרִים בָּאוּ שְׁעָרָיו וְעַל־יְרוּשָׁלַ‍ִם יַדּוּ גוֹרָל גַּם־אַתָּה כְּאַחַד מֵהֶם: יב וְאַל־תֵּרֶא בְיוֹם־אָחִיךָ בְּיוֹם נָכְרוֹ וְאַל־תִּשְׂמַח לִבְנֵי־יְהוּדָה בְּיוֹם אָבְדָם וְאַל־תַּגְדֵּל פִּיךָ בְּיוֹם צָרָה: יג אַל־תָּבוֹא בְשַׁעַר־עַמִּי בְּיוֹם אֵידָם אַל־תֵּרֶא גַם־אַתָּה בְּרָעָתוֹ בְּיוֹם אֵידוֹ וְאַל־תִּשְׁלַחְנָה בְחֵילוֹ בְּיוֹם אֵידוֹ: יד וְאַל־תַּעֲמֹד עַל־הַפֶּרֶק לְהַכְרִית אֶת־פְּלִיטָיו וְאַל־תַּסְגֵּר שְׂרִידָיו בְּיוֹם צָרָה: טו כִּי־קָרוֹב יוֹם־יְהוָה עַל־כָּל־הַגּוֹיִם כַּאֲשֶׁר עָשִׂיתָ יֵעָשֶׂה לָּךְ גְּמֻלְךָ יָשׁוּב בְּרֹאשֶׁךָ: טז כִּי כַּאֲשֶׁר שְׁתִיתֶם עַל־הַר קָדְשִׁי יִשְׁתּוּ כָל־הַגּוֹיִם תָּמִיד וְשָׁתוּ וְלָעוּ וְהָיוּ כְּלוֹא הָיוּ: יז וּבְהַר צִיּוֹן תִּהְיֶה פְלֵיטָה וְהָיָה קֹדֶשׁ וְיָרְשׁוּ בֵּית יַעֲקֹב אֵת מוֹרָשֵׁיהֶם: יח וְהָיָה בֵית־יַעֲקֹב אֵשׁ וּבֵית יוֹסֵף לֶהָבָה וּבֵית עֵשָׂו לְקַשׁ וְדָלְקוּ בָהֶם וַאֲכָלוּם וְלֹא־יִהְיֶה שָׂרִיד לְבֵית עֵשָׂו כִּי יְהוָה דִּבֵּר: יט וְיָרְשׁוּ הַנֶּגֶב אֶת־הַר עֵשָׂו וְהַשְּׁפֵלָה אֶת־פְּלִשְׁתִּים וְיָרְשׁוּ אֶת־שְׂדֵה אֶפְרַיִם וְאֵת שְׂדֵה שֹׁמְרוֹן וּבִנְיָמִן אֶת־הַגִּלְעָד: כ וְגָלֻת הַחֵל־הַזֶּה לִבְנֵי יִשְׂרָאֵל אֲשֶׁר־כְּנַעֲנִים עַד־צָרְפַת וְגָלֻת יְרוּשָׁלַ‍ִם אֲשֶׁר בִּסְפָרַד יִרְשׁוּ אֵת עָרֵי הַנֶּגֶב: כא וְעָלוּ מוֹשִׁעִים בְּהַר צִיּוֹן לִשְׁפֹּט אֶת־הַר עֵשָׂו וְהָיְתָה לַיהוָה הַמְּלוּכָה:

Finally, however, Edom will be repaid in kind. *On Mount Zion there shall be a remnant*: Despite all its suffering and persecutions, Israel and its land will survive and haughty Edom will be cast down. Israel will return to its land and its Temple Mount. It will judge Edom for its horrors and all the world will know that *the kingdom will be HASHEM's.*

left the young grapes. [6] How thoroughly scoured was Esau, how ransacked his hidden treasures! [7] Until the border all your confederates escorted you, those who seemed at peace with you seduced you and prevailed against you, those who eat your bread emplace sickness beneath you, who fail to discern it.

[8] Is there any doubt that on that day — the words of HASHEM — I will cause the wise men of Edom to be lost, and discernment from the mountain of Esau? [9] Your mighty ones to the south will be smashed, so that every man from Esau's mountain will be cut down through the slaughter. [10] For your violence to your brother Jacob, shame will cover you, and you will be cut down forever. [11] Because of the day you stood aloof, the day strangers plundered his wealth, foreigners entered his gates and they cast lots on Jerusalem — you were like one of them. [12] How dare you gaze on the day of your brother, the day he was exiled; how dare you rejoice over the children of Judah on the day of their destruction; how dare you speak arrogantly on the day of distress! [13] How dare you enter the gate of My people on the day of their disaster; how dare even you gaze upon its misfortune on the day of its disaster; how dare you put your hands on its wealth on the day of its disaster! [14] How dare you stand at the crossroads to cut down its refugees; how dare you imprison its survivors on the day of distress.

[15] For the day of HASHEM upon all the nations is near; as you did, so will be done to you, your recompense shall return upon your head. [16] For you have drunk on My holy mountain, so shall all the nations always drink, they shall drink and swallow and become as if they had never been.

[17] But on Mount Zion there shall be a remnant, and it shall become holy; and the House of Jacob will inherit its inheritors. [18] The House of Jacob will be a fire and the House of Joseph will be a flame — and the House of Esau will be like straw; they will kindle among them and consume them. There will be no survivor of the House of Esau, for HASHEM has spoken! [19] They shall inherit the southland, the mountain of Esau; and the lowland, Philistia; and they shall inherit the field of Ephraim and the field of Samaria, and Benjamin [shall inherit] the Gilead. [20] And this exiled force of the Children of Israel that were with Canaanites as far as France, and the exile of Jerusalem that is in Spain — they will inherit the cities of the south. [21] The saviors will ascend Mount Zion to judge Esau's mountain, and the kingdom will be HASHEM's.

הפטרת וישב

עמוס ב:ו - ג:ח

ו כֹּה אָמַר יהוֹה עַל־שְׁלֹשָׁה פִּשְׁעֵי יִשְׂרָאֵל וְעַל־אַרְבָּעָה לֹא אֲשִׁיבֶנּוּ עַל־מִכְרָם בַּכֶּסֶף צַדִּיק וְאֶבְיוֹן בַּעֲבוּר נַעֲלָיִם: ז הַשֹּׁאֲפִים עַל־עֲפַר־אֶרֶץ בְּרֹאשׁ דַּלִּים וְדֶרֶךְ עֲנָוִים יַטּוּ וְאִישׁ וְאָבִיו יֵלְכוּ אֶל־הַנַּעֲרָה לְמַעַן חַלֵּל אֶת־שֵׁם קָדְשִׁי: ח וְעַל־בְּגָדִים חֲבֻלִים יַטּוּ אֵצֶל כָּל־מִזְבֵּחַ וְיֵין עֲנוּשִׁים יִשְׁתּוּ בֵּית אֱלֹהֵיהֶם: ט וְאָנֹכִי הִשְׁמַדְתִּי אֶת־הָאֱמֹרִי מִפְּנֵיהֶם אֲשֶׁר כְּגֹבַהּ אֲרָזִים גָּבְהוֹ וְחָסֹן הוּא כָּאַלּוֹנִים וָאַשְׁמִיד פִּרְיוֹ מִמַּעַל וְשָׁרָשָׁיו מִתָּחַת: י וְאָנֹכִי הֶעֱלֵיתִי אֶתְכֶם מֵאֶרֶץ מִצְרָיִם וָאוֹלֵךְ אֶתְכֶם בַּמִּדְבָּר אַרְבָּעִים שָׁנָה לָרֶשֶׁת אֶת־אֶרֶץ הָאֱמֹרִי: יא וָאָקִים מִבְּנֵיכֶם לִנְבִיאִים וּמִבַּחוּרֵיכֶם לִנְזִרִים הַאַף אֵין־זֹאת בְּנֵי יִשְׂרָאֵל נְאֻם־יהוֹה: יב וַתַּשְׁקוּ אֶת־הַנְּזִרִים יָיִן וְעַל־הַנְּבִיאִים צִוִּיתֶם לֵאמֹר לֹא תִּנָּבְאוּ: יג הִנֵּה אָנֹכִי מֵעִיק תַּחְתֵּיכֶם כַּאֲשֶׁר תָּעִיק הָעֲגָלָה הַמְלֵאָה לָהּ עָמִיר: יד וְאָבַד מָנוֹס מִקָּל וְחָזָק לֹא־יְאַמֵּץ כֹּחוֹ וְגִבּוֹר לֹא־יְמַלֵּט נַפְשׁוֹ: טו וְתֹפֵשׂ הַקֶּשֶׁת לֹא יַעֲמֹד וְקַל בְּרַגְלָיו לֹא יְמַלֵּט וְרֹכֵב הַסּוּס לֹא יְמַלֵּט נַפְשׁוֹ: טז וְאַמִּיץ לִבּוֹ בַּגִּבּוֹרִים עָרוֹם יָנוּס בַּיּוֹם־הַהוּא נְאֻם־יהוֹה: ג א שִׁמְעוּ אֶת־הַדָּבָר הַזֶּה אֲשֶׁר דִּבֶּר יהוֹה עֲלֵיכֶם בְּנֵי יִשְׂרָאֵל עַל כָּל־הַמִּשְׁפָּחָה אֲשֶׁר הֶעֱלֵיתִי מֵאֶרֶץ מִצְרַיִם לֵאמֹר: ב רַק אֶתְכֶם יָדַעְתִּי מִכֹּל מִשְׁפְּחוֹת הָאֲדָמָה עַל־כֵּן אֶפְקֹד עֲלֵיכֶם אֵת כָּל־עֲוֹנֹתֵיכֶם: ג הֲיֵלְכוּ שְׁנַיִם יַחְדָּו בִּלְתִּי אִם־נוֹעָדוּ: ד הֲיִשְׁאַג אַרְיֵה בַּיַּעַר וְטֶרֶף אֵין לוֹ הֲיִתֵּן כְּפִיר קוֹלוֹ מִמְּעֹנָתוֹ בִּלְתִּי אִם־לָכָד: ה הֲתִפֹּל צִפּוֹר עַל־פַּח הָאָרֶץ וּמוֹקֵשׁ אֵין לָהּ

HAFTARAS VAYEISHEV

Amos 2:6-3:8

Lest these leaders continue to delude themselves that they were too powerful to be brought to justice, the prophet warns them that the Amorite inhabitants of Canaan were even more powerful, but God had swept them away when He wished to give the land to Israel. In 'gratitude,' Israel had prevented prophets from teaching God's word and nazirites from maintaining their holy standard of service — as if God's will could be ignored if it were not proclaimed openly. But the fleet-footed often cannot escape and the mighty cannot always prevail — should it not be clear that the power is God's alone?

The prophet closes with ringing rhetoric designed to wake up the people to the obvious. They use their logic to determine the significance of daily events. They *know* that a lion's roar means that prey is at hand, that a trap lifted from the sand means that a snared bird or animal is tugging vainly to free itself — should they not perceive that God is roaring for their repentance through His mastery of events?

⁶ So said HASHEM: For three wanton sins of Israel — but should I not exact retribution for the fourth? — for their having sold a righteous man for silver, and a destitute one for the sake of shoes? ⁷ Those who yearn that the dust of the earth be upon the head of the poor, who twist the way of the humble! A man and his father come to the same [betrothed] maiden, thereby profaning My Holy Name. ⁸ Next to every altar they recline on garments held as security, and they drink wine bought with [unjustly levied] fines in the temple of their gods.

⁹ Yet I destroyed the Amorite before them, whose height was like the height of cedars and who was as strong as oak trees; I destroyed its fruits from above and its roots from below. ¹⁰ And I brought you up from the land of Egypt and led you in the Wilderness for forty years to inherit the land of the Amorite. ¹¹ From among your children I raised up prophets, and nazirites from your lads — is this not so, O Children of Israel? — the words of HASHEM. ¹² But you caused the nazirites to drink wine, and you commanded the prophets, saying: 'Do not prophesy!'

¹³ Behold! — I press you down in your place, as a wagon is pressed down when it is filled with sheaves. ¹⁴ Flight will be lost to the fleet, the strong will not muster his courage, and the mighty will not be able to escape with his life; ¹⁵ he that grasps the bow will not stand fast, the fleet-footed one will not escape, and the horseman will not be able to escape with his life. ¹⁶ The most courageous of the heroes will flee naked on that day, the words of HASHEM.

3. ¹ Hear this thing that HASHEM has spoken about you, O Children of Israel, about the entire family that I have brought up from the land of Egypt, saying: ² Only you have I loved of all the families of the earth, therefore will I recall upon you all your iniquities. ³ Would two people walk together unless they have so arranged? ⁴ Would a lion roar in the forest if he had no prey? Would a young lion raise his voice in his den unless he had a catch? ⁵ Would a bird fall into a snare on the ground if there were no trap for it?

הַיַּעֲלֶה־פַּח֙ מִן־הָ֣אֲדָמָ֔ה וְלָכ֖וֹד לֹ֣א יִלְכּ֑וֹד ו אִם־
יִתָּקַ֤ע שׁוֹפָר֙ בְּעִ֔יר וְעָ֖ם לֹ֣א יֶחֱרָ֑דוּ אִם־תִּֽהְיֶ֤ה רָעָה֙
בְּעִ֔יר וַֽיהוָ֖ה לֹ֥א עָשָֽׂה: ז כִּ֣י לֹ֧א יַעֲשֶׂ֛ה אֲדֹנָ֥י יֱהוִ֖ה*
דָּבָ֑ר כִּ֚י אִם־גָּלָ֣ה סוֹד֔וֹ אֶל־עֲבָדָ֖יו הַנְּבִיאִֽים: ח אַרְיֵ֣ה
שָׁאָ֔ג מִ֖י לֹ֣א יִירָ֑א אֲדֹנָ֤י יֱהוִה֙ דִּבֶּ֔ר מִ֖י לֹ֥א יִנָּבֵֽא:

הפטרת מקץ
מלכים א' ג:טו-ד:א

טו וַיִּקַ֣ץ שְׁלֹמֹ֔ה וְהִנֵּ֖ה חֲל֑וֹם וַיָּב֣וֹא יְרוּשָׁלַ֗͏ִם וַֽיַּעֲמֹ֣ד ׀
לִפְנֵ֣י ׀ אֲר֣וֹן בְּרִית־אֲדֹנָ֗י וַיַּ֤עַל עֹלוֹת֙ וַיַּ֣עַשׂ שְׁלָמִ֔ים
וַיַּ֥עַשׂ מִשְׁתֶּ֖ה לְכָל־עֲבָדָֽיו: טז אָ֣ז תָּבֹ֗אנָה שְׁתַּ֛יִם
נָשִׁ֥ים זֹנ֖וֹת אֶל־הַמֶּ֑לֶךְ וַֽתַּעֲמֹ֖דְנָה לְפָנָֽיו: יז וַתֹּ֜אמֶר
הָאִשָּׁ֤ה הָֽאַחַת֙ בִּ֣י אֲדֹנִ֔י אֲנִי֙ וְהָאִשָּׁ֣ה הַזֹּ֔את יֹשְׁבֹ֖ת
בְּבַ֣יִת אֶחָ֑ד וָאֵלֵ֥ד עִמָּ֖הּ בַּבָּֽיִת: יח וַֽיְהִ֞י בַּיּ֤וֹם הַשְּׁלִישִׁי֙
לְלִדְתִּ֔י וַתֵּ֖לֶד גַּם־הָאִשָּׁ֣ה הַזֹּ֑את וַאֲנַ֣חְנוּ יַחְדָּ֗ו אֵֽין־זָ֤ר
אִתָּ֨נוּ֙ בַּבַּ֔יִת זֽוּלָתִ֥י שְׁתַּֽיִם־אֲנַ֖חְנוּ בַּבָּֽיִת: יט וַיָּ֛מָת
בֶּן־הָאִשָּׁ֥ה הַזֹּ֖את לָ֑יְלָה אֲשֶׁ֥ר שָׁכְבָ֖ה עָלָֽיו: כ וַתָּ֞קָם
בְּת֣וֹךְ הַלַּ֗יְלָה וַתִּקַּ֤ח אֶת־בְּנִי֙ מֵֽאֶצְלִ֔י וַאֲמָֽתְךָ֖ יְשֵׁנָ֑ה
וַתַּשְׁכִּיבֵ֣הוּ בְחֵיקָ֔הּ וְאֶת־בְּנָ֥הּ הַמֵּ֖ת הִשְׁכִּ֥יבָה בְחֵיקִֽי:
כא וָאָקֻ֥ם בַּבֹּ֛קֶר לְהֵינִ֥יק אֶת־בְּנִ֖י וְהִנֵּה־מֵ֑ת וָאֶתְבּוֹנֵ֤ן
אֵלָיו֙ בַּבֹּ֔קֶר וְהִנֵּ֛ה לֹֽא־הָיָ֥ה בְנִ֖י אֲשֶׁ֥ר יָלָֽדְתִּי:
כב וַתֹּ֩אמֶר֩ הָאִשָּׁ֨ה הָאַחֶ֜רֶת לֹ֣א כִ֗י בְּנִ֤י הַחַי֙ וּבְנֵ֣ךְ
הַמֵּ֔ת וְזֹ֤את אֹמֶ֙רֶת֙ לֹ֣א כִ֔י בְּנֵ֥ךְ הַמֵּ֖ת וּבְנִ֣י הֶחָ֑י
וַתְּדַבֵּ֖רְנָה לִפְנֵ֥י הַמֶּֽלֶךְ: כג וַיֹּ֣אמֶר הַמֶּ֔לֶךְ זֹ֣את אֹמֶ֗רֶת
זֶֽה־בְּנִ֤י הַחַי֙ וּבְנֵ֣ךְ הַמֵּ֔ת וְזֹ֤את אֹמֶ֙רֶת֙ לֹ֣א כִ֔י בְּנֵ֥ךְ
הַמֵּ֖ת וּבְנִ֣י הֶחָֽי: כד וַיֹּ֥אמֶר הַמֶּ֖לֶךְ קְח֣וּ לִי־חָ֑רֶב
וַיָּבִ֥אוּ הַחֶ֖רֶב לִפְנֵ֥י הַמֶּֽלֶךְ: כה וַיֹּ֣אמֶר הַמֶּ֗לֶךְ גִּזְר֛וּ
אֶת־הַיֶּ֥לֶד הַחַ֖י לִשְׁנָ֑יִם וּתְנ֤וּ אֶת־הַֽחֲצִי֙
לְאַחַ֔ת וְאֶֽת־הַחֲצִ֖י לְאֶחָֽת: כו וַתֹּ֣אמֶר הָאִשָּׁה֩ אֲשֶׁר־
בְּנָ֨הּ הַחַ֜י אֶל־הַמֶּ֗לֶךְ כִּֽי־נִכְמְר֣וּ רַחֲמֶ֘יהָ֮ עַל־בְּנָהּ֒

---

*Although the Divine Name יהוה is pronounced as if it were spelled אֲדֹנָי,
when it is vowelized יֱהוִה it is pronounced as if it were spelled אֱלֹהִים.

Like the *Sidrah,* the *Haftarah*
deals with royal dreams and
their aftermath. In the
Sidrah, Pharaoh had a portentous dream and Joseph
applied his God-given wisdom to its interpretation,
with the result that he became acknowledged as the
most qualified person to
rule Egypt. The *Haftarah* begins by saying that Solomon
awoke from a dream. It was
a dream that set the tone of
his reign and had implications for the future of the
Jewish people. In his
prophetic dream, the
twelve-year-old, newly
crowned Solomon had been
asked by God what blessing
he desired for his new position. Solomon had re-
quested wisdom so that he
could judge his people well.
Pleased that Solomon had
asked for wisdom, and not
for wealth or power, God
promised him not only
those gifts, but also un-
precedented wisdom, such
as had never been before
and would never be again.

Would a trap rise up from the ground unless it had made a catch? ⁶ If the shofar-alarm sounds in the city, would the people not tremble? Could there be misfortune in a city if HASHEM had not caused it? ⁷ For my Lord HASHEM/ELOHIM, will do nothing without having revealed his secret to His servants the prophets.

⁸ A lion has roared — who would not fear? My Lord HASHEM/ELOHIM has spoken — who would not prophesy?

HAFTARAS MIKEITZ
I Kings 3:15-4:1

Shortly after the dream, came proof of its fulfillment, in the form of a seemingly insoluble dilemma. Solomon's verdict gained the admiration and respect of the nation, and displayed a degree of wisdom that became the hallmark of his reign and an augury of the three inspiring and enlightening books he would contribute to Scripture: *Proverbs*, *Song of Songs*, and *Ecclesiastes*.

¹⁵ Solomon awoke and behold! — it had been a dream; he came to Jerusalem and stood before the Ark of the covenant of my Lord and he brought up elevation-offerings and he made peace-offerings, and he made a feast for all his servants.

¹⁶ Then two women, innkeepers, came to the king and stood before him. ¹⁷ One woman said: 'Please, my lord, I and this woman dwell in the same house, and I gave birth while with her in the house. ¹⁸ On the third day after I gave birth, this woman gave birth, as well: We were together, no outsider was with us in the house, only the two of us in the house. ¹⁹ The son of this woman died at night, because she lay upon him. ²⁰ She arose during the night and took my son from next to me, while your maidservant was asleep, and lay him in her bosom; and her dead son she lay in my bosom. ²¹ When I got up in the morning to nurse my son, behold! — he was dead. When I studied him in the morning, behold! — it was not the son to whom I had given birth.'

²² The other woman said: 'It is not so! My son is the live one and her son is the dead one.' But this one said: 'It is not so! Your son is the dead one and my son is the live one!' They went on speaking before the king.

²³ The king said: 'This one claims, "This is my son, who is alive, and your son is the dead one," and this one claims, "It is not so! Your son is the dead one and my son is the living one." ' ²⁴ So the King said: 'Fetch me a sword!' They brought a sword before the king.

²⁵ The king said: 'Cut the living child in two and give half to one and half to the other.'

²⁶ The woman whose son was alive spoke to the king — because her compassion was aroused for her son —

וַתֹּ֣אמֶר ׀ בִּ֣י אֲדֹנִ֗י תְּנוּ־לָהּ֙ אֶת־הַיָּל֣וּד הַחַ֔י וְהָמֵ֖ת
אַל־תְּמִיתֻ֑הוּ וְזֹ֣את אֹמֶ֗רֶת גַּם־לִ֥י גַם־לָ֛ךְ לֹ֥א יִֽהְיֶ֖ה
גְּזֹֽרוּ׃ כז וַיַּ֨עַן הַמֶּ֜לֶךְ וַיֹּ֗אמֶר תְּנוּ־לָהּ֙ אֶת־הַיָּל֣וּד הַחַ֔י
וְהָמֵ֖ת לֹ֣א תְמִיתֻ֑הוּ הִ֖יא אִמּֽוֹ׃ כח וַיִּשְׁמְע֣וּ כָל־
יִשְׂרָאֵ֗ל אֶת־הַמִּשְׁפָּט֙ אֲשֶׁ֣ר שָׁפַ֣ט הַמֶּ֔לֶךְ וַיִּֽרְא֖וּ
מִפְּנֵ֣י הַמֶּ֑לֶךְ כִּ֣י רָא֔וּ כִּֽי־חָכְמַ֧ת אֱלֹהִ֛ים בְּקִרְבּ֖וֹ
לַעֲשׂ֥וֹת מִשְׁפָּֽט׃ ד א וַֽיְהִי֙ הַמֶּ֣לֶךְ שְׁלֹמֹ֔ה מֶ֖לֶךְ
עַל־כָּל־יִשְׂרָאֵֽל׃

הפטרת ויגש
יחזקאל לז:טו־כח

טו וַיְהִ֥י דְבַר־יְהֹוָ֖ה אֵלַ֥י לֵאמֹֽר׃ טז וְאַתָּ֣ה בֶן־אָדָ֗ם
קַח־לְךָ֙ עֵ֣ץ אֶחָ֔ד וּכְתֹ֤ב עָלָיו֙ לִֽיהוּדָ֔ה וְלִבְנֵ֥י יִשְׂרָאֵ֖ל
חֲבֵרָ֑ו וּלְקַח֙ עֵ֣ץ אֶחָ֔ד וּכְת֣וֹב עָלָ֗יו לְיוֹסֵף֙ עֵ֣ץ אֶפְרַ֔יִם
וְכָל־בֵּ֥ית יִשְׂרָאֵ֖ל חֲבֵרָֽו׃ יז וְקָרַ֨ב אֹתָ֜ם אֶחָ֧ד אֶל־
אֶחָ֛ד לְךָ֖ לְעֵ֣ץ אֶחָ֑ד וְהָי֥וּ לַאֲחָדִ֖ים בְּיָדֶֽךָ׃ יח וְכַֽאֲשֶׁר֙
יֹאמְר֣וּ אֵלֶ֔יךָ בְּנֵ֥י עַמְּךָ֖ לֵאמֹ֑ר הֲלֽוֹא־תַגִּ֥יד לָ֖נוּ מָה־
אֵ֥לֶּה לָּֽךְ׃ יט דַּבֵּ֣ר אֲלֵהֶ֗ם כֹּֽה־אָמַר֮ אֲדֹנָ֣י יְהֹוָה֒ הִנֵּה֩
אֲנִ֨י לֹקֵ֜חַ אֶת־עֵ֣ץ יוֹסֵ֗ף אֲשֶׁ֤ר בְּיַד־אֶפְרַ֙יִם֙ וְשִׁבְטֵ֣י
יִשְׂרָאֵ֔ל חֲבֵרָ֑ו וְנָתַתִּי֩ אוֹתָ֨ם עָלָ֜יו אֶת־עֵ֣ץ יְהוּדָ֗ה
וַעֲשִׂיתִם֙ לְעֵ֣ץ אֶחָ֔ד וְהָי֥וּ אֶחָ֖ד בְּיָדִֽי׃ כ וְהָי֨וּ הָעֵצִ֜ים
אֲשֶׁר־תִּכְתֹּ֧ב עֲלֵיהֶ֛ם בְּיָדְךָ֖ לְעֵֽינֵיהֶֽם׃ כא וְדַבֵּ֣ר
אֲלֵיהֶ֗ם כֹּֽה־אָמַר֮ אֲדֹנָ֣י יְהֹוִה֒ הִנֵּ֨ה אֲנִ֤י לֹקֵ֙חַ֙ אֶת־בְּנֵ֣י
יִשְׂרָאֵ֔ל מִבֵּ֥ין הַגּוֹיִ֖ם אֲשֶׁ֣ר הָֽלְכוּ־שָׁ֑ם וְקִבַּצְתִּ֤י אֹתָם֙
מִסָּבִ֔יב וְהֵבֵאתִ֥י אוֹתָ֖ם אֶל־אַדְמָתָֽם׃ כב וְעָשִׂ֣יתִי
אֹ֠תָ֠ם לְג֨וֹי אֶחָ֤ד בָּאָ֙רֶץ֙ בְּהָרֵ֣י יִשְׂרָאֵ֔ל וּמֶ֧לֶךְ אֶחָ֛ד
יִֽהְיֶ֥ה לְכֻלָּ֖ם לְמֶ֑לֶךְ וְלֹ֤א יהיה־[יִֽהְיוּ־ קרי] עוֹד֙
לִשְׁנֵ֣י גוֹיִ֔ם וְלֹ֨א יֵחָ֥צוּ ע֛וֹד לִשְׁתֵּ֥י מַמְלָכ֖וֹת עֽוֹד׃
כג וְלֹ֧א יִֽטַּמְּא֣וּ ע֗וֹד בְּגִלּֽוּלֵיהֶם֙ וּבְשִׁקּ֣וּצֵיהֶ֔ם
וּבְכֹ֖ל פִּשְׁעֵיהֶ֑ם וְהוֹשַׁעְתִּ֣י אֹתָ֗ם מִכֹּ֤ל מוֹשְׁבֹֽתֵיהֶם֙
אֲשֶׁ֣ר חָטְא֣וּ בָהֶ֔ם וְטִֽהַרְתִּ֣י אוֹתָ֔ם וְהָיוּ־לִ֣י לְעָ֔ם

A *Sidrah* that tells of the reunification of Jacob's sons is followed by a *Haftarah* that prophecies the eventual unification of the twelve tribes of Israel. The prophet Ezekiel, like Jeremiah, was one of the main prophets of the Destruction, and he actually joined his exiled brethren in Babylonia. The destruction of the Temple took place 140 years after the exile of the twelve tribes, so that the prophecy of this *Haftarah* was a source of great comfort to the tribes of Judah and Benjamin, for if even their long-lost comrades of the Northern Kingdom were assured that they would again become part of the nation, surely the two southern tribes could be certain that God was not forsaking them.

According to *Maharal (Gur Aryeh, Genesis 45:14),* the tears that accompanied the embrace of Joseph and Benjamin when Joseph revealed himself in Egypt were tears of joy, because the long-separated brothers foresaw the prophecy of Ezekiel. Joseph was the father of Ephraim, leader of the Ten Tribes, and Benjamin's descendants remained loyal to the Davidic dynasty of Judah; thus their reunion in Egypt was a precursor of that foretold by Ezekiel.

and she said: 'Please, my lord, give her the living newborn, and do not put it to death!' And the other one said: 'Neither mine nor yours shall he be. Sever!'

²⁷ The king spoke up and said: 'Give her the living newborn and do not put it to death: She is his mother.'

²⁸ All Israel heard the judgment that the king rendered and they felt awe for the king, for they saw that the wisdom of God was within him, to do justice.

4. ¹ So King Solomon was king over all Israel.

HAFTARAS VAYIGASH
Ezekiel 37:15-28

¹⁵ The word of HASHEM came to me, saying: ¹⁶ Now you, son of man, Take yourself one wooden tablet and write upon it: 'For Judah and the Children of Israel, his comrades,' and take another wooden tablet and write upon it: 'For Joseph, Ephraim's tablet, and all the Children of Israel, his comrades.' ¹⁷ And bring close to yourself, one to the other, like a single wooden tablet, and they shall become one in your hand.

¹⁸ Now when the children of your people say to you, 'Will you not tell us what these are to you?' speak to them:

¹⁹ 'Thus says my Lord HASHEM/ELOHIM: Behold! — I take Joseph's wooden tablet, which is in Ephraim's hand, and of the tribes of Israel his comrades, and shall place them with it together with Judah's wooden tablet, and I will make them one wooden tablet, and they shall become one in my hand. ²⁰ And the wooden tablets upon which you will write shall be in your hand, in their sight.'

²¹ Then speak to them: 'Thus says my Lord HASHEM/ELOHIM: Behold! — I take the Children of Israel from among the nations to which they went, and I shall gather them from around and I shall bring them to their soil. ²² I shall make them into a single nation in the land upon Israel's hills, and a single king shall be for them all as a king; and they shall no longer be two nations, no longer divided into two kingdoms again. ²³ They will no longer be contaminated with their idols and their abhorrent things and with all their sins; and I shall save them from all their habitations in which they sinned, and I shall purify them, an they shall be a nation for Me, and

The *Haftarah* goes on to make clear what sort of unified nation the twelve tribes of the future would be. The prophecy speaks not of a mere political union, free from the wars and rivalry that marred the era of the First Temple. Rather, it speaks of an era under a king from the House of David, who will be a servant of God and who will unify the people in allegiance to the Torah. Idolatry will be gone and the Temple will stand; the standard of life will be obedience to the laws of the Torah and the result will be that the entire world will know that HASHEM is God.

*Although the Divine Name יהוה is pronounced as if it were spelled אֲדֹנָי, when it is vowelized יֱהוִה it is pronounced as if it were spelled אֱלֹהִים.

וַאֲנִי אֶהְיֶה לָהֶם לֵאלֹהִים: כד וְעַבְדִּי דָוִד מֶלֶךְ עֲלֵיהֶם וְרוֹעֶה אֶחָד יִהְיֶה לְכֻלָּם וּבְמִשְׁפָּטַי יֵלֵכוּ וְחֻקֹּתַי יִשְׁמְרוּ וְעָשׂוּ אוֹתָם: כה וְיָשְׁבוּ עַל־הָאָרֶץ אֲשֶׁר נָתַתִּי לְעַבְדִּי לְיַעֲקֹב אֲשֶׁר יָשְׁבוּ־בָהּ אֲבוֹתֵיכֶם וְיָשְׁבוּ עָלֶיהָ הֵמָּה וּבְנֵיהֶם וּבְנֵי בְנֵיהֶם עַד־עוֹלָם וְדָוִד עַבְדִּי נָשִׂיא לָהֶם לְעוֹלָם: כו וְכָרַתִּי לָהֶם בְּרִית שָׁלוֹם בְּרִית עוֹלָם יִהְיֶה אוֹתָם וּנְתַתִּים וְהִרְבֵּיתִי אוֹתָם וְנָתַתִּי אֶת־מִקְדָּשִׁי בְּתוֹכָם לְעוֹלָם: כז וְהָיָה מִשְׁכָּנִי עֲלֵיהֶם וְהָיִיתִי לָהֶם לֵאלֹהִים וְהֵמָּה יִהְיוּ־לִי לְעָם: כח וְיָדְעוּ הַגּוֹיִם כִּי אֲנִי יהוה מְקַדֵּשׁ אֶת־יִשְׂרָאֵל בִּהְיוֹת מִקְדָּשִׁי בְּתוֹכָם לְעוֹלָם:

הפטרת ויחי

מלכים א' ב:א-יב

ב א וַיִּקְרְבוּ יְמֵי־דָוִד לָמוּת וַיְצַו אֶת־שְׁלֹמֹה בְנוֹ לֵאמֹר: ב אָנֹכִי הֹלֵךְ בְּדֶרֶךְ כָּל־הָאָרֶץ וְחָזַקְתָּ וְהָיִיתָ לְאִישׁ: ג וְשָׁמַרְתָּ אֶת־מִשְׁמֶרֶת ׀ יהוה אֱלֹהֶיךָ לָלֶכֶת בִּדְרָכָיו לִשְׁמֹר חֻקֹּתָיו מִצְוֹתָיו וּמִשְׁפָּטָיו וְעֵדְוֹתָיו כַּכָּתוּב בְּתוֹרַת מֹשֶׁה לְמַעַן תַּשְׂכִּיל אֵת כָּל־אֲשֶׁר תַּעֲשֶׂה וְאֵת כָּל־אֲשֶׁר תִּפְנֶה שָׁם: ד לְמַעַן יָקִים יהוה אֶת־דְּבָרוֹ אֲשֶׁר דִּבֶּר עָלַי לֵאמֹר אִם־יִשְׁמְרוּ בָנֶיךָ אֶת־דַּרְכָּם לָלֶכֶת לְפָנַי בֶּאֱמֶת בְּכָל־לְבָבָם וּבְכָל־נַפְשָׁם לֵאמֹר לֹא־יִכָּרֵת לְךָ אִישׁ מֵעַל כִּסֵּא יִשְׂרָאֵל: ה וְגַם אַתָּה יָדַעְתָּ אֵת אֲשֶׁר־עָשָׂה לִי יוֹאָב בֶּן־צְרוּיָה אֲשֶׁר עָשָׂה לִשְׁנֵי־שָׂרֵי צִבְאוֹת יִשְׂרָאֵל לְאַבְנֵר בֶּן־נֵר וְלַעֲמָשָׂא בֶן־יֶתֶר וַיַּהַרְגֵם וַיָּשֶׂם דְּמֵי־מִלְחָמָה בְּשָׁלֹם וַיִּתֵּן דְּמֵי מִלְחָמָה בַּחֲגֹרָתוֹ אֲשֶׁר בְּמָתְנָיו וּבְנַעֲלוֹ אֲשֶׁר בְּרַגְלָיו: ו וְעָשִׂיתָ כְּחָכְמָתֶךָ וְלֹא־תוֹרֵד שֵׂיבָתוֹ בְּשָׁלֹם שְׁאֹל: ז וְלִבְנֵי בַרְזִלַּי הַגִּלְעָדִי תַּעֲשֶׂה־חֶסֶד וְהָיוּ בְּאֹכְלֵי שֻׁלְחָנֶךָ כִּי־כֵן קָרְבוּ אֵלַי בְּבָרְחִי מִפְּנֵי אַבְשָׁלוֹם אָחִיךָ:

Like the *Sidrah*, the *Haftarah* describes the last will and testament of one of the greatest figures in history. In the *Sidrah*, Jacob gives his final commands and blessings, first to Joseph and then to all the brothers, assigning each of them his specific role in Jewish history. David issues his commands to only one son, his anointed successor Solomon.

David's exhortations that Solomon follow the commandments of the Torah and that only thereby can he assure success for himself and his progeny are to be expected. So is his urging that Solomon show kindness to the family of Barzilai, who stood by David during the hardest period of his life. Obedience to the Torah is the *raison d'etre* of the Jewish people; without it the nation can look forward only to enmity, defeat, and exile. Acknowledging gratitude, too, is a basic Jewish value. But the rest of his will is surprising. David commanded Solomon to exact the death penalty against Joab and Shim'i. Was vengeance a prerequisite of Jewish leadership?

I will be God for them. ^{24} My servant David will be king over them, and there will be a single shepherd for all of them; they will go in My ordinances and they will observe My decrees and perform them. ^{25} They will dwell on the land that I gave to My servant Jacob, within which your forefathers dwelt, and they shall dwell upon it — they, their children and their children's children forever, and My servant David will be prince for them, forever.

^{26} 'I shall seal a covenant of peace with them, an eternal covenant shall it be with them; and I shall emplace them and I shall increase them, and I shall place My Sanctuary among them forever. ^{27} My dwelling place shall be upon them, and I shall be God for them, and they shall be My people. ^{28} Then the nations shall know that I am HASHEM, Who hallows Israel, when My Sanctuary is among them forever.'

HAFTARAS VAYECHI
I Kings 2:1-12

2 ^{1} King David's days drew near to die, and he instructed his son Solomon, saying:

^{2} I go the way of all the earth; be strong and become a man. ^{3} Safeguard the charge of HASHEM, your God, to walk in His ways, observe His decrees, commandments, ordinances, and testimonies, as written in the Torah of Moses, so that you will succeed in all that you do and wherever you turn. ^{4} So that HASHEM will uphold His word that He spoke regarding me, saying: 'If your children will safeguard their way to walk before Me sincerely with all their heart and with all their soul,' saying, 'no man of you will be cut off from upon the throne of Israel.'

^{5} Furthermore, you know what Joab son of Zeruiah did to me, what he did to two leaders of the armies of Israel, to Abner son of Ner and to Amasa son of Jether whom he killed, thereby shedding blood of war in peacetime, placing the blood of war on the girdle that is on his loins and on his shoes that were on his feet. ^{6} You shall act according to your wisdom and not let his white hair go down to the grave in peace.

^{7} To the children of Barzilai the Gileadite act with kindness, and they shall be among those who eat at your table, for so they befriended me during my flight from Absalom your brother.

It may be that David's last words were concerned with communicating to Solomon the attitudes he must have regarding such character traits as treachery, loyalty, and duplicity. As the commanding general of David's army, Joab was one of the most important people in the kingdom and in David's own accession to the throne. But in a cowardly and treacherous way, he had murdered Abner and Amasa after gaining their confidence. David had admitted that his position was not strong enough to permit him to punish Joab, but he urged Solomon not to permit the attitude to fester that the mighty have a different law than the weak, and to dispel the notion that David may have conspired with Joab to do away with the competing generals. Barzilai's loyalty, in contrast, must be rewarded in a public way, so that the people would draw the proper lessons for their own behavior.

ח וְהִנֵּה עִמְּךָ שִׁמְעִי בֶן־גֵּרָא בֶן־הַיְמִינִי מִבַּחֻרִים וְהוּא קִלְלַנִי קְלָלָה נִמְרֶצֶת בְּיוֹם לֶכְתִּי מַחֲנָיִם וְהוּא־יָרַד לִקְרָאתִי הַיַּרְדֵּן וָאֶשָּׁבַע לוֹ בַיהוה לֵאמֹר אִם־אֲמִיתְךָ בֶּחָרֶב: ט וְעַתָּה אַל־תְּנַקֵּהוּ כִּי אִישׁ חָכָם אָתָּה וְיָדַעְתָּ אֵת אֲשֶׁר תַּעֲשֶׂה־לּוֹ וְהוֹרַדְתָּ אֶת־שֵׂיבָתוֹ בְּדָם שְׁאוֹל: י וַיִּשְׁכַּב דָּוִד עִם־אֲבֹתָיו וַיִּקָּבֵר בְּעִיר דָּוִד: יא וְהַיָּמִים אֲשֶׁר מָלַךְ דָּוִד עַל־יִשְׂרָאֵל אַרְבָּעִים שָׁנָה בְּחֶבְרוֹן מָלַךְ שֶׁבַע שָׁנִים וּבִירוּשָׁלַ͏ִם מָלַךְ שְׁלֹשִׁים וְשָׁלֹשׁ שָׁנִים: יב וּשְׁלֹמֹה יָשַׁב עַל־כִּסֵּא דָוִד אָבִיו וַתִּכֹּן מַלְכֻתוֹ מְאֹד:

הפטרת שבת ראשונה של חנוכה

זכריה ב:יד–ד:ז

יד רָנִּי וְשִׂמְחִי בַּת־צִיּוֹן כִּי הִנְנִי־בָא וְשָׁכַנְתִּי בְתוֹכֵךְ נְאֻם־יהוה: טו וְנִלְווּ גוֹיִם רַבִּים אֶל־יהוה בַּיּוֹם הַהוּא וְהָיוּ לִי לְעָם וְשָׁכַנְתִּי בְתוֹכֵךְ וְיָדַעַתְּ כִּי־יהוה צְבָאוֹת שְׁלָחַנִי אֵלָיִךְ: טז וְנָחַל יהוה אֶת־יְהוּדָה חֶלְקוֹ עַל אַדְמַת הַקֹּדֶשׁ וּבָחַר עוֹד בִּירוּשָׁלָ͏ִם: יז הַס כָּל־בָּשָׂר מִפְּנֵי יהוה כִּי נֵעוֹר מִמְּעוֹן קָדְשׁוֹ: ג א וַיַּרְאֵנִי אֶת־יְהוֹשֻׁעַ הַכֹּהֵן הַגָּדוֹל עֹמֵד לִפְנֵי מַלְאַךְ יהוה וְהַשָּׂטָן עֹמֵד עַל־יְמִינוֹ לְשִׂטְנוֹ: ב וַיֹּאמֶר יהוה אֶל־הַשָּׂטָן יִגְעַר יהוה בְּךָ הַשָּׂטָן וְיִגְעַר יהוה בְּךָ הַבֹּחֵר בִּירוּשָׁלָ͏ִם הֲלוֹא זֶה אוּד מֻצָּל מֵאֵשׁ: ג וִיהוֹשֻׁעַ הָיָה לָבֻשׁ בְּגָדִים צוֹאִים וְעֹמֵד לִפְנֵי הַמַּלְאָךְ: ד וַיַּעַן וַיֹּאמֶר אֶל־הָעֹמְדִים לְפָנָיו לֵאמֹר הָסִירוּ הַבְּגָדִים הַצֹּאִים מֵעָלָיו וַיֹּאמֶר אֵלָיו רְאֵה הֶעֱבַרְתִּי מֵעָלֶיךָ עֲוֹנֶךָ וְהַלְבֵּשׁ אֹתְךָ מַחֲלָצוֹת: ה וָאֹמַר יָשִׂימוּ צָנִיף טָהוֹר עַל־רֹאשׁוֹ וַיָּשִׂימוּ הַצָּנִיף הַטָּהוֹר עַל־רֹאשׁוֹ וַיַּלְבִּשֻׁהוּ בְּגָדִים וּמַלְאַךְ יהוה עֹמֵד:

As to Shim'i, he was no ordinary citizen. He was Solomon's own teacher, and a man of considerable stature. But he was duplicitous. At first he was 'loyal' to David, but when Absalom rebelled and had the upper hand, Shim'i went out of his way to curse David and throw stones at him. As monarch, David had the right to order Shim'i's execution then and there, as indeed he was urged to do, but instead he displayed his astonishing humility by saying that the curse, like the rebellion, was a Divine punishment. When Absalom's rebellion collapsed, Shim'i once again attempted to ingratiate himself with the winners, David and Solomon. Such behavior could not be tolerated.

The *Haftarah* of Chanukah is read even if Rosh Chodesh falls on the same Sabbath.

On the Sabbath of Chanukah, the *Haftarah* speaks of an earlier Chanukah, when the Menorah of the Second Temple was inaugurated. The Kohen Gadol was Joshua, the leader of the nation was Zerubbabel, scion of the Davidic dynasty, and the prophet who conveyed this vision was Zechariah. The prophet begins by looking ahead to the times when all the world will acknowledge Israel's primacy as God's chosen people under the leadership of the tribe of Judah, the tribe of David.

Then the prophet turns to Joshua, who was victim of the same sin that plagued much of the nation in the wake of the Babylonian Exile: His sons had married gentile women, and Joshua had failed to chastise them. In his vision, Zechariah sees the Satan condemning

⁸ Behold! — with you is Shim'i son of Gera, the Benjaminite from Bachurim. He cursed me with a powerful curse on the day I went to Machanaim; but he came down to meet me at the Jordan, and I swore to him by HASHEM, saying, 'I will not put you to death by the sword.' ⁹ But now, you are not to hold him guiltless, for you are a wise man, and you will know what you are to do to him, and are to bring down his white hair to the grave in blood.

¹⁰ David lay with his forefathers, and he was buried in the City of David. ¹¹ The days that David reigned over Israel were forty years; in Hebron he reigned for seven years and in Jerusalem he reigned for thirty-three years. ¹² Solomon sat on the throne of David, his father, and his kingship was firmly established.

FIRST SHABBOS CHANUKAH
Zechariah 2:14-4:6

¹⁴ Sing and be glad, O daughter of Zion, for behold! — I come and I will dwell among you, the words of HASHEM. ¹⁵ Many nations will attach themselves to HASHEM on that day, and they shall become a people unto Me, but I will dwell among you — then you will realize that HASHEM, Master of Legions, sent me to you. ¹⁶ HASHEM shall take Judah as a heritage to Himself for His portion upon the holy soil, and He shall choose Jerusalem again. ¹⁷ Be silent, all flesh, before HASHEM, for He is aroused from His holy habitation!

3. ¹ He showed me Joshua the *Kohen Gadol* standing before an angel of HASHEM, and the Satan standing at his right to accuse him. ² And HASHEM said to the Satan: 'HASHEM shall denounce you, O Satan, and HASHEM Who chooses Jerusalem shall denounce you again; this is indeed a firebrand rescued from the flames.' ³ Joshua was dressed in soiled garments as he stood before the angel. ⁴ [The angel] spoke up and said to those standing before him, saying, 'Remove the soiled garments from upon him.' ⁵ Then he said to him, 'See, I have removed your sin from you and had you clothed in pure garments.'

⁵ Then I said, 'Let them place a pure turban on his head'; and they placed the pure turban on his head and they dressed him in garments, and the angel of HASHEM remained standing.

Joshua for this lapse, which was symbolized by the soiled garments he was wearing. But God defends Joshua on the grounds that he is a *firebrand rescued from the flames*; he was immersed in the flames of the exile's physical and spiritual destruction, and as such cannot be condemned for the past. The angel garbs him in the pure vestments and the turban of the high priesthood — but warns him that henceforth he must obey the commandments. Only then can he be assured that his heirs will succeed him as *Kohen Gadol*. And only then can he be assured constant progress among the angels, who are *immobile*, in the sense that they can do only what God commands them, but cannot choose and grow, as man can. Joshua's comrades — Chananiah, Mishael, and Azariah — will join him in welcoming Zerubbabel, *the flourishing one*, and in seeing the cornerstone of the Temple, which, figuratively, has all eyes upon it and which is adorned with beautiful carvings.

ו וַיָּעַד מַלְאַךְ יהוה בִּיהוֹשֻׁעַ לֵאמְר: זְ כְּה־אָמַר יהוה
צְבָאוֹת אִם־בִּדְרָכַי תֵּלֵךְ וְאִם אֶת־מִשְׁמַרְתִּי תִשְׁמֹר
וְגַם־אַתָּה תָּדִין אֶת־בֵּיתִי וְגַם תִּשְׁמֹר אֶת־חֲצֵרָי
וְנָתַתִּי לְךָ מַהְלְכִים בֵּין הָעֹמְדִים הָאֵלֶּה: חְ שְׁמַע־
נָא יְהוֹשֻׁעַ ׀ הַכֹּהֵן הַגָּדוֹל אַתָּה וְרֵעֶיךָ הַיֹּשְׁבִים
לְפָנֶיךָ כִּי־אַנְשֵׁי מוֹפֵת הֵמָּה כִּי־הִנְנִי מֵבִיא אֶת־
עַבְדִּי צֶמַח: טְ כִּי ׀ הִנֵּה הָאֶבֶן אֲשֶׁר נָתַתִּי לִפְנֵי
יְהוֹשֻׁעַ עַל־אֶבֶן אַחַת שִׁבְעָה עֵינָיִם הִנְנִי מְפַתֵּחַ
פִּתֻּחָהּ נְאֻם יהוה צְבָאוֹת וּמַשְׁתִּי אֶת־עֲוֹן הָאָרֶץ־
הַהִיא בְּיוֹם אֶחָד: יְ בַּיּוֹם הַהוּא נְאֻם יהוה צְבָאוֹת
תִּקְרְאוּ אִישׁ לְרֵעֵהוּ אֶל־תַּחַת גֶּפֶן וְאֶל־תַּחַת
תְּאֵנָה: ד א וַיָּשָׁב הַמַּלְאָךְ הַדֹּבֵר בִּי וַיְעִירֵנִי כְּאִישׁ
אֲשֶׁר־יֵעוֹר מִשְּׁנָתוֹ: בְ וַיֹּאמֶר אֵלַי מָה אַתָּה רֹאֶה
וַיֹּאמַר [וָאֹמַר קרי] רָאִיתִי ׀ וְהִנֵּה מְנוֹרַת זָהָב כֻּלָּהּ
וְגֻלָּהּ עַל־רֹאשָׁהּ וְשִׁבְעָה נֵרֹתֶיהָ עָלֶיהָ שִׁבְעָה
וְשִׁבְעָה מוּצָקוֹת לַנֵּרוֹת אֲשֶׁר עַל־רֹאשָׁהּ: גְ וּשְׁנַיִם
זֵיתִים עָלֶיהָ אֶחָד מִימִין הַגֻּלָּה וְאֶחָד עַל־שְׂמֹאלָהּ:
ד וָאַעַן וָאֹמַר אֶל־הַמַּלְאָךְ הַדֹּבֵר בִּי לֵאמֹר מָה אֵלֶּה
אֲדֹנִי: הְ וַיַּעַן הַמַּלְאָךְ הַדֹּבֵר בִּי וַיֹּאמֶר אֵלַי הֲלוֹא
יָדַעְתָּ מָה־הֵמָּה אֵלֶּה וָאֹמַר לֹא אֲדֹנִי: וְ וַיַּעַן וַיֹּאמֶר
אֵלַי לֵאמֹר זֶה דְּבַר־יהוה אֶל־זְרֻבָּבֶל לֵאמֹר לֹא
בְחַיִל וְלֹא בְכֹחַ כִּי אִם־בְּרוּחִי אָמַר יהוה צְבָאוֹת:
זְ מִי־אַתָּה הַר־הַגָּדוֹל לִפְנֵי זְרֻבָּבֶל לְמִישֹׁר וְהוֹצִיא
אֶת־הָאֶבֶן הָרֹאשָׁה תְּשֻׁאוֹת חֵן ׀ חֵן לָהּ:

Finally, Zechariah is shown a menorah, complete with a bowl containing oil, tubes bringing oil to its seven lamps, and even two olive trees to provide a continuous supply of fuel. This symbolizes that all man's needs are provided by God — man, however, must have the eyes to see it. Impassable mountains become hospitable plains if God so wills.

A fitting message for Chanukah, not only because of the Menorah, but because Chanukah, too, showed him that a small band of righteous warriors, putting their faith in God, were able to overcome the mountain of one of the world's superpowers and bring purity back to the Temple.

[6] Then the angel of HASHEM warned Joshua, saying: [7] 'So said HASHEM, Master of Legions: If you follow My ways and safeguard My charge, then you shall administer My Temple and safeguard My courtyards, and I shall permit you movement among these immobile [angels]. [8] Listen now, O Joshua the *Kohen Gadol* — you as well as your fellows sitting before you, for they are miracle workers — for behold! — I bring My servant, the flourishing one. [9] For behold! — the stone that I have placed before Joshua, seven eyes toward one stone; behold! — I am engraving its adornment, the words of HASHEM, Master of Legions, and I have removed the sin of that land in one day. [10] On that day, the words of HASHEM, Master of Legions, each man will invite his fellow beneath the vine and beneath the fig tree.'

4. [1] The angel who spoke with me returned and woke me, as a man is awakened from his sleep. [2] He said to me, 'What do you see?' I said, 'I see, and behold! — there is a menorah of pure gold with its bowl on its top, seven lamps are upon it and there are seven tubes to each of the lamps that are on its top. [3] And two olive trees are near it, one to the right of the bowl and one to its left.'

[4] And I spoke up and said to the angel that was speaking to me, saying, 'What are these, my lord?' [5] The angel who was speaking to me spoke up and said to me, 'Do you not know what they are?' I said, 'No, my lord.'

[6] He spoke up and said to me, saying, 'This is the word of HASHEM to Zerubbabel, saying, "Not through armies and not through might, but through My spirit," says HASHEM, Master of Legions. [7] Who are you, O great mountain — before Zerubbabel [you shall become] a plain!' He shall bring forth the main stone to shouts of 'Beauty, beauty to it!'

הפטרת שבת שניה של חנוכה

מלכים א׳ ז:מ-נ

מ וַיַּעַשׂ חִירוֹם אֶת־הַכִּיֹּרוֹת וְאֶת־הַיָּעִים וְאֶת־
הַמִּזְרָקוֹת וַיְכַל חִירָם לַעֲשׂוֹת אֶת־כָּל־הַמְּלָאכָה
אֲשֶׁר עָשָׂה לַמֶּלֶךְ שְׁלֹמֹה בֵּית יְהוָה: מא עַמֻּדִים
שְׁנַיִם וְגֻלֹּת הַכֹּתָרֹת אֲשֶׁר־עַל־רֹאשׁ הָעַמּוּדִים
שְׁתָּיִם וְהַשְּׂבָכוֹת שְׁתַּיִם לְכַסּוֹת אֶת־שְׁתֵּי גֻּלֹּת
הַכֹּתָרֹת אֲשֶׁר עַל־רֹאשׁ הָעַמּוּדִים: מב וְאֶת־
הָרִמֹּנִים אַרְבַּע מֵאוֹת לִשְׁתֵּי הַשְּׂבָכוֹת שְׁנֵי־טוּרִים
רִמֹּנִים לַשְּׂבָכָה הָאֶחָת לְכַסּוֹת אֶת־שְׁתֵּי גֻּלֹּת
הַכֹּתָרֹת אֲשֶׁר עַל־פְּנֵי הָעַמּוּדִים: מג וְאֶת־הַמְּכֹנוֹת
עָשֶׂר וְאֶת־הַכִּיֹּרֹת עֲשָׂרָה עַל־הַמְּכֹנוֹת: מד וְאֶת־
הַיָּם הָאֶחָד וְאֶת־הַבָּקָר שְׁנֵים־עָשָׂר תַּחַת הַיָּם:
מה וְאֶת־הַסִּירוֹת וְאֶת־הַיָּעִים וְאֶת־הַמִּזְרָקוֹת וְאֵת
כָּל־הַכֵּלִים הָאֹהֶל [הָאֵלֶּה קרי] אֲשֶׁר עָשָׂה חִירָם
לַמֶּלֶךְ שְׁלֹמֹה בֵּית יְהוָה נְחֹשֶׁת מְמֹרָט: מו בְּכִכַּר
הַיַּרְדֵּן יְצָקָם הַמֶּלֶךְ בְּמַעֲבֵה הָאֲדָמָה בֵּין סֻכּוֹת וּבֵין
צָרְתָן: מז וַיַּנַּח שְׁלֹמֹה אֶת־כָּל־הַכֵּלִים מֵרֹב מְאֹד
מְאֹד לֹא נֶחְקַר מִשְׁקַל הַנְּחֹשֶׁת: מח וַיַּעַשׂ שְׁלֹמֹה
אֵת כָּל־הַכֵּלִים אֲשֶׁר בֵּית יְהוָה אֵת מִזְבַּח הַזָּהָב
וְאֶת־הַשֻּׁלְחָן אֲשֶׁר עָלָיו לֶחֶם הַפָּנִים זָהָב: מט וְאֶת־
הַמְּנֹרוֹת חָמֵשׁ מִיָּמִין וְחָמֵשׁ מִשְּׂמֹאל לִפְנֵי הַדְּבִיר
זָהָב סָגוּר וְהַפֶּרַח וְהַנֵּרֹת וְהַמֶּלְקָחַיִם זָהָב:
נ וְהַסִּפּוֹת וְהַמְזַמְּרוֹת וְהַמִּזְרָקוֹת וְהַכַּפּוֹת
וְהַמַּחְתּוֹת זָהָב סָגוּר וְהַפֹּתוֹת לְדַלְתוֹת הַבַּיִת
הַפְּנִימִי לְקֹדֶשׁ הַקֳּדָשִׁים לְדַלְתֵי הַבַּיִת לַהֵיכָל זָהָב:

This *Haftarah* is the same as that of *Vayakhel*, which discusses the construction of the Tabernacle; thus it is appropriate for Chanukah, as well, when the Temple was rededicated. Much of the *Haftarah* describes the Temple vessels that were made by King Hiram of Tyre, a friend and collaborator of King Solomon. The Second Temple as a whole is often ascribed to King Cyrus, for he merited the privilege of giving permission for its construction, and even of contributing significant resources toward the work. In contrast, the desecration of the Temple prior to Chanukah was ordered by King Antiochus. This shows the contrast between the ideal state and the perverted one that has caused so much grief since the dawn of Jewish history. Israel was charged with the task of being a magnet to the nations, drawing them toward a recognition of God's majesty and service. Hiram and Cyrus saw and responded. Antiochus did not. When Israel is worthy, it is instrumental in leading society toward this state. Indeed, in the aftermath of Chanukah, when the family of Hasmoneans inspired the Jewish people to risk their lives to renew the glory and purity of the Temple, the result was that the Jewish commonwealth expanded, in size, wealth, and spiritual influence.

SECOND SHABBOS CHANUKAH

I Kings 7: 40-50

[40] Hiram made the lavers, the shovels, and the basins; and Hiram finished doing all the work that he did for King Solomon for the House of HASHEM. [41] The two columns and the two globes of the capitals that were atop the columns; and the two netted ornamentations to cover the two globes of the capitals that were atop the columns; [42] and the four hundred pomegranates for the two netted ornamentations, two rows of pomegranates for each netted ornamentation that are on the upper surface of the columns; [43] and the ten pedestals, and the ten lavers upon the pedestals; [44] and the one 'Sea,' and the twelve oxen under the 'Sea'; [45] and the pots, the shovels, and the basins; all these vessels that Hiram made for King Solomon for the House of HASHEM were of burnished copper.

[46] The king cast them in the Plain of the Jordan in firm clay, between Succoth and Zarthan. [47] Solomon left all the vessels unweighed because there were so very many; the weight of the copper was not calculated.

[48] Solomon made all the vessels that were in the House of HASHEM: the Golden Altar, and the Table — upon which was the showbread — was of gold; [49] and the candelabra, five to the right and five to the left, before the Holy of Holies, were of refined gold; and the blossoms, the lamps, and the tongs were of gold; [50] and the bowls, the knives, the basins, the spoons, the firepans were of refined gold; and the hinges for the innermost chamber of the House, the Holy of Holies, for the doors of the Hall of the House were of gold.

הפטרת שבת ערב ראש חדש

שמואל א׳ כ:יח-מח

יח וַיֹּאמֶר־לוֹ יְהוֹנָתָן מָחָר חֹדֶשׁ וְנִפְקַדְתָּ כִּי יִפָּקֵד מוֹשָׁבֶךָ: יט וְשִׁלַּשְׁתָּ תֵּרֵד מְאֹד וּבָאתָ אֶל־הַמָּקוֹם אֲשֶׁר־נִסְתַּרְתָּ שָּׁם בְּיוֹם הַמַּעֲשֶׂה וְיָשַׁבְתָּ אֵצֶל הָאֶבֶן הָאָזֶל: כ וַאֲנִי שְׁלֹשֶׁת הַחִצִּים צִדָּה אוֹרֶה לְשַׁלַּח־לִי לְמַטָּרָה: כא וְהִנֵּה אֶשְׁלַח אֶת־הַנַּעַר לֵךְ מְצָא אֶת־הַחִצִּים אִם־אָמֹר אֹמַר לַנַּעַר הִנֵּה הַחִצִּים | מִמְּךָ וָהֵנָּה קָחֶנּוּ וָבֹאָה כִּי־שָׁלוֹם לְךָ וְאֵין דָּבָר חַי־יְהוָה: כב וְאִם־כֹּה אֹמַר לָעֶלֶם הִנֵּה הַחִצִּים מִמְּךָ וָהָלְאָה לֵךְ כִּי שִׁלַּחֲךָ יְהוָה: כג וְהַדָּבָר אֲשֶׁר דִּבַּרְנוּ אֲנִי וָאָתָּה הִנֵּה יְהוָה בֵּינִי וּבֵינְךָ עַד־עוֹלָם: כד וַיִּסָּתֵר דָּוִד בַּשָּׂדֶה וַיְהִי הַחֹדֶשׁ וַיֵּשֶׁב הַמֶּלֶךְ עַל־[אֶל־ קרי] הַלֶּחֶם לֶאֱכוֹל: כה וַיֵּשֶׁב הַמֶּלֶךְ עַל־מוֹשָׁבוֹ כְּפַעַם | בְּפַעַם אֶל־מוֹשַׁב הַקִּיר וַיָּקָם יְהוֹנָתָן וַיֵּשֶׁב אַבְנֵר מִצַּד שָׁאוּל וַיִּפָּקֵד מְקוֹם דָּוִד: כו וְלֹא־דִבֶּר שָׁאוּל מְאוּמָה בַּיּוֹם הַהוּא כִּי אָמַר מִקְרֶה הוּא בִּלְתִּי טָהוֹר הוּא כִּי לֹא טָהוֹר: כז וַיְהִי מִמָּחֳרַת הַחֹדֶשׁ הַשֵּׁנִי וַיִּפָּקֵד מְקוֹם דָּוִד וַיֹּאמֶר שָׁאוּל אֶל־יְהוֹנָתָן בְּנוֹ מַדּוּעַ לֹא־בָא בֶן־יִשַׁי גַּם־תְּמוֹל גַּם־הַיּוֹם אֶל־הַלָּחֶם: כח וַיַּעַן יְהוֹנָתָן אֶת־שָׁאוּל נִשְׁאֹל נִשְׁאַל דָּוִד מֵעִמָּדִי עַד־בֵּית לָחֶם: כט וַיֹּאמֶר שַׁלְּחֵנִי נָא כִּי זֶבַח מִשְׁפָּחָה לָנוּ בָּעִיר וְהוּא צִוָּה־לִי אָחִי וְעַתָּה אִם־מָצָאתִי חֵן בְּעֵינֶיךָ אִמָּלְטָה נָּא וְאֶרְאֶה אֶת־אֶחָי עַל־כֵּן לֹא־בָא אֶל־שֻׁלְחַן הַמֶּלֶךְ: ל וַיִּחַר־אַף שָׁאוּל בִּיהוֹנָתָן וַיֹּאמֶר לוֹ בֶּן־נַעֲוַת הַמַּרְדּוּת הֲלוֹא יָדַעְתִּי כִּי־בֹחֵר אַתָּה לְבֶן־יִשַׁי לְבָשְׁתְּךָ וּלְבֹשֶׁת עֶרְוַת אִמֶּךָ: לא כִּי כָל־הַיָּמִים אֲשֶׁר בֶּן־יִשַׁי חַי עַל־הָאֲדָמָה לֹא תִכּוֹן אַתָּה וּמַלְכוּתֶךָ וְעַתָּה שְׁלַח וְקַח

The Sages teach that any love that is pure and not founded on selfishness will last forever. "And [which love] did not depend on a specific cause? — The love of David and Jonathan" (*Avos* 5: 19). Our *Haftarah* is the story that best demonstrates the nature of this quintessential friendship.

No two people were more natural rivals than David and Jonathan. Jonathan was the crown prince, the natural successor to his father Saul as king of Israel. And he was a man of great stature, beloved by the people, and righteous as well — he would have been a source of pride to the nation. David was the rival, the interloper who had been anointed by Samuel to take away the throne that should have been Jonathan's. And King Saul was incensed, overcome by a hatred that had brought him to hate and attempt to do away with David. Yet David and Jonathan were dear friends. In the story of the *Haftarah*, Jonathan ignores his selfish interests — even his father's fury — and devises a plan to warn David of danger and, as the narrative shows, to save his life.

SHABBOS EREV ROSH CHODESH
I Samuel 20:18-42

[18] Jonathan said to [David]: 'Tomorrow is the New Moon, and you will be missed because your seat will be empty. [19] For three days you are to go far down and come to the place where you hid on the day of the deed, and remain near the marker stone. [20] I will shoot three arrows in that direction as if I were shooting at a target. [21] Behold! — I will then send the lad, "Go, find the arrows." If I call out to the lad, "Behold! — the arrows are on this side of you!" then you should take him and return, for it is well with you and there is no concern, as HASHEM lives. [22] But if I say this to the boy, "Behold! — the arrows are beyond you!" then go, for HASHEM will have sent you away. [23] This matter of which we have spoken, I and you, behold! — HASHEM remains [witness] between me and you forever.'

[24] David concealed himself in the field. It was the New Moon and the king sat at the feast to eat. [25] The king sat on his seat as usual, on the seat by the wall; and Jonathan stood up so that Abner could sit at Saul's side, and David's seat was empty. [26] Saul said nothing on that day, for he thought, 'It is a coincidence that he must be impure, for he has not been cleansed.'

[27] It was the day after the New Moon, the second day, and David's place was empty; Saul said to Jonathan, his son, 'Why did the son of Jesse not come to the feast, yesterday or today?'

[28] Jonathan answered Saul, 'David asked me for permission to go to Bethlehem. [29] He said, "Please send me away, for we have a family feast in the city, and he, my brother, ordered me [to come]; so now, if I have found favor in your eyes, excuse me, please, and let me see my brothers." Therefore, he has not come to the king's table.'

[30] Saul's anger flared up at Jonathan, and he said to him, 'Son of a pervertedly rebellious woman, do I not know that you prefer the son of Jesse, for your own shame and the shame of your mother's nakedness! [31] For all the days that the son of Jesse is alive on the earth, you and your kingdom will not be secure! And now send and bring

אֹתוֹ אֵלַי כִּי בֶן־מָוֶת הֽוּא: לבוַיַּעַן יְהוֹנָתָן אֶת־
שָׁאוּל אָבִיו וַיֹּאמֶר אֵלָיו לָמָּה יוּמַת מֶה עָשָֽׂה:
לגוַיָּטֶל שָׁאוּל אֶת־הַחֲנִית עָלָיו לְהַכֹּתוֹ וַיֵּדַע
יְהוֹנָתָן כִּי־כָלָה הִיא מֵעִם אָבִיו לְהָמִית אֶת־דָּוִֽד:
לדוַיָּקָם יְהוֹנָתָן מֵעִם הַשֻּׁלְחָן בׇּחֳרִי־אָף וְלֹא־אָכַל
בְּיוֹם־הַחֹדֶשׁ הַשֵּׁנִי לֶחֶם כִּי נֶעְצַב אֶל־דָּוִד כִּי
הִכְלִמוֹ אָבִֽיו: להוַיְהִי בַבֹּקֶר וַיֵּצֵא יְהוֹנָתָן הַשָּׂדֶה
לְמוֹעֵד דָּוִד וְנַעַר קָטֹן עִמּֽוֹ: לווַיֹּאמֶר לְנַעֲרוֹ רֻץ
מְצָא־נָא אֶת־הַחִצִּים אֲשֶׁר אָנֹכִי מוֹרֶה הַנַּעַר רָץ
וְהֽוּא־יָרָה הַחֵצִי לְהַעֲבִרֽוֹ: לזוַיָּבֹא הַנַּעַר עַד־מְקוֹם
הַחֵצִי אֲשֶׁר יָרָה יְהוֹנָתָן וַיִּקְרָא יְהוֹנָתָן אַחֲרֵי הַנַּעַר
וַיֹּאמֶר הֲלוֹא הַחֵצִי מִמְּךָ וָהָֽלְאָה: לחוַיִּקְרָא יְהוֹנָתָן
אַחֲרֵי הַנַּעַר מְהֵרָה חוּשָׁה אַל־תַּעֲמֹד וַיְלַקֵּט נַעַר
יְהוֹנָתָן אֶת־הַחֵצִי [הַחִצִּים קרי] וַיָּבֹא אֶל־אֲדֹנָֽיו:
לטוְהַנַּעַר לֹֽא־יָדַע מְאוּמָה אַךְ יְהוֹנָתָן וְדָוִד יָֽדְעוּ
אֶת־הַדָּבָֽר: מוַיִּתֵּן יְהוֹנָתָן אֶת־כֵּלָיו אֶל־הַנַּעַר
אֲשֶׁר־לוֹ וַיֹּאמֶר לוֹ לֵךְ הָבֵיא הָעִֽיר: מאהַנַּעַר בָּא
וְדָוִד קָם מֵאֵצֶל הַנֶּגֶב וַיִּפֹּל לְאַפָּיו אַרְצָה וַיִּשְׁתַּחוּ
שָׁלֹשׁ פְּעָמִים וַיִּשְּׁקוּ אִישׁ אֶת־רֵעֵהוּ וַיִּבְכּוּ אִישׁ
אֶת־רֵעֵהוּ עַד־דָּוִד הִגְדִּֽיל: מבוַיֹּאמֶר יְהוֹנָתָן לְדָוִד
לֵךְ לְשָׁלוֹם אֲשֶׁר נִשְׁבַּעְנוּ שְׁנֵינוּ אֲנַחְנוּ בְּשֵׁם יהוה
לֵאמֹר יהוה יִֽהְיֶה | בֵּינִי וּבֵינֶךָ וּבֵין זַרְעִי וּבֵין זַרְעֲךָ
עַד־עוֹלָֽם:

him to me, for he is deserving of death.'

[32] Jonathan answered his father Saul and he said to him, 'Why should he die; what has he done?'

[33] Saul hurled his spear at him to strike him; so Jonathan realized that it was decided by his father to kill David. [34] Jonathan arose from the table in a burning anger; he did not partake of food on that second day of the month, for he was saddened over David and because his father had humiliated him.

[35] It happened in the morning that Jonathan went out to the field for the meeting with David, and a young lad was with him. [36] He said to his lad, 'Run — please find the arrows that I will be shooting.' [37] The lad ran, and he shot the arrow to make it go further. The lad arrived at the place of the arrow that Jonathan had shot, and Jonathan called out after the lad, and he said, 'Is not the arrow beyond you?'

[38] And Jonathan called out after the lad, 'Quickly, hurry, do not stand still!' The lad gathered the arrows and came to his master. [39] The lad knew nothing, only Jonathan and David understood the matter. [40] Jonathan gave his equipment to his lad and said to him, 'Go bring it to the city.'

[41] The lad went and David stood up from near the south [side of the stone], and he fell on his face to the ground and prostrated himself three times. They kissed one another and they wept with one another, until David [wept] greatly.

[42] Jonathan said to David, 'Go to peace. What the two of us have sworn in the Name of Hashem, saying, "Hashem shall be between me and you and between my children and your children — shall be forever!"'

הפטרת שבת ראש חדש

ישעיה סו:א–כד

סו א כֹּה אָמַר יְהוָה הַשָּׁמַיִם כִּסְאִי וְהָאָרֶץ הֲדֹם
רַגְלָי אֵי־זֶה בַיִת אֲשֶׁר תִּבְנוּ־לִי וְאֵי־זֶה מָקוֹם
מְנוּחָתִי: ב וְאֶת־כָּל־אֵלֶּה יָדִי עָשָׂתָה וַיִּהְיוּ כָל־
אֵלֶּה נְאֻם־יְהוָה וְאֶל־זֶה אַבִּיט אֶל־עָנִי וּנְכֵה־רוּחַ
וְחָרֵד עַל־דְּבָרִי: ג שׁוֹחֵט הַשּׁוֹר מַכֵּה־אִישׁ זוֹבֵחַ
הַשֶּׂה עֹרֵף כֶּלֶב מַעֲלֵה מִנְחָה דַּם־חֲזִיר מַזְכִּיר
לְבֹנָה מְבָרֵךְ אָוֶן גַּם־הֵמָּה בָּחֲרוּ בְּדַרְכֵיהֶם
וּבְשִׁקּוּצֵיהֶם נַפְשָׁם חָפֵצָה: ד גַּם־אֲנִי אֶבְחַר
בְּתַעֲלֻלֵיהֶם וּמְגוּרֹתָם אָבִיא לָהֶם יַעַן קָרָאתִי וְאֵין
עוֹנֶה דִּבַּרְתִּי וְלֹא שָׁמֵעוּ וַיַּעֲשׂוּ הָרַע בְּעֵינַי וּבַאֲשֶׁר
לֹא־חָפַצְתִּי בָּחָרוּ: ה שִׁמְעוּ דְּבַר־יְהוָה הַחֲרֵדִים
אֶל־דְּבָרוֹ אָמְרוּ אֲחֵיכֶם שֹׂנְאֵיכֶם מְנַדֵּיכֶם לְמַעַן
שְׁמִי יִכְבַּד יְהוָה וְנִרְאֶה בְשִׂמְחַתְכֶם וְהֵם יֵבֹשׁוּ:
ו קוֹל שָׁאוֹן מֵעִיר קוֹל מֵהֵיכָל קוֹל יְהוָה מְשַׁלֵּם
גְּמוּל לְאֹיְבָיו: ז בְּטֶרֶם תָּחִיל יָלָדָה בְּטֶרֶם יָבוֹא
חֵבֶל לָהּ וְהִמְלִיטָה זָכָר: ח מִי־שָׁמַע כָּזֹאת מִי
רָאָה כָּאֵלֶּה הֲיוּחַל אֶרֶץ בְּיוֹם אֶחָד אִם־יִוָּלֵד גּוֹי
פַּעַם אֶחָת כִּי־חָלָה גַּם־יָלְדָה צִיּוֹן אֶת־בָּנֶיהָ:
ט הַאֲנִי אַשְׁבִּיר וְלֹא אוֹלִיד יֹאמַר יְהוָה אִם־אֲנִי
הַמּוֹלִיד וְעָצַרְתִּי אָמַר אֱלֹהָיִךְ: י שִׂמְחוּ אֶת־
יְרוּשָׁלִַם וְגִילוּ בָהּ כָּל־אֹהֲבֶיהָ שִׂישׂוּ אִתָּהּ מָשׂוֹשׂ
כָּל־הַמִּתְאַבְּלִים עָלֶיהָ: יא לְמַעַן תִּינְקוּ וּשְׂבַעְתֶּם
מִשֹּׁד תַּנְחֻמֶיהָ לְמַעַן תָּמֹצּוּ וְהִתְעַנַּגְתֶּם מִזִּיז
כְּבוֹדָהּ: יב כִּי־כֹה | אָמַר יְהוָה הִנְנִי נֹטֶה־אֵלֶיהָ
כְּנָהָר שָׁלוֹם וּכְנַחַל שׁוֹטֵף כְּבוֹד גּוֹיִם וִינַקְתֶּם
עַל־צַד תִּנָּשֵׂאוּ וְעַל־בִּרְכַּיִם תְּשָׁעֳשָׁעוּ: יג כְּאִישׁ

This chapter is the last one in the stirring Book of *Isaiah*. It was chosen as the *Haftarah* of the Sabbath-Rosh Chodesh because its penultimate verse (which is repeated after the chapter is concluded) speaks of the homage that will be paid to God on every Sabbath and Rosh Chodesh.

The chapter gives hope and comfort to the Jewish people, as Isaiah foresees the ultimate downfall of the nations that will do battle against one another and against Israel in the climactic War of Gog and Magog, the war that will precede the final redemption. Isaiah speaks of the defeat of the nations and the universal recognition of the greatness of God and His people. But there are stern lessons for Israel, as well.

The chapter begins by declaring that all the world is but God's throne and His footstool. Can anyone think that the Jewish people can build a Temple that will encompass His Glory? Surely the purpose of the Temple is not to honor God — Who is above any honor we can render Him — but to serve as our vehicle to elevate ourselves. People who seek to appease God with insincere, meaningless service are considered like those who kill and maim people, and who offer unclean animals and contaminated blood upon His Altar. And they do so consciously, having *chosen* this form of blasphemous service. God will respond in kind, punishing those who ill serve Him. But that will not be the end. Those who are loyal to God will be acknowledged and rewarded in a miraculous manner. The rebirth of Israel will be as astounding as that of a nation being born in a single day, without even labor pains. If God decides to give new life to His people, can it be otherwise?

Thus, all who have been loyal to Jerusalem and mourned her will rejoice with her. Blessings will flow to them in torrents, but their enemies will suffer ignominious defeat, as God pours out His wrath upon them. The survivors will bring word of His greatness to the furthest corners of the world, and in the process they will bring back the straggling Jews who seemed to have been irretrievably lost in the long, hard exile.

Then all will come to the rebuilt Temple — the eternal Temple — to prostrate themselves in devout and loyal service to God. History will have reached its goal and those who were loyal to God will be vindicated.

SHABBOS ROSH CHODESH
Isaiah 66:1-24

66 [1] So said HASHEM, the heaven is My throne and the earth is My footstool; what House could you build for Me, and what could be My resting place? [2] My hand made all these and thus they came into being, the words of HASHEM — but it is to this that I look: to the poor and broken-spirited person who is zealous regarding My Word.

[3] He who slaughters an ox is as if he slays a man, he who offers a sheep is as if he breaks a dog's neck, he who brings up a meal-offering is as if he offers a swine's blood, one who brings a frankincense remembrance is as if he brings a gift of extortion; they have even chosen their ways, and their souls have desired their abominations.

[4] I, too, will choose to mock them and what they dread I will bring upon them — because I have called, but no one responded; I have spoken, but they did not hear; they did what is evil in My eyes and what I did not desire they chose.

[5] Listen to the Word of HASHEM, those who are zealous regarding His Word; your brethren who hate you and distance themselves from you say: 'HASHEM is glorified because of my reputation' — but we shall see your gladness and they will be shamed. [6] A tumultuous sound comes from the city, a sound from the Sanctuary, the sound of HASHEM dealing retribution to His enemies. [7] Before she will feel her labor she will have given birth, before the pain will come she will have delivered a son. [8] Who ever heard such a thing, who ever saw its like? Has a land gone through its labor in one day, has a nation been born at one time, as Zion went through labor and gave birth to her children? [9] Shall I bring [a woman] to the birthstool and not have her give birth? says HASHEM; shall I, Who causes birth, hold it back? says your God.

[10] Be glad with Jerusalem and rejoice in her, all who love her; exult with her exultation, all who mourned for her; [11] so that you may nurse and be sated from the breast of her consolations; so that you may suck and delight from the glow of her glory. [12] For so said HASHEM, Behold! — I shall direct peace to her like a river, and the honor of nations like a surging stream and you shall suckle; you will be carried on a shoulder and bounced on knees. [13] Like a man

אֲשֶׁר אִמּוֹ תְּנַחֲמֶנּוּ כֵּן אָנֹכִי אֲנַחֶמְכֶם וּבִירוּשָׁלַ͏ִם
תְּנֻחָמוּ: יד וּרְאִיתֶם וְשָׂשׂ לִבְּכֶם וְעַצְמוֹתֵיכֶם
כַּדֶּשֶׁא תִפְרַחְנָה וְנוֹדְעָה יַד־יְהוָה אֶת־עֲבָדָיו וְזָעַם
אֶת־אֹיְבָיו: טו כִּי־הִנֵּה יְהוָה בָּאֵשׁ יָבוֹא וְכַסּוּפָה
מַרְכְּבֹתָיו לְהָשִׁיב בְּחֵמָה אַפּוֹ וְגַעֲרָתוֹ בְּלַהֲבֵי־אֵשׁ:
טז כִּי בָאֵשׁ יְהוָה נִשְׁפָּט וּבְחַרְבּוֹ אֶת־כָּל־בָּשָׂר וְרַבּוּ
חַלְלֵי יְהוָה: יז הַמִּתְקַדְּשִׁים וְהַמִּטַּהֲרִים אֶל־הַגַּנּוֹת
אַחַר אֶחָד [אַחַת קרי] בַּתָּוֶךְ אֹכְלֵי בְּשַׂר הַחֲזִיר
וְהַשֶּׁקֶץ וְהָעַכְבָּר יַחְדָּו יָסֻפוּ נְאֻם־יְהוָה: יח וְאָנֹכִי
מַעֲשֵׂיהֶם וּמַחְשְׁבֹתֵיהֶם בָּאָה לְקַבֵּץ אֶת־כָּל־הַגּוֹיִם
וְהַלְּשֹׁנוֹת וּבָאוּ וְרָאוּ אֶת כְּבוֹדִי: יט וְשַׂמְתִּי בָהֶם
אוֹת וְשִׁלַּחְתִּי מֵהֶם | פְּלֵיטִים אֶל־הַגּוֹיִם תַּרְשִׁישׁ
פּוּל וְלוּד מֹשְׁכֵי קֶשֶׁת תֻּבַל וְיָוָן הָאִיִּים הָרְחֹקִים
אֲשֶׁר לֹא־שָׁמְעוּ אֶת־שִׁמְעִי וְלֹא־רָאוּ אֶת־כְּבוֹדִי
וְהִגִּידוּ אֶת־כְּבוֹדִי בַּגּוֹיִם: כ וְהֵבִיאוּ אֶת־כָּל־
אֲחֵיכֶם | מִכָּל־הַגּוֹיִם | מִנְחָה | לַיהוָה בַּסּוּסִים
וּבָרֶכֶב וּבַצַּבִּים וּבַפְּרָדִים וּבַכִּרְכָּרוֹת עַל הַר קָדְשִׁי
יְרוּשָׁלַ͏ִם אָמַר יְהוָה כַּאֲשֶׁר יָבִיאוּ בְנֵי יִשְׂרָאֵל
אֶת־הַמִּנְחָה בִּכְלִי טָהוֹר בֵּית יְהוָה: כא וְגַם־מֵהֶם
אֶקַּח לַכֹּהֲנִים לַלְוִיִּם אָמַר יְהוָה: כב כִּי כַאֲשֶׁר
הַשָּׁמַיִם הַחֲדָשִׁים וְהָאָרֶץ הַחֲדָשָׁה אֲשֶׁר אֲנִי עֹשֶׂה
עֹמְדִים לְפָנַי נְאֻם־יְהוָה כֵּן יַעֲמֹד זַרְעֲכֶם וְשִׁמְכֶם:
כג וְהָיָה מִדֵּי־חֹדֶשׁ בְּחָדְשׁוֹ וּמִדֵּי שַׁבָּת בְּשַׁבַּתּוֹ
יָבוֹא כָל־בָּשָׂר לְהִשְׁתַּחֲוֹת לְפָנַי אָמַר יְהוָה:
כד וְיָצְאוּ וְרָאוּ בְּפִגְרֵי הָאֲנָשִׁים הַפֹּשְׁעִים בִּי כִּי
תוֹלַעְתָּם לֹא תָמוּת וְאִשָּׁם לֹא תִכְבֶּה וְהָיוּ דֵרָאוֹן
לְכָל־בָּשָׂר:

וְהָיָה מִדֵּי־חֹדֶשׁ בְּחָדְשׁוֹ וּמִדֵּי שַׁבָּת בְּשַׁבַּתּוֹ יָבוֹא
כָל־בָּשָׂר לְהִשְׁתַּחֲוֹת לְפָנַי אָמַר יְהוָה:

whose mother consoled him, so will I console you, and in Jerusalem will you be consoled. [14] You shall see and your heart will exult, and your bones will flourish like grass; the hand of HASHEM will be known to His servants, and He will be angry with His enemies. [15] For behold! — HASHEM will arrive in fire and His chariots like the whirlwind, to requite His anger with wrath, and His rebuke with flaming fire. [16] For with fire HASHEM will judge, and with His sword against all flesh; many will be those slain by HASHEM.

[17] Those who prepare and purify themselves [to storm] the gardens go one after another to the midst [of the fray]; together will be consumed those who eat the flesh of swine, of abominable creatures and rodents — the words of HASHEM. [18] I [am aware of] their deeds and their thoughts; [the time] has come to gather in all the nations and tongues; they shall come and see My glory.

[19] I shall put a sign upon them and send some as survivors to the nations: Tarshish, Pul, and, Lud, the bow-drawers, Tubal, and Yavan; the distant islands, who have not heard of My fame and not seen My glory, and they will declare My glory among the nations. [20] They will bring all your brethren from all the nations as an offering to HASHEM, on horses, on chariots, on covered wagons, on mules, and with joyful dances upon My holy mountain, Jerusalem, said HASHEM; just as the Children of Israel bring their offering in a pure vessel to the House of HASHEM. [21] From them, too, will I take to be Kohanim and Levites, said HASHEM.

[22] For just as the new heaven and the new earth that I will make will endure before Me — the words of HASHEM — so will your offspring and your name endure. [23] And it shall be that, New Moon in and New Moon out, Sabbath in and Sabbath out, all flesh shall come to prostrate themselves to Me, said HASHEM.

[24] They shall go out and see the corpses of those who rebel against Me, for their worms will not die and their fire will not go out, and they shall be a disgrace for all flesh.

And it shall be that, New Moon in and New Moon out, Sabbath in and Sabbath out, all flesh shall come to prostrate themselves to Me, said HASHEM.

— the moving force of the teshuvah movement

• **NCSY** pioneered and gave rise to the near miraculous phenomenon of thousands of young Jews, intelligent and accomplished, searching and yearning for spirituality, Torah and roots.

• **NCSY** inspires more young people to become Sabbath observers than any other institution or program in North America and Jewish life.

• **NCSY** has given rise to a special group of yeshivos in the United States and Israel for the newly observant.

• **NCSY** serves as the only outreach program in scores of American and Canadian communities.

• **NCSY**, one of the largest and most effective Jewish movements in the world — a powerful and effective force for Jewish survival, revival and return — urgently requires your commitment and support in order to maintain and expand its activities and programs.

For further information contanct:
NATIONAL CONFERENCE OF SYNAGOGUE YOUTH
70 West 36th Street
New York, NY 10018
(212) 244-2011 • Fax (212) 268-4819

NCSY — The Youth Movement of the Orthodox Union